LITERAT
LOVER'S
COMPANION

LITERATURE LOVER'S COMPANION

THE ESSENTIAL REFERENCE TO THE WORLD'S GREATEST WRITERS–PAST AND PRESENT, POPULAR AND CLASSICAL

The Editors of Prentice Hall Press

Printed in the United States of America

10 9 8 7 6 5 4 3 2 1

ISBN 0-0-7352-0229-X

ATTENTION: CORPORATIONS AND SCHOOLS

Prentice Hall Press books are available at quantity discounts with bulk purchase for educational, business, or sales promotional use. For information, please write to: Prentice Hall, Special Sales, 240 Frisch Court, Paramus, NJ 07652. Please supply: title of book, ISBN, quantity, how the book will be used, date needed.

FOREWORD

The *Literature Lover's Companion* contains concise biographies of over 1,000 leading figures in the history of world literature. These writers from all over the world represent nearly 3,000 years of creative writing – from works of the ancient Greeks, through the recognized classics of world literature, and up to the famous blockbusters of today. Novelists, poets, playwrights, and short-story writers are included, and all literary forms are covered – from children's stories and fantasy to science fiction and thrillers.

The biography on each author includes an outline of the author's life and an introduction to the author's works. It is designed to give a clear and concise statement of what the author is best known for and to help the reader understand some of the influences that shaped the author's writing. For instance, it is interesting to learn that Cervantes, the author of *Don Quixote*, was captured by pirates and spent five years as a slave, and that when the crime writer James Ellroy was ten years old his mother was brutally murdered by a killer who was never found. You will discover that Charles Dickens was only 25 when he wrote the classic *Oliver Twist*, and Dodie Smith was 60 when she wrote the children's favorite *The Hundred and One Dalmations*.

Accompanying each author are his or her major works, listed in date order. The dates given are of first publication or, in the case of plays, of first performance. Titles of books, long poems, and other works published on their own are in italics (for example, *Bleak House*); short poems, short stories and other works not published on their own are in quotes (for example, "O Captain! My Captain!"). By consulting an author's date of birth and death and comparing these to dates of publications of other authors' works, you can discover that Thomas Hardy could have read *Gulliver's Travels* and *Robinson Crusoe* as a child.

The indexes at the back of the book will enable you to make connections between authors. For instance, from these lists you can discover at a glance that Virgil and Horace wrote in the same period, that Raymond Chandler and Jim Thompson wrote similar types of books, and that Anton Chekhov and Ivan Turgenev were both Russian writers. These links between authors will encourage you to find out about other writers and widen your knowledge of world literature.

ABE, Kobo

Japanese novelist, playwright and poet

Born Mar. 7, 1924
Died Jan. 22, 1993
Age at death 68

Kobo Abe explores the isolation and emptiness of modern life in a surrealistic style. His work, including the well-known novel *The Woman in the Dunes*, has been compared to that of the mysterious Czech author FRANZ KAFKA.

Abe was born in Tokyo but grew up in China – in the ancient city of Shenyang, Manchuria, then ruled by the Japanese. His father was a doctor.

After a brief stay in Tokyo when he was 17, Abe returned to Manchuria, where he stayed until World War II had ended. When his father died of typhoid, Abe returned to Japan. He took whatever odd jobs he could get, such as selling charcoal in the streets, so he could pay for his studies at medical school. He also started to write, and by the age of 24 Abe was a published poet and novelist. He never returned to medicine.

When he was 26, Abe won an important Japanese prize for *The Wall – The Crime of S. Karuma*. *The Woman in the Dunes*, perhaps his best-known work, was made into a prizewinning film. It is the bizarre tale of a young man who is held prisoner by a strange community that lives among the sand dunes. *Inter Ice Age 4*, published eight years later when Abe was 46, is a thriller about a computer that can predict the future. Abe also wrote many plays, including *Friends* and *The Man Who Turned into a Stick*.

Many of Abe's works explore the loss of identity and freedom and its effect on individuals. Abe was also fascinated by the isolation of modern urban living. This isolation was reflected in his own life; he never opened his post or answered his telephone.

Publications

1951	*The Wall – The Crime of S. Karuma*
1962	*The Woman in the Dunes*
1964	*The Face of Another*
1967	*The Ruined Map*
1967	*Friends*
1969	*The Man Who Turned into a Stick*
1970	*Inter Ice Age 4*
1977	*Secret Rendezvous*
1991	*Beyond the Curve*

ABRAHAMS, Peter

South African novelist and short-story writer

Born Mar. 19, 1919

Peter Abrahams is considered to be one of South Africa's best writers. Abrahams was born in a slum in Johannesburg, a large city in northeast South Africa. His father was from Ethiopia in East Africa, and his mother was officially labeled as Cape Colored – meaning that she was of mixed race. At that time, although most of South Africa's population was black, the whites controlled the government and all the major industries. Many of the rights of black people were restricted by law.

Abrahams spent part of his childhood with relatives and did not learn to read until he was 11 years old. Feeling the need to write, but unable to do so in South Africa, he left the country at age 20 aboard a ship on which he worked tending the furnace. After two years he settled in England, where he joined the staff of *The Daily Worker*, a communist newspaper. It was in England that he wrote his novel *Mine Boy*. Set in the South Africa he knew from his youth, it tells of a country boy's move to a large city and the problems he faces. This was one of the first books to explore the effects of South Africa's racist policies; it became one of the first by a black South African to earn international fame. Most of the novels that followed are set in South Africa. Abrahams's autobiography *Tell Freedom*, usually described as his best work, is the story of his early life in Johannesburg.

Since the 1950s, Abrahams has lived in Jamaica, where he worked as editor of the journal *West Indian Economist* until his decision in 1964 to write full time.

Publications

1946 Mine Boy
1948 The Path of Thunder
1950 Wild Conquest
1954 Tell Freedom
1956 A Wreath for Udomo
1965 A Night of Their Own
1966 This Island Now
1985 The View from Coyaba
1994 Lights Out
1995 The Fan

ACHEBE, Chinua

Nigerian novelist, short-story writer and poet

Born Nov. 16, 1930

Chinua Achebe is one of the greatest novelists of recent times; he is also probably Africa's most widely read writer. His novels are written in English but are all about Africans, especially his own people, the Igbo of eastern Nigeria. His books have brought African literature to the attention of the world.

Achebe was born in Ogidi, Nigeria. His father was a religious teacher and a committed Christian. As a child Achebe was introduced to English literature in missionary schools and soon became an avid reader. Although he loved the stories, he was disappointed that the characters came from a culture very different from his own. Later, he decided that he would write about characters that Africans could identify with.

Things Fall Apart was Achebe's first novel. It was published when he was 28 and was successful all over the world. Like much of his work, it is about the conflicts between African and European culture and between traditional ways of life and modern influences. He wrote three more successful novels over the next 12 years while also working for national radio, eventually becoming director of Nigeria's foreign broadcasting service.

In 1967, the Igbo of eastern Nigeria formed a separate country called Biafra. Achebe became a minister in the new government. The Biafran War followed, and Achebe's close friend, the poet CHRISTOPHER OKIGBO, was killed. After the war Achebe took up teaching positions in Nigerian and American universities. He produced poetry and short stories about the war and, in 1987, a fifth novel, *Anthills of the Savannah*.

Publications

1958 Things Fall Apart
1960 No Longer at Ease
1962 The Sacrificial Egg
1964 Arrow of God
1966 A Man of the People
1971 Christmas in Biafra
1971 Beware, Soul-Brother
1972 Girls at War
1987 Anthills of the Savannah
1988 Hopes and Impediments

ADAMS, Douglas

English fantasy writer

Born Mar. 11, 1952

Publications

1979 The Hitchhiker's Guide to the Galaxy
1980 The Restaurant at the End of the Universe
1982 Life, the Universe, and Everything
1987 Dirk Gently's Holistic Detective Agency
1988 The Long Dark Tea-Time of the Soul
1992 Mostly Harmless
1996 The Salmon of Doubt

Douglas Adams is a hugely popular author of comedy science fiction best known for his series of books beginning with *The Hitchhiker's Guide to the Galaxy*.

Adams was born in Cambridge, England. He studied at Cambridge University, where he became involved in drama productions, and after graduating he wrote radio and TV scripts for the BBC. For a while he wrote stories for the popular science fiction TV show *Doctor Who*.

The Hitchhiker's Guide to the Galaxy was originally a British radio series. Surprised by its popularity, Adams rewrote it as a novel, published when he was 27, that became popular all over the world. In this novel and the four sequels that follow, Adams recounts the incredible and extremely funny adventures of Arthur Dent, the only human being to survive the destruction of the planet Earth. Dent finds himself armed only with a towel, wandering the galaxy, which is inhabited by mad, bad, and dangerous aliens. His companions – Zaphod Beeblebrox (the two-headed former president of the galaxy), a mad computer, a depressed android and some superintelligent mice – are of little help.

Adams satirizes everything from annoying advertising campaigns to the search for immortality and knowledge; a supercomputer asked to solve the ultimate question of life, the Universe, and everything comes up with the answer "42" after several million years of calculations. In more recent novels, Adams has turned his humor to detective fiction, featuring Dirk Gently – a detective, philosopher and hat wearer.

ADAMS, Harriet Stratemeyer

American children's writer

Born Dec. 11, 1892
Died Mar. 27, 1982
Age at death 89

Harriet Stratemeyer Adams is best known as a writer of children's mystery books, including the bestselling Nancy Drew mystery series, which has inspired generations of young readers.

Adams was born in Pottersville, New Jersey. Her father, Edward Stratemeyer, was a writer and founder of a book business known as the Stratemeyer Syndicate. He created the characters for popular fiction series, including the Hardy Boys, the Bobbsey Twins, and Nancy Drew; other writers, under various pen names, then wrote the books for each of the series following his instructions.

Adams was 23 when she joined the syndicate as an editor. When her father died, the 38-year-old Adams – married and with four children – took charge of the syndicate and continued the production of her father's series. Adams provided the plots, settings and characters for each book and said how the books should be written. Of the 800 books produced by the syndicate, more than 180 were written by Adams herself, including 55 Nancy Drew books, written under the name Carolyn Keene.

Adams also modernized the series so that new generations of readers could identify with the characters. For example, she made Nancy Drew 18 (instead of the original 16) and more independent in her adventures as an amateur detective. Nancy became a feminist heroine for many readers: brave, smart and able to speak her own mind, she never relies on her boyfriend to get her out of scrapes.

Publications

More than 180 books in the following series:

Nancy Drew

The Hardy Boys

The Dana Girls

The Bobbsey Twins

Tom Swift, Jr.

Honey Bunch

ADAMS, Richard

English novelist

Born May 9, 1920

Richard Adams is best known for his novel *Watership Down*. An adventure novel, an animal story, and an exploration of the concept of community, *Watership Down* has been a favorite of both children and adults.

Born in the rural English town of Newbury and brought up in a nearby village where his father was the local doctor, Adams grew up in countryside like that featured in *Watership Down*. He studied at Oxford University, but his education was interrupted by service in the British Army during World War II. After the war, he married and worked in the civil service until his mid-50s, when he became a full-time writer.

Watership Down had its beginnings in stories Adams told his two daughters during long automobile journeys. It was originally published, when he was 52, as a children's book in a limited edition, but it soon gained a much wider audience and was published later as a book for adult readers.

Set in the English countryside with rabbits as the main characters, *Watership Down* is an adventure story that shows the rabbits as brave, loyal, and admirable creatures. Some of the rabbit characters are based on officers Adams knew in the army. The novel tells of a rabbit community's struggle to survive when property developers set out to destroy their home. It has been described as an epic about heroism and about the strength of good communities.

Adams's writing skill makes the reader believe in the animals as thinking beings in their own right rather than furry humans. More recent novels have dealt with human sexuality and have not been as popular with the critics or the public.

Publications

1972 Watership Down

1974 Shardik

1976 The Tyger Voyage

1977 The Ship's Cat

1977 The Plague Dogs

1980 The Girl in a Swing

1982 The Legend of Te Tuna

1984 Maia

1988 Traveler

1990 The Day Gone By

ADDISON, Joseph

English essayist, poet and playwright

Born May 1, 1672
Died Jun. 17, 1719
Age at death 47

Joseph Addison is best known for his essays. They had a great influence on the tastes and opinions of 18th-century middle-class English people and became a model for other writers.

Born in Wiltshire, in southern England, Addison was the son of a distinguished clergyman. He received a good education in London and at Oxford University, where he wrote Latin poetry and became a tutor. His ambition, however, was to be a politician.

At the age of 27, Addison accepted an offer to travel in Europe as training for the diplomatic service. He returned to London four years later and was commissioned to write a poem celebrating the British victory over the French at the Battle of Blenheim. The poem, called *The Campaign,* was so popular with government leaders that it secured Addison a place in parliament.

Addison became a member of parliament when he was 36, but he also found time to write. A year later he became a regular contributor to *The Tatler,* a newspaper founded by his lifelong friend Richard Steele. Addison and Steele then started another famous publication called *The Spectator,* to which Addison contributed more than 250 essays. His essays about social behavior, art, philosophy and morality were popular with the middle classes, who read them to improve their social position, sense of moral responsibility, and judgment of art. Addison's only play, a tragedy called *Cato,* was also a big success. It is full of sharp comments on the politics of the day.

At age 45, Addison became secretary of state but resigned the following year because of ill health.

Publications

1693 Account of the Greatest English Poets
1702 Dialogue on Medals
1704 The Campaign
1705 Remarks on Several Parts of Italy
1706 Rosamund
1713 Cato
1715 The Drummer

AESCHYLUS

Greek playwright

Born c. 524 BC
Died 456 BC
Age at death c. 68

Aeschylus was one of the greatest playwrights of ancient Greece. He is sometimes called the father of tragedy because he is said to have invented it as a form of theater.

Little is known about Aeschylus's life because he lived so long ago. Historians think that he was probably born at Eleusis, near Athens in Greece. He made several trips to Sicily in Italy during his lifetime, and it is thought that he died there.

Aeschylus fought in two of the most famous battles of ancient history: the Battle of Marathon in 490 BC and the Battle of Salamis in 480 BC. Both were desperate struggles in which the democratic Greek city-states defeated the armies of the powerful Persian Empire, which was trying to conquer them. Aeschylus's experience of these events can be seen in his vivid writing about war and suffering.

In Aeschylus's time, the theater was an important part of community life. Regular playwriting competitions were held, and the winners were highly regarded. Aeschylus first entered one of these competitions in 472 BC with his play *The Persians*, and he won first prize. Over the course of his career Aeschylus is thought to have written more than 80 plays, 52 of which won first prizes. Unfortunately, only seven of them have survived.

Aeschylus's plays have strong political messages. He used myths or old stories to make moral points about the events that he saw going on around him. They were so powerfully written that they are still performed today, almost 2,500 years later.

Publications

472 BC	*The Persians*
467 BC	*Seven Against Thebes*
c. 463 BC	*The Suppliants*
c. 460–456 BC	*Prometheus Bound*
458 BC	*Oresteia* – consisting of three plays: *Agamemnon, The Libation Bearers,* and *Eumenides*

AESOP

Greek writer

Born c. 620 BC
Died c. 560 BC
Age at death c. 60

According to tradition Aesop is the author of a collection of ancient Greek stories. These tales, known as *Aesop's Fables*, have been popular for thousands of years and are familiar all over the world.

It is not known whether Aesop ever actually lived or whether he is just a legendary figure. One ancient writer says that he was a slave in 6th-century BC Greece. According to this story Aesop was freed and became an adviser to a king because of his wisdom. The same source says he met his death when he was pushed over a cliff above the Greek city of Delphi.

For many years *Aesop's Fables* were handed down by word of mouth. The first time the fables were collected and written down is thought to be around 300 BC, when an Athenian politician named Demetrius of Phalerum collected about 200, which he called *Assemblies of Aesopic Tales*. Many new versions and translations of the fables followed over the years.

Aesop's Fables always have a moral and offer practical advice. Most of the characters are animals who behave like human beings; they have both the bad characteristics and the virtues of human nature. The story of the race between a hare and a tortoise is probably the most famous fable. Certain he is going to win, the hare decides to take a nap halfway through the race and continues to sleep as the tortoise plods by to win. The moral of the tale is that persistence can be more efficient than speed.

A famous version of *Aesop's Fables* was written in verse form by JEAN DE LA FONTAINE in the 17th century.

Publications

Aesop's Fables exist only in versions written by later authors. It is not known how many of the fables attributed to Aesop he actually wrote, or when he wrote them.

AGEE, James

American poet, novelist and screenwriter

Born Nov. 27, 1909
Died May 16, 1955
Age at death 45

James Agee was a leading American writer during his lifetime and became even better known after he died when his novel *A Death in the Family* was published.

Born in 1909 in Knoxville, Tennessee, Agee had a comfortable middle-class childhood, which was greatly saddened by the death of his father in an automobile accident. He was educated at church-run schools and Harvard University. After graduating, he became a film critic for the magazines *Time* and *The Nation*.

Agee's first book, a collection of poems called *Permit Me Voyage*, was published when he was 25. Later he wrote a study of the lives of poor agricultural workers known as sharecroppers who lived in Alabama during the Great Depression. His words appeared with pictures taken by the photographer Walter Evans. The book was called *Let Us Now Praise Famous Men* and earned Agee a reputation as a sensitive, passionate writer.

From 1948 until his death, Agee worked as a screenwriter in Hollywood. His best-known screenplay was for the 1951 Humphrey Bogart and Katharine Hepburn movie, *The African Queen*, which was based on a novel by the English writer C.S. FORESTER.

Agee's first novel, *The Morning Watch*, was published when he was 45. His second novel, *A Death in the Family*, was unfinished when he died, but it won the 1958 Pulitzer Prize for Fiction. Both of his novels are strongly autobiographical. They are about ordinary people living in the kinds of towns that Agee himself grew up in. Often he concentrates on describing the emotions of children who are caught up in circumstances they do not understand.

Publications

1934 Permit Me Voyage
1941 Let Us Now Praise Famous Men
1954 The Morning Watch

Published after he died

1957 A Death in the Family
1962 Letters to Father Flye

AGNON, S.Y.

Israeli novelist

Born Jul. 17, 1888
Died Feb. 17, 1970
Age at death 81

S.Y. Agnon is considered one of the greatest writers of modern Hebrew literature (Hebrew is the Jewish language). In 1966, he became the first Hebrew writer to receive the Nobel Prize for Literature.

Born in the Polish town of Buczacz, he was called Shmuel Yosef Czaczkes but adopted the pen name Agnon after his first book, the short novel *Forsaken Wives*, was published when he was 20. Both his parents were well educated, and his father earned his livelihood as a fur merchant.

Agnon moved to the ancient holy city of Jerusalem when he was 19. Then, at 25 he went to Berlin, Germany, where he worked as a teacher and researcher. There he began his studies of Jewish folklore, which features in many of his novels. He returned to Jerusalem 11 years later and settled down to write his first full-length novel, *The Bridal Canopy*. This book, published when he was 42, is the first in a series of several novels exploring Eastern European Jewish life through history and folklore. *A Guest for the Night* is an autobiographical novel about his hometown in Poland following World War I. It describes the spiritual decline that he witnessed when he revisited as a grown man. *The Day Before Yesterday* explores the problems facing a Westernized Jew who migrates to Israel and the conflicts he encounters between old and new ways of Jewish life.

Agnon wrote over 200 works of fiction, including many short stories. As he grew older, he wrote less about Europe and more about Israel.

Publications

1908 Forsaken Wives
1930 The Bridal Canopy
1931 Complete Stories
1933 In the Heart of the Seas
1939 A Guest for the Night
1945 The Day Before Yesterday
1966 Two Tales
1970 Twenty-One Stories

Published after he died

1971 Shira

AICKMAN, Robert

English horror writer

Born Jun. 27, 1914
Died Feb. 26, 1981
Age at death 66

Robert Aickman is best known as a writer of eerie and mysterious tales. Almost all of his books are collections of short stories.

Aickman was born in London. Although his family was not rich, his father was an architect and had many wealthy clients and friends. As a child Aickman often visited the huge London mansions that later became the spooky locations for many of his stories. In his autobiography Aickman describes his childhood as full of mental suffering and misery. He blames this on his lack of self-confidence.

Aickman did not begin to publish fiction until he was 37. The first book in which his stories appeared, *We Are for the Dark*, was not praised by reviewers, but Aickman found that he enjoyed writing supernatural short stories. He was soon recognized as a master of the supernatural short-story genre. Many of Aickman's stories have characters or plots that remind the reader of famous legends. An example is the story from the collection *Intrusions* called "No Time Is Passing," which has a plot similar to the legend of Rip Van Winkle.

Throughout his adult life Aickman enjoyed starting and joining societies. His interests included drama, opera, ballet, wildlife and railroads, but his greatest passion was for canals and rivers. Before he began to write fiction, he published two popular books about Britain's inland waterways. Aickman had very conventional beliefs and felt that much of modern society was in decline. He saw his attempts to conserve Britain's waterways as part of his desire to conserve the values of the past.

Publications

1951 We Are for the Dark
1964 Dark Entries
1966 Powers of Darkness
1968 Sub Rosa: Strange Tales
1975 Cold Hand in Mine
1977 Tales of Love and Death
1979 Painted Devils
1980 Intrusions

Published after he died

1985 Night Voices

AIDOO, Ama Ata

Ghanian playwright, novelist and poet

Born Mar. 23, 1942

Ama Ata Aidoo is one of Africa's best-known feminist writers. Born in Ghana, the daughter of an African chief, she had a privileged upbringing and received a European-style education at Ghanaian schools and later at the University of Ghana. Because of her family background she also learned all about African traditions. Her Western education and strong links to African culture have both influenced her writing.

Aidoo's stories often deal with the problems caused when ideas are introduced that disagree with the values of African society. One of her main themes is the problems faced by African women who try to rebel against their traditional roles. Aidoo's work also shows a great love and respect for African culture. In some of her stories she shows how traditional values like hospitality and concern for neighbors can solve people's problems.

Anowa, Aidoo's most famous play, was published when she was 28. It tells the tragic story of a strong-willed African girl living in the 19th century. Aidoo has also written short stories, poems and a novel that show her concerns about the role of women and the need to preserve African culture.

Aidoo was Professor of English at the University of Ghana between 1970 and 1982. In 1981, she was invited to become a member of the government. She served for two years as Minister of Education, but her plans to improve education for girls were considered too radical, and she had to resign. Aidoo continues to write and lecture full time.

Publications

1965 The Dilemma of a Ghost
1970 Anowa
1970 No Sweetness Here
1977 Our Sister Killjoy
1985 Someone Talking to Sometime
1986 The Eagle and the Chickens and Other Stories
1987 Birds and Other Poems
1991 Changes

AIKEN, Conrad

American poet, short-story writer and novelist

Born Aug. 5, 1889
Died Aug. 17, 1973
Age at death 84

Conrad Aiken is best known for the musical quality of his poetry.

Born in Savannah, Georgia, the young Aiken suffered the horror of finding the bodies of his parents – his father had killed his mother and then committed suicide. Aiken grew up with relatives in Massachusetts and was educated at public schools. He went on to attend Harvard University, where he made friends with the poet T.S. ELIOT.

At the age of 25 Aiken became famous with his first collection of poems, *Earth Triumphant and Other Tales in Verse.* Sixteen years later *Selected Poems* won him the 1930 Pulitzer Prize for Poetry. Like EDGAR ALLAN POE Aiken tried to make his poems resemble music, and he even described them as "symphonies." He used flowing rhythms and language that appealed to people's emotions rather than their powers of thought and intellect.

In his 30s and 40s, Aiken wrote short stories and novels. *Bring, Bring!*, his first collection of stories, explores people's thoughts and feelings. *King Coffin*, one of his successful novels, describes the experience of thinking about a murder that was never committed.

Much of Aiken's time was spent in England, and for a while he was the London correspondent for the *New Yorker* magazine, in which many of his fellow writers were published. As a critic he played an important role in introducing American poets to British readers. He also helped establish the literary reputation of poet EMILY DICKINSON.

Aiken's daughter, JOAN AIKEN, became a successful children's writer.

Publications

1914	*Earth Triumphant and Other Tales in Verse*
1920	*The House of Dust*
1925	*Bring, Bring!*
1929	*Selected Poems*
1935	*King Coffin*
1952	*Ushant*
1957	*Sheepfold Hills*
1963	*The Morning Song of Lord Zero*
1964	*A Seizure of Limericks*

AIKEN, Joan

English novelist and children's writer

Born Sep. 4, 1924

Joan Aiken has written novels for adults, stories for younger children, and many novels for older children. It is the latter for which she is best known – in particular for her series of "unhistorical" novels starting with *The Wolves of Willoughby Chase*.

Aiken was born in Rye in the south of England. Her father was the famous American poet CONRAD AIKEN. By the age of five, the young Aiken was writing poems and stories. She married when she was 21, but 10 years later her husband died, leaving Aiken with two children to provide for. She took a job as an editor on a literary magazine and revived a childhood dream to be a writer.

Aiken's first novel, *The Kingdom and the Cave*, came out when she was 36. The success of *The Wolves of Willoughby Chase*, which came out two years later, allowed Aiken to concentrate on writing full time. This was the first of a series of "unhistorical" books set in a period of 19th-century England that never really happened. In *The Wolves of Willoughby Chase* England is being terrorized by wolves that have entered the country through the Channel Tunnel. Aiken's boundless imagination has created a whole era for her adventurous stories. Although meant for children, they are equally enjoyed by adults.

Aiken has since written mystery stories, thrillers, romances and comedies, and all have been successful. Her shorter stories for younger children often feature fantastic animals that can talk or are superintelligent.

Publications

1960	*The Kingdom and the Cave*
1962	*The Wolves of Willoughby Chase*
1969	*Night Fall*
1972	*Arabel's Raven*
1972	*A Cluster of Separate Sparks*
1981	*The Stolen Lake*
1987	*If I Were You*
1994	*Eliza's Daughter*

AKHMATOVA, Anna

Russian poet

Born Jun. 23, 1888
Died Mar. 5, 1966
Age at death 77

Anna Akhmatova is one of the most important Russian poets of the 20th century.

Born in Odessa, Russia, Akhmatova was educated in Kiev. In 1910, while living in St. Petersburg, she married the poet Nikolai Gumilev. They became leading figures in a new literary movement called Acmeism, which encouraged art for art's sake. Between 1912 and 1921 Akhmatova published five very successful collections of poetry.

The Russian Revolution of 1917, which brought the communists to power, had a dramatic effect on Akhmatova's life. The new government became less and less tolerant of artistic expression as it tried to control every aspect of Russian society. Akhmatova was not allowed to publish anything between 1923 and 1940, and her poetry was criticized for being unpatriotic. Her marriage to Gumilev ended in 1918, and he was later shot as a traitor. In 1934 her only son, Lev, was arrested and sent into exile by Joseph Stalin. This inspired her to write the poem *Requiem*, which remained banned in the Soviet Union until long after her death.

During World War II Akhmatova lived in Tashkent in the far east of the Soviet Union. During this period she began work on a long poem about her life in Russia called *Poem Without a Hero*. She also published patriotic poems in official magazines. After the war she was again criticized by the government, and her poems were officially banned until the mid-1950s. Since the collapse of the Soviet Union in 1991, her poetry has been freely available.

Publications

1912	*Evening*
1914	*The Rosary*
1917	*The White Flock*
1918	*Ecstasy Collection*
1921	*Plantain*
1922	*Anno Domini MCMXXI*
1940	*From Six Books*
1960	*Poem Without a Hero*
1964	*Requiem*

AKINS, Zoë

American poet, playwright and screenwriter

Born Oct. 30, 1886
Died Oct. 29, 1958
Age at death 71

Zoë Akins was a popular American author who wrote simple, romantic plays full of glamour, humor, and the good things of life. Many of her plays were made into movies in the 1930s.

Akins was born in Humansville, Missouri. Her parents were wealthy, and they often took the young Akins to the theater. She fell in love with the stage at an early age, and when she was 12, wrote her first play. She published her first volume of poetry, *Interpretations*, at 26. However, it is for her playwriting and screenplays that Akins is remembered.

Papa was Akins's first performed play. It appeared at many theaters around the United States, but it only lasted 12 shows in New York in 1919. Her next play *The Magical City* did slightly better.

Akins finally received praise and fame with *Déclassée* ("Loss of Class"). Set among English high society, the play is about a wealthy woman's love affair with a man who has committed the sin of cheating at cards. The height of Akins's career came with the production of her play *The Old Maid*, which won the Pulitzer Prize in 1935.

By the 1920s, film companies began to buy the screen rights to Akins's plays. In 1928, Akins moved to California for health reasons, and within a couple of years she was writing films for Paramount. She lived in a mansion in Pasadena, attended by servants. Working for MGM in 1936, Akins adapted for the screen the French novel *Camille* by Alexandre Dumas (the younger). This tragic love story starring Greta Garbo and Robert Taylor was a great success. *Desire Me*, her last screenplay, was not so well received.

Publications

1912	*Interpretations*
1915	*The Magical City*
1919	*Papa*
1919	*Déclassée*
1921	*Daddy's Gone A-Hunting*
1928	*The Furies*
1930	*The Greeks Had a Word for It*
1931	*Women Love Once*
1935	*The Old Maid*

AKSENOV, Vasily

Russian novelist and short-story writer

Born Aug. 20, 1932

Vasily Aksenov is known as one of the foremost Russian novelists writing in the period following World War II.

Aksenov was born in Kazan, a town on the banks of the Volga River, in Russia. His parents had a terrible time under the dictator Stalin. Both were political prisoners for many years in concentration camps. His mother wrote a book about her husband's murder.

Aksenov was raised in a state-run orphanage. He worked hard, and at the age of 24 he qualified as a doctor. After the death of Stalin in 1953 there was greater freedom in Russia, and Aksenov turned to writing. In the late 1950s and early '60s he wrote short stories and three early novels. Although not political, these novels – especially *A Ticket to the Stars* – feature young rebels and social misfits. Their language is full of slang and jargon. They reveal the longing felt by young people for the kind of life that was then being enjoyed in America, and they made Aksenov a popular figure among Russian youth.

As his writing matured, Aksenov became more serious and more critical of the Russian government. By the late 1970s, much of his work remained unpublished because the authorities considered it dangerous. Aksenov and other writers then tried to publish a magazine without allowing government officials to cut out parts they didn't like. As a result, he had to leave the country. It was ten years before he was allowed to return. During that time Aksenov lived in the US. His book *In Search of Melancholy Baby* is a satirical look at American life and the author's own "Americanization."

Publications

1961	*Colleagues*
1961	*A Ticket to the Stars*
1963	*Oranges from Morocco*
1965	*It's Time, My Friend, It's Time*
1980	*The Burn*
1981	*The Island of Crimea*
1987	*In Search of Melancholy Baby*
1989	*Say Cheese!*
1994	*Generations of Winter*
1996	*The Winter's Hero*

ALBEE, Edward

American playwright

Born Mar. 12, 1928

Edward Albee is best known for his association with the theater of the absurd, a drama movement of the 1950s and early 1960s. Born in Washington, D.C., Albee was abandoned by his parents and adopted as a baby by a wealthy couple who owned a theater chain. Albee was an unhappy child despite his lavish home, servants and private tutors. At school he spent much of his time writing stories and poetry. After graduating at the age of 18, he attended Trinity College in Hartford, Connecticut, for one year.

Albee left home at the age of 20, and settled in Greenwich Village, New York City. He had various jobs and began to meet other authors, including W.H. AUDEN and THORNTON WILDER. It was Wilder who suggested that Albee should begin to write plays.

Albee wrote his first play, *The Zoo Story*, when he was 30. It took him just three weeks. Although the play failed to attract interest in New York, Albee's roommate sent it to a friend in Europe, where it had its premiere in 1959.

Who's Afraid of Virginia Woolf?, produced when Albee was 34, was his first full-length, three-act play and his greatest success. It won him international fame and several awards. Like many of Albee's plays, *Who's Afraid of Virginia Woolf?* concentrates on family relationships, but the characters and situations are more lifelike than in some of his earlier plays. The story centers on the complex relationship between a history professor and his wife.

Albee has won three Pulitzer Prizes – for *A Delicate Balance* in 1967, *Seascape* in 1975, and *Three Tall Women* in 1994.

Publications

1959 The Zoo Story
1960 The American Dream
1960 The Death of Bessie Smith
1962 Who's Afraid of Virginia Woolf?
1964 Tiny Alice
1966 A Delicate Balance
1968 Box-Mao-Box
1975 Seascape
1994 Three Tall Women

ALCOTT, Louisa May

American children's writer

Born Nov. 29, 1832
Died Mar. 6, 1888
Age at death 55

Louisa May Alcott is best known today as a children's author and especially for her novel *Little Women*.

Born in Germantown, Pennsylvania, Alcott suffered poverty and insecurity in her childhood. When she was only two years old, her father, Bronson Alcott, moved the family to Boston, where he ran a school. The school failed, and they moved again, this time to Concord, Massachusetts.

Alcott was taught mainly by her father, but she also learned a great deal from her neighbors, who included the writers RALPH WALDO EMERSON and HENRY DAVID THOREAU. Alcott's family had very little money, and she had to go to work. She decided that she would try to support her family by writing.

Alcott's first book, a collection of fairytales called *Flower Fables*, was written when she was just 16; it was published six years later in 1854. When Alcott was 30, she served as a nurse during the American Civil War. Her next book, *Hospital Sketches*, is about this experience.

Little Women, published when Alcott was 36, became her most popular work. Along with its sequel, *Good Wives*, *Little Women* tells the story of the March family. The book is a picture of family life, full of humor and loving relationships. It is based on Alcott's own home life. The main character, Jo March, is a self-portrait, and Jo's three sisters are based on Alcott's own beloved sisters.

Alcott felt strongly that women should have voting rights, and she became involved in movements that demanded changes in society. Her strong beliefs sometimes carry through into her writing.

Publications

1854 Flower Fables
1863 Hospital Sketches
1864 Moods
1868 Little Women
1869 Good Wives
1870 An Old-Fashioned Girl
1871 Little Men
1875 Eight Cousins
1886 Jo's Boys
1888 A Garland for Girls

Published after she died

1998 The Inheritance

ALDISS, Brian

English science fiction writer

Born Aug. 18, 1925

Brian Aldiss is one of Britain's foremost science fiction writers.

Aldiss was born in a small town in eastern England. His parents were shopkeepers. During World War II, Aldiss was drafted into the army, and after his discharge he worked in a bookstore. The job enabled him to catch up on his education, and he also began to write fiction. When he was 29, his first story, "Criminal Record," appeared in *Science Fantasy* magazine.

At age 30 Aldiss published his first novel. Three years later he published *Starship* (originally called *Non-Stop*), which tells the story of a people who have forgotten their origins and find that their world consists of a starship traveling through space. The novel attracted attention, but four years later he established his reputation with *Hothouse*, about the dying of the Earth as the Sun grows hotter. (This was many years before the idea of global warming had become common.)

Aldiss's stories and novels challenge accepted ideas about science fiction. His plots are often strange, and he relies more on imagination than on scientific explanation. He became part of the "New Wave" of British science fiction writers, including Michael Moorcock and J.G. Ballard, who experimented with new ideas and published their work in the magazine *New Worlds* from the 1960s onward.

In the 1980s Aldiss published his *Helliconia* series, an epic work that describes an imaginary alien world in great detail. In the US, he is best known for his history of science fiction writing, *Billion Year Spree*.

Publications

1955 The Brightfount Diaries
1958 Starship
1962 Hothouse
1964 Greybeard
1964 Report on Probability A
1969 Barefoot in the Head
1973 Billion Year Spree
1973 Frankenstein Unbound
1982 Helliconia Spring
1994 Somewhere East of Life
1998 Twinkling of an Eye

ALEGRÍA, Claribel

Nicaraguan-born Salvadoran writer

Born May 12, 1924

Claribel Alegría is known for her poems, novels and essays that describe the effects of political upheavals on the lives of the peoples of Nicaragua and El Salvador.

Although born in Esteli, Nicaragua, Alegría spent much of her childhood in neighboring El Salvador, where her family was forced to flee after her father supported a rebel leader who opposed the Nicaraguan government. She attended a convent school before going to the United States at age 19. At 24, she published her first volume of poetry.

The effects of political unrest in Central America during the 20th century feature strongly in Alegría's work. Her poetry, in blank verse, describes the violent and brutal treatment of ordinary men, women and children. Her first novel, *Ashes of Izalco*, depicts the massacre of thousands of peasants by government troops in 1932, an event that took place when Alegría was only eight years old. This book was condemned and publicly burned by the authorities in El Salvador. Alegría is now also famous for her "testimonial writing," which records the experiences of revolutionaries and political prisoners. Her novel *They Won't Take Me Alive* is based on these records.

Alegría has lived in several countries during her life but returned to Nicaragua in 1979 after the victory of the Sandinistas – the rebels who overthrew the country's repressive government. Besides her poetry and prose writing, she has translated works by other writers, including ROBERT GRAVES and SALMAN RUSHDIE.

Publications

1966 Ashes of Izalco
1978 I Survive
1982 Flowers from the Volcano
1983 They Won't Take Me Alive
1987 Luisa in Realityland
1989 Woman of the River
1989 Lovers and Comrades
1990 Family Album
1992 Fugues

ALGER, Horatio

American children's writer

Born Jan. 13, 1832
Died Jul. 18, 1899
Age at death 67

Horatio Alger was an extremely popular American children's author of the late 19th century.

Alger was born in Revere, Massachusetts. His father was a strict minister who taught his son prayer, hard work and discipline. Alger graduated from Harvard University in 1852. After five years as a schoolteacher and journalist, he returned to Harvard to become a minister like his father.

At age 28, before taking up his first post as a minister, Alger toured Europe. He returned to find America on the brink of the Civil War. Alger tried to enlist in the Union Army on the side of the anti-slavery north but was refused because of his asthma. While working as his father's assistant, he wrote his first book, *Marie Bertrand: The*

Felon's Daughter, an adult novel about life in the Paris slums.

In 1866, Alger moved to New York and became chaplain at the Newsboys' Lodging House, a home for orphans and other homeless boys. While there he wrote his first book for children. *Ragged Dick* was published when he was 35. It tells the story of a poor young boy who achieves wealth and fame through honesty, hard work and good luck. The book was an immediate success.

Over the next 30 years, Alger wrote more than 100 books on similar themes. They were so popular that people still say "It's a Horatio Alger story" when they hear about somebody who has risen from childhood poverty to wealth and fame. His books had a great influence on the way Americans thought for a long time after his death.

Publications

1864 Marie Bertrand: The Felon's Daughter
1864 Frank's Campaign
1867 Ragged Dick
1869 Luck and Pluck
1871 Tattered Tom
1879 The Young Miner
1881 From Canal Boy to President

ALGREN, Nelson

American novelist and journalist

Born Mar. 28, 1909
Died May 9, 1981
Age at death 72

Nelson Algren is best known for his stories about people in the Chicago slums. Algren was born in Detroit, the son of Jewish immigrants. He grew up in a poor area of Chicago and went to the University of Illinois, which he left in 1931 with a degree in journalism.

Algren then traveled all over America, hitching rides on the railroads and working as a salesman. His first short story, "So Help Me," was written when he found himself stranded one day outside an abandoned gas station in Texas. Later, Algren worked for the Chicago Board of Health and during World War II served in the army's medical corps.

Algren's first important novel, *Never Come Morning*, was published when he was 33. It is set in the Polish area of downtown Chicago and describes the hard lives of the people who live there. Algren used this kind of neighborhood as the background to many of his novels. He tried to make his stories give a picture of real life. Among the characters in his novels are drug addicts, gamblers and criminals. Many readers disliked Algren's work because of this, but he was admired by other writers, such as ERNEST HEMINGWAY, who also tried to make their work reflect real life.

Algren wrote little after *A Walk on the Wild Side*, published when he was 47, and he became a university lecturer. Two of his books, *The Man with the Golden Arm*, which won the first National Book Award in 1949, and *A Walk on the Wild Side*, were made into successful movies.

Publications

1935 Somebody in Boots
1942 Never Come Morning
1947 The Neon Wilderness
1949 The Man with the Golden Arm
1951 Chicago: City on the Make
1956 A Walk on the Wild Side
1963 Who Lost an American?
1973 The Last Carousel

ALLEN, Paula Gunn

American poet, novelist and critic

Born 1939

Poet and novelist Paula Gunn Allen explores the rich heritage of Native American traditions in her work, and she combines her interest in spirituality with her commitment to political action.

Allen was born in Cubero, an ethnically mixed town in New Mexico. Her father was Lebanese American, and her mother was Native American, with both Laguna and Sioux ancestry. Allen became interested in other Native American groups, particularly Pueblo, which she views as a woman-centered culture. She also loved the work of women poets, in particular DENISE LEVERTOV and AUDRE LORDE, and as a young, aspiring writer she read and was greatly impressed by GERTRUDE STEIN. Allen left New Mexico to study at the University of Oregon, where she received her undergraduate degree in 1966 and a Master's degree in 1968. She later received a Ph.D. from the University of New Mexico.

At age 35, Allen published her first collection of poems, *The Blind Lion*. She went on to publish several more volumes of poetry over the next 15 years, and when she was 44, her first novel appeared. *The Woman Who Owned the Shadows* features a woman of mixed heritage who has a mental breakdown and heals herself by embracing the traditions and rituals of her Native American ancestry. Allen's work examines "tribal" ties of all kinds, not just Native American but those of other cultures also.

Allen is a highly respected critic and is currently a professor of Native American Studies at the University of California at Berkeley.

Publications

1974 The Blind Lion
1978 Coyote's Daylight Trip
1981 Starchild
1981 A Cannon Between My Knees
1982 Shadow Country
1983 The Woman Who Owned the Shadows
1986 The Sacred Hoop
1994 Women in American Indian Mythology

ALLENDE, Isabel

Chilean novelist

Born Aug. 2, 1942

Isabel Allende is a prominent South American novelist.

Born in Lima, Peru, Allende was the daughter of a diplomat who worked for the Chilean government. When she was three, her parents divorced, and she went back to Chile with her mother. Much of her childhood was spent happily in her mother's parents' house in Santiago.

Allende attended public schools in Chile and traveled widely in Europe and the Middle East after her mother married another diplomat. In her 20s, she worked as a television news reporter and documentary filmmaker. She married at age 21, and has a son and a daughter. Throughout this period she wrote short plays and contributed regularly to feminist magazines.

In 1970, Allende's uncle, Salvador Allende, was elected president of Chile. His socialist policies – which, among other things, discouraged personal wealth – were unpopular, and in 1973 he was killed in a military coup. The harsh dictatorship that followed imprisoned many intellectuals and artists; Allende and her family fled to Venezuela.

After ten years in exile, Allende began to write her first novel, *The House of the Spirits*. It was published when she was 40, and was a great success. Inspired by her own life and the political unrest in Chile, the novel combines harsh realism, surrealist fantasy, and politics. It is written in a style known as magic realism, also used by South American novelist GABRIEL GARCÍA MÁRQUEZ. Her criticism of the Chilean government made it impossible for her to return home for many years.

Publications

1982 The House of the Spirits
1984 Of Love and Shadows
1987 Eva Luna
1989 The Stories of Eva Luna
1993 The Infinite Plan
1995 Paula
1998 Aphrodite
1998 Enduring Spirit

ALLINGHAM, Margery

English crime writer

Born May 20, 1904
Died Jun. 30, 1966
Age at death 62

Margery Allingham, along with AGATHA CHRISTIE and DOROTHY L. SAYERS, is one of the greatest writers of the "whodunit" – a mystery story in which the reader has to figure out from clues which character in the story committed the crime.

Allingham was born in London, the daughter of a writer. She began writing at age 16 and published her first novel, *Blackerchief Dick*, when she was just 17. Most of her books are set in and around London, and she wrote vividly of the city and its people. The hero of her early stories is Albert Campion, a detective modeled on such classic mystery story heroes as Sherlock Holmes and the Scarlet Pimpernel. Like these heroes, Campion is a romantic, glamorous figure who works as a detective for the fun of it rather than to earn a living.

During World War II, Allingham was involved in war work in London. She became familiar with areas of the city where there was a great deal of poverty, and as a result of this experience her perspective as a writer changed. Instead of enjoyable mystery stories, she began to write more serious novels that deal with the reality of death and cruelty in the world of crime. In keeping with this darker vision, the role of Albert Campion becomes less important in her later stories. He is on the scene more as an observer than as an amusing character in his own right.

Allingham's most famous novel, *The Tiger in the Smoke*, was filmed in 1956 and is still regarded as a classic work of crime fiction today.

Publications

1929 The Black Dudley Murder
1931 The Gyrth Chalice Mystery
1934 Death of a Ghost
1936 Flowers for the Judge
1937 The Case of the Late Pig
1941 Traitor's Purse
1945 Pearls Before Swine
1952 The Tiger in the Smoke
1958 Hide My Eyes
1965 The Mind Readers

ALVARO, Corrado

Italian novelist and journalist

Born Apr. 15, 1895
Died Jun. 11, 1956
Age at death 61

Corrado Alvaro is noted for the courage with which his writings criticized the fascist regime of the Italian dictator Benito Mussolini. This was a dangerous activity, since critics of the government could end up in prison or suffer a worse fate.

Alvaro was born in the town of Reggio, Calabria, in the extreme south of Italy, and worked as a journalist. For a time he was editor of the important Italian newspaper *Il Mondo*. He was a well-educated and sophisticated man who had a strong attachment to his homeland, Calabria.

Alvaro's best-known novels are *Revolt in Aspromonte, The Masters of the Flood* and *The Strong Man*. The last two are set in Soviet Russia rather than in Italy. They were not banned in Italy because the fascist censors thought the books were a criticism of Soviet communism. In fact, Alvaro was attacking all dictatorships. *The Strong Man* is about a young man who returns to his country to find everyone living in fear of a cruel dictator. Critics generally regard *Revolt in Aspromonte* as Alvaro's finest work. It illustrates the hard life of the peasants in Calabria and the contrasts between town and country life.

Alvaro's work is in the realist tradition of writers such as HONORÉ DE BALZAC and ÉMILE ZOLA in France. Alvaro's aim was to present life as it really is lived by ordinary people, using direct, simple language, realistic dialogue and clear descriptions. Alvaro is also known for his published diary, *Almost a Life*, which reveals his ethical and literary concerns.

Publications

1922 Man in the Labyrinth
1930 Revolt in Aspromonte
1934 The Strong Man
1935 The Masters of the Flood
1951 Almost a Life

AMBLER, Eric

English thriller writer

Born Jun. 28, 1909
Died Oct. 22, 1998
Age at death 89

Eric Ambler was one of the first writers to make the hero of his books a spy and to set his stories against the backdrop of politics and current affairs.

Born and educated in London, Ambler studied engineering before going to work in advertising. He began by writing plays but then turned to writing thrillers. At that time a British writer called Sapper was producing popular adventure stories about a character called Bulldog Drummond. The stories were badly written, full of old ideas and prejudiced views about other cultures. Ambler set out to write a better class of adventure story and published his first, *The Dark Frontier*, when he was 27.

With his first six novels, written between the ages of 27 and 31,

Ambler established his reputation as a great thriller writer. Although his novels have exciting adventure plots, they are also about serious political subjects. Novels like *A Coffin for Dimitrios* are set in Europe and generally involve ordinary Englishmen caught up in the rise of the fascist movement just before World War II.

During World War II, Ambler worked for the British Army's film-making unit. After the war, he became a scriptwriter and continued to write novels that involve current political events. *Judgment on Deltchev*, for example, is set against the background of the beginnings of the Cold War. These stories set the scene for spy novelists like John Le Carré and Len Deighton. *The Light of Day*, a comedy thriller, was later made into a film. Ambler's work helped show that popular literature can be considered art.

Publications

1936	*The Dark Frontier*
1938	*Cause for Alarm*
1939	*A Coffin for Dimitrios*
1940	*Journey into Fear*
1951	*Judgment on Deltchev*
1962	*The Light of Day*
1964	*A Kind of Anger*
1969	*The Intercom Conspiracy*
1972	*The Levanter*
1977	*Send No More Roses*

AMICHAI, Yehuda

German-born Israeli poet, playwright and novelist

Born May 3, 1924

Yehuda Amichai is best known as an Israeli poet, but he has also written short stories, novels and plays, all in Hebrew (the Jewish language).

Born in Würzburg, Germany, Amichai was 12 when his family – which was Jewish – decided to emigrate after the Nazis came to power. The family settled in Jerusalem. Amichai served with the British Army during World War II and later served in the infantry of the Israeli Army during the War of Independence. After his military service, he earned his living by teaching the Bible and Hebrew literature in secondary schools in Jerusalem, where he still lives with his wife and son.

Amichai's first collection of poems, *Now and in Other Days*, was published when he was 31. The poems from this and other collections are recognized for introducing modern terms from technology, law and war into the ancient Hebrew language. *Not of This Time, Not of This Place*, Amichai's first novel, came out when he was 39. It is about a young German Jew living in Israel after World War II and struggling to come to terms with the idea that humanity is capable of an act as terrible as the Holocaust – the German genocide of European Jews. His second novel, *O That I Had a Lodging*, is about an Israeli poet in New York, and was published while Amichai was the visiting poet at an American college. Much of Amichai's fiction writing is autobiographical and explores the contrasts between the past – including the hopes and dreams of his childhood – and the less hopeful present.

Publications

1955	*Now and in Other Days*
1963	*Not of This Time, Not of This Place*
1966	*Bells and Trains*
1971	*O That I Had a Lodging*
1973	*Poems of Jerusalem*
1984	*The World Is a Room*
1986	*Travels*
1991	*Even a Fist Was Once an Open Palm with Fingers: Recent Poems*

AMIS, Kingsley

English novelist and poet

Born Apr. 16, 1922
Died Oct. 22, 1995
Age at death 73

Publications

1954 Lucky Jim
1955 That Uncertain Feeling
1958 I Like It Here
1966 The Anti-Death League
1969 The Green Man
1973 The Riverside Villas Murder
1979 Collected Poems 1944–1979
1984 Stanley and the Women
1986 The Old Devils
1991 Memoirs

Kingsley Amis was among the group of British writers known as Angry Young Men. The group – which included JOHN OSBORNE and ALAN SILLITOE, among others – emerged in the 1950s and shocked readers with their rage and rejection of middle-class values. Amis is best known for his witty novels satirizing the class system.

Born on the outskirts of London, Amis won a scholarship to study English at Oxford University when he was 19. He served as an officer during World War II, then at 25 he completed his English degree. That year he became a college teacher in Wales and published his first book of poetry, *Bright November*.

Amis continued to teach and to publish poetry for several years, while also working on what was to become his first and most famous novel, *Lucky Jim*. Published when Amis was 32, *Lucky Jim* is a funny story about a young man from a lower-middle-class background who becomes a college teacher and grows to hate what he sees as the cultural and class snobbery of the academic world. The novel was a huge success, striking a chord among readers who felt angry about society's pressure on people to move up through the social classes – to "better themselves." In addition to his novels satirizing British social values, Amis wrote a ghost story, *The Green Man*; a detective novel, *The Riverside Villas Murder*; and spy novels. He was also a gifted poet and was lifelong friends with the famous poet PHILIP LARKIN.

Amis was awarded a knighthood in 1990, making him Sir Kingsley Amis. His son, MARTIN AMIS, is also a respected novelist.

AMIS, Martin

English novelist, literary critic and short-story writer

Born Aug. 25, 1949

Martin Amis is widely considered to be one of Britain's leading writers of the late 20th century. He burst onto the literary scene at the age of 24 with the publication of his first novel, *The Rachel Papers*. It caused a stir in Britain for its frank and detailed but hilarious analysis of a self-absorbed teenager's sex life. Amis was instantly recognized as a young writer of great promise, and he launched his career as a modern-day satirist who mocks the nastier side of life.

Amis was born in Oxford, England. His father was the famous novelist KINGSLEY AMIS. Amis's family moved around a lot while he was growing up, so in all he attended 13 different schools in various countries, including England, Spain and the US. He graduated from Oxford University in 1971 with a top-class degree in English literature. He then moved to London and worked as a journalist for most of the 1970s. He reviewed books before becoming an editor for the *Times Literary Supplement* in 1972, and then for the *New Statesman* from 1975 to 1979. Since 1980 he has concentrated on writing books full time but also writes articles for newspapers.

Since *The Rachel Papers,* Amis has written many other darkly comic and satirical novels. Some, such as *Dark Secrets* (at first called *Dead Babies*), have shocked many with their extreme portrayals of bizarre sex and violence. Amis has also been criticized for being antiwomen, but he claims that he is simply mocking the men who are. Amis's unique style and command of English have impressed many, while others find his work difficult to follow. All this has made Amis one of the most talked about of British authors.

Publications

1973	*The Rachel Papers*
1975	*Dark Secrets*
1978	*Success*
1981	*Other People: A Mystery Story*
1984	*Money: A Suicide Note*
1986	*The Moronic Inferno*
1987	*Einstein's Monsters*
1989	*London Fields*
1991	*Time's Arrow*
1995	*The Information*
1997	*Night Train*

ANDERSEN, Hans Christian

Danish writer

Born Apr. 2, 1805
Died Aug. 4, 1875
Age at death 70

The 19th-century Danish writer Hans Christian Andersen is known for his fairy tales, which are among the most widely read works in literature.

Andersen was born in Odense, Denmark, into a poor family and attended the city's school for poor children. When he was 14, he left Odense, hoping to earn a living as an actor or singer in the capital city, Copenhagen. After three hard years of minor acting roles and barely enough to eat, Andersen became friendly with a theater director who raised money for him to continue his education.

At the age of 23, Andersen went to the University of Copenhagen and a year later produced his first important work, *A Walk from Holmen's Canal to the East Point of the Island of Amager*. This fantastic tale about a journey was an instant success.

Andersen wrote 168 fairy tales between 1835 and 1872. The first few were published in *Tales Told for Children* when he was 30. Stories such as "The Princess and the Pea," "The Ugly Duckling," "The Emperor's New Clothes," and "The Snow Queen" won him worldwide fame. Some of his tales are based on Danish folklore, and some are based on his own unhappy experiences at school and later. Many have a serious moral message. His use of dialogue in the stories makes them very direct and enjoyable to read. CHARLES DICKENS admired them greatly.

Andersen fell deeply in love three times but never married. He traveled throughout Europe and wrote plays, novels and travel books about his experiences.

Publications

1829	*A Walk from Holmen's Canal to the East Point of the Island of Amager*
1830	*Poems*
1835	*The Improvisatore*
1835	*Tales Told for Children*
1835	*72 Fairy Tales*
1836	*O.T.*
1847	*The True Story of My Life*
1851	*In Sweden*
1854	*The Fairy Tale of My Life*

ANDERSON, Maxwell

American playwright and poet

Born Dec. 15, 1888
Died Feb. 28, 1959
Age at death 70

Maxwell Anderson was a writer of serious drama who tried to make a place in American theater for tragic plays written in verse.

He was born in Atlantic, Pennsylvania. After studying at the University of North Dakota and at Stanford, he became a schoolteacher and a journalist.

With another writer, Laurence Stallings, Anderson wrote a comedy called *What Price Glory?*, which gives a realistic picture of life as a soldier. When he was 36, this play was produced in New York City, and its success made him famous. Three years later *Saturday's Children*, which he wrote on his own, was also highly praised. Anderson went on to write many more plays, including some with music. He also published essays on theater and helped found the Playwrights' Company, which presented many notable plays.

Most of his later plays were written in verse. Several are about historical personalities such as Queen Elizabeth I of England and Joan of Arc. One of his prose plays, *Both Your Houses*, is a satire on corruption in the United States Congress. It won a Pulitzer Prize in 1933.

Winterset, Anderson's most powerful play, was also inspired by contemporary events – in this case the execution for murder of two Italian immigrants called Sacco and Vanzetti. They were both anarchists, and many people thought that their political views and the fact that they were immigrants had prejudiced the court against them. The play is fictional, but everyone saw the similarities with the real-life case.

Publications

1924	*What Price Glory?*
1927	*Saturday's Children*
1930	*Elizabeth the Queen*
1933	*Mary of Scotland*
1933	*Both Your Houses*
1935	*Winterset*
1938	*Knickerbocker Holiday*
1939	*Key Largo*
1947	*Joan of Lorraine*
1954	*The Bad Seed*

ANDERSON, Poul

American science fiction writer

Born Nov. 25, 1926

Poul Anderson is one of the most versatile and skilled writers of American science fiction. He has written more than 70 books.

Born in Bristol, Pennsylvania, Anderson lived briefly in Denmark as a child and was fascinated by Scandinavian sagas about the brave deeds of ancient warriors. He graduated with a physics degree from the University of Minnesota. His knowledge of science and of folklore later inspired his science fiction writing.

Anderson's first published story, "Tomorrow's Children," appeared when he was 21. His career as a writer was slow at first, but when he was 28, his novel *Brain Wave* appeared, immediately establishing his reputation. In the story, the Earth moves out of range of a cloud that has inhibited the intelligence of its living beings. Animals develop human intelligence, and human beings are able to think in a superhuman way. Anderson describes the effects of such a change down to the last detail and raises the question of how much intelligence is ideal for human society.

Anderson then wrote a "future history" series of novels – the *Technic Civilization* series – in which he describes how human beings of the future establish a huge empire across the Universe. Two central characters emerge from this world, Nicholas van Rijn and Dominic Flandry. They are both traditional American heroes – brave, independent and self-reliant. Since then, Anderson has written a huge variety of science fiction. The common theme in his work is a faith in the human spirit and awe in the face of the Universe.

Publications

1954 Brain Wave
1956 Star Ways
1958 War of the Wing-Men
1959 The War of Two Worlds
1970 Tau Zero
1973 The Queen of Air and Darkness
1978 The Avatar
1989 The Boat of a Million Years
1993 Harvest of Stars
1996 All One Universe

ANDERSON, Sherwood

American novelist, short-story writer, and journalist

Born Sep. 13, 1876
Died Mar. 8, 1941
Age at death 64

Sherwood Anderson is best known for his short stories and novels about small-town life in America's Midwest. He was born and grew up in Camden, Ohio, just the kind of small town that he later wrote about.

Anderson was the third of seven children. His father worked as a harness maker, and the family was very poor. Anderson had to leave school when he was 14 to find work. He did all kinds of jobs and, aged 22, served in the army during the Spanish-American War. After the war he worked in an advertising agency and then became the manager of a small factory in Elyria, Ohio.

Anderson began to write fiction when he was in his early 30s. However, the strain of writing and working to support his family became too great, and when he was 36, Anderson suffered a mental breakdown. He recovered, but abandoned his family and his life in Ohio, and went to live in Chicago. There he met other writers like THEODORE DREISER and CARL SANDBURG, who encouraged him to continue with his novels.

Anderson's first important work and the one that is still considered to be his best is *Winesburg, Ohio*, published when Anderson was 43. It is a sequence of 14 interrelated short stories about the dreams, passions and sorrows of people living in Winesburg, an imaginary small town in the Midwest. The book made Anderson famous. His next two novels, *Poor White* and *The Triumph of the Egg*, are both on the same theme but were less successful. The best of Anderson's later work is his short stories, especially the collection *Horses and Men*.

Publications

1916 Windy McPherson's Son
1917 Marching Men
1919 Winesburg, Ohio
1920 Poor White
1921 The Triumph of the Egg
1923 Horses and Men
1924 A Story Teller's Story
1925 Dark Laughter
1927 Tar
1935 Puzzled America

ANDREWS, Virginia

American novelist

Born Jun. 6, 1933
Died Dec. 19, 1986
Age at death 53

Virginia Andrews became one of America's fastest selling authors with the publication of her seven modern-day gothic tales. These gloomy and sinister books have not received much critical attention but have been hugely popular with readers, in particular with young women. Andrews's books have now sold over 30 million copies, and most have become bestsellers.

Andrews was born in Portsmouth, Virginia. She spent most of her life on crutches or in a wheelchair after being crippled at an early age by medical neglect. Nevertheless, she managed to finish secondary school and complete a four-year art course. After this, Andrews worked as a reasonably successful portrait painter, commercial artist and fashion illustrator.

Andrews had been writing for years before *Flowers in the Attic* – her first and probably most famous published novel – came out when she was 46. Before this many of her books had been rejected by publishers. One was considered promising, however, but too long, so she pared it down to produce an early version of *Flowers in the Attic.* Readers suggested Andrews give full rein to her imagination, and she rewrote it to include all the "unsavory" elements such as child abuse, rape and incest that were originally left out. Four children, the Dollangangers, are kept hidden in an attic by their mother and abused by their grandmother. They gradually unravel the blighted story of their lives and look to each other for love and affection. Their story is continued in *Petals on the Wind* and *If There Be Thorns*.

Publications

1979 Flowers in the Attic
1980 Petals on the Wind
1981 If There Be Thorns
1982 My Sweet Audrina
1984 Seeds of Yesterday
1985 Heaven
1986 Dark Angel

ANDRIC, Ivo

Bosnian novelist, short-story writer and poet

Born Oct. 10, 1892
Died Mar. 13, 1975
Age at death 82

Ivo Andric is famous for his trilogy of powerfully written tales about his native Bosnia. He was awarded the Nobel Prize for Literature in 1961.

Andric was born to Bosnian Serb parents near Travnik in Bosnia. As a young man he went to Vienna, Austria, to study philosophy. At the time Bosnia was part of the Austro-Hungarian Empire, and while in Vienna, Andric became involved in the campaign for Bosnian independence. In 1914, however, Europe was plunged into World War I, and Andric and other Bosnian activists were imprisoned. It was during this time that he wrote his first important works, *Prison Meditations* and a collection of poetry called *Inquietudes*, both published when he was in his late 20s. This period of imprisonment had a profound effect on Andric. His later novels are dominated by images of fear and isolation as individuals are caught up in events beyond their control.

After the war, Bosnia became part of Yugoslavia, and Andric joined the diplomatic service, eventually becoming the Yugoslav ambassador to Berlin in Germany. With the outbreak of World War II, Andric and his wife found themselves trapped in the city of Belgrade, which was occupied by the German Army. Although he avoided prison, this was an extremely traumatic time for him.

While in Belgrade, Andric wrote the novels that made him famous: *A Bosnian Story*, *The Woman from Sarajevo* and *The Bridge on the Drina*. These three works, all published when he was in his 50s, span many centuries of Bosnia's rich history, with Bosnia used to symbolize the world in miniature.

Publications

1918	*Prison Meditations*
1919	*Inquietudes*
1945	*A Bosnian Story*
1945	*The Woman from Sarajevo*
1945	*The Bridge on the Drina*
1948	*New Tales*
1948	*The Vizier's Elephant*
1952	*Under the Hornbeam*
1960	*Faces*
1962	*Devil's Yard*

ANGELOU, Maya

American poet and writer

Born Apr. 4, 1928

Maya Angelou is one of America's best-loved writers. Her books are all about her adventurous life.

Born in St. Louis, Missouri, Angelou was originally called Marguerite Johnson. Most of her childhood was spent with her grandparents after her parents divorced when she was three.

When she was eight years old, Angelou was raped by her mother's boyfriend. The experience was so terrifying that she was unable to speak for five years. Eventually, a teacher helped her regain her speech through reading and reciting literature. It was at this time that Angelou's love for literature was born.

Angelou moved to San Francisco in 1940 to attend secondary school and to live with her mother. While still at school, she was the first African-American woman in the city to become a streetcar conductor. After graduating at age 16, Angelou gave birth to a son.

By the time she was 25, Angelou had married, divorced and begun a career as a cabaret entertainer. It was at this time that she changed her name. Five years later, she was living in New York City and had begun to write. Her performing career was successful; she toured Europe and performed on Broadway. While in New York, she also became involved with the civil rights movement.

After working in Africa between 1961 and 1966, Angelou began the first volume of her autobiography. *I Know Why the Caged Bird Sings* was published when she was 42. Its optimism and vigor made it an instant success. Angelou has written further books about her experiences as well as volumes of poetry such as *Just Give Me a Cool Drink of Water 'fore I Diiie*.

Publications

1970	*I Know Why the Caged Bird Sings*
1971	*Just Give Me a Cool Drink of Water 'fore I Diiie*
1974	*Gather Together in My Name*
1981	*The Heart of a Woman*
1986	*All God's Children Need Traveling Shoes*
1990	*I Shall Not Be Moved*
1993	*Wouldn't Take Nothing for My Journey Now*
1998	*Even the Stars Look Lonesome*

ANOUILH, Jean

French playwright

Born Jun. 23, 1910
Died Oct. 3, 1987
Age at death 77

Jean Anouilh gained an international reputation as a playwright in the years following World War II. He was born in Bordeaux, southwestern France. After studying law, he worked in advertising and for a time was secretary to a famous French actor. He started writing drama after seeing a play by the French writer Jean Giraudoux, and he later acknowledged the influence of both Giraudoux and MOLIÈRE on his work.

The Ermine, his first play, was staged when he was 22, but it was not until he was 27 that he achieved a real hit with *Traveler without Luggage*. The following year he wrote *Thieves' Carnival*, which is about the romantic exploits of three charming crooks during a costume party. It became so popular that French theaters regularly revived it when they needed a sure-fire success.

During World War II, when France was occupied by Germany, Anouilh wrote *Antigone*, based on a play written by the ancient Greek playwright SOPHOCLES. *Antigone* shows the clash between a person's individual loyalties and his or her duty to the law. Many people saw the play as a symbol of resistance to the Germans, but others thought it supported them. It was only because the play could be interpreted in this way that it wasn't banned by the German authorities.

Nearly all Anouilh's plays show innocent people finding out about the harsh realities of life. They show the compromises people have to make in search of happiness. He called some of his plays "rose-colored" and others "black plays"; the black plays are the serious ones, and the rose plays are the comedies.

Publications

1932 The Ermine
1937 Traveler without Luggage
1938 Thieves' Carnival
1941 Legend of Lovers
1942 Antigone
1946 Medea
1949 Ardèle
1952 Waltz of the Toreadors
1953 The Lark
1959 Becket

APOLLINAIRE, Guillaume

French poet, novelist and playwright

Born Aug. 26, 1880
Died Nov. 9, 1918
Age at death 38

Guillaume Apollinaire was the pen name of Wilhelm Apollinaris de Kostrowitzki, whose work inspired the surrealist movement.

Little is known about Apollinaire, mainly because he deliberately kept the facts about his life vague. From his own accounts his father was an Italian church official and his mother a Polish aristocrat. Moving to Paris, France, when he was 20, Apollinaire soon became known as an outspoken supporter of new "modernist" ideas. Friends with many of the artists based in Paris, including Pablo Picasso, he argued for a move away from traditional art and literature toward more spontaneous art forms.

Apollinaire's first literary success came with the prose poem *The Decaying Magician*, published when he was 29. The poem features many of the fantastical elements for which his work became known. His masterpiece, *Alcools*, followed four years later; it contains his famous poem "Song of the Poorly Loved."

With the start of World War I in Europe, Apollinaire enlisted. He was wounded several times and eventually discharged. While convalescing he wrote some of his best work, including *The Poet Assassinated* – a strange, partly autobiographical novel.

In 1917, Apollinaire wrote the play *The Breasts of Tirésias*, which he called "surrealist" – an attempt to express the workings of the mind by creating art without deliberate control. Because of this many surrealist works seem strange or confusing.

Publications

1909 The Decaying Magician
1910 The Heresiarch and Co.
1913 Alcools
1913 Cubist Painters
1916 The Poet Assassinated
1917 The Breasts of Tirésias
1918 Calligrammes

Published after he died

1946 The New Spirit and the Poets

APULEIUS, Lucius

Roman novelist and satirist

Born c. 123
Died c. 150
Age at death c. 27

Lucius Apuleius is best known for his story *The Metamorphoses*, the only complete Latin novel that has survived from Roman times.

Apuleius was born in Madaura in North Africa, an area that was then part of the vast Roman Empire. As the son of an important official, he was given an excellent education in Carthage, North Africa, and then in Athens, Greece. He used the fortune his father left him to travel to far-off places in Asia.

On his travels, Apuleius learned about many different religious and magical practices, and he put this knowledge to use in *The Metamorphoses*, the novel that became known as *The Golden Ass*. This satire on the vices of the Roman age, especially those of priests and quacks (doctors), incorporates a romantic tale of adventure based on the ancient Egyptian story of Isis and Osiris. In Apuleius's version, the hero, who appears as an ass, is restored to human shape by the beautiful Isis. The most poetic episode of the book is the love story of Cupid and Psyche, which Apuleius adapted from popular legend.

Apuleius married a wealthy, middle-aged widow, but her relatives disapproved and accused him of using magic to make her fall in love with him. *The Apology* is the entertaining speech Apuleius gave in court to defend himself. After his acquittal he returned to Carthage to teach philosophy and rhetoric (the art of persuasion, especially in public speaking). Statues erected in his honor in Carthage and elsewhere show that he was a successful and prosperous member of Roman society.

Publications

2nd century
The Metamorphoses (later known as *The Golden Ass*)
The Apology
The Florida
Essays on the Greek philosopher Plato, including "On the God of Socrates"

ARIOSTO, Ludovico

Italian poet and playwright

Born Sep. 8, 1474
Died c. Jul. 6, 1533
Age at death 58

Ludovico Ariosto was an important poet and playwright of the Italian Renaissance of the 1500s. He wrote the remarkable poem *The Frenzy of Orlando*, which has been called the most perfect Italian poem ever written.

Ariosto was born in Reggio Emilia, northern Italy. At that time, Italy was divided into small kingdoms and city-states run by important families, such as the Medici family in Florence. Ariosto's family were minor aristocrats linked to the Este family, which ruled the city of Ferrara. When Ariosto was still young, his family moved to Ferrara, and his father ran the administration. After five years of hated legal studies, Ariosto convinced his father to let him study ancient Roman literature when he was 21. Three years later, however, he had to begin working for the Este family as a courtier and servant. On the death of his father in 1500, Ariosto became responsible for the care of his family. Until much later in his life, Ariosto battled with poverty while working for different members of the Este family.

Ariosto became interested in literature at an early age. Ferrara was a cultural center during the Italian Renaissance, and Ariosto first went to the theater at an early age. His masterpiece, *The Frenzy of Orlando*, was first published when he was 42, but the final, perfected version was not finished until 16 years later. This long, romantic poem details the adventures of heroic knights, in particular of one called Orlando. He is driven mad by love before regaining his reason. Ariosto also wrote several plays, including satires, comedies and serious dramas.

Publications

1508	*The Coffer*
1509	*The Pretenders*
1516	*The Frenzy of Orlando (I)*
1521	*The Frenzy of Orlando (II)*
1528	*Lena*
1529	*The Necromancer*
1532	*The Frenzy of Orlando (III)*

Published after he died

1534	*The Satires*
1545	*Five Cantos*

ARISTOPHANES

Greek playwright

Born c. 450 BC
Died c. 385 BC
Age at death c. 65

Aristophanes was the greatest comic playwright of ancient Greece. His comedies are the earliest roots of the film, theater and television comedies we enjoy today. Other ancient writers list over 40 plays by Aristophanes; only 11 of these have survived to the present.

Very little is known about the life of Aristophanes. Born in the city-state of Athens, he started writing before he was 20. Aristophanes lived through a period of great political and social change. For 27 years, Athens fought a bitter war against its archrival, the city of Sparta. The eventual defeat of Athens brought to an end the greatest period of ancient Greek civilization, and was followed by a time of political instability during which Athens was ruled by dictators and corrupt governments. Aristophanes wrote plays about the changes he saw going on around him.

Many of Aristophanes's plays are satires. He criticizes political leaders by making them seem ridiculous; often the leaders are outwitted by the hero of the play, who is portrayed as an ordinary citizen. Aristophanes also made fun of people such as philosophers, teachers and lawyers, who he felt corrupted society. Nobody was safe from his sharp words; even the most famous and respected figures of the time are made to look foolish. In his play the great Greek philosopher and teacher, Socrates, is portrayed as a madman who has an evil influence on the young people of Athens.

Publications

425 BC	*The Acharnians*
424 BC	*The Knights*
423 BC	*The Clouds*
422 BC	*The Wasps*
421 BC	*The Peace*
414 BC	*The Birds*
411 BC	*Lysistrata*
411 BC	*Thesmophoriazusae*
405 BC	*The Frogs*
388 BC	*Plutus*

ARNOLD, Matthew

English poet and critic

Born Dec. 24, 1822
Died Apr. 15, 1888
Age at death 65

Matthew Arnold was a leading Victorian poet and critic who believed art served a moral purpose.

Arnold was born near London and went to Rugby School. His father, Thomas Arnold – the school's principal – was famous for reforming teaching on firm Christian lines. Arnold studied at Oxford University, and at 28, he became an inspector of schools, a post that he held until retiring 35 years later. Also at 28, he married Frances Wightman. They lived at Laleham near London. Sadly, only three of their six children outlived their father.

Matthew Arnold was 26 when his first book of poetry appeared. *The Strayed Reveler* was a surprisingly gloomy and thoughtful book from a man his friends had believed not to be serious. He wrote in an age when people were losing their religious beliefs and wondering what really mattered in life. Many of Arnold's verses are about people feeling lonely and confused. His longest and maybe best poem, *Empedocles on Etna*, tells of an ancient Greek philosopher driven by self-doubt to suicide. Arnold used such characters to explore his own fears and uncertainties.

Between the ages of 34 and 44, Arnold held the mainly unpaid post of Professor of Poetry at Oxford University. He wrote critical essays that praise ancient Greek and Roman authors and proclaim the noble purpose of art. In *Culture and Anarchy,* he argued that culture could save society from depending on material possessions for happiness. In *Essays in Criticism,* he argued for poetry to replace religion as the way to show people how to lead a good life.

Publications

1849	*The Strayed Reveller*
1852	*Empedocles on Etna*
1853	*Poems*
1861	*On Translating Homer*
1865	*Essays in Criticism* (1st series)
1867	*New Poems*
1869	*Culture and Anarchy*
1871	*Friendship's Garland*
1875	*God and the Bible*
1888	*Essays in Criticism* (2nd series)

ASHBERY, John

American poet, novelist and playwright

Born Jul. 28, 1927

John Ashbery is one of America's most distinguished modern poets and has won many awards over the years.

Ashbery was born in Rochester, New York, the son of a farmer and a biology teacher. He studied at Deerfield Academy, Massachusetts, and at Harvard and Columbia universities. When he was 28, he was awarded a scholarship that allowed him to travel to Europe. He settled in Paris, France, and stayed there for ten years, working as an art critic and journalist and studying experimental writers and artists. Since 1965, he has lived in New York City.

Ashbery's first volume of poetry, *Turandot and Other Poems*, came out when he was 26. His second volume, *Some Trees*, published when he was 29, was chosen by the poet W.H. AUDEN to be included in a Yale University series on modern poets.

Many people find Ashbery's poetry difficult to understand. His work has been influenced by his interest in art. Some critics have said that his poems are like abstract paintings in words. He does not write about the world we see or things that happen but about what goes on in the poet's mind as he lives his life from day to day. The title poem of the collection *Self-Portrait in a Convex Mirror* examines the relationship between artists and poets and is, perhaps, easier to understand than Ashbery's earlier work. The collection won several awards, including a Pulitzer Prize in 1976. Ashbery has also published one novel, *A Nest of Ninnies*, and several poetic plays.

Publications

1953	*Turandot and Other Poems*
1956	*Some Trees*
1962	*The Tennis Court Oath*
1969	*A Nest of Ninnies*
1975	*Self-Portrait in a Convex Mirror*
1986	*Selected Poems*
1991	*Flow Chart*
1992	*Hotel Lautreamont*
1994	*And the Stars Were Shining*

ASHTON-WARNER, Sylvia

New Zealand novelist

Born Dec. 17, 1908
Died Apr. 28, 1984
Age at death 75

Sylvia Ashton-Warner was one of New Zealand's leading writers. She is famous for her autobiographical books about teaching.

Ashton-Warner was born in a small town in New Zealand, one of nine children. Her father was an invalid, and her mother a schoolteacher in country schools. After attending Auckland Teachers' Training College, she married a fellow teacher and went with him to teach in remote rural schools. Many of her pupils were Maoris – the original inhabitants of New Zealand – and she developed new teaching methods that avoided emphasizing European culture. Her experiences form the basis for most of her novels.

In 1958, when Ashton-Warner was 50, her first novel, *Spinster*, was published to great acclaim. Her earlier novel, *Teacher*, which had been rejected in 1953, was finally published in 1963. Both of these novels are based on her experiences of teaching.

Ashton-Warner was concerned about the racism she saw in New Zealand's European-dominated educational program, and she felt that children must be educated in a way that allows them to make sense of all their cultural influences.

After her husband's death in 1969, Ashton-Warner lived and worked in North America, teaching for some time in Aspen, Colorado, and then in Vancouver, Canada. She returned to New Zealand on retirement to devote herself to music and painting. Her memoirs, *I Passed This Way*, won the New Zealand Book Award in 1980.

Publications

1958 Spinster
1960 Incense to Idols
1963 Teacher
1964 Bell Call
1967 Greenstone
1967 Myself
1970 Three
1972 Spearpoint: Teacher in America
1980 I Passed This Way

ASIMOV, Isaac

Russian-born American science fiction writer

Born Jan. 2, 1920
Died Apr. 6, 1992
Age at death 72

Isaac Asimov was one of the most outstanding US science fiction writers of the 1940s, '50s and '60s. Although born in Russia, he went to the US with his family when he was three and became a citizen at the age of eight.

As a child Asimov read literature and science avidly. In 1929, he persuaded his father, who disapproved of comics, to let him read a new magazine called *Science Wonder Stories* because it had the word "science" in the title. The magazine was full of science fiction stories, and Asimov soon became addicted.

At the age of 17, Asimov wrote a short science fiction story, which his father suggested he send to a prestigious magazine called *Astounding Stories*. Although it was not published, Asimov met the editor of the magazine, John W. Campbell, who guided him through his early years as a writer and published many of his short stories.

At school, Asimov had always shown a talent for science. He received a Ph.D. from Columbia University in 1948, and from 1949 until 1979 taught biochemistry at Boston University. Asimov's first novel, *Pebble in the Sky*, was published when he was 30. In the same year he published *I, Robot*, a collection of his famous robot stories. Altogether he published more than 400 books. Many were nonfiction works in which he tried to explain science to the general public. He is as highly regarded for these books as for his fiction.

Asimov's knowledge of science allowed him to write science fiction stories that seemed realistic and possible. He received many awards.

Publications

1950 Pebble in the Sky
1950 I, Robot
1951 The Stars, Like Dust
1951–53 Foundation (3 vols.)
1954 The Caves of Steel
1957 The Naked Sun
1969 Nightfall and Other Stories
1972 The Gods Themselves
1976 The Bicentennial Man
1986 Foundation and Earth

ASTURIAS, Miguel Angel

Guatemalan novelist and poet

Born Oct. 19, 1899
Died Jun. 9, 1974
Age at death 74

Miguel Angel Asturias was one of Central America's most important and admired writers. He won the 1967 Nobel Prize for Literature.

Asturias was born in Guatemala. After studying law at the University of Guatemala, he went to live in Paris. There he studied the Mayan civilization, which ruled Central America before the arrival of the Spaniards. Asturias's lifelong fascination with Mayan culture can be seen in his stories, which often contain references to their folklore.

Asturias began writing his first novel, *The President*, when he was 23. It was at a time in Guatemala's history when ordinary people had little political freedom, and Native Americans lived almost like slaves. The novel was a powerful attack on dictatorship, and had no chance of being published in Guatemala. When he returned from Paris, Asturias worked in radio and wrote several books of poetry. The first, *Sonnets*, was published when he was 37.

Following a period of political unrest in Guatemala, a new liberal constitution was adopted in 1945. *The President* was published the next year and was an immediate success. The same year Asturias began a career as a diplomat for the Guatemalan government. He traveled widely in South and Central America. This was Asturias's most creative period. Between 1966 and 1970, he returned to Paris as Guatemalan ambassador to France, and when he retired, he settled there permanently.

Publications

1930	*Legends of Guatemala*
1936	*Sonnets*
1946	*The President*
1949	*Men of Corn*
1950	*The Cyclone*
1954	*The Green Pope*
1956	*Weekend in Guatemala*
1960	*The Eyes of the Interred*
1963	*Mulatta*

ATWOOD, Margaret

Canadian novelist, poet and short-story writer

Born Nov. 18, 1939

Margaret Atwood is a Canadian writer with an international reputation. Her poetry, novels and short stories combine storytelling with political and social criticism. She is also a political activist involved in causes supporting human rights.

Atwood was born in Ottawa, Canada. Her childhood summers were spent in the Canadian wilderness, where her father – a scientist – did research on insects. At age 22, she graduated from the University of Toronto, and in the same year she published her first book, a poetry collection called *Double Persephone*. She earned a Master's degree and began work on a Ph.D. at Harvard University. In 1967, she married, and that same year her book *The Circle Game* won a major Canadian award for the year's best book of poetry. In

1973, Atwood divorced. She now lives with her partner and their daughter in Toronto, where she writes full time and also teaches.

Among her best-known early works are *The Edible Woman* and *Surfacing*, both of which explore the changing roles of women in modern society. Atwood's writing displays her inventive feel for language. Novelist ANNE TYLER wrote about *Dancing Girls*, Atwood's first book of short stories, that Atwood "clearly writes with an ear cocked for the way her words will sound when read back." This love of language is often combined with a bleak vision of society, especially of its treatment of women. *The Handmaid's Tale* describes a society in the future in which women are used as baby machines and kept under strict control. This award-winning book was made into a popular film.

Publications

1966 The Circle Game
1969 The Edible Woman
1970 Journals of Susanna Moodie
1972 Surfacing
1976 Lady Oracle
1977 Dancing Girls
1982 Bodily Harm
1985 The Handmaid's Tale
1988 Cat's Eye
1996 Alias Grace
1998 Eating Fire: Selected Poetry 1965-95

AUCHINCLOSS, Louis

American novelist and short-story writer

Born Sep. 27, 1917

Louis Auchincloss has written almost 30 novels and several collections of short stories, nearly all of which are about the lives of rich, "high-society" New Yorkers.

Born in Lawrence, Long Island, Auchincloss comes from a wealthy, upper-class family. His father was a lawyer on Wall Street, the financial center of the United States, but the family's money originally came from a successful textile business founded by a Scottish immigrant ancestor in 1803.

Auchincloss studied law at the University of Virginia and then returned to New York City to practice law, like his father. In 1941, he joined the navy and served in World War II. After the war, Auchincloss returned to New York and combined his law career with his writing. His first novel, *The Indifferent Children*, was published when he was 30.

Auchincloss writes about the world he knows so well – wealthy New Yorkers who live in their own special society apart from the everyday lives of ordinary people. They have their own rules and regulations about how they should behave. Auchincloss sees himself as an observer of his characters, watching what they do and say. He follows in the tradition of HENRY JAMES and EDITH WHARTON, who first began to write in this way about American society. (Auchincloss has also written nonfiction about both these authors.) Auchincloss's best-known novels are *Portrait in Brownstone*, *The Rector of Justin*, and *The Embezzler*, which is based on a real financial scandal.

Publications

1947 The Indifferent Children
1952 Sybil
1954 The Romantic Egoists
1958 Venus in Sparta
1959 Pursuit of the Prodigal
1962 Portrait in Brownstone
1964 The Rector of Justin
1966 The Embezzler
1986 Diary of a Yuppie
1989 Fellow Passengers

AUDEN, W.H.

English-American poet and playwright

Born Feb. 21, 1907
Died Sep. 28, 1973
Age at death 66

The poetry of W.H. Auden is regarded as among the best English poetry of the 20th century.

Wystan Hugh Auden was born in York. He went to Oxford University, where he established a reputation as a leading young poet. His first poetry collection was published when he was 23 and was an immediate success.

After graduating, Auden traveled widely. He lived in Germany, volunteered as an ambulance driver in the Spanish Civil War, and also visited China and Iceland. In this period, he collaborated with the writer and former schoolfriend CHRISTOPHER ISHERWOOD on a number of plays and with the poet LOUIS MACNEICE on *Letters from Iceland*. Although Auden had been aware from an early age that he was a homosexual, when he was 29 he married Erika Mann, the daughter of the German novelist THOMAS MANN, so that she could escape Nazi Germany.

In 1939, Auden emigrated to the US and later became an American citizen. While living in New York, he met and fell in love with Chester Kallman, who remained Auden's partner for the rest of his life and inspired some of his best love poetry. He also became a committed Anglican Christian, and religious questions feature in much of his work of the 1940s. Auden continued to write poetry throughout the following decades. In 1948, his long poem *The Age of Anxiety* won the Pulitzer Prize.

Auden believed that the poetry of his day was tired and unimaginative. He set out to make poetry relevant to the 20th century by writing about everyday modern objects and using simple, direct language.

Publications

1930 Poems
1932 The Orators
1935 The Dog beneath the Skin
1936 The Ascent of F6
1937 Letters from Iceland
1938 On the Frontier
1939 Journey to a War
1945 Collected Poetry of W.H. Auden
1947 The Age of Anxiety
1955 The Shield of Achilles

AUSTEN, Jane

English novelist

Born Dec. 16, 1775
Died Jul. 18, 1817
Age at death 41

Jane Austen is considered by many to be the first outstanding woman novelist. She was one of the first writers to describe ordinary people in a believable way. Her subtle stories tell of young, well-bred heroines, and the manners and snobbery of their country-house families.

Austen was a clergyman's daughter, born in a village in southern England. Tutored at home with some outside schooling, Austen received a broader education than many women of her time. Her parents were avid readers, and the family performed plays in the rectory barn. She lived with her parents for most of her life and never married or traveled far, though she visited London and Bath. Contacts with friends and relatives helped her understand and write about minor landed gentry, country clergymen and their families.

Austen wrote her first book, *Love and Friendship,* when she was 14. She finished several novels before any were published. *Sense and Sensibility* appeared when she was 35. She kept its author's name secret, for in those days people thought writing was not a ladylike occupation.

Her best-known books include *Pride and Prejudice* and *Emma.* In *Pride and Prejudice* a young man and woman begin by disliking each other but at last fall in love. In *Emma* a snobbish, headstrong young woman develops into someone capable of feeling and love. In all her novels the heroines end happily married.

Critics praise Austen for her dry humor and elegant style. She built excitement from simple misunderstandings and from characters torn between their feelings and family duty.

Publications

1811	*Sense and Sensibility*
1813	*Pride and Prejudice*
1814	*Mansfield Park*
1816	*Emma*

Published after she died

1818	*Northanger Abbey*
1818	*Persuasion*
1922	*Love and Friendship*

AWOONOR, Kofi

Ghanaian poet, novelist and playwright

Born Mar. 13, 1935

Kofi Awoonor is widely thought to be one of the finest English-language poets in Africa.

He was born in Ghana (West Africa), which was then the British-ruled colony of the Gold Coast. Educated to university level in Ghana, Awoonor went on to teach African literature at the University of Ghana. During this time he wrote his first book of poetry, *Rediscovery*. Like the rest of his work, these poems are based on African oral poetry, which is spoken rather than written down.

After managing the Ghana Film Corporation and founding the Ghana Play House at age 32, he studied literature at London University in England. While there, he wrote several radio plays for the BBC. Awoonor spent the early 1970s in the United States, where he studied and taught at various universities. His time there was a period of great creativity; he wrote major pieces such as *This Earth, My Brother* (a cross between a novel and a long poem) and *Night of My Blood* – poems in which Awoonor explores his roots and the impact that foreign rule has had on Africa.

Awoonor returned to Ghana in 1975 to head the English department at the University of Cape Coast. Within months, he was arrested for helping a soldier accused of trying to overthrow the military government. Imprisoned without trial, he was found guilty ten months later and then released. *The House by the Sea* tells of his time in jail. Since then, Awoonor has become politically active and has written mostly nonfiction. In the 1990s, he has represented Ghana as ambassador to the United Nations.

Publications

1964	*Rediscovery*
1970	*Ancestral Power*
1971	*This Earth, My Brother*
1971	*Night of My Blood*
1973	*Ride Me, Memory*
1975	*The Breast of the Earth*
1978	*The House by the Sea*
1984	*The Ghana Revolution*
1987	*Until the Morning After*
1992	*Comes the Voyager at Last*

AYCKBOURN, Alan

English playwright

Born Apr. 12, 1939

Publications

1975 The Norman Conquests
1977 Bedroom Farce
1977 Absurd Person Singular
1979 Joking Apart
1982 Way Upstream
1986 A Chorus of Disapproval
1986 Woman in Mind
1987 A Small Family Business
1988 Henceforward
1990 Man of the Moment

Alan Ayckbourn is one of the most successful British playwrights working today. He is best known for his comedies.

Ayckbourn was born in London and educated at a public school. He first worked in theater as a stage manager and also occasionally as an actor.

In his early 20s, Ayckbourn got a job with a small theater in the seaside town of Scarborough, in northern England. The theater was run by Stephen Joseph, who encouraged Ayckbourn to write plays. Joseph's theater was unusual; it was a theater-in-the-round, which means that the audience sat all around the stage instead of just in front of it. When he was 20, Ayckbourn had his first play, *The Square Cat*, produced at Joseph's theater.

After Joseph died, Ayckbourn became the new director of his theater, a position he still holds. Today, he is known as a successful director as well as a playwright; among the plays he has directed are works by ARTHUR MILLER.

Most of Ayckbourn's plays are about ordinary, middle-class people living in the suburbs. A typical Ayckbourn play is a comedy of manners, in which things that could happen to anyone lead to comical situations or uncover hidden truths about people's lives. His plays often have an unusual structure. One of his best-known works, *The Norman Conquests*, is a group of three plays that show the same events at a weekend party seen from three different parts of the house.

BÂ, Mariama

Senegalese novelist

Born 1929
Died 1981
Age at death c. 51

Mariama Bâ's novel *So Long a Letter* is a classic of African literature.

Bâ was born in Dakar, the capital of Senegal, which was then part of the French West Africa colony. Her mother died when she was young, and her father was often away, so Bâ was brought up by her mother's parents. The family was wealthy, but did not see the need for a girl to be educated beyond primary school. Her father insisted, however, and Bâ received a good education. While still at school, she published two essays. One created a stir for its rejection of French policies in Africa.

After leaving school, Bâ worked as a teacher and school inspector. She married a politician, and they had nine children together. The marriage broke up, however, and Bâ raised their children alone. She became a champion of women's rights, making speeches and writing newspaper articles.

Bâ's first novel, *So Long a Letter*, shot her to fame at the age of 30. This prizewinning book, written in French, is in the form of a letter from a widow to a childhood girlfriend. Both women's husbands had taken a second wife, but the widow had stayed in her marriage and suffered, while the other had left and started a new life. Although the book was not based on Bâ's own life, she drew from her experiences in writing it. She wanted to make people aware of the difficulties that women face in a society that treats them as inferior. Bâ died after a long illness just as her second novel, *Scarlet Song*, was about to be published. It is about the marriage between a European woman and an African man.

Publications

1979 So Long a Letter

Published after she died

1981 Scarlet Song

BABEL, Isaac

Russian short-story writer and playwright

Born Jul. 13, 1894

Died Mar. 17, 1941

Age at death 46

Isaac Babel is one of the greatest short-story writers. A leading literary figure in the period just after the Russian Revolution, he eventually became a victim of the dictator Joseph Stalin.

Born in the Russian port of Odessa, Babel was raised in the Jewish faith and learned Yiddish, the language of European Jews, as a child. He was to become the first major Jewish author to write in Russian, but he also wrote stories in Yiddish, and many of his Jewish characters use Yiddish phrases. When he was 21, Babel settled in St. Petersburg and dedicated himself to writing. There he became friends with the novelist MAKSIM GORKY, who helped Babel publish his early stories.

Babel served as a soldier during World War I and during the Russian Revolution; he also worked as a war correspondent for Russian papers. These experiences formed the basis for *Red Cavalry*, his famously realistic collection of stories about army life, published when he was 32. The book was opposed by political groups who considered his descriptions of the brutalities carried out by Russian soldiers to be unpatriotic. In *Odessa Tales*, another of Babel's story collections, he uses humor and irony to describe life in the Jewish neighborhood of his hometown.

In the 1930s, Stalin, the new leader of Russia, set about crushing any opposition to his power. This included writers and other thinkers who had strong views. Babel was arrested in 1939 and disappeared soon after. Only recently have scholars learned that he died in a prison camp in 1941.

Publications

1924 Odessa Tales

1926 Red Cavalry

1927 Benya Krik, the Gangster and Other Stories

1928 Sunset

1935 Maria

Published after he died

1955 Collected Stories

1969 You Must Know Everything: Stories 1915–1937

BAGNOLD, Enid

English novelist and playwright

Born Oct. 27, 1889
Died Mar. 31, 1981
Age at death 91

Enid Bagnold is best known for her novel *National Velvet*. It also became a play and, in 1944, was made into a Hollywood movie starring Elizabeth Taylor.

The daughter of an army officer, Bagnold was born in Kent, southern England, but spent her early years abroad.

Bagnold was aged 28 and serving in the British Women's Auxiliaries during World War I when her first book, *A Diary without Dates*, was published. It tells of her experience in a war hospital in such realistic detail that it upset the military authorities, and she was removed from her post. In 1920, she married Sir Roderick Jones, the head of a news agency in London, and became Lady Jones.

National Velvet was published when she was 46. It is the story of a young girl, Velvet, who rides to victory in the Grand National, a famous horse race. Although *National Velvet* became a favorite with young readers, Bagnold wrote the story with adult readers in mind. Like *National Velvet*, most of her stories have women as central characters. Her books recreate events with great detail and vividness.

In 1929, her novel *Serena Blandish*, which Bagnold had published anonymously, was turned into a play by the American dramatist S.N. Behrman. Bagnold made her own stage versions of *Lottie Dundass* and *National Velvet*, and at age 62 she wrote *Poor Judas*, her first original play.

Bagnold's most successful play was *The Chalk Garden*, which is about a governess who is gradually revealed to have been in jail for murder.

Publications

1917 A Diary without Dates
1924 Serena Blandish
1935 National Velvet
1938 The Door of Life
1943 Lottie Dundass
1951 The Loved and Envied
1951 Poor Judas
1955 The Chalk Garden
1964 The Chinese Prime Minister
1975 A Matter of Gravity

BAINBRIDGE, Beryl

English novelist

Born Nov. 21, 1934

Beryl Bainbridge is an English novelist known for her stories of strange characters and events.

Bainbridge was born in Liverpool. From an early age she was aware of the English class system and of the fact that her father, a salesman, was working class, while her mother came from a middle-class background. Bainbridge was encouraged to write by both parents. Her mother bought her notebooks to write in, while her father read her stories by CHARLES DICKENS. She became a child actor in radio and theater plays, and she continued to act into her 40s.

At 22 she married a painter, and together they had three children before divorcing in 1959. Bainbridge began to write seriously when her children were young. Her first novel, *Harriet Said*, was rejected

Publications

1967 A Weekend with Claude

by publishers, who were outraged at her story of two schoolgirls who murder their neighbor. It wasn't published until 14 years later.

In her late 30s, Bainbridge, with two successful novels to her credit, managed to publish *Harriet Said*. She went on to publish many more books over the next two decades. Her books are distinguished by their sharp and entertaining wit. Many explore the grim lives of working-class people in Liverpool, her native city. Her own childhood experiences – including her fear of her father's temper – also feature. Some are adventure stories, for example, *The Birthday Boys* is a tale about a South Pole expedition.

Bainbridge has adapted several of her novels for the movies. Since the 1970s, she has also written television plays.

1968 Another Part of the Wood
1972 Harriet Said
1975 Sweet William
1977 Injury Time
1984 English Journey, or, The Road to Milton Keynes
1989 An Awfully Big Adventure
1991 The Birthday Boys
1996 Every Man for Himself
1998 Master Georgie

BALDWIN, James

James Baldwin was a leading American writer. His novels and short stories express the anger of a generation of African Americans in the 1950s and '60s civil rights movement.

Baldwin was born in Harlem, New York City, the son of a domestic worker. When he was three, his mother married a preacher whose fanatical religious beliefs and strictness had a strong influence on the young Baldwin. He grew up in poverty and in fear of his stepfather and the violence of the city. From an early age he turned to literature as an escape; he had read HARRIET BEECHER STOWE's novel *Uncle Tom's Cabin* before he was eight. Between 14 and 17, Baldwin also turned to religion and became a preacher in small evangelical churches. At about the same time, he discovered that he was homosexual.

When he was 20, Baldwin began to write his first novel. An early version was rejected by publishers, and he began to despair at ever achieving success in his home country. At age 24, following the suicide of a friend, Baldwin decided to leave America and live in France.

Go Tell It on the Mountain, Baldwin's first novel, was finally published when he was 29. Like his later novels, it explores the prejudice that Baldwin encountered as a black man and a homosexual, and the terrible effects of that prejudice on society. In the late 1950s, Baldwin returned to the US to witness the progress of antiracism laws. He became a spokesman for the civil rights leader Martin Luther King, and published many articles about the political position of African Americans.

American novelist, short-story writer and playwright

Born Aug. 2, 1924
Died Dec. 1, 1987
Age at death 63

Publications

1953 Go Tell It on the Mountain
1955 Notes of a Native Son
1956 Giovanni's Room
1960 Nobody Knows My Name
1962 Another Country
1968 Tell Me How Long the Train's Been Gone
1974 If Beale Street Could Talk
1979 Just Above My Head
1987 Harlem Quartet

BALLARD, J.G.

English science fiction writer, novelist and short-story writer

Born Nov. 15, 1930

J.G. Ballard is an important English novelist, perhaps best known for his book *Empire of the Sun*. He is also one of the most original writers in science fiction today; his work brings out the strangeness of this world rather than of imaginary alien planets.

James Graham Ballard was born in Shanghai, China, where his father was the manager of a British textile factory. The family was wealthy, living in luxury with many servants. Then, in 1937, war broke out between the Chinese and the Japanese. The family was sent to a prison camp, an experience Ballard later recalled in his novel *Empire of the Sun*, filmed by Steven Spielberg in 1987. Ballard's memories of the camp were not all bad; one aspect of life he enjoyed was the number of playmates he had – around 500 children.

When Ballard was 16, he returned to England with his family. He went on to study medicine at Cambridge University and then joined the Royal Air Force. While in the air force he discovered science fiction magazines, and he soon began to write short stories for publication.

Ballard's unusual childhood experiences had given him a sense of the strange and absurd. In Shanghai he had witnessed the collapse of a civilized way of life, and this awareness of how easily order can break down into chaos is a strong theme in all his writing.

The Wind From Nowhere, Ballard's first novel, was published when he was 32. In the same year he published his second novel, *The Drowned World*, which established him as a successful writer. Since then he has written many novels and short stories; one of these, *Crash*, became a controversial film in 1996.

Publications

1962	*The Drowned World*
1966	*The Crystal World*
1970	*The Atrocity Exhibition*
1972	*Crash*
1974	*Concrete Island*
1975	*High-Rise*
1979	*The Unlimited Dream Company*
1984	*Empire of the Sun*
1991	*The Kindness of Women*
1995	*Rushing to Paradise*

BALZAC, Honoré de

French novelist and short-story writer

Born May 20, 1799
Died Aug. 17, 1850
Age at death 51

Honoré de Balzac was a great French novelist. Some people say that he was the greatest novelist of all time. His works have had a huge influence on the development of the modern novel, and his colorful and hectic life has become part of literary legend.

Balzac was born in the French city of Tours. His prosperous, middle-class family moved to Paris when he was 15, and he was forced by his father to study law, which he hated. Eventually he persuaded his family to support him so that he could be a writer. From the age of 22, Balzac wrote tirelessly. He regularly worked 16 hours a day, producing stories, magazine articles and plays, and writing many letters.

Balzac's first plays and novels are not very good and earned him no money. Then, when he was 30, he produced his first important novel, *The Chouans*, about peasants during the French Revolution. Around this time he also got into some disastrous business ventures that left him with huge debts. For the rest of his life, Balzac was pursued by creditors; this was mostly because he insisted on living like a wealthy man while earning very little. His large appetite for food, wine and fun was legendary.

The great work for which Balzac is remembered is his sequence of novels called *The Human Comedy* (the word "comedy" also meant "story" in Balzac's time). He described it as an attempt to create a complete picture of French society. When he died, he had completed nearly 100 books in the series, many of which were individual masterpieces. He included over 2,000 characters from all sections of society, some of whom appear at different stages of their lives.

Publications

1829 The Chouans
1831 The Wild Ass's Skin
1831–34 The Thirty-Year-Old Woman
1832–37 Droll Stories
1833 Eugénie Grandet
1835 Pere Goriot
1837–43 Lost Illusions
1846 Cousin Bette

BAMBARA, Toni Cade

American novelist and short-story writer

Born Mar. 25, 1939
Died Dec. 9, 1995
Age at death 56

Toni Cade Bambara was a community worker as well as a writer. Her concern for the African-American community is present in all of her writings.

Bambara, born in New York City, was given the name Toni Cade. Her mother encouraged her children to write, daydream and use their imaginations. By the time she was 20, Cade had published her first short story, "Sweet Town." That year she also graduated and began working as a social worker in Harlem. In the 1960s, she worked on several community projects and as a college professor.

In 1970, Cade adopted the name Bambara, which she discovered in a sketchbook belonging to her great-grandmother. That year she edited a book called *The Black Woman*, which ushered in a new era of African-American women's writing. Among the contributors to *The Black Woman* were ALICE WALKER, NIKKI GIOVANNI, AUDRE LORDE and PAULE MARSHALL, as well as Bambara herself. It provided an opportunity for black women to express their views on a range of issues from the civil rights movement to feminism, relationships, education and housing.

Bambara's writing is set in urban African-American culture. The stories in her collection, *Gorilla, My Love*, published when she was 33, feature characters who challenge stereotypes of what it is to be a young black woman. At age 41, she published her first novel, *The Salt Eaters*, which won the 1980 National Book Award.

In the last decade of her life, Bambara lived in Philadelphia. In 1996, TONI MORRISON edited a collection of Bambara's unpublished work called *Deep Sightings and Rescue Missions*.

Publications

1959 "Sweet Town"
1970 The Black Woman
1972 Gorilla, My Love
1977 The Sea Birds are Still Alive
1980 The Salt Eaters
1987 If Blessing Comes
1990 Raymond's Run

Published after she died

1996 Deep Sightings and Rescue Missions

BANKS, Iain

Scottish novelist and science fiction writer

Born Feb. 16, 1954

Iain Banks ranks among the most original Scottish authors of the late 20th century.

Banks was born in Fife, Scotland. Interested in writing from an early age, he began submitting articles to newspapers and magazines when he was just 16. After graduating from college, he spent some time traveling. During this period he took various jobs, including working as a technician for the computer giant, IBM.

Banks had already written a number of science fiction novels that hadn't been published, but at age 30, he finally succeeded with *The Wasp Factory* – a bizarre and gruesome black comedy in which the main character is a disturbed, murderous teenager. As in many of his works, the novel blends traditional literary styles and uses clever plot twists to surprise and entertain the reader. It is probably still his most talked-about novel.

The Wasp Factory was followed by two more groundbreaking books, which show a wide range of influences from FRANZ KAFKA to EDGAR ALLAN POE.

At age 33, Banks published *Consider Phlebas*, an epic science fiction novel. It was the first in an ever-growing series of highly successful science fiction novels that demonstrate Banks's talent for creating believable worlds. To distinguish his science fiction from his other work, Banks uses his middle initial – M for "Menzies."

Since *Consider Phlebas,* Banks has written one book a year, alternating between his science fiction and other novels. His works are increasingly being adapted for stage, TV and radio.

Publications

1984 The Wasp Factory
1985 Walking on Glass
1987 Consider Phlebas
1988 The Player of Games
1989 Canal Dreams
1990 Use of Weapons
1993 Complicity
1995 Whit
1996 Excession
1997 A Song of Stone
1998 Inversions

BARAKA, Amiri

American writer

Born Oct. 7, 1934

As a playwright, poet, novelist, political activist and essayist, Amiri Baraka (known as LeRoi Jones until 1967) has long been a leader of African-American culture and, in particular, of revolutionary theater.

Baraka was born in Newark, New Jersey, and studied at Howard University in Washington, DC. After graduating in 1954, he joined the US Air Force but was discharged in 1957, apparently for his growing black nationalist views. The black nationalist movement fostered pride in African-American culture. Some of its more radical followers sought an independent African-American nation.

After his discharge Baraka settled in New York City. He helped found the literary magazine *Yugen* (an African word meaning "beauty" or "grace") and started a publishing company, Totem Press.

Baraka's first collection of poetry, *Preface to a Twenty Volume Suicide Note*, was published when he was 27. His later poetry was more political. With the assassination of Malcolm X in 1965, Baraka became convinced that blacks and whites could not live together, and he felt the need to create a uniquely black way of writing poetry that reflected his black nationalist views. Baraka's radical plays also reflect his political views. The award-winning *Dutchman* tells of the encounter between a young black man and a middle-class white girl that ends in violence.

Later in his career Baraka became less sure about the value of black nationalism. He began to believe that big business capitalism was the cause of social problems.

Publications

1961	*Preface to a Twenty Volume Suicide Note*
1964	*The Dead Lecturer*
1964	*Dutchman*
1965	*The System of Dante's Hell*
1969	*Black Magic*
1969	*Four Black Revolutionary Plays*
1975	*Hard Facts*
1994	*Thornton Dial*

BARKER, Clive

English horror writer

Born 1952

Clive Barker is one of the world's most successful horror writers.

Born in Liverpool, Barker was inspired to become a writer when a local horror author, Ramsey Campbell, gave a talk at his school. At university, Barker developed a lifelong interest in drawing, although he graduated in English literature and philosophy. He then moved to London, where he lived on unemployment benefit and wrote plays with a horror theme for his theater group, The Dog Company. During this time he began to write short stories.

The first publisher Barker sent his stories to was impressed by his work and asked for more. At age 32, Barker published his stories over the next two years in six volumes titled *Books of Blood*. The collection sold well, and he was hailed as a major new horror writer. The following year he published his first novel, *The Damnation Game*. It is the story of two criminals with superhuman abilities who chase each other across Europe for many years.

Barker's first major film was *Hellraiser*. It was based on a short novel he had written, *The Hellbound Heart*, and introduced an evil character nicknamed "Pinhead" by audiences. There were two sequels to the film, and Barker went on to write, direct and produce more films based on his fiction.

Barker's work is graphic in its descriptions of violence, and he has been praised by the master of horror, STEPHEN KING. Recently, Barker's work has veered toward fantasy rather than horror. One of his most popular books is a fantasy story for children, *The Thief of Always*, which includes his own illustrations.

Publications

1984	*Books of Blood (Vols. 1–3)*
1985	*The Damnation Game*
1985	*Books of Blood (Vols. 4–6)*
1987	*Weaveworld*
1988	*Cabal*
1988	*The Hellbound Heart*
1989	*The Great and Secret Show*
1991	*Imajica*
1992	*The Thief of Always*
1996	*Sacrament*
1998	*Galilee*

BARNES, Djuna

American novelist and playwright

Born Jun. 12, 1892
Died Jun. 18, 1982
Age at death 90

With her two groundbreaking novels *Ryder* and *Nightwood,* Djuna Barnes had a major impact on 20th-century literature. Despite this, she is little known today and has been called the unknown legend of American literature. This is mostly because she was a very private person who willingly stepped out of the spotlight after becoming famous. Almost 300 articles, plays, stories, books and poems are known to have been written by her during the 1920s and '30s, making her one of the most important American writers of the time. The full extent of her writing is not known, since she did not always sign her work.

Barnes was born in Cornwall-on-Hudson, New York, to an American father and a British mother. Her wealthy father was a free-spirited man who ran a farm on Long Island to ensure that he could remain independent from society. Barnes was educated at home before studying art at a Brooklyn college.

At age 21, she began publishing her first short stories in various journals and became a reporter and illustrator. She first attracted attention as a writer with the staging of three of her plays in 1919–20. In the 1920s she lived in Europe, mostly in Paris, working as a journalist. She became part of the post-World War I literary invasion from the US, and her friends included JAMES JOYCE, T.S. ELIOT, GERTRUDE STEIN and EZRA POUND. Her first novel, *Ryder*, came out when she was 36. Both *Ryder* and *Nightwood* are comic, experimental novels that break with the traditions of plot, character and dialogue. They feature people leading lives that do not conform to "normal" society and are now cult classics.

Publications

1915 The Book of Repulsive Women
1923 A Book
1928 Ladies' Almanack
1928 Ryder
1929 A Night Among the Horses
1936 Nightwood
1958 The Antiphon
1962 Spillway
1974 Vagaries Malicieux Two Stories

BARNES, Julian

English novelist and essayist

Born Jan. 19, 1946

Julian Barnes's witty, ironic novels use a range of styles and display great imagination and curiosity.

Barnes was born in Leicester. After studying at Oxford University, he helped compile the *Oxford English Dictionary Supplement*. In his 30s, he was a television critic and literary editor with leading British newspapers and magazines. He settled in London with his wife, Pat Kavanagh.

At 34, Barnes published his first novel, *Metroland*. It describes a smart young man's memories of growing up in the peaceful suburbs to which he later returns. Four years later he made his reputation with *Flaubert's Parrot*. This is about a retired English doctor obsessed with the writings of the French author GUSTAVE FLAUBERT.

Into his story Barnes weaves facts about Flaubert, Flaubert's books, and the area of France where Flaubert lived. France also figures in *Cross Channel*, Barnes's recent collection of short stories.

One of his most inventive efforts is *A History of the World in 10½ Chapters*, which links ideas about art, love, death and religion in a series of tales – part fable, part history – beginning with one based on the biblical story of Noah's ark. Parts that seem more fact than fiction helped earn such writing the nickname "faction." The problems of love reappeared two years later in *Talking It Over*.

Barnes's clever, sensitive stories have won him a number of literary awards, especially in France. He has also written essays for the *New Yorker* magazine and published several detective novels under the pen name of Dan Kavanagh.

Publications

- 1980 *Metroland*
- 1980 *Duffy*
- 1982 *Before She Met Me*
- 1984 *Flaubert's Parrot*
- 1986 *Staring at the Sun*
- 1989 *A History of the World in 10½ Chapters*
- 1991 *Talking It Over*
- 1992 *The Porcupine*
- 1996 *Cross Channel*
- 1998 *England, England*

BARNES, Margaret Ayer

American novelist and playwright

Born Apr. 8, 1886
Died Oct. 26, 1967
Age at death 81

Margaret Ayer Barnes won a Pulitzer Prize in 1931 for her novel *Years of Grace*. It traces the life of a Chicago woman from the 1890s to the new freedom of the 1920s. Barnes's work comments on the changing lifestyles of women during this period.

Born Margaret Ayer in Chicago, she graduated from Bryn Mawr College, Pennsylvania, in 1907. Three years later she married a lawyer, Cecil Barnes. While at Bryn Mawr, she was inspired by the college's feminist president and became interested in promoting higher education for women. In the early 1920s, she helped set up the Working Women's College at Bryn Mawr, which taught industrial workers during the summer months. Many of the college's students went back to their home towns and set up similar colleges.

Barnes began her writing career when she was in her 40s. After a serious automobile accident in 1925, she was expected to spend the rest of her life as an invalid. She fought to become active again and while recovering was encouraged by her childhood friend, the playwright Edward Sheldon, to write short stories. These were published in various journals and later appeared in her first published work, *Prevailing Winds*, which came out when she was 42. In the same year, she turned EDITH WHARTON's novel *Age of Innocence* into a successful play. Then, with Sheldon she wrote two other plays: the comedy *Jennie* and *Dishonored Lady*, based on the trial of a woman accused of murdering her lover.

Years of Grace, Barnes's most famous novel, was published when she was 44.

Publications

- 1928 *Prevailing Winds*
- 1929 *Jennie* (with E. Sheldon)
- 1930 *Dishonored Lady* (with E. Sheldon)
- 1930 *Years of Grace*
- 1931 *Westward Passage*
- 1933 *Within This Present*
- 1935 *Edna, His Wife*
- 1938 *Wisdom's Gate*

BARRIE, J.M.

Scottish children's writer, playwright and novelist

Born May 9, 1860
Died Jun. 19, 1937
Age at death 77

J.M. Barrie is best known as the creator of *Peter Pan*, the much-loved fairy tale celebrating childhood.

James Matthew Barrie was born in Kirriemuir, Scotland, the son of handloom weavers. He had a strict upbringing, and at the age of six he suffered the tragedy of his brother's death, which plunged his adored mother into grief. For years he longed to return to the happy childhood he had known when his brother was alive.

After graduating from the University of Edinburgh, Barrie left Scotland and settled in England. He worked as a journalist and then began to write fiction. His first successful novel, *Auld Licht Idylls*, was published when he was 28. It is about his experience of Scottish village life. A few years later, the dramatized version of *The Little Minister*, his novel about love and adventure, brought him fame and wealth.

Barrie wrote 35 plays in all. Some are social satires, for example, *The Admirable Crichton*, which makes fun of a group of upper-class English people shipwrecked on an island. *Peter Pan* – first performed when Barrie was 44 – grew from stories he invented for the five sons of his friends Arthur and Sylvia Llewelyn Davies. The tale is a mixture of fantasy and adventure and is about everlasting childhood. The main character, a boy named Peter Pan who refuses to grow up, has become a folklore hero.

Barrie suffered greatly from several tragedies in his life. His childless marriage to actress Mary Ansell came to an end, and his friends the Davies both died. They left their five sons for Barrie to look after, but later two of the boys were killed.

Publications

1888	*Auld Licht Idylls*
1891	*The Little Minister*
1892	*The Professor's Love Story*
1900	*The Wedding Guest*
1902	*Quality Street*
1902	*The Admirable Crichton*
1904	*Peter Pan*
1908	*What Every Woman Knows*
1917	*Dear Brutus*
1920	*Mary Rose*

BARTH, John

American novelist

Born May 27, 1930

John Barth is one of America's most distinguished and successful novelists.

Barth was born in Cambridge, Maryland, and has spent most of his life around the East Coast. He showed an early talent for music and was accepted as a student at Juilliard School of Music in New York. But he only stayed there for a short time before leaving to go to Johns Hopkins University. He graduated in 1951 with a degree in creative writing.

In 1953, Barth became an English teacher at Pennsylvania State University. Apart from a brief period when he earned his living as a professional drummer, he has spent his working life as a college lecturer, writing novels in his free time.

Barth is recognized today as one of America's leading experimental novelists, which means that he likes to try and find new ways of writing fiction. In his first two novels, *The Floating Opera*, published when he was 26, and *The End of the Road*, Barth attempts to describe what goes on in his characters' heads as they try to make a vital decision – for example, should they take their own lives or not?

However, his third novel, *The Sot-Weed Factor*, is completely different. It was modeled on the long, comic, fantastic style of 18th-century adventure novels. *Giles Goat-Boy*, Barth's next novel, is considered by many to be his most important. It is set in an imaginary world consisting of one vast computer-run university.

Barth continues to experiment with different ways of writing fiction. In his later work he even puts himself in some of his stories as a character called The Author.

Publications

1956	*The Floating Opera*
1958	*The End of the Road*
1960	*The Sot-Weed Factor*
1966	*Giles Goat-Boy*
1972	*Chimera*
1982	*Sabbatical*
1991	*The Last Voyage of Somebody the Sailor*
1994	*Once upon a Time*

BARTHELME, Donald

American novelist and short-story writer

Born Apr. 7, 1931
Died Jul. 23, 1989
Age at death 58

Donald Barthelme is best known for experimenting with language in his books; he relies much more on language than on plot or characters to tell his stories.

Barthelme was born in Philadelphia, Pennsylvania, where his parents were in university, but moved at an early age to Houston, Texas, where he later worked as a reporter, editor and art museum director. At age 32, he went to New York City to become a full-time writer. His career began when the *New Yorker* magazine started to publish his work. *Come Back, Dr. Caligari*, his first book of short stories, was published when Barthelme was 33.

Barthelme believes that the everyday language used in modern fiction cannot capture modern life. In using the sometimes absurd language and images that he does, he tries to make the reader aware of how language has been changed by advertising and politics. In one story from his collection *Unspeakable Practices, Unnatural Acts*, for example, he uses realistic-sounding nonsense to get his point across. In the story a group of military scientists invent such weapons as "rots, blights and rusts capable of destroying [the enemy's] alphabet." In another book, *Snow White*, he gives boxes of cereal accurate sounding but ridiculous names such as "Chix," "Rats" and "Fear."

Barthelme's genius was to recognize that we have become so accustomed to hearing or reading something that we have heard or read so often before that its true meaning has been lost. In the course of his distinguished career, he received several prestigious awards.

Publications

1964	*Come Back, Dr. Caligari*
1967	*Snow White*
1968	*Unspeakable Practices, Unnatural Acts*
1970	*City Life*
1974	*Guilty Pleasures*
1975	*The Dead Father*
1976	*Amateurs*
1986	*Paradise*
1987	*Forty Stories*

BASHO, Matsuo

Japanese poet

Born 1644
Died 1694
Age at death c. 50

Although he did not create the haiku, Matsuo Basho is considered to have had the greatest impact on the development of this Japanese poetic form and to be one of its best practitioners. Haiku poems can have only 17 syllables arranged in a strict pattern of 5-7-5. (A syllable is a word or part of a word that forms one unit of sound when spoken.) Basho raised the haiku from the status of an entertaining pastime to a major literary genre. His masterpiece – variously translated as, for example, *Narrow Road to the Interior* or *Narrow Road to the Deep North* – is considered to be one of the greatest works of Japanese literature.

Basho was born near modern Kyoto in southern Japan. It is thought that he became the companion of a young relative of the local military ruler while still quite young. He formed a close relationship with his young master, and the two often composed poetry together. Written when Basho was just 18, the earliest surviving example of his work dates from this period. After the death of his friend in 1666, the course of Basho's life changed. He became a wanderer before moving to Edo (modern Tokyo) in his late 20s. He continued to write poetry, competing in and judging contests at which haiku were composed on the spot, and he became a respected poet and teacher.

In 1689, Basho went on a journey, not his first, to the wilds north of Edo. It lasted for five months, covered 1,233 miles, and Basho visited many religious and historical sites. *Narrow Road to the Interior* tells of this journey in haiku and other verse forms. Its richly suggestive but light style earned this work praise from the start and has made it the classic it is today.

Publications

1672	*The Seashell Game*
1685	*The Records of a Weather-Exposed Skeleton*
1687	*A Visit to Kashima Shrine*
1687	*The Records of a Travel-Worn Satchel*
1687	*A Visit to Sarashina Village*
1691	*The Saga Diary*
1694	*Narrow Road to the Interior*

BATES, H.E.

English novelist, short-story writer and playwright

Born May 16, 1905
Died Jan. 29, 1974
Age at death 68

During his lifetime, H.E. Bates received critical acclaim for his short stories, but is now known to a wider audience for his novel, *The Darling Buds of May*.

Born in the small town of Rushden, Herbert Ernest Bates grew up among "simple country folk," as he later described his family. After finishing school, he worked as a reporter on a country newspaper and later as a clerk. When he was 21, his first novel, *The Two Sisters*, was published. Bates completed his education by reading the works of authors who came to have a big influence on him, such as ANTON CHEKHOV, GUSTAVE FLAUBERT and GUY DE MAUPASSANT. He worked in a London bookstore, but began to write full time in his 20s.

In 1931, Bates married Marjorie Cox and went to live in southeast England, where he remained for the rest of his life – apart from during World War II, when he served in the Royal Air Force in Burma. He loved the British countryside and was inspired by it as THOMAS HARDY had been. Successful both in America and Britain, he published mainly short stories at the beginning of his career, and his essay *The Modern Short Story* is now respected as a classic. During the war, he wrote novels based on his experiences and followed those with one of his best-known works, *The Jacaranda Tree*, set in Burma.

At age 53, he published the comic story about the countryside adventures of the vulgar but good-natured Larkin family, *The Darling Buds of May*. In the 1990s, the novel received new life as a popular television series.

Publications

1926 The Two Sisters
1935 The Poacher
1939 My Uncle Silas
1940 The Beauty of the Dead
1941 The Modern Short Story
1944 Fair Stood the Wind for France
1947 The Purple Plain
1949 The Jacaranda Tree
1952 Love for Lydia
1958 The Darling Buds of May

BAUDELAIRE, Charles

French poet

Born Apr. 9, 1821
Died Aug. 31, 1867
Age at death 46

Charles Baudelaire was a radical and influential French poet. He introduced the themes of loneliness, decay and hopelessness, which came to dominate much of modern poetry.

Paris was the city of Baudelaire's birth, his lifelong home, and the setting for most of his poems. The death of his father left him set to inherit a large fortune, but his mother's marriage to a strict soldier made his childhood unhappy.

After graduating from university, Baudelaire went on a sea voyage to India. His journey was interrupted on the island of Mauritius, where he fell in love with a woman named Jeanne Duval, who became the inspiration for his early poetry. He called her the Black Venus.

Returning to Paris four years later, Baudelaire, now 22, inherited his father's fortune and settled into a life of luxury and artistic pursuits. He became well known for his writings about painting, and also his poetry. His great masterpiece, the poetry collection *The Flowers of Evil*, was published when he was 36. Its 101 poems, including many sonnets, are among the greatest works of French literature. They are full of beautiful poetic images created from a bleak and ugly view of modern urban life. Baudelaire's descriptions of the undesirable side of human nature shocked readers. He was convicted of immorality, and six of his poems were banned from publication.

Baudelaire later suffered from illness and drug use and wrote little. He was the first to translate the eerie tales of EDGAR ALLAN POE into French.

Publications

1847 La Fanfarlo
1857 The Flowers of Evil
1860 Artificial Paradises

Published after he died

1869 Little Prose Poems

BAUM, L. Frank

American children's writer and playwright

Born May 15, 1856
Died May 6, 1919
Age at death 62

L. Frank Baum wrote *The Wonderful Wizard of Oz*. Although he wrote many other popular children's books during his lifetime, the land of Oz took on a life of its own and is now more famous than its creator, who came to be known as the "Royal Historian of Oz." The 1939 movie of his book, starring Judy Garland, is a classic.

Lyman Frank Baum was born in Chittenango, New York. His parents got rich from oil, and Baum spent years drifting from one job or failed business venture to another. He acted, set up a theater that burned to the ground, sold axle grease, ran a newspaper, and even set up a doomed department store selling fancy goods in a frontier town. Finally his mother-in-law encouraged him to write down the stories that he told his four sons.

Baum's first book, *Mother Goose in Prose*, was published when he was 41. His first success, however, came two years later with the bestselling and beautifully illustrated *Father Goose: His Book*. Baum and the illustrator also worked together on *The Wonderful Wizard of Oz*, published when Baum was 44.

Written with the aim of amusing children, *The Wonderful Wizard of Oz* became one of the first modern American fairy tales. It stars the Tin Woodman, the Cowardly Lion, the Scarecrow and Dorothy (one of the first positive female role models in young fiction), and is set in the fantastical land of Oz. The book was a huge success, and Baum went on to write several more books about Oz, Dorothy and her friends. Even after Baum's death, stories about Oz continued to be written by other authors.

Publications

1897 Mother Goose in Prose
1899 Father Goose: His Book
1900 The Wonderful Wizard of Oz
1901 Dot and Tot of Merryland
1901 American Fairy Tales
1904 The Marvellous Land of Oz
1908 Dorothy and the Wizard of Oz
1914 Tik-Tok Man of Oz
1915 The Scarecrow of Oz

BAUM, Vicki

Austrian-born American novelist

Born Jan. 24, 1888
Died Aug. 29, 1960
Age at death 72

Vicki Baum is most famous as the author of the bestselling novel *Grand Hotel*, which became a successful play and an Academy Award-winning movie, starring Greta Garbo.

Baum was born in Vienna, the capital city of Austria, into a middle-class Jewish family. Her mother insisted that Baum have a career, so she began harp lessons when she was eight and attended the Vienna Conservatory, a famous music school, until she was 22. She began playing in leading orchestras while still a teenager.

During World War I, Baum gave up music to raise her two sons and began publishing stories she had written in her teens to earn extra money. Early versions of her novel *Grand Hotel* appeared as a serial in a German magazine when Baum was in her early 30s. It tells the interconnected stories of a group of people who happen to be staying in the same hotel at the same time. Published as a book when Baum was 41, *Grand Hotel* was a great success. She rewrote it as a play, which appeared in New York in 1931. She then moved to America, settling in Los Angeles, where she worked as a screenwriter. Although she wrote a screenplay of her novel, it was not used for the famous 1932 movie version.

Baum wrote several more novels that used ideas similar to *Grand Hotel*, including *Shanghai '37* and *Hotel Berlin '43*, but none was as popular as her original. Tired of being expected to write the same kind of book again and again, she turned to other themes in her later novels.

Publications

1929 Grand Hotel
1934 Falling Star
1939 Shanghai '37
1944 Hotel Berlin '43
1948 Headless Angel
1951 Danger from Deer
1953 The Mustard Seed
1958 Theme for Ballet

Published after she died

1962 It Was All Quite Different

BEAUMARCHAIS

French playwright

Born Jan. 24, 1732
Died May 18, 1799
Age at death 67

Pierre Augustin Caron, who took the name Beaumarchais in 1757, is best known today as the author of *The Barber of Seville* and its sequel *The Marriage of Figaro*. These two plays were adapted into even more famous operas, the first composed by Gioacchino Rossini, the second by Wolfgang Amadeus Mozart. They are typical of the light comedies popular in Europe in the 18th century.

Beaumarchais was born in Paris. He was the son of a watchmaker and learned the trade himself. He even invented a new form of escapement (the mechanism that controls the speed of watches). Beaumarchais led a varied and exciting life. He became music teacher to the daughters of King Louis XV, he was sent as a secret agent to Britain, and his business speculations included supplying guns to the American revolutionaries for their fight against the British.

The Barber of Seville and *The Marriage of Figaro*, first produced when Beaumarchais was 43 and 52 respectively, are satires that show clever servants outwitting their aristocratic employers. Beaumarchais was critical of the nobility and showed great sympathy for the lower classes. Opposition to aristocratic privilege was growing in France at the time and was soon to explode in the French Revolution. It has been said that a performance of *The Marriage of Figaro* was the final spark that set off the revolution.

Even though he supported the revolution, the revolutionaries forced Beaumarchais to go into exile in 1792. His wealth and former association with the royal court made them suspect that he favored the old order.

Publications

1767 Eugénie
1770 The Two Friends
1775 The Barber of Seville
1784 The Marriage of Figaro
1787 Tarare
1792 The Guilty Mother

BEAUVOIR, Simone de

French novelist, essayist and short-story writer

Born Jan. 9, 1908
Died Apr. 14, 1986
Age at death 78

Simone de Beauvoir is regarded as one of the leading feminist writers of the 20th century.

Beauvoir was born in central Paris, where she lived for most of her life. Her father was a lawyer, and her mother was a devout Catholic. Beauvoir later rejected their traditional, religious values in search of a new and freer way of life. While studying at the Sorbonne, she met the young philosopher JEAN-PAUL SARTRE. They became lifelong partners but never married, believing marriage to be an outdated idea.

Beauvoir published her first novel, *She Came to Stay*, when she was 35. It is about the relationships between a trio of two women and one man and was based on her experience of living with Sartre and another woman. She wrote two more novels and several works of philosophy, based on ideas she developed with Sartre, before publishing her most famous book, *The Second Sex*, when she was 41.

The Second Sex has been described as the most important work in the history of feminist writing. In it, Beauvoir attempts to describe exactly what it means to be a woman. Its central idea is summed up in the famous phrase "One is not born a woman, one becomes one" – Beauvoir believed that it is only tradition and social constraints that put women in an inferior position. Although this idea is widely accepted today, at the time many people believed women were born inferior.

Beauvoir's ideas shocked many people, but brought inspiration and hope to millions of women who recognized their own lives in her writing.

Publications

1943 She Came to Stay
1949 The Second Sex
1954 The Mandarins
1958 Memoirs of a Dutiful Daughter
1960 The Prime of Life
1972 All Said and Done
1979 When Things of the Spirit Come First
1981 A Farewell to Sartre

BECKETT, Samuel

Irish playwright and novelist

Born Apr. 13, 1906
Died Dec. 22, 1989
Age at death 83

Samuel Beckett was one of the most important and influential writers of the 20th century. He is best known as the leading dramatist of the 1950s movement called the theater of the absurd. He won the Nobel Prize for Literature in 1969.

Born in Dublin, Beckett was brought up in a middle-class Protestant household. After graduating from Trinity College, Dublin, he taught English in Paris, where he first met his lifelong friend, JAMES JOYCE. He returned to Trinity College at the age of 24, but decided that he disliked academic life and set off on his travels around Europe. Several years later, he settled in Paris hoping to earn a living as a writer. During World War II, Beckett was a member of the French Resistance, which fought against the German occupation of France.

Beckett's first full-length novel, *Murphy*, was written in English and published when he was 32. Most of the works that followed were written in French and then translated into English, including the important trilogy of novels *Molloy*, *Malone Dies* and *The Unnameable*. His play *Waiting for Godot* brought him international fame. Beckett's works are very complex and deal with difficult questions. His characters often seem to be full of despair about death and people's failure to communicate with each other. Despite this dark side to his work, Beckett often used absurd humor. *Waiting for Godot* has a despairing message, but is also one of the theater's greatest comedies.

As Beckett grew older his plays became stranger: *Breath*, written when he was 64, consists of a pile of rubbish, a breath and a cry.

Publications

1938 Murphy
1951 Molloy
1951 Malone Dies
1953 The Unnameable
1953 Waiting for Godot
1957 Endgame
1961 Happy Days
1970 Breath
1973 Not I
1981 Ill Seen Ill Said

BEHAN, Brendan

Irish playwright, novelist and journalist

Born Feb. 9, 1923
Died Mar. 20, 1964
Age at death 41

Brendan Behan was a famous Irish playwright, though he published only two plays in his lifetime. His plays had a powerful impact when they first appeared because they dealt with tough political issues of the day. Behan was a heavy drinker, and he sometimes turned up at performances of his plays to argue with the audience. This colorful behavior helped make him famous, but it also led to his early death.

Behan was born in Dublin. Ireland was then part of Britain, but most Irish people wanted independence. There was a civil war in Ireland just before Behan was born. Throughout his childhood, the Irish Republican Army (IRA) continued the fight to get rid of the British. Behan's father was a member of the IRA, and at the age of 14, Behan also joined. Two years later, he was caught trying to blow up a British battleship and was put in jail. He was in and out of jail until 1946.

In his mid-20s, Behan began earning a living as a journalist and also began to write plays for radio. For his first stage play, *The Quare Fellow*, produced when Behan was 37, he drew on his own experience. The play is set in a prison on the eve of an execution. His books *Borstal Boy* (a borstal is a jail for young people) and *Confessions of an Irish Rebel* are also autobiographical.

The Hostage, Behan's second play, was first produced in Irish as *An Gaill*. It is about an English soldier held by the IRA. Further work was left unfinished when Behan died from diabetes and a liver condition caused by his heavy drinking.

Publications

1954 The Quare Fellow
1958 The Hostage
1958 Borstal Boy
1958 The Big House
1962 Brendan Behan's Island

Published after he died

1964 Hold Your Hour and Have Another
1964 The Scarperer
1965 Confessions of an Irish Rebel

BEHN, Aphra

English playwright, novelist and poet

Born Jul. 1640
Died Apr. 16, 1689
Age at death 48

Aphra Behn was probably the first Englishwoman to earn a living as a writer. Details about her place of birth and her parents are not clear, but historians are certain that she spent her childhood in Suriname in South America, which was then ruled by the British.

After returning to England, Behn married a merchant who died a few years later in 1666, leaving her with no money. At that time, England was at war with the Dutch, and Behn volunteered to work as a spy in Holland. Her spy name was Astrea, which she later also used as a pen name for her poetry. Unfortunately, the English government did not pay her for her services, and she was thrown into prison because of her debts.

Behn next turned to writing as a way to earn money. When she was 30, she wrote her first play, *The Forced Marriage*, which was a big success. Following the restoration of the English monarchy in 1660, laws restricting drama were abolished, and playwrights took full advantage of the new freedom to write satirical, rude and outrageous plays. Behn was one of the most popular writers of what is now known as Restoration Drama.

Behn's plays attacked the conventions that prevented women from living as equals to men. Although they contain a strong message, her plays are above all funny, entertaining and profitable. She also wrote a novel based on her childhood memories of South America. *Oroonoko*, published just one year before her death, is a romantic adventure story about a slave revolt led by an African prince. It was one of the first books to criticize the slave trade.

Publications

1670 The Forced Marriage
1677–81 The Rover
1678 Sir Patient Fancy
1682 The Roundheads
1682 The City Heiress
1688 Oroonoko

Published after she died

1690 The Widow Ranter

BELLOC, Hilaire

French-born British writer

Born Jul. 27, 1870
Died Jul. 16, 1953
Age at death 82

Hilaire Belloc was a versatile writer who wrote more than 100 books on a variety of subjects, but he is now remembered for his books of children's verse such as *The Bad Child's Book of Beasts*.

Belloc was born near Paris, to an English mother and French father, but the family moved to London shortly after Belloc's birth. His father died when Belloc was only two years old, and the family stayed on in England, spending many holidays in France. Belloc did military service in the French Army but, at age 22, he returned to England to study history at Oxford University. He was raised a Roman Catholic and remained in that faith all his life.

The Bad Child's Book of Beasts, Belloc's first book of comic verse, came out when he was 26. It was an instant success. He then married and, a few years later, became a British citizen. This made it possible for him to enter politics, and for four years he was a member of parliament.

Belloc wrote books on many of his numerous interests, including history, politics, religion and travel (*The Path to Rome* is about a walk he made from France to Rome when he was 30). He was an outspoken critic of society and, in *Cautionary Tales*, published when he was 37, he made fun of Victorian values. This book of humorous poems for children includes characters such as Matilda, who tells terrible lies and comes to a nasty end, and Jim, who wanders away from his nurse and gets eaten up by a lion. The writer G.K. CHESTERTON was friends with Belloc and illustrated many of his books.

Publications

- *1896 The Bad Child's Book of Beasts*
- *1901 Robespierre*
- *1902 The Path to Rome*
- *1907 Cautionary Tales*
- *1912 The Servile State*
- *1925–31 History of England*
- *1928 Belinda*
- *1932 The Postmaster General*
- *1934 Cromwell*

BELLOW, Saul

Canadian-born American novelist and short-story writer

Born Jun. 10, 1915

Saul Bellow is considered to be one of America's finest living writers. He has won many awards for his work, including the Nobel Prize for Literature in 1976.

Bellow was born in Montreal, Canada. His parents were Russian Jews who had recently arrived as immigrants from St. Petersburg. Bellow's father was a businessman, but he was not always successful. When Bellow was nine, his father moved the family to the United States, settling in Chicago. Here Bellow, who could speak English, French, Hebrew and Yiddish, grew up and went to school. Later, he studied at universities in Chicago and Illinois and, after graduating when he was 21, he decided to become a writer. By this time, Bellow had married his first wife and needed to earn money. He began working as a teacher and also helped compile the literature section of the *Encyclopaedia Britannica*, as well as writing novels.

During World War II, Bellow joined the merchant marine. He used this experience as the basis for his first novel, *Dangling Man*, published when Bellow was 29. It is about the thoughts and feelings of a man waiting to be drafted into the army. After the war, Bellow returned to his life of teaching and writing.

Bellow often writes about people who feel that they do not fit in with the world they live in, who feel that they are outsiders and do not belong. Many of his stories are both sad and funny at the same time. Typical of this is his novel *Humboldt's Gift* – a comic book about death that won the Pulitzer Prize in 1976.

Publications

- *1944 Dangling Man*
- *1947 The Victim*
- *1953 Adventures of Augie March*
- *1956 Seize the Day*
- *1959 Henderson the Rain King*
- *1964 Herzog*
- *1975 Humboldt's Gift*
- *1982 The Dean's December*
- *1987 More Die of Heartbreak*
- *1997 The Actual*

BELY, Andrei

Russian novelist and poet

Born Oct. 26, 1880
Died Jan. 7, 1934
Age at death 53

Andrei Bely was a leading figure in Russia's symbolist movement, which emphasized spiritual and mystical elements in art, during the early 20th century. He is best known for his novel *Petersburg*, which has been compared to the masterpieces of James Joyce and Franz Kafka.

Bely was born Boris Nikolayevich Bugayev in Moscow. Although he had a deep interest in romantic music, philosophy and religion, Bely studied science at the University of Moscow before focusing on literature. His first collection of poems, *Gold in Azure*, was published when he was 24. Bely's third volume of verse, *The Urn*, contains love poems inspired by an affair with the wife of his friend and fellow poet, Aleksandr Blok. There was such long-running bitterness between the two poets that they had challenged each other to several duels before Bely fell in love with another woman.

Bely's reputation as an outstanding writer rests on his novels. His first, *The Silver Dove*, published when he was 29, is the story of a young poet who thinks he will be spiritually revived by spending time among simple rural people. His second novel, *Petersburg*, is considered to be his masterpiece. Set during the unsuccessful Russian revolution of 1905, it tells of a group of radicals planning an assassination. It has a bizarre humor: the bomb is camouflaged as a can of sardines, and one of the radicals is the son of the intended victim. Like *Ulysses* by James Joyce, *Petersburg* plays with language, making it difficult to grasp. It also explores themes of identity and history.

Publications

1904 Gold in Azure
1908 Ashes
1909 The Urn
1909 The Silver Dove
1913 Petersburg
1921 First Meeting
1921 Diary of an Eccentric
1922 Kotik Letayev
1923 Reminiscences about Blok
1934 Gogol's Mastery

BENAVENTE, Jacinto

Spanish playwright and poet

Born Aug. 12, 1866
Died Jul. 14, 1954
Age at death 87

Jacinto Benavente was a popular Spanish playwright and poet. He won the Nobel Prize for Literature in 1922.

Benavente was born in Madrid, where his father was a wealthy doctor. After school and university he ran a circus and toured with it around Europe. Soon he became bored, and turned to writing instead. In 1892, he published a book of plays and, the next year, a collection of poems. He had his first success at age 28 with his comedy play, *Another's Nest*.

When Benavente started writing, Spanish drama was in a state of decline. Spanish audiences were used to plays written in verse in which characters acted with extreme, unrealistic emotion. Benavente's characters were witty, and spoke and behaved more like real people. Many of his plays were satires attacking Spanish society, which Benavente believed had become corrupt and outdated. His play *For Heaven and the Highest* was banned by the government because it looked forward to a time when the Spanish monarchy no longer existed.

In 1936, Spain was torn apart by the Spanish Civil War. The monarchy had already ended, as Benavente had predicted, but he supported the losing side in the war, and was imprisoned for a time. After the war finished in 1939, Benavente was released and he re-established his popularity.

Benavente wrote over 170 plays. He translated the plays of William Shakespeare and Molière into Spanish, and he toured North and South America with his own theater company. He also wrote plays for children and established a children's theater.

Publications

1894 Another's Nest
1896 People You Know
1903 Saturday Night
1905 The Evil Doers of Good
1905 Autumnal Roses
1907 The Bonds of Interest
1908 Señora Ama
1913 The Passion Flower
1928 For Heaven and the Highest
1945 The Noblewoman

BENEDETTI, Mario

Uruguayan writer

Born Sep. 14, 1920

Mario Benedetti is regarded as one of the greats of South American literature. A political radical, he is also one of Uruguay's most popular writers.

Benedetti was born in Pasa de Los Toros in Uruguay and moved with his family to the capital city, Montevideo, when he was four. He attended a German school there and later moved to Buenos Aires, Argentina, where he worked as a journalist. When he was 25, he published his first collection of poems, *The Ineffaceable Eve*.

At age 36, Benedetti published *Office Poems*, a collection of verse about working in an office. Its unusual theme made the book a success. Benedetti followed it up with short stories, his first novel and a book of essays, and he soon became the most widely read author in Uruguay.

The main theme of Benedetti's novels and stories over the next 20 years is the decay and corruption of Uruguayan society. For example, in his third novel, *Thank You for the Light*, he contrasts the liveliness of US society with the old-fashioned opinions and customs of Uruguay through the story of a group of Uruguayans in New York City.

In 1973, the Uruguayan government was taken over by the military. The new regime did not tolerate any criticism and used censorship, torture and murder to crush its political opponents. Like many other writers and thinkers, Benedetti left the country and lived in exile. His writings over the next ten years drew the world's attention to the injustices in Uruguay. When the regime collapsed in 1985, Benedetti returned to live in Montevideo.

Publications

1949 This Morning
1955 Which One of Us
1956 Office Poems
1959 Montevideanos
1960 The Truce
1965 Thank You for the Light
1968 Death and Other Surprises
1977 The House and the Brick
1982 Spring with a Broken Corner
1984 Diverse Geography

BENÉT, Stephen Vincent

American poet and short-story writer

Born Jul. 22, 1898
Died Mar. 13, 1943
Age at death 44

Stephen Vincent Benét is remembered today for his American Civil War poem *John Brown's Body* and his popular short stories.

Benét was born in Bethlehem, Pennsylvania. His father was an army colonel, and the family frequently moved from one military posting to another, eventually settling in New York. By the time Benét graduated from Yale University, he had published two volumes of verse, including *Five Men and Pompey* when he was only 17.

Benét made his living solely from writing. He was influenced by his father's books on military subjects, and his writing was distinguished by its patriotism and historical detail. Benét was also influenced by folktales and ballads. His long narrative poem, *John Brown's Body*, won him the Pulitzer Prize in 1929 and remains a classic of American literature. In it he tried to give a full picture of the Civil War, from the earliest events leading up to the conflict to actual battlefield scenes. The action is seen from the point of view of various characters, including a farmer, a slave and an abolitionist. Benét's short story "The Devil and Daniel Webster" is also a classic and has been made into a movie. It is a humorous retelling of an event in New England history.

Much of Benét's work explores the American experience. He and his wife, Rosemary Carr, worked together on a book of poetry celebrating well-known historical figures. At the time he died he was writing *Western Star*, a verse epic about the American West. It won a Pulitzer Prize after his death.

Publications

1915 *Five Men and Pompey*
1923 *King David: The Ballad of William Sycamore, 1790–1880*
1923 *Jean Huguenot*
1928 *John Brown's Body*
1937 "The Devil and Daniel Webster"

Published after he died

1944 *Western Star*

BENNETT, Alan

English playwright and screenwriter

Born May 9, 1934

Playwright Alan Bennett came to public attention with his use of satire, which became increasingly popular in England in the 1950s.

Bennett was born in Leeds and educated at Oxford University. He began his career as an actor, performing and co-writing a series of comical sketches, *Beyond the Fringe*. *Forty Years On*, Bennett's first solo work, is typical of his satirical comedies. Set in an English public school, the play pokes fun at the Bloomsbury Group.

Some of Bennett's later work dwells on the subject of alienation. *The Old Country* tells the story of an ex-English spy living in the Soviet Union. Exile as a central theme is also developed in one of his most famous plays for television, *An Englishman Abroad*. It recounts the true story of a meeting between the English spy Guy

Burgess, who defected to the Soviet Union in 1951, and the English actress Coral Browne, on tour in Moscow.

When he was 60, Bennett published *Writing Home*, a collection of essays, speeches and sketches. These give an insight into his humor, which appears to derive from his Protestant upbringing and his family's almost painful obsession with class. The British class system is also the theme of his first screenplay, *A Private Function* (1984). With his writing for films Bennett gained a wider audience. Among his other screenplays are *The Madness of King George* (1994), based on an earlier play, and *Prick Up Your Ears* (1987), a biography of the playwright, Joe Orton.

Publications

1960 Beyond the Fringe
1968 Forty Years On
1971 Getting On
1973 Habeas Corpus
1977 The Old Country
1982 An Englishman Abroad
1991 The Madness of King George
1992 Talking Heads
1994 Writing Home
1998 Talking Heads 2
1999 The Lady in the Van

BENNETT, Arnold

English novelist and playwright

Born May 27, 1867
Died Mar. 27, 1931
Age at death 63

Arnold Bennett is best known for his early novels depicting, in gritty realism, life in the part of industrial England known as the "Potteries."

Bennett was born in Staffordshire, the son of a solicitor and the eldest of nine children. Encouraged by his father, Bennett became a lawyer's clerk after attending London University, but his real passion, writing, was soon to take him down a very different career path. He worked as a journalist, and before age 30 he had become editor of the women's magazine *Woman*.

Bennett's first novel, *A Man from the North*, was published when he was 31. Following his father's death in 1902, Bennett moved to Paris, France, where he was heavily influenced by the work of French novelists Gustave Flaubert and Honoré de Balzac. Although he produced his best-known work in Paris, Bennett's roots were firmly planted in industrial England. *Anna of the Five Towns*, *The Old Wives' Tale* and *Clayhanger*, for example, are all set in the "Potteries," an area so named because it was known for its production of china and earthenware. Many of the titles refer to the "five towns" of the area, which are now part of the modern city of Stoke-on-Trent. *The Old Wives' Tale* is considered one of the best English novels of the 20th century.

In total, Bennett wrote more than 30 novels and plays. During the 1920s, his literary reputation declined, but this was reversed with the publication in three volumes of *The Journals of Arnold Bennett* just after his death.

Publications

1898 A Man from the North
1902 Anna of the Five Towns
1902 The Grand Babylon Hotel
1908 The Old Wives' Tale
1910 Clayhanger
1911 The Card
1915 These Twain
1924 Riceyman Steps

Published after he died

1932–33 The Journals of Arnold Bennett

BERRYMAN, John

American poet and critic

Born Oct. 25, 1914
Died Jan. 7, 1972
Age at death 57

John Berryman is one of America's best-known modern poets. Born in McAlester, Oklahoma, he was given the name John Smith. His father shot and killed himself at the family home when Berryman was 12 years old. When Berryman's mother married again, John took his stepfather's name.

Berryman was a gifted student, and after studying at Columbia University in New York and at Cambridge University, he became a university lecturer. Berryman's first important work, *Homage to Mistress Bradstreet*, was published when he was 42 years old. This long poem is a kind of imaginary conversation between the poet and ANNE BRADSTREET, the first woman poet of the American colonies. In Berryman's next poem, the Pulitzer Prize-winning *77 Dream Songs*, he writes about an imaginary character – a middle-aged American called Henry – whose life is full of sorrows, problems and disappointments. Berryman completed his examination of Henry's life in *His Toy, His Dream, His Rest*. These two works are notable for Berryman's use of ordinary, everyday American speech, including the rhythms of Black English, which was unusual in poetry at the time.

The sad and confused Henry is generally understood to be a representation of the poet himself. Berryman was a deeply unhappy and insecure man who struggled for many years against an addiction to alcohol. His alcoholism, combined with his misery, led to increasing mental instability and, in 1972, Berryman took his own life by jumping off a bridge in Minneapolis into the frozen Mississippi River.

Publications

1942 Poems
1948 The Dispossessed
1956 Homage to Mistress Bradstreet
1964 77 Dream Songs
1968 His Toy, His Dream, His Rest
1970 Love and Fame

Published after he died

1972 Delusions, etc
1973 Recovery

BETI, Mongo

Cameroonian novelist

Born Jun. 30, 1932

Mongo Beti is the pen name used by Alexandre Biyidi. He is one of the most famous and most important African authors writing in French.

Beti was born near Yaoundé, the capital of Cameroon, which was then a part of the French West Africa colony. Although expelled from the local school at the age of 14 for being a rebel, he went on to study French at the University of Yaoundé. Later, he studied at the famous Sorbonne University in Paris.

By age 26, Beti had produced four novels. He believes that French rule had harmed African society and used satire and humor to show this in his work. *The Poor Christ of Bomba*, his most famous book, is about a well-meaning missionary who comes to realize that he is just a servant of French rule in Africa. Beti's best work, *Mission Accomplished*, is about a young man who finds that his French education has left him with no place in African society.

Beti moved to France at age 27, and stopped writing for more than 15 years. During this time he took an active role in Cameroon's struggle for independence. His interest in politics led to his next published book, *Rape of Cameroon,* which was banned in both France and Africa. A nonfiction work, it accused the rulers of independent Cameroon of serving the interests of France. The same accusation was worked into his next novel, *Remember Ruben*.

Considered together, Beti's work imaginatively and humorously charts the 20th-century history of Africa from European rule to independence – a time of great change that he himself has lived through.

Publications

1954	*Cruel City*
1956	*The Poor Christ of Bomba*
1957	*Mission Accomplished*
1958	*King Lazarus*
1972	*Rape of Cameroon*
1974	*Remember Ruben*
1979	*The Almost Laughable Downfall of a Buffoon*
1985	*Lament for an African Pol*

BETJEMAN, John

English poet and essayist

Born Aug. 28, 1906
Died May 19, 1984
Age at death 77

John Betjeman was a popular English poet. He was given the honorary title "Sir" in 1969 and was made Poet Laureate of England in 1972. He wrote his autobiography, *Summoned by Bells*, in verse. His prose works include guides to several English regions.

Betjeman was born in London. After studying at Oxford University, which he left without graduating, he taught school for a while and then began writing for an architectural journal. His poems first appeared in magazines when he was 24. At age 25, he published his first book of poems, *Mount Zion*, and two years later his first book on architecture, *Ghastly Good Taste*.

Many of Betjeman's poems can be described as "light verse" – they have strong rhythms and are full of wit and humor. But his poetry has its savage moments, as in the poem written during World War II beginning "Come, friendly bombs and fall on Slough," an English town whose modern architecture he detested. Betjeman was an authority on historical architecture and did much to preserve beautiful ancient buildings.

Betjeman published several volumes of verse, including the very successful *Collected Poems*. Thanks to its "popular" style his poetry was not favored by the critics, but the British people loved it because he wrote about the everyday things they knew, such as railroad stations and suburban life. His recollections of life before World Wars I and II pleased a public that had suffered from the hardships brought about by those wars.

Publications

1931	*Mount Zion*
1933	*Ghastly Good Taste*
1945	*New Bats in Old Belfries*
1952	*First and Last Loves*
1958	*Collected Poems*
1960	*Summoned by Bells*
1966	*High and Low*
1975	*A Nip in the Air*
1981	*Church Poems*
1982	*Uncollected Poems*

BIERCE, Ambrose

American horror writer

Born Jun. 24, 1842
Died Jan. 11, 1914
Age at death 71

Ambrose Bierce was an influential figure in the history of horror fiction.

Bierce was born into a poor family in Ohio. His father was an eccentric who gave all his 13 children names beginning with the letter "A." Bierce was raised in a strict religious atmosphere and grew up hating his family. As a young man he fought in the American Civil War. The horrors he experienced in war added to his negative outlook.

After the war, Bierce moved to California and became a journalist, writing witty newspaper columns. He also began to write stories that shocked his readers – tales of cruelty and death told in a cold and distant voice. His most famous story is "An Occurrence at Owl Creek Bridge," published when he was 49 in *In the Midst of Life*. It begins as a war story about a condemned prisoner waiting to be hanged but turns into a tale of supernatural horror. The prisoner thinks that a miracle of time travel has saved him but returns to reality just as he is about to be hung.

Time travel is a frequent theme in Bierce's work. In his story "An Inhabitant of Corcosa," he imagines a man wandering through a desert where he finds his own grave. Bierce's view was that life is horrific and the afterlife even more so. Although his stories are bleak, they also display an absurd sense of humor.

Bierce was known as a bitter man who generally disliked people. In his 60s, he compiled *The Devil's Dictionary*, a collection of pessimistic, satirical word definitions that convey his views of human nature. His life ended mysteriously when he went to Mexico on a reporting assignment and was never heard of again.

Publications

1872 The Fiend's Delight
1874 Cobwebs from an Empty Skull
1891 In the Midst of Life
1893 Can Such Things Be?
1906 The Devil's Dictionary
1909–12 The Collected Works of Ambrose Bierce

BIRNEY, Earle

Canadian poet, novelist and playwright

Born May 13, 1904
Died Aug. 27, 1995
Age at death 91

Earle Birney has had a huge influence on Canadian literature both as a writer and as a teacher. He wrote a great deal of award-winning poetry as well as popular fiction and drama.

Birney was born in Calgary, Alberta. He grew up in the mountainous wilderness of Canada's British Columbia before studying at British Columbia and Toronto universities. As a student he supported the communist followers of the Russian revolutionary, Leon Trotsky. After graduating, he taught English at Toronto University from 1936 to 1942, when he published his first book of poetry.

During World War II, Birney was an administrator in the army in Canada and later in Europe. The war was a turning point for Birney. He expressed his political concerns in the poems of his first collection, *David and Other Poems*, which was published when he was 38. The famous title poem compares the death wish of a young mountain climber who has been paralyzed by a fall to the fate of Canada following the war.

After the war, Birney taught for 19 years at the University of British Columbia. During his summer breaks, he produced many poetical works and also his first novel, *Turvey,* a comedy based on his time in the army. At first banned for its use of swearing, *Turvey* is now considered a Canadian classic. Birney also set up Canada's first creative writing department at his university. At the age of 61, he retired and committed himself to writing while taking various short-term, but influential, teaching jobs.

Publications

1942 David and Other Poems
1945 Now Is Time
1948 The Strait of Anian
1949 Turvey
1952 Trial of a City
1955 Down the Long Table
1973 The Bear on the Delhi Road
1980 The Mammoth Corridors
1985 The Copernican Fix
1991 Last Makings

BISHOP, Elizabeth

American poet and short-story writer

Born Feb. 8, 1911
Died Oct. 6, 1979
Age at death 68

Elizabeth Bishop is now considered to be one of America's best poets. During her lifetime she won many awards, including a Pulitzer Prize in 1956 for *Poems: North & South – A Cold Spring*.

Bishop was born to Canadian parents in Worcester, Massachusetts. Her father died when she was only months old, and her mother was placed in a mental institution when Bishop was only four. She went to school in Worcester, living with her father's parents, and spent the summers with her mother's parents in Nova Scotia, Canada. Bishop was often absent from school due to ill health, but she read widely. From 1930 to 1934, she attended Vassar College in New York, where she met the poet MARIANNE MOORE, who influenced her own decision to become a poet.

After graduating, Bishop embarked on her many travels. She went to France, North Africa, Spain and Key West in Florida, where she lived between 1937 and 1942. She spent most of 1943 in Mexico and from 1951 to 1969 lived mostly in Brazil.

North & South, Bishop's first book of poems, came out when she was 35. It was well received, and her reputation as a leading poet grew the more she published. She wrote in a polished but natural style about places and ordinary events that had unusual meanings for her. Her poems are carefully written and witty, drawing inspiration from the places she lived and visited, in particular Nova Scotia, Key West and Brazil. In her later years, she taught writing at Harvard University and at the Massachusetts Institute of Technology.

Publications

1946 North & South
1953 In the Village
1955 Poems: North & South – A Cold Spring
1965 Questions of Travel
1969 Complete Poems
1976 Geography III

Published after she died

1983 Complete poems 1927–79
1984 Collected Prose

BJØRNSON, Bjørnstjerne

Norwegian writer

Born Dec. 8, 1832
Died Apr. 26, 1910
Age at death 77

Bjørnson is often called Norway's national poet, and he was certainly the most important Norwegian writer of the 19th century. He was awarded the Nobel Prize for Literature in 1903.

The son of a Lutheran clergyman, Bjørnson was born in Kvikne in scenic southeast Norway. At the age of 18, he went to the University at Oslo but left without a degree to become a journalist. When he was 25, he published his first volume of stories, and from then on a seemingly endless stream of plays, stories, novels, travel books and poems flowed from his pen.

A fine public speaker, Bjørnson was a lifelong champion of liberal views and political freedom. He became a national hero as a result of the major part he played in bringing about Norway's independence from Sweden in 1905. Although always busy writing novels, he developed his interest in the theater and directed some of his own plays. He also worked as an editor and traveled widely.

Bjørnson's writing was inspired by Scandinavian sagas and rural life in contemporary Norway. Some of his best lyrical writing about Norwegian rural life belongs to early novels like *Sunny Hill*. His plays include *Sigurd Slembe*, a historical and patriotic tale, and *The Editor*, which addresses social and political problems. *Beyond Our Power*, perhaps his greatest play, is about a religious man who can perform miracles but is unable to respond to the love of his wife.

His poem "Yes, We Love This Land" is the text of the Norwegian national anthem.

Publications

1857 Sunny Hill
1858 Arne
1860 The Happy Boy
1862 Sigurd Slembe
1868 The Fisher Girl
1870 Poems and Songs
1874 The Editor
1883–85 Beyond Our Power
1889 In God's Way
1898 Paul Lange

BLACKMORE, R.D.

English novelist and poet

Born Jun. 7, 1825
Died Jan. 20, 1900
Age at death 74

Although he wrote more than a dozen novels that during his lifetime made him an important writer about the English countryside, R.D. Blackmore is remembered today only as the author of *Lorna Doone*. This historical romantic adventure was one of Britain's most popular books in the second half of the 1800s and is still in demand today. It has been made into a film, a television series and a comic.

Richard Doddridge Blackmore was born in a rural village in the south of England. His mother died when he was just months old and his father, a clergyman, sent him to live with an aunt in a remote part of southwest England. As a child he was bullied at school, but did well when he studied classical literature at Oxford

University. He graduated aged 22, and two years later began to study law in London. He qualified, but poor health prevented him from practicing, so he turned to teaching. When Blackmore was 32, an uncle left him enough money to buy a farm just outside London. He spent the rest of his days growing fruit and writing fiction.

Lorna Doone, Blackmore's fourth published work, came out when he was 44. It is a tale of murder, highwaymen, bandits, rebellions, smuggling and troubled love. Set in the late 1600s, it is based on the legend of the outlawed Doone family, which terrorized the remote landscape of moors that Blackmore knew as a child. The hero's father is killed by a Doone, and he later falls in love with a young girl they have abducted called Lorna. The successful, unique mix of humor and poetic descriptions proved to be one that Blackmore was not to achieve again.

Publications

1854 Poems by Melanter
1869 Lorna Doone
1872 The Maid of Sker
1875 Alice Lorraine
1876 Cripps, the Carrier
1880 Mary Anerley
1881 Christowell
1887 Springhaven
1894 Perlycross
1897 Dariel

BLAKE, William

English poet

Born Nov. 28, 1757
Died Aug. 12, 1827
Age at death 69

William Blake was a poet, artist and visionary. In his day, many people thought he was insane, but since his death he has been recognized as one of the most original and important English poets.

Blake was born in London, the son of a simple tradesman. He never attended school but despite this acquired a wide knowledge of languages, the Bible and English poetry. In his early teens, he was apprenticed to an engraver, from whom he learned the skills that were to earn him his living.

Blake was an intensely spiritual man. He often had visions of angels and ancient figures from the Bible. He believed that imagination was the most important human experience and should be encouraged.

In his engravings and in his writing, Blake broke all the conventions of his day, searching for imaginative originality. His most famous collections of poems, *Songs of Innocence*, published when he was 32, and *Songs of Experience*, published five years later, are beautifully simple and honest expressions of spiritual and emotional feelings. They include some of his best-loved poems, such as "The Tyger" and "The Rose."

Later in his life, Blake concentrated on a series of poetical works known as the *Prophetic Books*. In these he sketches out the whole history and future of humanity, using an invented mythology inspired by the Bible. As with his earlier books, they were not popular and earned him virtually no money. Only his work as an illustrator was respected in his own time.

After 1818, Blake wrote nothing, but created some of his greatest illustrations for editions of DANTE's *Divine Comedy* and the biblical Book of Job.

Publications

1783 Poetical Sketches
1784 An Island in the Moon
1789 Songs of Innocence
c. 1790–93 The Marriage of Heaven and Hell
1794 Songs of Experience
1794 The Book of Urizen
1797 The Four Zoas
c. 1804–08 Milton
c. 1804–20 Jerusalem

BLISH, James

American science fiction writer

Born May 23, 1921
Died Jul. 30, 1975
Age at death 54

James Blish is known for the deep ideas about science and morality that he put forward in his science fiction.

Blish was born in Orange, New Jersey, and educated at Rutgers and Columbia colleges, where he studied biochemistry. His studies gave him a lifelong interest in genetic engineering (changing the inherited information contained in the cells of plants, animals and humans to breed new kinds of living beings).

As a student, Blish wrote science fiction stories. When he was 19, his first published story, called '"Emergency Refueling," appeared in the magazine *Super Science Stories*. With the outbreak of World War II, Blish was drafted into the army. He began to write again after the war, becoming part of a radical writers' group called The Futurians. But it was not until he was 31 that his work began to attract attention with the publication of "Surface Tension," a story about human beings who have been genetically engineered into microscopic beings that live like fish underwater. This story later appeared in *The Seedling Stars*.

Blish went on to write many more stories and novels, including a series known as *Cities in Flight*, in which whole cities like New York take off into space. The series was inspired by the German philosopher Oswald Spengler, who had written about the decline of culture in the West. Blish's other masterpiece, *A Case of Conscience*, is a novel that explores the concept of sin.

In later life, Blish wrote stories based on the TV series *Star Trek* to earn a living.

Publications

1952	*Jack of Eagles*
1955	*Earthman, Come Home*
1957	*The Seedling Stars*
1958	*The Triumph of Time*
1958	*A Case of Conscience*
1962	*A Life for the Stars*
1964	*Doctor Mirabilis*
1970	*The Day after Judgment*
1970	*Cities in Flight*
1972	*Midsummer Century*

BLOCK, Lawrence

American crime writer

Born Jun. 24, 1938

Lawrence Block is one of the most versatile American crime writers working today.

Born in Buffalo, New York, Block began his literary career by writing "pulp" fiction – stories and novels printed on cheap paper for the commercial market. He worked for a short time in a publishing company, but his skill at writing short stories and novels meant that very soon he was able to earn a living as a writer. He wrote under his own name and under pen names such as Paul Kavanagh and Chip Harrison.

Block is best known for two series of novels that he began when in his 30s. The first describes the adventures of a New York City burglar, Bernie Rhodenbarr, who by day has a job selling secondhand books. These stories are lighthearted, funny and entertaining. The second series is about a New York private detective, Matt Scudder, who practices without a license. Scudder is an ex-policeman who is addicted to alcohol. Block based aspects of Scudder's character on his own experience of being an alcoholic in the 1970s. Block himself eventually went into a recovery program and began to rebuild his life; his character Scudder also goes through this experience.

Unlike the Bernie series, the Matt Scudder books show the dark side of Block's writing. Block is one of the few crime novelists to write in both a humorous and a hard-boiled style – that is, a realistic style that describes the seamy side of life in America's big cities.

Since 1977, Block has written a column for *Writer's Digest* magazine in which he tries to explain the skill of writing to his readers.

Publications

1961	*Mona*
1967	*Tanner's Twelve Swingers*
1976	*In the Midst of Death*
1979	*The Burglar Who Liked to Quote Kipling*
1982	*Eight Million Ways to Die*
1986	*When the Sacred Ginmill Closes*
1991	*A Dance at the Slaughterhouse*
1995	*The Burglar Who Thought He Was Bogart*

BLOK, Aleksandr

Russian poet, playwright, and essayist

Born Nov. 28, 1880
Died Aug. 7, 1921
Age at death 40

Aleksandr Blok was a great Russian poet. He believed that the artist's role was to reveal to humanity the meaning of life.

Blok was born into an intellectual family in St. Petersburg, Russia, and began writing poetry at an early age. His first volume of poetry, *Verses about the Beautiful Lady*, concerns his vision of the "Beautiful Lady" as a force for good. Published when he was 24, the book's success confirmed Blok as one of the foremost poets of the time. The Beautiful Lady became a major poetic symbol. She existed in reality as well: the poems were dedicated to and inspired by his future wife, Lyobov Mendeleyeva, whom he married in 1903.

By 1906, Blok's ideal had been shattered both by the failure of his marriage and the failure of an uprising against the government in 1905. His writing became bitter until the image of Russia itself became his new ideal. From 1908 until the Russian Revolution of 1917, his poetry and plays explored the difference between his idealized Russia and the reality of a country in political and economic turmoil. In 1918, his long poem *The Twelve* generated controversy. For Blok, *The Twelve* was both a celebration of the revolution and his own interpretation of that chaotic period. In the same year he published *The Scythians*, calling for Western support of the new socialist government. Disillusioned by the violence and devastation following 1917, Blok wrote little else and died a broken man.

Publications

1904	*Verses about the Beautiful Lady*
1906	*The Puppet Show*
1907	*The King in the Square*
1907	*Unexpected Joy*
1909	*The Song of Fate*
1913	*The Rose and the Cross*
1918	*The Twelve*
1918	*The Scythians*

Published after he died

1968	*Selected Poems*

BLUME, Judy

American young-adults' writer

Born Feb. 12, 1938

Publications

1970 Are You There God? It's Me, Margaret
1972 It's Not the End of the World
1972 Tales of a Fourth Grade Nothing
1974 Blubber
1975 Forever
1980 Superfudge
1984 Smart Women
1990 Fudge-a-mania
1993 Here's to You, Rachel Robinson
1998 Summer Sisters

Judy Blume is America's most popular writer for teenagers. She is known for her humorous novels that deal in a very frank way with the problems faced by young adults. Since she began writing in the 1970s, Blume has won many awards and sold over 30 million copies of her books.

Blume was born in Elizabeth, New Jersey. Her father was a dentist and her mother a homemaker. She studied early childhood education at New York University. While still a student in 1959, she married and, after graduating, started a family. She did not begin writing until she was in her 30s and her children had begun nursery school.

Are You There God? It's Me, Margaret, Blume's first important work, was published when she was 32. It is about an 11-year-old girl's fears and doubts as her body changes during puberty and about her search for God. It was highly praised for its natural style. As with most of Blume's books, it is written as if told by the child herself.

In other books Blume writes about common problems such as divorce (*It's Not the End of the World*) and being overweight (*Blubber*). While her readers respond well to her writing, some parents dislike the direct way in which she deals with topics such as sex, romance and drugs. Many attempts have been made to restrict the sale of her books. Blume believes that bringing dilemmas into the open can help young people find solutions. With this in mind she has established The Kids Fund – an educational charity that addresses the needs of children.

BLYTON, Enid

English children's writer

Born Aug. 11, 1897
Died Nov. 28, 1968
Age at death 71

Enid Blyton has been called the world's most successful children's author. She created such famous characters as Noddy, the Famous Five, and the Secret Seven. She wrote more than 600 books for children and is one of the most frequently translated English writers.

Blyton was born in London. From an early age she had a great interest in writing. She trained to become a teacher of young children because she felt this would be useful for her planned writing career. Her first published work was a poem that came out in a children's magazine when she was 20 and still training to be a teacher. Five years later, she published her first book of verse, *Child Whispers*.

Over the next two decades, Blyton wrote many poems, stories and educational articles. Her work was popular at first, partly because there was not much children's literature to choose from at that time. In the 1940s, she created some of her most memorable characters: Noddy and his friend Big Ears and, for older children, the adventurous Famous Five and Secret Seven, who are ever busy solving mysteries.

In the 1950s, Blyton's work fell out of favor. She wrote in a simple style that was easy for children to read but was criticized for this by some adults. Many people now feel, however, that her stories get young children into reading. Blyton has also been criticized for snobbery, racism, sexism and for including too strong a Christian message in her work. Nevertheless, her books are still popular today and continue to be read worldwide.

Publications

1922	*Child Whispers*
1927	*A Little Book of Plays*
1937	*Adventures of a Wishing Chair*
1942	*Five on a Treasure Island*
1945	*Mystery of the Secret Room*
1949	*Little Noddy Goes to Toyland*
1949	*The Secret Seven*
1959	*Bom and the Clown*
1965	*The Secret Island*

BOCCACCIO, Giovanni

Italian writer

Born 1313
Died Dec. 21, 1375
Age at death c. 62

Giovanni Boccaccio, an important Italian Renaissance writer, is remembered in particular for his great work *The Decameron*. Many English writers, including GEOFFREY CHAUCER and WILLIAM SHAKESPEARE, were inspired by his prose and poetry.

Boccaccio was the son of a wealthy merchant in Florence, Italy. He studied law at Naples, but his real interest was in writing. As a young man, he entered the court of King Robert of Anjou in western France, where he fell in love with a beautiful noblewoman. From then on this lady inspired his writings, appearing constantly as the character Fiammetta.

In 1340, his father's business failed, and Boccaccio was recalled to Florence. At the time, a bubonic plague, known as the Black Death, was spreading over Europe and approaching Italy. This inspired Boccaccio to write the prose work for which he has ever since been famous – *The Decameron* ("Ten Days' Work"). Its setting is a villa outside Florence, where a group of people have gathered to escape the plague, and it consists of 100 stories told by members of the group over a period of ten days. These stories deal mainly with every aspect of love, from the most pure to the most down-to-earth. The principal character is Fiammetta. *The Decameron* is one of the most popular books ever written and led to a revolution in Italian literature, helping to overthrow the solemn writing of earlier authors.

Boccaccio also wrote much fine poetry. Encouraged by his friend PETRARCH, Boccaccio developed his scholarly interest in the work of ancient Greek and Roman writers and of the great Italian poet, DANTE.

Publications

c. 1338	*Filostrato*
1343	*Fiammetta*
1345	*The Nymph of Fiesole*
1348–53	*The Decameron*
c. 1350–60	*The Genealogy of the Gentile Gods*
c. 1355–74	*Concerning Mountains*
c. 1360–74	*Concerning Famous Women*
1362	*Life of Dante*

BÖLL, Heinrich

German novelist

Born Dec. 21, 1917
Died Jul. 16, 1985
Age at death 67

Publications

1951 Adam, Where Art Thou?
1954 The Unguarded House
1962 Billiards at Half-past Nine
1963 The Clown
1971 Group Portrait with Lady
1974 The Lost Honor of Katharina Blum
1979 Safety Net
1984 What's to Become of the Boy?

Published after he died

1992 The Silent Angel

Heinrich Böll's stories show what life was like for soldiers and ordinary people in Germany during World War II and after, when millions of Germans were homeless and there was not enough to eat. He was awarded the Nobel Prize for Literature in 1972.

Before World War II, Böll worked as a bookseller and went to university for one semester. When the war started in 1939, he was called up into the army and served as an infantryman for six years. He was wounded four times and was briefly a prisoner-of-war.

Böll's early books deal with the horrors of war and the difficulties Germany experienced in recovering from Nazism. *The Unguarded House*, written when he was 37, is about what happens to a group of boys orphaned during these times.

During the late 1950s and '60s, West Germany became increasingly wealthy. Böll was critical of West German society and attacked Germans for what he saw as their endless pursuit of money and lack of morals, and for trying to block out their Nazi past. In the 1970s, when terrorists bombed buildings and people in Germany, Böll argued that the terrorists should be treated fairly by the courts. For saying this he was attacked by many German newspapers. Böll turned these events into a novel, *The Lost Honor of Katharina Blum*.

Böll was a strong supporter of human rights. When the Russian novelist ALEKSANDR SOLZHENITSYN was expelled from Russia, Böll met and befriended him when he arrived in Germany.

BOLTON, Sarah Knowles

American poet, biographer and novelist

Born Sep. 15, 1841
Died Feb. 21, 1916
Age at death 74

Sarah Knowles Bolton used her writing to protest against inequalities in 19th-century America. She promoted social reform for workers and showed that women, who were often held back by society, should be respected for their intelligence and hard work.

Bolton was born in Farmington, Connecticut. Her father died when she was just 11, and she moved with her mother to Hartford, Connecticut, where they stayed with her uncle. As a young woman in Hartford, Bolton met the writer HARRIET BEECHER STOWE, who had a big influence on her.

After graduating from a local girls' school, Bolton became a teacher. Her first job was in Natchez, Mississippi. The American Civil War broke out almost as soon as she got there, so she returned home to teach. In her early 20s she married and settled in Cleveland, Ohio. She became involved with groups campaigning for a ban on alcoholic drinks and wrote a history of the campaign.

Bolton's first collection of poetry, *Orlean Lamar and Other Poems*, came out when she was 23. In 1873, her husband's business went bankrupt, and she supported the family with her writing. She published stories, poetry and a series of biographies for children.

Bolton was ahead of her time in recognizing that women could combine successful careers with raising a family. Much of her fiction is sentimental and has an obvious moral message. But her biographies are models of concise style. *Famous Leaders among Women*, and other books in the series, demonstrate her belief that women can earn respect through education and careers.

Publications

1864	*Orlean Lamar and Other Poems*
1865	*Wellesley*
1874	*The Present Problem*
1885	*Lives of Poor Boys Who Became Famous*
1886	*Lives of Girls Who Became Famous*
1887	*From Heart and Nature*
1895	*The Inevitable and Other Poems*
1895	*Famous Leaders among Women*

BONTEMPS, Arna

American poet, novelist and children's writer

Born Oct. 13, 1902
Died Jun. 4, 1973
Age at death 70

As a writer, historian and librarian Arna Bontemps helped to bring African-American culture and history to the attention of readers and scholars. He was also a major poet in the Harlem Renaissance. Seeking to develop black pride, this 1920s artistic and literary movement produced the first large body of work in the US written by African Americans.

Bontemps was born in Alexandria, Louisiana, but his family moved to Los Angeles when he was three to escape the racism of the South. His father wanted Bontemps to forget the fact that he was black; so they lived in a white area, and Bontemps went to a white boarding school. At this and other schools, he found that African history was hardly taught at all.

After graduating from Pacific Union College, California, Bontemps began his writing career while teaching at various schools. One year later, when he was 21, he published his first poem, "Hope." This and many other fine poems he wrote in the 1920s appear in *Personals*. Bontemps's first novel, *God Sends Sunday*, the story of a famous black jockey, was published when he was 29. His most popular novel was *Black Thunder*, the tale of a slave revolt in the 1800s. He also wrote many children's stories that provide role models for young African Americans.

In 1943, Bontemps became head librarian at Fisk University in Nashville, Tennessee. Over the next 20 years he greatly expanded the library's material on African-American culture, history and personalities. It is now a major resource center. He left Fisk in 1965 to teach at the University of Illinois and then at Yale. He died while writing his life story.

Publications

1931	*God Sends Sunday*
1932	*Popo and Fifina*
1934	*You Can't Pet a Possum*
1936	*Black Thunder*
1940	*Drums at Dusk*
1955	*Lonesome Boy*
1963	*Personals*
1970	*Mr. Kelso's Lion*
1973	*The Old South; 'A Summer Tragedy' and Other Stories of the 1930s*

BORGES, Jorge Luis

Argentinian short-story writer and poet

Born Aug. 24, 1899
Died Jun. 14, 1986
Age at death 86

Publications

1923	*Fervor of Buenos Aires*
1935	*A Universal History of Infamy*
1944	*Fictions*
1949	*The Aleph*
1957	*The Book of Imaginary Beings*
1960	*Dreamtigers*
1962	*Labyrinths*
1970	*Dr. Brodie's Report*
1986	*Atlas*

Jorge Luis Borges is one of the most famous South American writers of the 20th century. He is remembered for writing short stories that explore the boundaries between what is real and what is fiction.

Borges was born in Argentina into an established and wealthy family. He was educated in the capital city, Buenos Aires, and in Switzerland, where his family lived for several years. He read widely in Spanish, French, German, Latin and English.

As a young man Borges lived in Spain and became involved with a group of radical young poets who wanted to revolutionize Spanish poetry. After returning to Buenos Aires, aged 22, Borges became the center of a revival in Argentinian literature. He published his first poetry collection, *Fervor of Buenos Aires*, two years after his return.

In the 1930s, Borges turned his attention to writing short stories. His first important work in this genre was *A Universal History of Infamy*, published when he was 36. This is a collection of criminals' biographies, some of whom are real people and some made up. This mixture of reality and fiction became an important feature of Borges's work.

Borges published his most famous stories in his 40s. Two of his best-known collections, *The Aleph* and *Fictions*, include tales about an infinite library and an infinitely small point in space from which the whole universe can be seen.

Later in life, Borges slowly became blind, and he returned to writing poetry as well as short stories.

BOSWELL, James

Scottish writer and biographer

Born Oct. 29, 1740
Died May 19, 1795
Age at death 54

James Boswell is best known for his biography of his close friend, the English literary figure, DR. JOHNSON.

Born in Edinburgh, the eldest son of a judge, Boswell attended Edinburgh High School then studied law at the universities of Edinburgh and Glasgow. He was already keeping a detailed journal and writing poems when he was 18. At 19, he made his first visit to London and developed a taste for wild living. On his second visit a few years later, he met Dr. Johnson, then at the height of his fame. Boswell was a great admirer of the author of the first English dictionary, and the two became friends.

Boswell went to Holland to continue his legal studies, but after one term he left for a tour of Europe, continuing with his riotous lifestyle, and boldly introducing himself to the French writers VOLTAIRE and JEAN JACQUES ROUSSEAU. At age 28, he published *An Account of Corsica*, which was an immediate success. The following year he married his cousin, Margaret Montgomerie.

At age 33, Boswell was elected to Johnson's literary club, the members of which included some of the most famous men of the time. Boswell took Johnson on a tour of the remote Scottish Hebrides (Johnson described him as "the best travelling companion in the world") and later published *The Journal of a Tour to the Hebrides*. This was so successful that he was encouraged to write his long, detailed and entertaining biography of his friend. *The Life of Johnson* continues to be admired and respected as a brilliant piece of biographical writing.

Publications

1761	*An Elegy on the Death of an Amiable Young Lady*
1761	*An Ode to Tragedy*
1762	*The Cub, at Newmarket*
1767	*The Essence of the Douglas Cause*
1768	*An Account of Corsica*
1786	*The Journal of a Tour to the Hebrides*
1791	*The Life of Johnson*

BOWERING, George

Canadian poet and satirist

Born Dec. 1, 1935

George Bowering, one of Canada's most interesting poets, has won many awards for his unique, playful poetry. There has been some confusion as to exactly where and when he was born, in part created by Bowering himself, who also tries to disrupt his reader's sense of time and place in his work. It is now known that he was born in 1935 in Penticton, British Columbia.

When he was 19, Bowering joined the Royal Canadian Air Force and served as an aerial photographer for three years. He then went to the University of British Columbia, where he studied history and creative writing and then English. After his studies, he lived in various places in Canada before returning to the west as Professor of English at Simon Fraser University in British Columbia.

Bowering started writing as a teenager but was at first more interested in prose than poetry. As a college student, however, he came across a collection of poems by WILLIAM CARLOS WILLIAMS that jolted him into a new awareness of what poetry could do.

Bowering was inspired by the idea that poetry need not be raised above daily life but could instead record seemingly ordinary events and give them new and deeper associations. He published his first collection of poetry, *Sticks & Stones*, when he was 28, and he went on to write many successful and witty poems that break the traditional rules of poetry. He has also written several satirical works of fiction, including *A Short Sad Book*, which makes fun of Canadian art, politics and history while exploring the nature of time.

Publications

1963	*Sticks & Stones*
1970	*A Discovery Poem*
1971	*Touch: Selected Poems*
1971	*Genève*
1972	*Autobiology*
1976	*Allophanes*
1977	*A Short Sad Book*
1980	*Uncle Louis*
1984	*Kerrisdale Elegies*
1985	*Craft-Shoes*

BRADBURY, Ray

American science fiction writer

Born Aug. 22, 1920

Publications

1947 Dark Carnival
1950 The Martian Chronicles
1951 The Illustrated Man
1953 The Golden Apples of the Sun
1953 Fahrenheit 451
1957 Dandelion Wine
1962 Something Wicked This Way Comes
1964 The Machineries of Joy
1969 I Sing the Body Electric!
1988 The Toynbee Convector

Ray Bradbury is one of the founders of modern science fiction.

Bradbury was born in Waukegan, Illinois. His father was a telephone lineman. The family moved to Los Angeles in 1934, and after graduating from secondary school, Bradbury got a job selling newspapers on street corners. He began to write short stories and even set up his own magazine, but it was not until he was 21 that he made any money from his writing. His first paid publication was a story called "Pendulum," published in the magazine *Super Science Stories*. That same year he gave up his newspaper job and became a full-time writer.

The publication of *The Martian Chronicles* in 1950 established Bradbury as an important science fiction writer. In these stories, Bradbury imagines what it would be like if people from Earth tried to invade and settle on Mars. He also imagines what the effects of a huge nuclear war on Earth would be.

As well as short stories, Bradbury has published several novels. The most famous of these is *Fahrenheit 451*, which describes a future society in which books are forbidden. Another of his novels, *Dandelion Wine*, had a crater on the Moon named after it.

Bradbury's stories are not really based on science. Instead, he paints a picture of the future that expresses the hopes and fears of many Americans: the hope for a return to the simple life of a small town, like the one Bradbury grew up in, and the fear of state control and modern technology.

BRADSTREET, Anne

English-born American poet

Born c. 1612
Died Sep. 16, 1672
Age at death c. 60

One of the most important early American poets, Anne Bradstreet is considered to be the first English poet in America. She was a devout Puritan, and much of her poetry reflects her religious views.

Born in the English city of Northampton, she was the daughter of Thomas Dudley, an aristocratic and wealthy Puritan. Her father made sure that she was well educated, and while he worked for the Earl of Lincoln, she was allowed to use the earl's large library. Before the age of 17, she was married to a Puritan minister, Simon Bradstreet. Puritans wanted to reform the Church of England but were often oppressed.

In 1630, with her husband and father, Bradstreet left England for America in search of religious freedom and new opportunities. Her father became governor of Massachusetts Bay Colony. The Bradstreets settled in Ipswich, a relatively large town near Boston, in 1635. Ten years later they moved to the frontier town of Andover, where Bradstreet lived until her death.

Although she raised eight children, Bradstreet managed to write many poems. Her brother-in-law secretly took some to England and published them as *The Tenth Muse Lately Sprung up in America* when Bradstreet was in her late 30s. Her poetry reflects her learning, wit, spirit and discomfort with the inferior status given to women at the time. In her best work she seemed to find ways of overcoming the problems of being a Puritan, a woman and a poet in 17th-century America.

Publications

1650 The Tenth Muse Lately Sprung up in America

1664 Meditations

Published after she died

1678 Several Poems Compiled with Great Variety of Wit and Learning

BRECHT, Bertolt

German playwright and poet

Born Feb. 10, 1898

Died Aug. 14, 1956

Age at death 58

Bertolt Brecht was a German playwright who developed a form of drama called epic theater in which ideas, rather than characters, are important.

Brecht was born in Augsburg, Germany. When he was 19, he enrolled at Munich University to study medicine, but soon after beginning the course he was conscripted into the army. At 20, he wrote his first play, *Baal*. In stark contrast to World War I then raging in Europe, *Baal* celebrates life and sexuality. It was a great success and established Brecht's reputation. At age 24, he won Germany's main literary prize for his play *Drums in the Night.*

Brecht wrote his most popular work, *The Threepenny Opera*, when he was 30. It is based on *The Beggar's Opera* by 18th-century English playwright John Gay. Five years later he was forced to leave Germany because of his anti-Nazi political beliefs. He settled in California in 1941.

The plays written during Brecht's years living outside Germany show clearly the development of his ideas. Brecht believed that the capitalist method of wealth creation oppressed the poor, and he wanted to use theater to make people think about society. Many of his plays use techniques that aim to prevent audiences from becoming too involved in the drama and so miss the message.

While in America Brecht wrote *The Caucasian Chalk Circle*, which the poet W.H. Auden helped translate. In 1947, during the McCarthy era, Brecht was questioned by the government committee investigating communist activity in Hollywood. He left for Europe soon after.

Publications

1918 Baal

1922 Drums in the Night

1928 The Threepenny Opera

1930 The Rise and Fall of the City of Mahogonny

1941 Mother Courage and Her Children

1943 Galileo

1943 The Good Woman of Setzuan

1948 The Caucasian Chalk Circle

BRETON, André

French poet and novelist

Born Feb. 18, 1896
Died Sep. 28, 1966
Age at death 70

André Breton was a French poet who helped found surrealism, one of the most influential artistic movements of the 20th century.

At medical school, Breton was introduced to the new theories of Sigmund Freud, the founder of psychoanalysis. He became fascinated with the workings of the mind and began to experiment with new ways of writing, hoping to reveal the hidden parts of the mind that Freud called the unconscious. At age 25, he wrote a work called *Magnetic Fields,* inspired by words and phrases written down without deliberate thought, a technique that became known as "automatic writing."

Breton became involved with a group of artists called the Dadaists. Although they believed that society and the world had no meaning, Breton felt that a new, meaningful way of thinking could be developed. This new way of thinking became known as surrealism and, in 1924, Breton published the *Manifesto of Surrealism* setting out these beliefs.

Surrealism became very influential. In the 1920s, many writers and artists felt that the death and destruction that Europe had suffered during World War I showed that civilization was sick. They saw surrealism as a new hope for a better world.

Breton became known as "the pope of surrealism" because he had such a strong influence on its ideas. His 1928 novel *Nadja* challenged accepted ideas of what makes us call one person mad and another one sane. Most of Breton's surrealist poetry remained unpublished until after his death.

Publications

1921 Magnetic Fields
1924 Manifesto of Surrealism
1928 Nadja
1932 The Community Vessels
1934 What Is Surrealism?
1937 Mad Love
1948 Poems

Published after he died

1969 Selected Poems
1982 Poems of André Breton

BREYTENBACH, Breyten

South African poet

Born Sep. 16, 1939

Breyten Breytenbach has been called South Africa's finest living poet writing in Afrikaans (the Afrikaner language). He has won many literary prizes.

Breytenbach was born into an Afrikaner family in Cape Province, South Africa – the Afrikaners are descended from 17th-century Dutch settlers. Although most of South Africa's people are black, at the time Breytenbach was born, white South Africans controlled the government and all the major industries. Laws restricted where people could live and whom they could marry.

Breytenbach studied art at college in Cape Town. While still a student he began to write poems that attracted attention for their originality. When he was 20, he left Africa to travel around Europe, settling in Paris, in 1961. He published his first book of poetry, *The Iron Cow Must Sweat*, three years later when he was just 25. It was followed by several more collections.

While in France, Breytenbach married a Vietnamese woman, which would have been illegal in South Africa. In 1973, he visited South Africa with his wife, causing great outrage. He returned illegally the following year and was arrested in 1975 for setting up an antiapartheid movement. He was sentenced to nine years for "terrorism." Even in prison he did not stop writing: *A Season in Paradise* tells of his return home; *The True Confessions of an Albino Terrorist*, written in English, tells of his arrest and imprisonment; and *Mourior* was written while he was locked up alone. Since his release after seven years in prison, Breytenbach has become a French citizen.

Publications

1964	*The Iron Cow Must Sweat*
1967	*The House of the Deaf*
1976	*A Season in Paradise*
1983	*YK*
1983	*Mourior*
1984	*The True Confessions of an Albino Terrorist*
1986	*In Africa Even the Flies Are Happy*
1993	*Return to Paradise*

BRINK, André

South African novelist, short-story writer and playwright

Born May 29, 1935

André Brink is one of the most popular Afrikaner novelists and playwrights working today. He writes in English and in Afrikaans – the language of South African-born people who are descended from 17th-century Dutch settlers.

Brink was born in central South Africa in the Orange Free State. Although most of the population was black (and still is), white South Africans controlled the government and all the major industries. Laws restricted what black people could do. As Brink grew up, the power of whites, and in particular Afrikaners, increased.

Brink went to university in South Africa and began his writing career in his 20s but received little attention at first. For three years, he studied at the famous Sorbonne University in Paris, then returned to South Africa to study and teach at Rhodes University. In the 1960s, Brink was one of a group of Afrikaans writers called the *Sestigers* ("Writers of the 1960s"), who were linked by their radical views. Brink described in his work the evils of the government's racist system, known as apartheid. At age 33, he returned to Paris. He thought he would have to remain there because he was unpopular with the South African rulers, but the 1968 student uprisings in France inspired him to return to his homeland and fight apartheid. Brink's seventh novel, *Looking on Darkness*, was the first Afrikaans book to be banned in South Africa. It made him internationally famous. Many of Brink's later books were banned up until the end of apartheid in the early 1990s.

Publications

1962	*The Price of Living*
1963	*The Ambassador*
1973	*Looking on Darkness*
1978	*Rumors of Rain*
1979	*A Dry White Season*
1983	*Mapmakers: Writing in a State of Siege*
1988	*States of Emergency*
1991	*An Act of Terror*
1993	*On the Contrary*

BRODSKY, Joseph

Russian-American poet and critic

Born May 24, 1940
Died Jan. 28, 1996
Age at death 55

Joseph Brodsky is one of the most respected Russian poets of the 20th century. He was awarded the Nobel Prize for Literature in 1987.

Brodsky was born in Leningrad (now St. Petersburg) just as World War II was beginning. At that time, Russia was ruled by a communist government that strictly controlled all aspects of culture and society. When Brodsky was 15, he left school, determined to educate himself more widely than the state system would allow. He began reading all kinds of literature and taught himself Polish so he could read poetry that had never been translated into Russian.

At age 18, Brodsky began to write poetry. Two years later he met the great Russian poet ANNA AKHMATOVA, who praised and encouraged his work. In 1964, when Brodsky was 24, he was arrested by the authorities and charged with being a useless member of society. Although he had never directly criticized the government in his work, the authorities thought his individualistic style and interest in Western literature were dangerous and sentenced him to five years of hard labor.

The following year a collection of Brodsky's poems was published in America – his work had never been published in Russia. Released after just one year, Brodsky continued to write, although very little of his work was printed. In 1972, after years of persecution, the authorities forced him to leave Russia. He eventually settled in America, where he lectured in universities and continued to write. In 1991, Brodsky was made America's Poet Laureate.

Publications

1965 Poems and Narrative Verse
1967 Elegy to John Donne and Other Poems
1973 Selected Poems
1977 In England
1986 Less Than One: Selected Essays
1988 To Urania: Selected Poems
1988 Marbles
1992 The Form of Time

BROMFIELD, Louis

American novelist, short-story writer and playwright

Born Dec. 27, 1896
Died Mar. 18, 1956
Age at death 59

Louis Bromfield wrote novels and short stories about rural and small-town life at a time when American society was changing rapidly.

Bromfield was born in Mansfield, Ohio, to a farming family. He studied at local schools before trying, unsuccessfully, to rebuild the failing family farm with his father and grandfather. At the age of 18 he went to study agriculture at New York's Cornell University, but switched to studying journalism at Columbia. During World War I Bromfield joined the US Army Ambulance Service. He survived some of the bloodiest battles in Europe and was awarded France's highest medal, the Croix de Guerre ("Cross of War").

Bromfield returned to New York in 1918 to become a writer.

During his lifetime the US economy had become increasingly industrial, with machines doing jobs once done by people. This conflict between old and new featured in much of his work. After destroying the first four novels he wrote, he finally published *The Green Bay Tree* when he was 28. Like much of his work, it is based on his experiences of Ohio at a time when people were leaving the land and moving to the towns to work in industry. The following year Bromfield and his family moved to France, where he finished his novel *Early Autumn*, which won the 1927 Pulitzer Prize. Bromfield spent the next 11 years in France working as a journalist, then returned to Ohio in 1938 to set up a new farm, which he ran as a model in natural farming.

Publications
1924 The Green Bay Tree
1925 Possession
1926 Early Autumn
1927 A Good Woman
1929 Awake and Rehearse
1930 Twenty-Four Hours
1933 The Farm
1937 The Rains Came
1943 Mrs. Parkington
1955 From My Experience

BRONTË, Charlotte, Emily, and Anne

The three Brontë sisters are almost as famous for their short, tragic lives as for their passionate novels, which include two of the most widely read books in the English language – *Jane Eyre* and *Wuthering Heights*.

The Brontë family lived in the north of England on the bleak Yorkshire moors. After Anne's birth their mother died, leaving five sisters and a brother to be raised by their clergyman father and a strict, religious aunt. Both eldest sisters died in their early teens. The others grew up at home, playing on the moors, reading avidly, and writing in tiny books about imaginary kingdoms. They attended school only briefly. Later, however, they worked as teachers or governesses.

In 1846, Charlotte, Emily and Anne published a book of poems together. The finest poems were Emily's. After only a few copies sold, the Brontës tried writing fiction instead. A novel by each sister appeared in 1847: *Agnes Grey* by Anne, aged 27; *Wuthering Heights* by Emily, aged 29; and *Jane Eyre* by Charlotte, aged 31. All three books drew on their authors' own experiences and intense feelings, but the last two are the most striking. *Jane Eyre* tells of a poor but brave girl who falls in love with a harsh landowner. *Wuthering Heights* is a powerful story of love, hate and revenge set on the Yorkshire moors. No other Victorian novel shares its wild, savage spirit. Sadly, by mid-1849 Emily, Anne and their brother had died of tuberculosis. In 1854, Charlotte married a clergyman and died giving birth the next year.

Charlotte Brontë
English novelist
Born Apr. 21, 1816
Died Mar. 31, 1855
Age at death 38
Publications
1847 Jane Eyre
1849 Shirley
1853 Villette
Published after she died
1857 The Professor

Emily Brontë
English novelist and poet
Born Jul. 30, 1818
Died Dec. 19, 1848
Age at death 30
Publications
1847 Wuthering Heights

Anne Brontë
English novelist
Born Jan. 17, 1820
Died May 28, 1849
Age at death 29
Publications
1847 Agnes Grey
1848 The Tenant of Wildfell Hall

BROOKE, Rupert

English poet

Born Aug. 3, 1887
Died Apr. 23, 1915
Age at death 27

Rupert Brooke's poetry stirred patriotism among the English and inspired optimism in the period before World War I.

Brooke was born in Rugby. He won a scholarship to Cambridge University, where he became a prominent figure in literary circles. At age 22, he began to publish his poetry. Four years later he suffered a nervous breakdown and set out on his travels to the United States, Canada and the Pacific. In Tahiti, he wrote what many regard as his best lighter work, including "Tiare Tahiti" and "The Great Lover."

When Brooke returned to England in 1914, World War I had begun. He volunteered to serve in the British forces and continued to write while he was in the army. His collection *1914 and Other Poems* – containing his well-known "war sonnets," including the famous "The Soldier" – was received enthusiastically by the public. Soon after, however, Brooke developed blood poisoning on an expedition to confront the Turkish army and died. He was buried on the Greek island of Scyros.

Brooke's early death, his good looks, and the patriotic ideals of his war poetry contributed to his reputation as England's national poet. As time passed, however, and the works of WILFRED OWEN, SIEGFRIED SASSOON and others began to appear, Brooke's appeal began to wane. The senseless brutality of war overwhelmed the boyish and simplistic appeal of what appeared to be Brooke's call to arms. As time passed, more emphasis was placed on his lighter verse.

Publications

1911 Poems
1915 Lithuania
1915 1914 and Other Poems

Published after he died

1916 Letters from America
1918 Collected Poems

BROOKS, Gwendolyn

American poet and novelist

Born Jun. 7, 1917

The poet Gwendolyn Brooks was the first African American to receive the Pulitzer Prize, which she won in 1950 for her poetry collection *Annie Allen*.

Born in Topeka, Kansas, Brooks was raised in Chicago and has strong ties to the city. Her mother, a teacher, encouraged her love of language and learning and, by age 11, the young Brooks was writing poetry. She was first published when she was 13, and at 16, she met the poet LANGSTON HUGHES. His encouragement was a boost to the young Brooks, who, it is said, hoped that one day her poems would save the world.

After graduating from university in 1936, Brooks married fellow poet Henry Blakely in 1939, and together they had two children.

At age 28, she published *A Street in Bronzeville*, which focuses on the lives of ordinary African Americans and their struggles. Soon after this she began to receive a number of grants and to gain widespread recognition, leading to the Pulitzer Prize. At 36, she wrote her first novel, *Maud Martha*, which is partly based on her own life. Selections from her book *The Bean Eaters* are used in literature classes today.

In the 1960s, Brooks's writing was influenced by the civil rights movement and became more powerful and intense, focusing on issues such as racism and black solidarity. She began to reach out for a wider black audience and to work only with black publishers.

In 1968, Brooks was Poet Laureate of Illinois. In addition to writing, she has held poetry workshops, including one with members of a Chicago gang.

Publications

1945	*A Street in Bronzeville*
1949	*Annie Allen*
1953	*Maud Martha*
1956	*Bronzeville Boys and Girls*
1960	*The Bean Eaters*
1969	*Riot*
1972	*Report from Part One*
1986	*The Near Johannesburg Boy*
1988	*Winnie*
1993	*Report from Part Two*

BROWN, William Wells

American novelist

Born c. 1813
Died Nov. 6, 1884
Age at death c. 71

William Wells Brown was America's first African-American novelist. Born a slave on a plantation in Kentucky, Brown escaped slavery when he was about 20 and settled in Ohio. There he learned to read and write and assisted in the Underground Railroad, helping fugitive slaves get to safety in Canada. In 1836, he moved to Buffalo, New York, where he founded a society for freed slaves and became an antislavery lecturer.

In his mid-30s, Brown published his memoir, the *Narrative of William W. Brown, A Fugitive Slave.* It is a moving account of his cruel treatment under slavery and his escape to freedom. An immediate success, it made Brown a prominent figure in the antislavery movement. Fearful that he might be captured and returned to slavery, Brown moved to England in 1849, where he worked as an antislavery lecturer. While there he published *Clotel; or, The President's Daughter*, the first novel by an African American. The book is about the adventures of Thomas Jefferson's alleged slave daughter. Its dramatic descriptions of slave auctions and escapes to freedom made it a popular antislavery work. The novel's success led Brown to produce several revisions, each with the same basic story but with different characters.

In addition to his novels, Brown also wrote several plays with antislavery themes. *The Escape; or, A Leap for Freedom*, which came out when he was in his mid-40s, was the first play published by an African American.

Publications

1847	*Narrative of William W. Brown, A Fugitive Slave*
1848	*The Antislavery Harp*
1853	*Clotel; or, The President's Daughter*
1858	*The Escape; or, A Leap for Freedom*
1863	*The Black Man: His Antecedents, His Genius, and His Achievements*

BROWNING, Elizabeth Barrett

English poet

Born Mar. 6, 1806
Died Jun. 29, 1861
Age at death 55

Publications

1838	*The Seraphim and Other Poems*
1844	*Poems*
1850	*Sonnets from the Portuguese*
1851	*Casa Guidi Windows*
1856	*Aurora Leigh*
1860	*Poems Before Congress*

Published after she died

1862	*Last Poems*

People once thought Elizabeth Barrett Browning was the finest woman poet in England. Now she is best remembered for her love poems inspired by ROBERT BROWNING.

Elizabeth Barrett was the eldest of 12 children of a rich British owner of Jamaican estates. She grew up in the west of England. Taught at home by a tutor, she quickly learned Latin and Greek and read and wrote avidly. By ten years old she had written a long poem and plays that were acted out in the family nursery. When she was 14, her father privately published her poem *The Battle of Marathon*.

Tuberculosis damaged Browning's spine when she was 15, and she spent much of her life as an invalid. When she was 29, the Barretts moved to a London house, where she kept to her room, becoming deeply depressed by the death of a brother in 1840.

At 32, however, Browning's poetry was making her famous. Critics praised *The Seraphim and Other Poems*, while *Poems* (1844) brought praise from a young British poet, Robert Browning, and the American writer, EDGAR ALLAN POE. Robert Browning and Elizabeth met and fell in love. Against her father's wishes they secretly married and moved to Italy. There they had a son, and she lived happily for her last 15 years. Her famous *Sonnets from the Portuguese* – 44 poems about her love for the man she married – appeared in 1850. "The Portuguese" was Robert Browning's nickname for dark-haired Elizabeth.

BROWNING, Robert

English poet

Born May 7, 1812
Died Dec. 12, 1889
Age at death 77

Robert Browning was a great Victorian poet. In his best poems, people from the past reveal their thoughts and lives as if speaking or thinking aloud.

Browning was born in London. His father was a clerk at the Bank of England. His mother's parents were German. At the family home he read many books in his father's huge library. Reading poems by writers such as PERCY BYSSHE SHELLEY and JOHN KEATS made Browning determined to become a poet himself. Fortunately he was well off, with no need to earn money from better-paid work.

Browning's first poem, "Pauline," appeared when he was 21. Later, he wrote plays and long story-poems such as "The Pied Piper of Hamelin." But his best works are the long speechlike poems in

Dramatic Lyrics, *Men and Women*, *Dramatis Personae*, and *The Ring and the Book* – the work that at last made him famous.

A typical Browning poem tells of a key moment in the life of a prince, priest or painter of the Italian Renaissance. Whether good or wicked, Browning disliked anyone who let life slip away instead of striving to achieve something. He believed that even failures found happiness in Heaven. He often wrote about obscure people and places, and crammed his meaning into so few words that many readers could not grasp what he meant. It was because of this that he was over 50 before he became better known than his wife, ELIZABETH BARRETT BROWNING. Their secret wedding and elopement to Italy in 1846 is a famous love story. After his wife died, he returned to live in England.

Publications

1835 Paracelsus
1840 Sordello
1842 Dramatic Lyrics (including "The Pied Piper of Hamelin")
1845 Dramatic Romances and Lyrics
1855 Men and Women
1864 Dramatis Personae
1868–69 The Ring and the Book
1879–80 Dramatic Idyls
1889 Asolando

BRUNHOFF, Jean de

French children's writer

Born Dec. 9, 1899
Died Oct. 16, 1937
Age at death 37

Jean de Brunhoff created one of the best-loved characters in children's fiction – Babar the Elephant. Brunhoff's books have been translated into at least 15 languages, and Babar continues to appear in books written by Brunhoff's son, Laurent, as well as in films, cartoons and even a ballet.

Brunhoff was born in Paris. His father published art magazines. After finishing school, Brunhoff served in the army for a brief period during World War I before becoming a moderately successful artist. When he was 25, he married a pianist, and they eventually had three sons. Brunhoff's wife told her sons a story about a small elephant. The boys liked it so much that they demanded their father draw some pictures of the elephant. Brunhoff expanded and reworked the tale, added pictures, and named the character "Babar." Friends were so impressed with Brunhoff's creation that they urged him to publish it.

The beautifully illustrated *The Story of Babar, the Little Elephant* was published when Brunhoff was 32. It was a great success, and Brunhoff followed it with six other Babar books. Several were written in Brunhoff's final years during which he spent some time convalescing in a Swiss hospital because he suffered from tuberculosis. Brunhoff's books follow Babar from his childhood in the Great Forest to his manhood as the father of three children and the king of Celesteville, an ideal city. With easy-to-read text and pictures filled with details to catch the eye of small children, the Babar series changed the style of children's books.

Publications

1931 The Story of Babar, the Little Elephant
1932 The Travels of Babar
1933 Babar the King
1934 ABC of Babar
1934 Zephir's Holidays

Published after he died

1938 Babar and His Children
1941 Babar and Father Christmas

BRUTUS, Dennis

South African poet

Born Nov. 28, 1924

Dennis Brutus has been called the "Poet Laureate of South Africa" – he is one of that country's most respected and important poets.

Brutus was born in Zimbabwe to South African parents. The family returned to South Africa shortly after his birth. His parents, who were both teachers, were officially classified as "colored" – meaning that they were of both African and European ancestry. At the time Brutus was growing up, the white South Africans controlled the government and all the major industries. Laws restricted where black and "colored" people could live and what work they could do.

After studying in university, Brutus worked for many years as a teacher. He became active in the fight against the government's racist apartheid policies. He was banned from holding political and social meetings and fired from his job in 1961. Two years later, he was arrested for going to a meeting. While on bail he fled, but was soon caught. He was shot in the back during an escape attempt. He survived, only to spend 18 months doing hard labor in prison. His first collection of poetry, *Sirens, Knuckles, Boots*, was published while he was in jail. Brutus was 39 at the time. Like much of his work, it attacks apartheid. Not allowed to publish after his release, Brutus wrote a series of poems about his time in prison disguised as letters to his sister-in-law Martha. In 1966, he was forced to leave the country, and after a few years in England, he settled in the US. Since 1986, he has taught at the University of Pittsburgh. Brutus has continued to write and to campaign for civil rights in the US and elsewhere.

Publications

1963 Sirens, Knuckles, Boots
1968 Letters to Martha
1970 Poems from Algiers
1973 A Simple Lust
1975 Thoughts Abroad
1975 Strains
1975 China Poems
1978 Stubborn Hope
1984 Salutes and Censures
1989 Airs and Tributes

BRYANT, William Cullen

American poet and journalist

Born Nov. 3, 1794
Died Jun. 12, 1878
Age at death 83

William Cullen Bryant was America's first great poet. He was born in the Berkshire hills of Massachusetts, where he developed an early love of nature that never left him. Bryant always wanted to be a poet and had his first poem published when he was 13. After studying law privately, he opened his practice in Great Barrington, Massachusetts, when he was 22.

Bryant began writing his most famous poem, "Thanatopsis," when he was only 16. The poem is about the meaning of death. It immediately established him as America's leading poet. He was often compared to the English Romantic poet William Wordsworth because of the importance of nature in his writing. Many of Bryant's most significant poems, including "To a Waterfowl," "Inscription for the Entrance to a Wood" and "Green River," describe nature as a symbol of God's power and as a moral force affecting humankind. His later works often deal with religion and humanitarian concerns.

Bryant, who never liked being a lawyer, moved to New York City when he was 31 to become a writer. The following year he became editor of the *New York Post*. For nearly 50 years, from 1829 until his death, he was editor-in-chief and part owner. Under his direction the *Post* became one of the country's most important newspapers. It supported religious freedom, defended organized labor, and opposed slavery. Bryant backed Abraham Lincoln in his campaign for presidency and was one of the founders of the Republican Party.

Publications

1808	"The Embargo"
1817	"Thanatopsis"
1818	"To a Waterfowl"
1821	"Inscription for the Entrance to a Wood"
1821	"Green River"
1821	"The Yellow Violet"
1832	"The Death of the Flowers"
1832	"To the Fringed Gentian"
1834	"The Prairies"

BUCHAN, John

Scottish novelist and biographer

Born Aug. 26, 1875
Died Feb.11, 1940
Age at death 64

John Buchan is famous for his adventure novels, especially *Prester John* and *The Thirty-Nine Steps*. The latter was made into a film by Alfred Hitchcock in 1935, although there have been many other adaptations since then.

Buchan was born in Perth, Scotland, the son of a Protestant minister, and he studied at Glasgow and Oxford universities. He published his first novel at the age of 20. Between 1901 and 1903, he worked in South Africa with the reconstruction commission following the Boer War.

Writing was a hobby for Buchan. He was an active politician and, in 1927, was elected to the British parliament. In 1935, King George V made him a lord (he took the title Baron Tweedsmuir) and appointed him governor-general of Canada. In this position, he represented the king in that country in the monarch's absence.

Although Buchan wrote many nonfiction works, including histories and biographies, his worldwide reputation rests on his adventure stories. These feature a recurring group of heroes (Richard Hannay, Sandy Arbuthnot, Edward Leithen) and are often set in Scotland, southwest England or South Africa. His exciting tales contain all the elements of action-packed movies, with simple characterization, fast-moving plots, and dramatic endings. There are almost always cross-country chases, with magnificent descriptions of the landscape.

Buchan's last novel, *Mountain Meadow,* is set in the icy wastes of Canada, a country he came to love.

Publications

1895	*Sir Quixote of the Moors*
1910	*Prester John*
1915	*The Thirty-Nine Steps*
1916	*Greenmantle*
1921–22	*History of the Great War*
1926	*The Dancing Floor*
1932	*Sir Walter Scott*

Published after he died

1940	*Pilgrim's Way*
1941	*Mountain Meadow*

BUCK, Pearl S.

American novelist

Born Jun. 26, 1892
Died Mar. 6, 1973
Age at death 80

Publications
1930 East Wind: West Wind
1931 The Good Earth
1932 Sons
1935 A House Divided
1936 The Exile
1936 Fighting Angel
1943 Water Buffalo Children
1960 The Christmas Ghost
1969 The Three Daughters of Madame Liang

Pearl S(ydenstricker) Buck was a person of remarkable intelligence and energy. She earned three university degrees, adopted nine children of different nationalities, and wrote more than 80 books. In 1938, she became the first American woman to win the Nobel Prize for Literature.

Buck was born in Hillsboro, West Virginia. Her parents worked as missionaries in China, and she moved there when she was only a few months old. Their lives were sometimes in danger because many of the Chinese had become suspicious of foreigners, but they stayed on, living among local people. Buck learned to speak Chinese before English and didn't return to America until she was 18.

After graduating from university, she moved back to China with her missionary husband, John Buck, whom she married in 1917. They had one child, a daughter, who was born disabled.

When she was 38, Buck's first novel, *East Wind: West Wind*, was published. A year later her most famous book, *The Good Earth*, appeared. It is a novel about the struggles of a poor Chinese farmer and became a bestseller, winning a Pulitzer Prize in 1932. She was the first person from a Western country to write about Chinese people in a sympathetic and understanding way.

Following the breakdown of her marriage in 1934, Buck returned to America for good, later remarrying and setting up a charity to help disadvantaged Asian-American children.

BUCKLER, Ernest

Canadian novelist, short-story writer and essayist

Born Jul. 19, 1908
Died Mar. 4, 1984
Age at death 75

Ernest Buckler was an important Canadian writer, and his book *The Mountain and the Valley* is now considered a classic of Canadian literature. Buckler's writing has a lyrical, poetic quality, and he excels at capturing family scenes and at describing characters.

Born in Dalhousie West, Nova Scotia, Buckler worked for ten years after leaving school to put himself through university. He spent his summers employed at a vacation hotel in Greenwich, Connecticut. His experiences there probably inspired his second novel, *The Cruelest Month* – the story of a group of people who come to stay at a guest house seeking peace of mind from the troubles in their lives. After attending the University of Toronto and Dalhousie University, Buckler returned to Nova Scotia in 1936 to write and indulge in his other great love, farming. He found the isolation of farming ideal because it left his mind free to invent stories and characters.

Buckler's first novel, *The Mountain and the Valley*, published when he was 44, was his most celebrated. Like most of his novels, it is set in Nova Scotia. It is a complex story about a sensitive young man, David Canaan, and his journey toward adulthood. It also deals with how his childhood world in the country is being destroyed by modern city values and ideas. This theme appears again in *Ox Bells and Fireflies*, a memoir of Buckler's own childhood. In it, he captures the atmosphere of Nova Scotia and describes how rural ways were rapidly disappearing.

Publications

1952	*The Mountain and the Valley*
1963	*The Cruelest Month*
1968	*Ox Bells and Fireflies*
1973	*Nova Scotia: Window on the Sea*
1975	*The Rebellion of Young David and Other Stories*
1977	*Whirligig: Selected prose and Verse*

BUCKLEY, William F.

American essayist and novelist

Born Nov. 24, 1925

William F(rank) Buckley, an influential political essayist, was the voice of the conservative right wing in the US during the 1950s and '60s.

Buckley was born in New York City, one of ten children of a self-made oil millionaire. His immigrant father's example of making his own way in the world was a major influence on Buckley's political thinking. The young Buckley was educated first at home and later in public schools in England. He spent a year at the University of Mexico and then served in the US Army during World War II. Afterward he attended Yale University, graduating with honors.

Buckley first came to the public's notice with *Man and God at Yale*, his criticism of the political liberalism that he felt was widespread in higher education. A contributor to numerous magazines and newspapers, Buckley was running a political column in over 200 newspapers before he was 40. In his book *Rumbles Left and Right,* he gave an intelligent and witty voice to the large group of people who were suspicious of the government intervening in their everyday lives. The *National Review*, which he founded in 1955, campaigned for isolationism in foreign policy – which placed America's interests before those of other countries – and against governments providing costly social support, such as benefit payments.

Buckley has also written several spy novels. *A Very Private Plot* is the tenth book in his Blackford Oakes series, which features a CIA agent working during the Cold War years of the 1950s and '60s.

Publications

1951	*Man and God at Yale*
1954	*McCarthy and His Enemies*
1963	*Rumbles Left and Right*
1976	*Saving the Queen*
1978	*Stained Glass*
1985	*Right Reason*
1986	*High Jinx*
1993	*Happy Days Were Here Again*
1994	*A Very Private Plot*
1995	*Brothers No More*
1997	*Nearer, My God: An Autobiography of Faith*

BULGAKOV, Mikhail

Russian novelist and playwright

Born May 15, 1891
Died Mar. 10, 1940
Age at death 48

Mikhail Bulgakov is best known for his satirical stories about life in Russia under communist rule.

Bulgakov was born in the city of Kiev. He studied medicine and briefly worked as a doctor. In 1921, he settled in Moscow and gave up medicine to write.

Bulgakov's first important book was *The White Guard*, which was published when he was 34. Written with humor and sympathy, it is about a group of anticommunists in Kiev. The following year Bulgakov turned it into a play, *The Days of the Turbins*, which was performed at the Moscow Art Theater, where he later worked as an assistant producer. Other plays and stories followed, including *Flight*, a play about rebellious generals, and *The Crimson Island*, a satirical comedy about censorship.

Bulgakov's work was popular, but the authorities increasingly criticized his attacks on the communist system, and his stories were banned. In 1930, he wrote to the leader of Russia, Joseph Stalin, asking for permission to leave the country. Stalin refused, and Bulgakov continued writing, although his work was no longer published. He also worked with the Moscow Art Theater and then the Bolshoi Theater until he went blind in 1939.

During those years Bulgakov worked on his masterpiece, *The Master and Margarita*. Set in Moscow, the novel is a fantasy about the Devil, disguised as a professor, who causes havoc in the city. The manuscript was smuggled out of Russia but was not published until nearly 30 years after Bulgakov's death. Bulgakov was writing *Black Snow*, a novel based on his experiences in the theater, when he died.

Publications

1925 The White Guard
1926 The Days of the Turbins
1928 The Crimson Island
1936 Molière

Published after he died

1957 Flight
1966–67 The Master and Margarita
1967 Black Snow
1968 The Heart of a Dog

BULLINS, Ed

American playwright

Born Jul. 2, 1935

Ed Bullins is a radical African-American playwright. He is known for his intense and angry plays about the lives of black people in the United States.

Bullins was born in Philadelphia, Pennsylvania. He attended business school before joining the US Navy at 17. After serving three years at sea, he went to university in Los Angeles and San Francisco. As a student, Bullins became involved in ghetto drama projects that gave underprivileged people the chance to watch and perform plays.

In the 1950s and '60s, black Americans were fighting for equal rights. Bullins became deeply involved with the civil rights movement. He edited magazines promoting black literature and became cultural adviser to an extreme political group, the Black Panthers.

Bullins also began writing plays in the '60s. He had experimented with poetry and written a novel, but his experience with ghetto drama projects persuaded him that theater was the most effective way of reaching a black audience. Bullins finished his first important play, *Clara's Ole Man*, in 1965, when he was 30. This short one-act play was popular with black audiences, who recognized the problems and frustrations it dramatized.

Bullins's 1968 play *In the Wine Time* is about a group of young black people growing up in the '50s and discovering that society offers them few opportunities. In later plays, Bullins follows the lives of these and other African-American characters and their descendants and forebears to give a complete picture of black life in the 20th century.

Publications

1965	*Clara's Ole Man*
1968	*In the Wine Time*
1968	*The Electronic Nigger*
1970	*The Duplex*
1971	*In New England Winter*
1971	*The Fabulous Miss Marie*
1975	*The Taking of Miss Janie*
1977	*Daddy*
1980	*American Griot*
1980	*Steve and Velma*

BUNIN, Ivan

Russian writer

Born Oct. 22, 1870
Died Nov. 8, 1953
Age at death 83

Ivan Bunin is considered one of the most important figures in Russian literature before the Russian Revolution of 1917. In 1933, he became the first Russian to be awarded the Nobel Prize for Literature.

Bunin was born in the village of Voronezh, central Russia, into a poor but aristocratic family. He studied at Moscow University, then worked as a journalist. He also traveled widely through Europe and Asia.

When Bunin was 21, he published his first volume of poetry, and some years later he received a literary prize. In St. Petersburg he joined a group of young writers founded by MAKSIM GORKY, and when he was 40, he published his first novel, *The Village*. The story, set in Bunin's birthplace, is about two peasant brothers – one a cruel drunk, the other a gentler, more sympathetic character. For Bunin they symbolized the two sides of the Russian peasantry. Bunin was fascinated by the decay of the Russian aristocracy in the years before the Russian Revolution finally swept away their power and wealth. He hated the blind pursuit of wealth that he saw in the ruling classes and in the countries of the West. *The Village* made him famous in Russia.

One of Bunin's best-known stories, "The Gentleman from San Francisco," deals with his favorite themes. The gentleman is an American millionaire who cares only about making money. He dies in a luxury Italian hotel and is shipped home in the hold of a luxury liner. Bunin makes us realize how pointless the man's life has been.

Bunin left Russia after the 1917 Revolution and settled in Paris.

Publications

1897	*To the Edge of the World*
1898	*Under the Open Sky*
1910	*The Village*
1916	*The Gentleman from San Francisco and Other Stories*
1917	*The Temple of the Sun*
1933	*The Well of Days*
1935	*Mitia's Love*
1939	*Lika*
1952	*The Life of Arsenev*

BUNYAN, John

English writer

Born Nov. 30, 1628
Died Aug. 31, 1688
Age at death 59

John Bunyan was a great English prose writer. His books are powerful expressions of his religious beliefs.

Born near London in a village where his family had been farmers for generations, Bunyan received virtually no education and seemed destined to lead a simple life until two events changed everything.

The first came in 1642, when England was plunged into civil war as Oliver Cromwell fought to overthrow the king (English Civil War). On his 16th birthday, Bunyan joined Cromwell's army. He met people he would never have encountered otherwise and was introduced to new ideas. Like many others he became interested in the message of Puritanism, a strict kind of Christianity that was very popular among Cromwell's men.

The second event came a few years after the end of the war; Bunyan became a committed Christian. He began preaching whenever he could, but in 1660, the English monarchy was returned to power, and Puritan worship was banned. Bunyan continued preaching, however, and he was soon arrested and put in jail.

Bunyan spent the next 11 years in jail, where he began to write. His first book, *Grace Abounding to the Chief of Sinners*, is the story of his own conversion to Christianity. He also began work on his masterpiece, *The Pilgrim's Progress*, which was completed when he was 50, following a second short term in jail. *The Pilgrim's Progress* describes the journey of its hero, Christian, from the City of Destruction to the Celestial City. It is an allegory of a soul's journey. The story is so powerfully told that it has remained a favorite long after the religious age in which Bunyan lived.

Publications

1666	*Grace Abounding to the Chief of Sinners*
1678	*The Pilgrim's Progress*
1680	*The Life and Death of Mr. Badman*
1682	*The Holy War*
1684	*The Pilgrim's Progress, Part II*
1686	*A Book for Boys and Girls*

BURGESS, Anthony

English novelist and critic

Born Feb. 25, 1917
Died Nov. 25, 1993
Age at death 76

Anthony Burgess is best known for his novel *A Clockwork Orange*, a disturbing portrayal of a violent youth who feels rejected by society.

Burgess was born in Manchester, into a Catholic family. His father was a pianist, and his mother was a musical comedy performer who died when Burgess was only a year old. Burgess studied at Manchester University before serving in the Army Education Corps in World War II. He spent several years abroad working as an education officer for the British government. In his late 30s, he began writing as a hobby, and many of his early novels were inspired by his experiences in Southeast Asia.

In 1942, Burgess, who was doing his army service, received news from London that his wife Llewela had been so badly assaulted that she was in a hospital, having miscarried their expected first child. This incident is thought to have given him the idea for the most violent scene in *A Clockwork Orange*, in which a writer and his wife are attacked. *A Clockwork Orange*, first published when Burgess was 45, uses made-up slang language and is set in an England of the near future. It tells of a young, violent thug who, after serving time in prison, is brainwashed into becoming an acceptable member of society. Its random violence – heightened in the film version made in 1971 – provoked controversy.

At 42, Burgess was diagnosed as having a brain tumor, and in an effort to provide for his wife after his death, he wrote an amazing five novels in one year. He survived the tumor and wrote more than 50 novels in all.

Publications

1956 Time for a Tiger
1960 The Doctor Is Sick
1961 The Worm and the Ring
1962 A Clockwork Orange
1964 The Long Day Wanes
1968 Enderby Outside
1978 Ernest Hemingway and His World
1980 Earthly Powers
1989 You've Had Your Time

BURKE, James Lee

American crime writer and novelist

Born Dec. 5, 1936

James Lee Burke is best known for his crime novels set in and around the city of New Orleans.

Burke was born in Houston, Texas. He went to secondary school in Houston and then college in Lafayette, Louisiana. When Burke was 19, his father was killed in an automobile accident. Around this time, Burke began to drink heavily and spent a brief period in prison. He later wrote several novels that drew on his experience of life as a prisoner.

By the time Burke was 33, three of his novels had been published. However, he had a falling out with his agent, and for many years he could not find a publisher for his books. Since he was married with four children to support, he had to work at a variety of other jobs: English teacher, land surveyor, social worker and newspaper reporter.

The turning point came for Burke when he stopped drinking and entered a recovery program. A new publisher produced *The Lost Get-Back Boogie*, a poetic novel about an ex-convict; it won Burke a nomination for the Pulitzer Prize. He then began work on a series of crime novels set in New Orleans and around the bayous of southern Louisiana. The series features a courageous but hot-tempered cop, Dave Robicheaux, who, like his author, is a recovering alcoholic. The first novel in the series, *The Neon Rain*, was published when Burke was 51 and established him as a major American crime writer.

Burke's novels are as much about an individual's struggle with his own problems as they are about combating the forces of evil in society.

Publications

1986 The Lost Get-Back Boogie
1987 The Neon Rain
1988 Heaven's Prisoners
1989 Black Cherry Blues
1990 A Morning for Flamingos
1992 A Stained White Radiance
1994 Dixie City Jam
1995 Burning Angel
1996 Cadillac Jukebox
1997 Cimarron Rose

BURNETT, Frances Hodgson

Anglo-American children's writer

Born Nov. 24, 1849
Died Oct. 29, 1924
Age at death 74

Frances Hodgson Burnett wrote novels and plays for adults, but is best remembered as the author of the classic children's books *Little Lord Fauntleroy* and *The Secret Garden*.

Burnett was born in Manchester. When she was 16 years old, she moved with her family to the United States and settled in Knoxville, Tennessee. Burnett had always loved storytelling, and she began writing short stories for magazines to help support the family. After the polluted industrial city she had come from, Tennessee seemed like paradise, but she remained strongly attached to England, and her most popular books are set in the English countryside.

It wasn't until Burnett had married and given birth to two sons that she began to write children's books. Her first success, *That Lass o' Lowrie's*, published when she was 28, was about a mining family. Ten years later, she became famous as the author of *Little Lord Fauntleroy*. The book was so popular that there was a craze of mothers dressing their sons to look like the hero, a lovable orphan who is adopted by an aristocratic family. Burnett based the character of Little Lord Fauntleroy on her young son, Vivian.

Burnett's two marriages ended unhappily. Living alone, she divided her time between England and Long Island, New York. It was in the rose garden of her English home that she wrote her famous book *The Secret Garden*, published when she was in her 60s. It has captivated generations of children with its simple tale of courage, friendship and finding happiness.

Publications

1877	*That Lass o' Lowrie's*
1879	*Haworth's*
1880	*Louisiana*
1886	*Little Lord Fauntleroy*
1888	*Editha's Burglar*
1894	*Piccino and Other Child Stories*
1905	*A Little Princess*
1911	*The Secret Garden*
1915	*The Lost Prince*

BURNETT, W.R.

American crime writer and screenwriter

Born Nov. 25, 1899
Died Apr. 26, 1982
Age at death 82

W.R. Burnett created the American gangster novel. Although his books are not widely read today, he is one of the most influential writers in crime fiction.

William Riley Burnett was born in Springfield, Ohio. After studying journalism for a year at Ohio State University, he worked for the state government as a statistician. During this time, he began writing to keep from becoming bored, but it was only when he moved to Chicago that his career as a writer took off.

Chicago in the 1920s and '30s was the home of organized crime. Laws had been passed to ban the drinking of alcohol, but the unfortunate result of this was to create a huge network of gangsters who were involved in supplying illegal liquor. The violence of these gangsters, such as Al Capone, was legendary.

Burnett found work in a Chicago hotel. He made friends with the hobos, boxers and gangsters he met there and listened carefully to the way they talked. He even had one of the gangsters explain all the slang words to him. He then wrote a novel, *Little Caesar*, about the criminal underworld in Chicago. It was an overnight success, and at the age of 30, Burnett became one of the most sought-after writers in Hollywood.

Burnett went on to write 36 books and 60 screenplays. He wrote the screenplays of several classic films, including *High Sierra*, starring Humphrey Bogart.

During the 1960s, Burnett's style of writing went out of fashion, and for many years he was almost forgotten. Today, he is better known in Europe than he is in America.

Publications

1929 Little Caesar
1933 Dark Hazard
1936 King Cole
1940 High Sierra
1943 Nobody Lives Forever
1945 Tomorrow's Another Day
1949 The Asphalt Jungle
1952 Vanity Row
1954 Captain Lightfoot
1968 The Cool Man

BURNEY, Fanny

English novelist

Born Jun. 13, 1752
Died Jan. 6, 1840
Age at death 87

Fanny Burney was one of the first popular female novelists. Her success ensured that women writers could take their place in literature. During her lifetime, Burney was famed as a comic novelist. Now she is best remembered for her diary, which was published after her death. Begun when Burney was 16 and continued over the next 70 years, the diary details English social life of the era and describes the famous people that Burney knew.

Burney was born in King's Lynn, Norfolk, in the east of England. Her family moved to London, and her mother died soon afterward. Burney began writing when she was 10, but her father disapproved, so she burned her poems, essays, plays and stories when she was 15. When she was 26, however, Burney secretly published *Evelina*, the story of a good but simple country girl who comes into contact with London society. With humor and accurate social observation Burney shows how Evelina discovers the low value society gives to women. It was a great success, as was her next novel, *Cecilia* – the story of a girl whose inheritance is wasted by her male guardians.

From 1786 to 1791, Burney held a court post as a keeper of the robes to the queen on the insistence of her father, who did not consider writing a proper career. Burney hated her new role. She resigned and then married a French refugee, General Alexandre d'Arblay, after which she was known as Madame d'Arblay. Her most feminist novel, *The Wanderer*, published when she was 62, has been called her best work. It depicts the difficulties faced by women.

Publications

1778 Evelina
1782 Cecilia
1796 Camilla
1814 The Wanderer
1832 Memoirs of Dr. Burney

Published after she died

1842–54 Diary and Letters of Madame d'Arblay (7 vols.)
1889 The Early Diary of Frances Burney, 1768–78 (2 vols.)

BURNS, Robert

Scottish poet

Born Jan. 25, 1759
Died Jul. 21, 1796
Age at death 37

Robert Burns is celebrated today as national poet of Scotland. His work, which was often in Scots dialect, rescued Scottish culture from being swamped by the growing influence of English culture.

Burns was born at Alloway in Ayrshire, western Scotland. His father, a poor farmer, did his best to give his sons a good education. In due course, Burns and his brother Gilbert set up as farmers. But their rented land was poor, and they struggled to make a living. Freed from his father's watchful eye, Burns set about wooing girls and writing poems. He fathered several children by different women. He wanted to marry one of his loves, Jean Armour, but her parents disapproved.

Burns had been taught the formal, very English poetry of the day. He found, however, that Scottish dialect was the ideal way to express himself and his rebellious attitude to the severe Scottish Church. When he was 27, Burns had many of his poems published as *Poems, Chiefly in the Scottish Dialect*. The book was a great success, and Burns moved to Edinburgh for a year and a half and mixed with high society. The success made Jean's parents relent, and Burns married her in 1788. He returned to farming, but then gave it up for a secure job as a tax collector.

Burns wrote nearly all his long narrative poems between 1784 and 1786. After that he took to writing the songs for which he is chiefly remembered, such as "A Red, Red Rose" and "Auld Lang Syne." He wrote and edited hundreds of songs for collections before dying of heart disease at an early age.

Publications

1786 Poems, Chiefly in the Scottish Dialect

Published after he died

1834–86 The Works of Robert Burns
1938 Robert Burns's Commonplace Book, 1783–85

BURROUGHS, Edgar Rice

American fantasy writer

Born Sep. 1, 1875
Died Mar. 19, 1950
Age at death 74

Edgar Rice Burroughs is famous for his Tarzan series and for his stories about the planet Mars, known as the Barsoom series. His jungle hero, Tarzan, modeled on the virtues of the classical hero, is one of the most memorable characters in modern popular literature.

Burroughs was born in Chicago. His father was an army major with a strong belief in discipline. Burroughs attended the Harvard School in Chicago, where he learned about the classical world of ancient Greece and Rome. After leaving school, he was sent to live on his brother's cattle ranch. This was in the days of the Wild West, when life was tough and arguments could end in a shootout.

After two years of life as a cowboy, Burroughs was enrolled at a scholarly academy but was expelled for laziness. Following training at Michigan Military Academy, he joined the US 7th Cavalry and fought the Apaches in Arizona. He returned to Chicago and did various jobs, including selling stationery.

Burroughs was 36 when his first story was published in *All-Story Weekly*, a science fiction magazine. His first Tarzan book came out when he was 39. The hero – an infant son of an English aristocrat – is abandoned in the African jungle, brought up by apes, and becomes Tarzan, lord of the jungle. Burroughs's popular novels have sold over 25 million copies worldwide. His life as a scholar, cowboy and soldier helped him to create a simple world of good and evil.

Publications

1914 Tarzan of the Apes
1915 The Return of Tarzan
1917 The Son of Tarzan
1917 A Princess of Mars
1918 The Gods of Mars
1922 At the Earth's Core
1924 The Land That Time Forgot
1928 Tarzan, Lord of the Jungle
1939 Carson of Venus
1946 Escape on Venus

BURROUGHS, William S.

William S. Burroughs was a founder of the 1950s beat generation, which experimented with new ways of writing and developed an alternative culture in the process. Burroughs's most famous novel, *Naked Lunch*, is a vivid account of the nightmarish world of drug addiction and a satire on human weaknesses and modern society.

William Seward Burroughs was born in St. Louis. Educated at public schools, he went on to study at Harvard. After graduating, he traveled and studied in Europe, then worked for an advertising agency in New York City, joined the army, and took various odd jobs in Chicago. At age 29, Burroughs returned to New York, married, and through his wife met Jack Kerouac and Allen Ginsberg. Together, the three friends launched the beat generation. They also experimented with drugs, and Burroughs became addicted to heroin. He often had to move to avoid the police and fled to Mexico City after a drug raid. While there he shot and killed his wife by accident. He moved to London in the mid-1960s before settling in Lawrence, Kansas.

Burroughs's first novel, *Junkie*, was published under the pen name William Lee when he was 39. It gives a realistic account of a drug addict's life. His later novels also explore addiction (to drugs, sex or power) but are more dreamlike and experimental. He has pioneered the use of "cutting up" and "folding in," in which he actually cut up the text or folded pages in on themselves to produce unusual effects.

American novelist and short-story writer

Born Feb. 5, 1914
Died Aug. 2, 1997
Age at death 83

Publications

1953 Junkie
1959 Naked Lunch
1962 The Ticket That Exploded
1964 Nova Express
1966 The Soft Machine
1981 Cities of the Red Night
1982 Letters to Allen Ginsberg
1985 Queer
1986 The Cat Inside
1991 Ghost of a Chance

BUSCH, Wilhelm

German satirist and poet

Born Apr. 15, 1832
Died Jan. 9, 1908
Age at death 75

Publications

1865 Max and Moritz
1868 Bushel of Merry-Thoughts
1869 Buzz-a-buzz
1870 The Holy Antonius of Padua
1872 Jack Huckaback, the Scapegrace Raven
1873 Pater Filucius
1876 Mr. and Mrs. Knopp
1878 Hookey-Beak, the Raven, and Other Tales

The German illustrator and poet Wilhelm Busch is famous for the way he used his varied talents to satirize German culture of the late 19th century – to laugh at the snobbery of the newly rich, the pompous pride of the military, and the self-satisfaction of the Catholic Church. He could also be described as the originator of the modern comic strip.

Busch was born near Hanover, Germany. At the age of 27, he joined the staff of the leading German comic weekly and remained there for 12 years. His job was to write "nonsense" verse and to draw cartoons. He adopted a deliberately simplistic style of drawing that immediately became popular. At age 33, he published his first book of humorous illustrated poetry, *Max and Moritz.* With comic strips and short funny rhymes, it is a clever observation of mischievous childish behavior. It was enormously popular, selling over half a million copies in Germany by 1910. Five years after *Max and Moritz,* the poem *The Holy Antonius of Padua* was published. This is a powerful satire against the priesthood and the exaggerated middle-class German respect for their role.

Busch had been encouraged in these anticlerical activities by the policy of the German leader, Otto von Bismarck. But in time he regretted the savagery of his satire and toned it down. From 1884 onward, he published a yearly album of his work in which he maintained a good-humored and gently ironic survey of the human condition and its shortcomings. He also wrote serious poetry, but his nonsense verse is much more widely read.

BUTLER, Octavia E.

American science fiction writer

Born Jun. 22, 1947

Octavia E. Butler is the first African-American woman to become well known as a writer of science fiction. Her tales of future and past worlds offer a unique voice in contemporary science fiction.

Octavia Estelle Butler grew up in Pasadena, California. Her father died when she was a baby, and her mother worked as a maid. A lonely child, Butler found comfort in reading, especially science fiction magazines. At 12, she began writing stories and then won a short-story contest at university. When she was 23, she took part in a writers' workshop and managed to sell two stories.

For the next five years, Butler had no success as a writer and supported herself by doing menial jobs. When she became unemployed, she took the opportunity to complete her first novel,

Patternmaster, which was published when she was 29.

Patternmaster is the first in a series of novels about a future world in which people are divided into two classes: "patternists," who rule society, and "clayarks," mutant humans infected by a disease from outer space. While writing this series, Butler also wrote a novel, *Kindred*, about an African-American woman who travels back in time to the slave plantations of the South.

In the 1980s, Butler produced a series of novels known as the Xenogenesis Sequence. These describe how aliens try to help human survivors after a nuclear war on Earth. A more recent novel, *Parable of the Sower*, explores a future world in which water supplies have dried up, causing social chaos.

Publications

1976 Patternmaster
1977 Mind of My Mind
1978 Survivor
1979 Kindred
1980 Wild Seed
1984 Clay's Ark
1987 Dawn
1988 Adulthood Rites
1989 Imago
1993 Parable of the Sower

BUTLER, Robert Olen

American novelist and short-story writer

Born Jan. 20, 1945

Robert Olen Butler's novels explore the impact of the Vietnam War on individuals, both in Vietnam during the war and in the US after the war ended.

Butler was born in Granite City, Illinois. His father was a college professor, and his mother was a secretary. After graduating from Northwestern University, Butler received a Master's degree in playwriting from the University of Iowa. He served with military intelligence in the army in Vietnam, an experience that shaped his writing. After his discharge in 1972, he worked as an editor and reporter while writing novels and short stories.

Butler was 36 when he published his first novel, *The Alleys of Eden*. It is the story of an American army deserter and a Vietnamese woman trying to cope with the clash between American and Vietnamese cultures.

The pain and suffering caused by US participation in the Vietnam War are the themes of his next novel, *Sun Dogs*. It is about a former prisoner of war who comes to terms with his experience.

Butler's most successful book so far is *A Good Scent from a Strange Mountain*, published when he was 47. This collection of 15 short stories is set in Louisiana, where many Vietnamese immigrants settled after the end of the Vietnam War. It tells of the new arrivals and the native Louisianans trying to balance two conflicting cultures and the traditions that go with them. Butler, who was a translator in the war, writes sympathetically of the immigrants' efforts to preserve their Vietnamese culture. The book was awarded the Pulitzer Prize in 1993.

Publications

1981 The Alleys of Eden
1982 Sun Dogs
1983 Countrymen of Bones
1985 On Distant Ground
1987 Wabash
1989 The Deuce
1992 A Good Scent from a Strange Mountain
1994 They Whisper

BUTLER, Samuel

English novelist and essayist

Born Dec. 4, 1835
Died Jun. 18, 1902
Age at death 66

Samuel Butler was an English writer famous for his satires, in particular, the novel *Erewhon*.

Born in Nottinghamshire, Butler was the eldest son of the local vicar. After he graduated from Cambridge University, his family assumed that he would join the church, but Butler had doubts about this career. His father then agreed to send his son to New Zealand to farm sheep. It was here that Butler began to write.

When Butler was 27, he wrote his first essay, "Dialogue," which was a response to *The Origin of Species* by the naturalist, Charles Darwin. This essay shows many of Butler's developing ideas. He argued that evolution is controlled by a "life force" rather than being random, as Darwin believed. These views greatly influenced the work of the playwright GEORGE BERNARD SHAW. Butler's collection of letters home from New Zealand, *A First Year in Canterbury Settlement*, appeared the following year.

After five years, Butler returned to London. While in New Zealand, he had made his fortune and now had the money to pursue his interests. A man of many talents, he began to paint, compose and write on a range of topics from philosophy to science.

When he was 37, Butler published the utopian novel *Erewhon*, which has been called the greatest satire in the English language. Like JONATHAN SWIFT's *Gulliver's Travels*, it mocks English society, and it imagines a better world where poverty and ill-health are crimes.

The Way of All Flesh, which criticizes Victorian family life and is based on Butler's own rather unhappy childhood, was published a year after his death.

Publications

1863 A First Year in Canterbury Settlement
1872 Erewhon
1873 The Fair Haven
1879 Evolution, Old and New
1886 Luck or Cunning
1897 The Authoress of the "Odyssey"
1901 Erewhon Revisited

Published after he died

1903 The Way of All Flesh

BYATT, A.S.

English novelist, biographer, and critic

Born Aug. 24 1936

A.S. Byatt is respected as a scholar and literary critic as well as a successful novelist. She comes from a literary family: her father, a sister and several of her aunts are also novelists.

Born in the northern city of Sheffield, Antonia Susan Drabble was a very bright child who spent a lot of time reading because she suffered from asthma. She went to university on a scholarship, graduating with honors, then spent a postgraduate year at Bryn Mawr, Pennsylvania. She married at 23, combining raising a family with part-time teaching. Byatt divorced and then remarried in 1969.

Byatt's first novel, *The Shadow of a Sun*, was published when she was 28, but she had been working on it for nearly 15 years. It is about the hopes and dreams of a sensitive young writer determined to carve a career for herself. Her writing in this novel was strongly influenced by the works of Marcel Proust. An influence on her later work has been the novelist Iris Murdoch, about whom she wrote a critical work, *Degrees of Freedom*.

Byatt's critical and scholarly writings were already much admired when her third novel, *The Virgin in the Garden*, won praise. This book, planned to be the first of a series of four, is based on the character of the 16th-century queen of England, Elizabeth I, who was called "the Virgin Queen" because she never married. Byatt's fifth novel, *Possession*, won the Booker Prize. Byatt's novels take a long time to write, and they each go through several versions. Her interests in art history, social history and philosophy can all be seen in her fiction.

Publications

1964 The Shadow of a Sun
1965 Degrees of Freedom
1978 The Virgin in the Garden
1986 Still Life
1987 Sugar and Other Stories
1990 Possession
1992 Angels and Insects
1995 The Djinn in the Nightingale's Eye
1996 Babel Tower
1998 Elementals

BYRON, Lord

English poet

Born Jan. 22, 1788
Died Apr. 19, 1824
Age at death 36

Lord Byron was a leading poet of the 19th-century English Romantic movement. His life was almost as colorful as those of the moody, mysterious heroes of his poems.

George Gordon Noel Byron was born in London, but spent his first troubled years in Scotland. When Byron was three, his father died, after spending his mother's fortune, and Byron and his mother faced hardships. But at ten, he inherited a great uncle's title and estates. Later, he attended the prestigious Harrow School and Cambridge University. Byron's first published poems, *Hours of Idleness*, appeared when he was 19 and were strongly criticized. Byron responded with *English Bards and Scotch Reviewers*, a satirical poem attacking the major literary figures of the time.

At 21, Byron began a two-year grand tour through southern Europe to Turkey. These travels inspired *Childe Harold's Pilgrimage*, a long poem about a world-weary young lord's journey through a Europe in need of reforms. The handsome author's gloomy passion and pleas for justice and liberty attracted women admirers. At 26, Byron married Annabella Milbanke. She soon left him, though, shocked by news of Byron's affair with his half-sister, Augusta. The disgrace made Byron leave England, aged 28.

In Italy he had new love affairs and wrote his masterpiece, *Don Juan*, a long, witty poem about a handsome man's adventures with women. Byron also began ardently supporting Italian and Greek freedom from foreign control. He joined an Italian nationalist secret society and was leading Greek troops against Turks when he caught a fever and died.

Publications

1807 Hours of Idleness
1809 English Bards and Scotch Reviewers
1812–18 Childe Harold's Pilgrimage
1813 The Bride of Abydos
1817 Manfred
1818 Beppo
1819–24 Don Juan
1821 Cain
1822 The Vision of Judgment

CABRERA INFANTE, Guillermo

Cuban-British novelist and short-story writer

Born Apr. 22, 1929

Publications

1960	*In Peace as in War: Stories*
1965	*View of Dawn in the Tropics*
1967	*Three Trapped Tigers*
1979	*Infante's Inferno*
1985	*Holy Smoke*
1993	*Writes of Passage*
1995	*Mea Cuba*

Guillermo Cabrera Infante writes experimental fiction that mixes elements of life in his native Cuba with comic puns on the English language. Now a British citizen, he writes in both English and Spanish.

Cabrera Infante was born in Gibara, Cuba. His parents were radical communists imprisoned by the anti-Russian regime when he was only seven years old. His family had to move around the country in search of work. When he was 12, they moved to Havana. While still a student, Cabrera Infante cofounded the national film archive. A year later, he was fined and jailed for publishing obscenities – although the offending words were in English.

In 1958, the communist leader, Fidel Castro, took power in Cuba. Cabrera Infante became director of the National Council for Culture, and for many years he was a leading figure in Castro's government. After an incident involving the banning of a film made by his brother, however, he became unhappy with the Castro regime, and moved to London, aged 38.

Cabrera Infante's first novel, published a year after leaving Cuba, is an experimental work about nightclub life in Cuba before Castro. It shows the author's love of puns – using, for example, "Shame's Choice" for the writer James Joyce. One of the themes of *Three Trapped Tigers* is betrayal, and the novel is seen as strongly anti-communist. *Holy Smoke*, written in English, is less controversial: it tells the story of the cigar.

CAIN, James M.

American crime writer

Born Jul. 1, 1892
Died Oct. 27, 1977
Age at death 85

James M. Cain is best known for two novels, *The Postman Always Rings Twice* and *Double Indemnity*.

Born in Annapolis, Maryland, the son of the president of Washington College, Chestertown, James Mallahan Cain studied singing after leaving school. He then tried several jobs, including coal miner and reporter. He joined the army when he was 26, and served in France during World War I. After the war, he returned to the United States and became a journalist. When he was 39, he went to Hollywood to become a screenwriter. He was not very successful writing scripts for films, but during this time he began to write novels, and these were much more popular.

Cain's first novel, *The Postman Always Rings Twice,* was published when he was 42. It is the story of a love affair between a man and a married woman that leads to murder and betrayal. The story is told by the criminal himself in his own words, and this helps to make it very dramatic and colorful. Cain used the same style in his later novel *Double Indemnity*, which was published when he was 51. Again, this is the story of a love affair involving greed, murder and disillusion.

Cain wrote his stories in a fast-paced, realistic style, which is often compared to that of two other famous crime writers of the time, Dashiell Hammett and Raymond Chandler, although Cain did not write about private detectives and gangsters as they did. The film versions of *The Postman Always Rings Twice* and *Double Indemnity* are now regarded as classic movies.

Publications

1934	*The Postman Always Rings Twice*
1937	*Serenade*
1941	*Mildred Pierce*
1943	*Career in C Major*
1943	*Double Indemnity*
1946	*Past All Dishonor*
1947	*The Butterfly*
1948	*The Moth*
1951	*The Root of His Evil*

CALDWELL, Erskine

American novelist and short-story writer

Born Dec. 17, 1903
Died Apr. 11, 1987
Age at death 83

Erskine Caldwell is best known for his novels *Tobacco Road* and *God's Little Acre*.

Caldwell was born in White Oak – a remote part of Georgia. He was the son of a Presbyterian minister who moved constantly from place to place, taking his family with him. Caldwell rarely stayed anywhere for more than six months at a time. This wandering lifestyle affected his education, and he seldom attended school. Instead, he was taught at home by his mother.

At the age of 14, Caldwell left home and traveled around the South. He took any job he could find and lived in poor communities. When he was 18, Caldwell went to Erskine College in South Carolina but left without finishing the course to go on a boat taking illegal guns to South America. He later enrolled at the universities of Virginia and Pennsylvania but failed to complete a course at either, returning again to casual work. His jobs ranged from bodyguard to professional football player.

When he was 29, Caldwell's first successful book, *Tobacco Road*, was published. *Tobacco Road* and Caldwell's next novel, *God's Little Acre*, are about the harsh, difficult lives of the poor whites and African Americans in the Deep South. Caldwell wrote about the everyday lives of his characters in a realistic way, but his detailed descriptions of their sex lives shocked many people, and some tried to have his books banned. These two books made Caldwell rich and successful. He continued to write about the South, although the quality of his work declined in later years.

Publications

1929	*The Bastard*
1930	*Poor Fool*
1932	*Tobacco Road*
1933	*God's Little Acre*
1943	*Georgia Boy*
1947	*Sure Hand of God*
1952	*A Lamp for Nightfall*
1954	*Love and Money*
1962	*Close to Home*
1967	*Miss Mama Aimée*

CALVINO, Italo

Italian novelist and essayist

Born Oct. 15, 1923
Died Sep. 19, 1985
Age at death 61

Italo Calvino, a major Italian 20th-century writer of fantasy, fairy tale, allegory and science fiction, has had all of his significant works translated into English.

Calvino was born in Cuba of Italian parents, but grew up in San Remo, Italy. He studied at Turin University and in 1940, greatly against his wish, was drafted into a fascist youth organization. Calvino hated extreme right-wing politics and, in 1943, joined the resistance to fight against the German Nazis, who were Italy's allies. During this period and for the rest of the 1940s, he wrote articles for the communist press.

Calvino's first novel, *The Path to the Nest of Spiders*, was published when he was 24. It was a fairly traditional, realistic work about wartime resistance and excited little interest. Later works were more experimental, and he came to combine fantasy, folklore, fairy tales and science fiction to produce something new in contemporary fiction. During the 1950s, he became a member of a Turin publishing firm and wrote three fantasy novels based in history under the general title *Our Ancestors*. The second of these stories, called *The Baron in the Trees*, is about a nobleman who rejects normal life and makes a home in the trees. Soon Calvino was regarded as one of the most original, inventive and imaginative writers of the time.

Other good works by Calvino published in the 1970s show a remarkable combination of fantasy, humor, complexity, and depth. By then he was well known not only in Italy, but throughout the Western world. In 1973, he was awarded the prestigious Italian literary prize, the Premio Feltrinelli award.

Publications

1947 The Path to the Nest of Spiders
1949 Adam, One Afternoon, and Other Stories
1956 Italian Folktales
1960 Our Ancestors (3 parts)
1972 Invisible Cities
1973 Castle of Crossed Destinies
1979 If on a Winter's Night a Traveler
1983 Mr. Palomar

CAMUS, Albert

French novelist, journalist and playwright

Born Nov. 7, 1913
Died Jan. 4, 1960
Age at death 46

Albert Camus was a major and influential French author of the 20th century who, in 1957, received the Nobel Prize for Literature.

Camus was born into a poor working-class family in Algeria, North Africa, which at that time belonged to France and which was the setting for much of his work. After his father was killed in World War I, he was raised by his mother in the capital city, Algiers. He studied at local schools and, despite suffering from the lung disease tuberculosis, obtained a degree in philosophy from the University of Algiers.

Camus went to France and, in 1942, joined the French Resistance, which fought against Nazi occupation in World War II. He then became a journalist and made his reputation as a novelist with the publication, when he was 29, of *The Stranger*. The main theme of the book is the absurd and pointless nature of human existence.

The next major novel from Camus, *The Plague*, published when he was 34, called on people to fight against injustice. Unlike other left-wing authors, such as JEAN-PAUL SARTRE, Camus believed in the need for a moral rather than a political revolt to change society. His essay "The Rebel" was about the need for people to take moral responsibility for their actions. Camus's last great novel was *The Fall*, published when he was 43. It shows how human beings should solve by effort and moderate behavior the problem of being an individual and, at the same time, part of a community. Camus's plays were not as popular as his novels. He died in an automobile accident in France.

Publications

1938 Caligula
1942 The Stranger
1942 The Myth of Sisyphus
1944 Cross Purpose
1947 The Plague
1948 State of Siege
1951 The Rebel
1956 The Fall
1958 Exile and the Kingdom

CANETTI, Elias

Bulgarian novelist, playwright and essayist

Born Jul. 25, 1905
Died Aug. 14, 1994
Age at death 89

Elias Canetti is chiefly remembered for two books, *Auto-da-fe* and *Crowds and Power*. Regarded as one of the 20th century's truly original thinkers, Canetti was awarded the Nobel Prize for literature in 1981.

Canetti was born in Ruse, a small port in Bulgaria on the Danube River. His family of Spanish Jews encouraged his interest in a wide range of cultures. By the time Canetti was ten, he could speak four languages, including German. This was the language that his parents spoke to each other in private; because of this the young Canetti came to see it as "magical." He eventually chose to write in German and retained a lasting love of German culture.

When he was 18, Canetti enrolled at the University of Vienna, Austria. While in Austria, he had an experience that would affect all of his future work. Angry protesters burned down the Palace of Justice. Canetti, caught up in the crowd, later described how he felt himself "dissolving" and becoming part of the mob. From this moment, Canetti dedicated himself to understanding the human mind, in particular the behavior of people in crowds.

When he was 30, Canetti published the novel that made him famous, *Auto-da-fe*. The story deals with obsessive characters who ultimately become victims of their own thoughts. It was an instant success, but was banned by Nazi censors.

In 1939, Canetti moved to England to escape growing anti-Jewish feelings in Germany. It was there that he wrote his most respected work, *Crowds and Power*, a nonfiction study of the psychology of crowds.

Publications

1935 Auto-da-fe
1956 The Numbered
1960 Crowds and Power
1975 The Conscience of Words
1977 The Tongue Set Free
1980 The Torch in My Ear
1985 The Play of the Eyes
1992 The Agony of the Flies

CAPEK, Karel

Czech playwright and novelist

Born Jan. 9, 1890
Died Dec. 25, 1938
Age at death 48

Publications

1921	*R.U.R.*
1921	*The World We Live In*
1922	*The Makropoulos Secret*
1922	*The Absolute at Large*
1924	*Krakatit*
1929	*Tales from One Pocket*
1934	*The Meteor*
1936	*War with the Newts*
1937	*Power and Glory*
1938	*The Mother*

Karel Capek is best known for his play *R.U.R.*, about a race of robots that become human.

Capek was born in Male Svatonovice, Czechoslovakia (now the Czech Republic). As a young man he was educated at the University of Prague and wrote newspaper articles, plays, political essays and novels. He then set up and ran his own theater in Prague.

Capek had a liberal political outlook and was very much involved in the political affairs of his country. After World War I, he worked closely with his friend the president to unify Czechoslovakia.

Today Capek is remembered for his plays, whose themes were in many ways ahead of their time. His most famous play, *R.U.R*, which stands for Rossum's Universal Robots, was first produced when he was 31. It introduced a new word, "robot," to describe a race of humanlike machines created in order to perform repetitive, boring tasks in factories but which develops human characteristics and emotions. A satire about a society that has become over technologized, the play tells the story of how the worker-robots rebel against their masters, causing complete chaos and anarchy. The story ends on a note of hope, however.

Capek went on to write more plays, several novels and many short stories. Two of his best-known plays are *The World We Live In* and *Power and Glory*. Both are about how too much power can corrupt political leaders.

Karel Capek died shortly before the invasion of Czechoslovakia by German Nazis in 1939.

CAPOTE, Truman

American novelist and journalist

Born Sep. 30, 1924
Died Aug. 25, 1984
Age at death 59

Truman Capote is best known for his fictionalized account of a true-life murder, *In Cold Blood*.

Capote was born in New Orleans, the son of a salesman and a 16-year-old beauty queen. His parents divorced when he was four years old, and he went to live with a series of different relatives. When he was 15, he was adopted by his mother's second husband, a Cuban businessman, and he took his stepfather's name.

Capote started to write stories when he was only eight and, although he won several prizes at school for his fiction, he left when he was 17 and became a journalist.

Capote's first novel, *Other Voices, Other Rooms*, was published when he was 24. This story and his later novel *The Grass Harp* are about growing up in the Deep South and were very successful.

At age 35, Capote became fascinated by the real-life murder of a wealthy farming family in Kansas. He closely followed the arrest, trial, conviction and eventual execution of the murderers – two drifters who had no real reason for their crime. The killers were executed in 1965, and the following year Capote's book *In Cold Blood* was published. In this book, Capote recreates, in great detail, the lives of all the people involved in the crime. He called it a "nonfiction novel," a mixing of fact and fiction. This was a new kind of writing at the time, and Capote claimed to have invented it. *In Cold Blood* is said to be his masterpiece, and it became an international bestseller.

Publications

1948 *Other Voices, Other Rooms*
1949 *A Tree of Night*
1951 *The Grass Harp*
1958 *Breakfast at Tiffany"s*
1965 "A Christmas Memory"
1966 *In Cold Blood*
1968 "The Thanksgiving Visitor"
1980 *Music for Chameleons*

Published after he died

1986 *Answered Prayers*

CARDENAL, Ernesto

Nicaraguan poet

Born Jan. 20, 1925

For Ernesto Cardenal poetry and politics are closely connected. With his poetry, which ranges from romantic verse to religious epic, he aims to bring about social change in Latin America.

Cardenal was born in Granada, Nicaragua, during one of the many periods of anti-American political violence in the country. He was a college student in Mexico City, then continued his postgraduate studies at Columbia University in New York. He published his first collection of poems at age 23.

Given the grinding poverty of his native land and the influence of the Catholic faith on his upbringing, it is no surprise that political radicalism and religious devotion are the main themes of Cardenal's work. At age 29, he took part in a failed uprising against the Nicaraguan dictator Somoza, who was assassinated two years later.

Instead of pursuing a political path, Cardenal underwent a religious conversion. He spent several years studying silent mysticism with monks in the US, Mexico and Colombia before becoming a priest at age 40.

Cardenal helped found a community on the island of Solentiname, in Lake Nicaragua, whose members led a life of prayer, writing poetry and music in a search for inner peace. In 1977, the community was destroyed by the forces of Anastasio Somoza, son of the previous dictator. Two years later, the rebel army, the Sandinistas, took power in Nicaragua, and Cardenal was made Minister of Culture.

Publications

1965 *Marilyn Monroe and Other Poems*
1969 *Homage to the American Indians*
1971 *Zero Hour*
1972 *In Cuba*
1975 *The Gospel in Solentiname*
1990 *The Music of the Spheres*
1992 *Golden UFOs/The Indian Poems*

CARDUCCI, Giosuè

Italian poet and critic

Born Jul. 28, 1835
Died Feb. 16, 1907
Age at death 71

Because of his patriotic vision and his striving for a revival of standards in Italian thought and literature, Giosuè Carducci was regarded in his day as Italy's national poet. In 1906, he was awarded the Nobel Prize for Literature.

The son of a doctor, Carducci was born in Valdicastello on the west coast of northern Italy near the Leaning Tower of Pisa. His studies of the classical literature of ancient Greece and Rome persuaded him that Italian literature had declined, and he longed to bring about a new Italian Renaissance. When he was 25, he was appointed Professor of Italian Literature at Bologna University, where he remained for 44 years.

During this time Carducci wrote many lyrical poems, such as the notable *Barbarian Odes*. Based on classical models and concerned mainly with political and historical subjects, these poems reflect his determination to promote classical ideals and oppose Romanticism. He also wrote criticism of Italian literature. He was convinced that the state of Italian literary affairs was partly due to Christianity, and he was not afraid to outrage public opinion by promoting the values of a pre-Christian time. His poetry was deeply influenced by the Greek and Latin classics, but has been criticized for its tendency to preach. Much of it, however, is beautifully lyrical and displays his deep sensitivity to the Italian landscape throughout the changing seasons.

In 1876, he became a member of parliament and, in 1890, he was appointed senator. Carducci was a prolific writer, and his complete works were published in 30 volumes in 1940.

Publications

1865 Hymn to Satan
1861–71 Light and Serious Poems
1867–79 Iambics and Epodes
1877–87 Barbarian Odes
1887 New Poems
1899 Poems

CAREY, Peter

Australian novelist and short-story writer

Born May 7, 1943

Peter Carey is one of Australia's best known modern authors. He is famous for writing stories full of bizarre characters and surreal situations.

Carey was born in the Australian city of Victoria. After leaving school, Carey began a career as an advertising agent and lived in London for a short time.

It wasn't until he was 31, almost ten years after he had begun to write, that Carey published *The Fat Man in History*. This collection of short stories was highly praised by critics and his second collection, *War Crimes*, published five years later, won a major Australian literary prize. It was with these works that Carey established his unique style. Although they contain extraordinary characters and incredible situations the reader cannot help but believe that they could just be true. It was this feature that was to make his novels so successful.

Carey's first novel *Bliss* was published when he was 38. It is the story of a man who, after waking up from a serious operation, believes he has, in fact, died and gone to hell. Disaster upon disaster befalls him making his belief all the stronger and tempting the reader to think that he may be right. Carey's second novel *Illywhacker* follows its 139-year-old central character, an outrageous conman and joker, on his comic adventures through the history of Australia. His third, *Oscar and Lucinda* is about the incredible adventures of an Englishman obsessed with gambling, and his Australian lover, a woman who builds a cathedral made from glass.

Publications

1974	*The Fat Man in History*
1979	*War Crimes*
1981	*Bliss*
1985	*Illywhacker*
1988	*Oscar and Lucinda*
1997	*Jack Maggs*

CARLE, Eric

American children's writer and illustrator

Born Jun. 25, 1929

Eric Carle is the author and illustrator of the immensely popular children's book *The Very Hungry Caterpillar*.

Carle was born in Syracuse, New York. His parents had moved to America from Germany before he was born. He remembers his early years in Syracuse as a happy time. When he was six, the family returned to Germany because Carle's mother was homesick. They shared a house in Stuttgart with other family members. Carle was beaten on his third day at the local school; from that time on he hated school and wished he were back in America. The good things the Carles had heard about Adolf Hitler, Germany's Nazi leader, proved to be untrue. Hitler led the country into World War II, and Carle's father was drafted into the German army. Even teenage Carle had to dig trenches on the battle front and was wounded.

After the war, Carle studied art in Stuttgart, then worked as a magazine art director. He returned to the US in 1952, but was drafted into the US Army and sent back to Stuttgart for two years! His military service over, Carle returned to the US for good in 1954 and became a commercial artist. After illustrating a children's book, he decided to write one of his own. His second book, written when he was 40, was *The Very Hungry Caterpillar*, whose star eats his way through the book, leaving a trail of holes before becoming a butterfly. The book has sold over ten million copies worldwide. Carle has written many other children's books, featuring such memorable creatures as spiders, ladybugs and fireflies.

Publications

1968	*1, 2, 3, to the Zoo*
1969	*The Very Hungry Caterpillar*
1973	*Have You Seen My Cat?*
1975	*The Mixed-up Chameleon*
1977	*The Grouchy Ladybug*
1984	*The Very Busy Spider*
1989	*Animals, Animals*
1990	*The Very Quiet Cricket*
1991	*Dragons, Dragons*
1995	*The Very Lonely Firefly*

CARLYLE, Thomas

Scottish novelist and essayist

Born Dec. 4, 1795
Died Feb. 5, 1881
Age at death 85

Thomas Carlyle was a Scottish writer who wrote many influential books on history, philosophy and society.

Carlyle was born in Dumfriesshire, Scotland, and at 15 went to Edinburgh University. There he studied to become a minister and developed an interest in German philosophy, which greatly affected his thinking.

At age 24, Carlyle supported himself by working as a private tutor. During this time he began contributing articles to magazines. His essays on German philosophy introduced many new ideas to the British public. He also produced a translation of a work by JOHANN WOLFGANG VON GOETHE, which was highly acclaimed.

After marrying in 1826, Carlyle settled at his wife's farm and concentrated on his writing. He established his reputation at age 38 when he published *Sartor Resartus*. Part autobiography, part philosophy, it is written using an energetic, complex language that came to be called "Carlylese." The first half of the book is about the ideas of a made-up philosopher who believes everything can be explained in terms of clothes!

Later, after moving to London, Carlyle wrote his most famous work, *The French Revolution*. With its rich, dramatic language, the book brings the history of the French Revolution alive in a way that few historians have ever done. When he had finished the manuscript, it was accidentally burned by a domestic servant. Remembering much of what he had written, Carlyle rewrote the book. It was published when he was 42.

Publications

1833 Sartor Resartus
1837 The French Revolution
1839 Chartism
1841 On Heroes and Hero Worship
1843 Past and Present
1845 Oliver Cromwell's Letters and Speeches
1850 Latter-Day Pamphlets
1858–65 Frederick the Great

CARPENTIER, Alejo

Cuban novelist and journalist

Born Dec. 26, 1904
Died Apr. 24, 1980
Age at death 75

Alejo Carpentier was one of Latin America's leading writers. His novels are in the tradition of magic realism.

Carpentier was born to a French father and Russian mother in Havana, Cuba. He came from a family with a tradition in music criticism, and after attending Havana University, he wrote a music column for a local newspaper. Music features in much of Carpentier's writing, including the novel *The Lost Steps*, about a musician in the jungle.

Carpentier spent much of his life traveling around South and Central America and the Caribbean, working as a newspaper and radio journalist. A revolutionary leftist, he was a supporter of the 1958 revolution that brought the communist leader Fidel Castro to power in Cuba. Carpentier became director of the new regime's state publishing house before his appointment as cultural attaché to the Cuban embassy in France in 1968. Unlike some of his fellow writers, Carpentier managed to remain on good terms with the Cuban government.

With his French-Russian background, Carpentier was among those writers who incorporated elements of European literary traditions into their work. His writing is nevertheless always firmly rooted in the settings and concerns of Latin America. *The Lost Steps*, considered by some to be his masterpiece, is about a voyage into the South American jungle. Like his other novels, it is partly an exploration of history. *Reasons of State* depicts a South American dictator who tries to rule the fictitious Nueva Cordoba from his home in France.

Publications

1932 *Poems of the Antillies*
1946 *Music in Cuba*
1949 *The Kingdom of This World*
1953 *The Lost Steps*
1958 *The War of Time*
1962 *Explosion in a Cathedral*
1974 *Reasons of State*

CARROLL, Lewis

English children's writer

Born Jan. 27, 1832
Died Jan. 14, 1898
Age at death 65

Lewis Carroll was a 19th-century English author of children's stories and poems. His real name was Charles Lutwidge Dodgson, and he wrote one of the funniest and most famous of all children's books, *Alice's Adventures in Wonderland*.

Carroll came from a wealthy family. He was well educated at a famous boarding school and attended Oxford University, where he studied mathematics. He was a brilliant student and, in 1855, he joined the university as a teacher.

Photography had recently been invented in the mid-19th century, and Carroll became an early pioneer of this new art form. He produced superb photographs of young children, with whom he was able to talk and develop warm and close friendships. Carroll entertained his young friends with stories. The stories he told to one young girl, Alice Liddell, became the beginnings of his first book for children, *Alice's Adventures in Wonderland*. The book, when it was published, was loved by children everywhere and also by adults. Unlike other children's books of the time it did not try to teach a moral message but aimed only to amuse its readers with Alice's incredible adventures and ridiculous characters, such as the Mad Hatter and the grinning Cheshire Cat.

Carroll led a happy life living quietly at the university and continuing to produce popular tales for children. He published *Through the Looking-Glass*, about the further adventures of Alice, when he was 39. He also wrote very funny poetry known as nonsense poetry because it has no real meaning.

Publications

1865 *Alice's Adventures in Wonderland*
1869 *Phantasmagoria and Other Poems*
1871 *Through the Looking-Glass*
1876 *The Hunting of the Snark*
1883 *Rhyme? and Reason?*
1889–93 *Sylvie and Bruno* (2 vols.)

Published after he died

1929 *The Collected Verse*

CARTER, Angela

English novelist and short-story writer

Born May 7, 1940
Died Feb. 16, 1992
Age at death 51

Angela Carter was an English writer whose novels and short stories explore dark and disturbing ideas. She is often described as a writer of modern gothic horror or of fairy tales for adults.

Carter was born in London. Her father was a journalist, and after leaving school, she also worked for a short time in this field. At 20, she got married and, two years later, went to Bristol University to study English. After graduating, she settled in the city of Bristol and began writing.

Carter's first novel, *Honeybuzzard*, was published when she was 26. It is a sort of detective story and introduces many of the elements that were to become a familiar part of her writing. The main characters are odd, unstable people who live beyond the edges of "normal" society in a world of decay and menace. *Honeybuzzard* and her next two novels, *The Magic Toyshop* and *Several Perceptions*, established Carter as a respected writer.

In 1970, having separated from her husband, Carter went to live in Japan for two years. Her experience of this radically different culture had a strong influence on her work, and was the inspiration for her 1972 novel, *The War of Dreams*.

Carter returned to England and continued writing novels and short stories. She also wrote nonfiction, including *The Sadeian Woman*, a look at the work of the MARQUIS DE SADE from a feminist perspective. In 1984, she wrote the screenplay for the film *A Company of Wolves*, a bloodthirsty retelling of the Little Red Riding Hood story.

Publications

1966 Honeybuzzard
1967 The Magic Toyshop
1968 Several Perceptions
1972 The War of Dreams
1974 Fireworks
1979 The Bloody Chamber
1979 The Sadeian Woman
1991 Wise Children

Published after she died

1995 Burning Your Boats

CARVER, Raymond

American short-story writer and poet

Born May 25, 1938
Died Aug. 2, 1988
Age at death 50

Raymond Carver's main characters are working-class Americans; his spare, tense prose reflects their attempts to express themselves. Several of his short-story collections were nominated for prestigious prizes, including Pulitzer Prizes.

Carver was born in Clatskanie, Oregon, but his family moved to Yakima, Washington, when he was three. His alcoholic, storytelling father was a millworker. At 19, Carver married Maryann Burke and was soon struggling to support a young family. He took odd jobs, and the family drifted to California. It was there that Carver realized he wanted to write and eventually earned a degree in English from Humboldt State University. He received a fellowship to the prestigious Iowa Writers' Workshop, but financial pressure drove him back to California, where he finally found a job editing textbooks.

Carver's story "Will You Please Be Quiet, Please?" appeared in *The Best American Short Stories 1967* collection when he was 29. It is also the title story of his first short-story collection, which received critical acclaim when Carver was in his late 30s. Carver's stories focus sympathetically on people coping with divorce, joblessness, loss or humiliation. His characters are often people who have just realized they are not in control of their lives and who struggle to find the language to describe that situation.

In 1976, after being treated for alcoholism, Carver stopped drinking. In the 1980s, he and his second wife, the poet Tess Gallagher, taught creative writing at Syracuse University, spending summers in Washington state.

Publications

1976 Will You Please Be Quiet, Please?
1977 Furious Seasons
1981 What We Talk about When We Talk about Love
1983 Cathedral
1988 Where I'm Calling From
1988 Elephant and Other Stories

Published after he died

1989 A New Path to the Waterfall

CATHER, Willa

American novelist and short-story writer

Born Dec. 7, 1873
Died Apr. 24, 1947
Age at death 73

Willa Cather is best known for her novels about immigrants struggling to make a living in the Midwest during the late 1800s. Unlike many writers of the time, Cather created strong, determined female characters who have the courage and vision to make the most of their difficult lives.

Born in Virginia, where her parents had a farm, Cather was nine when they moved to a ranch in Nebraska. She was homesick at first, but she grew to love roaming the wide open spaces and visiting her neighbors, who mostly came from Scandinavia and other parts of Europe. The ranch was not a success, however, and, in 1884, the family moved a short distance away to the small railroad town of Red Cloud, where her father opened an insurance business. In early childhood, Cather was educated at home, but she later attended Red Cloud High School and the University of Nebraska.

At age 23 Cather went to Pittsburgh, Pennsylvania, working there as a journalist and writing short stories before moving to New York City in 1906. Her first successful novel, *O Pioneers!*, was published when she was 40. It was one of several books Cather wrote about newcomers to the prairies and the sacrifices that women, especially, had to make. Later, Cather became interested in American deserts, and her book *The Professor's House* tells of the amazing discovery of an ancient New Mexican cliff city.

In 1923, Cather won the Pulitzer Prize for her novel *One of Ours.* It is the story of a young Nebraskan man who leaves home to fight in World War I.

Publications

1912 Alexander's Bridge
1913 O Pioneers!
1915 The Song of the Lark
1918 My Antonia
1922 One of Ours
1923 A Lost Lady
1925 The Professor's House
1926 My Mortal Enemy
1927 Death Comes for the Archbishop
1935 Lucy Grayheart

CATULLUS

Roman poet

Born c. 84 BC
Died c. 54 BC
Age at death c. 30

Catullus was one of the greatest poets of ancient Rome. He is best known for his love poems to a mysterious woman he called Lesbia.

Very little is known about Catullus's life except that he was born in the city of Verona in Italy and settled in Rome when he was about 18. Catullus's family was probably wealthy; his father was a friend of the great Roman leader, Julius Caesar, and Catullus owned villas in Rome and in the Italian countryside.

In Rome, Catullus soon became the leader of a group of young writers called the New Poets. His poetry imitated the style and subject matter of the earlier poets of ancient Greece. He wrote intensely about his personal feelings and relationships with other people. This kind of writing had never been attempted before in Latin (the Roman language), but Catullus was so successful that poets long after his death admired and followed his style.

Scholars believe that Lesbia, the subject of Catullus's love poems, may have been the wife of a wealthy Roman politician and that her real name was Clodia. Catullus probably called her Lesbia, a Greek name, because of his love for the poetry of the Greek poet, SAPPHO of Lesbos. Catullus's love poems, written over a period of several years, vividly show his feelings for Lesbia as their relationship grew and then broke up.

After his affair with Lesbia ended, Catullus went on a long journey to Asia Minor (modern-day Turkey). He visited the grave of his brother, who had died there, and wrote a moving poem about the experience. Catullus died very young, soon after his return to Rome.

Publications

116 poems survive, all probably written between c. 61 BC and 54 BC

CELA, Camilo José

Spanish novelist, poet and playwright

Born May 11, 1916

Camilo José Cela is one of Spain's leading novelists, specializing in highly original and satirical works of realism. In 1989, he was awarded the Nobel Prize for Literature.

Cela was born in Iria Flavia, Spain, and literature was in his blood. His father was a part-time author, and his brother was also a novelist. When he was 17, Cela enrolled at the University of Madrid, but his education was interrupted by the Spanish Civil War. After serving as a corporal in the fascist-controlled Nationalist Army, he resumed his studies, finally graduating at age 27.

When he was 26, Cela published his first and most popular novel, *The Family of Pascual Duarte*, which has since been made into a film. The novel was labeled "tremendismo," a literary style Cela is credited with inventing. Tremendismo works deal with the darker side of life and often include unexpected or violent scenes that are intended to shock the reader. The violence of *The Family of Pascual Duarte* did shock, and the novel was briefly banned.

As Cela's work has progressed, it has become more experimental. His main aim is to change the way novels are written. In most books, the important element is the story, told in correct date order – past, present, then future. Cela's concern is with characters. In his masterpiece, *The Hive*, there are more than 300 characters, whose stories are told in loosely connected "snapshots." In *Toboggan of Hungry People* events from the future and past are mixed together in no specific order. Cela's works have done much to introduce new literary ideas.

Publications

1942	*The Family of Pascual Duarte*
1948	*Journey to the Alcarria*
1951	*The Hive*
1953	*Mrs. Caldwell Speaks to Her Son*
1962	*Toboggan of Hungry People*
1969	*San Camilo, 1936*
1973	*Ministry of Darkness 5*
1983	*Mazurka for Two Dead Men*
1988	*Cristo Versus Arizona*

CELLINI, Benvenuto

Italian writer

Born Nov. 3, 1500
Died Feb. 13, 1571
Age at death 70

Benvenuto Cellini was a well-known troublemaker in the Middle Ages. He was a talented goldsmith, silversmith and sculptor, but he is also remembered for his colorful autobiography, which gives a lively picture of 16th-century Italy.

Cellini was born in Florence in Italy. His father wanted him to be a musician, but he wanted to work as a goldsmith. By age 16, he was already in trouble – after being involved in a duel he was told to leave town. Cellini's autobiography, begun when he was 58 but not published until 170 years later, covers his life up to the age of 62. It tells of the violent sword fights, duels, murders, beatings and political scrapes that led to his being thrown out of one town after another. Most of his life, as a result, was spent moving between several towns in Italy and France.

Cellini was dangerously unbalanced mentally but immensely talented, and he had the knack of gaining the support of the most important people. Kings, popes, cardinals and members of the nobility supported him when he was in favor and imprisoned or exiled him when his outrageous behavior became too much for them. He had numerous children, some illegitimate and some born in marriage.

The Life of Benvenuto Cellini is a lively and interesting work that gives a unique picture of Italy and the Renaissance and recounts the extraordinary adventures and misdeeds of this remarkable man. It is a major classic of Italian literature and has, in the past, been one of the most popular books ever written. It has been continuously in print since its first publication and was first translated into English in 1822.

Published after he died

1728	*The Life of Benvenuto Cellini*

CERVANTES, Miguel de

Spanish writer

Born Sep. 29, 1547
Died Apr. 23, 1616
Age at death 68

Miguel de Cervantes was the greatest writer in the history of Spanish literature. He is famous worldwide as the author of *The Ingenious Gentleman Don Quixote of La Mancha* (known as *Don Quixote*).

Cervantes lived an unsettled life of adventure and hardship. He was born near Madrid, Spain, into an aristocratic but poor family, and spent much of his childhood moving from town to town while his father, a doctor, sought work. Years spent in study with a famous humanist scholar gave him a passion for the principles of the humanist movement: learning and tolerance.

In his early 20s, Cervantes became a soldier. He fought at the Battle of Lapanto, one of the greatest sea battles in history. When he was 28, he was captured by North African pirates and spent five years as a slave until his family could raise enough money to buy his release. Returning to Spain, Cervantes found his family in poverty. He had several temporary jobs and turned to writing as a way of earning money. Among his works in this period were a pastoral novel, poetry and several plays.

During a period of particularly bad luck Cervantes found himself in jail for fraud. It was here that he had the idea for his masterpiece. The first volume of *Don Quixote* was published when he was 58, and it was an immediate success. It follows the adventures of a slightly insane Spanish nobleman and his loyal servant. The Don sees himself as a knight in shining armor and sets out to right the wrongs of the world. Scholars describe *Don Quixote* as one of the world's first novels.

Publications

1585 Galatea: A Pastoral Romance
c. 1585 Comedy of Confusion
1605–15 Don Quixote
1613 Exemplary Novels
1615 Eight New Plays and Eight New Interludes

Published after he died

1617 The Exploits of Persiles and Sigismunda

CHANDLER, Raymond

American crime writer

Born Jul. 23, 1888
Died Mar. 26, 1959
Age at death 70

Raymond Chandler is one of the best-known writers of detective stories.

Chandler was born in Chicago, but moved to England as a child. He returned to the US when he was 24, and did many different jobs, such as working on a ranch and in the oil business, until he became a full-time writer at age 45.

Starting with *The Big Sleep*, which he published when he was 51, the hero of Chandler's novels is Philip Marlowe, a private investigator who seems like a tough guy but who has a soft heart. Chandler's stories are set in Los Angeles, a city that was growing fast in the 1930s. It was an exciting place to be, and Chandler's books are full of characters like gangsters, movie stars and rich bankers. The stories are also fun to read because they are full of wisecracks and lively, sarcastic humor about these people.

Crime novels, which were increasingly popular in the 1940s, were sometimes called "pulp fiction" because they were printed on cheap paper. Many of them were badly written and have been forgotten. But Raymond Chandler, along with authors like JAMES M. CAIN and DASHIELL HAMMETT, is recognized today as an important writer.

Chandler was a well-educated man who was familiar with serious literature. His hard-boiled novels are full of realistic street life, and Philip Marlowe always has a strong sense of right and wrong. Chandler also wrote film scripts, and many movies have been made of his stories, the most famous being *The Big Sleep*, in which the actor Humphrey Bogart played Marlowe.

Publications

1939 *The Big Sleep*
1940 *Farewell, My Lovely*
1942 *The High Window*
1943 *The Lady in the Lake*
1944 *Double Indemnity*
1949 *The Little Sister*
1950 *The Simple Art of Murder*
1953 *The Long Goodbye*
1953 *Smart Aleck Kill*
1958 *Playback*

CHASE, Mary

American playwright

Born Feb. 25, 1907
Died Oct. 20, 1981
Age at death 74

American dramatist Mary Chase won a Pulitzer Prize in 1945 for her classic play *Harvey* – the story of a drunk whose friend is an invisible six-foot-tall rabbit called Harvey. The play had one of the longest runs ever on Broadway. Five years after winning the Pulitzer, it was made into a successful film starring James Stewart. *Harvey* is still performed in many parts of the world and often shown on American television.

Chase was born Mary Coyle in Denver, Colorado. She studied at the universities of Colorado and Denver before becoming a reporter when she was 18. In 1928, she married Robert L. Chase. After three years with the *Rocky Mountain News*, she then went freelance, collecting stories that were bought by the International News Service and United Press.

Chase's first play, *Me, Third*, was produced when she was 29. This comedy is about a young man who is helped by a prostitute to become a politician. It came out in New York as *Now You've Done It* but lasted only a few weeks. *Harvey* – Chase's first success – was produced eight years later. As a story of faith triumphing over reality, it appealed widely. Harvey's invisibility is central to the success of the play; the one time an actor in a rabbit costume appeared, the play was not as good.

Although none of Chase's work was ever as popular as *Harvey*, she again displayed her gift for combining comedy and fantasy in *Mrs. McThing*. This children's play is about a girl whose mother is a witch and a rich boy who is kidnapped. She also tried more serious drama with *The Next Half Hour*, but this failed at the box office.

Publications

1936 *Me, Third*
1939 *Sorority House*
1944 *Harvey*
1945 *The Next Half Hour*
1952 *Mrs. McThing*
1952 *Bernadine*
1954 *Lolita*
1961 *Midgie Purvis*
1963 *The Dog Sitters*
1973 *Cocktails with Mimi*

CHASE, Mary Ellen

American novelist

Born Feb. 24, 1887
Died Jul. 28, 1973
Age at death 86

Mary Ellen Chase was a highly popular novelist whose work features the landscape and people of Maine.

One of eight children, Chase grew up in Blue Hill, on Maine's east coast. Her father was a lawyer and her mother a teacher. While in college at the University of Maine, Chase began to sell her stories to magazines, and she published three children's books while still in her 20s. After graduating, she taught history, then earned a Master's degree and Ph.D. For nearly 30 years she was Professor of English at Smith College.

Although she had already published novels and stories, Chase was in her late 40s before she became well known as a writer after publishing two historical novels, *Mary Peters* and *Silas Crockett*. Set in the Maine coastal communities that she knew and loved, they describe the lives of seafaring families at the time of the introduction of steamships.

With these novels Chase became known as a regionalist, a writer of "local color" whose work vividly describes the land and people of a particular place. She has been compared to SARAH ORNE JEWETT, another local-color writer whom Chase had met as a child and who had inspired the younger writer to use Maine as the setting for her books.

Other books include studies of the Bible and English literature and several autobiographical works, including *A Goodly Fellowship*, which describes her childhood and her experiences as a teacher. She is well loved by some readers today for the way her writing preserves a fondly remembered time in America's past, a way of living that has now disappeared.

Publications

1915	*His Birthday*
1927	*Uplands*
1934	*Mary Peters*
1935	*Silas Crockett*
1939	*A Goodly Fellowship*
1941	*Windswept*
1949	*The Plum Tree*
1954	*The White Gate*
1957	*The Edge of Darkness*
1960	*Lovely Ambition*

CHATEAUBRIAND, François René

French novelist and essayist

Born Sep. 4, 1768
Died Jul. 4, 1848
Age at death 79

Francois René, Viscount of Chateaubriand, was the most influential writer of his generation in France. He is considered by some to have been the founder of the Romantic movement.

Chateaubriand was born in Saint-Malo, France, into an aristocratic but poor family. He spent much of his childhood living in the family's rundown castle, an experience that provided rich material for his romantic and literary mind. Later, he became a soldier, and in 1791, during the French Revolution, he traveled extensively in North America. His novel *The Natchez*, published when he was 58, was based on his experiences among the Native Americans.

After Chateaubriand was wounded fighting for the side of the royalty in France, he fled to England, where he wrote a book about the

French Revolution. He returned to France and achieved great critical acclaim at age 34 with *The Genius of Christianity*. This book brought him to the attention of the French leader, Napoleon Bonaparte, who made him a diplomat and sent him to Rome, Italy. However, Chateaubriand soon resigned in protest at the execution of a prominent French aristocrat. He remained opposed to Napoleon until the leader's final fall in 1815.

In 1811, Chateaubriand was elected to the prestigious French Academy for his literary achievements. His lyrical prose had influenced many other writers. Now he is remembered mainly for his autobiography, *Memoirs from Beyond the Grave*.

Publications

1797 Essay on the Revolutions
1801 Atala
1802 The Genius of Christianity
1802 René
1809 The Martyrs
1826 The Natchez
1827 Travels in America

Published after he died

1848–49 Memoirs from Beyond the Grave

CHAUCER, Geoffrey

English poet

Born c. 1343
Died Oct. 25, 1400
Age at death c. 57

Geoffrey Chaucer was the greatest English poet of the Middle Ages. He is remembered as the author of *The Canterbury Tales*, one of the most important books in the history of English literature.

Chaucer was born in London into a prosperous trade family. At 16, he took part in a military expedition to France, part of the Hundred Years' War. He was captured by the French and held prisoner until the English king and Chaucer's friends paid the ransom for his release.

Between 1370 and 1387, Chaucer was sent on diplomatic missions throughout Europe. He was also granted privileges and incomes by the king and gained status and wealth. This was a period of great creativity for Chaucer, during which he produced most of his best poetry. His best-known work from this time is *Troilus and Cressida*, a long poem based on a love story told by the Italian writer, GIOVANNI BOCCACCIO.

Chaucer did not begin his greatest work, *The Canterbury Tales*, until he was in his early 40s, and it was left unfinished when he died. The book is made up of 24 stories told by a group of pilgrims on their way to Canterbury Cathedral. The rhyming verse is written in what is called Middle English, an old form of the language that is very different from the English we use today. The stories are humorous, thoughtful, rude and moralizing. Many of them were told by other writers of the time, but Chaucer's versions have been enjoyed for centuries because of the beauty of his poetry and the colorfulness of his characters.

Publications

c. 1369 The Book of the Duchess
c. 1374–85 The House of Fame
c. 1380 The Parliament of Fowls
c. 1385 Troilus and Cressida
c. 1386–1400 The Canterbury Tales
c. 1387–94 The Legend of Good Women

CHAYEFSKY, Paddy

American television playwright and screenwriter

Born Jan. 29, 1923
Died Aug. 1, 1981
Age at death 58

Paddy Chayefsky was one of American television's foremost writers during the 1950s.

The son of Russian immigrants, Chayefsky was raised in a traditional Jewish household in the Bronx, New York. He graduated from City College of New York and enlisted in the army. There he gained his nickname "Paddy" because of his frequent request to attend Catholic Mass rather than serve on kitchen duty. After the war he began writing plays for television during a time when most of the prime-time shows were live dramas. His works depicted the lives of ordinary people he had known while growing up.

Chayefsky gained national fame when he was 30 for the TV drama *Marty*, a sympathetic love story about two lonely, unattractive people. In 1955, the movie version won an Academy Award. Several other TV plays, including *The Bachelor Party* and *The Catered Affair*, became successful films. Chayefsky's work was noted for using details about everyday life to explore universal themes.

When filmed dramas replaced live works on TV, Chayefsky began writing Broadway plays, including *The Tenth Man*, the traditional Jewish tale of the Dybbuk (the wandering soul of a dead person), set in the Bronx. Other plays were *Gideon*, a story about a man's refusal to accept God's assurances, and *The Passion of Josef D.*, about the Russian Revolution. He also wrote screenplays for movies such as *The Hospital* and *Network*, both of which won Academy Awards. His only novel, the science fiction story *Altered States*, was also made into a film.

Publications

1953 Marty
1954 The Bachelor Party
1954 Middle of the Night
1955 The Catered Affair
1959 The Tenth Man
1961 Gideon
1964 The Passion of Josef D.
1971 The Hospital
1976 Network
1978 Altered States

CHEEVER, John

American novelist and short-story writer

Born May 27, 1912
Died Jun. 18, 1982
Age at death 70

John Cheever is best known for his stories that satirize the lives of middle-class Americans.

Cheever was born in Quincy, Massachusetts. At age eight, he was already entertaining his classmates with stories he had made up. His father was relatively wealthy until he lost his business in the 1929 stock market crash. This sudden loss led to the breakdown of his parents' relationship, which deeply upset young Cheever. He left home at 17 after being expelled from school for smoking. Soon afterward, he sold his first short story.

During most of the 1930s, Cheever lived in New York City, where he became friends with other writers such as James Agee and John Dos Passos. He also began a long-standing association with the *New*

Yorker magazine. At age 31, he published his first volume of short stories, *The Way Some People Live*. Some of these stories had already appeared in the *New Yorker*.

In the mid-1950s, Cheever began writing novels. His first, *The Wapshot Chronicle*, is autobiographical and tells of the breakdown of a family. The novel won the National Book Award in 1958 and remains his most famous work.

Although often funny and filled with irony, Cheever's novels and stories also have a darker side, exploring the isolation of modern American life. He is concerned with social institutions, such as the family, and the morals and hidden emotions of ordinary suburban people. In 1979, *The Stories of John Cheever* was awarded a Pulitzer Prize.

Publications

1943 The Way Some People Live
1953 The Enormous Radio
1957 The Wapshot Chronicle
1964 The Brigadier and the Golf Widow
1964 The Wapshot Scandal
1969 Bullet Park
1977 Falconer
1978 The Stories of John Cheever
1982 Oh What a Paradise It Seems

CHEKHOV, Anton

Russian short-story writer and playwright

Born Jan. 29, 1860
Died Jul. 14, 1904
Age at death 44

Anton Chekhov was a great Russian author. His plays and short stories are famous for their realistic examination of the lives of ordinary Russians at the end of the 19th century.

Chekhov was born in Taganrog, a small port in southern Russia. When he was 15, his father went bankrupt, and the family left for Moscow to avoid paying debts. Chekhov stayed behind to finish school, but was deeply affected by the separation.

When he was 19, Chekhov joined his family in Moscow. While studying medicine, he began writing stories, and by the time he became a doctor, he had published hundreds of them. At 28, he began to be taken seriously as a writer, and he was awarded a literary prize. Four years later, he became the physician for a poor area outside Moscow. While there, he wrote some of his best short stories. With the proceeds from his writing, he bought a home in the area and worked hard to improve conditions for the people living there.

Chekhov had been suffering from tuberculosis for some time, and by his late 30s he had to move to the warmer climate of the Crimea, in southern Russia. There he wrote his most famous plays: *Uncle Vanya*, *The Seagull*, *The Three Sisters* and *The Cherry Orchard*.

In all his work Chekhov created dramatic tension through mood and setting rather than action or dramatic events. His works were never openly political, but they have been seen as critical of life under the Russian monarchy, or the czars. Chekhov's main concern was for the people and their hopes, dreams and disappointments.

Publications

1884 Melpomene
1886 Motley Stories
1888 The Bear
1888 Ivanov
1889 The Wood Demon
1893–94 Sakhalin Island
1896 The Seagull
1897 Uncle Vanya
1901 The Three Sisters
1903 The Cherry Orchard

CHESNUTT, Charles Waddell

American novelist and short-story writer

Born Jun. 20, 1858
Died Nov. 15, 1932
Age at death 74

Charles Waddell Chesnutt was the first important African-American fiction writer to effectively use standard publishing houses to reach a white audience. His aim was to write stories that would educate white readers about black people. His characters were strong, complex and diverse; he refused to create simple stereotypes, but instead tried to write about real people.

Chesnutt was born in Cleveland, Ohio. His parents were "free Negroes" who had moved from Fayetteville, North Carolina. The family moved back there after the American Civil War brought an end to slavery. When he was 13, his mother died, so he took a teaching job to help support the family. Although unable to continue his studies, he read widely. In 1883, he left his position as school principal and set up a profitable business in Cleveland.

Although Chesnutt started writing stories when he was 14, his work was not noticed until he was 41, when the collections *The Conjure Woman* and *The Wife of His Youth and Other Stories of the Color Line* came out. *The Conjure Woman* stories are his versions of Southern folklore. A year later he published his first novel, *The House behind the Cedars*, a story about a young black woman who tries to pass as white.

In his books Chesnutt tried to show why some felt forced by a racist society to deny their color. He continued to make speeches and write articles supporting civil rights until his death.

Publications

1899 The Conjure Woman
1899 The Wife of His Youth and Other Stories of the Colour Line
1900 The House behind the Cedars
1901 The Marrow of Tradition
1905 The Colonel's Dream

CHESTERTON, G.K.

English novelist, poet and journalist

Born May 29, 1874
Died Jun. 14, 1936
Age at death 62

Publications

1900 The Wild Knight
1904 The Napoleon of Notting Hill
1905 The Club of Queer Trades

G.K. Chesterton was a famous English personality whose novels, poetry and journalism were witty and popular.

Gilbert Keith Chesterton was born in London, where at St. Paul's School he made his name as a poet. When he was 26, he published a book of verse, *The Wild Knight*, and began his long career as a journalist. He wrote articles for newspapers and magazines.

Chesterton had strong views on just about everything. He criticized big business, government interference in people's lives, and technology. His views were largely shared by his great friend HILAIRE BELLOC. The playwright GEORGE BERNARD SHAW gave the pair of them the nickname 'Chesterbelloc'.

Chesterton's first novel was *The Napoleon of Notting Hill*, a fantasy set in a future in which London is ruled by a mad king. Other fantasty novels followed, including *The Man Who Was Thursday*, about a plot to overthrow the world's governments. He also wrote a series of detective short stories featuring Father Brown, a gentle Roman Catholic priest whose understanding of human nature helps him to solve baffling crimes. Chesterton was deeply interested in religion and, in 1922, he became a Roman Catholic himself. He wrote widely on religious subjects.

Another major field of Chesterton's writing was literary criticism, and he wrote fine books and articles about authors such as CHARLES DICKENS and ROBERT LOUIS STEVENSON.

Chesterton was a tubby, jolly man with a loud, jolly laugh. His humor appears in most of his verse, though he did write serious poems as well.

1908	*The Man Who Was Thursday*
1911	*The Innocence of Father Brown*
1914	*The Wisdom of Father Brown*
1926	*The Incredulity of Father Brown*
1927	*The Secret of Father Brown*
1929	*New and Collected Poems*
1935	*The Scandal of Father Brown*

CHILDRESS, Alice

American novelist and playwright

Born Oct. 12, 1920
Died Aug. 14, 1994
Age at death 73

Alice Childress was the first African American to have a play, *Gold through the Trees*, professionally staged in the United States. She is now more famous, however, as the author of the novel and screenplay *A Hero Ain't Nothin' but a Sandwich*. This story of a 13-year-old heroin user was one of the first books for young-adult readers to deal with issues such as drug abuse.

Childress was born in Charleston, South Carolina, but moved to one of the poorest blocks in Harlem, New York City, when she was just five. She was raised by her grandmother, whose ability as a storyteller first awakened her interest in the theater. Childress had to leave school at the age of 16. While working in low-paid jobs, she educated herself at public libraries. Her interest in the stage grew, and although still in her teens, she helped found Harlem's American Negro Theatre (ANT) in 1939.

Over the next decade Childress directed and acted in many plays at ANT before writing her first play, *Florence*, when she was 29. It explores racism through the conversation of two women – one black, one white – who meet by chance at a train station. Although performed in a loft, it got a lot of attention. Childress wrote many more plays throughout the 1960s. She was not slow to attack stereotypes about race and poverty, and she often portrayed black women as brave survivors. Despite her lack of formal schooling, she also taught at many colleges and universities, including Harvard. Childress later wrote plays and stories for young people and novels for adults. Her novel *A Hero Ain't Nothin' but a Sandwich* was published when she was 53.

Publications

1949	*Florence*
1950	*Just a Little Simple*
1952	*Gold through the Trees*
1955	*Trouble in Mind*
1966	*Wedding Band*
1969	*Wine in the Wilderness*
1970	*Mojo*
1973	*A Hero Ain't Nothin' but a Sandwich*
1977	*Sea Island Song*

CHOPIN, Kate

American novelist and short-story writer

Born Feb. 8, 1851
Died Aug. 22, 1904
Age at death 53

Kate Chopin's best-known work, *The Awakening*, aroused a storm of criticism and abuse when it was published. Today the novel is considered a classic feminist work.

Chopin was born Kate O'Flaherty and raised in St. Louis, Missouri. Her parents were prominent members of St. Louis society, and her upbringing was relatively privileged.

When she was 19, she married Oscar Chopin and moved with him to his native New Orleans. In her mid-30s, she began to write stories after experiencing several family tragedies. Her husband's death in 1883 and that of her mother two years later, combined with the early deaths during her childhood of her father and beloved great-grandmother, had caused Chopin considerable grief. Her doctor advised her to try writing as a form of therapy.

Chopin set all her fiction in Louisiana, depicting the complex Creole and Cajun society in which she lived. She published her first novel, *At Fault*, at age 39. In it she explored what became one of her main themes: the conflict between women's sexual passions and the restrictions placed on women by society. Throughout the 1890s she wrote more than 100 short stories, published in two collections.

At age 48, Chopin published what was to become her great work. The heroine of *The Awakening* struggles to identify herself beyond her roles as wife and mother, and in so doing she awakens a sexual longing that cannot be fulfilled because of society's restraints. She ends up committing suicide. It is a bleak portrayal of 19th-century attitudes toward women.

Publications
1890 At Fault
1894 Bayou Folk
1897 A Night in Acadie
1899 The Awakening

CHRÉTIEN de TROYES

French poet

Born c. 1130
Died c. 1185
Age at death c. 55

Chrétien de Troyes was a French poet who lived in the early medieval period. He was the first to write down the legendary stories of King Arthur and his knights of the Round Table.

Very little is known about Chrétien's life. Scholars do know that he lived and worked at the court of a powerful aristocrat in eastern France called Marie, Countess of Champagne. It is also likely that Chrétien was a priest or monk because in medieval times members of the Church were almost the only people who learned to read and write.

Chrétien wrote long narrative poems – poems that tell an ongoing story. They are full of adventure, romance and religious feeling. One of his works, *Perceval* (also called *The Tale of the Grail*), is the earliest known version of the legend of the Holy Grail. It is the story of a magical holy object – the Grail – that tests the worthiness of the knights who are on a quest to find it.

An important part of Chrétien's stories is the idea of courtly love, an idea inspired by the Roman poet, OVID. This was a kind of ideal romance between a knight and a noblewoman, often the wife of his king or lord. It was seen as a test of the knight's ability to resist temptation and as a test of his obedience to the king or lord. The story of the knight Lancelot and Guinevere, the wife of King Arthur, is a famous example of courtly love.

Chrétien's poems remained popular for a hundred years after his death, and his work has had a lasting influence on the often retold tales of the court of King Arthur.

Publications

c. 1160–64	*Eric and Enide*
c. 1160–64	*Cliges*
1164–72	*Yvain*
1164–72	*Lancelot*
c. 1180	*Perceval*

CHRISTIE, Agatha

English crime writer

Born Sep. 15, 1890
Died Jan. 12, 1976
Age at death 85

Agatha Christie is probably the most famous of all crime writers. Her books have been translated into many languages and sell millions of copies worldwide. She is the queen of the "whodunit" – a type of crime story in which the reader can puzzle out from clues which of the characters in the story is guilty of a murder. Her stories are known for their clever, surprising twists of plot.

Born Agatha Miller in the southern English coastal town of Torquay, she was educated privately at home and went on to study music in Paris. During World War I, she worked as a nurse for the Red Cross in Torquay. In 1914, she married Colonel Archibald Christie and had a daughter, but the couple divorced in 1928. She then married archeologist Max Mallowan and accompanied him on many trips to Syria and Iraq, which gave her the setting for several of her novels.

When she was 30, Christie's first book, *The Mysterious Affair at Styles*, came out. It introduced the dapper Belgian detective Hercule Poirot. Christie came from an upper-middle-class background, and it is this world that she wrote about in her books. She has a simple writing style and a good ear for dialogue. The stories usually involve a murder that takes place among ordinary people with ordinary lives. There are also memorable characters, such as Poirot and the quiet but inquisitive, elderly Miss Marple.

Christie also wrote plays. One of these, *The Mousetrap*, has been running continuously in London since 1952. In 1954, she won the New York Drama Critics' Circle Award and, in 1971, she was made a Dame.

Publications

1920	*The Mysterious Affair at Styles*
1926	*The Murder of Roger Ackroyd*
1930	*Murder at the Vicarage*
1934	*Murder on the Orient Express*
1937	*Death on the Nile*
1938	*Appointment with Death*
1952	*They Do It With Mirrors*
1952	*The Mousetrap*
1964	*A Caribbean Mystery*
1975	*Curtain*

CHRISTINE de PIZAN

Italian-born French writer

Born 1364
Died c.1430
Age at death c. 66

Publications

c. 1400 The Letter of Othéa
1401–02 The Letters on the Romance of the Rose
1404 The Book of the Mutations of Fortune
1405 The Book of the City of Ladies
1405 The Book of the Three Virtues
1410 The Book of the Deeds of Arms and of Chivalry
1429 The Song of Joan of Arc

Christine de Pizan was probably the first professional woman writer and one of the first feminists.

Born in Venice, the daughter of an Italian academic, Tommaso di Pizzano, Christine went with him to France when he became astrologer and physician to the French king, Charles V. Although limited in her formal education by the social opinions of the time concerning women, she did learn Latin and have access to the court's wonderful library. She was married at age 15 to Étienne de Castel, who had a bright future as an official in the royal government. He died in an epidemic when she was 25, leaving her with three children and an elderly mother to support.

Christine began to write poetry to express her grief and loneliness, and she broadened her education by reading books of philosophy. Her first long work, *The Letter of Othéa*, is a poem describing the proper moral and spiritual education for a young knight. Education would remain a favorite topic.

Christine supported her family by her writing and took part in a literary debate concerning the most popular poem of the time, *The Romance of the Rose*, about the art of love. She attacked its attitude to women and went on to write two other works in defense of her sex, *The Book of the City of Ladies* and *The Book of the Three Virtues*. During the Hundred Years' War, after the French were defeated by the English at Agincourt in 1415, she entered the convent of Poissy, where her daughter was a nun. She published one more work, a song to celebrate the victory of Joan of Arc over the English at Orleans.

CICERO

Roman writer

Born Jun. 3, 106 BC
Died Dec. 7, 43 BC
Age at death 63

Cicero was a Roman statesman, orator and writer. He is considered to be the greatest Roman prose writer and is particularly remembered for his speeches, which have survived in written form. Cicero's work did a lot to make the Roman language, Latin, the language of learning and culture in Europe for the next 1,000 years.

Cicero came from a wealthy, middle-class family and received an excellent education in Rome. He started his career as a lawyer and soon became famous for his skill at public speaking and debating. When Cicero was about 30, he was elected to the Senate, the government of Rome. He was ambitious and wanted to become consul, the highest office in government. Usually this would have been impossible for a man who did not come from an aristocratic background, but Cicero's public-speaking skills won the Senate's support, and he was elected consul in 63 BC.

While consul, Cicero defeated a plot to overthrow the government and had some of the conspirators executed. Julius Caesar, the future dictator of Rome, persuaded the Senate that Cicero had acted unfairly and had him sent into exile for a year. After returning to Rome, Cicero lived quietly and devoted himself to literature. He wrote many works on society, philosophy and oration during this period.

After the assassination of Caesar in 44 BC, Cicero became involved in a power struggle between the consul, Mark Antony, and the future Emperor Augustus. He made speeches attacking Mark Antony. These, known as the *Philippics*, cost him his life when the two rivals later joined forces to rule together.

Publications

63 BC Orations Against Catiline
55 BC On Oratory
52 BC On the Republic
c. 52 BC On the Laws
46 BC Brutus
c. 44 BC On Old Age
c. 44 BC On Friendship
c. 44 BC On the Nature of the Gods
c. 44 BC On Duty
44–43 BC Philippics

CLAMPITT, Amy

American poet

Born Jun. 15, 1920
Died Sep. 10, 1994
Age at death 74

Amy Clampitt burst onto the literary scene at the age of 63 with the publication of her third collection of poems, *The Kingfisher*. She then became a major American poet in fewer than ten years.

Clampitt was born in a small farming village in Iowa. Her grandfather had written an account of his life on the prairies. This inspired her to try writing, and she started to compose poems when she was just nine. Later, she studied English at Grinnell College, Iowa. After graduating in 1941, Clampitt began further studies at Columbia University, New York, but left within a year to start work. Her career that followed often involved books. She promoted college textbooks for the Oxford University Press, worked as a librarian, and, between the years 1960 and 1982, earned a living as a freelance editor.

While working as an editor, Clampitt began writing poetry again. Her first collection *Multitudes, Multitudes* was published when she was 54. This and her second collection, *The Isthmus*, showed talent, but received little attention. Some well-known literary figures, however, did notice her work and, from 1982, she was able to support herself by writing, reading poetry, teaching and living off grants.

With the publication of *The Kingfisher* and other collections Clampitt's reputation and fame grew. While her poems are highly descriptive of the Maine coast and other places she visited, she also used her considerable knowledge of science, history, nature, art, religion and literature to explore many ideas.

Publications

1974 Multitudes, Multitudes
1981 The Isthmus
1983 The Kingfisher
1983 The Summer Solstice
1984 A Homage to John Keats
1985 What the Light Was Like
1988 Archaic Figure
1990 Westward

Published after she died

1998 Collected Poems

CLARE, John

English poet

Born Jul. 13, 1793
Died May 20, 1864
Age at death 70

John Clare was a peasant poet who wrote about the English countryside. He produced some of his best verses while suffering from mental illness.

Clare was born in eastern England in the rural village of Helpstone. His father was a needy farm worker; his mother could neither read nor write. They were so poor that at age seven John had to herd cattle. He received little schooling but had a keen eye, a good memory, and a gift for using words. As a boy, he began writing verses in pencil on his mother's used sugar bags. He read few books, but James Thomson's long 18th-century nature poem "Seasons" inspired him to write about the local countryside. When Clare was 26, a London publisher produced his first book, *Poems Descriptive of Rural Life and Scenery*. Three more books of poems followed. Some of Clare's best word-pictures of countryside scenes appeared in *The Shepherd's Calendar*, published when he was 34.

For a time, Clare found himself almost famous. Important writers, including SAMUEL TAYLOR COLERIDGE and CHARLES LAMB, became friends. But only his first book sold well, and the small income paid to him by rich poetry lovers left him too poor to keep his wife Martha and seven children in their cottage. Money worries helped to bring on a mental illness.

Clare spent most of his last 26 years in asylums. Even then his confused mind produced striking poems about plants and animals. These verses of John Clare's madness were published long after he died.

Publications

1820 Poems Descriptive of Rural Life and Scenery
1821 The Village Minstrel
1827 The Shepherd's Calendar
1835 The Rural Muse

Published after he died

1949 Poems of John Clare's Madness

CLARK, Mary Higgins

American crime writer

Born Dec. 24, 1929

Mary Higgins Clark is one of America's most popular crime and mystery writers.

Born and educated in New York City, Clark married in 1949 and has had five children. She began her career in advertising, worked for a while as an air hostess, and then worked in radio. During the 1950s she wrote some suspense stories for women's magazines but did not return to this type of fiction until 1975, when her first novel, *Where Are the Children?*, was published.

Although not a traditional mystery story – it is clear from the start who the murderer is – Clark's first novel was an immediate success. The plot was based on the true case of Alice Crimmins, a woman

Publications

1975 Where Are the Children?
1978 A Stranger is Watching

who reported the disappearance of her children to the police and who was later found to have murdered them.

Clark's next novel was on a similar theme, but she went on to write many different kinds of thrillers, including medical stories and romantic mystery tales. She has also written novels set in the glamorous worlds of film, television and fashion.

Clark's books are full of suspense and usually involve frightening things happening to ordinary people in ordinary situations. *Loves Music, Loves to Dance* is about meeting a murderer through a newspaper personal advertisement. She often writes stories about children in danger, as well as stories about women living in isolated places. Her work is to some degree in the tradition of female writers like the BRONTËS and DAPHNE DU MAURIER – full of mystery and romance.

Publications

1980	*The Cradle Will Fall*
1982	*A Cry in the Night*
1989	*While My Pretty One Sleeps*
1989	*The Anastasia Syndrome*
1991	*Loves Music, Loves to Dance*
1994	*Remember Me*
1995	*Let Me Call You Sweetheart*
1996	*Moonlight Becomes You*
1999	*We'll Meet Again*

CLARKE, Arthur C.

English science fiction writer

Born Dec. 16, 1917

Arthur C. Clarke is one of the most popular science fiction writers of the 20th century.

Clarke was born in the seaside town of Minehead, in southwest England. As a young man he became fascinated with the idea of space travel and, at 19, he moved to London to join the British Interplanetary Society. There he wrote technical papers for the society's bulletin.

During World War II, Clarke served in the Royal Air Force and was in charge of the first radar equipment designed to help airplanes land. In 1945, while still in the Air Force, he wrote a magazine article describing how satellites could be launched into fixed positions around the earth and used to form a worldwide communications network. Many scientists thought the idea was absurd, but 20 years later it became a reality. The year after this article appeared Clarke, aged 29, published his first science fiction story, "Rescue Mission."

After he returned to civilian life, Clarke went to university,, graduating in mathematics and physics. He then began writing seriously. His first novel, *Prelude to Space*, was published when he was 34. A series of science fiction books, novels and collections of short stories followed. The main theme of Clarke's work is the idea that humanity is constantly advancing toward a new and better world, and that with science we can conquer anything.

Clarke became world famous with the release of the 1968 film *2001: A Space Odyssey*, which is based on his 1950 short story "The Sentinel."

Publications

1951	*Prelude to Space*
1953	*Childhood's End*
1955	*Earthlight*
1963	*Dolphin Island*
1968	*2001: A Space Odyssey*
1973	*Rendezvous with Rama*
1979	*The Fountains of Paradise*
1990	*The Ghost from The Grand Banks*
1993	*The Hammer of God*
1997	*3001: The Last Odyssey*

CLARK-BEKEDEREMO, John Pepper

Nigerian playwright and poet

Born Apr. 6, 1935

John Pepper Clark-Bekederemo is one of Nigeria's most important literary figures. For decades, he wrote under the name John Pepper Clark, but in the mid-1980s he began to use his full family name, Clark-Bekederemo.

Clark was born in Nigeria in West Africa, which was then a British colony. His father was an African chief, and Clark received a good education. While still a student at the University of Ibadan, he wrote his first book of verse. He also began his first play, *Song of a Goat,* a family tragedy, and founded a poetry magazine. After graduating, Clark worked as a journalist. He studied at Princeton University for one year and then brought out his book *America, Their America*, which harshly criticizes American society.

When Clark returned home, he began a 15-year project to record the legend of Ozidi, an African epic poem that he recalled from his childhood. This project produced his best play, *Ozidi*, which was made into a film in 1975 called *Tides of the Delta*. He also wrote *A Reed in the Tide* – the first poetry book by a single African author to be published internationally.

Much of Clark's work is based on recent Nigerian history. His play *The Raft* is about four men stuck on a raft drifting down a river. It represents the fate of newly independent Nigeria cast adrift in the modern world. *Casualties* is about the human cost of the Biafran War – a civil war in Nigeria in which his friend the poet CHRISTOPHER OKIGBO died.

Publications

1961	*Song of a Goat*
1962	*Poems*
1964	*The Raft*
1964	*America, Their America*
1965	*A Reed in the Tide*
1966	*Ozidi*
1970	*Casualties: Poems 1966–68*
1981	*A Decade of Tongues*
1985	*State of the Union*
1991	*Collected Plays and Poems*

CLAVELL, James

Australian born English-American novelist and screenwriter

Born Oct. 10, 1925
Died Sep. 6, 1994
Age at death 68

James Clavell was an enormously popular Australian-born author of sweeping historical adventure novels.

Clavell was the son of a British Royal Navy captain and was brought up on tales of adventure told by his father and grandfather – also a seaman. As soon as he was able, Clavell joined the British Army and, in 1941, not long before the start of World War II in the Far East, he was stationed in Malaysia.

During fierce jungle fighting with the Japanese, Clavell was wounded and, after hiding out in a local village for several months, was captured and sent to a notorious prisoner-of-war camp near Singapore called Changi. Of the 150,000 men sent to the prison, only 10,000 survived. Clavell later said that his three and a half years there gave him a strength that most other people do not have.

Returning to England after the defeat of the Japanese, Clavell was involved in a motorcycle accident that ended his military career. He soon became fascinated with the world of movies and determined to get involved in the business. He moved to America and sold his first screenplay, a science-fiction story entitled *The Fly*, at the age of 33. Clavell went on to write screenplays for several more successful films, including the classic 1963 war movie, *The Great Escape*.

Clavell's first novel *King Rat*, published when he was 37, is based on his experiences in Changi. He followed it with a series of historical novels about the Far East, the most famous being *Shogun* – the tale of an Elizabethan sailor shipwrecked in Japan.

Publications

1958 The Fly
1962 King Rat
1963 The Great Escape
1966 Tai-Pan
1969 To Sir With Love
1975 Shogun: A Novel of Japan
1981 Noble House
1986 James Clavell's "Whirlwind"
1993 James Clavell's Gai-Jin: A Novel of Japan

CLIFTON, Lucille

American poet and children's writer

Born Jun. 27, 1936

Lucille Clifton grew up loving family stories, and her poems – for both children and adults – are rooted in her ties to family and to the African-American community.

Clifton was born Thelma Lucille Sayles in Depew, New York, and grew up in a loving but poor family. At 17, she went to Howard University in Washington, D.C., on a scholarship but left after two years to attend Fredonia State Teachers' College in New York. There she met her husband, writer Fred Clifton. At age 33, she published her first book, *Good Times*. Its poems use free verse to describe the experience of being black and female. *Good Times* was chosen by the *New York Times* as one of the ten best books of 1969. That year she was also given the Discovery Award for promising poets.

With six children – all under age ten – Clifton was, as she herself says, "too busy to take [getting published] terribly seriously." Yet this is also perhaps why she has been able to write for children as successfully as for adults. She doesn't believe that poetry must be complex or difficult for it to be true.

Her poems convey the importance of self-valuing, of taking responsibility for one's actions, and of having pride in being black. In 1969, she wrote the first of a children's series featuring a character named Everett Anderson, a boy growing up with his mother and exploring what it means to be African American.

Generations is a memoir tracing her family's history, starting with her great-great-grandmother, who was born in Africa in 1822. Clifton has been twice nominated for the Pulitzer Prize.

Publications

1969 Good Times
1970 Some of the Days of Everett Anderson
1970 The Black BCs
1972 Good News About the Earth
1974 An Ordinary Woman
1974 Everett Anderson's Year
1976 Generations
1980 Two-Headed Woman
1993 Book of Light

COCTEAU, Jean

French writer

Born Jul. 5, 1889
Died Oct. 11, 1963
Age at death 74

Jean Cocteau was one of the leading literary figures in France in the early 20th century.

Cocteau was born near Paris into a cultured middle-class family. At age 20, he published his first volume of poetry, *Aladdin's Lamp*. That year he also met Russian ballet-master Sergei Diaghilev, who famously challenged the young Cocteau to write for the ballet.

From then Cocteau embarked on his long career in search of new forms of artistic expression. In his 30s he wrote several important works, including the play *Orpheus* and the novels *Thomas the Impostor* and *The Infernal Machine*, which is based on *Oedipus Rex* by the ancient Greek playwright, SOPHOCLES. His most famous novel, *Children of the Game* (also known as *Les Enfants Terribles*), was published when he was 40. It is a terrifying story of four children who become trapped in their own spooky world. Later, Cocteau turned to filmmaking. In addition to films of some of his earlier work, including *Children of the Game* and *Orpheus*, he created a number of surrealist films, including *Beauty and the Beast*, for which he is well known today.

Cocteau's own life was rich with experience. He served as an ambulance driver at the front in World War I. After the war, he became involved with a young man, also a writer. When his lover died, however, Cocteau became addicted to opium and spent many years in a drug-induced state. He eventually recovered from his addiction, an experience he wrote about in *Opium*. He was also an accomplished artist and illustrated much of his own work.

Publications

1909 Aladdin's Lamp
1923 The Miscreant
1923 Thomas the Impostor
1925 The Angel Heurtebise
1926 Orpheus
1929 Children of the Game
1930 The Human Voice
1930 Opium
1934 The Infernal Machine
1946 The Eagle Has Two Heads

COETZEE, J.M.

South African novelist

Born Feb. 9, 1940

J(ohn) M(axwell) Coetzee is one of South Africa's most important writers. His novels have earned him international fame and won many prizes.

Coetzee was born in Cape Town, South Africa; his mother was a schoolteacher, and his father a lawyer. Although an Afrikaner (descended from 17th-century Dutch settlers), Coetzee writes in English; he grew up speaking English at home and Afrikaans (the Afrikaner language) with other relatives.

Coetzee studied at the University of Cape Town. In the 1960s, he went to Britain, where he worked with computers for IBM. At the age of 25, Coetzee left Britain for the United States, where he studied literature and languages at the University of Texas. At the State

University of New York he taught English and wrote most of *Dusklands,* his first book. He returned to South Africa when he was 32 to teach literature at the University of Cape Town.

South Africa's history and politics have provided the raw material for much of Coetzee's work. He attacks Afrikaner legends that call their conquest of South Africa "God's work." *Dusklands* depicts the brutal activities of early Afrikaner settlers, and *In the Heart of the Country* tells of a white-settler girl's descent into madness. As Coetzee grew up, the power of whites (and in particular Afrikaners) in South Africa increased at the expense of the rights of black people. In *Waiting for the Barbarians* he depicts a brutal state that justifies its actions by holding up the threat of an imagined enemy. Coetzee's view of the end of the racist apartheid system is told in *Age of Iron*, the story of a dying white woman.

Publications

1974	*Dusklands*
1977	*In the Heart of the Country*
1980	*Waiting for the Barbarians*
1983	*Life and Times of Michael K.*
1987	*Foe*
1990	*Age of Iron*
1994	*The Master of St. Petersburg*
1997	*Boyhood: A Memoir*

COFFIN, Robert Peter Tristram

American poet

Born Mar. 18, 1892
Died Jan. 20, 1955
Age at death 62

Robert Peter Tristram Coffin was an American poet who firmly believed that the purpose of poetry was to highlight all that was wonderful in life.

Coffin was born into an old Nantucket whaling family in Brunswick, Maine. He graduated from Bowdoin College at the top of his class, went on to complete a Master's degree at Princeton University, and was a Rhodes Scholar at Oxford University. He described his active service in World War I as his "two years' vacation from civilization." On his return in 1918, he married Ruth Philip, with whom he had four children.

Although he taught for more than a decade at a college in New York, in his 40s, Coffin returned to Maine to teach at Bowdoin College, his former school. He lived in a house close to where he was born and spent time during the summers on his two farms. Late at night he would sit down to write.

Coffin's pastoral poetry was greatly influenced by his boyhood in rural Maine. In fact, he bought his old red-brick schoolhouse in order to preserve it for posterity and to remind him of his youth. His poetry is optimistic, lively and full of the sights and sounds of his Maine farms.

In 1936, Coffin was awarded a Pulitzer Prize for his poetry collection *Strange Holiness*. Three years later in *Collected Poems* he expressed his love of New England using blank verse and ballad forms. Coffin's writing ranged very widely, covering history and literary criticism as well as novels and autobiography.

Publications

1929	*Golden Falco*
1932	*The Yoke of Thunder*
1933	*Ballads of Square-Toed Americans*
1934	*Lost Paradise*
1935	*Strange Holiness*
1936	*John Dawn*
1938	*Maine Ballads*
1948	*Collected Poems*
1950	*Apples by the Ocean*

COHEN, Leonard

Canadian poet and novelist

Born Sep. 21, 1934

Leonard Cohen was the most popular Canadian poet and songwriter of the 1960s and is still popular today.

Born into a Jewish family in Montreal, Canada, Cohen grew up there, later attending McGill University. He abandoned further studies at Columbia University, New York, and returned to Montreal, where he read his poetry in nightclubs and worked in the family clothing business.

When he was just 22, Cohen's career took off with *Let Us Compare Mythologies*, a series of emotional poems comparing Jewish and Christian traditions. This had a great impact on the Canadian public and won Cohen the 1956 McGill Literary award. With his prize money he traveled to England, where he wrote his first novel, *The Favorite Game.*

For the next few years Cohen lived on the Greek island of Hydra, where he wrote a second novel, *Beautiful Losers*, and several more books of poetry, including *Flowers for Hitler*. These works show that Cohen had started to move away from talking of gentleness and romantic love to describing human suffering. Although he had been writing songs for years, it wasn't until the late 1960s that he made a recording, *The Songs of Leonard Cohen.* It was a huge hit with audiences in the Montreal coffee houses where he performed his songs of love and protest, and it also brought him international fame.

Cohen considers himself "a teacher of the heart." Both his early love poetry and his later work, in which he explores human suffering and social issues of the time, are characterized by their energy and sensuality and have a strong spiritual element.

Publications

1956 Let Us Compare Mythologies
1961 The Spice-Box of Earth
1963 The Favorite Game
1964 Flowers for Hitler
1966 Beautiful Losers
1968 Selected Poems 1956–68
1972 The Energy of Slaves
1978 Death of a Lady's Man
1984 Book of Mercy

COLERIDGE, Samuel Taylor

English poet and critic

Born Oct. 21, 1772
Died Jul. 25, 1834
Age at death 61

Samuel Taylor Coleridge was a pioneer of the English Romantic movement in poetry. He is best remembered for his poem "The Rime of the Ancient Mariner."

Coleridge was a clergyman's son, born in the rural southwest of England. At school in London, he made friends with CHARLES LAMB, and at Cambridge University he met the poet ROBERT SOUTHEY, with whom he planned to found an ideal community in Pennsylvania. The plan collapsed but, in 1795, Coleridge married the sister of Southey's fiancée.

In 1797, Coleridge became a close friend of WILLIAM WORDSWORTH. The next year, at age 25, Coleridge with Wordsworth brought out the poetry collection *Lyrical Ballads*. These poems set an exciting new style by using everyday language and fresh ways of looking at nature. Coleridge's main contribution was his most famous poem, "The Rime of the Ancient Mariner." It tells of a sailor who kills an albatross – an enchanted bird – and for that crime against nature endures terrible punishments. This and other famous poems by Coleridge, like "Kubla Khan" and "Christabel," have a strange sense of mystery and wonder. Coleridge said that he heard the words to "Kubla Khan" in a dream.

Coleridge began suffering personal problems. He left his family and became addicted to opium. Despite these difficulties he continued to write and lecture about art. In *Biographia Literaria* he argued that it was the job of the poet to create something new and beautiful out of existing ideas.

Publications

1796 Poems on Various Subjects
1798 Lyrical Ballads (with William Wordsworth)
1802 Dejection: An Ode
1816 "Christabel"
1816 "Kubla Khan"
1817 Biographia Literaria
1825 Aids to Reflection

Published after he died

1895 Anima Poetae

COLETTE

French novelist and short-story writer

Born Jan. 28, 1873
Died Aug. 3, 1954
Age at death 81

Colette was one of the most popular French novelists of the first half of the 20th century. She is remembered in particular for her clear expression of feelings toward animals and flowers, and her insights into human behavior, especially the behavior of women in love.

Born in St.-Sauveur-en-Puisaye, Burgundy, France, Colette was the daughter of a tax collector. She was brought up and educated by her down-to-earth mother "Sido." When she was 20, she married the popular novelist and music critic Henry Gauthier-Villars ("Monsieur Willy"). He took her to Paris and forced her to publish her work under his name. The result was the successful *Claudine* series of four novels about a teenage girl's improper adventures.

Colette left her first husband when she was 31 (she was married three times altogether). She joined the music-hall theater, and started writing her own stories, which often drew heavily on her understanding of animals and on her rural upbringing. The best-known books are the two *Chéri* novels about a tragic love affair, which appeared between 1920 and 1926; *Sido*, based on her mother and published when Colette was 56; and *Gigi*, which was published when she was 72. *Gigi* was made into a film in 1958.

The writing in Colette's novels is often full of life and humor. Two French institutions honored her for her achievements. She was the first woman to be admitted to the important Goncourt Academy, and she became a grand officer of the Legion of Honor in 1953, the year before her death. Her state funeral was attended by thousands of mourners.

Publications

1900–03 Claudine series
1904 Creatures Great and Small
1911 The Vagabond
1920 Chéri
1923 The Ripening
1926 The Last of Chéri
1929 Sido
1933 The Cat
1945 Gigi

COLLINS, Wilkie

English crime writer

Born Jan. 8, 1824
Died Sep. 23, 1889
Age at death 65

Wilkie Collins wrote mystery and crime novels. He helped pioneer the modern detective story.

Born in London, William Wilkie Collins was the son of a landscape painter. He began thinking up stories as a boy while at a private boarding school. Later, he briefly went into business, then became a lawyer at 27. Collins never practiced law, but put his legal knowledge to work in crime writing. His first book, though, was a biography of his father. *Memoirs of the Life of William Collins* appeared when Wilkie Collins was 24. Two years later came his first novel, *Antonina*, a historical romance set in ancient Rome. At 28, he produced *Basil*, his first novel based on crime, mystery and suspense.

In his 30s, Collins was writing stories for CHARLES DICKENS's magazines. Dickens helped Collins bring humor and believable characters into his books. In turn, Collins's clever plots and use of suspense influenced Dickens.

Collins was 36 when his first major novel appeared. *The Woman in White* is a mystery involving two almost identical women. Eight years later came *The Moonstone*, the first English detective novel and one of the best of all time. In it, Sergeant Cluff interviews people at a country house to discover who stole a huge Asian diamond supposed to carry a curse. The story unfolds through the words of its various characters.

The characters in Collins's detective stories each give their own distinctive version of events. The plots are often far-fetched yet ingenious.

Publications

1848	*Memoirs of the Life of William Collins*
1850	*Antonina*
1852	*Basil*
1857	*The Dead Secret*
1860	*The Woman in White*
1862	*No Name*
1866	*Armadale*
1868	*The Moonstone*
1873	*The New Magdalen*

COLLODI, Carlo

Italian children's writer and journalist

Born Nov. 24,1826
Died Oct. 26,1890
Age at death 63

Carlo Collodi was the creator of the character Pinocchio, the lovable wooden boy puppet who came to life.

Collodi's real name was Carlo Lorenzini. He was born in Florence, Italy, and he trained to be a priest. He found politics more interesting, however, and when he was 22, he founded a newspaper of political satire in support of the unification of Italy. He also edited newspapers and wrote comedies using the pen name Collodi, from the name of the town where his mother was born and where he spent time as a boy.

In 1861, when Italy became a united nation, Collodi gave up journalism and turned to translation, producing Italian versions of the tales of the French writer CHARLES PERRAULT. It was Perrault who reintroduced such half-forgotten tales as "Little Red Riding Hood," "Sleeping Beauty," and "Puss in Boots." Collodi also began to write his own children's stories, including a series about a character named Giannettino. When he was 54, he began work on a new set of stories, published in parts in a children's magazine. *History of a Puppet* was an immediate success and was soon reissued as *The Adventures of Pinocchio*. The story is about Pinocchio, a wooden puppet carved by a friendly old man called Geppetto. Pinocchio comes to life, but has to learn how to work hard and be generous. The book became a classic and was soon delighting children all around the world.

Collodi had discovered that children identify with stories that portray children realistically, that embody children's values, and that depict the kind of behavior adults deplore.

Publications

1876	"Giannettino"
1880	*The Adventures of Pinocchio*

CONGREVE, William

English playwright and poet

Born Jan. 24, 1670
Died Jan. 19, 1729
Age at death 58

William Congreve was an English playwright and poet who is remembered most for his comedies, which are among the best Restoration dramas written in the period after 1660.

Born near the city of Leeds, Congreve was educated in Ireland, where his father commanded a garrison of soldiers. At school and college, he was a friend of JONATHAN SWIFT.

In 1691, Congreve moved to London to study law. He had already started writing and soon found that he preferred this to law. *Incognito*, a romantic novel that he had written at age 17, was published in 1692. The following year, he became instantly famous with the success of his first comedy drama, *The Old Bachelor*. JOHN DRYDEN recognized Congreve's talent and encouraged him in his early career.

When he was just 25, Congreve became the joint manager of a new theater. He wrote a new play for the theater every year until 1700, the year he completed *The Way of the World*. Although not a success at the time, it is Congreve's best-known comedy today.

Congreve was one of the leading figures in a style of drama known today as Restoration comedy. This style, which is based on making fun of fashionable people and includes clever, funny and lively speeches, was developed after the monarchy was restored in England in 1660. Theaters that had been closed by the previous religious and Puritan government of the republic were reopened, and there was a new flowering of English drama, particularly comedy.

Publications

1692	*Incognito*
1693	*The Old Bachelor*
1693	*The Double Dealer*
1695	*Love for Love*
1697	*The Mourning Bride*
1700	*The Way of the World*

CONNELLY, Marc

American playwright and novelist

Born Dec. 13, 1890
Died Dec. 21, 1980
Age at death 90

Marc Connelly is most famous as the author of the play *The Green Pastures*, which won a Pulitzer Prize in 1930, and as GEORGE S. KAUFMAN's playwriting partner.

Connelly was born in McKeesport, Pennsylvania. His parents had been traveling actors until a year before his birth, when they had settled down to manage a hotel. Family friends included notable actors of the day, and Connelly grew up with a great admiration for the theater. When he was 12, his father died, and a few years later he had to give up school and find work to help his mother. He held a variety of jobs on newspapers in Pittsburgh, including writing a light-hearted column.

Connelly first worked for the theater in 1914, when he wrote the lyrics for a musical. This was followed, however, by several unsuccessful plays. A turning point came in his 30s when he met Kaufman. Both were journalists at the time. They were among the founders of the *New Yorker* magazine and members, along with DOROTHY PARKER, of the Round Table group of writers, who met at New York's Algonquin Hotel. Together Kaufman and Connelly wrote successful comedies that cleverly made fun of the manners of the upper-middle classes. Of these plays *Dulcy*, the tale of a meddling businessman's wife, and *Merton of the Movies*, a satire about Hollywood, were the most popular.

The two writers parted company in 1924. Six years later, Connelly, aged 40, wrote his masterpiece, *The Green Pastures*. It used fantasy and African-American actors and folklore to retell Bible stories. Nothing that he wrote after this was as popular.

Publications

With George S. Kaufman
1921 Dulcy
1922 To the Ladies!
1922 Merton of the Movies
1923 Helen of Troy, New York

By Connelly alone
1926 The Wisdom Tooth
1930 The Green Pastures
1942 The Flowers of Virtue
1965 A Souvenir from Qam

CONRAD, Joseph

Polish-born British novelist and short-story writer

Born Dec. 3, 1857
Died Aug. 3, 1924
Age at death 66

Joseph Conrad did not learn English until he was 20, yet he became a great English novelist. He was christened Józef Teodor Konrad Nalecz Korzeniowski and was born in what was then part of Russian-occupied Poland. As a boy, he read Polish and French versions of English novels with his father, a poet and translator.

Tales of the sea made the young Conrad restless. At 16, he left Poland to work on French ships. At 20, he began 16 years with the British Merchant Navy, making adventurous voyages and rising from deckhand to command a ship of his own. Meanwhile, he learned English and became a British subject.

When he was 36, Conrad settled down in England and began writing. His life at sea was a great source of stories. Faraway settings for his books include Southeast Asia, the Caribbean, and Africa. At 37, he published his first novel, *Almayer's Folly*. That year he also married; he and his wife had two sons.

Conrad used exotic locations as a backdrop for stories about characters fighting powerful destructive forces or who are torn between the good and evil in themselves. One of Conrad's finest short stories is "Heart of Darkness," based on his experiences in what was then the Belgian Congo (now the Democratic Republic of Congo) in Africa.

Conrad gained the respect of famous writers such as JOHN GALSWORTHY, HENRY JAMES and H.G. WELLS. He did not become successful with a wider audience until his novel *Chance* came out when he was 56. By then, two of his best works – *Lord Jim* and *Nostromo* – had also been published.

Publications

1895 Almayer's Folly
1897 The Nigger of the "Narcissus"
1900 Lord Jim
1902 "Heart of Darkness"
1903 Typhoon
1904 Nostromo
1907 The Secret Agent
1911 Under Western Eyes
1913 Chance

COOKSON, Catherine

English novelist

Born Jun. 20, 1906
Died Jun. 11, 1998
Age at death 91

Catherine Cookson is one of the most popular contemporary women English novelists. She is famous for her family sagas set against the backdrop of England in the 19th century.

Cookson was born in South Shields, an industrial city in the northeast of England. Her mother was poverty-stricken and unmarried – both a great disadvantage in the society of the time. For many years, Cookson believed that she had been abandoned as a baby and that her mother was actually her older sister. She received little formal education and began work as a maid in the houses of the rich and powerful. These early experiences of the great divide between wealthy society and the hard lives of the ordinary working class were later to become the inspiration for her novels.

Cookson moved to the south of England and was married to a school teacher at the age of 34. Encouraged by her husband and with more free time, she began to write about the culture she had known in the northeast. Her first novel *Kate Hannigan*, about a girl not unlike her young self, was published when she was 44.

Soon Cookson's novels began to win a reputation as chronicles of the social history of industrial England. Her 1968 novel *The Round Tower* won an award as the best regional novel of the year. Despite the strong local flavor of her stories, Cookson's work began to win an international readership. Today, her novels are translated into 15 languages and top bestseller lists all over the world.

Publications

1950 Kate Hannigan
1954 Maggie Rowan
1960 Fenwick Houses
1963 The Blind Miller
1968 The Round Tower
1978 Tilly Trotter
1981 Tilly Wed
1982 Tilly Alone
1987 The Harrogate Secret
1996 The Bonny Dawn

COOPER, James Fenimore

American novelist

Born Sep. 15, 1789
Died Sep. 14, 1851
Age at death 61

James Fenimore Cooper, often regarded as America's first major novelist, is important for his sea novels and stories about the American frontier.

Cooper, the son of a wealthy businessman and politician, grew up in Cooperstown, New York, a frontier town his father had founded. He was expelled from Yale University and went to sea before becoming a gentleman farmer.

Cooper began his literary career when his wife challenged him to write a book better than the one Cooper was reading. His first novel, *Precaution*, was a failure. His second book, *The Spy*, an exciting adventure tale about the American Revolution, was so successful that Cooper gave up farming to become a professional writer at age 32.

When he was 34, Cooper published two important books in American literature. *The Pilot* was the first American sea tale. *The Pioneers* was the first of his "Leatherstocking Tales." In this adventure series, Cooper contrasts the lives of frontiersman Natty Bumppo and his Native American friends with those of the pioneer settlers. Bumppo lives free, close to nature, while the settlers bring "civilization" that destroys the wilderness. The other Leatherstocking Tales are *The Last of the Mohicans*, *The Prairie*, *The Pathfinder* and *The Deerslayer*. Cooper's books were the first to give an accurate description of the American wilderness and pioneer life. They helped shape the 19th-century view of the American character and society and sparked interest in America's history.

Publications

1821 The Spy
1823 The Pilot
1823 The Pioneers
1826 The Last of the Mohicans
1827 The Prairie
1828 The Red Rover
1838 Home as Found
1840 The Pathfinder
1841 The Deerslayer
1845 Satanstoe

COOPER, Jilly

English novelist and nonfiction writer

Born Feb. 21, 1937

Jilly Cooper is a highly popular English author who has moved from light-hearted nonfiction works that examine her greatest fascination – the English class system – to popular novels stuffed full of glamour, sex and humor.

Cooper was born in a small town not far from London. Her father was an engineer and ex-military man. She was educated at a public girls' school in the historic city of Salisbury.

After finishing her education, Cooper began a career as a journalist and later worked in advertising and publishing. She began to write her popular nonfiction guides to society in the late 1960s – a period of profound social change in England. Her first book *How to Stay Married* was published when she was 32 and had

Publications

1969 How to Stay Married

herself been married for eight years. She followed up this success with a series of similar titles, such as *How to Survive From Nine to Five*, about the world of office work, and *Women and Super Women*, about the changing role of women and the pressures placed on them. The most famous of Cooper's books from the period was *Class: A View From Middle England*, published when she was 42. Throughout this time Cooper produced weekly columns for popular English newspapers that brought her views about English society to a vast readership.

Cooper began writing romantic novels in the mid-1970s. They became more and more raunchy and outrageously plotted until she produced titles such as *Riders* and *The Man Who Made Husbands Jealous,* which became notorious bestsellers.

Publications

1969 How to Stay Married
1970 How to Survive from Nine to Five
1974 Women and Super Women
1975 Emily
1979 Class: A View From Middle England
1985 Riders
1991 Polo
1993 The Man Who Made Husbands Jealous
1996 Appassionata
1999 Score

CORMIER, Robert

American young-adults' writer

Born Jan. 17, 1925

Robert Cormier is one of America's leading writers of fiction for young adults.

Cormier was born into a large family in Leominster, Massachusetts. His father was a factory worker, and the family had to move to a larger home each time a new child came along. Cormier was a shy child and spent a lot of time reading and writing. One of his teachers secretly sent a story of his to a magazine that published it when Cormier was still in his teens.

For many years, Cormier worked as a reporter, becoming a top editor and columnist at the *Fitchburg Sentinel*. All the time, however, he was writing fiction at night. He published several short stories but did not publish his first novel, *Now and at the Hour* (about a man dying from cancer) until he was 35. Cormier wrote it to help himself cope with his father's death.

The Chocolate War was Cormier's first book for young adults and has become his most famous work. It is the story of a young boy who tries to make a stand for what he believes in but gets caught between a corrupt principal and the evil leader of a school gang. Some loved the direct way Cormier explores issues about good and evil and the abuse of power; others hated the frank language and the fact that the good guy doesn't win.

Cormier insists that he does not write for young adults but for intelligent readers; it just so happens that most of these are teenagers. His thought-provoking novels cover themes not often dealt with in books for young people, such as terrorism and betrayal in *After the First Death,* and government corruption in *I Am the Cheese*.

Publications

1960 Now and at the Hour
1974 The Chocolate War
1977 I Am the Cheese
1979 After the First Death
1980 Eight Plus One
1983 The Bumblebee Flies Anyway
1985 Beyond the Chocolate War
1988 Fade
1992 Tunes for Bears to Dance To
1995 In the Middle of the Night

CORNEILLE, Pierre

French playwright

Born Jun. 6, 1606
Died Oct. 1, 1684
Age at death 78

Pierre Corneille was one of France's greatest playwrights. He has been called the father of French tragedy, although he wrote many different kinds of plays.

Corneille was born in the northern French city of Rouen. He was educated at a Jesuit school in the city where he learned to love ancient Roman literature and to believe in the values of humanism – reason and the nobility of the human spirit. As was the tradition in his family, he studied law and became a judge, a position that had to be bought rather than earned in 17th-century France.

Corneille's first play, *Mélite*, was written when he was in his early 20s. His early plays are romantic comedies in which the heroes prefer to avoid passion and rely on reason. Like many of his plays, *Médée*, his first tragedy, was based on a story from classical literature. Corneille caused a sensation with the first production of *The Cid* when he was 31. Based on the story of the legendary 11th-century Spanish soldier, El Cid, Corneille's version broke the traditional rules of French theater, which demanded that a play should be set in one place and over the course of a single day.

Although *The Cid* was a popular success, Corneille was discouraged by the criticisms of other writers and waited three years before producing his other three great tragic dramas: *Horace*, *Cinna* and *Polyeucte*. Corneille's reputation rests on these four plays. They are remarkable for their heroic central characters who forge their own destinies through strength of character, reason and ambition.

Publications

c. 1629 Mélite
1635 Médée
1637 The Cid
1640 Horace
1641 Cinna
1643 Polyeucte
1644 Rodogune
1651 Nicoméde
1660 Discourses on Tragedy
1674 Suréna

CORNWELL, Patricia

American crime writer

Born Jun. 9, 1956

Patricia Cornwell is one of the most popular crime writers in America today.

Cornwell's father was a solicitor, and the family lived in Miami. However, when she was seven, her parents divorced, and she moved with her mother and brothers to Montreat, North Carolina. There she met the preacher Billy Graham and his wife Ruth, who encouraged her to write.

After graduating from university, Cornwell first became a crime reporter and then worked as a computer analyst at the Virginia Medical Examiner's office. She began to write novels based on her experiences at the morgue, but they were all rejected. One editor suggested she get rid of her male hero and make a minor female character, Kay Scarpetta, the main investigator. Cornwell took her advice, and the resulting novel, *Postmortem,* was published to great acclaim when Cornwell was 34.

All Cornwell's novels draw on her knowledge of forensic medicine: how doctors and scientists study evidence to find the cause of a person's death. In the stories, Dr. Scarpetta, along with her policeman colleague Pete Marino, use their wits and training to solve complicated murders. Dr. Scarpetta is often helped in her investigations by her niece Lucy, a whizzkid on computers. In later books, Lucy grows up and takes on a more important role in the novels.

Not surprisingly, some of the morgue scenes in Cornwell's books are gruesome. However, Cornwell tries to balance the horror by showing her compassion for the victims of crime and their relatives.

Publications

1990 Postmortem
1991 Body of Evidence
1992 All That Remains
1993 Cruel and Unusual
1994 The Body Farm
1995 From Potter's Field
1996 Cause of Death
1997 Hornet's Nest
1997 Unnatural Exposure

CORTÁZAR, Julio

Argentinian novelist and short-story writer

Born Aug. 26, 1914
Died Feb. 12, 1984
Age at death 69

Julio Cortázar's experimental novel *Hopscotch* is considered one of the greatest Latin American novels. It achieved worldwide success and brought wider recognition of Latin American literature.

Cortázar was born in Brussels, Belgium, of Argentinian parents. When he was still a child, the family returned to Argentina, and Cortázar grew up in a suburb of Buenos Aires. At 21, he became a secondary school teacher and worked in several small Argentinian towns. In his 30s, he worked as a translator. He was unhappy with the government in Argentina, however, so he moved to Paris, France, where he remained for the rest of his life.

At age 37, he published his first book of short stories, *Bestiary*. These are fantasy stories in the style of JORGE LUIS BORGES. His first novel, *The Winners* – published when he was 46 – was in the same style. One of his short stories, "The Devil's Drivel," was the basis for the popular 1966 film, *Blow-Up*.

The work generally considered to be Cortázar's masterpiece is *Hopscotch*, published when he was 49. This is an experimental work that can be read in a number of different chapter orders. Cortázar provides "instructions" to the reader explaining the ways the book can be read.

Cortázar was accused of being unconcerned about the political oppression suffered by many Latin Americans. Late in his life, however, he became an activist, and many of his later works – such as *A Manual for Manuel* – address the need for radical political change.

Publications

1951 Bestiary
1959 Secret Weapons
1960 The Winners
1963 Hopscotch
1966 All Fires the Fire
1967 End of the Game
1968 62: A Model Kit
1969 Cronopios and Famas
1973 A Manual for Manuel
1980 We Love Glenda So Much

COWARD, Noël

English playwright

Born Dec. 16, 1899
Died Mar. 26, 1973
Age at death 73

Noël Coward was one of the most famous figures of 20th-century theater. His comedies still define the way many people think of England and the English. They are part of a tradition of witty English comedy that began with WILLIAM CONGREVE and continued with OSCAR WILDE.

Coward was born near London. Encouraged by his mother, he started working in theater very young, acting in his first play at 12 and selling his first comedy, *The Last Trick*, at 19. His first big success came when he was 25 with the production of *The Vortex*. Coward acted in the main role of this serious story about an irresponsible mother and her drug-addicted son.

Throughout the 1920s, '30s, and '40s, Coward wrote a succession of popular and very funny plays. Comedies such as *Hay Fever*, *Private Lives*, and *Blithe Spirit* still amuse and delight audiences today with their absurd, lovable characters, witty dialogue and sophistication. At the time, these plays were thought daring because the main characters had unconventional moral values. Usually in Coward's comedies he includes characters who are shocked at these unconventional attitudes but who are shown to be much less clever and witty than those who shock them.

In 1942, as Britain faced invasion in World War II, Coward wrote *This Happy Breed*, a patriotic story about the fortunes of a working-class family. Later in life, Coward wrote and acted in films and worked on more serious dramas for the theater. He was given the honorary title "Sir" in 1970.

Publications

1918 The Last Trick
1925 The Vortex
1925 Hay Fever
1929 Bitter Sweet
1930 Private Lives
1931 Cavalcade
1936 Tonight at Eight-Thirty
1939 Present Laughter
1941 Blithe Spirit
1943 This Happy Breed

COWPER, William

English poet

Born Nov. 26, 1731
Died Apr. 25, 1800
Age at death 68

William Cowper (pronounced "cooper") wrote verse in a simple, natural style instead of the high-flown manner most poets used in his day. He is best known for *The Task*, a long poem praising the simple joys of the countryside.

Cowper was the son of the parson in a village in Hertfordshire. He went to private schools and, at 22, became a lawyer. But his mother's early death, bullying at his school, an unhappy love affair, and strict religious beliefs unsettled his mind. Unable to hold down a job, he lived on a small private income. At age 33, he moved in with Morley and Mary Unwin, a retired clergyman and his wife. Morley soon died, and William and Mary moved to the village of Olney. There, with the village clergyman, Cowper wrote *Olney Hymns*.

Mary encouraged William's poetry writing to help him recover from bouts of depression. In his 50s, he wrote *Poems* and "The Diverting History of John Gilpin," an amusing ballad about an uncontrolled horseback ride. Then came his long, unrhymed verse masterpiece, *The Task*. Preferring country to town, he wrote 5,000 lines about such everyday rural scenes as the garden, a ploughed field, and the postman arriving.

Mary's death in 1796 deeply depressed Cowper. He showed his despair in his last and most powerful poem, "The Castaway."

Cowper's verses range from funny to deeply religious and include strongly felt attacks against hunting and slavery. His simple language and affection for nature foreshadow the Romantic poetry of WILLIAM WORDSWORTH.

Publications

1779 *Olney Hymns*
1782 *Poems*
1783 "The Diverting History of John Gilpin"
1785 *The Task*
1799 "The Castaway"

COZZENS, James Gould

American novelist

Born Aug. 19, 1903
Died Aug. 9, 1978
Age at death 74

James Gould Cozzens is best known for his Pulitzer Prize-winning novel *Guard of Honor*.

Cozzens was born in Chicago but grew up in Staten Island, New York City. While still in school, he decided to become a writer. His first novel, *Confusion*, was published while he was a 21-year-old student at Harvard. This prompted him to leave university without graduating. He then traveled widely, working as a private tutor to the children of Americans living in Cuba and Europe, while continuing to write and publish novels based on his experiences.

Cozzens returned to America in the late 1920s and began to concentrate on the theme that is at the heart of all his best work: what do ordinary, respectable people do when something happens that makes them question all their beliefs and moral standards? This eventually resulted in his most popular work, *By Love Possessed*, which came out when he was 54. This novel is about a well-respected, small-town lawyer who suddenly finds himself at the center of a dramatic and potentially destructive conflict. The story turns on how far he is prepared to compromise his ideals and beliefs to resolve the situation.

During World War II, Cozzens joined the US Air Force. After the war he drew on his experiences to write *Guard of Honor*. The action of the novel takes place over three days on an air-force base and centers on the inquiry that follows after two planes almost crash on the runway. Cozzens uses this event to explore the conflict between human and military values and loyalties as the men involved are forced to take responsibility for their actions.

Publications

1924 *Confusion*
1925 *Michael Scarlett*
1931 *S.S. San Pedro*
1934 *Castaway*
1936 *Men and Brethren*
1940 *Ask Me Tomorrow*
1942 *The Just and the Unjust*
1948 *Guard of Honor*
1957 *By Love Possessed*
1968 *Morning Noon and Night*

CRANE, Stephen

American novelist, short-story writer and poet

Born Nov. 1, 1871
Died Jun. 5, 1900
Age at death 28

Publications

1893 Maggie: A Girl of the Streets
1895 The Black Riders
1895 The Red Badge of Courage
1896 George's Mother
1898 The Open Boat and Other Tales
1899 War Is Kind
1899 Active Service
1900 Wounds in the Rain

Published after he died

1903 The O'Ruddy (completed by Robert Barr)

Stephen Crane's use of realism in his stories profoundly influenced future American writers.

The 14th child of a New Jersey minister, Crane began writing when he was 8; at 16, he was writing articles for the *New York Tribune*. His literary career did not flourish until he went to Syracuse University, New York, in 1890. While supporting himself as a freelance journalist, he lived among the poor in the Bowery slums to research his first novel, *Maggie: A Girl of the Streets*, completed when he was 22. Crane had to print the book at his own expense as publishers found its realism too "ugly." When he was only 24, he had completed his most important work, *The Red Badge of Courage*, a novel about the horrors of the American Civil War.

The success of this novel, now a classic of American literature, led to assignments as a war correspondent. During the last half of the 1890s, he traveled to Mexico, to Greece to cover the Greco-Turkish War, and also to Cuba to report on the Spanish-American War. In 1896, he was shipwrecked for several days, an experience that inspired his short story "The Open Boat." During these years, Crane refined his use of realism to expose social ills such as poverty and war. In the same year, he completed *George's Mother*, detailing life in the Bowery. A year later, he published *Active Service*, a novel based on the Greco-Turkish War.

After the war in Cuba, Crane settled in England. He contracted tuberculosis and died when he was only 28. His work was neglected for many years after his death until rediscovered by other writers such as AMY LOWELL and WILLA CATHER.

CRICHTON, Michael

American science fiction writer

Born Oct. 23, 1942

Michael Crichton is one of the most popular writers in America today. He is known for his ability to write bestselling novels using his specialist knowledge on a range of subjects.

Born in Chicago, Crichton was a gifted student and graduated at the top of his class from Harvard University. By the age of 23, he was teaching anthropology at Cambridge University. He then returned to the US and trained as a doctor. To help pay for his training, he began to write thrillers under a pen name.

By the time Crichton finished his studies, he had written his first bestseller, *The Andromeda Strain*, a science fiction novel about an American desert community infected by an alien microorganism. The novel sold well and was made into a film.

His science fiction, thrillers and fantasy novels cover a wide range of subjects from economics to genetics. He is a pioneer of a new genre of popular fiction: the "techno-thriller." Eight of his novels have been filmed, including the hugely successful *Jurassic Park* and its sequel, *The Lost World*. In both these stories Crichton uses his scientific knowledge to imagine an experiment in which dinosaurs come to life in the present. Crichton has also directed movies and created the popular television series *ER*.

During the 1980s, Crichton became an expert on computers. He was one of the first popular writers to realize the impact of new information technology. He has also set up his own computer software company and designed a computer game, *Amazon*.

Publications

1969 The Andromeda Strain
1972 The Terminal Man
1975 The Great Train Robbery
1980 Congo
1987 Sphere
1990 Jurassic Park
1992 Rising Sun
1994 Disclosure
1995 The Lost World
1996 Airframe
1999 Timeline

CRISTOFER, Michael

American playwright

Born Jan. 22, 1945

Michael Cristofer is most famous as the author of the play *The Shadow Box*, which won a Pulitzer Prize in 1977. It is the sensitive and humorous story of three dying patients and how they deal with their approaching deaths.

Cristofer was born Michael Procaccino in White Horse, New Jersey. When he was 19, he dropped out of the Catholic University of America, Washington, DC, after three years of studies to begin an acting career. During the 1960s, he lived in a commune in San Francisco before landing his first major acting position at the Arena Stage in Washington, DC, when he was just 23. He changed his name to Michael Cristofer because he felt his own name had prevented him from getting some roles. Over the next decade his acting career progressed. Since 1972, he has worked mostly for the Mark Taper Forum in Los Angeles. In the 1970s, Cristofer also appeared in many televison roles and won several acting awards.

Cristofer has described his acting career as "homework" for his playwriting. When he was just 23, his first play, *The Mandala*, was performed in Philadelphia, but it received little attention. Two more of his plays were staged before the hugely successful *The Shadow Box* appeared on Broadway. A later play, *Black Angel*, tells the story of a German Nazi, Engel, who killed many people during World War II. Engel returns to the scene of his crimes seeking forgiveness. Although Cristofer was criticized for treating Engel with too much understanding, the play was well received.

Publications

1968 The Mandala
1971 Plot Counter Plot
1973 Americomedia
1975 The Shadow Box
1976 Ice
1978 Black Angel
1978 C.C. Pyle and the Bunyon Derby
1980 The Lady and the Clarinet
1989 Love Me or Leave Me

CRONIN, A.J.

Scottish novelist

Born Jul. 19, 1896
Died Jan. 6, 1981
Age at death 84

A.J. Cronin wrote bestselling novels about people with "real-life" problems. Several tales feature knowledge he gained as a doctor.

Archibald Joseph Cronin was born in Cardross in Dumbartonshire, Scotland. He studied medicine at Glasgow University. In World War I, he became a surgeon-lieutenant in the Royal Navy. Later he worked as a doctor in Glasgow, a medical inspector of mines in South Wales, and as a physician in London.

At 34, ill health made him give up medical work, and he began writing. The following year he achieved instant success with his first novel. *Hatter's Castle* tells a Scottish story of doomed love and a poor man's relentless ambition. While still in his 30s, Cronin wrote *The Stars Look Down*, about a politically ambitious miner. At 41, he published his best-known book; *The Citadel* describes a young doctor so busy getting rich that he neglects the people he loves. Cronin's story strongly hinted at the need for a free national health service of the kind later created in Britain. Four years later came *The Keys of the Kingdom*, the tale of a missionary's life. Cronin's other books include his autobiography, *Adventures in Two Worlds*. Published when he was 56, this covers the time the author spent working in medicine.

Cronin wrote his last novels in Switzerland, where he had moved to avoid paying Britain's high taxes. Some critics think his last books are too sentimental, perhaps because he had lost touch with the places and people they were about.

Many of Cronin's novels have been made into movies or adapted for television.

Publications

1931 Hatter's Castle
1935 The Stars Look Down
1937 The Citadel
1941 The Keys of the Kingdom
1945 The Green Years
1950 Shannon's Way
1952 Adventures in Two Worlds
1961 The Judas Tree
1964 A Song of Sixpence
1975 The Minstrel Boy

CULLEN, Countee

American poet and novelist

Born May 30, 1903
Died Jan. 9, 1946
Age at death 42

The poet Countee Cullen was a leading figure in the Harlem Renaissance. Seeking to develop black pride, this 1920s artistic movement produced the first large body of work in the United States written by African Americans. As well as writing books himself, Cullen promoted the work of other black writers.

The details of Cullen's early life are vague, in part kept that way by Cullen himself. He was brought up in New York City by his father's mother. After she died when Cullen was 15, he was looked after by a local reverend and his wife, whom Cullen came to consider as his parents. His real mother did not contact him until he became famous in the 1920s.

Cullen began writing prizewinning poetry while still in secondary school and continued to do so while at New York University. When he was just 22, his first collection, *Color*, was published. Written in a careful, traditional style inspired by poets such as W.B. YEATS, Cullen's verse celebrates black beauty and deplores the effects of racism. *Color* was praised by both black and white critics.

After studying literature at Harvard University, Cullen published two more collections, *The Ballad of the Brown Girl* and *Copper Sun*, on similar themes as *Color*. They were criticized for being less intense than *Color*, but Cullen's response was that he did not want to be forced to write a certain way because of his race. After spending two years in France in his late 20s, he wrote his only novel, *One Way to Heaven*, about life in Harlem. In 1934, he took a job teaching creative writing at an all-black secondary school in New York, where he worked until his early death.

Publications

1925 Color
1927 The Ballad of the Brown Girl
1927 Copper Sun
1929 The Black Christ and Other Poems
1932 One Way to Heaven
1935 The Medea and Some Poems
1940 The Lost Zoo

Published after he died

1947 On These I Stand

CUMMINGS, E.E.

American poet

Born Oct. 14, 1894
Died Sep. 3, 1962
Age at death 67

E.E. Cummings, a 20th-century lyric poet, is best known for his individual and inventive style. One well-known characteristic was his use of only lower-case letters in his poetry, even for his own name. His style reflected his belief in the importance of the individual.

Edward Estlin Cummings was born in Cambridge, Massachusetts. He graduated from Harvard University with a Master's degree when he was 32. During World War I, he joined the volunteer Ambulance Corps and was stationed in France, but he was arrested in 1917 and sent to a prison camp where he was held prisoner for three months. Later, he found out he had been accused of treason, but the charges were never proved. These experiences inspired a prose work, *The Enormous Room*.

Cummings was a gifted artist, painting still-life pictures and landscapes to a professional level. As a poet he used varied styles and forms as well as unusual arrangements and punctuation. His overriding concern was to express individuality. He believed that modern mass society was a threat to the rich and varied experiences of individuals. Nearly all his work – from *Tulips and Chimneys*, his first book of poetry, to *I x I* and the collections *95 Poems* and *73 Poems* – deals with this overall subject.

In 1952, Cummings returned to Harvard, and there he gave the Charles Eliot Norton lecture series, *i: six nonlectures*. In 1957, he won the Bollingen Prize for poetry.

Publications

1922 The Enormous Room
1923 Tulips and Chimneys
1927 him
1933 Eimi
1940 50 Poems
1944 I x I
1953 i: six nonlectures
1954 Poems 1923–54
1958 95 Poems

Published after he died

1963 73 Poems

CYRANO de BERGERAC

French writer

Born Mar. 6, 1619
Died Jul. 28, 1655
Age at death 36

Cyrano de Bergerac was a talented and controversial author in 17th-century France who also achieved fame for his legendary exploits.

Born in Paris, Cyrano spent his early years in an intense study of science and philosophy. In about 1638, he became an officer in a regiment of guards, where he earned a reputation for his bravery and for his big nose. He was twice wounded in a war against the Germans and retired from the army in 1641.

Cyrano was in the habit of telling tall tales. The story spread that he defeated 100 men in a fight, and this and other feats were fictionalized in the French writer Edmond Rostand's play *Cyrano de Bergerac*, published 250 years later in 1897.

Cyrano de Bergerac wrote a number of plays that attacked the religious, educational and political authorities in France. These included the tragic play *The Death of Agrippine*, which was performed when he was 34. The next year, he published the comedy *The Pedant Imitated*, which the famous French playwright MOLIÈRE thought was so brilliant that he stole some of the ideas for one of his own plays.

Cyrano de Bergerac died after being hit on the head by a falling wooden beam. Following his death, a friend published his two great science fiction works, describing imaginary voyages to the Moon and the Sun. It is only in the 20th century, with the republication of his plays, that Cyrano de Bergerac's true originality has come to be widely appreciated.

Publications

1653 The Death of Agrippine
1654 The Pedant Imitated

Published after he died

1657 The Other World, or the States and Empires of the Moon
1662 The States and Empires of the Sun

DAHL, Roald

Welsh children's writer and short-story writer

Born Sep. 13, 1916
Died Nov. 23, 1990
Age at death 74

Roald Dahl was a 20th-century British writer of short stories and children's books. He wrote *Charlie and the Chocolate Factory*, *James and the Giant Peach*, and many other favorite children's stories.

Dahl was born in Wales, although his parents came from Norway. When Dahl was only four years old, his father died, and Dahl was sent away to boarding school. The harsh treatment he received there later inspired him to write stories in which children take revenge on cruel adults in authority.

After leaving school, Dahl gave up an opportunity to go to university and went to work in Africa for an oil company instead. When World War II began in 1939, he joined the Royal Air Force with the same spirit of adventure that had taken him to Africa. Dahl became a fighter pilot but was seriously injured in a plane crash and spent the rest of the war as a spy. While he was recovering from his injuries, he had strange dreams, and it was these that inspired his first short stories.

After the war, Dahl began to publish collections of his short stories for adults. They were extremely popular, and many were later made into screenplays for television. His stories have unexpected endings and strange, menacing atmospheres.

Dahl became a regular writer of books for children when he was married and had children of his own. His first big success was with *James and the Giant Peach*, published when he was 44. Children love his books because they are full of outrageous fun and rudeness to adults. Parents and teachers often disapprove of them for exactly the same reasons.

Publications

1953 Someone Like You
1959 Kiss, Kiss
1961 James and the Giant Peach
1964 Charlie and the Chocolate Factory
1970 Fantastic Mr. Fox
1975 Danny: The Champion of the World
1982 The BFG
1983 The Witches
1988 Matilda

D'ANNUNZIO, Gabriele

Italian poet, playwright and novelist

Born Mar. 12, 1863
Died Mar. 1, 1938
Age at death 74

Gabriele D'Annunzio, the colorful adventurer and political leader in the era of fascism, wrote many controversial works that had a major impact on 20th-century Italian literature.

The son of a noble Italian family, D'Annunzio was born in Pescara in central Italy on the Adriatic coast. His writing career started with poetry, and at the age of 16, he started to publish volumes of verse. He then moved to Rome, where he got a job on the staff of the paper *Tribuna* and wrote short stories in the manner of the popular French writer GUY DE MAUPASSANT.

Inspired by FRIEDRICH NIETZSCHE, he then wrote two novels that made his reputation outside Italy. He became a parliamentary deputy in 1897, had a passionate affair with a celebrated actress, Eleonora Duse, and wrote several plays in which she starred. The love affair also prompted the novel *The Flame of Life*. At age 41, D'Annunzio produced his masterpiece, the drama *The Daughter of Jorio*, which set new standards for contemporary writing in Italian. More fine poetry followed.

During World War I, D'Annunzio served in the Italian Air Force and lost an eye in aerial combat. In 1919, annoyed that Italy had lost the town of Fiume, he led a force to occupy it and declared Fiume annexed to his country. He was forced to surrender the town in 1920, and he retired from politics.

Such was his literary reputation that the Italian government published an official version of his complete works. This eventually ran to 49 volumes.

Publications

1879 Primo vere
1889 The Child of Pleasure
1894 The Triumph of Death
1895 The Virgins of the Rocks
1898 The Flame of Life
1898 The Dead City
1899 La Gioconda
1901 Francesca da Rimini
1904 Alcyone
1904 The Daughter of Jorio

DANTE

Italian poet

Born c. Jun. 1265
Died Sep. 14, 1321
Age at death c. 56

Dante is one of the most important writers in the history of world literature. He is Italy's most celebrated poet, and his masterpiece *The Divine Comedy* is the greatest Italian poem.

Dante Alighieri was born in the Italian city of Florence. At the age of 12, he was promised to his future wife, although he had already fallen in love with another girl whom he called Beatrice. Although they would never be together, Dante's love for Beatrice was to inspire his greatest poetry.

As a young man, Dante fought in the wars that were always going on between rival cities and became involved in the struggle for political power in Florence. Beatrice married another man, and then, when she was just 24, she died. Dante was heartbroken. He withdrew into intense study and began composing poems dedicated to her memory. In 1295, Dante's political enemies won power in Florence, and he had to leave the city forever.

Now a political exile, Dante wandered from city to city. He began to write *The Divine Comedy*, a long story-poem that describes an imaginary journey made by Dante through the three worlds of the afterlife – Hell, Purgatory and Heaven. His guide for most of the journey is the ancient Roman poet, VIRGIL, but in Heaven he is reunited with the long-dead Beatrice.

As well as providing a fascinating insight into the beliefs of people living in medieval Europe, *The Divine Comedy* has inspired generations of writers and other artists with its beautiful language and moving love story.

Publications

1292–94 The New Life
1309–c. 1321 The Divine Comedy

DARÍO, Rubén

Nicaraguan poet, journalist, and short-story writer

Born Jan. 18, 1867
Died Feb. 6, 1916
Age at death 49

Rubén Darío was the pen name used by the Nicaraguan poet Félix Rubén García-Sarmiento. He is known as the founder of Latin-American modernism, a literary movement characterized by simple but strong imagery and language.

Darío was born in San Pedro de Metapa in Nicaragua. He came from humble origins in what could be called "small-town" Nicaragua. At 19, however, he moved to Chile and so began what would become a lifetime of travel.

On moving to Buenos Aires, Argentina, Darío established a literary society that became the origin of the Latin American modernist movement. He had been writing poetry since childhood, and his reputation spread throughout the world when, at age 21, he published his first collection of poems, *Blue*. This book marked a turning point in Latin-American literature, moving away from Romanticism, and was praised for its experimental use of language and blending of European and Latin American influences. His next collection, *Profane Hymns and Other Poems*, came out eight years later. These works use simple and direct language and inventive verse structures typical of Latin American modernism.

Darío moved to Europe and worked as a journalist, while writing poetry on Spanish culture, most notably in *Songs of Life and Hope*. This dual interest in Latin America and Spain is represented in much of his writings. Darío was also a diplomat and was Colombian consul in Buenos Aires and Nicaraguan consul in Paris, France.

Publications

1888 Blue
1893 The Rare Ones
1896 Profane Hymns and Other Poems
1905 Songs of Life and Hope
1907 The Wandering Song
1910 Poem of Autumn
1914 Song to Argentina

Published after he died

1917 The World of Dreams
1965 Selected Poems

DAVIS, H.L.

American novelist and poet

Born Oct. 18, 1896
Died Oct. 31, 1960
Age at death 64

H.L. Davis is best known for his novels set in the American West. His first, *Honey in the Horn*, won a Pulitzer Prize in 1936.

Born in Rone's Mill, Oregon, Harold Lenoir Davis's father was a schoolteacher whose job moved the family around a lot, giving young Davis many different views of rural life in Oregon. Davis later used this experience in his writing.

After graduating from secondary school in 1912, Davis tried to earn enough money to attend Stanford University, but before he could afford it, he was drafted into the army, aged 22. During this time Davis sent poems to *Poetry* magazine that were published when he was 23. He worked at various jobs for some years, then turned to writing fiction.

In 1932, Davis went to Mexico on a Guggenheim fellowship intending to write an epic poem. Instead, he wrote his first novel, *Honey in the Horn*, which was published when he was 39. It is the story of an orphaned teenager, Clay Calvert, who goes on a journey through rural Oregon. Working at various jobs, Calvert learns about good and evil, love and hate, and starts to feel less out of place in society.

Davis liked to use a journey as a symbol of a person's search for their own place in society. He used it in *Beulah Land*, the story of a half-Cherokee, half-white girl who leaves her Cherokee home and ends up in Oregon, where she discovers love and its cost.

Davis's poetry and novels are primarily set in Oregon and are full of frontier humor and folklore. They often deal with people trying to understand themselves or helping others to do so.

Publications

1935 Honey in the Horn
1942 Proud Riders and Other Poems
1947 Harp of a Thousand Strings
1949 Beulah Land
1952 Winds of Morning
1953 Team Bells Woke Me and Other Stories
1957 The Distant Music
1959 Kettle of Fire

DAY-LEWIS, Cecil

British poet, crime writer and translator

Born Apr. 27, 1904
Died May 22, 1972
Age at death 68

Cecil Day-Lewis was a leading poet from the 1930s through to the '60s. He also wrote detective novels.

Born in southern Ireland, then part of the United Kingdom, Day-Lewis was the son of a minister of the Church of Ireland. A year after he was born, the family moved to England. At Oxford University, he met the poet W.H. AUDEN and adopted left-wing political views; these views are the subject of his early poems.

After college Day-Lewis became a schoolteacher but abandoned that career when he was 31. He then joined the Communist Party, but soon became disappointed with it and left three years later in 1939. His years of involvement with communism are described in his autobiography, *The Buried Day*. His revolutionary interests are also the focus of his early verse, especially the collections *From Feathers to Iron* and *The Magnetic Mountain.* After his rejection of communism he gave up writing political poems, and his verse became more lyrical and traditional.

During World War II, he worked for the Ministry of Information. By the time the war ended, his views had become far from left wing, and he was regarded as his country's leading poet. He became Professor of Poetry at Oxford University and later taught at Harvard University. He was Britain's Poet Laureate from 1968 to 1972.

In 1935, using the pen name Nicholas Blake, he wrote *A Question of Proof*, the first of about 20 detective novels. These ranged from straightforward murder puzzles to the partly autobiographical *The Private Wound*.

Publications

1932	*From Feathers to Iron*
1933	*The Magnetic Mountain*
1935	*A Question of Proof*
1936	*The Friendly Tree*
1940	*Poems in Wartime*
1947	*The Poetic Image*
1954	*The Whisper in the Gloom*
1960	*The Buried Day*
1965	*The Room and Other Poems*
1968	*The Private Wound*

DEFOE, Daniel

English novelist, journalist and satirist

Born 1660
Died Apr. 24, 1731
Age at death c. 71

Daniel Defoe is known as the father of the English novel. He wrote one of the best-known books in English literature – *Robinson Crusoe*, an early example of a novel. Before Defoe's time stories were usually written as long poems or dramas. Defoe was one of the first to write stories about believable characters in realistic situations using simple prose.

Defoe was born in London, the son of a butcher. After completing his education, he traveled in Europe and then settled into a life as a businessman and trader. As a young man he was involved in many different business ventures, all of which failed, leaving him with large debts. He turned to writing as a way of earning money and to criticize things that he felt were unfair or unjust in society.

During his life, Defoe wrote hundreds of pamphlets on a huge range of subjects from politics and religion to geography, travel and the supernatural. His political writing, often in the form of satires, was popular with the public but made him powerful enemies. More than once his attacking style got him into trouble, including a term in jail.

It wasn't until Defoe was in his 40s that he gave up politics and began writing the books for which he is remembered today. *Robinson Crusoe*, the story of a man shipwrecked alone on an island, was published when Defoe was 59. It was based on the real-life adventures of a man called Alexander Selkirk and was an immediate and huge success. Defoe's second great novel, *Moll Flanders*, was also much loved. Both have become classics of English literature.

Publications

1719 Robinson Crusoe
1719 Farther Adventures of Robinson Crusoe
1720 Memoirs of a Cavalier
1720 Captain Singleton
1722 Moll Flanders
1722 A Journal of the Plague Year
1722 Colonel Jack
1724 Roxana

DEIGHTON, Len

English thriller writer

Born Feb. 18, 1929

Len Deighton is one of the most popular writers of modern spy fiction.

Born to Anglo-Irish parents and educated in London, Deighton went to art school and then did his military service in the Royal Air Force. A variety of jobs followed: as a pastry cook, as a waiter, as a teacher, as a photographer, in advertising agencies, and as an air steward. He published his first book, *The Ipcress File*, when he was 33.

Like JOHN LE CARRÉ, Deighton wrote realistic stories about the world of espionage and explored the moral issues of the Cold War: was it right for British spies to lie, cheat and even kill in order to gain important information that might help protect their country from communist aggression?

Deighton also introduced a new element into the spy novel. The main character of his first four novels is a sharp-witted young man who comes from a working-class background. Previously, spies in fiction had always been from rich backgrounds. One such character, Harry Palmer, was later played on film by Michael Caine. Caine also starred in the film versions of Deighton's bestselling books *Funeral in Berlin* and *Billion-Dollar Brain*.

Deighton was part of the "swinging sixties" in London – that period of the 1960s when young people were creating a new fashion and music scene. With his cockney accent, Deighton helped sweep away the idea that only the upper classes in Britain had a culture. As well as his novels, he has written cookery books, historical novels, and nonfiction books, mostly about World War II.

Publications

1962 The Ipcress File
1964 Funeral in Berlin
1966 Billion-Dollar Brain
1974 Spy Story
1983 Berlin Game
1984 Mexico Set
1985 London Match
1988 Spy Hook
1992 City of Gold
1995 Hope

De la MARE, Walter

English poet, novelist and short-story writer

Born Apr. 25, 1873
Died Jun. 22, 1956
Age at death 83

The English writer Walter de la Mare is remembered for poetry and stories that have an element of mystery and magic about them. He wrote for both children and adults.

De la Mare was born in the south of England. He studied at St. Paul's Cathedral Choir School in London, which he left at age 16 to work in the London office of an oil company. There he stayed for 18 years until he was given a government pension and could concentrate on writing full time. He published his first book of poems, *Songs of Childhood*, when he was 29, using the pen name Walter Ramal. His first adult novel, *Henry Brocken*, was published when he was 31. It is a fantastic story in which the hero meets a series of long-dead writers. *Memoirs of a Midget*, perhaps his best-known novel, is also a strange and fantastic tale.

One of de la Mare's most successful books for children is *The Three Mulla Mulgars*, which tells of the adventures of three royal monkeys on a long journey. The book, published when he was 37, was later retitled *The Three Royal Monkeys*.

De la Mare had written most of his poetry by age 54, and he wrote most of his stories and novels in the 20 years after that. His reputation as a leading poet of the time was firmly established with *The Listeners*. The title poem of this collection is often considered one of his best. In 1923, he produced a collection of other people's poetry, *Come Hither*. In it, he writes highly entertaining notes of explanation about each poem and often includes another verse that is related to it in some way.

Publications

1902 Songs of Childhood
1904 Henry Brocken
1910 The Three Royal Monkeys
1912 The Listeners
1913 Peacock Pie
1921 Memoirs of a Midget
1921 The Veil
1930 On the Edge
1941 Bells and Grass
1953 O Lovely England

DELANY, Martin Robinson

American writer

Born May 6, 1812
Died Jan. 24, 1885
Age at death 72

Martin Robinson Delany has been described as the founder of black nationalism – a political movement that aimed to establish an independent country for African Americans.

Delany was born in Charles Town, West Virginia. He and and his parents were free, but most African Americans at the time were slaves. His mother was the daughter of a West African prince, and Delany grew up proud of his heritage. Later, the family moved to Pittsburgh, Pennsylvania, to escape constant racial harassment.

Delany became involved in politics. He joined secret societies that helped slaves escape to the North and made a tour of southern plantations, where he witnessed the full horrors of slavery. He also edited one of the earliest black newspapers, *Mystery*, and made speeches demanding the end of slavery and full civil rights for African Americans. During the American Civil War, Delany became the first African-American major in the US Army.

At age 40, Delany published *The Condition, Elevation, Emigration, and Destiny of the Colored People of the United States*, in which he argued for the setting up of an independent black state. Seven years later, Delany's novel *Blake; or the Huts of America* appeared as a serial in a magazine. It is an angry tale of rebellion and revenge featuring Blake, an escaped slave who has been described as the first fully-developed African-American character in American literature.

Publications

1852	*The Condition, Elevation, Emigration, and Destiny of the Colored People of the United States*
1854	*Political Destiny of the Colored Race on the American Continent*
1859	*Blake; or the Huts of America*
1879	*Principia of Ethnology*

DELANY, Samuel R.

American science fiction writer

Born Apr. 1, 1942

Samuel R(ay) Delany is one of the most original voices in science fiction today. With J.G. BALLARD, he was among the group of "New Wave" writers who, beginning in the 1960s, worked toward making science fiction accepted as literature.

Delany was born in Harlem, New York City, to an African-American family. His father was the wealthy owner of a funeral business and made sure that his son had a first-rate education. Delany was a bright student, and by age 20 had published his first novel, *The Jewels of Aptor*. He went on to publish several more novels that were full of ideas about communication and language. *Babel-17*, for example, is the story of a future world in which a poet heroine tries to understand the language of aliens who broadcast on radio. In real life, Delany was married to poet Marilyn Hacker.

One of Delany's most important early works is *The Einstein Intersection*. The novel describes a future in which aliens have taken over the Earth and are trying to make sense of human culture. After two more novels and a gap of several years, Delany published his controversial novel *Dhalgren*. Although it is a long, difficult book, it sold well. The story, set in the present, concerns a young man's adventures in a violent city. Since its publication Delany's opinion has been sought on issues of race, gender and sexuality in modern society.

Delany's later works have become more complex and difficult to read, with the exception of his Nevèrÿon series of short stories set in the distant past.

Publications

1962	*The Jewels of Aptor*
1966	*Babel-17*
1967	*The Einstein Intersection*
1968	*Nova*
1975	*Dhalgren*
1979	*The Tales of Nevèrÿon*
1985	*Flight from Nevèrÿon*
1992	*They Fly at Ciron*
1994	*Atlantis: Three Tales*
1995	*The Mad Man*

De la ROCHE, Mazo

Canadian novelist and children's writer

Born Jan. 15, 1879
Died Jul. 12, 1961
Age at death 82

Mazo de la Roche is best known for her award-winning novel *Jalna* and its sequels, which together comprise a romantic saga describing several generations of a wealthy Canadian family.

Mazo Roche (she later added the 'de la' to her name) was born and raised in rural Ontario, the setting for most of her fiction. Although her family wasn't rich, she spent some years as a child living on a "gentleman's farm" – one owned by a wealthy man who farmed as a hobby. While there she began to develop her fantasy world of rural aristocracy.

De la Roche spent most of her life with her cousin, Carolyn Clement, and together they adopted two children. They lived in England for ten years, but returned to Canada before the start of World War II.

De la Roche published her first story when she was 23, but her career took off with *Jalna*, published when she was 48. Set in Clarkson, Ontario, the novel describes the Whiteoak family and their grand estate. It was highly popular and also well received by the critics. It earned de la Roche an important $10,000 literary prize.

De la Roche hadn't foreseen the success of *Jalna*. Readers demanded more of the Whiteoak family, and de la Roche found herself producing one after another in the series, creating a long-running story eventually stretching to 16 volumes. Today her work is admired for its strong characters and sense of place, but it has been criticized for not addressing social issues. With *Jalna* and its sequels de la Roche created a rich fantasy world that fed readers' longing for a romantic past.

Publications

1922 Explorers of the Dawn
1923 Possession
1925 Low Life and Other Plays
1926 Delight
1927 Jalna
1938 Growth of a Man
1951 Renny's Daughter
1957 Ringing the Changes: An Autobiography
1960 Morning at Jalna

DELEDDA, Grazia

Italian novelist and short-story writer

Born Sep. 27, 1871
Died Aug. 16, 1936
Age at death 64

Grazia Deledda wrote nearly 50 novels, many of them concerned with the hard lives of the peasants in her native island of Sardinia to the west of Italy. She was a member of the "verismo," or realist, school of literature. In 1926, she became the first Italian woman to be awarded the Nobel Prize for Literature.

Deledda, who had hardly any real schooling, wasted no time in getting down to a career as a writer and produced her first stories at the age of 17. These are gentle, emotional versions of folklore. She also married when very young and moved to Rome but made frequent visits to her place of birth to get inspiration for her books.

When she was 29, Deledda published a novel, *The Old Man of the Mountain*, which was the first of many books dealing with simple characters and illustrating the destructive and tragic effects of sexual temptation and other "sinful" conduct. Her novels are often bleak and painful but lyrical, romantic and intense. The early novel *Elias Portolu*, for instance, is about a released convict's love for his brother's wife; *The Mother* is a tragic tale of a woman whose dream of seeing her son become a priest is shattered when he gives in to sexual desire. The later novels have a wider setting than Sardinia but continue to deal with the same moral and ethical themes.

Deledda also wrote an autobiographical novel, *Cosima*, which discusses the subject of breast cancer. The book was published the year after she died.

Publications

1900 The Old Man of the Mountain
1902 After the Divorce
1903 Elias Portolu
1904 Ashes
1905 Nostalgia
1913 Reeds in the Wind
1920 The Mother
1928 Annalena Bilsini

Published after she died

1937 Cosima

DeLILLO, Don

American novelist, short-story writer and playwright

Born Nov. 20, 1936

Don DeLillo is best known for writing novels that expose the concerns and manias of modern Americans. His fantastic imagination and ear for sharp and witty dialogue make his one of the most bitingly funny voices to comment on present-day life in America.

DeLillo was born in New York City; he spent most of his childhood in Pennsylvania and in the South Bronx and graduated from Fordham University. His first novel, *Americana*, was published when he was 35. It describes a TV executive's spiritual search in America's heartland and involves some very memorable characters.

DeLillo uses his fiction to explore the inner workings of the many underground cultures that exist in American life. Using bright, funny language, he creates stories about the myth-making process that surrounds American obsessions such as football, rock music, terrorism and technology. Once his characters – often ordinary people – become involved in these underground cultures, they begin to shed their old values and behave in new and sometimes dangerous ways.

One of DeLillo's most widely praised novels, *Libra*, is about the many theories that still surround the assassination of President John F. Kennedy. The highly praised *White Noise* explores the fear of death in American suburbia. Another important theme in DeLillo's novels is the power of the electronic media, such as television and radio, to manipulate public opinion.

Publications

1971 Americana
1972 End Zone
1976 Ratner's Star
1977 Players
1978 Running Dog
1982 The Names
1985 White Noise
1988 Libra
1991 Mao II
1997 Underworld

De QUINCEY, Thomas

English writer

Born Aug. 15, 1785
Died Dec. 8, 1859
Age at death 74

Thomas De Quincey was part of the 19th-century English Romantic movement. He wrote about drug addiction, nightmares and other dark subjects.

De Quincey was born in Manchester. He was the son of a wealthy tradesman and was well educated at private schools. At age 17, he ran away from school and spent months wandering homeless in the countryside and in the slum districts of London. He later wrote about this experience in his famous autobiographical book *Confessions of an English Opium Eater*.

While studying at Oxford University, De Quincey became addicted to the drug opium, which he started taking to relieve the pain caused by a nerve disease. He became a friend of the poet SAMUEL TAYLOR COLERIDGE. Through Coleridge, De Quincey met his hero, the poet WILLIAM WORDSWORTH, who was the leading figure of the English Romantic movement. De Quincey became very close to Wordsworth's family and eventually moved into their old home in the remote Lake District in northern England.

De Quincey married and settled down to support his family by writing articles for magazines. His most famous book, *Confessions of an English Opium Eater*, first appeared as a magazine serial when he was 36. The book is a strange mix of stories about his life and descriptions of his experiences with opium. It was very successful and became an important inspiration for other writers, including CHARLES BAUDELAIRE and EDGAR ALLAN POE. De Quincey also wrote fiction and was a noted essayist.

Publications

1821	*Confessions of an English Opium Eater*
1825	*Walladmor*
1827	*Murder Considered as One of the Fine Arts*
1832	*Klosterheim*
1845	*Suspiria de Profundis*
1847	*Joan of Arc*
1849	*The English Mail Coach*
1853	*Autobiographic Sketches*

DESAI, Anita

Indian novelist and short-story writer

Born Jun. 24, 1937

Anita Desai is best known for her detailed portrayals of life in modern India.

Desai was born in Mussoorie, Uttar Pradesh, India, which was then a British colony. Her father was Bengali and her mother German. She started writing early. "I have been writing," she has said, "since the age of seven, as instinctively as I breathe." She graduated from Delhi University at age 20 with a degree in English.

Desai's first novel, *Cry, the Peacock*, was published when she was 26. It describes a woman who finds it difficult to be independent because of the constraints of Indian society. This is a theme Desai returns to in later works.

Desai says that writing is essential for her; it enables her to think and feel and discover truth. She does not attempt simply to portray Indian society or politics – her novels are part of a private effort to impose some kind of order on what she calls "the shapeless, meaninglessness, and lack of design of the raw material of life." Much of Desai's writing explores the changes that have occurred since India became independent from Britain in 1947. Her earlier novels deal with the undermining of traditional religious values in upper-class Indians by modern attitudes and concepts, and the resulting spiritual collapse. In later novels, such as *Journey to Ithaca*, she describes the confusion of outsiders – Westerners – when faced with the complexities of Indian culture. She has been particularly praised for her use of imagery and her ability to convey the richness of Indian life.

Publications

1963 Cry, the Peacock
1965 Voices in the City
1975 Where Shall We Go This Summer?
1977 Fire on the Mountain
1978 Games at Twilight
1980 Clear Light of Day
1982 The Village by the Sea
1984 In Custody
1989 Baumgartner's Bombay
1995 Journey to Ithaca
1999 Fasting, Feasting

DHLOMO, Herbert

South African poet and playwright

Born c. 1905
Died Oct. 23, 1956
Age at death c. 51

Herbert Dhlomo, sometimes called the father of black drama, was the first black South African to publish a play, *The Girl Who Killed to Save*, in English.

Dhlomo was born in what was then the British-ruled colony of Natal and is now the South African province of KwaZulu/Natal. Dhlomo's father was a Christian preacher, and his brother was the famous writer R.R.R. DHLOMO. The Dhlomos were Zulus, members of one of the largest ethnic groups in South Africa.

Dhlomo studied at local schools before completing a teacher-training course in 1924. He then taught for several years at schools in Natal. In the 1930s, ill health forced him to take a job as a librarian in the "non-European" section of a library near Johannesburg. Not long after this he became assistant editor of the Zulu newspaper *Natal Sun*, where he worked until his death.

Dhlomo's many plays, written in Zulu and in English, celebrated black African history at a time when few whites realized Africa had a past. Dhlomo's poetry mourns the descent of black South Africans from independence to white rule. His plays *Shaka* and *Cetshwayo* relate the adventures of these two famous Zulu kings; *Moshoeshoe* tells the story of the founder of the Kingdom of Lesotho. Dhlomo's first successful play, *The Girl Who Killed to Save*, was published when he was in his early 30s. It is based on a tragedy in South African history. A young girl promised her people – the Xhosa – that if they killed all their cattle, the white invaders would be swept into the sea. Two hundred thousand cattle were killed, poverty and starvation followed, and the whites seized the Xhosa's land.

Publications

1935 The Girl Who Killed to Save
1936 Cetshwayo
1937 Dingane
1937 Moshoeshoe
1940 The Workers
1941 The Valley of a Thousand Hills
1942 Shaka

DHLOMO, R.R.R.

South African novelist and journalist

Born 1901
Died 1971
Age at death c. 70

R.R.R. Dhlomo published the first English novel by a black African – *An African Tragedy*.

Rolfus Reginald Raymond Dhlomo was born in what was then the British-ruled colony of Natal and is now the South African province of KwaZulu/Natal. Dhlomo's father was a Christian preacher, and his brother was the famous playwright and poet HERBERT DHLOMO. The Dhlomos were Zulus, members of one of the largest ethnic groups in South Africa.

Dhlomo studied at local schools before completing a teacher-training course in his 20s. He spent a short time working as a clerk for a mining company near Johannesburg before taking up a career as a journalist. The first job in his new career was on the journal *The Sjambok*. Working as an assistant to the editor, he contributed stories and sketches. He then worked on the Zulu newspaper *Natal Sun*. For ten years, he worked at *The Bantu World* newspaper before returning to *Natal Sun*, where he stayed until his retirement. Many of his novels first appeared as serials – published in parts – in this newspaper.

Dhlomo's first novel, *An African Tragedy*, was published when he was 27. It describes the move of a young rural couple to a big city and the impact it has on their morals. It is set in Dhlomo's lifetime – a period of great upheaval in South Africa. At that time, although most of the population was black, the white South Africans controlled the government and all the major industries. The lives of black people were severely restricted by laws. His later works, most written in Zulu, tell the story of historic Zulu kings such as Shaka and Cetshwayo.

Publications

1928 An African Tragedy
1934 Nomalanga
1935 Dingane
1936 Mpande
1936 Knowledge Improves One
1936 Shaka
1952 Cetshwayo
1962 The Path of the Wicked
1968 Dinuzulo

DICK, Philip K.

American science fiction writer

Born Dec. 16, 1928
Died Mar. 2, 1982
Age at death 53

Philip K(indred) Dick is one of the most influential science fiction writers of the 20th century.

Dick was born in Chicago, one of twins. His twin sister, Jane, died just a few weeks after the birth, and his parents divorced when he was four. As a teenager, he lived in Berkeley, California, and began to write science fiction stories for the local paper. He started working in a record store when he was 18, and he wrote stories for science fiction magazines in his spare time. Encouraged by his success as a short-story writer, he produced several novels but failed to find a publisher until he was 27, when *Solar Lottery* was published.

Dick went on to write nearly 50 more novels, including his early masterpiece, *The Man in the High Castle*, which is about an alternative world where the Nazi leader of Germany, Adolf Hitler, has won World War II. In another bleak novel, *Do Androids Dream of Electric Sheep?*, he describes a future Los Angeles of decaying slums and street violence. The 1982 movie *Blade Runner* was based on this novel.

Dick's personal life was a turbulent one. He married five times, suffered bouts of mental illness, and became addicted to drugs. Before his death he believed he was receiving messages from higher beings. However, in his novels his pessimistic view of the human condition remained intelligent and persuasive. He has been a profound influence on a new generation of science fiction writers, such as William Gibson, who comment on the dehumanizing aspects of modern urban life.

Publications

1955 Solar Lottery
1962 The Man in the High Castle
1965 The Three Stigmata of Palmer Eldritch
1967 Counter-Clock World
1968 Do Androids Dream of Electric Sheep?
1970 A Maze of Death
1977 A Scanner Darkly
1981 VALIS

DICKENS, Charles

English novelist

Born Feb. 7, 1812
Died Jun. 9, 1870
Age at death 58

Charles Dickens is the most famous of all British novelists. People remember him for his lively inventions of good, bad and comic characters in tales set in 19th-century London.

Dickens was born in Portsmouth during the new industrial age that made businessmen rich but brought great hardships to millions of low-paid workers. His own father was a badly paid clerk sent to a debtors' prison of the kind Dickens later described in *Little Dorrit*. Dickens left school at 14, and he soon became a newspaper reporter in London. A sharp ear for conversation helped him reveal characters through their own words. At only 24, he became famous for *The Pickwick Papers*. These stories about a group of rather odd individuals and their amusing adventures came out in monthly parts, as did most of his later novels.

In 1836, he married Catherine Hogarth, though some people think he was more fond of her sister, who died in 1837. Catherine and Charles Dickens had ten children, but parted in 1858. Besides writing novels, from 1850, Dickens edited weekly magazines and traveled in Britain and America, giving public readings of his works.

Among the best known of Dickens's books is *A Christmas Carol*, about a cruel miser who becomes kind and generous. His finest novel is arguably *Bleak House*, which attacks long, dragged-out lawsuits, ill-treatment of the poor, and other injustices. The books reveal great humor and warmth, and by pointing out social evils they helped bring about laws that improved poor people's working and living conditions.

Publications

1836–37 The Pickwick Papers
1837–39 Oliver Twist
1838–39 Nicholas Nickleby
1843 A Christmas Carol
1849–50 David Copperfield
1852–53 Bleak House
1854 Hard Times
1855–57 Little Dorrit
1859 A Tale of Two Cities
1860–61 Great Expectations

DICKINSON, Emily

American poet

Born Dec. 10, 1830
Died May. 15, 1886
Age at death 55

Although she died more than 100 years ago, people are still fascinated by the mysterious life of Emily Dickinson, now considered to be one of the finest poets in the English language.

Dickinson was born in the Massachusetts village of Amherst, where her father was a successful lawyer. She went to school locally and then spent a year away from home at a ladies' college. On her return, she and her younger sister took over the running of the house because her mother was often sick. During the day, she baked bread, sewed, worked in the garden and walked her dog. But at night, when the rest of the family had gone to bed, Dickinson read, thought and wrote deeply emotional poems about love, life, death, nature and pain.

The more important her poetry became to her, the less she wanted to mix with people. By the time she was 40, Dickinson had become a recluse, never venturing beyond her garden gate and refusing to meet strangers. Only seven of her poems appeared in print during her life, and they were so unusual for their time, few people understood them. Spare in words but rich in meaning and unusual ideas and images, Dickinson's poems lack the flowery phrases and sentimentality popular at that time.

After Dickinson died, her sister was astounded to discover a box containing almost 2,000 poems. They were not published in full until 1955. Since then Dickinson's life and work have been the subjects of many plays, books, and TV and radio programs. In 1964, her home in Amherst was named a National Historic Landmark.

Published after she died

1890 Poems by Emily Dickinson
1891 Poems: Second Series
1896 Poems: Third Series
1914 The Single Hound
1955 The Complete Poems of Emily Dickinson (3 vols.)
1958 The Letters of Emily Dickinson (3 vols.)
1961 Final Harvest

DIDION, Joan

American novelist, journalist and screenwriter

Born Dec. 5, 1934

Joan Didion's novels describe her vision of a modern America in which culture and morality are disappearing.

Didion was born in Sacramento, California, and has lived in California all her life. After graduating from the University of California in Berkeley, she worked for several years for *Vogue* magazine, becoming a features editor. She married fellow writer John Gregory Dunne when she was 30; they have an adopted daughter.

Run River, Didion's first novel, was published when she was 29. It describes the falling-apart of a couple's orderly life and, like many of her books, involves characters who find themselves in chaotic situations beyond their control. A sharply critical observer of modern American life and American politics, Didion has written some clearly political stories, for example, *Salvador*, a personal account of the civil war in that country. Most of her novels are set in California, but *A Book of Common Prayer*, one of her best-known works, is centered on a fictional Central American republic run by a dictator and on the verge of a civil war.

Didion has written for the *Saturday Evening Post* and *Esquire*, among other magazines, and her columns are collected in *Slouching Toward Bethlehem* and *The White Album*. She has also written Hollywood screenplays in collaboration with her husband, including *Panic in Needle Park*, based on her novel *Play It As It Lays*, and the 1970s version of *A Star Is Born*, starring Barbra Streisand. More recently they worked on the film *Up Close and Personal*, starring Robert Redford and Michelle Pfeiffer.

Publications

1963 Run River
1968 Slouching Toward Bethlehem
1970 Play It As It Lays
1977 A Book of Common Prayer
1979 The White Album
1983 Salvador
1984 Democracy
1987 Miami
1992 After Henry
1996 The Last Thing He Wanted

DINESEN, Isak

Danish writer

Born Apr. 17, 1885
Died Sep. 7, 1962
Age at death 77

Isak Dinesen, who was born Karen Dinesen, is famous for her short stories and accounts of her experiences in Kenya, East Africa.

Born in Rungsted, Denmark, she was the daughter of the writer William Dinesen and was educated at home, in Switzerland, and in England. When she started to write stories, she adopted the name Isak and chose English as her literary language, but later translated some of her work back into Danish.

At age 29, she married her cousin Baron Bror Blixen-Finecke and went to live with him on a coffee plantation in Kenya. Her time there is recounted in the autobiographical work *Out of Africa*, which was published when she was 52 and which reveals the depth of her love for the continent. This highly successful book was the basis of a 1985 Hollywood film starring Meryl Streep. Dinesen then had an unhappy period. She divorced her husband, she lost her lover, the English hunter Denys Finch-Hatton when he was killed in a plane crash, and she lost her farm, which had failed commercially. So she returned to Denmark to write.

When she was 59, she produced her only novel, *The Angelic Avengers*, which Danish readers recognized as a satire on Nazi-occupied Denmark. She then embarked on a series of romantic tales that won her worldwide recognition. These stories are concerned with the problems of personal identity and with destiny. The story "Babette's Feast," which is in a lighter, more humorous vein, also made a successful film. In the book *Shadows on the Grass* she returned to Kenya for her inspiration.

Publications

1934 Seven Gothic Tales
1937 Out of Africa
1942 Winter's Tales
1944 The Angelic Avengers
1950 "Babette's Feast"
1957 Last Tales
1961 Shadows on the Grass

Published after she died

1981 Letters from Africa, 1914–31

DING LING

Chinese novelist and short-story writer

Born Oct. 12, 1904
Died Mar. 4, 1986
Age at death 81

Ding Ling (or Ting Ling) is the pen name of Jiang Bingzhi, one of China's most popular authors.

Ding Ling was born in Hunan Province, China. Her father died when she was three, and her mother then became a teacher. She was educated at Shanghai and Beijing colleges, where she developed a dislike of traditional Chinese values. In her early 20s, she started to publish stories, such as *The Diary of Miss Sophia*, that seemed scandalous to many, dealing as they did with sexual desire and women's rights. These stories, however, made her famous and enabled her to support her mother. At 26, she became editor of the journal of the League of Left-Wing Writers. Her partner, by whom she had a son in 1930, was executed by the right-wing government, and Ding Ling joined the Chinese Communist Party.

Ding Ling's writing was initially acclaimed as a model of socialist fiction by the communists. In 1933, she was kidnapped by right-wing agents and imprisoned for three years. She escaped dressed as a soldier and rejoined the communist forces. She made friends with Mao Zedong, leader of the communists, and had a romantic association with one of his generals. She was too independent to not question party policies, however, and was formally criticized by Mao. But her land-reform novel, *The Sun Shines over the Sanggan River*, restored her to favor. She remained a maverick and, in 1958, she was banished to raise chickens in northern China. In the 1970s, she was expelled from the party and imprisoned for five years. She was later reaccepted by the communists.

Publications

1928 The Diary of Miss Sophia
1929 Birth of an Individual
1930 A Woman
1931 The Flood
1948 The Sun Shines over the Sanggan River
1979 Comrade Du Wanxiang

DIOP, Birago

Senegalese poet and short-story writer

Born Dec. 11, 1906
Died Nov. 25, 1989
Age at death 82

The prizewinning poet Birago Diop's greatest achievement was the popularization of West African folklore.

Diop was born in Dakar, Senegal (West Africa), which was then part of the French West Africa colony. His father died when he was young, and he grew up with his mother's side of the family. He went first to school in Dakar and later to a multiracial school in Saint Louis, then the capital of Senegal. In Toulouse, France, he trained as a vet, completing his studies in Paris at age 32.

It was in Paris that Diop met fellow countryman and poet LÉOPOLD SÉDAR SENGHOR. Diop was inspired by Senghor's literary and philosophical movement, Negritude ("Blackness"), which began as a protest against French rule in Africa and celebrated African history and culture. He began to write verse, in French, exploring African culture, and most of the poems that appear in *Lures and Glimmerings* were produced while in France. In 1936, he married a white French woman at a time when such marriages were rare.

Diop worked as a vet in several African countries. During his travels he met his old family griot (professional storyteller), Amadou Koumba. The stories in *Tales of Amadou Koumba* and other books are based on African folktales such as those told by Koumba. Diop's aim was to record African oral literature, which is spoken rather than written down, for French readers and for other Africans.

In 1960, Senegal became independent, with Senghor as president. Diop was made ambassador to Tunisia.

Publications

1947 Tales of Amadou Koumba
1958 New Tales of Amadou Koumba
1960 Lures and Glimmerings
1963 Tales and Commentaries
1978 Tales of Awa

DOCTOROW, E.L.

American novelist and playwright

Born Jan. 6, 1931

E.L. Doctorow weaves historical figures and events into his fiction, which examines serious moral issues in America's past.

Doctorow's best-known novel is *Ragtime*, in which real people such as Harry Houdini, Henry Ford, and Sigmund Freud mingle with fictional characters. Set in the 1930s just before World War II, the novel demonstrates how historical events can affect people's lives.

Edgar Laurence Doctorow was born in New York City, went to the Bronx High School of Science, and later received a degree from Kenyon College. At age 29, while working as an editor for the publishing company New American Library, he wrote his first novel, *Welcome to Hard Times*. It is a Western, depicting life in America's Wild West of frontier days, but it was not a success. Nor was his second book, the science fiction novel *Big as Life,* which describes the reactions of ordinary New Yorkers when two enormous, naked human figures suddenly appear above the city skyline.

It was not until his third novel, *The Book of Daniel*, that Doctorow found success. The book explores the reactions of the children of Julius and Ethel Rosenberg, two real people who were executed as communist spies in the 1950s.

Doctorow is highly regarded for his ability to identify the causes of social problems and to draw clear lines between the forces of good and the forces of evil. Several of his books have been made into Hollywood movies.

Publications

1960 Welcome to Hard Times
1966 Big as Life
1971 The Book of Daniel
1975 Ragtime
1978 Drinks Before Dinner
1980 Loon Lake
1985 World's Fair
1989 Billy Bathgate
1994 Waterworks

DONNE, John

English poet

Born 1572
Died Mar. 31, 1631
Age at death c. 59

Publications

1601 Progress of the Soul
1611–12 Anniversarie (parts1 and 2)
1618 Holy Sonnets
1624 Devotions upon Emergent Occasions
1631 Death's Duel

Published after he died

1644 Biathanatos
Satires (date unknown)
Songs and Sonnets (date unknown)
Divine Poems (date unknown)

John Donne was the leading figure of a group of 17th-century English writers who are known as the Metaphysical Poets.

Donne was born in London into a prosperous Roman Catholic family. He went to Oxford University, even though Roman Catholics were usually banned from attending, and then, at 19, returned to London to study law. In his 20s, Donne took part in military expeditions to Spain and the Azores; England and Spain were in a state of almost constant war in the 16th century. Donne seemed set to enjoy a successful career as a diplomat until he secretly married the niece of a powerful aristocrat for whom he was working. The aristocrat had Donne thrown into jail for a while, and his ambitions for a career in politics were finished.

Donne wrote poetry all his life. In his 20s and 30s, he wrote some of his most famous lyric poems, including the collections *Satires* and *Songs and Sonnets*. His first work to be published, *Anniversarie*, did not appear until he was 39, and most of his other poetry was not published until after his death. His poems were widely read and admired among aristocratic and literary circles. Younger poets were influenced by Donne's style, with its distinctive rhythms and images and its highly personal and spiritual nature. One well-known phrase and image is "No man is an island," which appears in his book *Devotions upon Emergent Occasions*.

In 1615, Donne converted to the Anglican faith and became a priest. Later, he became chaplain to the king and, in 1621, head of St. Paul's Cathedral in London.

DOOLITTLE, Hilda

American poet and novelist

Born Oct. 9, 1886
Died Sep. 27, 1961
Age at death 74

Hilda Doolittle, who wrote under the initials H.D., was an important American poet. She lived most of her life in Europe, and her work was influential in the development of modern poetry in the 1920s.

H.D. was born in Bethlehem, Pennsylvania. She always felt that the contrasting careers of her parents – her mother was an artist and her father an astronomer – played a role in the development of her work and ideas. For two years she attended Bryn Mawr College, where she met the poet MARIANNE MOORE. She went to London alone and there met the American poet EZRA POUND. Pound helped get her work noticed and suggested that she publish it using just her initials, H.D., as a pen name. Her first poetry collection, *Sea Garden*, came out when she was 30.

In 1913, H.D. married, and three years later she became coeditor, with the poet T.S. ELIOT, of *The Egoist*, a British literary journal. In 1919, she almost died in childbirth. She began a long-term relationship with an English woman named Winnifred Ellerman, also known as the poet "Bryher." Her marriage was over, but she did not divorce until 1937, after which she settled in Switzerland.

Much of H.D.'s work explores female sexuality and creativity. She was also interested in the ways that individuals discover and define themselves. After being treated by the famous Austrian psychoanalyst Sigmund Freud in the 1930s, she often included dream analysis and other techniques of Freudian theory in her work.

Publications

1916 Sea Garden
1921 Hymen
1925 Collected Poems
1926 Palimpsest
1944 The Walls Do Not Fall
1960 Bid Me to Live
1961 Helen in Egypt

Published after she died

1972 Hermetic Definition
1982 Collected Poems 1912–44

DOS PASSOS, John

American novelist, playwright, and poet

Born Jan. 14, 1896
Died Sep. 28, 1970
Age at death 74

John Dos Passos is best known for his trilogy *USA*. This immense personal, historical, and social account of American society from 1900 until 1930 is regarded as a masterpiece.

Dos Passos was the son of a wealthy Portuguese-American lawyer and a widow from Maryland. His parents did not marry until Dos Passos was 12, and he spent much of his childhood traveling in Europe and Mexico with his family. He graduated from Harvard when he was 20 and went to Spain to study architecture. Once there, however, he became caught up in World War I. He joined the French forces as a volunteer ambulance driver, and later he joined the US Army Medical Corps.

Dos Passos witnessed the full horrors of the battlefield and developed strong antiwar views. These are expressed in his first two novels, *One Man's Initiation*, published when he was 21, and *Three Soldiers*, published four years later. After the war he returned to America, but his experiences in Europe had changed his feelings about American society.

Dos Passos believed that the pursuit of money was at the root of all America's social problems and would eventually lead to the decay of society. He was a committed socialist, and, together with other left-wing writers, he supported the two anarchists in the controversial Sacco-Vanzetti case in 1927. Dos Passos expressed his beliefs in his three major novels, *The 42nd Parallel*, *1919* and *The Big Money*. They were collected and published as a single volume, *USA*. In later years, Dos Passos's politics became more conservative and right wing.

Publications

1917 One Man's Initiation
1921 Three Soldiers
1925 Manhattan Transfer
1930 The 42nd Parallel
1932 1919
1936 The Big Money
1938 USA (3 parts)
1939–49 District of Columbia (3 vols.)
1961 Midcentury
1966 The Best Years

DOSTOEVSKY, Fyodor

Russian novelist

Born Nov. 11, 1821
Died Feb. 9, 1881
Age at death 59

Fyodor Dostoevsky was one of the world's greatest writers. He wrote about the nature of good and evil as he had experienced them in his own life.

Dostoevsky was born in Moscow, Russia, the son of an army surgeon. He trained as a military engineer, but when he was about 22 decided to earn money by writing. His first novel, *Poor Folk*, appeared when he was 25, and he was hailed as an important new writer. He joined a socialist writers' group that read and discussed banned books and, in 1849, the group was arrested. Dostoevsky was nearly executed, but at the last moment the death sentence was changed. The experience of coming so close to death made a lasting impression on him, and he often wrote about murder and cruelty. Dostoevsky spent the next eight years in Siberia, first in a prison camp, then he had to serve as a soldier. He rejected socialism and became strongly religious.

Dostoevsky was nearly 40 when he returned from Siberia. He wrote *The House of the Dead*, a powerful novel about his prison experiences. Constantly in debt thanks to his gambling, he spent time in Europe. On his return to Russia, he wrote at frenzied speed to clear his debts, producing his first great masterpiece, *Crime and Punishment*, at the age of 45. It is about a student who is driven mad with guilt after he murders an old woman just because he thought she was inferior. Other brilliant novels followed: *The Idiot*, *The Devils* – a bitter attack on revolutionaries – and his final novel, *The Brothers Karamazov*, which explores the effect on four brothers of the murder of their evil father.

Publications

1846	*Poor Folk*
1859	*Uncle's Dream*
1859	*The Friend of the Family*
1860–61	*The House of the Dead*
1864	*Notes from the Underground*
1866	*Crime and Punishment*
1866	*The Gambler*
1868	*The Idiot*
1872	*The Devils*
1880	*The Brothers Karamazov*

DOUGLASS, Frederick

American writer

Born Feb. 7, 1817
Died Feb. 20, 1895
Age at death 78

Frederick Douglass was the most important African-American leader and writer of the 19th century.

Originally named Frederick Augustus Washington Bailey, he was born a slave in Tuckahoe, Maryland. He escaped slavery when he was 21 and settled in New Bedford, Massachusetts. There he changed his name to Douglass to avoid capture and return to the South.

Following an impassioned speech to the Massachusetts Antislavery Society in 1841, Douglass became a spokesperson for the organization. In response to charges that no slave could be such a good speaker he wrote his autobiography, *Narrative of the Life of Frederick Douglass, an American Slave*. It is a powerful account of his struggle for identity and freedom. He described the cruelty he suffered as a slave and denounced the ideas used to justify slavery. Douglass's work was published when he was 28; it became the most popular of the many slave narratives written at the time.

Fearing that he might be captured and returned to slavery, Douglass went to England in 1845, where he continued to lecture. His admirers bought his freedom in 1846, and Douglass returned to the United States in 1847 and settled in Rochester, New York. There he founded an antislavery newspaper, the *North Star*. He also worked with the Underground Railroad, helping escaped slaves to reach freedom in Canada. During the 1850s, Douglass became the leading spokesman for northern blacks, urging equal opportunities and an end to racial discrimination. He was a valued adviser to President Abraham Lincoln.

Publications

1845	*Narrative of the Life of Frederick Douglass, an American Slave*
1851	*The Heroic Slave*
1855	*My Bondage and My Freedom*
1881	*Life and Times of Frederick Douglass*

DOVE, Rita

American poet, novelist and short-story writer

Born Aug. 28, 1952

Rita Dove is a renowned poet who became, in 1993, the first African American to be named Poet Laureate of the United States.

Dove was born and raised in Akron, Ohio. She says that it was books themselves – the feel of them in her hand, the crisp pages – that made her want to be a writer. Her first piece of writing, done at about age 11, was a novel, *Chaos*, about robots who take over the planet. Dove went on to graduate from Miami University (in Oxford, Ohio) in 1973 and later earned a Master's degree at the University of Iowa. She now teaches at the University of Virginia. She is married and has one daughter.

When she was named Poet Laureate at age 41 she became the youngest person ever to hold that position. But Dove's star had already been on the rise for several years. Dove's first book, *Ten Poems*, was published when she was 25, and it was followed by four more collections of poems and a collection of short stories. Then, in 1987, she received the Pulitzer Prize for her poetry collection *Thomas and Beulah* – she was just 34. In it Dove tells a fictionalized history of her grandparents, inspired by a story told to her by her grandmother. Dove has also published a novel, a play in verse, and essays.

Dove believes that poetry should be easily accessible and available, not an elite art form. She is even said to have argued that poetry should appear on MTV. In 1996, her popularity was rewarded with a high honor: she was asked to write the text for the symphony that opened the Summer Olympic Games in Atlanta, Georgia.

Publications

1980	*The Yellow House on the Corner*
1983	*Museum*
1985	*Fifth Sunday*
1986	*Thomas and Beulah*
1992	*Through the Ivory Gate*
1993	*Selected Poems*
1994	*The Darker Face of the Earth*
1995	*Mother Love*

DOYLE, Arthur Conan

Scottish crime writer

Born May 22, 1859
Died Jul. 7, 1930
Age at death 71

Arthur Conan Doyle was the creator of Sherlock Holmes, perhaps the most famous fictional detective of all time. Conan Doyle was born in Edinburgh and studied medicine at university there. He based part of Holmes's character – his wide knowledge and his ability to reason from the tiniest clue – on some of the professors he met at university.

Conan Doyle became an army doctor and worked in South Africa during the Boer War. Returning to England, he wrote two books explaining the war, for which he was knighted in 1902. Still in his 20s and while working as a doctor, he began to write mystery stories featuring the character of Sherlock Holmes, a brilliant detective who uses reasoning to solve crimes that stump the police. The stories are told through the voice of Dr. Watson, Holmes's good-natured friend. The two amateur detectives – they solve crimes for fun and not for money – share living quarters in Baker Street in London.

The success of the Sherlock Holmes stories gave Conan Doyle the chance to become a full-time writer at age 32. But he soon grew tired of the series. He even tried to kill off Holmes in one of his stories but had to bring him back by popular demand. Conan Doyle was more interested in writing on serious subjects; during his lifetime he published many books on history, politics, and spiritualism. He also wrote historical romances. However, today he is best remembered for his adventure stories about Sherlock Holmes.

Publications

1887 A Study in Scarlet
1890 The Sign of Four
1892 The Adventures of Sherlock Holmes
1894 The Memoirs of Sherlock Holmes
1902 The Hound of the Baskervilles
1905 The Return of Sherlock Holmes
1914 The Valley of Fear

DREISER, Theodore

American novelist, playwright and short-story writer

Born Aug. 27, 1871
Died Dec. 28, 1945
Age at death 74

Theodore Dreiser is best known for his novel *An American Tragedy*. Dreiser was born in Terre Haute, Indiana, the ninth of ten children. His father was an intensely religious German immigrant weaver. The family was poor, moving constantly from place to place, so Dreiser had little formal education. He left home when he was 16 and worked at whatever jobs he could find. One of his former teachers was shocked to find him working in a hardware store in Chicago and agreed to pay for Dreiser to attend the University of Indiana.

Dreiser left after only a year. He then became a newspaper reporter and magazine editor, finally settling in New York. Dreiser knew from his own experience how difficult it is for someone from a poor, disadvantaged background to make his or her way in the world. He also knew that a ruthless desire to become rich and successful could lead to corruption and crime. He explored these themes in his first novel, *Sister Carrie*, which came out when he was 29, and in two later novels about unscrupulous businessmen, *The Financier* and *The Titan*.

In *An American Tragedy* Dreiser follows the rise and fall of an ambitious young man who is determined to acquire wealth and status, even if he must commit murder to do so. Based on a real murder case, the story strongly supports Dreiser's argument that society's emphasis on the value of material success leads only to immorality, greed and destruction. *An American Tragedy* is still widely read today and has become a classic of American literature.

Publications

1900 Sister Carrie
1911 Jennie Gerhardt
1912 The Financier
1914 The Titan
1915 The "Genius"
1918 Free and Other Stories
1919 Twelve Men
1925 An American Tragedy

Published after he died

1947 The Stoic

DRURY, Allen

Allen Drury is regarded as a master of the political novel. Through his fiction he exposes what he considers the bad parts of liberal American politics.

Drury was born in Houston, Texas. After graduating from Stanford University he wrote for several California newspapers before serving in the army during World War II. During the late 1940s and '50s, he worked as a Washington political reporter, covering the Senate for a variety of newspapers, news services and journals, including the United Press International, Pathfinders, the *New York Times*, and *Reader's Digest*.

Drury's experiences of politics in Washington inspired his first novel, *Advise and Consent*, which was published when he was 41. Based on the true story of a Senate battle over the confirmation of a liberal nominee for secretary of state, it shows the corrupt nature of congressional politics. The book became a bestseller and received the Pulitzer Prize in 1960. It was made into a movie two years later, and its success encouraged Drury to leave journalism and write full time.

Drury followed his initial success with a series of political novels. *Anna Hastings: The Story of a Newspaperperson!* is a criticism of 1970s liberalism. In *The Hill of Summer* he writes about a conservative government dealing with the liberal press. His political stories are full of tension, sharp dialogue, and clever tactics. Among his most recent works are *Into What Far Harbor* and *A Thing of State*. None of his later books has achieved the popularity of *Advise and Consent*.

American novelist and journalist

Born Sep. 2, 1918
Died Sep-1998
Age at death 80

Publications

1959 Advise and Consent
1962 A Shade of Difference
1978 Anna Hastings: The Story of a Newspaperperson!
1979 Mark Coffin
1981 The Hill of Summer
1986 Pentagon
1990 Toward What Bright Glory?
1993 Into What Far Harbor
1995 A Thing of State

DRYDEN, John

English poet and playwright

Born Aug. 9, 1631
Died May 1, 1700
Age at death 68

John Dryden was the leading English writer of the Restoration period – the time when poetry and drama flourished following the return to the throne of the English monarchy in 1660.

Dryden was born into a well-off rural family. He was educated at Westminster School in London and Cambridge University, where he enjoyed studying science as well as the arts. While he was still a child, the English Civil War was fought. Dryden's family supported Oliver Cromwell and the Parliamentarians, who won the struggle to overthrow King Charles I and make England a republic.

Dryden was more concerned that the country should have a stable government than with who was in charge. When he was 28, he produced his first important poem, *Heroic Stanzas on the Death of Cromwell*. It was a celebration of the life of Cromwell, who had died the previous year after ruling the country since the end of the war. A year later, Dryden welcomed the return of a new king, Charles II, and the end of the republic with his poem *Astraea Redux*.

During Cromwell's dictatorship many theaters had been closed. With the return of the monarchy they were reopened and the period of great theater known today as Restoration Drama began. Dryden wrote his first play in 1663. He soon discovered that plays earned him a lot more money than poems, and over the next 20 years he wrote more than 20. He wrote both comedies and tragedies in verse. *All For Love*, a version of the story of Antony and Cleopatra, was his most successful tragedy. His comedy *Marriage à-la-Mode* is still popular today.

Publications

1659	*Heroic Stanzas on the Death of Cromwell*
1660	*Astraea Redux*
1663	*The Wild Gallant*
1667	*Annus Mirabilis*
1667	*Secret Love*
1672	*Marriage à-la-Mode*
1677	*All For Love*
1681–82	*Absolom and Achitophel*
1687	*The Hind and the Panther*

Du BOIS, W.E.B.

American essayist and novelist

Born Feb. 23, 1868
Died Aug. 27, 1963
Age at death 95

The writings of W.E.B. Du Bois were influential in both black literature and in the struggle for African-American civil rights. He was the author of 22 books, including five novels.

William Edward Burghardt Du Bois was born in Massachusetts into a family of Puritans, in which hard work and achievement were stressed. He attended the then all-black Fisk University in Nashville, Tennessee, and later earned a Ph.D. at Harvard with a dissertation on the African slave trade. It was published as his first book when he was 28.

After studying in Germany and teaching in Ohio, Du Bois conducted a study in Pennsylvania about black life, published as *The Philadelphia Negro*. He became increasingly involved with the emerging civil rights movement and produced a collection of essays called *The Souls of Black Folk*. Du Bois believed that an educated "talented tenth" could lead the black masses to political and social equality. He disagreed with Booker T. Washington, the recognized spokesman for black opinion, who advocated nonpolitical development toward economic power.

In 1909, Du Bois was a cofounder of the National Association for the Advancement of Colored People (NAACP). His disagreements with black leaders and flirtations with socialism and then communism during the McCarthy era meant, however, that his views became increasingly out of step with mainstream black opinion.

Late in life, he was invited to oversee the production of *Encyclopedia Africana* by Ghana's president. He became a citizen of Ghana, and later he died there.

Publications

1896 The Suppression of the African Slave Trade to the USA.
1899 The Philadelphia Negro
1903 The Souls of Black Folk
1928 The Dark Princess
1935 Black Reconstruction in America
1940 Dusk of Dawn

DU FU

Chinese poet

Born 712
Died 770
Age at death c. 58

Du Fu (also spelled Tu Fu) is regarded by many as the greatest poet in Chinese literature. He lived more than a thousand years ago, when China had one of the most advanced civilizations in the world.

Du Fu was born in what is now Henan Province, north-central China. His family, although once wealthy and influential, had fallen on hard times, and Du Fu was expected to make a career as a minor official in the civil service. At that time, China had a highly organized government that employed thousands of civil servants of different ranks to represent the authority of the emperor. A series of examinations had to be passed in order to become a civil servant – Du Fu failed these examinations several times.

For several years, Du Fu wandered China, experiencing the great variety of that vast country and writing poems about what he saw. Eventually, he managed to get a minor position at the emperor's court through his growing reputation as a poet. Shortly afterward, a rebellion forced the emperor and his government to leave the area, and Du Fu found himself trapped in enemy territory. After a period of great hardship, poverty and danger, he managed to return home.

Most of Du Fu's more than 1,400 surviving poems were written during the last 12 years of his life. He wrote about the hardships he had witnessed during the rebellion, about ordinary people, and about the timeless human concerns of love and death. Everything he wrote has a tone of compassion and moral sense.

Publications

8th century
"Song of the War Chariots"
"The Ballad of Beautiful Women"
"The Newlyweds' Parting"
"Three Farewells"
"Three Officials"

Du MAURIER, Daphne

English novelist, short-story writer and biographer

Born May 13, 1907
Died Apr. 19, 1989
Age at death 81

Daphne du Maurier was a writer of romantic suspense novels, mostly set on the coast of Cornwall. This is a wild, stormy area, with a wild, stormy past, and she spent most of her life there.

Born in London, du Maurier came from an artistic family. Her father was an actor-manager, and her grandfather was an artist and novelist. She was married to a lieutenant-general in the British Army.

Du Maurier's first novel, *The Loving Spirit*, was published when she was 24. A string of other novels, some with historical settings, followed. Her most famous book is the gothic bestseller *Rebecca*, whose hero is unable to forget his tragic first marriage while trying to be happy in his second. It was made into a movie in 1940, starring Laurence Olivier and Joan Fontaine, and was voted the best picture of that year. It was directed by Alfred Hitchcock, who also directed the film of du Maurier's frightening story "The Birds."

Other bestsellers that were also made into motion pictures include: *Jamaica Inn*, a blood-and-thunder tale of smugglers; *Frenchman's Creek*, a pirate romance; and *My Cousin Rachel*, a sensational romance.

Du Maurier also wrote biographies of members of her family and of Francis Bacon (an English statesman in the 1500s and 1600s). Her plays include *September Tide*. She was made a Dame of the British Empire in 1969. At age 70, she published her autobiography, *Myself When Young*.

Publications

1931 The Loving Spirit
1936 Jamaica Inn
1938 Rebecca
1941 Frenchman's Creek
1948 September Tide
1951 My Cousin Rachel
1952 Kiss Me Again, Stranger (including "The Birds")
1957 The Scapegoat
1977 Myself When Young

DUGAN, Alan

American poet

Born Feb. 12, 1923

With his first volume of published poetry, Alan Dugan won a Pulitzer Prize in 1962, a Prix de Rome from the American Academy, and the National Book Award.

Dugan was born in Brooklyn, New York City. He grew up and was educated in both Brooklyn and Jamaica, Queens. After finishing secondary school, he began studying at Queens College, New York, but was drafted into the army before he had completed his degree. Following World War II, Dugan finished his studies at Mexico City College and then moved back to New York, where he lived for most of the next ten years. During the 1950s, he spent as much time as he could writing poetry while holding a variety of jobs to support himself.

At age 38, Dugan published *Poems*, his first collection. While some criticized it for being too "clever" – they thought the emotions did not seem genuine and found it wordy – others praised Dugan for his original and distinctive voice and for his ability to convey strong feelings of grief, love, hate and fear. Despite these mixed reviews, *Poems* became a great success and marked a turning point in his career. Supported by various literary grants, reading tours and teaching jobs, he found that his new role as an accepted poet allowed him to travel: to Paris; around the United States; through South and Central America; and in Mexico.

Dugan has since written many equally good poems, though none of his collections has received as much attention as *Poems*. Since 1969, he has worked mostly for the Fine Arts Work Center in Provincetown, Massachusetts.

Publications

1961 Poems
1963 Poems 2
1967 Poems 3
1969 Collected Poems
1974 Poems 4
1976 Sequence
1985 New and Collected Poems, 1961–83

DUMAS, Alexandre

French novelist and playwright

Born Jul. 24, 1802
Died Dec. 5, 1870
Age at death 68

Alexandre Dumas was a popular 19th-century French writer. He is remembered today as the author of two famous adventure novels: *The Three Musketeers* and *The Count of Monte Cristo*.

Dumas was born in a rural town, the son of a general and an innkeeper's daughter. His father was later killed fighting in the army of Napoleon Bonaparte, the future emperor of France. His death left the family in poverty, and Dumas moved to Paris to find work. It was while working as a clerk in the capital city that he began writing.

At the age of 27, Dumas had his first success with *Henry III*, a historical drama. He followed this with more popular plays and soon established a reputation as one of France's leading writers. He wrote constantly, producing a steady stream of plays, novels, and short stories. When the pressure of work got too much for him, he would take long holidays in the countryside.

Dumas wanted to write a series of books covering the whole history of France. Two parts of this series were the novels *The Count of Monte Cristo* and *The Three Musketeers*, historical adventure stories that became his best-known works.

Although many of his books brought him great wealth, Dumas was as talented at spending money as he was at telling stories. He often found himself in debt, only to rebuild his fortunes soon after. He and his mistress had a son, also called Alexandre. Dumas the younger is remembered for writing *Camille*, a tragic love story set in Paris, first performed in the theater in 1852.

Publications

1829 Henry III
1830 Christine
1831 Napoleon Bonaparte
1831 Antony
1832 The Tower of Nesle
1836 Kean
1844 The Three Musketeers
1844 The Count of Monte Cristo
1845 Twenty Years After
1850 The Black Tulip

DUNBAR, Paul Laurence

American poet, short-story writer and novelist

Born Jun. 27, 1872
Died Feb. 9, 1906
Age at death 33

Paul Laurence Dunbar is widely recognized to have been the first important African-American poet. He is best remembered as a writer of poems in Black English.

Born in Dayton, Ohio, Dunbar was the son of escaped slaves. When he was 17, he published his first poems in a local African-American newspaper, the *Dayton Herald*. Dunbar had hoped to become a law clerk after graduating from secondary school but, because he was black, he was unable to get a job and worked as an elevator operator while writing poetry.

Dunbar published his first collection of poetry, *Oak and Ivy*, at his own expense when he was 21. He became a national celebrity with the publication of *Majors and Minors* and *Lyrics of Lowly Life* by the time he was 24. The poems, written in Black English, portray the hardships and joys of African-American life. They were based on his own experience and on the stories told him by his mother. The public enjoyed his sentimentality and wit, while critics praised his use of language to express the qualities of African-American culture.

Dunbar lived during a period of increasing segregation and racism, yet his poetry avoided these issues. Writing primarily for a white audience, he was forced to limit himself to praising African Americans rather than attacking whites. He did, however, address the issue of prejudice in his essays and novels, in which he bitterly and mockingly pointed out racial injustice. These were never as popular as his poems though. Dunbar died at an early age from tuberculosis.

Publications

1893 Oak and Ivy
1895 Majors and Minors
1896 Lyrics of Lowly Life
1898 The Uncalled
1899 Lyrics of the Hearthside
1900 The Strength of Gideon and Other Stories
1902 The Sport of the Gods
1905 Lyrics of Sunshine and Shadow

DUNCAN, Robert

American poet and essayist

Born Jan. 7, 1919
Died Feb. 3, 1988
Age at death 69

Robert Duncan is most famous for being one of the poets who made the San Francisco Bay area a major center for poetry in America. He taught for a time at Black Mountain College in western North Carolina, and he is also known as one of the most important Black Mountain poets.

Duncan was born in Oakland, California. His mother died soon after his birth, and he was adopted and raised mainly in Bakersfield, California. He attended the University of California, Berkeley, for two years between the ages of 17 and 19; after a period in New York, he went back to Berkeley, where he studied medieval and Renaissance civilizations. He published his first poems in school magazines.

Few poets have written more clearly about the meaning of their poetry and their understanding of poetry. One of the themes running through Duncan's work is the world as seen through the wondering eyes of a child. Some of his later poetry poses questions about the state of American politics in the era of the Cold War; he even denounced President Lyndon Johnson for leading the nation deeper into the Vietnam conflict. At age 41, Duncan published his most important book, *The Opening of the Field*. It contains the poem "Passages," which speaks out against the Vietnam War; it also contains his best-known poem, "My Mother Would Be a Falconress."

Duncan's poetry was influenced by the writing of another American poet, EZRA POUND. In his own work, Duncan has maintained the age-old tradition of the poet as a revolutionary prophet.

Publications

1947	*Heavenly City, Earthly City*
1950	*Medieval Scenes*
1959	*Selected Poems*
1960	*The Opening of the Field*
1964	*Roots and Branches*
1966	*The Years as Catches*
1968	*Derivations: Selected Poems, 1950–56*
1970	*Tribunals: Passages 31–35*
1985	*The Regulators*

DUNNE, John Gregory

American novelist

Born May 25, 1932

John Gregory Dunne is an American novelist known for his stories exploring the Irish Catholic experience in America.

The son of a physician, Dunne grew up in the wealthy town of West Hartford, Connecticut. He graduated from Princeton University, then was a staff writer for *Time* magazine before moving to California to become a freelance writer at age 22. With his wife, novelist JOAN DIDION, he developed several screenplays.

Dunne initially wrote nonfiction works. These include *Delano: The Story of the California Grape Strike*, published when he was 35, and *The Studio*, an in-depth portrait of the workings of a Hollywood film studio.

When he was 42, Dunne turned to writing fiction. *Vegas: A Memoir of a Dark Season*, his first novel, is a fictionalized account of a summer he spent in Las Vegas. He has also created crime novels in which his characters are shaped by the Irish Catholic moral sense and the Irish experience in America. Dunne's first bestseller was *True Confessions*, published when he was 45. It is a murder mystery that focuses not on solving the crime but on exploring the relationship between two Irish Catholic brothers who are involved in the case. *True Confessions* was made into a movie in 1981. Dunne's next novel, *Dutch Shea, Jr.*, revolves around the theme of corruption among Irish Catholics. More recent works include *The Red White and Blue* – a complex web of characters creating a darkly funny portrait of America – and an autobiography, *Harp*.

Publications

1967	*Delano: The Story of the California Grape Strike*
1969	*The Studio*
1974	*Vegas: A Memoir of a Dark Season*
1977	*True Confessions*
1982	*Dutch Shea, Jr.*
1987	*The Red White and Blue*
1989	*Harp*
1994	*Playland*

DUNSANY, Lord

Anglo-Irish fantasy writer and playwright

Born Jul. 24, 1878
Died Oct. 25, 1957
Age at death 79

Publications

1905 The Gods of Pegana
1906 Time and the Gods
1908 The Sword of Welleran
1909 The Glittering Gate
1912 The Book of Wonder
1916 A Night at the Inn
1926 The Charwoman's Shadow
1924 The King of Elfland's Daughter
1933 The Curse of the Wise Woman
1936 Rory and Bran

Lord Dunsany was one of the first fantasy writers of the 20th century.

He was born Edward Plunkett into an Anglo-Irish family. His traditional upper-class education at Eton and Sandhurst was followed by military service in the Boer War, South Africa. In 1899, his father died, and he inherited the title Baron Dunsany. He went to live in the family castle in County Meath, Ireland, and married the daughter of the Earl of Jersey. When World War I broke out, he again served as a soldier. After the war, he taught English literature at Athens University in Greece.

Dunsany wrote more than 60 books. He disliked anything modern or mechanical such as a typewriter and always wrote with a quill pen. He was inspired by romantic myths and legends from Europe, and he also became fascinated with art and ideas from India and the Muslim world. In his novels, plays, poems and stories he created imaginary lands full of gods, witches, spirits and magic. These fairytale worlds are for adults rather than children.

Dunsany's first book of short stories, *The Gods of Pegana*, was published when he was 27. Pegana was the first of many fantasy worlds that Dunsany wrote about. His idea of creating complete "other worlds" influenced many later fantasy writers, including J.R.R. TOLKIEN and H.P. LOVECRAFT.

Most of Dunsany's books were illustrated by the artist S.H. Sime, who captured the spirit of the worlds that Dunsany described as "beyond the fields we know."

DURAS, Marguerite

French novelist, screenwriter and playwright

Born Apr. 4, 1914
Died Mar. 3, 1996
Age at death 81

Marguerite Duras wrote more than 50 novels, screenplays and plays and is France's most famous woman author of the late 20th century.

Duras was born Marguerite Donnadieu in Gia Dinh, French Indochina (now Vietnam). Her father died when she was four, and her mother, a teacher, struggled hard to bring up three children. Duras's upbringing was to provide her with much material for her later writing. She went to study in Paris at age 17, later married, and had a son in 1942. During World War II, she joined the Communist Party and fought with the French Resistance against the Nazi German occupation of France. She also began writing under the name of Duras, taken from the name of a village in France near where her father had owned property.

At age 29, Duras published her first novel, *The Impudent Ones*, written in a style that was influenced by Ernest Hemingway. Her first real success, however, was *The Sea Wall*, published when she was 36. This autobiographical novel is about a poor French family in Indochina. It was Duras's growing talent for dialogue that led her, at 45, to write the screen scenario for Alain Renais's famous film *Hiroshima, Mon Amour* – about the brief love affair between a French actress and a Japanese businessman. The theme of love between people of different races runs through many of her other works, including her prizewinning novel *The Lover*. This book was made into a film in 1992, making Duras known to a wider audience.

Publications

1943 The Impudent Ones
1950 The Sea Wall
1952 The Sailor from Gibraltar
1958 Moderato Cantabile
1959 Hiroshima, Mon Amour
1972 Love
1974 India Song
1984 The Lover
1992 The North China Lover
1995 That's All

DURRELL, Gerald

English writer

Born Jan. 7, 1925
Died Jan. 30, 1995
Age at death 70

Gerald Durrell, a renowned naturalist, wrote amusing books about the wild animals and people he knew.

Durrell was born to English parents in Jamshedpur, India, the youngest of four children; his brother Lawrence Durrell became a famous novelist. Gerald's passion for wildlife began almost in the cradle – he claimed the first word he spoke was "zoo." When he was ten, his widowed mother took her family to live on the Greek island of Corfu. Private tutors taught Durrell, and for five years he roamed free, catching and keeping as pets all sorts of small creatures. In his early 20s, he traveled to Africa and South America, collecting animals for British zoos. At 33, he founded the Jersey Zoological Park on one of the British Channel Islands off northwest France. With his second wife Lee – an American-born conservationist – Durrell bred rare species for eventual return to the wild. Many of his books were written to earn money for this work.

Durrell's most famous book appeared when he was 31. *My Family and Other Animals* tells hilarious tales about his own unconventional family and the oddly delightful islanders on Corfu. Durrell's anecdotes read like slapstick comedy, though he claimed all were true. Durrell also described animal-collecting expeditions, as in *The Drunken Forest* and *Three Tickets to Adventure*. Later books include *The Stationary Ark*, about his now world-famous zoo, and *The Aye-Aye and I*, about Durrell's attempts to save a mammal that had become rare in the wild. His novels include *Rosy Is My Relative*, the comical tale of a drunken elephant.

Publications

1954 Three Tickets to Adventure
1956 My Family and Other Animals
1956 The Drunken Forest
1960 A Zoo in My Luggage
1968 Rosy Is My Relative
1972 Catch Me a Colobus
1976 The Stationary Ark
1979 The Picnic and Suchlike Pandemonium
1992 The Aye-Aye and I

DURRELL, Lawrence

English novelist, poet and short-story writer

Born Feb. 27, 1912
Died Nov. 7, 1990
Age at death 78

Publications

1935 Pied Piper of Lovers
1938 The Black Book
1945 Prospero's Cell
1957 Bitter Lemons
1957 Justine
1958 Balthazar
1958 Mountolive
1960 Clea
1974–85 The Avignon Quintet (5 vols.)
1980 Collected Poems 1931–74

Lawrence Durrell earned worldwide fame on the publication of *The Alexandria Quartet*. On the surface a story of love, espionage and mystery set in Alexandria, Egypt, this series of four experimental novels is actually an exploration of memory. A young writer tells of a love affair in the first novel, *Justine*, but his point of view is contradicted by the recollections of others in the second book, *Balthazar*. *Mountolive* gives the facts, and *Clea* tells of the writer's journey of self discovery.

Durrell, brother of GERALD DURRELL, was born of British parents in India, where he spent the first 11 years of his life. He had little feeling for England and the English, and spent most of his life traveling or living in Mediterranean countries. His first published work, the novel *Pied Piper of Lovers*, came out when he was 23.

During World War II, he was on the staff of the British embassy in Egypt, working in Cairo and Alexandria. After the war, Durrell held various diplomatic and teaching jobs in places as diverse as Greece, Cyprus, Argentina and Yugoslavia. He finally settled in Provence, southern France. There he wrote another multivolume work, *The Avignon Quintet*. He also produced several travel books describing the places he had visited. His poems, published over many years, were gathered in a collected edition in 1980. Other publications include humorous short stories and plays in verse.

In his writing, Durrell was influenced by the American writer HENRY MILLER, and the two kept up an exchange of letters over 45 years.

DÜRRENMATT, Friedrich

Swiss playwright and novelist

Born Jan. 5, 1921
Died Dec. 12, 1990
Age at death 69

Friedrich Dürrenmatt is best known for his role in the revival of German theater after World War II.

Born near Bern, in Switzerland, Dürrenmatt was the son of a pastor. He was educated in Bern and Zürich. Although he originally wanted to be a painter, he turned to writing, and when he was 26, his first play, *It Is Written*, was produced. This play is about the persecution of a religious group, the Anabaptists, in 16th-century Germany. The same year his play *The Blind Man* was also produced.

Dürrenmatt quickly developed a modern style of writing for the stage. His plays often have off-beat settings. Following the example of BERTOLT BRECHT, he included comedy and tragedy in the same work. His actors often step out of their roles to make comments on what is going on in the play. He makes the point that life is absurd and full of tragedy but must be lived with courage. Believing that tragedy is an unavoidable part of human life, he makes people's attempts to avoid tragic events seem comic.

Dürrenmatt wrote many plays. With one of these, *The Marriage of Mr. Mississippi*, he became known outside Europe. (It was produced in New York as *Fools Are Passing Through*.) It is a play about human nature and the impossibility of changing the world. Later, he wrote *The Physicists*, a play that considers the moral implications of science. Many critics think this is his best work.

At the age of 49, Dürrenmatt gave up writing and devoted himself to adapting important works for the stage. He also wrote detective novels and radio plays.

Publications

1947 It Is Written
1947 The Blind Man
1952 The Marriage of Mr. Mississippi
1952 The Judge and His Hangman
1953 The Quarry
1956 The Dangerous Game
1956 The Visit
1958 The Pledge
1962 The Physicists

DWORKIN, Andrea

American writer

Born Sep. 26, 1946

Andrea Dworkin is one of the best-known feminist writers in America today.

Dworkin was born in Camden, New Jersey. She was greatly influenced by her parents: her mother, a teacher, encouraged her to read widely. Her father, a postal worker and teacher, instilled in his daughter a strong sense of human rights. Since she is Jewish, Dworkin objected to having to sing Christmas carols in primary school, an early sign of her radicalism and rebellion. Many of her parents' relatives had been killed in the Holocaust in World War II, and so from an early age she took hate and discrimination seriously.

After attending Bennington College in Vermont, Dworkin went to the Greek island of Crete where, at age 20, a collection of her poems was published. Her marriage to a political radical ended after three years during which she suffered violent abuse. She spent some years afterward as a prostitute, an experience that contributed to her later radical politics.

Dworkin believes that writing and legislation really change society. Her first political writings of the mid-1970s appeared at the height of the feminist and antiwar movements. *Woman Hating* and *Our Blood* argue passionately and angrily against male dominance of society and blame this for the existence of sexual violence. In the 1980s, she was involved in fighting pornography, which she believes violates women's rights. Her fiction – including a short story collection, *The New Woman's Broken Heart*, and two novels, *Ice and Fire* and *Mercy* – has always been informed by her politics.

Publications

1974 Woman Hating
1976 Our Blood
1979 The New Woman's Broken Heart
1981 Pornography
1983 Right-Wing Women
1986 Ice and Fire
1987 Intercourse
1989 Letters from a War Zone
1990 Mercy

EBERHART, Richard

American poet

Born Apr. 5, 1904

Richard Eberhart is a major 20th-century American poet whose work is often concerned with change and death. He was awarded a Pulitzer Prize in 1966 for *Selected Poems 1930–65*.

Eberhart was born in Austin, Minnesota, and had a happy upbringing until the age of 17; his parents had been comfortably well off, and his devoted mother had encouraged him to write. In 1921, however, his father left his job after trouble in the company, and his mother, nursed by Eberhart, died slowly from lung cancer.

These events changed Eberhart from a confident high achiever to a quieter student. While in college, he wrote poetry and had some of his work published. He then went to Cambridge University, where he finished his first major work. *A Bravery of Earth*, begun when Eberhart was 24, is a long autobiographical poem dealing with life and death.

Eberhart then moved to New York, where he worked in a slaughterhouse and as a tutor to pay his way through graduate school at Harvard. He left to teach at a school in Massachusetts, where he met other writers such as W.H. AUDEN and FORD MADOX FORD.

Eberhart's best-known poem, "The Groundhog," was inspired by the poet's reaction to seeing a dead groundhog and published when he was 30. The themes found in this poem – living and dying, mind and body, childhood and adulthood – appear in most of his later work. He also describes simple images from nature and uses them to discuss wider issues of life and death.

Publications

1930	*A Bravery of Earth*
1934	"The Groundhog"
1947	*Burr Oaks*
1950	*An Herb Basket*
1964	*The Quarry: New Poems*
1965	*Selected Poems 1930–65*
1972	*Fields of Grace*
1976	*Poems to Poets*
1976	*Collected Poems 1930–76*
1990	*New and Selected Poems*

ECHEGARAY, José

Spanish playwright

Born Apr. 19, 1832
Died Sep. 4, 1916
Age at death 84

José Echegaray was a leading Spanish playwright of the late 19th and early 20th centuries. He was joint winner of the Nobel Prize for Literature in 1904.

Born in Madrid, the capital city of Spain, Echegaray trained as an engineer. At the age of only 22, he became Professor of Mathematics and Physics at the Madrid Engineering School. He taught there until 1868, when he was elected to the Cortés, the Spanish parliament. In 1874, he was appointed Minister of Finance. Later, he was Minister of Commerce and Minister of Education and, in 1905, became Minister of Finance again.

Echegaray's first play, *The Checkbook*, was not published until he was 42, the same year he first became finance minister. Then, despite his very busy political career, he found time to write two plays a year for the rest of his life. Altogether, he produced more than 60 plays.

The early plays were popular but conventional romantic stories. Later, influenced by the work of the great Norwegian dramatist, Henrik Ibsen, Echegaray began to explore more difficult social issues. *Madman or Saint* shows how society might treat somebody who always tells the truth. *The World and His Wife*, finished in 1881 and today considered his best work, was one of the first plays to criticize Spanish society.

Although Echegaray's plays are rarely performed or read today, he was very popular in his time. His work opened the way for later playwrights, such as Jacinto Benavente, to revolutionize Spanish drama.

Publications

- *1874 The Checkbook*
- *1877 Madman or Saint*
- *1877 Either Madness or Holiness*
- *1881 The World and His Wife*
- *1892 The Son of Don Juan*
- *1892 Mariana*
- *1900 The Mad God*

ECO, Umberto

Italian novelist

Born Jan. 5, 1932

Italian writer Umberto Eco is best known for his highly successful novel *The Name of the Rose*, which became an international bestseller and was made into a popular movie.

Eco was born in a small town in northwest Italy. He studied philosophy at Turin University and was awarded a Ph.D. at the age of 22 for a thesis on the early philosopher and religious thinker, St. Thomas Aquinas. Eco then worked as an editor on cultural programs for Italian radio and television. In his 20s, he taught philosophy at the University of Turin.

At the early age of 39, Eco was appointed Professor of Semiotics at Bologna University in the north of Italy. Semiotics is the study of signs and symbols of all kinds. It deals especially with how written or spoken signs relate to the real world and the world of ideas. One of Eco's theories is that modern art, especially in the forms of music, poetry and fiction, often expresses deliberately uncertain messages. This allows the reader or listener to take an active part in deciding the meaning of a work of art.

At age 48, Eco published his first novel, *The Name of the Rose*. It is an extraordinary story of crime detection in a medieval Italian monastery, featuring a detective who is an English Franciscan monk. The book, however, is far more than a straightforward thriller. It is a scholarly quest for all kinds of "truth" and a brilliant illustration of semiotics in action. Since then, he has written two more successful novels: *Foucault's Pendulum*, also a bestseller, is another murder mystery; *The Island of the Day Before* is a story about an Italian castaway.

Publications

- *1962 The Open Work*
- *1965 The Bond Affair*
- *1976 A Theory of Semiotics*
- *1980 The Name of the Rose*
- *1986 Travels in Hyper Reality*
- *1988 Foucault's Pendulum*
- *1993 Misreadings*
- *1994 How to Travel with a Salmon and Other Essays*
- *1994 The Island of the Day Before*

EKWENSI, Cyprian

Nigerian novelist, short-story writer and children's author

Born Sep. 26, 1921

Cyprian Ekwensi, considered to be the father of the modern Nigerian novel, is also one of Africa's best short-story writers and most popular authors. His *People of the City* was one of the first modern African novels.

Ekwensi was born in northern Nigeria (West Africa), which was then a British colony. He was educated in Nigeria, where he studied forestry.

In his early 20s, finding himself alone a lot as a forestry officer, Ekwensi began to write short stories. After he had left forestry and was working as a teacher, he read his stories on a weekly radio show. When he traveled to England in 1951 to study pharmacy at London University, he composed his first novel, *People of the City*, during the two-week journey aboard ship. Written at a time when the fight for independence was growing in Nigeria, it is about the confusion of city life in a country seeking a new order. This book led to a short career in broadcasting until he became Nigeria's Director of Information in 1961.

Ekwensi writes in a popular style that appeals to the ordinary Nigerian. He has traveled all over Nigeria, making notes and recording his observations for use in his books. For this reason, he has been called a reporter of modern African life, in particular city life. *Jagua Nana,* his best work, tells of the troubles of newly independent Nigeria through the story of a city prostitute. *Iska* predicted the Biafran War – a civil war that divided Nigeria in the late 1960s. Since the war, Ekwensi has continued to write (he has had over 40 books published). He also manages a publishing company and runs a pharmacy.

Publications

- 1947 *Ikolo the Wrestler and Other Igbo Tales*
- 1954 *People of the City*
- 1961 *Jagua Nana*
- 1962 *Burning Grass*
- 1963 *Beautiful Feathers*
- 1966 *Iska*
- 1966 *Lokotown and Other Stories*
- 1980 *Divided We Stand*
- 1991 *Gone to Mecca*

ELIOT, George

English novelist and short-story writer

Born Nov. 22, 1819
Died Dec. 22, 1880
Age at death 61

George Eliot was the pen name of Mary Ann (or Marian) Evans. She is best known for her novels *Adam Bede*, *The Mill on the Floss*, *Silas Marner* and *Middlemarch*. Her reputation as one of the greatest English novelists continues to this day.

Eliot was born in Warwickshire in the Midlands at a time when the country was changing very rapidly in the new industrial age of steam engines, factories and railroads. She was educated at good schools. After her father died in 1849, she traveled around Europe before settling in London. There she worked as assistant editor on a magazine.

In 1854, she went to Germany with the writer George Henry Lewes. Although he was already married and could not get a divorce, she lived with him in London until his death 24 years later. Such a situation was very shocking in those days. Eliot was nearly 40 when her first short stories were published in a book later called *Scenes of Clerical Life*. She used the pen name George Eliot because in those days writing was considered to be a male profession.

Eliot's first full-length novel, *Adam Bede*, was published when she was 40. It is a tragic love story in which the model for the title character is Eliot's father. It was an instant success, and she became known as a leading writer. Two years later, *Silas Marner* was published. It is the well-known story of a miser saved from his lonely and selfish life by the love of a young girl. *Middlemarch*, generally considered to be her greatest novel, came out ten years later. Noted for their realism, Eliot's novels are about the lives of ordinary people and their everyday problems.

Publications

1858 Scenes of Clerical Life
1859 Adam Bede
1860 The Mill on the Floss
1861 Silas Marner
1863 Romola
1866 Felix Holt, the Radical
1868 The Spanish Gypsy
1871–72 Middlemarch
1876 Daniel Deronda

ELIOT, T.S.

American-British poet and critic

Born Sep. 26, 1888
Died Jan. 4, 1965
Age at death 76

T.S. Eliot is one of the most important figures in 20th-century literature. Works like his famous poem *The Waste Land* revolutionized the way poetry was written. He was awarded the Nobel Prize for Literature in 1948.

Thomas Stearns Eliot was born in St. Louis, the youngest of seven children. He studied at Harvard University, where he was recognized as a brilliant student and where he began work on his poem "The Love Song of J. Alfred Prufrock," one of his best-known works. After graduating, he continued his studies in Germany, France and at Oxford University.

When he was 27, Eliot moved to England for good. He worked in a bank and also began editing literary magazines. He quickly became a member of London's literary scene – after the publication of his first poetry collection, *Prufrock, and Other Observations*, he was introduced to members of the Bloomsbury Group. Later, he joined the publishing company Faber and Faber, where he worked for the rest of his life.

Eliot's most famous work is *The Waste Land*, written when he was 34. It is a long poem that caught the mood of despair and confusion felt by many in the years between the two World Wars, when everything in society seemed to be changing. The poem is a mix of references to modern life and great literature of the past, written in a style that combines slang with scholarly language. Although very difficult to understand, it remains one of the great works of 20th-century literature.

Publications

1917 Prufrock, and Other Observations
1919 Poems
1922 The Waste Land
1934 The Rock
1935 Murder in the Cathedral
1939 Old Possum's Book of Practical Cats
1943 Four Quartets
1949 The Cocktail Party

ELLISON, Harlan

American science fiction writer

Born May 27, 1934

Harlan Ellison is a controversial and outspoken writer best known for his science fiction short stories.

Ellison was born in Cleveland, Ohio, the youngest son of a dentist. The Ellisons were the only Jewish family in the neighborhood, and Harlan was often bullied by local children. After leaving university, he moved to New York with the idea of becoming a writer. He decided to find out about life on the streets of the city and spent time with young criminals in Brooklyn. He later wrote about this experience in *Memos from Purgatory*.

Ellison was then drafted into the army and on his release began to sell stories to science fiction and mystery magazines. *The Man with Nine Lives*, his first novel, was published when Ellison was 26. His work soon established him as one of the major science fiction writers of his generation. Of all his short stories, critics and fans single out "'Repent Harlequin!' Said the Ticktockman" as his best. It is one of the ten most reprinted stories in the English language. Ellison's science fiction stories are disturbing, violent and often offensive. Many are critical of the US government.

As well as stories, Ellison wrote newspaper columns, essays and film reviews for national newspapers. He became known for his controversial views and his political activities. In the 1960s, he was involved in the civil rights movement and opposed the Vietnam War. He is also a great self-publicist: one of his stunts is to write short stories in public while sitting in a shop window.

Publications

- *1960* *The Man with Nine Lives*
- *1961* *Memos from Purgatory*
- *1965* *Paingod and Other Delusions* (includes "'Repent Harlequin!' Said the Ticktockman")
- *1967* *I Have No Mouth and I Must Scream*
- *1969* *The Beast That Shouted Love at the Heart of the World*
- *1994* *Slippage*

ELLISON, Ralph Waldo

American novelist and essayist

Born Mar. 1, 1914
Died Apr. 16, 1994
Age at death 80

Ralph Waldo Ellison is best known for his novel *Invisible Man*. This study of racism and its effect on a person's identity became a classic of modern American literature.

Ellison was born in Oklahoma City. He won a state scholarship and was educated at what became Tuskegee University. A music major, he played the trumpet. Music was a big influence in Ellison's life. He was a friend of the blues singer Jimmy Rushing and knew members of Count Basie's band.

At age 22, Ellison went to New York City, where he met RICHARD WRIGHT, who encouraged him to become a writer. Writing reviews and short stories to begin with, he then embarked on what was to become his best-known work, *Invisible Man*. It was published when Ellison was 38, and it received the National Book Award for fiction. The book tells the story of a young Southern black man's search for identity in a world in which he is virtually "invisible" to white people. The novel was one of the first to describe the modern racial problems in the US from an African-American point of view.

The success of *Invisible Man* troubled Ellison. To a great extent it overshadowed his other achievements, which included awards and lectureships as well as other writing. His essay collections *Shadow and Act* and *Going to the Territory* commented on different aspects of American culture. He was also criticized by the African-American community for failing to be an outspoken leader of the civil rights movement. For many years he referred to his work on a second novel, but it remained unfinished when he died.

Publications

1952 *Invisible Man*
1964 *Shadow and Act*
1986 *Going to the Territory*

ELLROY, James

American crime writer

Born Mar. 4, 1948

James Ellroy's novels are known for their violent, vivid picture of Los Angeles from the 1940s to the present.

Ellroy was born in Los Angeles. His parents divorced when he was six, and he remained with his mother. However, when he was ten, she was brutally murdered, and the killer was never found. Ellroy then went to live with his father, a former Hollywood accountant who was then unemployed.

As a teenager and young man, Ellroy drifted into a life of petty crime and heavy drinking. He did various jobs, including working as a caddie in a golf club. He then sobered up and turned to writing. His first novel, *Brown's Requiem*, published when he was 33, is a story about private detectives and uses his experiences as a golf caddie. Three years later, he became a full-time writer.

Much of Ellroy's writing is dominated by the traumatic event of his mother's murder when he was a child. His books are very dark, full of horror and fear. Most of his stories are set in Los Angeles, a city he describes as corrupt and chaotic. Many of his characters – from politicians to gangsters – are violent, evil people gripped by twisted passions.

The publication of *The Black Dahlia* established 39-year-old Ellroy as a major crime writer. The book was the first of his L.A. Quartet, four novels that describe the city in the 1940s and '50s. Another novel, *American Tabloid*, concerns the assassination of President John F. Kennedy. In 1996, Ellroy wrote an autobiographical account of his search for his mother's killer, *My Dark Places*.

Publications

1981 *Brown's Requiem*
1982 *Clandestine*
1984 *Blood on the Moon*
1985 *Because the Night*
1987 *The Black Dahlia*
1988 *The Big Nowhere*
1990 *L.A. Confidential*
1992 *White Jazz*
1995 *American Tabloid*
1996 *My Dark Places*
1999 *Crime Wave*

ELYTIS, Odysseus

Greek poet and critic

Born Nov. 2, 1911
Died Mar. 18, 1996
Age at death 84

Odysseus Elytis was a Greek surrealist poet who was awarded the Nobel Prize for literature in 1979.

Born Odysseus Alepoudelis in Heraklion on the island of Crete, he was educated at Athens University, Greece, and at the Sorbonne in Paris. His parents came from the Greek island of Lesbos, home of the ancient Greek poet, Sappho. It is seldom that a poet, however distinguished, can live comfortably on earnings from writing, and Elytis worked as a literary and art critic and in broadcasting. He was also a talented painter.

Elytis's career started with the publication of his first book of poems, *Orientations*, when he was 25. In it he celebrates his love of Greece and his delight in the sun, the sea, and the air. At an early stage he was influenced by surrealism but, during World War II, he was involved in the fighting in Albania, and a new note of violence and sudden death became apparent in his work. His poem *A Heroic and Mournful Song for the Lost Second Lieutenant of the Albanian Campaign* has been described as one of the most moving to come out of the war.

Elytis's greatest achievement is the poetic cycle of prose and verse *The Axion Esti*. It took him 14 years to write and combines the biblical story of the creation with modern Greek history. This magnificent work compares humankind's suffering in the war with the suffering of Christ. This and other works led to the award of the Nobel Prize.

Publications

1936 Orientations
1945 A Heroic and Mournful Song for the Lost Second Lieutenant of the Albanian Campaign
1959 The Axion Esti
1960 Six and One Regrets for the Sky
1978 Maria the Cloud
1985 The Little Mariner

Published after he died

1997 Collected Poems

EMECHETA, Buchi

Nigerian novelist

Born Jul. 21, 1944

Buchi Emecheta is probably Africa's most widely read woman writer. She was born near Lagos, the capital of Nigeria in West Africa. Her parents died when she was young, and she was sent to a missionary school. She married at the age of 16 and moved to London, England, with her student husband two years later. It was in London that Emecheta began writing, while struggling to support her husband and five children and earn a sociology degree at London University. The marriage broke up in 1966.

The first novel Emecheta wrote, *The Bride Price*, was not published until she was 32, since her husband burned the original version. Set in Nigeria, it explores marriage customs through the story of Aku-nna, who marries an "unsuitable" man. *In the Ditch* and

Second-Class Citizen are based on Emecheta's experiences as a wife and as a lone mother in London. They describe the struggle of Adah to support her family and pursue a writing career in the face of racism, sexism and poverty. Like Emecheta herself, the heroine triumphs and becomes a success. In *The Joys of Motherhood*, her best-known novel, Emecheta draws on her experiences as a mother and on her time spent in British-ruled Nigeria. It mocks idealized concepts of motherhood by contrasting the life of Nnu Ego, who tries to be the perfect wife and mother, with that of Adaku, who rebels. Nnu Ego dies alone on a roadside, while Adaku lives happily in Lagos. It tells how women became burdened by both British rule – which changed the position of women for the worse – and the attitudes of men. Emecheta has since established her own publishing company in London.

Publications

1972 In the Ditch
1974 Second-Class Citizen
1976 The Bride Price
1977 The Slave Girl
1979 The Joys of Motherhood
1982 Destination Biafra
1982 Double Yoke
1983 The Rape of Shavi
1986 Head above Water
1989 The Family

EMERSON, Ralph Waldo

American essayist and poet

Born May 25, 1803
Died Apr. 27, 1882
Age at death 78

Ralph Waldo Emerson was an important 19th-century American poet and essayist. His ideas had a strong influence on the development of American culture.

Emerson, the son of a minister, was born and raised in Boston. Like his father, he attended Harvard and then entered the ministry. He was appointed pastor of the important Second Unitarian Church in Boston, but three years later, at the age of 29, he had a crisis of faith and left the church. That same year, Emerson visited England, where he became a close friend of the writer THOMAS CARLYLE.

Back in America, Emerson settled in Concord, Massachusetts, and began a successful career as a lecturer and essayist. His first book *Nature*, published when he was 33, summed up his ideas. He emphasized individualism and self-reliance and rejected traditional authority. He also believed that people should rely on their reason to learn what is right and should try to live a simple life in harmony with nature and with others.

Emerson became famous for his lectures. He encouraged American scholars to break free of European influences and create a new American culture. His first collection of essays, in which he explored his ideas more fully, was published when he was 38. They were widely read and further collections followed. At the age of 44, he published his first collection of poetry. Later, he became involved in the antislavery movement and worked for women's rights.

Publications

1836 Nature
1841 Essays
1844 Essays
1847 Poems
1850 Representative Men
1856 English Traits
1860 The Conduct of Life
1867 May Day and Other Pieces
1870 Society and Solitude
1893 Natural History of Intellect

ERASMUS

Dutch writer

Born Oct. 27,1469
Died Jul. 12,1536
Age at death 66

Erasmus was one of the most influential men of his time and a major figure in promoting the Renaissance in Europe.

Born in Rotterdam, Holland, Eramus was the son of a priest. At the age of 17, after both his parents died of the plague, he was sent to a monastery. By the time he became a priest six years later, however, he was already unhappy with monastic life. His problem was solved the following year when the Bishop of Cambrai appointed him as his secretary and even allowed him to study in France and England. Erasmus was a brilliant scholar and met several of the most scholarly men of the day.

When he was 40, Erasmus was appointed Professor of Divinity at Cambridge University. There he produced an edition of the New Testament and established an unmatched reputation for his studies of the Bible. He also wrote a witty satire called *The Colloquies,* which drew attention to the unworthy conduct of many of the clergy and became one of the most widely read books of its day.

In his early 50s, Erasmus moved to Switzerland to avoid the controversy then raging about the reform of the Church. He wanted peace and unity and hoped that change could come about through reading rather than violence. But he was pressured into taking a stand against the reformer Martin Luther, publishing a short work, *On Free Will*, explaining his position. In the end, Luther and his supporters won. Although still respected as a writer and humanist, Erasmus spent his remaining years isolated from the sweeping changes that followed.

Publications

1500 Proverbs or Adages
1503 Manual of a Christian Knight
1511 In Praise of Folly
1518 The Colloquies
1523 On Free Will

ERDRICH, Louise

American novelist and short-story writer

Born Jun. 7, 1954

Louise Erdrich is one of the best-known modern Native American novelists.

Erdrich was born in Little Falls, Minnesota, the oldest of seven children. Her mother is a Chippewa Indian, and her father is German American. Both parents taught at a boarding school run by the Bureau of Indian Affairs in North Dakota, where Erdrich was raised. The family was close, and Erdrich recalls her parents' stories about their community, which inspired the characters in her work.

At Dartmouth College, New Hampshire, Erdrich began to take writing seriously and to explore her Native American identity. After graduating, she worked at odd jobs, then received a Master's degree and returned to Dartmouth to teach. In 1981, she married writer

Michael Dorris, who had been her teacher at Dartmouth. Also part Native American, Dorris had three adopted children; together Erdrich and Dorris had another three children. They worked closely on a number of books, including *Crown of Columbus*, about the meaning for Native Americans and Europeans of Columbus's "discovery" of America.

Erdrich published *Jacklight*, a poetry collection at age 30. But it is for her novel *Love Medicine* that she has become internationally known. The novel weaves together stories of several Chippewa families who live on a North Dakota reservation. This and her next two novels, *The Beet Queen* and *Tracks*, tell the stories of several generations of these families and explore the pressures on modern Native American society and the struggle to preserve the traditions and values of old.

Publications

1984	*Jacklight*
1984	*Love Medicine*
1986	*The Beet Queen*
1988	*Tracks*
1991	*Crown of Columbus* (with Michael Dorris)
1991	*Baptism of Desire*
1994	*The Bingo Palace*
1995	*The Bluejay's Dance*
1996	*Grandmother Pigeon*
1997	*Tales of Burning Love*

ESQUIVEL, Laura

Mexican novelist and screenwriter

Born Sep. 30, 1950

Mexican novelist Laura Esquivel is best known for her first novel, *Like Water for Chocolate*, a tale about love, pain and the healing power of food written in the style known as magic realism.

Esquivel was born in Mexico and worked as a teacher for eight years. Her writing career began in her early 30s when, working in conjunction with her film-director husband, Alfonso Arau, she wrote the screenplay for the movie *Chido One.* The film was directed by Arau and was a success.

Inspired by her lifelong interest in cooking, Esquivel then wrote the novel *Like Water for Chocolate*. It was published when she was 39 and was a bestseller in Mexico before being translated into many languages and becoming a worldwide success. In 1993, Esquivel adapted her novel for the screen; the resulting movie became one of the most popular foreign films in the US.

The book is a strange and original blend of ingredients that includes cooking recipes, folklore, magic, sex and fables. The title is a Mexican saying that roughly translates as "excited" or "agitated." The story is about Tita, the youngest of three sisters, who is destined by tradition never to marry but to care for her strict mother. She expresses her sorrow through her cooking. Said to have been influenced by JORGE LUIS BORGES and GABRIEL GARCÍA MÁRQUEZ, *Like Water for Chocolate* has been described as showing "a deeply feminist-humanist sensitivity" and as portraying "the secrets of love and life as revealed by the kitchen."

Publications

1989	*Like Water for Chocolate*
1995	*An Appetite for Passion Cookbook*
1996	*The Law of Love*

EURIPIDES

Greek playwright

Born c. 485 BC
Died 406 BC
Age at death c. 79

Publications

431 BC Medea
c. 426 BC Andromache
c. 422 BC The Suppliants
415 BC The Trojan Women
c. 413 BC Electra
412 BC Helen
c. 410 BC The Phoenician Women
408 BC Orestes

Published after he died

c.405 BC The Bacchae

Euripides was one of the great playwrights of ancient Greece; he continued the development of tragic drama that had begun with AESCHYLUS and SOPHOCLES. The ancient Greek philosopher Aristotle called him the most tragic of the tragic poets.

Born in Athens into a fairly wealthy family, Euripides was well educated. He became friendly with Socrates and other leading philosophers of the day. Their influence made him one of the most thoughtful writers of the age. Great intellectual advances were being made in Athens during Euripides's life, and he embraced the new spirit of learning and inquiry that questioned the traditional beliefs of Athenian society.

Drama was an important part of ancient Greek society. Regular playwriting competitions were held, and the winners were highly regarded. Euripides first entered one of these competitions when he was 30, but he did not win first place until 14 years later.

Euripides's plays caused great controversy when they were first performed. He used characters and situations from mythology, just as other playwrights did, but shocked audiences by representing them as real people instead of symbolic heroes. He tried to show what it would be like for real people to find themselves in the extreme circumstances of the mythological stories that were so familiar. His best plays have a strong, passionate woman as the central character – an example is *Medea*.

Although Euripides wrote 92 plays, he won first prize only four times. After his death his reputation grew, and many of his plays have survived intact to this day because they were copied and read for centuries.

EVANS, Mari

American poet and playwright

Born Jul. 16, 1923

Mari Evans considers herself a political writer and believes that African-American authors like herself must use their talents to promote political change and to contribute to community affairs.

Evans was born and raised in Toledo, Ohio. Her father – "an oak of a man" whom Evans much admired – proudly saved her first published story, written when she was in the fourth grade. This act encouraged her to realize the power of the printed word.

The greatest influence on her as a writer, however, came from LANGSTON HUGHES, in whose poetry she saw reflected her own experience. Hughes later advised and inspired Evans as a poet, and she says he gave her confidence to view writing as a craft – as a profession, not a hobby.

After graduating from the University of Toledo, Evans worked as a journalist, then as an editor and in television. During this time she also wrote, but it wasn't until she was 45 that she published her first volume of poetry. The poems in *Where Is All the Music?* are mostly on personal themes such as love and loneliness. In her second, and perhaps most celebrated volume, *I Am a Black Woman*, Evans writes about more public and political concerns, such as children, black communities and the strength of African-American unity.

Evans has taught at universities and edited a critical evaluation of black women writers. She has also published several children's books and plays, including an adaptation, *River of My Song*, of Zora Neale Hurston's classic *Their Eyes Were Watching God*.

Publications

1968 Where Is All the Music?
1970 I Am a Black Woman
1973 Rap Stories
1974 I Look at Me!
1976 Singing Black
1977 River of My Song
1979 Whisper
1979 Jim Flying High
1980 Nightstar
1984 Black Women Writers 1950–80

FALKNER, John

English children's writer and poet

Born May 8, 1858
Died Jul. 22, 1932
Age at death 74

John Falkner wrote only three novels, but one of them, *Moonfleet*, became a children's classic.

Falkner was born in southwestern England, the son of a clergyman. He was educated at a private school and at Oxford University before getting a job as a tutor to the children of a wealthy businessman. Falkner so impressed his employer that he was offered a good job in his employer's firm, a successful weapons manufacturer.

Falkner was quickly promoted in the company and was soon traveling the world representing its interests to foreign governments. Despite his commitment to work, Falkner kept up his interest in books and learning. In whichever country or city he visited, he would always try to find time to study ancient manuscripts in libraries and museums.

When Falkner was 37, he published his first novel. *The Lost Stradivarius* is a ghost story set in Oxford and Italy. His most famous novel, *Moonfleet*, was published three years later. It is about the adventures of a teenage boy living in the 18th century who becomes involved with smugglers. Its fast-moving story, memorable characters and spooky atmosphere have made it a favorite of children's literature. After the publication of his third novel, *The Nebuly Coat*, a mystery story involving a timid architect, Falkner wrote a fourth, but sadly he lost the only copy of the manuscript on a train!

Falkner also wrote poetry, and a collection of his medieval-style verse was published after his death.

Publications

1895 The Lost Stradivarius
1898 Moonfleet
1903 The Nebuly Coat

Published after he died

1933 Poems

FARAH, Nuruddin

Somalian novelist, short-story writer and playwright

Born Nov. 24, 1945

Nuruddin Farah is Somalia's leading modern writer. He was born in the Italian Somalia colony, East Africa. The fourth son in a family of ten, Farah was educated at schools in Somalia and neighboring Ethiopia. He studied English as well as Italian. From 1966 to 1970, he lived in India, studying literature and philosophy at Panjab University in Chandigarh. While there he wrote *From a Crooked Rib*, the story of a Somalian girl's search for independence in a country where women have little control over their lives.

Farah returned to Somalia in 1970. A military coup had brought the dictator Muhammad Siad Barre to power. He ruled with no mercy, and the state police imprisoned people without trial and used torture. Farah spent four years teaching in Mogadishu, the capital. He witnessed the troubles there and was forced to leave Somalia when he criticized Siad Barre. Farah's novel *A Naked Needle* compares the state of Somalia at this time to a man eaten up with hate.

From 1974 to 1976, Farah lived in the south of England and studied at the universities of London and Essex. In his spare time, he wrote plays for the BBC and began writing short stories. In 1976, he moved to Rome, Italy, where he produced a set of three novels – *Sweet and Sour Milk*, *Sardines* and *Close Sesame* – about dictatorship. Much of Farah's work has been banned in Somalia.

Since 1979, Farah has lived and taught in Nigeria, West Africa. Continuing instability in Somalia has prevented him from returning home.

Publications

1970 From a Crooked Rib
1976 A Naked Needle
1979 Sweet and Sour Milk
1981 Sardines
1982 Close Sesame
1986 Maps
1990 Gifts

FARJEON, Eleanor

English children's writer, novelist and poet

Born Feb. 13, 1881
Died Jun. 5, 1965
Age at death 84

Eleanor Farjeon was one of the most outstanding children's writers of the 20th century.

Farjeon was born into an artistic household in London. Her father was a popular British novelist of the day, and her American mother was descended from a long line of actors. Their house was a meeting place for artists, writers, musicians and actors. Farjeon was taught at home by governesses and by her father, who encouraged all his children to read and write stories.

Farjeon wrote her first short story, "Kitty's Dream," when she was just six. She wrote stories for journals produced by her brothers, Bertie and Harry, and later wrote lyrics for Harry's music. It was not until Farjeon was 22, when her father's death threatened the family with poverty, that she seriously began trying to make a living from writing. Her first major success, *Martin Pippin in the Apple-Orchard*, did not come until 18 years later. A fantasy story for adults about a wandering minstrel trying to unite two lovers, it brought Farjeon fame for the first time.

Over the next 40 years she wrote many other works of fiction, including short stories for adults and children, poems for children, musical plays and novels. By the end of her life she had published over 80 works. *The Little Book-Room* is a collection of what she considered to be the best of her short stories. Over 300 poems for children appear in *The Children's Bells*, including "Morning Has Broken." In her writing for children Farjeon did a very difficult thing – she created new fairy tales without being sentimental or trying to lecture her readers.

Publications

1921 Martin Pippin in the Apple-Orchard
1928 Kaleidoscope
1934 The Children's Bells
1934 Jim at the Corner
1937 Martin Pippin in the Daisy-Field
1946 The Glass Slipper
1955 The Little Book-Room
1958 Then There Were Three

FARMER, Philip José

American science fiction writer

Born Jan. 26, 1918

Philip José Farmer is famous for his humorous, unconventional and sometimes shocking science fiction stories.

Farmer was born in North Terre Haute, Indiana, and grew up in Peoria, Illinois, where his father worked for the local power company. As a boy he devoured adventure stories about superheroes such as EDGAR RICE BURROUGHS's Tarzan. As a young man he enrolled in university, but lack of money forced him to take a job in a steel and wire company. He worked there for 11 years, attending night school until he finally gained a degree in English when he was 34.

During those years Farmer wrote many stories, all of which were rejected. Then, when he was 34, his story *The Lovers* was accepted by the magazine *Startling Stories*. It tells of a man sent to an alien planet to exterminate the inhabitants. However, he falls in love with an alien who looks human but turns out to be an insect. The story's publication caused a sensation, and its subject matter was widely copied by other writers.

Farmer's best novels are known as the Riverworld Series and feature good superhumans called "ethicals." A 19th-century explorer wakes up in a large tank to find that everyone who has ever lived in the history of the world is now stored on an alien planet; 12 people are chosen to be woken up, and in *To Your Scattered Bodies Go* they try to find the source of a river that is 10 million miles long.

Farmer has written many other novels and stories and received science fiction awards for his work.

Publications

1952 The Lovers
1957 The Green Odyssey
1960 Flesh
1965 Dare
1969 A Feast Unknown
1971 To Your Scattered Bodies Go
1977 The Dark Design
1981 The Magic Labyrinth
1983 Gods of Riverworld

FARQUHAR, George

Irish playwright

Born 1678
Died Apr. 29, 1707
Age at death c. 28

George Farquhar wrote some of the best comedies of manners in the English theater of the early 1700s.

Farquhar was a clergyman's son, born in Londonderry (now in Northern Ireland). At 16, he entered Trinity College, Dublin, but left to go on the stage. In one performance, he stabbed another player with a real sword he mistook for a blunt, prop sword. The accident made Farquhar give up acting, but an actor friend persuaded him to try comedy writing instead. The Drury Lane Theater in London produced his first play, *Love and a Bottle*, when he was 21. In the early 1700s, he wrote other popular plays, mostly about silly young men who reform after leading wild lives.

At 24, Farquhar became an army lieutenant and wrote no plays for a year or more. Then came his two last and best plays. His own army experience probably helped him write *The Recruiting Officer*. Set in an English country town, it shows the antics of an army captain who flirts with women to make their lovers enlist. In *The Beaux' Stratagem* two friends have farcical adventures in a country town as they try winning rich wives to restore fortunes they have frittered away.

Farquhar himself was often hard up. At 25, he married a woman, wrongly believing she was rich. He wrote *The Beaux' Stratagem* while suffering from the illness that killed him, and he died poor before learning about its success.

His finest plays are as witty as the Restoration Dramas of the late 1600s, but lively language and middle-class characters make Farquhar's seem more realistic.

Publications

1699 Love and a Bottle
1699 The Constant Couple
1701 Sir Harry Wildair
1702 The Inconstant
1702 The Twin-Rivals
1706 The Recruiting Officer
1707 The Beaux' Stratagem

FARRELL, James T.

American novelist, short-story writer and critic

Born Feb. 27, 1904
Died Aug. 22, 1979
Age at death 75

James T. Farrell is famous as the author of the Studs Lonigan trilogy, which is now considered a classic of American literature.

Farrell was born into a working-class Irish-American family on Chicago's South Side. His parents had many children, but because they were too poor to look after them all, he was sent to live with his grandparents. Farrell went to local Catholic schools, and by working at a petrol station, he paid his way through the University of Chicago. After graduating, he spent a year in France. Returning to America in 1932, he finally settled in New York City, where he lived for much of the rest of his life.

Young Lonigan, Farrell's first novel, was published when he was 28. In this and the other two novels in the series, *The Young*

Manhood of Studs Lonigan and *Judgment Day*, he follows the fortunes of the title character as he grows up in the tough world of 1920s and '30s Chicago. Much of Farrell's work was based on his own experiences of growing up as a poor Irish American. Using a realistic and natural style, Farrell tried to write about how social forces affect people's lives. He attacked the "American Dream," which says that anyone can do well if they work hard.

Farrell's books fell out of favor in the 1940s, and he found it difficult to make ends meet again. He continued to write, however, producing over 50 books, including a series of five novels about Danny O'Neill in the same style as the Studs Lonigan books.

Publications

1932 Young Lonigan
1934 The Young Manhood of Studs Lonigan
1935 Judgment Day
1936 A World I Never Made
1938 No Star Is Lost
1940 Father and Son
1943 My Days of Angel
1946 Bernard Clare
1953 The Face of Time

FAULKNER, William

American novelist and short-story writer

Born Sep. 25, 1897
Died Jul. 6, 1962
Age at death 64

William Faulkner is one of the most important American novelists of the 20th century. He was awarded the Nobel Prize for Literature in 1949.

In his stories about Yoknapatawpha County, an imaginary rural Southern community based on his own hometown, he used various writing styles to explore family relationships and to depict racial tensions in the South. For Faulkner, writing when the South was still legally racially segregated, slavery was a great crime that lay like a curse on the land and its people.

When Faulkner was five, his family settled in Oxford, Mississippi, the town where he lived for most of his life. He liked to ride horses and read, but found school boring and left aged 17. He tried to join the army but was rejected because he was too short. When World War I was raging in Europe, Faulkner went to Canada and trained as a fighter pilot, but the war ended before he saw any action. After the war, he studied at the University of Mississippi for a short time and, aged 27, published his first book *The Marble Faun*, a collection of poems. For a while he lived in New Orleans, where he met SHERWOOD ANDERSON and completed his first novel, *Soldier's Pay.* In 1929, he married and took a nightshift job in a power plant. Here he wrote *As I Lay Dying* in six weeks, writing from midnight until four each morning.

In novels such as *The Sound and the Fury* and *As I Lay Dying*, Faulkner employed the new stream-of-consciousness technique to illustrate the conflicting feelings of his characters. He was awarded the Pulitzer Prize in 1955 for his novel *A Fable,* and another in 1963 for *The Reivers*.

Publications

1929 The Sound and the Fury
1930 As I Lay Dying
1931 Sanctuary
1932 Light in August
1936 Absalom, Absalom!
1940 The Hamlet
1948 Intruder in the Dust
1954 A Fable
1957 The Town
1962 The Reivers

FAUSET, Jessie Redmon

American novelist and short-story writer

Born Apr. 27, 1884
Died Apr. 30 1961
Age at death 77

Jessie Redmon Fauset was a writer of the Harlem Renaissance who argued that creating African-American characters whose lives were like those of whites in literature was the best way to bring about an end to racism. She was criticized, however, for her unrealistic portrayal of middle-class black people.

Fauset was born near Philadelphia, Pennsylvania, where her father, a minister, campaigned for racial justice. Her mother died when Fauset was still a child. Although poor, the family valued education, and the young Fauset achieved honors in secondary school. She applied to university at Bryn Mawr but was rejected because she was black; instead, she went to Cornell University, from which she graduated in 1905.

Fauset wanted to teach, but once again racism was a barrier. Denied a job in the segregated Philadelphia state schools, she moved to Washington, DC, to teach. There she took a Master's degree in French.

At age 35, Fauset was offered a job as literary editor of *Crisis*, the journal of the National Association for the Advancement of Colored People (NAACP). She had been contributing stories to *Crisis* for several years, and its general editor, W.E.B. Du Bois, recognized her talents as a writer and educator.

It was not until 1924, when Fauset was 40, that she published her first novel. *There Is Confusion* describes the racial barriers to advancement that limited the choices of many young African Americans, in particular women. Her third novel, *The Chinaberry Tree*, criticizes social rules while exploring the attitudes of African Americans toward interracial relationships.

Publications

1924 There Is Confusion
1929 Plum Bun
1931 The Chinaberry Tree
1933 Comedy, American Style

FERBER, Edna

American novelist, short-story writer and playwright

Born Aug. 15, 1885
Died Apr. 17, 1968
Age at death 82

The name Edna Ferber may not be widely known these days, but *Show Boat*, the title of her 1926 blockbuster novel, is still familiar. The book, which was turned into a popular musical, brought her so much money she called it her "oil well."

Born in Kalamazoo, Michigan, into a Jewish family, Ferber got a job on a local newspaper when she finished secondary school, shocking readers who thought reporting was "men's work." Her first novel, *Dawn O'Hara*, published when she was 26, was based on her experiences as a journalist and was fairly successful. But Ferber's career really took off with the publication of the "Emma McChesney" stories, which appeared between 1913 and 1915. Like most of her later writing, the stories feature a strong female character who has to work for a living to support her family.

In 1925, Ferber won the Pulitzer Prize for *So Big*, her novel about the struggles of a young, widowed farm woman. That same year she began work on her most famous book, *Show Boat*, a story based on the floating theaters that traveled the Mississippi River during the late 19th century. The theme of fulfillment through hard work again features in this book.

Ferber wrote more than 20 novels. Most of them were bestsellers, and all are celebrations of American culture. She concentrated on the lives of ordinary people, setting them against a backdrop of different regions. But Ferber upset the citizens of Texas with her unflattering portrait of their state in her 1952 book *Giant*, later made into a movie starring James Dean and Elizabeth Taylor.

Publications

1911 Dawn O'Hara
1915 Emma McChesney and Co.
1917 Fanny Herself
1924 So Big
1926 Show Boat
1930 Cimarron
1939 A Peculiar Treasure
1941 Saratoga Trunk
1952 Giant
1958 Ice Palace

FERLINGHETTI, Lawrence

American poet

Born Mar. 24, 1920

Lawrence Ferlinghetti believes that poetry should move the reader to action. A member of the beat generation of writers in the 1950s, Ferlinghetti was also responsible for publishing many of the beat writers, including Jack Kerouac and Allen Ginsberg.

Born in Yonkers, New York, Ferlinghetti lived in France with a relative until he was four because his father had died before he was born, and his mother was in a mental hospital. He returned to the US and graduated from the University of North Carolina. During World War II, he served as a US naval officer before doing graduate study in New York and Paris.

Ferlinghetti was a major force in the beat generation. Like the 19th-century poet Walt Whitman, Ferlinghetti believed that poetry needed to speak to the masses of people ignored by writers of earlier generations. Using experimental techniques and language that shocked, he created poems celebrating the beat ideals of freedom, love and sex. His most famous volume, *A Coney Island of the Mind*, was published by his own company, City Lights, when he was 38 and became one of the all-time poetry bestsellers. In *Christ Climbed Down,* the beat ideals were reflected in his criticism of the materialistic society he perceived in modern America. His political criticism also appeared in later works, such as *Who Are We Now?* and *Wild Dreams of a New Beginning*.

Ferlinghetti published the work of young poets and sold their books through City Lights Bookstore in San Francisco: the first paperback bookstore in the world.

Publications

1955 Pictures of the Gone World
1958 A Coney Island of the Mind
1961 Starting from San Francisco
1965 Christ Climbed Down
1967 An Eye on the World
1976 Who Are We Now?
1988 Wild Dreams of a New Beginning
1993 These Are My Rivers: New & Selected Poems 1955–93

FIELD, Eugene

American children's writer and journalist

Born Sep. 2, 1850
Died Nov. 4, 1895
Age at death 45

Eugene Field, a popular humorist and newspaper columnist, is best remembered today as a writer of children's poetry.

Born in St. Louis, Missouri, Field was the son of the lawyer who represented Dred Scott, the fugitive slave whose suit for freedom eventually led to an historic Supreme Court decision. Field's mother died when he was six, and he was raised by a cousin in Amherst, Massachusetts. He loved pranks and had a bold sense of humor that made him very popular. Field attended several universities, but, because he was more interested in having fun than studying, he failed to graduate.

From 1873 to 1883, Field worked as a journalist in Missouri and Colorado, where he gained a reputation as a humorist. When he was 33, he moved to Chicago to write a newspaper column called "Sharps and Flats" for the *Chicago Morning News*. He was one of the first newspaper humorists to have a national reputation, and his column strongly influenced the development of humorous newspaper writing in America. Field's satirical essays formed the basis for his numerous books. His favorite subjects were book collecting and Chicago's culture and politics.

While working at the newspaper, Field wrote many poems for and about children that earned him the title "Poet of Childhood." His works include some of the most famous children's poems in American literature, among them "Wynken, Blynken, and Nod," a whimsical lullaby that first appeared in *With Trumpet and Drum*, and "Little Boy Blue," a sentimental poem about a boy who dies in his sleep.

Publications

1888	"Little Boy Blue"
1889	*A Little Book of Western Verse*
1891	*Echoes from the Sabine Farm*
1892	*With Trumpet and Drum*
1892	*Second Book of Verse*
1893	*The Holy Cross and Other Tales*
1894	*Love-Songs of Childhood*

Published after he died

1897	*Lullaby Land*
1900	*Sharps and Flats*

FIELDING, Henry

English novelist and playwright

Born Apr. 22, 1707
Died Oct. 8, 1754
Age at death 47

Henry Fielding was a popular author in his lifetime, best known for his plays. Today, he is remembered as one of the first English novelists.

Fielding was born into a wealthy and respected family in southwest England. He was educated at Eton College, a famous private school, where he learned to love ancient Greek and Roman literature and decided to become a playwright.

After a year spent at a university in Holland, he returned to England and settled in London, where his literary career began to take off. When he was 23, four of his plays were produced in one year. One of them was *Tom Thumb*, which was to become his most famous and popular drama.

For several years Fielding's life was happy and prosperous, and his plays continued to be successful. Like many dramatists of the time, Fielding wrote plays with strong political messages. Unfortunately, those he wrote attacking the government of the day were so effective at influencing public opinion that in 1737 a law was passed giving the authorities control over the theaters, and Fielding's career as a playwright was ended.

Fielding qualified as a lawyer but did not make a success of this new profession, so he turned to writing for magazines to support himself. When another English writer, SAMUEL RICHARDSON, published his first novel, *Pamela*, Fielding was inspired to write a comic version called *Shamela*. Encouraged by its success, he wrote several more comic novels, including *Tom Jones*, which is regarded as one of the finest early English novels.

Publications

1728	*Love in Several Masques*
1730	*The Author's Farce*
1730	*Tom Thumb*
1730	*Rape upon Rape*
1732	*The Modern Husband*
1736	*Pasquin*
1741	*Shamela*
1742	*Joseph Andrews*
1749	*Tom Jones*
1751	*Amelia*

FINE, Anne

English young-adults' writer

Born Dec. 7, 1947

Anne Fine has written many books for young adults that explore family relationships in a sensitive but comic way. Her most successful book so far is *Alias Madame Doubtfire*, which was made into a very popular 1993 film, *Mrs. Doubtfire*, starring Robin Williams. She has also written books for adults.

Fine was born Anne Laker in the English city of Leicester. Her father was a scientist and her mother a housewife. She grew up in the countryside with her four sisters. From an early age she was interested in how the members of a family get on or don't get on.

After graduating from the University of Warwick in 1968, she got married almost immediately to a professor and became known as Anne Fine. Over the next decade she held a variety of jobs and raised two daughters. She worked as a teacher at a girls' school for two years, for a charity concerned with famine relief, taught at a Scottish jail, and worked as a volunteer for the human rights organization Amnesty International for several years.

When Fine was 31, her first book, *The Summer-House Loon*, came out. It follows one day in the life of Ione Muffet, who is trying to match her father's secretary with a shy student. Fine managed to make her book mischievous and funny yet wise and understanding. It was very well received. In a similar fashion, *Alias Madame Doubtfire*, published when Fine was 40, deals with divorce. The father, an actor, disguises himself as the ultra-efficient Madame Doubtfire and lands a job as housekeeper for his ex-wife – all so that he can spend more time with his children.

Publications

1978	*The Summer-House Loon*
1979	*The Other, Darker Ned*
1980	*The Stone Menagerie*
1983	*The Granny Project*
1987	*Alias Madame Doubtfire*
1987	*The Killjoy*
1989	*Bill's New Frock*
1991	*The Worst Child I Ever Had*
1993	*Flower Babies*
1996	*Tulip Touch*
1998	*Telling Liddy*

FITZGERALD, F. Scott

American novelist and short-story writer

Born Sep. 24, 1896
Died Dec. 21, 1940
Age at death 44

F. Scott Fitzgerald is best known for his novel *The Great Gatsby*, which captured the spirit of the decade known as the Roaring Twenties.

Francis Scott Fitzgerald was born in St. Paul, Minnesota. He went to Princeton University but left to join the army and then spent most of his time writing his first novel, *This Side of Paradise*. Published when he was 24, it was a great success. That year Fitzgerald married the beautiful Zelda Sayre and began a life that was like one of those described in his books. This was the start of the Jazz Age, a period after World War I when America was booming and people tried to live as if life were one long party. It was an age of new freedoms, new music, short skirts, new dances and wild, unconventional behavior.

The Fitzgeralds, with other carefree, rich Americans, often went to France for the pleasures of Paris and the French Riviera. Fitzgerald wrote other novels and many short stories to pay for his glamorous, expensive lifestyle. Zelda – herself a writer and painter – became mentally ill, and Fitzgerald began to drink, increasing their need for money. He described his struggles to save Zelda and to overcome his own problems in *The Crack-Up*.

After the economic crash in America in 1929, when banks and businesses went bankrupt, Fitzgerald lost his popularity, and sales of his book slumped. Zelda was now in a mental hospital, and Fitzgerald got a job as a screenwriter in Hollywood, living there, almost unknown, until he died at the age of 44.

Publications

1920 This Side of Paradise
1921 Flappers and Philosophers
1922 Tales of the Jazz Age
1922 The Beautiful and Damned
1925 The Great Gatsby
1926 All the Sad Young Men
1934 Tender Is the Night

Published after he died

1941 The Last Tycoon (unfinished)
1945 The Crack-Up

FLAUBERT, Gustave

French novelist

Born Dec. 12, 1821
Died May 8, 1880
Age at death 58

Gustave Flaubert is regarded, especially by other writers, as one of the greatest and most influential novelists.

Flaubert was born near Paris, France, into a highly respectable middle-class family of doctors. He rebelled against his background and was expelled from school, completing his education privately in Paris. It was there that he showed signs of considerable talent as a writer. After Flaubert developed a nervous condition that could have been epilepsy and failed his law exams, his father bought him a house at Croisset, on the River Seine between Paris and Rouen, where he settled down to write. At age 25, he was joined by his mother and his niece, following the death of his father and his sister.

Flaubert was a perfectionist as a writer, and he would work on the drafts of novels again and again until he got them right. His first and best-known novel is *Madame Bovary*, which was published when he was 36. The main character, Emma Bovary, is a bored and unhappy housewife living in a small French town. She has an affair and is betrayed. The novel ends with her suicide. The book shocked French society with its realistic depiction of middle-class life and was the subject of a court case. It made Flaubert famous, and he mixed with other great writers of the period, including GEORGE SAND. Another fine novel *A Sentimental Education*, published when Flaubert was 48, is the account of a young man's affair with an older woman. The book was not such a hit. Flaubert became very bitter about life and died before he could complete his last novel.

Publications

1857 Madame Bovary
1862 Salammbô
1869 A Sentimental Education
1874 The Temptation of Saint Antoine
1877 Three Tales

Published after he died

1881 Bouvard and Pécuchet

FLAVIN, Martin

American novelist and playwright

Born Nov. 2, 1883
Died Dec. 27, 1967
Age at death 84

Martin Flavin is best known for his novel *Journey in the Dark*, for which he won a Pulitzer Prize in 1944.

Flavin was born in San Francisco but grew up in Chicago. He studied at the University of Chicago for two years. While working nights for the *Chicago Tribune*, he began writing short stories. However, seeing no financial future in writing, he concentrated on a business career for 12 years, rising through the ranks of workers in a wallpaper company.

As a successful businessman in his mid-30s, Flavin began to write again. This time he wrote plays. He was 40 when *Children of the Moon*, a play about madness, became the first of his works to be staged on Broadway. It ran for more than 100 performances and later appeared in London and in Dublin, where it became the first American play to be translated into Gaelic. After this success, Flavin retired from his positions as president of one wallpaper firm and vice-president of another. He continued to write plays for the next ten years; some were successful and others were not. In the 1930s, five of his plays were made into movies.

At the age of 57 Flavin turned to writing novels. By far the most successful was *Journey in the Dark*. Partly based on his own life, it traces a young boy's rise from childhood poverty to millionaire businessman. While praised for its honest descriptions of the trials of growing up, it has also been criticized for its lack of power and depth. Flavin went on to write four more books, including two travel books.

Publications

1923 Children of the Moon
1929 The Criminal Code
1929 Broken Dishes
1937 Around the Corner
1940 Mr. Littlejohn
1941 Corporal Cat
1943 Journey in the Dark
1947 The Enchanted
1957 Cameron Hill
1962 Red Poppies and White Marble

FLEMING, Ian

English novelist

Born May 28, 1908
Died Aug. 12, 1964
Age at death 56

Ian Fleming is famous as the creator of secret agent James Bond, whose adventures feature in a series of novels and movies. He also wrote the children's book *Chitty-Chitty-Bang-Bang*, a modern fairy tale that has been made into a classic movie.

Fleming was born in Canterbury, southeast England. His father died in World War I. Fleming was educated at Eton. He was not an outstanding student but was a good athlete. After a short time at Sandhurst Military Academy, he left to study languages in Europe.

Fleming's first job, as the Moscow correspondent for Reuters news agency, brought him into contact with the world of espionage. On his return to London, he worked as a merchant banker and stockbroker. During World War II, he served as a senior naval intelligence officer.

It was during the war that Fleming decided to take up writing. The first Bond novel, *Casino Royale*, came out nine years after the war ended – when Fleming was 46.

The 12 novels and 7 short stories featuring James Bond, British secret service agent 007, were immensely popular. When the first Bond movie, *Dr. No*, came out in 1963, Fleming's fame spread worldwide. The books combine plots involving international spy rings, exotic locations, beautiful women and the dynamic character of Bond to produce exciting, escapist stories. Although some aspects of them, particularly Bond's attitude to women, now seem dated, they have remained popular long after Fleming's death.

Publications

1954	*Casino Royale*
1954	*Live and Let Die*
1955	*Moonraker*
1956	*Diamonds are Forever*
1957	*From Russia, with Love*
1958	*Dr. No*
1959	*Goldfinger*
1961	*Thunderball*
1964	*You Only Live Twice*
1964	*Chitty-Chitty-Bang-Bang*

FLETCHER, John Gould

American poet

Born Jan. 3, 1886
Died May 20, 1950
Age at death 64

John Gould Fletcher began his literary career as an experimental poet involved in finding new ways of writing verse. Later, he wrote poetry in more traditional forms and, in 1939, he won the Pulitzer Prize for his *Selected Poems*.

Fletcher was born into a wealthy family in Little Rock, Arkansas. He was educated at private schools and studied French, German, English and Latin literature at Harvard. He quit in his final year, however, and never completed his degree.

Like many American writers of the time, Fletcher went to Europe and lived in Paris and London, then the leading cultural centers of the West. In Paris he met the American poet EZRA POUND and became inspired by his new ideas about writing.

Fletcher began to write poetry that combined ideas from painting and music. His first important collection, *Irradiations, Sand and Spray*, came out when he was 29. After falling out with Pound, Fletcher became a close friend of another American poet, Amy Lowell, who was to become famous for her efforts to modernize American poetry.

At age 47, Fletcher returned to America for good. He became involved with a group of poets who criticized the values of a modern world obsessed with machinery and moneymaking. In *The Epic of Arkansas* and *South Star* he expressed the hope that a return to a simple farming life could heal humanity and prevent future wars. His Pulitzer Prize-winning collection of poems from throughout his career came out when he was 52. Fletcher drowned himself in Little Rock 12 years later.

Publications

1915	Irradiations, Sand and Spray
1916	Goblins and Pagodas
1922	Preludes and Symphonies
1925	Parables
1926	Branches of Adam
1935	XXIV Elegies
1936	The Epic of Arkansas
1938	Selected Poems
1941	South Star
1946	The Burning Mountain

FO, Dario

Italian playwright

Born Mar. 24, 1926

Dario Fo is an Italian writer known for his satirical plays. He was awarded the Nobel Prize for Literature in 1997.

Fo was born in a small town near the northern Italian city of Milan. His father worked on the railroad and was also a part-time actor. During World War II, Fo helped his father, who was a member of the resistance against German forces in Italy, to take escaped Allied soldiers across the border to Switzerland. All his life, Fo has opposed fascism and unjust governments.

After studying at art school and training to become an architect, Fo turned to playwriting to express his political views. He was already a committed communist, and the plays he wrote used satire to attack the values of capitalist society. The Italian government often censored his work, and he has been jailed, beaten up, and threatened with assassination because of his outspoken views.

Between 1959 and 1968 Fo ran a theater company in Milan with his actress wife Franca Rame. Fo – a great comic actor – often performed in his plays alongside his wife. In 1962, he presented a satirical television show, which was closed down after just seven weeks on air.

Fo's most famous plays are *Accidental Death of an Anarchist* – about the police murder of a political activist – and *Can't Pay? Won't Pay!* – about citizens refusing to pay taxes to a corrupt government. Written in the 1970s, they were very popular in Italy and have since been translated into many languages and performed in many countries.

Publications

1969	Mistero Buffo
1970	Accidental Death of an Anarchist
1970	Can't Pay? Won't Pay!
1977	All Home Bed and Church
1983	The Open Couple
1984	Elizabeth, Almost by Chance a Woman
1989	The Pope and the Witch
1991	Johan Padan and the Discovery of America

FOOTE, Horton

American playwright and screenwriter

Born Mar. 14, 1916

Horton Foote has written many successful plays and screenplays about contemporary life in America.

Foote was born in the small town of Wharton, Texas. After graduating from the local secondary school, he followed a theatrical career. Between the ages of 17 and 23, he studied at the Pasadena Playhouse in California and at the Tamara Daykarhanova Theater School in New York. He acted in many Broadway plays after graduating and then switched to managing a production company in Washington DC, where he also taught playwriting.

Foote's first professional play, *Texas Town*, was produced when he was 26. Five years later, he began writing plays for television. With great realism he explored American society through the lives of characters in small towns, often the imaginary small town of Harrison, Texas, which is similar to Wharton – Foote's own home town.

Foote's first screenplay, *Storm Fear*, was made into a film when he was 40. It was not a success. However, his second screenplay, for HARPER LEE's novel *To Kill a Mockingbird*, won an Academy Award. This led to several of Foote's own plays being made into movies, though none was as popular as *To Kill a Mockingbird*. His screenplay of WILLIAM FAULKNER's *Tomorrow* has, however, been called one of the best film versions of a Faulkner work.

In 1995, Foote's play *The Young Man from Atlanta* won a Pulitzer Prize. Set in 1950s Houston, Texas, it is about an elderly couple faced with several crises that rock their faith in God, in their country and in themselves.

Publications

1942 Texas Town
1944 Only the Heart
1952 The Chase
1953 The Trip to Bountiful
1954 The Traveling Lady
1956 Storm Fear
1962 To Kill a Mockingbird
1973 Tomorrow
1983 Tender Mercies
1995 The Young Man from Atlanta

FORD, Ford Madox

English novelist, critic and poet

Born Dec. 17, 1873
Died Jun. 26, 1939
Age at death 65

Ford Madox Ford was a leading figure, both as a literary critic and a writer, in the development of modern English literature in the early 20th century.

Ford was born Ford Madox Hueffer in London. In 1919, he officially changed his name. Both his grandfather and his mother were artists, and his father was an author and a music critic for *The Times* newspaper, so Ford grew up in a creative environment. His first published works were fairy stories – *The Brown Owl*, for example, which came out when he was just 18.

When he was 25, Ford met the great novelist JOSEPH CONRAD. They became good friends and together wrote several novels, including *The Inheritors* and *Romance*, but after 1901 their relationship faltered. Ford later wrote a personal memoir in which he recalled the years of their friendship.

In all, Ford published over 80 books of fiction and nonfiction as well as some poetry. A frequent theme is the conflict between traditional civilized values and those of modern industrial life. His greatest novels are *The Good Soldier* and the multivolume *Parade's End*. *The Good Soldier* is about a man who discovers his wife has committed suicide over an affair. It is written in a style that tries to recreate real thoughts – a technique that was groundbreaking at the time. In *Parade's End,* the honest Tietjens escapes from his wife's lies and betrayals by serving in World War I. The novels illustrate the changes in English society brought by the war. Ford also founded two influential literary journals, the *English Review* (in 1908) and the *Transatlantic Review* (in 1924).

Publications

1891 The Brown Owl
1892 The Feather
1901 The Inheritors (with Joseph Conrad)
1903 Romance (with Joseph Conrad)
1906–08 The Fifth Queen (3 vols.)
1915 The Good Soldier
1924 Joseph Conrad
1924–28 Parade's End (4 vols.)
1936 Collected Poems
1937 Portraits from Life

FORESTER, C.S.

English novelist and journalist

Born Aug. 27, 1899
Died Apr. 2, 1966
Age at death 66

C.S. Forester is remembered as the author of a popular series of sea tales about the adventures of Horatio Hornblower. One of his other novels, *The African Queen*, was made into a film in 1951.

Cecil Scott Forester studied medicine but abandoned a medical career in favor of writing. He worked for *The Times* as a correspondent in the Spanish Civil War and in the German occupation of Czechoslovakia of 1938.

Payment Deferred, Forester's first novel, came out when he was 27. It was an instant success. He followed it with a number of novels on varying themes, including another popular psychological thriller, *Plain Murder*.

At age 38, Forester produced the first of his tales of the Napoleonic Wars featuring the fictional British naval hero, Horatio Hornblower. *The Happy Return* was inspired by three volumes of a naval journal published between 1790 and 1820 that Forester had bought secondhand. The Hornblower saga eventually grew to 12 volumes, tracing the hero's career from midshipman to admiral. The endearing character of Hornblower – forever calm in tricky situations and a romantic at heart – appealed to a wide audience.

Forester also wrote naval histories and travel books. During a visit to the Bering Sea to research a book on the US Navy during World War II, Forester suffered a disease of the arteries that left him permanently crippled. In later life he moved to California, where the climate suited him better.

Publications

1926 Payment Deferred
1929 Brown on Resolution
1930 Plain Murder
1933 The Gun
1935 The African Queen
1937 The Happy Return
1939 Captain Hornblower, R.N.
1964 Hornblower Companion

Published after he died

1967 Hornblower During the Crisis

FORSTER, E.M.

English novelist, short-story writer and essayist

Born Jan. 1, 1879
Died Jun. 7, 1970
Age at death 91

E.M. Forster's five famous novels, all written before he was 45, put him among the leading English writers of the 20th century.

Edward Morgan Forster was born in London. His father, an architect, died the year after Forster was born. He loathed his school days but was happy at Cambridge University, where he became a member of The Apostles, an intellectual debating society. Soon he became linked to the Bloomsbury Group, whose members were writers and artists in revolt against old-fashioned ideas.

As a young man, Forster traveled in Italy and Greece with his mother and later paid two long visits to India. His first novel, *Where Angels Fear to Tread*, was published when he was 26. It was soon followed by *The Longest Journey*, *A Room with a View* and *Howard's End*, all published before he was 32. *Howard's End* deals with the clash between two families, one interested in art and literature, the other only in business. It established his reputation as an important novelist.

A Passage to India, Forster's best-known novel, came out in 1924 when he was 45. It is a vivid account of India under British rule, the clash between Hindus and Muslims, and the problems of the Hindu caste system of class divisions.

Forster also wrote essays, short stories and literary criticism, and lectured on literature at Cambridge University, where he finally settled as a teacher.

Forster's early novel *Maurice* has a homosexual theme. Written in 1913, it was not published until after Forster's death.

Publications

1905 Where Angels Fear to Tread
1907 The Longest Journey
1908 A Room with a View
1910 Howard's End
1911 The Celestial Omnibus
1922 Alexandria: A History and a Guide
1924 A Passage to India
1936 Abinger Harvest

Published after he died

1971 Maurice

FORSYTH, Frederick

English thriller writer and journalist

Born Aug. 25, 1938

Frederick Forsyth is best known for his nail-biting political thrillers, most of which have been made into movies.

Forsyth was born in Ashford, Kent, and educated at Tonbridge School, where he excelled in foreign languages. Later, he served in the Royal Air Force before becoming a journalist and a radio and television reporter.

Forsyth's work as a journalist taught him how to dig out technical facts that few people know. By working these into his fictional stories he helped make them believable and intriguing. Forsyth was 33 when he published his first and most famous novel. *The Day of the Jackal* tells how a ruthless hit man known as the "Jackal" plans to kill President Charles de Gaulle of France and so alter the direction of world history. Forsyth's careful research into such subjects as snipers' rifles and bullets and how to obtain a false passport made his tale read more like a real-life news story than a novel. Also, he cleverly built up suspense as the Jackal dodges French security forces to get within shooting distance of his victim.

Further patient research went into Forsyth's more recent political thrillers, including *The Odessa File*, *The Fourth Protocol* and *The Fist of God* – the tale of a terrible secret threat to the Allied forces planning to free Kuwait from its Iraqi invaders during the Gulf War.

Besides novels, Forsyth has written short stories and *The Biafra Story*, about the Biafran War – the bloody Nigerian civil war of 1967–70 when eastern Nigeria tried forming a breakaway nation, Biafra.

Publications

1969 The Biafra Story
1971 The Day of the Jackal
1972 The Odessa File
1974 The Dogs of War
1975 The Shepherd
1980 The Devil's Alternative
1984 The Fourth Protocol
1989 The Negotiator
1991 The Deceiver
1993 The Fist of God

FOWLES, John

English novelist

Born Mar. 31, 1926

John Fowles is best known for his dramatic and complex novels.

Born in a suburb of London, Fowles served in the Royal Marines before studying French at Oxford University. After graduation he taught first in France and then on the island of Spetsai, Greece. The beauty of the island had a strong effect on him, and he began to write poetry. He also met Elizabeth Whitton, whom he married three years later.

Returning to London to teach, Fowles worked on many projects, including a novel (*The Magus*) that he continued to revise for 13 years. His first published novel, *The Collector*, came out when he was 37 and was an immediate success. He became a full-time writer, moving with his wife and stepdaughter to a cliff-top house by the sea in a southern town called Lyme Regis. It was here that Fowles set his most famous novel, *The French Lieutenant's Woman*. Published when he was 43, it was an outstanding critical and popular success and was made into an equally successful film in 1981, with a screenplay written by Harold Pinter. Part love story, part historical novel, the book is a portrait of a young woman who, as a social outcast, has freed herself from the constraints of strict Victorian society. It is an experimental novel with a complex plot and three different endings.

The themes of freedom and of self-determination – making one's own choices – are key in Fowles's work. In his novels and short stories his main characters are on a quest for an ideal, struggling to come to terms with the reality of existence.

Publications

1963 The Collector
1964 The Aristos
1966 The Magus
1969 The French Lieutenant's Woman
1973 Poems
1974 The Ebony Tower
1977 Daniel Martin
1978 Islands
1982 Mantissa
1985 A Maggot
1998 Wormholes: Essays and Occasional Writings

FRANCE, Anatole

French novelist, poet and essayist

Born Apr. 16, 1844
Died Oct. 12, 1924
Age at death 80

Anatole France was one of the major figures of French literature in the late 19th and early 20th centuries. He was awarded the Nobel Prize for Literature in 1921.

Born in Paris, the son of a bookseller, France loved books and reading from an early age. His real name was Jacques Anatole François Thibault. He took the name under which he wrote from his father's shop, the Librairie (Bookshop) de France.

In his 20s and 30s, France wrote verse and articles for newspapers and magazines on literary subjects. He also worked as a librarian. In his 40s, he wrote influential essays on books and writers for the newspaper *Le Temps*.

France's first novel, *The Crime of Sylvestre Bonnard*, was published when he was 37. Like his other works, it looks back to the 18th century as a golden age. It was praised for its elegant prose, irony, and sympathetic portrayal of characters – features that would become characteristic of France's best work.

During the 1890s and early 1900s, France wrote novels with political themes. As a humanist he attacked the shortcomings of contemporary society and the Church, and argued for social reforms. The fourth volume of *A Contemporary Tale* deals with the Dreyfus affair. France, with other writers such as the novelist ÉMILE ZOLA, had supported Captain Dreyfus, a Jewish army officer wrongly convicted of treason.

Later France wrote on wider themes. *Penguin Island* is a fanciful, satirical description of the way society has evolved, and *The Gods Are Athirst* is set during the most frightening years of the French Revolution.

Publications

1872 Golden Verses
1881 The Crime of Sylvestre Bonnard
1885 My Friend's Book
1889 Balthasar
1890 Thaïs
1897–1901 A Contemporary Tale (4 vols.)
1908 Penguin Island
1912 The Gods Are Athirst
1914 The Revolt of the Angels

FRANCIS, Dick

English crime writer

Born Oct. 31, 1920

Dick Francis is one of the most popular crime writers working today. Many of his books are set in the exciting world of horse racing, but he has also written about the worlds of the movies, of computers and of air travel.

Francis was brought up in the south of England. The son of a jockey, he spent much of his early life riding horses at the stables where his father worked. As a young man he joined the Royal Air Force and fought in World War II as a pilot. After the war he became a champion steeplechase jockey, racing horses owned by the British royal family. Following several falls and injuries Francis decided to stop racing and write about it instead. He became racing correspondent for the *Sunday Express* and soon began to write fiction as well.

Dead Cert, Francis's first novel, like his other early books, is set in the world of racing. Settings for later works are more varied. His stories are fast paced and full of action and intrigue. But Francis is also a serious writer: his central characters are always complex, and he tries to show what motivates them. The stories also reflect something of real life: although the villains always lose in the end, there are few neat happy endings. In many cases, the heroes are left with problems and difficulties as a result of their decisions to do the right thing. The backgrounds to the novels are carefully researched, which helps to make the stories realistic.

Francis's books have been translated into over 30 languages, and after 30 years of writing he is still a bestselling author.

Publications

1962 Dead Cert
1965 For Kicks
1967 Blood Sport
1970 Rat Race
1973 Slay Ride
1975 High Stakes
1979 Whip Hand
1987 Hot Money
1990 Longshot
1995 Come to Grief
1996 To the Hilt
1997 10-lb Penalty
1998 Field of 13

FRANK, Anne

German writer

Born Jun. 12, 1929
Died Mar. 1945
Age at death 15

Anne Frank was a young Jewish girl who died during World War II. She was a victim of the Holocaust; like millions of other Jews, she was killed by German Nazis who were trying to exterminate the Jewish race. Anne Frank is remembered today because she wrote a diary about her experiences. Her voice has come to represent the voices of millions of children who were lost in this terrible time.

Anne Frank was born in Germany four years before Adolf Hitler, the leader of the Nazi Party, came to power. Like many other Jewish families, the Franks were terrified by threats made by the Nazis, and they left Germany to live in Amsterdam, Netherlands.

Hitler's ambition did not end with power in Germany; he wanted to rule the world. In 1939, World War II began and German soldiers marched across Europe. By 1941, Amsterdam was under Hitler's control, and the Frank family was in danger again. Hitler ordered his armies to begin the total extermination of all Jews.

Anne Frank and her family went into hiding in July 1942. They spent the next two years locked in a secret attic, unable ever to go outside and in constant terror of being found by the Nazi secret police. Anne began to write a diary about her life in hiding. She kept writing diligently until the last entry, on August 1, 1944. Three days later Nazi police burst in. The family was split up. Anne and her sister were sent to Bergen-Belsen concentration camp, where they both died of typhoid. Anne was 15 years old. After the war, Anne's father, the only member of the family to have survived, published her diary for the world to read.

Published after she died

1947 The House Behind (translated and published in English as *Anne Frank: The Diary of a Young Girl*)
1959 The Works of Anne Frank
1962 Tales from the House Behind

FREELING, Nicolas

English crime writer

Born Mar. 3, 1927

Nicolas Freeling is best known for his stories about Dutch detective Piet van der Valk.

Freeling was born in London, and educated in England, Ireland and France. He did his military service in the Royal Air Force and then worked as a cook in hotels and restaurants throughout Europe. His experience of living and working in many different countries gives his writing a strong continental European flavor.

Freeling's first novel, *Love in Amsterdam*, was published when he was 35, and it set the tone for his future stories. Freeling describes the Dutch city in detail, giving the reader a vivid sense of its atmosphere. In later novels he writes about other cities with equal skill.

Love in Amsterdam also introduced Freeling's main character, Inspector Van der Valk, a man who is caring and decent but also streetwise and wary about human behavior. In a later series of novels, Freeling introduced a French detective, Henri Castang, who has a similar personality.

Freeling's Van der Valk novels were very successful and became the basis for a popular TV series in Britain. However, Freeling then shocked his fans by killing off Inspector Van der Valk and using the detective's widow, Arlette, as the main character.

Freeling's work has often been compared to that of GEORGES SIMENON. In recent years, Freeling's novels have taken a different direction. They have become less action based and more concerned with conveying general ideas about the nature of justice, morality and the human condition.

Publications

1962 Love in Amsterdam
1963 Because of the Cats
1966 The King of the Rainy Country
1969 Tsing-Boum
1971 A Long Silence
1974 Dressing of Diamond
1979 The Widow
1989 Sand Castles
1994 You Who Know
1996 A Dwarf Kingdom

FRENEAU, Philip

American poet and essayist

Born Jan. 2, 1752
Died Dec. 18, 1832
Age at death 80

Philip Freneau is remembered as the poet of the American Revolution.

Freneau was born in New York City and educated at Princeton University, from which he graduated at the age of 19. At age 20, he and a classmate published a long patriotic poem, *The Rising Glory of America*. He then worked as a schoolteacher and studied to become a minister. This ambition was interrupted by the outbreak of the American Revolution, and Freneau wrote a series of blistering satirical poems against the British. These revolutionary war satires made him famous. They were also highly effective in stirring up hatred against the British.

Freneau didn't fight in the revolution until he was 26 and had spent two years in the Caribbean, working as a planter's secretary. He then joined the New Jersey militia and, as a privateer, sailed to the West Indies. He was captured by the British in 1780 and briefly made a prisoner of war. When released, he wrote the bitter poem *The British Prison-Ship*, published when he was 29.

Freneau seems to have acquired a taste for the sea, however, and continued as a sea captain. But he did not neglect his writing and became a regular contributor to *Freeman's Journal*, published in Philadelphia. In 1791, he became editor of Philadelphia's *National Gazette*, a strongly republican paper. His later poems – graceful romantic lyrics – had some influence on 19th-century writing.

Freneau continued to alternate sea voyages with newspaper work until he retired to his farm in New Jersey, where he spent the rest of his life.

Publications

1772	*The Rising Glory of America*
1772	*The American Village*
1779	*The House of Night*
1781	*The British Prison-Ship*
1786	*The Wild Honeysuckle*
1786	*Poems*
1788	*Miscellaneous Works*
1794	*The Village Merchant*

FRIEDAN, Betty

American writer and journalist

Born Feb. 4, 1921

The writer and feminist Betty Friedan is best known for her groundbreaking book *The Feminine Mystique*.

Friedan was born Elizabeth Naomi Goldstein in Peoria, Illinois. In 1942, she graduated in psychology from Smith College. She did graduate research at Berkeley but left to work on a newspaper. In 1947, she married Carl Friedan (they divorced in 1969). They had three children, and during her second pregnancy Friedan was fired from her job for asking for maternity leave. She became a freelance writer for women's magazines but was annoyed that her references to women's careers were edited out of her articles.

Friedan found that middle-class women like herself were dissatisfied, and she began to write *The Feminine Mystique*. In it, Friedan analyzed the situation of American women and argued that they had been trapped through the media and social pressure into thinking that women could find happiness only in marriage and motherhood. She claimed that domesticity is not enough; women need work. *The Feminine Mystique* was published when Friedan was 42 and was an instant bestseller. Millions of women identified with the message, and the book has been described as marking the start of the modern women's movement.

In 1966, Friedan cofounded the National Organization for Women (NOW) and through the early 1970s campaigned actively for equal rights. Her recent book, *The Fountain of Age*, deals with the rights of older people.

Publications

1963	*The Feminine Mystique*
1976	*It Changed My Life: Writings on the Women's Movement*
1981	*The Second Stage*
1993	*The Fountain of Age*

FROST, Robert

American poet

Born Mar. 26, 1874
Died Jan. 29, 1963
Age at death 88

The American writer Robert Frost is one of the finest of rural New England's 20th-century pastoral poets.

Frost's family moved from San Francisco to Massachusetts when he was 11, following his father's death. He completed his education in New England, attending both Dartmouth College and Harvard University without graduating. Over the next ten years, he held a number of jobs while running a farm. In 1895, he married a former schoolmate, with whom he had four children. Frost sold the farm in 1912 and took his family to England, devoting himself entirely to poetry. His first book of verse, *A Boy's Will*, was published when he was 39. It was followed a year later by *North of Boston*.

While in England, Frost was greatly influenced by the nature poems of English poets such as RUPERT BROOKE. Frost shared the same interest in natural themes, but his work showed a more down-to-earth appreciation of nature. He wrote about a natural world that is full of hardship and difficulty but which is mastered by ordinary practically-minded people who are greatly aware of their environment.

Returning to the United States in 1915, Frost settled on a farm in New Hampshire and continued writing, supplementing his income with teaching and lecturing. His adaptation of blank verse styles to the rhythms and everyday vocabulary of New England won him four Pulitzer Prizes between 1924 (for his collection *New Hampshire*) and 1943 (for *A Witness Tree*). Frost also composed a poem, "The Gift Outright," for the inauguration of President John F. Kennedy after his election in 1960.

Publications

1913	*A Boy's Will*
1914	*North of Boston*
1923	*New Hampshire*
1928	*West-Running Brook*
1930	*Collected Poems*
1936	*A Further Range*
1942	*A Witness Tree*
1947	*A Masque of Mercy*
1947	*Steeple Bush*
1962	*In the Clearing*

FRY, Christopher

English playwright and screenwriter

Born Dec. 18, 1907

Christopher Fry was recognized as a major figure in British drama with the production of his play *The Lady's Not for Burning*.

Fry was born in Bristol. He became a schoolmaster for five years, then served for three years as a founding director of a theater company that produced *Youth and the Peregrines*, a play he had written as a schoolboy.

Fry's serious professional career began with *The Boy with a Cart*, first produced when he was 31; like all his later plays, it was written in verse. In its first London performance 12 years later, a young Richard Burton starred as Saint Cuthman, the play's central character.

It was, however, the London production of *The Lady's Not for*

Burning that brought Fry lasting fame at age 41. The main characters in the play are a young soldier who appears to be so disillusioned with life that he seeks death and a young woman – on the verge of being arrested for witchcraft – who loves life and is determined not to die. What begins as a simple story turns into a plot full of cunning, wit and mystery.

Fry made a lasting impression on English theater with his elegant use of words in verse form to explore the truth of human nature. In addition to writing plays, composing music and successfully adapting foreign-language plays, he has written several major film scripts as well as television and radio plays for the BBC's famous Children's Hour programs.

Publications

1934	*Youth and the Peregrines*
1938	*The Boy with a Cart*
1946	*A Phoenix Too Frequent*
1948	*The Lady's Not for Burning*
1948	*The Firstborn*
1950	*Venus Observed*
1954	*The Dark Is Light Enough*
1970	*A Yard of Sun*
1986	*One Thing More, or Caedmon Construed*

FUENTES, Carlos

Mexican writer

Born Nov. 11, 1928

Carlos Fuentes is one of Mexico's greatest novelists. In 1987, he received the MIGUEL DE CERVANTES Award, one of the highest honors for a writer in the Spanish language.

Fuentes was born in Mexico City, and his upbringing was privileged. His father was a diplomat who traveled all over the world, so in his youth Fuentes lived in South America, North America and in Europe. He attended school in Washington, DC, and in Chile, and he studied law at the National University of Mexico. He was a member of the Mexican delegation to the International Labor Organization from 1950 to 1952.

In the years following World War II, Fuentes began to reject his family background. He joined the Communist Party and worked as a journalist for most of the 1950s. However, when he was 30, he went back to a job with the Mexican civil service.

Fuentes then began to concentrate on his writing, and his early works were mostly short stories. In the same year, he published his first novel, *Where the Air Is Clear*. Written in an experimental style never seen before in his country's literature, it tells of people and events in Mexico City since the revolution of 1910. Fuentes's intense interest in the history of Mexico combined with his unusual use of flashbacks create an interesting but complicated way of telling a story. These new techniques and his constant use of themes from Spanish and Mexican history are repeated in his other books, notably his most important novel, *The Death of Artemio Cruz*, which brought him international acclaim.

Publications

1958	*Where the Air Is Clear*
1962	*The Death of Artemio Cruz*
1967	*A Change of Skin*
1969	*The New Latin American Novel*
1975	*Terra Nostra*
1980	*Distant Relations*
1985	*The Old Gringo*
1989	*Constancia and Other Stories for Virgins*

FUGARD, Athol

South African playwright

Born Jun. 11, 1932

Athol Fugard is the best-known white African dramatist writing today and one of the leading playwrights and directors in the world. He is known for his fierce criticism of racial injustices in South Africa.

Fugard was born in the South African city of Middleburg. His parents were wealthy, and he grew up in a household with black servants. When Fugard was still a teenager, the South African government introduced laws that separated the white and black populations of the country at the expense of the black majority. This was the system known as apartheid. It caused great hardship and suffering for the black people of South Africa. Fugard recognized that it was wrong.

After studying at university but failing to take a degree, Fugard became a merchant seaman. He returned to South Africa after two years at sea, married an actress, and became interested in theater. His first play, *No-Good Friday*, was performed privately in South Africa when he was 26.

Almost all of Fugard's plays are set in South Africa and are about the injustices of apartheid. His play *The Blood Knot* was censored by the then white minority government because it criticized apartheid. The play had to be performed secretly because Fugard illegally used both black and white actors in his production.

Many of Fugard's plays were first performed outside South Africa because of their critical message. They have been very popular in the United States and Europe, where they encouraged international demands for change in South Africa.

Publications

1958 No-Good Friday
1961 The Blood Knot
1968 Boesman and Lena
1972 Sizwe Banzi Is Dead
1972 The Island
1982 "Master Harold"... and the Boys
1984 The Road to Mecca
1987 A Place with the Pigs
1995 Valley Song

FULLER, Charles

American playwright

Born Mar. 5, 1939

Charles Fuller is an African-American playwright best known for the realistic way he deals with human relationships, particularly between different races. He was awarded the Pulitzer Prize in 1982 for his drama *A Soldier's Play*, which was later filmed.

Fuller, the son of a printer, was born in Philadelphia, Pennsylvania. His interest in writing began when his father asked him to help check some proofs for errors. He went to a Roman Catholic secondary school and Villanova University before spending four years in the army as a laboratory technician in Japan and Korea. When he returned to civilian life, he attended LaSalle University in 1965-68. He began to write short, simple plays for the Afro-American Theater of Philadelphia, which he helped found.

Fuller's first major play, produced when he was 30, was *The Village: A Party*. It is about a community of interracial couples who live in harmony until their black leader falls in love with a black woman, thus threatening the preferred racial mix. National recognition came to Fuller with *The Brownsville Raid*, produced when he was 37. Based on a true incident in 1906, it tells the story of an entire black regiment in the US Army that was dishonorably discharged because none of the 167 soldiers would admit to being guilty of starting a riot in the town of Brownsville, Texas. The whole regiment was later cleared of all charges.

A Soldier's Play was Fuller's most successful play. Again, it has an army setting and concerns the murder of an unpopular black sergeant.

Publications

1969 The Village: A Party
1974 The Candidate
1974 In the Deepest Part of Sleep
1974 First Love
1976 The Brownsville Raid
1978 Sparrow in Flight
1980 Zooman and the Sign
1981 A Soldier's Play
1988 We
1990 Jonquil

FULLER, Margaret

American writer

Born May 23, 1810
Died Jul. 19, 1850
Age at death 40

Margaret Fuller was one of the great American thinkers of the 19th century. She was an early feminist who argued for women's rights.

Fuller was born in Cambridgeport, Massachusetts, and from an early age she was taught Latin and Greek by her lawyer father. Her parents believed that women should be educated and self-reliant – an uncommon attitude at the time.

When Fuller was 25, her father died, and she became a teacher to help support the family. About the same time she met the poet Ralph Waldo Emerson and joined the Boston-based group known as Transcendentalists – a group of writers and philosophers who believed in an ideal spiritual world that could be reached through experience and natural insight. For several years she edited *The Dial*, the group's magazine. An essay she wrote for *The Dial* was later expanded into *Woman in the Nineteenth Century*, her influential book arguing for women's rights, which was published when she was 35.

After getting a job on the *New York Tribune*, Fuller became the first female professional journalist and, eventually, the first female foreign correspondent. The *Tribune* sent her to Europe, where she became active in the Italian liberation movement. She also met the Marquis d'Ossoli; they had a child and later married. In 1850, they set sail for America, but their ship hit a sandbar outside New York, and all three were drowned.

Fuller's memoirs, edited by Emerson, were published after her death. Lost in the shipwreck was her manuscript of a book on the Italian revolution.

Publications

1844 Summer on the Lakes
1845 Woman in the Nineteenth Century
1846 Papers on Literature and Art

Published after she died

1852 Memoirs of Margaret Fuller Ossoli
1856 At Home and Abroad
1858 Life Without and Life Within
1903 Love Letters of Margaret Fuller

GAINES, Ernest J.

American novelist and short-story writer

Born Jan. 15, 1933

Ernest J(ames) Gaines's best-known novel is *The Autobiography of Miss Jane Pittman*, in which a 100-year-old woman recounts the history of rural Louisiana African Americans from slavery to the civil rights movement of the 1960s.

Gaines was born in marshland and lake country near Oscar, Louisiana. Until he was 15, he worked as a laborer on a local plantation. After finishing junior college in California, he received a degree from San Francisco State University and was awarded a fellowship to study creative writing at Stanford University, also in California.

Although Gaines never moved back to his birthplace, all his stories are set there – in an imaginary place called Bayonne, Louisiana. The subject of his fiction is the conflict between the world of the old, traditional South and the forces of change that began with the American Civil War and continued into the civil rights era. His first two novels, *Catherine Carmier* – published when he was 31 – and *Of Love and Dust*, are basically love stories; each features a love affair doomed by the racial prejudices of others. It was, however, the fictional autobiography of a black slave named Jane Pittman that brought him fame. Pittman's harsh life, her refusal to be beaten, and her ability to endure hardship make hers one of the most moving narrative voices in American literature.

Gaines has been compared with other writers, like MARK TWAIN and WILLIAM FAULKNER, who also set their stories in a particular region in the South. Like them, he creates characters who are "alive" and with whom his readers can identify.

Publications

1964 Catherine Carmier
1967 Of Love and Dust
1968 Bloodline
1971 The Autobiography of Miss Jane Pittman
1971 A Long Day in November
1978 In My Fathers House
1983 A Gathering of Old Men
1993 A Lesson before Dying

GALE, Zona

American novelist and playwright

Born Aug. 26, 1874
Died Dec. 27, 1938
Age at death 64

Zona Gale won a Pulitzer Prize in 1921 for her play *Miss Lulu Bett*, based on her novel of the same name.

Born in Portage, Wisconsin, Gale had a happy upbringing as the only child of loving parents. She graduated from the University of Wisconsin in 1895 and led a successful career as a journalist. By age 27, she was a reporter on the *New York World*. In New York City, she published her first short story when she was 29. A year later she moved back to Portage and began writing full time. Gale lived there for the rest of her life, marrying a local man when she was 54.

Much of Gale's work is set in small-town America. Her earliest fiction is sentimental and gives an ideal view of small-town life. Later, the series of books set in the imaginary place called *Friendship*

Village shows a growing awareness of the negative side of village life.

In her 40s, Gale began to write about her social and political concerns. She was an early supporter of movements that were trying to bring the vote to women, to improve social conditions, and to promote racial equality. Although many scorned Gale's ideas, her expression of these views improved her fiction. Her novel *Miss Lulu Bett*, published when she was 46, was praised for its realistic depiction of the life of a woman trapped in her job as a servant. *Faint Perfume*, perhaps her best work, is the story of another woman mistreated by life.

During the final period of Gale's writing career her works were influenced by her growing religious beliefs.

Publications

1906 Romance Island
1908 Friendship Village
1909 Friendship Village Love Stories
1915 Heart's Kindred
1918 Birth
1920 Miss Lulu Bett
1923 Faint Perfume
1925 Mr. Pitt
1930 Bridal Pond
1932 Evening Clothes

GALLANT, Mavis

Canadian short-story writer, novelist and playwright

Born Aug. 11, 1922

Mavis Gallant is one of Canada's leading short-story writers.

Gallant was born in Montreal, Canada, to English-speaking parents. As a child, however, she was sent to a French-speaking school and has since been able to speak both French and English perfectly. Her father died when she was young, and she spent the rest of her schooling being moved from place to place. At age 18, she returned to Montreal and soon began work as a reporter for the *Montreal Standard*. At 28, she decided she wanted to be a full-time writer, left Canada, and traveled around Europe for many years before settling in Paris in the 1960s. She has lived in Paris ever since.

With the publication of the short story "Madeline's Birthday" in the famous *New Yorker* magazine when she was 29, Gallant began a long relationship with the magazine. Most of her stories were published there, earning her enough money to write full time. In Canada her work was not published until the 1970s. However, *Home Truths*, her prizewinning collection of stories about Canada, eventually guaranteed her fame at home.

Gallant's stories have a dreamlike quality and can be confusing like a dream, but can also be very funny. As in real life, the reader has to search for meaning. She often explores the relationship between individuals and history; in the short novel *The Pegnitz Junction,* Germans give their views of World War II. She has also written a play, *What Is to Be Done?*, and two novels, *Green Water, Green Sky* and *A Fairly Good Time*.

Publications

1951 "Madeline's Birthday"
1953 "The Other Paris"
1959 Green Water, Green Sky
1970 A Fairly Good Time
1973 The Pegnitz Junction
1979 From the Fifteenth District
1981 Home Truths
1983 What Is to Be Done?
1985 Overhead in a Balloon
1989 In Transit

GALLICO, Paul

American novelist and short-story writer

Born Jul. 26, 1897
Died Jul. 15, 1976
Age at death 78

Paul Gallico wrote over 40 books and hundreds of short stories. He is best known for his short novel *The Snow Goose* and for *The Poseidon Adventure*, which was the first "disaster" novel.

The son of immigrant parents from Italy, Gallico was educated in New York City. To pay his way through Columbia College, he worked at many jobs, including translator, gym instructor and dock laborer. He graduated at age 24, after taking time out to serve as a navy gunner in World War I. After university, he went to work at the *New York Daily News* as sports editor and columnist for more than a decade. During this time he took part in sports of all kinds and started the Golden Gloves tournament for amateur boxers.

When he was 39, Gallico retired from full-time work but continued to write on a freelance basis. His books and stories were very popular because many of his heroes and heroines are strong, determined people who succeed in spite of overwhelming odds against them. *The Snow Goose*, set in World War II, is about a hunchback's love for a beautiful girl and the mysterious snow goose that flies over his boat as he helps British soldiers escape from Dunkirk. *The Poseidon Adventure*, which was made into a film, was the first of the "disaster" genre of books and films – and perhaps the most inventive. It tells of the capsize and sinking of a great cruise ship and the passengers' struggles to survive.

At age 53, Gallico settled in Europe, where he wrote one book a year for the rest of his life. He prided himself on being a professional writer and entertainer – in other words, a storyteller.

Publications

1939 The Adventures of Hiram Holiday
1941 The Snow Goose
1947 The Lonely
1953 The Foolish Immortals
1958 Mrs. 'Arris Goes to Paris
1963 Love, Let Me Not Hunger
1969 The Poseidon Adventure
1971 The Zoo Gang
1972 Honorable Cat

GALSWORTHY, John

English novelist, playwright and poet

Born Aug. 14, 1867
Died Jan. 31, 1933
Age at death 65

John Galsworthy was an English writer who became famous for his series of novels about the fortunes of the Forsyte family, known as *The Forsyte Saga*. He was awarded the Nobel Prize for Literature in 1932.

Born into a wealthy family, Galsworthy received an expensive education. He became a lawyer, but during a round-the-world voyage to gain experience of sea law, he met and became friendly with the great novelist, JOSEPH CONRAD. This experience convinced him to give up law and become a writer instead.

Galsworthy's first book, a collection of short stories called *From the Four Winds*, came out when he was 30. It was published under the pen name John Sinjohn. In 1905, after a ten-year affair, he married Ada, the wife of his first cousin. She became the inspiration for many of Galsworthy's leading female characters.

The Forsytes, the fictional upper-class English family that was to become Galsworthy's best-known creation, first appeared in an early short story. The first of *The Forsyte Saga* novels, *The Man of Property*, came out when he was 39 and was later included in *The Forsyte Saga* trilogy. In this and other volumes in the series, Galsworthy examined the way that the wealthy English upper-class and its position in society was changing as the Victorian era came to an end and the 20th century began.

In his books, Galsworthy did not hesitate to criticize the injustices he saw in society. He also wrote a series of plays that deal directly with the unequal division of wealth and the unfair treatment of poor people by the legal system. His first play appeared in the same year that he began writing *The Forsyte Saga*.

Publications

1901 Man of Devon
1904 The Island Pharisees
1906 The Silver Box
1909 Strife
1910 Justice
1920 The Skin Game
1922 The Forsyte Saga (3 vols.)
1929 A Modern Comedy (3 vols.)
1931–32 End of the Chapter (3 vols.)

Published after he died

1934 Collected Poems

GARCÍA LORCA, Federico

Spanish poet and playwright

Born Jun. 5, 1898
Died Aug. 19, 1936
Age at death 38

Federico García Lorca was a great Spanish playwright and poet. He is known as the "poet of blood" because of the violence in his plays and his own tragic death.

García Lorca was born near the Spanish city of Granada into a wealthy family. He attended college in Madrid but took little interest in his studies and decided to become a writer. Through recitals of his poetry he became well known even before the publication of his *Book of Poems* when he was 23. Many of his poems were strongly influenced by Spanish gypsy songs and the rhythms of flamenco music. *Gypsy Ballads* became his best-known collection.

García Lorca's plays use the same powerful imagery and language as his poetry. His most successful dramas were written after a year spent in New York in 1929. Plays such as the tragedies *Blood Wedding* and *The House of Bernarda Alba* are good examples of his fascination with the conflict between human instincts and the restrictions forced on people by society. García Lorca tried to express emotions and comment on modern society by using strange and unexpected images and ideas in his writing.

In 1936, the Spanish Civil War began. Although García Lorca had no real involvement in politics, the right-wing forces that seized control in the south of Spain saw him as an enemy and a friend of communism. García Lorca hid from the soldiers but was soon found and arrested. On August 19 at age 38, he was executed by a firing squad and buried in a grave that he had been forced to dig for himself.

Publications

1921 Book of Poems
1928 Gypsy Ballads
1933 Blood Wedding
1934 Yerma
1935 Lament for the Death of a Bullfighter
1935 Doña Rosita the Spinster

Published after he died

1945 The House of Bernarda Alba

GARCÍA MÁRQUEZ, Gabriel

Colombian novelist and short-story writer

Born Mar. 6, 1928

Publications

- *1955 Leafstorm and Other Stories*
- *1958 No One Writes to the Colonel*
- *1967 One Hundred Years of Solitude*
- *1975 The Autumn of the Patriarch*
- *1979 In Evil Hour*
- *1981 Chronicle of a Death Foretold*
- *1985 Love in the Time of Cholera*
- *1989 The General in His Labyrinth*
- *1995 Of Love and Other Demons*

Gabriel García Márquez is one of South America's most respected and famous writers; he was awarded the Nobel Prize for Literature in 1982.

García Márquez was born in Aracataca, a small town in Colombia. His childhood home and large, extended family became the inspiration for much of his later work. After studying law in college, García Márquez became a newspaper journalist and began to publish stories and articles in various periodicals. His work as a journalist took him to Europe and to other South American countries, where he witnessed the oppression and violence suffered by people living under dictatorships. His own country, Colombia, also suffered from political violence.

At age 27, García Márquez published his first book, *Leafstorm and Other Stories*. Macondo, the fictional Colombian town that is the setting for the title story, later became the setting for his most famous book, *One Hundred Years of Solitude.* García Márquez wrote it during a stay in Mexico several years later, and it was published when he was 39. The story follows the fortunes of the Buendía family and the town in which they live from the earliest days of European settlement to the present. It is an allegory of the history of Colombia.

One Hundred Years of Solitude became internationally famous. García Márquez's style of writing mixed politics and everyday life in a setting that was full of larger-than-life characters, sex, violence and magical events. His work is a good example of magic realism.

GARDNER, Erle Stanley

American crime writer

Born Jul. 17, 1889
Died Mar. 11, 1970
Age at death 80

Publications

- *1933 The Case of the Velvet Claws*
- *1933 The Case of the Sulky Girl*
- *1934 The Case of the Curious Bride*

Erle Stanley Gardner is known all over the world as the creator of the brilliant American lawyer-detective, Perry Mason.

Gardner was born in Malden, Massachusetts, the son of a mining engineer. The family moved from town to town as his father searched for work, and Gardner's education was disrupted. He managed to finish secondary school, however, and after a period as a professional boxer he decided to study law. When he was only 22, he began to practice as a defense lawyer and quickly became successful, often using unusual methods to win his cases.

In his early 30s, Gardner began to write short stories based on his courtroom experiences, and many of these were published in detective magazines. But it was his creation of Perry Mason that was the turning point in his writing career. Perry Mason appeared for the first time in *The Case of the Velvet Claws*, which Gardner wrote in only three days when he was 44.

A total of 82 novels followed over the years, all written to the same formula: each story features a different court case for the super-sleuth Perry Mason, who, with a little help from his loyal secretary Della Street and his faithful assistant Paul Drake, astonishes the courtroom with a dramatic, last-minute revelation of the truth that proves his client's innocence.

Gardner eventually gave up the law to concentrate on writing, but he retained an interest in justice and founded The Court of Last Resort, an organization that took on apparently hopeless cases.

1938 The Case of the Shoplifter's Shoe
1941 The Case of the Haunted Husband
1944 The Case of the Black-Eyed Blonde
1948 The Case of the Lonely Heiress
1952 The Case of the Grinning Gorilla
1962 The Case of the Ice-Cold Hands
1968 The Case of the Careless Cupid

GARDNER, John

American novelist, short-story writer and poet

Born Jul. 21, 1933
Died Sep. 14, 1982
Age at death 49

John Gardner was a prolific and successful novelist, poet and educator best known for *Grendel*, his reworking of the 8th-century Anglo-Saxon *Beowulf* story.

John Chaplin Gardner, Jr., grew up on a farm near Rochester, New York. Both his parents – his teacher mother and farmer father – fostered in him a love of literature. He also loved music, and on Saturdays his father gave him time off from working on the farm so he could listen to opera on the radio. At age 20, he married pianist Joan Patterson. After graduating from Washington University in St. Louis, Gardner earned a Master's degree and Ph.D from Iowa State University. He was a respected academic and taught medieval literature and writing at several American universities. He died in a motorcycle accident.

Gardner's first novel, *The Resurrection*, was published when he was 33. It was not successful, but five years later *Grendel* established his literary reputation. In this book Gardner gave the *Beowulf* epic poem a new twist by writing it from the point of view of the monster, Grendel, thus creating sympathy for a character who is usually seen as a brute. Key themes in Gardner's work are the exploration of the meaning of life and social values in modern fiction, as set out in *On Moral Fiction*. The award-winning *October Light* discusses politics and philosophy, and in *The Sunlight Dialogues* a police chief learns to accept new values while pursuing a criminal known as the Sunlight Man. Gardner also wrote fairy tales for children and epic poetry.

Publications

1966 The Resurrection
1970 The Wreckage of Agathon
1971 Grendel
1972 The Sunlight Dialogues
1973 Nickel Mountain
1976 October Light
1978 On Moral Fiction
1980 Freddy's Book
1981 The Art of Living
1982 Mickelsson's Ghosts

GASKELL, Elizabeth

English novelist, short-story writer and biographer

Born Sep. 29, 1810
Died Nov. 12, 1865
Age at death 55

Publications

1848	*Mary Barton*
1850	*The Moorland Cottage*
1853	*Cranford*
1853	*Ruth*
1854–55	*North and South*
1857	*The Life of Charlotte Brontë*
1863	*Sylvia's Lovers*
1863	*Cousin Phillis*

Published after she died

1866	*Wives and Daughters*

Elizabeth Gaskell's novels stress differences between rich and poor, town and country, and young and old.

She was born in London. Her mother died when she was an infant, and she was raised by an aunt in the village of Knutsford near the northern city of Manchester. Later, she attended a boarding school in the Midlands. For a while she lived with her father, a civil servant who had remarried.

When she was 22, she met and married William Gaskell, a preacher who taught English literature. They lived in the fast-growing, industrial city of Manchester and felt deeply for its working poor, who suffered great hardships. They wrote verses together called *Sketches among the Poor*.

Gaskell's first novel appeared when she was 38. She wrote it to help herself recover from the death of her infant son, but also to highlight the struggles of factory workers. *Mary Barton* tells of class hatred that drives a working-class father to murder. The book's realistic characters and scenes were praised by CHARLES DICKENS.

Gaskell later wrote short stories and sketches for Dickens's magazine *Household Words*, some of which formed the basis of her novel *Cranford*. Her memories of Knutsford's villagers inspired this novel of life in a quiet country town. Country families also figure in *Wives and Daughters*, her last book.

Gaskell's sympathy for the poor and for ill-treated women won many friends, including CHARLOTTE BRONTË. After Brontë died in 1855, Gaskell wrote her biography.

GAY, John

English poet and playwright

Born Jun. 30, 1685
Died Dec. 4, 1732
Age at death 47

John Gay was an English writer famous for his comical plays and satires. He was born in Barnstaple, southwest England, and went to school there. After leaving school, he went to London and soon made friends with leading literary figures of the day, including JONATHAN SWIFT and ALEXANDER POPE.

In London, Gay supported himself by working as a journalist. When he was 28, he had his first success with *Rural Sports*. This long poem comically glorifies descriptions of hunting and fishing and has amusing sections in the style of the ancient Roman poet, HORACE.

Gay's first play was a satirical farce called *The What D'ye Call It*, which he finished at age 30. Although successful, it was nothing compared with his most famous work, *The Beggar's Opera*, first performed when he was 43. *The Beggar's Opera* is a comic play with songs composed in the style of popular ballads of the day. It is a story of highwaymen and corrupt lawkeepers and satirizes the government of the then prime minister, Robert Walpole. The play is still performed today, and in the 1920s it inspired BERTOLT BRECHT'S *The Threepenny Opera.* Gay wrote a sequel, *Polly*, which was banned by Walpole and not performed until 1777.

With the money he made from *The Beggar's Opera*, Gay invested in the South Sea Company, which was promising to bring in huge profits from new trade routes to South America. Everyone rushed to buy its shares, but suddenly the market collapsed, and Gay, like many other people, was ruined. He died a poor man only four years after achieving his greatest success.

Publications

1713	*Rural Sports*
1714	*The Shepherd's Week*
1715	*The What D'ye Call It*
1716	*Trivia: or, the Art of Walking the Streets of London*
1717	*Three Hours after Marriage* (with Alexander Pope and John Arbuthnot)
1727	*Fables*
1728	*The Beggar's Opera*
1729	*Polly*

GELLHORN, Martha

American journalist, novelist and travel writer

Born 1908
Died Feb.15 1998
Age at death 90

Martha Gellhorn was best known as a journalist who covered wars all over the world, but she also wrote novels and short stories based on her experiences.

Gellhorn was born and raised in St. Louis, Missouri. Her mother was a campaigner for equal rights, and her father was a doctor. The young Gellhorn, an only child, went to a private school in St. Louis before attending Bryn Mawr College. At age 26, she published her first novel, *What Mad Pursuit*. Partly autobiographical, it was followed two years later with *The Trouble I've Seen*, four short novels based on her observations as a reporter for the Federal Emergency Relief Program, set up to help deal with poverty created by the Great Depression.

In the late 1930s, Gellhorn moved to Spain and as a correspondent with *Collier's* magazine reported on the Spanish Civil War. She lived with the writer ERNEST HEMINGWAY; they married in 1940 and endured a famously stormy marriage for five years before divorcing. During this time, Gellhorn published a collection of stories called *The Heart of Another* and two novels, *A Stricken Field* and *Liana*.

Gellhorn covered dramatic events in World War II, including the Russian invasion of Finland, the Allied landings in Normandy and the postwar Nuremberg trials of Nazis. She also reported on the Vietnam War and wars in the Middle East and Central America. Her fiction has been described as journalistic, featuring sharp observations of lives during wartime. Without sentimentality, she also conveys her concern for the damage caused to people by wars and social injustice.

Publications

1934	*What Mad Pursuit*
1936	*The Trouble I've Seen*
1940	*A Stricken Field*
1941	*The Heart of Another*
1944	*Liana*
1948	*The Wine of Astonishment*
1953	*The Honeyed Peace*
1958	*Two by Two*
1959	*The Face of War*
1980	*The Weather in Africa*

GENET, Jean

French playwright, novelist and poet

Born Dec. 19, 1910
Died Apr. 15, 1986
Age at death 75

Jean Genet is considered one of the most influential and controversial of writers of the 20th century.

Born in Paris, France, Genet was given to an orphanage by his mother when he was seven months old and was raised by foster parents. He started on a life of petty crime at 10 and was sent to a reformatory when he was 16. After his release at age 19, he joined the Foreign Legion but deserted and was imprisoned several times for various crimes before being given a life term at age 37.

Genet maintained that he began to write in prison. His first novel, *Our Lady of the Flowers*, published when he was 33, caused a sensation. The violent underworld of criminals is described in a way that uses religious forms to create beauty from horror. Other novels explore the same themes of suffering, alienation and death, and show his sympathy for the outcasts of society. He was also writing poetry and plays. His first play, *The Maids*, was produced when he was 37, and it made a significant contribution to the theater of the absurd. The French writers JEAN COCTEAU and JEAN-PAUL SARTRE valued his work, and they sponsored a successful petition to the French president in 1948 for his release from prison. Other writers, like FRANÇOIS MAURIAC, hated his subject matter and felt he was abusing French literature. Genet's later plays, such as *The Balcony* and *The Blacks*, deal with social and political struggles. When he first wrote them, they were too controversial to be performed in France.

After 1966, Genet largely gave up writing. He spent his time lecturing and supporting radical causes.

Publications

1943 Our Lady of the Flowers
1946 Miracle of the Rose
1947 Funeral Rites
1947 Querelle of Brest
1947 The Maids
1949 The Thief's Journal
1954 Deathwatch
1956 The Balcony
1958 The Blacks
1961 The Screens

GEORGE, Jean Craighead

American children's writer

Born Jul. 2, 1919

Jean Craighead George is the author of many popular children's books that include people and animals as the main characters.

George was born Jean Craighead in Washington, DC. Her father was a scientist who studied insects, and she was brought up to have love and respect for nature. George studied science and English at Pennsylvania State University and Louisiana State University and art at the University of Michigan. She was employed as a reporter for several years and then as a magazine artist before becoming a teacher in the 1960s. After that, she worked for *Reader's Digest* for 11 years, first as a writer and later as an editor.

George wrote and illustrated her first six books with her husband. *The Hole in the Tree*, the first book she wrote on her own, was published when she was 38. Six years later, she divorced her husband, but she has continued to write and to raise their three children to have a love for nature.

In her books, George often compares a stage in the life of an animal with the growth of a child into an adult, showing the relationship between the two. *Julie of the Wolves* is the story of a young Eskimo woman who manages to live with a pack of wolves. Her most famous children's book, *My Side of the Mountain*, is about a boy who learns to survive in the wild and discovers important things about himself and about nature. She has also written a series of "Moon" books, with titles such as *The Moon of the Bears*. Each story deals with a season in the life of a particular animal.

Publications

1956	*Dipper of Copper Creek* (with John Lothar George)
1957	*The Hole in the Tree*
1959	*My Side of the Mountain*
1965	*Spring Comes to the Ocean*
1967	*The Moon of the Bears*
1971	*All Upon a Stone*
1971	*Who Really Killed Cock Robin?*
1972	*Julie of the Wolves*
1982	*Journey Inward*

GIBRAN, Kahlil

Lebanese-American poet and philosopher

Born Jan. 6, 1883
Died Apr. 10, 1931
Age at death 48

Kahlil Gibran's book *The Prophet* – an exploration of love, spirituality, and self-fulfillment – has remained popular throughout the world since it was published in the 1920s. Its mystical poetry is frequently read at weddings even today.

Gibran was born in Bsherri, Lebanon. A talented child, he was modeling, drawing, and writing at an early age. It is said that he was impressed by the drawings of Leonardo da Vinci and Michelangelo when he was only eight. He went with his mother to Boston when he was 12 but only stayed for 3 years before returning to Lebanon to study Arabic. Later, he studied drawing in Paris. Eventually, however, he settled in New York City. After his mother died when he was 20, his sister supported him while he established himself as a writer and painter.

Gibran published his first book, a collection of short stories set in Lebanon called *Nymphs of the Valley*, when he was 23. His earliest works were in Arabic, and their beauty and spirituality made a tremendous impact throughout the Arabic-speaking world – so much so that his style and themes became known as "Gibranism." Later, he wrote mostly in English. He was concerned with spiritual questions that he tried to work out through his art. He believed that if a sensible way of living and thinking could be found, people would have mastery over their own lives.

The Prophet, for which Gibran also drew the illustrations, was published when he was 40 and became a bestseller in 20 languages. Partly autobiographical, it is about a man's search for spiritual self-fulfillment.

Publications

1914	*Tears and Laughter*
1920	*The Forerunner: His Parables and Poems*
1923	*The Prophet*
1928	*Jesus the Son of Man*

Published after he died

1932	*The Wanderer: His Parables and His Sayings*
1933	*The Garden of the Prophet*
1957	*The Broken Wings*

GIBSON, William

American-born Canadian science fiction writer

Born Mar. 17, 1948

William Gibson is best known as the originator of "cyberpunk" – science fiction that combines elements of crime fiction, computer technology and the alternative rock music scene.

Gibson was born in Conway, South Carolina. His father was in the construction business and helped build the facility that manufactured the first atomic bomb. When his father died, Gibson moved with his mother to southwestern Virginia. At 19, he left the US for Canada to avoid the draft for the Vietnam War. He still lives in Canada.

Gibson began to write science fiction while studying for a degree in English literature. When he was 28, his first story, "Fragments of a Hologram Rose," was published; it explored the idea of virtual reality – a computer-generated world – well before the term became generally known. This was followed by "Johnny Mnemonic," a short story that was later made into a film. Gibson's first novel, *Neuromancer*, came out when he was 36, and established him as a writer with a sharp understanding of the way information technology is changing modern life.

In *Neuromancer* and its sequels, *Count Zero* and *Mona Lisa Overdrive*, Gibson uses the term "cyberspace" to describe a parallel universe of information that in its way is as real as the world we know. Computer technology gives us access to a whole new field of information, such as the Internet. However, for Gibson this parallel universe of cyberspace is a frightening place, controlled by big corporations and capable of polluting our minds with meaningless information and mindless slogans.

Publications

1983 "Johnny Mnemonic"
1984 *Neuromancer*
1986 *Count Zero*
1986 *Burning Chrome*
1988 *Mona Lisa Overdrive*
1990 *The Difference Engine* (with Bruce Sterling)
1992 *Agrippa: A Book of the Dead*
1993 *Virtual Light*
1996 *Idoru*

GIDE, André

French novelist, playwright and essayist

Born Nov. 22, 1869
Died Feb. 19, 1951
Age at death 81

Throughout his long career André Gide used his writing to examine personal moral conflicts and the way people should behave in modern society. He was a leading French writer and in 1947 was awarded the Nobel Prize for Literature.

Gide's childhood was a lonely one. He was ill for long periods and was mostly educated at home. His mother was protective but also very strict. When he was 13, Gide fell in love with his cousin Madeleine. They married 12 years later. Although they lived apart for long periods – Gide also felt strongly attracted to men and had a daughter by another woman – she provided the security he needed all his life.

At 22, Gide published his first book, *The Notebooks of André*

Walter. Based on his own childhood, it tells the story of an unhappy young man. Two years later, Gide traveled to North Africa for the first time; he often returned there throughout his life.

Gide wrote more than 50 books. He modestly described most of his novels as "tales." Only the most ambitious of them, *The Counterfeiters,* did he refer to as a "novel." The central character in *The Counterfeiters* is a novelist writing a novel about a novelist who is writing a novel about forging. Gide also wrote plays and translated into French some of WILLIAM SHAKESPEARE's plays and poems by WILLIAM BLAKE and WALT WHITMAN.

In 1909, Gide helped found the influential literary magazine *The New French Review*. For more than 60 years, he wrote a journal in which he put down his experiences, thoughts and feelings. These were published toward the end of his life.

Publications

1891	The Notebooks of André Walter
1897	Fruits of the Earth
1902	The Immoralist
1909	Strait Is the Gate
1914	Lafcadio's Adventures
1919	The Pastoral Symphony
1925	The Counterfeiters
1929	The School for Wives
1931	Oedipus
1939–51	Journals

GILMAN, Charlotte Perkins

American novelist, poet and short-story writer

Born Jul. 8, 1860
Died Aug. 17, 1935
Age at death 75

Charlotte Perkins Gilman was a feminist writer and social reformer remembered for her masterpiece *Herland*.

Gilman was born in Hartford, Connecticut. Her father left the family, and she and her brother were raised by their mother. Gilman was mostly self-taught. Among her role models was her great aunt, the writer HARRIET BEECHER STOWE.

She married in 1884, and after the birth of her daughter three years later she suffered from depression, which at that time was treated with a long period of enforced rest. This experience led to her most famous story, "The Yellow Wallpaper," written when she was 32. It describes the cruel confinement of a woman who is thought to be going insane because she resists society's restraints.

In 1894, Gilman divorced and began to travel around the country speaking on women's issues. *In This Our World*, published when she was 33, is a collection of poetry about the women's movement. She believed that women needed fulfilling work and that confining women to the home made them feeble. She examined the economic causes of women's dependence on men in several nonfiction works.

Gilman's writing often uses humor to convey important social messages. In stories such as "If I Were a Man" she swaps men's and women's traditional roles. The novel *Herland* is a celebration of women's strength; it is set in a future society where women live without men.

Publications

1892	"The Yellow Wallpaper"
1893	In This Our World
1898	Women and Economics
1900	Concerning Children
1904	The Home
1911	The Man-Made World
1915	Herland
1916	With Her in Ourland
1935	The Living of Charlotte Perkins Gilman

GINSBERG, Allen

American poet

Born Jun. 3, 1926
Died Apr. 5, 1997
Age at death 70

Allen Ginsberg was a leading figure of the beat generation, a movement which revolutionized American literature in the late 1950s and early '60s. Much of Ginsberg's writing focuses on what he saw as the struggle of the human spirit against a materialistic, money-seeking society.

Ginsberg was born in Newark, New Jersey. His father, a teacher, also wrote poetry. Ginsberg was very close to his Russian-born mother, who died in a mental hospital when he was 30. Her life and death are the subject of his moving poem "Kaddish" (kaddish is the Jewish prayer of mourning).

In 1948, Ginsberg graduated from Columbia University, where he had met Jack Kerouac and William S. Burroughs, both of whom became important writers of the beat generation. After working at a few boring office jobs, he decided to devote himself to writing poetry.

Ginsberg's early poems were inspired by the mystical poetry of William Blake, but it was his poem "Howl," published when he was 30, that made him famous. "Howl" was an attack on American society, which Ginsberg felt destroyed people's spirituality.

Ginsberg was open about his homosexuality and experimental drug-taking. He was influenced by Zen Buddhist beliefs and formally became a Buddhist in 1972. In the 1960s, he was a prominent protestor for artistic freedom and against the Vietnam War, among other causes. He performed his own and Blake's poetry set to music before huge audiences.

Ginsberg won the National Book Award in 1972 for *The Fall of America*.

Publications

1956 Howl and Other Poems
1961 Kaddish and Other Poems
1963 Reality Sandwiches
1968 Planet News
1972 The Fall of America
1978 Mind Breaths
1982 Plutonium Ode and Other Poems
1984 Collected Poems
1987 White Shroud

GIOVANNI, Nikki

American poet

Born Jun. 7, 1943

Nikki Giovanni became popular in the turbulent 1960s, when her poetry spoke of the rage of African Americans and of the need to end racist oppression. Over the years her tone softened, and her militancy was replaced by a rejection of violence as the way to achieve equality.

Born in Tennessee, Giovanni was raised in a middle-class family near Cincinnati, Ohio. She says she has "always been a lover of books and the ideas they contain." When she went to Fisk University aged 17, she was politically conservative; she supported a right-wing Republican presidential candidate named Barry Goldwater. But after a break from Fisk she returned aged 21 with a change in her politics and became a militant activist. In 1967, the year she graduated, she took part in a poetry reading with, among others, SONIA SANCHEZ, which marked the emergence of a new generation of black poets.

The year 1967 was also the year of Giovanni's first poetry collection, *Black Feeling, Black Talk*, which she published herself aged 24. This early work calls for violent revolution with lines such as "Nigger / Can you kill?" Later work, such as the poems in *My House*, are more personal and include her love life and a celebration of African-American women.

Giovanni also writes essays and poems for children. She has one son, and in 1972 she received an honorary doctorate in literature from Wilberforce University. In 1971, she was named Woman of the Year by *Mademoiselle* magazine. She has performed on television, and she continues to give readings that draw large crowds.

Publications

1967	*Black Feeling, Black Talk*
1968	*Black Judgment*
1970	*Re: Creation*
1971	*Spin a Soft Black Song*
1971	*Gemini*
1972	*My House*
1978	*Cotton Candy on a Rainy Day*
1983	*Those Who Ride the Night Winds*
1994	*Knoxville, Tennessee*
1994	*Grand Mothers*

GJELLERUP, Karl A.

Danish novelist and playwright

Born Jun. 2, 1857
Died Oct. 11, 1919
Age at death 62

Karl Adolph Gjellerup is best known for his novels with religious themes. He was awarded the Nobel Prize for Literature in 1917.

Gjellerup was born in Roholte, Denmark. The son of a parson, he was expected to have a career in the church, and so he studied theology. Soon, however, he discovered the works of Charles Darwin and Georg Brandes. Darwin's book *The Origin of Species* was not against religion, but it showed that the account of the creation of the world in the Bible could not be true. Brandes, an influential figure in Scandinavian literature, attacked religion in his book *Jesus, a Myth*. These influences convinced Gjellerup to become an atheist – someone who doesn't believe in God. His break with religion is the subject of two novels. *An Idealist, A Description of Epigonus*, published when he was 21, explains his loss of religious faith. *The Teutons' Apprentice* follows the life of a young theologian who becomes a freethinker and develops his own beliefs and rules of behavior.

Gjellerup then went to Germany and became involved in German idealist philosophy. This is the theory that the physical world does not exist independently of the human mind but is "created" by the mind. Gjellerup never really lost his longing for a religion, and he later turned to Buddhism and other Indian faiths. His changing interests and beliefs inspired two novels: *Minna*, set in the Germany of his day, and *The Pilgrim Kamanita*, set in India and based on the idea that after a person dies their soul is reborn into another body (known as reincarnation).

Publications

1878	*An Idealist, A Description of Epigonus*
1882	*The Teutons' Apprentice*
1884	*Brynhild*
1888	*Hagbard and Signe*
1889	*Minna*
1896	*The Mill*
1906	*The Pilgrim Kamanita*
1916	*God's Friends*
1917	*The Golden Bough*

GLASPELL, Susan

American playwright and novelist

Born Jul. 1, 1882
Died Jul. 27, 1948
Age at death 66

Susan Glaspell was an American experimental playwright whose work concentrates on the sufferings and triumphs of women.

Glaspell was born in Davenport, Iowa. She graduated from Drake University in 1899 and worked as a journalist until devoting herself full time to her writing. She published short stories in magazines and produced her first novel when she was 27. *The Glory of the Conquered* earned Glaspell enough money to spend a year in Paris. Two years later, she published a second novel, *The Visioning*, followed by a collection of short stories, *Lifted Masks*.

Glaspell married when she was 25, and she and her husband George Cook – together with American playwright Eugene O'Neill – established the Provincetown Players. Glaspell was one of the main writers and directors of this experimental theater group, which produced the work of O'Neill and others and started what became known as "little theater" in New York.

Glaspell's own plays, including *Trifles*, *Bernice* and *The Verge*, are feminist in their depiction of the ways that women support each other. *The Verge*, set in a greenhouse, is about a strange woman who invents new plants; the hopeful message seems to be that women need not be limited by their biology.

In the early 1920s, Glaspell and her husband lived in Greece. She remarried in 1925 (later to divorce), and in 1930 she wrote her best-known play, *Alison's House*, which won her a Pulitzer Prize. The play is based on the family of the great American poet Emily Dickinson many years after her death.

Publications

1909 The Glory of the Conquered
1911 The Visioning
1912 Lifted Masks
1915 Fidelity
1916 Trifles
1919 Bernice
1921 The Verge
1928 Brook Evans
1930 Alison's House
1942 Norma Ashe

GLÜCK, Louise

American poet

Born Apr. 22, 1943

Loss and death are present in much of the work of Louise Glück, a contemporary American poet who is often compared to Robert Lowell. In 1993, she was awarded the Pulitzer Prize for her poetry collection *The Wild Iris*.

Glück was born in New York City and attended Sarah Lawrence College before studying poetry at Columbia University. By age 23, she was teaching poetry to young people and had been awarded a prize by the Academy of American Poets.

Glück secured her reputation as an important poet at age 25 with the publication of *Firstborn*. Many of the poems in this volume are reflections by female characters on important stages in their lives: marriage and pregnancy, for example. In this sense, Glück's themes are like those of other American female poets such as SYLVIA PLATH and ANNE SEXTON, whose observations of women's lives and roles were found to be unexpectedly negative: in the 1950s, women were expected to be thrilled by a pregnancy, not depressed. By the late 1960s, when Glück was writing, this honesty was not so shocking to readers.

For the following seven years, Glück published nothing. Then she produced *The House on Marshland*, a volume focusing on loss and mourning, particularly the pain in relationships between men and women. There was some debate about whether the experiences she describes are her own or imagined. The conclusion now is that they are not necessarily autobiographical.

Glück has been married twice and has one son. She has taught at a number of colleges.

Publications

1968	*Firstborn*
1975	*The House on Marshland*
1976	*The Garden*
1976	*Teh*
1980	*Descending Figure*
1985	*The Triumph of Achilles*
1990	*Ararat*
1992	*The Wild Iris*

GOETHE, Johann Wolfgang von

German poet, playwright and novelist

Born Aug. 28, 1749
Died Mar. 22, 1832
Age at death 82

Johann Wolfgang von Goethe is considered one of the greatest German writers.

Born in the German city of Frankfurt to an influential family, Goethe had a comfortable childhood. Educated at home, he was greatly influenced by his mother, an artistic and sensitive woman who encouraged his love of literature. When he was 16, Goethe went to Leipzig University. Two years later, he began an unhappy love affair that inspired his first play, *The Lover's Caprice*.

After a period of illness, Goethe resumed his studies. He then fell in love with a woman who was engaged to someone else. In an attempt to express his anguish, he wrote *The Sorrows of Young Werther*, a novel that made him famous throughout Europe and influenced the development of modern German literature.

Back in Frankfurt, the 24-year-old Goethe joined a group called *Sturm und Drang* ("Storm and Stress"), which wrote emotionally intense works that were part of the Romantic movement. A few years later Goethe accepted an appointment to the court of the Duke of Saxe-Weimar. For the next ten years he wrote little, but pursued his scientific and political work.

Goethe then traveled to Italy, long regarded by him as the center of culture. He returned a changed man and left his post to concentrate on writing. His masterpiece, *Faust*, which he began years earlier, was completed just before his death. An epic work, it shows Goethe's development, as well as that of European society.

Publications

1767	*The Lover's Caprice*
1774	*The Sorrows of Young Werther*
1774	*Clavigo*
1775	*Stella*
1787	*Iphigenia: A Tragedy*
1788	*Egmont*
1798	*Hermann and Dorothea*
1808–32	*Faust*
1816–17	*Italian Journey*
1821–29	*Wilhelm Meister's Travels*

GOGOL, Nikolai

Russian novelist, playwright and short-story writer

Born Mar. 31, 1809
Died Mar. 4, 1852
Age at death 42

Nikolai Gogol is noted as being one of a small group of outstanding Russian novelists of the 19th century. He tried to expose the injustices of life in Russia and often wrote about the mistreated "underdog."

Gogol was born in Sorochintsy in the Ukraine into a well-to-do landowning family. After leaving school, he went to St. Petersburg to look for a job, and he had already published a book by the time he was 20. He worked as a civil service clerk, a job he hated, and then as a college lecturer in history. But he had neither the knowledge nor the skills to succeed in this and resigned in little over a year.

Happily, by then Gogol was established as a writer of Ukrainian tales and plays. Many of his stories have a macabre, nightmarish element. One of his plays, *The Inspector General*, which was intended to ridicule the Russian government, was heavily criticized and the furious author left the country. The play was, however, a brilliant piece of work. At age 31, Gogol produced the satirical novel *Dead Souls*, which was a resounding success. This epic, his masterpiece, is one of the few great works of fiction and is read all over the world. The novel's "hero" is a conman who tries to get rich quick by buying and selling serfs (peasants who were treated as slaves by landowners).

Later in his life Gogol became mentally unstable. He burned manuscripts, developed a religious mania, had visions, and believed that he was about to be attacked so he always walked sideways with his back to a wall. He returned to Moscow, where he starved himself to death.

Publications

1829 Hans Küchelgarten
1831–32 Evenings on a Farm Near Dikanka
1835 Arabesques
1835 Mirgorod
1835 Diary of a Madman, and Other Stories
1836 "The Nose"
1836 The Inspector General
1842 Dead Souls
1842 "The Overcoat"
1842 The Marriage

GOLDING, William

English novelist, poet and playwright

Born Sep. 19, 1911
Died Jun. 19, 1993
Age at death 81

William Golding is one of the 20th century's greatest novelists. He is best known for his novel, *Lord of the Flies*. In 1983, he was awarded the Nobel Prize for lLiterature and, in 1988, he was knighted. He was humble about his achievements, pointing out in his Nobel Prize acceptance speech that he was insignificant in the larger scheme of things.

Golding was born in Cornwall in the southwest of England. After graduating from Oxford University, he worked as an actor and theatrical producer then spent a year teaching. At age 24, he published a book of poems.

When Golding was 28, he joined the navy and rose to the rank of commander. He saw active service during World War II, which included involvement in the sinking of the German battleship *Bismarck* and the D-day landings in Normandy. After the war, he returned to teaching and writing, but with a dark view of people's ability to destroy one another.

Lord of the Flies, published when Golding was 43, was an immediate success and made enough money to allow him to give up teaching. It is a terrifying story that tells how a group of British schoolboys stranded on a desert island lapse into tribal battles and murder once they are away from society. Like much of Golding's work, the book deals with what it describes as "the darkness of man's heart." It has been filmed twice, in 1963 and 1990.

Golding's work earned him many accolades. The novel *Rites of Passage*, published when he was 69, won the Booker Prize.

Publications

1934 Poems
1954 Lord of the Flies
1955 The Inheritors
1956 Pincher Martin
1959 Free Fall
1964 The Spire
1979 Darkness Visible
1980 Rites of Passage
1987 Close Quarters
1989 Fire Down Below

GOLDSMITH, Oliver

Irish playwright and novelist

Born Nov. 10, 1730
Died Apr. 4, 1774
Age at death 43

Oliver Goldsmith is the author of one of the best comedies ever written – the play *She Stoops to Conquer*. His only novel, *The Vicar of Wakefield*, became one of the most popular fiction works of the time and is now a classic of English literature.

Goldsmith was born in Ballymahon, Ireland. His father was a clergyman, and at first Goldsmith also wanted to join the Church. He graduated from Trinity College in Dublin in 1750 and tried to join the Church, but was rejected. He then studied medicine for a few years in Edinburgh, but did not complete his degree. In his mid-20s, Goldsmith abandoned his studies to travel around Europe for a year. He soon ran out of money, so he paid his way by playing his lute and generally living off his wits.

In 1756, Goldsmith arrived in London, with no money. He tried, unsuccessfully, to make a living as a doctor before becoming a journalist. He reviewed books and wrote essays for various periodicals. In the 1760s, he met the famous writer Dr. Johnson, who became his friend and an admirer of Goldsmith's work. The first literary piece by Goldsmith to attract attention was his poem *The Traveler*, which came out when he was 34. *The Vicar of Wakefield* was published two years later. It is a lively, charming tale of the ups and downs of a vicar's family. Goldsmith's masterpiece, *She Stoops to Conquer*, was not produced until he was 43. On his way to visit the family of his future wife, the hero arrives at their country mansion. He mistakes it for an inn, however, and treats the father as the innkeeper and the daughter as a servant.

Publications

1764 The Traveler
1766 The Vicar of Wakefield
1768 The Good Natur'd Man
1770 The Deserted Village
1773 She Stoops to Conquer
1774 Retaliation (unfinished)

GONCHAROV, Ivan

Russian novelist

Born Jun. 6, 1812
Died Sep. 15, 1891
Age at death 79

Ivan Goncharov is best known for his novel *Oblomov*, a masterpiece of world literature.

Goncharov was born in Simbirsk, the son of a wealthy merchant. As a child he was fascinated by the slow and easy lives of the traditional Russian upper class, so different from his own background. He later used what he had learned in his novels.

Goncharov graduated from Moscow University, then worked as a government official for more than 30 years while secretly training himself to write. His first novel, *A Common Story*, was published when he was 35. It describes the clash between the decaying Russian nobility and the new merchant classes. Goncharov began his second novel, *Oblomov*, but his life was interrupted in 1852, when he went as official secretary on a Russian navy ship sailing to Japan.

When Goncharov returned, he published an account of his travels, *The Frigate Pallas*, then went back to his novel. *Oblomov* was published when he was 47 and became known as his greatest book. The hero, Oblomov, is a young, intelligent, but dreamy nobleman who cannot be bothered to do much with his life. He rarely leaves his room or his bed. He is a generous person but incapable of action or decision-making. He loses the woman he loves to a friend and gradually slips into complete apathy.

The book was an enormous success and was praised as a satirical portrait of a group of people, the Russian aristocracy, who no longer had a useful role in society. Oblomov became a world famous literary character, and the term "Oblomovism" came to refer to inaction or lack of interest.

Publications

1847	*A Common Story*
1858	*The Frigate Pallas*
1859	*Oblomov*
1869	*The Precipice*

Published after he died

1924	*An Uncommon Story*

GORDIMER, Nadine

South African novelist and short-story writer

Born Nov. 20, 1923

In 1991, Nadine Gordimer, one of Africa's best writers, became the first South African to win the Nobel Prize for Literature.

Gordimer was born into a well-off, English-speaking white family in a small mining town in northeastern South Africa. Although most South Africans are black, the whites controlled all the major industries and the government at that time, and additional laws restricted what black people could do. As Gordimer grew up, white power increased at the expense of the rights of black people.

Gordimer, whose father was Jewish, went to a local convent school run by nuns and then the University of Witwatersrand, Johannesburg – but for only one year. Although not a great student, she began writing at the age of nine; and at the age of 15, she published her first story, "Come Again Tomorrow." Her work did not receive a great deal of attention, however, until the publication of *The Lying Days* when she was 30. Based largely on Gordimer's own life, it is the story of a white girl who attempts to escape the racism of small-town life. Much of Gordimer's work is concerned with the effects on individuals – black and white – of the former South African government's racist apartheid policies.

Since 1948, Gordimer has lived in the South African city of Johannesburg, the setting for most of her work. Several of Gordimer's works were banned by the government, including *Burger's Daughter*. This book deals with the 1976 Soweto riots and the failure of white liberals to force government reforms.

Publications

1953 The Lying Days
1958 A World of Strangers
1965 Not for Publication
1966 The Late Bourgeois World
1970 A Guest of Honor
1974 The Conservationist
1979 Burger's Daughter
1981 July's People
1987 A Sport of Nature
1994 None to Accompany Me
1998 The House Gun

GORDONE, Charles

American playwright

Born Oct. 12, 1925
Died Nov. 17, 1995
Age at death 70

With his play *No Place to Be Somebody*, Charles Gordone became the first African-American playwright to be awarded the Pulitzer Prize.

Gordone was born in Cleveland but grew up in Indiana. Race was an issue for him in his youth: his family – of mixed Indian, European and African-American heritage – was considered black but lived in a predominantly white part of town. Shunned by both blacks and whites, Gordone left to go to university in Los Angeles. There he studied music and drama and worked as a calypso singer to support himself. After graduating, he moved to New York City.

Gordone started his career as an actor, landing his first Broadway part when he was in his late 20s. Over the next two decades he starred in a number of productions, including JOHN STEINBECK'S *Of Mice and Men* in 1953 (for which he gave an award-winning performance). Between jobs he worked as a waiter.

The turning point from actor to writer came in the 1960s. Inspired by *The Blacks* by the French playwright JEAN GENET (in which Gordone performed with the poet MAYA ANGELOU), he wrote *No Place to Be Somebody*. The characters, loosely based on customers in the Greenwich Village bar in which he worked, include a petty criminal, a prostitute, a musician, a retired gangster and a light-skinned black man – a writer and actor like Gordone – who speaks at the beginning of each act, and who represents the search for racial identity.

The play was a huge success and earned the 45-year-old author the Pulitzer Prize in 1970 and several prestigious drama awards.

Publications

1964 Little More Light Around the Place
1969 No Place to Be Somebody
1970 Willy Bignigga
1970 Chumpanzee
1970 Gordone Is a Muthah
1975 Baba-Chops
1977 The Last Chord
1979 Anabiosis

GORKY, Maksim

Russian novelist, journalist and playwright

Born Mar. 28, 1868
Died Jun. 18, 1936
Age at death 68

Maksim Gorky became famous as a spokesman for the downtrodden in his novels. From personal experience, he wrote with sympathy and optimism about the Russian poor.

Gorky was born in the Russian town of Nizhny Novgorod, later renamed Gorky in his honor. His real surname was Peshkov, but he used the pen name Gorky, meaning "bitter," in memory of his early years. His father died when Gorky was five, and by the age of nine he was on his own. He wandered through Russia, working on a river steamer (where he learned to read), as a baker, street peddler and railroad worker. When he was 21, he became a hobo.

Despite having no formal education – Gorky said that life was his school – he became a journalist. His first short story "Makar Chudra" was published when he was 24. In 1895, he scored an immediate success with "Chelkash," the story of a harbor thief. Over the next few years, Gorky produced a stream of stories, novels and plays, including *Twenty-Six Men and a Girl* and his best-known play, *The Lower Depths*. In all of them, he wrote about the gypsies, hobos and down-and-outs whom he knew so well.

Gorky's work became increasingly political as he attacked the society that caused such hardship. He lived in exile for many years, and during that time he wrote *The Mother*, a novel about the revolutionary movement later dramatized by Bertolt Brecht. Between 1913 and 1923 he published his best-known work, a three-part autobiography, beginning with *My Childhood*. His emphasis on the worker as hero and his realism made him the leader of writers in the Soviet period.

Publications

1892	"Makar Chudra"
1895	"Chelkash"
1899	*Twenty-Six Men and a Girl*
1899	*Foma Gordeyev*
1902	*The Lower Depths*
1906–07	*The Mother*
1913–14	*My Childhood*
1915	*In the World*
1923	*My Universities*
1925	*The Artamonov Business*

GOWER, John

English poet

Born 1330
Died 1408
Age at death c. 78

John Gower was a medieval English poet with a gift for storytelling who in his day was as popular as his friend, Geoffrey Chaucer.

Gower came from a well-to-do English family. He held lands in eastern England but lived in London, probably as a court official. He wrote verses for kings Richard II and Henry IV. Gower held strong religious beliefs and made generous gifts to churches. Although not a priest, he was living in a priory when he married or remarried, aged about 67.

In a century when plague, famine, revolution and war upset orderly ways of life, Gower tried through his poetry to show people the right way to live. He put his strong moral message across in allegories and by making human characters out of vices (for example, treating sins such as greed as if they were people).

Each of his three major poems appeared in a different language. Gower completed *Mirror of Man* in French when he was aged about 49. This work is about seven vices and seven virtues fighting to rule humankind. About three years later *Voice of Complaint,* written in Latin, describes the terrible effects of the then recent Peasants' Revolt of 1381. Finally, his masterpiece was completed when he was about 60. *A Lover's Confession* is a group of stories written in English about the vices and virtues of love. Tales from the Roman poet, Ovid, the Bible, and medieval writers figure in this long allegory. Its simple style helped pioneer the use of plain English.

Publications

1376–79 Mirror of Man
1377–81 Voice of Complaint
1386–93 A Lover's Confession

GRAFTON, Sue

American crime writer

Born Apr. 24, 1940

Sue Grafton is one of the most popular female detective novelists in America today. She has sold more than 20 million books in the US alone.

Grafton's father was a crime novelist and her mother a teacher. She was born and educated in Louisville, Kentucky. In her 20s, she worked as an administrator in the medical field. During this time she published two novels. She then moved to Santa Barbara, California, and turned to writing screenplays for television. She was a successful TV writer for over 15 years, writing episodes of *Murder She Wrote* and adapting Agatha Christie crime novels for television.

Grafton's first crime novel, *"A" Is for Alibi*, was published when she was 42. The book marked a turning point in her career and was the first in a long running series – *"B" Is for Burglar*, *"C" Is for Corpse*, and so on – that made her main character, a female private detective called Kinsey Millhone, a household name.

Up until the 1980s there were few female private detectives in crime fiction. Grafton, along with Sara Paretsky, was among the first crime writers to introduce a woman as the main investigator – especially in the genre of hard-boiled crime writing made famous by Raymond Chandler. Kinsey Millhone, Grafton's detective, is a tough, intelligent and very self-reliant California woman in her 30s. She is a compassionate person who often forms an emotional bond with her clients, but she can protect herself in a physically threatening situation. She also has a strong, wisecracking sense of humor.

Publications

1969 The Lolly-Madonna War
1982 "A" Is for Alibi
1985 "B" Is for Burglar
1986 "C" Is for Corpse
1989 "F" Is for Fugitive
1990 "G" Is for Gumshoe
1993 "J" Is for Judgment
1994 "K" Is for Killer
1995 "L" Is for Lawless
1996 "M" Is for Malice
1998 "N" Is for Noose

GRAHAME, Kenneth

Scottish children's writer

Born Mar. 8, 1859
Died Jul. 6, 1932
Age at death 73

Publications

1893 Pagan Papers
1895 The Golden Age
1898 Dream Days
1908 The Wind in the Willows

Published after he died

1938 The Reluctant Dragon
1949 Bertie's Escapade

Kenneth Grahame was the author of *The Wind in the Willows*, a great classic of children's literature.

Grahame was born in Edinburgh. When he was five years old, his mother died of scarlet fever. His father was deeply upset by her death and felt unable to cope with bringing up their children. Grahame and his brothers and sisters were sent to live with their grandmother in England.

Grahame had a happy childhood in the English countryside. The children were left to do more or less what they wanted. They explored, had adventures, and learned about the world through their own experiences. Later, when Grahame began writing, his characters shared the same carefree, adventurous spirit that he had enjoyed as a child.

After leaving school, Grahame began working for the Bank of England in London. In his spare time he wrote articles for magazines and began a series of stories about a group of orphaned children; the stories were later published in his first book, *Pagan Papers*. This book and his next two, *The Golden Age* and *Dream Days*, were about children but were written for adults. He was highly praised for his skill at recreating the thoughts and feelings of childhood.

Grahame began writing the stories that became *The Wind in the Willows* for his young son, Alastair. The adventures of the lovable woodland animals – shy little Mole, clever Ratty, and crazy Toad – were published when Grahame was nearly 50. Although the book was not liked by critics, children loved it, and it had become a classic within a few years of Grahame's death.

GRASS, Günter

German novelist, playwright and poet

Born Oct. 16, 1927

Günter Grass is one of Germany's most important living writers.

Grass, born in Danzig (now the Polish city of Gdansk), was the son of a grocery store owner. At the age of 16, he was drafted into the German army to fight in World War II. He was wounded in the fighting and taken prisoner. After the war he tried various occupations, including jazz drumming, farm laboring, potash mining, black-market trading, painting and, eventually, writing.

When he was 32, Grass published his first novel, *The Tin Drum*, which recounts the wartime experiences of the people of Danzig and the way German society was damaged by the extremist Nazi Party. The main character is three-year-old Oskar, who plays a tin drum given to him on his birthday. He refuses to grow up in protest against the adult world. While many recognized the novel as a work of great literary importance, others found it difficult or shocking. Grass quickly became known by many as "the conscience of Germany" because he writes about things in German history that many Germans find difficult to face.

Grass has written many other books, poems and plays. His work is often hard to understand and contains mockeries of what he sees to be the faults of Germany and the German people. In his books, Grass has ruthlessly savaged many aspects of German culture. His recent novel, *Wide Field*, was the first major literary work to deal with the reunification of East and West Germany after the Berlin Wall was removed. Grass's reputation and the importance of the subject caused enormous interest in the book worldwide.

Publications

1959 The Tin Drum
1961 Cat and Mouse
1963 Dog Years
1969 Local Anesthetic
1972 From the Diary of a Snail
1977 The Flounder
1980 Danzig Trilogy
1986 The Rat
1992 The Call of the Toad
1995 Wide Field

GRAU, Shirley Ann

American novelist and short-story writer

Born Jul. 8, 1929

Shirley Ann Grau writes about the American South. Her novel *The Keepers of the House* earned her a Pulitzer Prize in 1965.

Grau was born and raised in New Orleans, where she studied at Tulane University. While at university, where she worked on the literary journal, she decided to be a writer, and she had her first story published when she was 25. Her first book, the short-story collection *The Black Prince*, was published the following year. It describes life among the blacks and whites who live in the Louisiana bayou, a swampy, beautiful part of the country. One of its themes is relations between the races. Although the book was well received, she has been criticized for creating black characters who are depicted as primitive stereotypes.

The Hard Blue Sky, Grau's first published novel, focuses on a community of French and Spanish descendants who live on an island in the Gulf of Mexico. Their lives are made difficult by the harshness of nature, in particular the hurricanes that sweep through the area with regular violence.

Grau's finest work so far is her Pulitzer Prize-winning novel *The Keepers of the House*, which she published when she was 35. It tells of a Southern family in which an interracial marriage, kept secret for many years, causes problems for a family member who has become a politician and a member of the racist organization the Ku Klux Klan.

Grau went on to produce several more novels and short-story collections. She is married, has four children, and still lives in New Orleans.

Publications

1955 The Black Prince
1958 The Hard Blue Sky
1961 The House on Coliseum Street
1964 The Keepers of the House
1971 The Condor Passes
1973 The Wind Shifting West
1977 Evidence of Love
1986 Nine Women
1994 Roadwalkers

GRAVES, Robert

English poet, novelist and critic

Born Jul. 26, 1895
Died Dec. 7, 1985
Age at death 90

Robert Graves was considered the best writer of love poetry in his generation, which spanned both of the world wars.

Graves was born in London. His father was a school inspector, scholar and minor Irish poet. The family were reasonably wealthy, and Graves's childhood was a happy one, although he hated his school. Later, he studied at Oxford University but did not graduate. In 1914, he joined the British Army, and his first volume of poetry was published while he was serving in World War I.

Throughout his life, Graves produced many volumes of poetry, essays, fiction, children's works and biographies. Although he saw himself primarily as a poet, his best-known work is his powerful autobiography, *Goodbye to All That.* It describes his unhappy time at school, the horrors of World War I, and the breakdown of his first marriage.

Among Graves's many historical novels, *I, Claudius* and *Claudius the God* are the most famous. His research for the novel *Hercules, My Shipmate* spurred his interest in myths and history. *The White Goddess*, his most important work of nonfiction, is an imaginative reconstruction of an ancient myth.

Early in his career Graves was recognized as a poet who wrote conventional poetry and maintained a late-Romantic style. However, he strived to avoid being identified with any particular school of poetry throughout his life. He wanted to maintain his own distinct style. His love poetry, for example, is both gloomy and romantically passionate. Although extremely personal, his work has universal appeal.

Publications

1929	*Goodbye to All That*
1934	*I, Claudius*
1934	*Claudius the God*
1943	*The Story of Marie Powell, Wife to Mr. Milton*
1944	*Hercules, My Shipmate*
1946	*King Jesus*
1948	*The White Goddess*
1955	*The Greek Myths*
1959	*Collected Poems*

GRAY, John

English poet

Born 1866
Died 1934
Age at death c. 68

John Gray was an English poet of the late 19th and early 20th centuries. He is best known for his friendship with the English writer OSCAR WILDE. Many scholars have suggested that the hero of Wilde's famous novel, *The Picture of Dorian Gray* (which is about the corruption of a handsome, intelligent young man) was based on John Gray.

Born into a poor family in London, Gray did well at school but had to leave when he was 15 and get a job to help support his seven brothers and sisters. While working at a shipyard, Gray continued to study, teaching himself Latin, French and German. When he was 18, he passed exams that allowed him to get a job in the civil service.

Gray's work in the civil service left him plenty of time to pursue his interest in literature. It was at this time that his friendship with Oscar Wilde began. At 27, Gray published his first and most famous collection of poems, *Silverpoints*.

Gray became tired of literary society in London and turned to the Catholic Church for a new direction in life. His second collection, *Spiritual Poems*, published just three years after *Silverpoints*, shows his growing devotion to a religious way of life. When he was 32, Gray went to Rome and studied to become a priest. Two years later the Catholic Church sent him to Edinburgh, where he served as a priest for the rest of his life. He published nothing for 20 years, then returned to writing with a long autobiographical poem, *The Long Road*, and a fantasy set in a future England called *Park: A Fantastic Story*.

Publications

1893 Silverpoints
1894 The Blackmailers
1894–96 The Blue Calendar
1896 Spiritual Poems
1904 Ad Matrem
1905 Verses for Tableaux Vivants
1922 Vivis
1926 The Long Road
1931 Poems
1932 Park: A Fantastic Story

GRAY, Thomas

English poet

Born Dec. 26, 1716
Died Jul. 30, 1771
Age at death 54

Thomas Gray wrote few poems, but his *Elegy Written in a Country Churchyard* has become one of the most famous and often quoted in the English language.

Gray was born in London into a prosperous family. His 11 brothers and sisters died young, and his mentally unstable father tormented his mother. Her hat-making business helped pay for her son's education at the prestigious Eton College and Cambridge University.

At 22, Gray began a tour of France, Switzerland and Italy with his friend the novelist HORACE WALPOLE. Later he made trips through the wilder parts of Great Britain. He loved romantic scenery, ancient monuments and legends.

Gray began writing some of his best poems at age 25, when his emotions were stirred by the death of his friend Richard West. *Ode on a Distant Prospect of Eton College*, his first published piece, came out when he was 31. *Elegy Written in a Country Churchyard* appeared four years later. In this famous poem, Gray reminds us that everyone shares the fate of the forgotten villagers buried in the churchyard. In a direct and simple way it expresses a conflict – between the advantages of education and the values of simple rural life. He also wrote lighter pieces such as "Ode on the Death of a Favorite Cat, Drowned in a Tub of Goldfishes."

Gray led a quiet, scholarly life at Cambridge. At 51, he became a professor of modern history. He never married. He was buried in the graveyard he made famous in his poem.

Publications

1747 Ode on a Distant Prospect of Eton College
1748 "Ode on the Death of a Favorite Cat, Drowned in a Tub of Goldfishes"
1751 Elegy Written in a Country Churchyard
1753 Six Poems By Mr. T. Gray
1757 Odes
1768 Poems by Mr. T. Gray

GREEN, Paul

American playwright and novelist

Born Mar. 17, 1894
Died May 4, 1981
Age at death 87

Paul Green's work explores relationships between people of different races and classes, usually in rural settings. His comedies and tragedies show sympathy for people on the margins of society and recognize that they have the same hopes and ambitions as everyone else.

Green was born on a farm near Lillington, North Carolina. He served as a school principal for two years before attending the University of North Carolina in Chapel Hill. His first play, *Surrender to the Enemy*, was performed there when Green was 22. After serving in France in World War I, he graduated from university and married fellow playwright, Elizabeth Lay.

Green first wrote one-act "folkplays" inspired by the people and folklore of his region. Many of these appeared in two collections, *The Lord's Will* and *Lonesome Road*. The tragedy *In Abraham's Bosom* describes an African-American man who struggles against racism in the South; it won the Pulitzer Prize for drama in 1927. A supporter of the civil rights movement, Green adapted RICHARD WRIGHT's novel *Native Son* for the stage in 1941.

In the 1930s, Green began to write "symphonic dramas," for which he is now best known. These outdoor plays incorporate music, dance and poetry, and their plots are often derived from the life and history of people in a particular area. His first symphonic drama, *The Lost Colony*, about the early colonization of North Carolina, is still annually presented at the place where the settlers first landed. These plays helped fulfill Green's dream of creating theater "for the people."

Publications

1925 The Lord's Will
1926 Lonesome Road
1926 In Abraham's Bosom
1928 In the Valley
1931 The House of Connelly
1935 This Body the Earth
1937 The Lost Colony
1948 The Common Glory
1976 The Land of Nod and Other Stories

GREENE, Graham

English novelist, short-story writer and journalist

Born Oct. 2, 1904
Died Apr. 3, 1991
Age at death 86

Graham Greene was one of the greatest and most popular English writers of the 20th century. His novels and short stories deal with moral issues, and many have exotic settings. Greene gathered material for these settings during his travels all over the world.

Greene began his career at age 21 as a journalist in London. At 25, he published his first novel, *The Man Within*; its success allowed him to leave journalism. Later he was employed by the Foreign Office during World War II. In the 1950s and '60s, he was involved with Britain's Secret Intelligence Service. Many of Greene's novels feature political intrigue.

Greene's first popular success was the spy story *Stamboul Train*, published when he was 28. Other thrillers – Greene called them "entertainments" – include *A Gun for Sale* (1936), *The Confidential Agent* (1939) and *The Third Man*, all of which are among his many novels that were made into movies.

In 1926, Greene became a Roman Catholic, and his religion became an important element in several novels, including: *Brighton Rock*, the story of a teenage criminal in an English seaside resort; *The Power and the Glory*, about a hunted, drunken priest in Mexico; and *A Burnt-Out Case*, whose hero is a Roman Catholic architect in central Africa.

Greene's life was complicated, and he did his best to make it more so by playing practical jokes, especially to fool journalists. He pretended that the manuscript of his novel *The Tenth Man* had suddenly been found after 40 years – though all the time he knew where it was. It was published in 1985 but is not one of his best.

Publications

1935	*The Basement Room and Other Stories*
1938	*Brighton Rock*
1940	*The Power and the Glory*
1948	*The Heart of the Matter*
1950	*The Third Man*
1951	*The End of the Affair*
1955	*The Quiet American*
1958	*Our Man in Havana*
1961	*A Burnt-Out Case*
1966	*The Comedians*

GREGORY, Lady

Irish playwright

Born Mar. 15, 1852
Died May 22, 1932
Age at death 80

Lady Gregory is remembered for the many comedies she wrote for the Abbey Theater in Dublin, Ireland. She was a director of the theatre from its foundation in 1904 through to 1932.

Born Isabella Augusta Persse into a wealthy landowning family in County Galway, Ireland, she married Sir William Gregory, one-time British governor of Ceylon (now Sri Lanka). She took up writing after he died in 1892, when she was 40.

With the poet and playwright W.B. YEATS, Lady Gregory set up the Irish Literary Theater in 1899. This was the organization that began the revival of Irish drama. When the Abbey Theater opened in 1904, Lady Gregory, Yeats and JOHN MILLINGTON SYNGE became codirectors. Their plays were the first to be performed there.

Lady Gregory and Yeats collaborated on two plays: a patriotic drama and a comedy. Her first work on her own, the one-act play *Spreading the News*, was performed when she was 52. It is now considered one of her greatest works.

Most of Lady Gregory's best plays are light comedies, featuring Irish peasant ways of life and tricks of speech. She wrote them in a dialect known as "Kiltartan." Many of them are short. She also wrote fantasies and made dramas out of ancient Irish sagas. She translated several dramas by the French writer MOLIÈRE and set them in western Ireland.

Lady Gregory was a tireless worker for the Abbey Theater and, in 1911, she took the theater company on a successful visit to America.

Publications

1904	*Spreading the News*
1906	*Hyacinth Halvey*
1906	*The Gaol Gate*
1907	*The Rising of the Moon*
1910	*The Image*
1911	*Grania*
1912	*Damer's Gold*
1916	*The Golden Apple*
1920	*The Dragon*
1921	*Aristotle's Bellows*

GREY, Zane

American novelist

Born Jan. 31, 1872
Died Oct. 23, 1939
Age at death 67

Zane Grey is one of the most popular writers of this century. He wrote 63 novels, mainly Westerns, which have sold over 130 million copies worldwide. His most popular novel is *Riders of the Purple Sage*.

Pearl Zane Grey was born in Zanesville, Ohio, where from an early age he dreamed of being a writer. Nine years after receiving a degree in dentistry from the University of Pennsylvania, he married Lina Elise Roth. Encouraged by her belief in his talent, he gave up dentistry to concentrate on writing. His first book, *Betty Zane* – based on a diary of pioneer life written by one of his ancestors – was published when he was 31, but it was not a success. Just when their money began to run out and he thought he would have to return to dentistry, Grey met "Buffalo" Jones, an Arizona rancher, who invited him back to his ranch to see what the real "Wild West" was like. From that time on, Grey was fascinated by Western life. He joined Jones in chasing buffalo, roping wild horses and exploring Native-American ruins. When he was 36, he wrote about his experiences in his first success, a nonfiction book called *The Last of the Plainsmen*.

The plots of Grey's novels are relatively simple: his heroes are Easterners who do not know the ways of the West. As they face hardships such as sandstorms and stampedes, and battle with rustlers and gunmen, they lose their innocence and become expert at surviving in their new surroundings. Although Grey's novels were never well received by critics, he was popular with readers because he allowed them to escape into unfamiliar and romantic settings. More than 100 feature films have been based on his stories.

Publications

1903 Betty Zane
1908 The Last of the Plainsmen
1912 Riders of the Purple Sage
1915 The Lone Star Ranger
1922 To the Last Man
1924 The Call of the Canyon
1934 The Code of the West

Published after he died

1941 Twin Sombreros
1957 The Fugitive Trail

GRIMM, The Brothers

German writers

Jacob Grimm

Born Jan. 4, 1785
Died Sep. 20, 1863
Age at death 78

Wilhelm Grimm

Born Feb. 24, 1786
Died Dec. 16, 1859
Age at death 73

The brothers Jacob and Wilhelm Grimm first made famous what are today some of the best-known stories in the world. They collected and published folktales and legends that might otherwise have been forgotten and lost forever. Stories such as "Snow White," "Rumplestiltskin" and "Sleeping Beauty" have been retold countless times and have inspired numerous writers, but they were first written down by the Brothers Grimm.

Jacob and Wilhelm were born in the German city of Hanau. Their father died when they were young, and their family struggled to pay for their education at Marburg University. After they left, the brothers worked in a variety of jobs in libraries, universities and government offices.

Between 1812 and 1822, the brothers raised extra money by publishing three volumes of folktales; these were the stories that were to become world famous as *Grimm's Fairy Tales*. At that time Germany was not a single country but a collection of many independent kingdoms and principalities. The Brothers Grimm, like many other Germans, wanted Germany to unite into one strong country. They had studied folklore and the history of the German language to show how all Germans shared a similar culture, and it was this research that formed the basis of *Grimm's Fairy Tales*.

The brothers were strongly influenced by the ideas of Romanticism; they retold the tales in a way that emphasized a mystical idea of ancient wisdom and magic living in the land and people.

Publications

1812–22 Grimm's Fairy Tales (3 vols.)

GRISHAM, John

American thriller writer

Born Feb. 8, 1955

John Grisham is one of America's bestselling novelists.

Born in Jonesboro, Arkansas, Grisham graduated from the University of Mississippi and went on to practice law for ten years. His experiences as a lawyer not only helped him to understand the way the law works in the courtroom, but also brought him into contact with criminals and their social world. All Grisham's novels are based on his experiences as a lawyer.

Grisham took three years to complete his first novel, *A Time to Kill*. He got up at 5 a.m. every morning to write before going to work. He had difficulty in finding a publisher, and when the book finally came out when Grisham was 34, it did not sell many copies. However, his next novel, *The Firm* – published when he was 36 – was a huge success and was made into a movie starring Tom Cruise. Six bestselling novels followed, making Grisham a rich man. His success led to *A Time to Kill* being reissued, selling five million copies. It and *The Pelican Brief* were also filmed, starring Susan Sarandon and Julia Roberts, respectively.

A Time to Kill is regarded by Grisham as his best novel. Set in the South, it tells the story of a young black girl who is viciously raped; her father then kills her attackers. The story is a comment on the racism of the American justice system and has been compared to HARPER LEE's classic novel, *To Kill a Mockingbird*. Grisham's later novels all have a similar storyline in which a courageous individual pits himself or herself against a corrupt institution such as the government, big business or organized crime.

Publications

1989 A Time to Kill
1991 The Firm
1991 The Gingerbread Man
1992 The Pelican Brief
1993 The Client
1994 The Chamber
1995 The Rainmaker
1996 The Runaway Jury
1997 The Partner
1998 The Street Lawyer

GUNN, Thom

English-born American poet

Born Aug. 29, 1929

Thom Gunn is one of the major poets of the late 20th century.

Thomson Gunn was born in Gravesend. His parents were journalists, and he had a happy childhood in London, where he lived with his mother after his parents divorced. When he was 15, however, his mother committed suicide. Gunn studied at Cambridge University and did national service in the Army, afterwards living briefly in Paris, Cambridge and Rome before going to Stanford University on a fellowship at age 25. He has lived mostly in California since then.

Gunn's first collection of poems, published when he was only 25, was written while he was at Cambridge. His traditional use of rhyme and rhythm, influenced by his reading of WILLIAM SHAKESPEARE and JOHN DONNE, is combined with lively modern language that makes the poems popular with young people. His choice of subject is influenced by French writers such as JEAN-PAUL SARTRE and ALBERT CAMUS and includes relationships, the difficulties of communication, and the lack of meaning in life. While his early poems are cynical and tough, the more recent ones are gentler. His style changes from traditional to free verse, but he has never abandoned the traditional form.

A favorite subject to which Gunn often returns is the rebel or outsider, as in "Elvis Presley" and "On the Move." Another theme is love. In *The Passages of Joy* he writes about his homosexuality, and *The Man with Night Sweats* includes poems written to friends who have died of AIDS.

Publications

1954	*Fighting Terms*
1957	*The Sense of Movement*
1961	*My Sad Captains and Other Poems*
1967	*Touch*
1971	*Moly*
1975	*Jack Straw's Castle*
1982	*The Passages of Joy*
1992	*The Man with Night Sweats*
1994	*Shelf Life*

GUTHRIE, A.B.

American novelist

Born Jan. 13, 1901
Died Apr. 26, 1991
Age at death 90

A.B. Guthrie was famous for his unsentimental and realistic tales of the American frontier from the end of the 19th century to the outbreak of World War II.

Alfred Bertram Guthrie was born in Bedford, Indiana, but grew up in Montana, where he went to school. He attended the University of Washington for a year but then moved to the University of Montana, graduating with a degree in journalism. He worked up through the ranks in journalism, first as a reporter on a local Montana newspaper and finally as executive editor of the *Leader* in Lexington, Kentucky. At age 46, he became Professor of Creative Writing at the University of Kentucky.

Guthrie began writing his famous Western novels in his early 40s.

His first novel, *Murders at Moon Dance*, was published when he was 42. The best-known novels are *The Big Sky*, *The Way West* – which won a Pulitzer Prize in 1950 – and *These Thousand Hills*. These stories were a new kind of fiction about the American West written by someone who lived there. At a time when most people could only imagine life in the "Wild West" with the help of Hollywood movies or TV programs, Guthrie wrote accurate accounts that combined historical fact and sensitive writing. His novels did not feature the stereotype of the gun-toting, lawless West so often exploited by earlier writers in the genre.

Guthrie also wrote the screenplay for the movie *Shane*, which was produced in 1951 and became a Hollywood classic. He received numerous special prizes for his writings, including the National Cowboy Hall of Fame Wrangler Award in 1970.

Publications

1943	*Murders at Moon Dance*
1947	*The Big Sky*
1950	*The Way West*
1951	*Shane*
1956	*These Thousand Hills*
1965	*The Blue Hen's Chick*
1971	*Arfive*
1975	*The Last Valley*
1981	*The Genuine Article*
1982	*Fair Land, Fair Land*

HAGGARD, H. Rider

English fantasy writer

Born Jun. 22, 1856
Died May 14, 1925
Age at death 68

H. Rider Haggard's romantic adventure stories with their fantastic plots made him very famous, and many have been made into successful movies.

Henry Rider Haggard was born in Norfolk, England, into an established and respected family. His father ended his education at 17, thinking him slow and a dreamer. Haggard was sent age 19 to British-ruled Natal, South Africa, where he held different government positions. During the next five years he learned about the African people, landscape and animals. He returned to England, married in 1880, and took over the running of his wife's estate.

Haggard then studied law, but just as he graduated, aged 29, his successful fourth book was published. *King Solomon's Mines* is a heroic adventure set in Africa about three friends who, with a Zulu warrior called Umbopa, go in search of the legendary mines of King Solomon and the diamonds hidden there. They cross terrifying deserts, nearly freeze in the mountains, and narrowly escape death in many ways before eventually finding the lost jewels. The book has never been out of print over the last hundred years.

Haggard's other famous story is *She*. A beautiful 2,000-year-old queen called Ayesha lives in the city of Kor in Africa. The novel's hero finds out about her from words on a pot left to him in his father's will. He sets out on the dangerous mission to find Ayesha. When he eventually does, she promises to make him live forever if they walk together into a pillar of flame. When she goes ahead of the hero, however, she ages rapidly, turning into a pile of dust and then nothing.

Publications

1885	*King Solomon's Mines*
1886	*She*
1887	*Allan Quartermain*
1888	*Maiwa's Revenge*
1894	*The People of the Mist*
1895	*Heart of the World*
1905	*Ayesha: the Return of She*
1911	*Red Eve*
1916	*The Ivory Child*
1921	*She and Allan*

HALEY, Alex

American novelist

Born Aug. 11, 1921
Died Feb. 10, 1992
Age at death 70

Alex Haley is best known for his historical novel *Roots: The Saga of an American Family.*

Haley was born in Ithaca, New York, and brought up in the small town of Henning in Tennessee while his parents continued their studies. It was here that his grandmother and other relatives first told him stories about his African ancestor, Kunta Kinte.

Haley did not excel at school or university, and at age 18 he enlisted in the US Coast Guard as a messboy. He spent much of his time writing articles for newspapers and magazines. After retiring 20 years later and determined to make a living by writing, he moved to New York. Following years of poverty he achieved success by working with black activist Malcolm X to produce *The Autobiography of Malcolm X*. It was published in 1965 just before the controversial black leader was assassinated. Soon after, in the era of the civil rights movement, Haley began to research his own family background, a task that took 12 years. The result was *Roots*, published when Haley was 55. It is the story of an African slave who so valued his heritage that he never accepted the ways of his slave masters and insisted on being called by his real name Kinte, not by his slave name Toby. Within two years of publication, *Roots* had won 276 awards, including a special Pulitzer Prize in 1977.

Haley was the first black American to trace his ancestry back to Africa in a popular book combining elements of fact and fiction. The huge success of the book and the two television series (*Roots* and *Roots: The Next Generation*) had an enormous impact on race relations in America.

Publications

1965 The Autobiography of Malcolm X
1976 Roots: The Saga of an American Family

HALL, Radclyffe

English novelist, poet and short-story writer

Born Aug. 12, 1886
Died Oct. 7, 1943
Age at death 57

Radclyffe Hall was the pen name used by the English writer Marguerite Radclyffe-Hall. She is remembered today for her novel *The Well of Loneliness*, which was partly based on her own life.

Hall was born in Bournemouth in southern England. She had an unhappy childhood. Her father left home shortly after her birth, and her mother remarried and moved to London, where Hall was educated by a series of governesses and in various schools. This unsettled education, together with the constant fighting between her mother and stepfather, made her feel lonely and rejected. She took comfort in writing poetry.

Hall's father died when she was 16, and she inherited his fortune. The money allowed her to concentrate on writing and, at age 20, she published a book of poems, *'Twixt Earth and Stars*.

About this time Hall fell in love with an older woman, Mabel Batten. The couple lived together until Batten's death in 1916. Soon afterward Hall met Una Trowbridge, the wife of an admiral. Una left her husband and lived with Hall until Hall's death.

The Well of Loneliness was published when Hall was 42 and at the height of her fame. The novel tells the story of a wealthy young woman who falls in love with another woman, and it calls for tolerance toward homosexuals. The book caused an immediate scandal for its frank portrayal of a lesbian relationship. Hall and her publisher were prosecuted, and the novel was banned in Britain until 1949.

Publications

1906	*'Twixt Earth and Stars*
1908	*A Sheaf of Verses*
1915	*The Forgotten Island*
1924	*The Forge*
1924	*The Unlit Lamp*
1925	*A Saturday Life*
1926	*Adam's Breed*
1928	*The Well of Loneliness*
1932	*The Master of the House*
1934	*Miss Ogilvy Finds Herself*

HAMMETT, Dashiell

American crime writer

Born May 27, 1894
Died Jan. 10, 1961
Age at death 66

Dashiell Hammett was the first author to write crime stories in a hard-boiled style – that is, realistic stories set in rough areas of American cities. Instead of writing amusing mystery stories for middle-class readers, he wrote about "low life" and the brutal world of criminals on the city streets.

Hammett was born in St. Mary's County, Maryland. He left school at 13, and traveled across America, working as a clerk, a yardman, and an advertising manager. He then worked as a private detective for the Pinkerton Agency and later based many of his stories on this experience, creating the first realistic private detective in fiction. Sam Spade was the hero of his most famous novel, *The Maltese Falcon* (also a famous film starring Humphrey Bogart as Spade). Hammett's four great novels were all written by the time he was 36 and had met the writer LILLIAN HELLMAN. He lived with her for the rest of his life and worked in Hollywood.

In the 1940s and '50s, the government in America was very anti-communist. This period is known as the McCarthy Era, after Senator Joe McCarthy, who led the hunt for communists. Hammett was suspected of being a communist and in 1951 was called to testify in court against some of his colleagues. He refused and was sentenced to six months in prison.

Hammett's stories show a cynical attitude toward society, but there is also a strong moral content in his work. His hero, private detective Sam Spade, is a tough man, but he has a strong sense of justice. Hammett set the standard for all the crime writers who followed him.

Publications

1929	*Red Harvest*
1929	*The Dain Curse*
1930	*The Maltese Falcon*
1931	*The Glass Key*
1934	*The Thin Man*
1943	*Blood Money*
1944	*The Adventures of Sam Spade and Other Stories*
1945	*The Continental Op*
1948	"The Big Knockover"

HAMMON, Jupiter

American poet and essayist

Born Oct. 17, 1711
Died c. 1800
Age at death c. 89

Publications

- *1760 An Evening Thought: Salvation by Christ with Penetential Cries*
- *1778 An Address to Miss Phillis Wheatley*
- *1779 An Essay on the Ten Virgins*
- *1782 A Winter Piece*
- *1783 An Evening's Improvement*
- *1787 An Address to the Negroes in the State of New-York*

Jupiter Hammon was the first black writer in slavery to publish work in the United States. A slave all his life, Hammon wrote poetry that was praised by fellow blacks and some white critics. He was also known as an essayist and a preacher.

Hammon was born into slavery. His slave father is believed to have been nicknamed "Opium," and his slave mother was probably sold when Jupiter was young. Hammon lived in the North, where some slaves were needed as clerks and skilled craftsmen, so he may have received some education along with his master's children. At the age of 19, he became very ill and nearly died. He bought a Bible and developed a strong interest in religion that eventually led him to become a writer and preacher.

Hammon's first poem, *An Evening Thought*, was published when he was 49. It appears to be about salvation of the soul, a common theme in 18th-century literature, but is actually about freedom for slaves. The family who "owned" Hammon left Long Island during the American Revolution to escape the fighting and settled in Hartford, Connecticut. There Hammon's next three surviving works were published. One of them was dedicated to PHILLIS WHEATLEY, a fellow slave and the first black American woman poet.

Much of Hammon's work has a religious theme, such as *A Winter Piece*, which compares the American black people to the Samaritans in Palestine – fellow racial outcasts. He used religious images and stories to challenge slave laws and propose freedom and equality for all.

HAMSUN, Knut

Norwegian novelist

Born Aug. 4, 1859
Died Feb. 19, 1952
Age at death 92

For most of the early 20th century Knut Hamsun was the leading literary figure in Norway. He is considered to be one of Scandinavia's greatest novelists.

Hamsun is an example of how a writer can succeed despite humble beginnings and a lack of formal education. His parents were peasants, and he spent his boyhood with an uncle, a fisherman who treated him cruelly. Hamsun did odd jobs as a shoemaker, a coal miner, a clerk and a teacher.

When he was 30, he submitted a story to a Danish magazine. *Hunger* was well received and was published as a book the following year. It is a study of how a man's character is destroyed by hardship and deprivation. It struck a new note in Scandinavian literature and made Hamsun famous. A long succession of novels followed, all dealing with important subjects and revealing Hamsun's personal view of life. This view contained conflicting elements. Hamsun's inclination was to avoid human commitment and retire to enjoy nature in solitude. But at the same time he was aware of his responsibility to attack the evils of modern living. In the period between World War I and World War II he became a virtual recluse.

Among many novels was one, *The Growth of the Soil*, in which he achieved a resolution to his dilemma. This book, considered to be his masterpiece, earned him the Nobel Prize for Literature in 1920. He lost popularity for his support for the Nazis during World War II, but since his death there has been renewed interest in his work.

Publications

1890 Hunger
1892 Mysteries
1893 Shallow Soil
1894 Pan
1898 Victoria
1917 The Growth of the Soil
1927 Vagabonds
1930 August
1933 The Road Leads On
1936 The Circle Is Closed

HANSBERRY, Lorraine

American playwright

Born May 19, 1930
Died Jan. 12, 1965
Age at death 34

With her classic drama *A Raisin in the Sun* Lorraine Hansberry became the first black woman to have a play produced on Broadway and the first to win the New York Drama Critics' Circle Award, in 1959.

Hansberry grew up in Chicago, the daughter of middle-class African Americans who sent her to public schools rather than private ones as a protest against the segregation laws. They also protested the segregation of communities. When Hansberry was eight, her parents bought a house in a white neighborhood. Their experience of discrimination there led to a civil rights case that her parents fought all the way to the Supreme Court, where they won.

Hansberry studied art at the University of Wisconsin and later in Mexico but gave it up to move to New York City at age 20. There she worked as a waitress and cashier and wrote short stories and plays; she also wrote for an African-American newspaper called *Freedom*, where she met writer LANGSTON HUGHES. In 1953, she married a Jewish songwriter.

A line in a Langston Hughes poem gave her the title of her best-known work, *A Raisin in the Sun*. It is based loosely on her childhood experiences and tells the story of a black family who confront racism when they move into a white neighborhood. The play was hugely successful. It opened on Broadway when she was 29, and ran for nearly two years; later, it was made into a film starring the young Sidney Poitier.

Hansberry died of cancer at age 34 after completing only one more play. Her husband completed an unfinished play and published a collection of her letters and other writings after her death.

Publications

1959 A Raisin in the Sun
1964 The Movement: Documentary of a Struggle for Equality
1964 The Sign in Sidney Brustein's Window

Published after she died

1969 To Be Young, Gifted, and Black
1970 Les Blanc (The Collected Last Plays of Lorraine Hansberry)

HARDWICK, Elizabeth

American critic, short-story writer and novelist

Born Jul. 27, 1916

Elizabeth Hardwick is a successful short-story writer, novelist, and literary and social critic. In 1963, she cofounded the *New York Review of Books*, which is now one of America's leading literary journals.

Hardwick was born in Lexington, Kentucky. Her father ran a heating and plumbing business, while her mother raised their 11 children. Hardwick earned a degree in English literature from the University of Kentucky. At age 23, she moved to New York to study further at Columbia University.

In New York, Hardwick began her first novel, *The Ghostly Lover*, which was published when she was 29. It is the story of a lonely young Southern woman in New York and of her unhappy relationship with her mother. While some praised *The Ghostly Lover* for its beautiful writing, others criticized it for lacking a clear story. Hardwick did not publish another novel for ten years. During this decade she was asked to contribute essays to the *Partisan Review*, beginning her hugely successful career as a literary and social critic. She also married, in 1949, the poet ROBERT LOWELL; the marriage lasted 23 years, and they traveled widely together.

After Hardwick settled in Boston in 1954, her second novel, *The Simple Truth*, was published. Praise for her fiction was not widespread, however, until her third novel, *Sleepless Nights*, came out. Partly based on Hardwick's own life, this is the story of a woman remembering people she had met or known, including her mother, a doctor, and a maid. The characters she remembers are often lonely or unhappy, but brave in the face of trouble.

Publications

1945	*The Ghostly Lover*
1955	*The Simple Truth*
1962	*A View of My Own: Essays in Literature and Society*
1974	*Seduction and Betrayal: Women and Literature*
1979	*Sleepless Nights*
1983	*Bartleby in Manhattan and Other Essays*

HARDY, Thomas

English novelist and poet

Born Jun. 2, 1840
Died Jan. 11, 1928
Age at death 87

Thomas Hardy wrote novels about country people living in Wessex, his name for the quiet, rural county of Dorset in southwest England. He also wrote more than ten volumes of poetry and short stories.

Hardy was a stonemason's son born in a Dorset village. His parents encouraged him to love music and reading. He went to school in Dorchester, the county town, and then trained as an architect. For a while he worked in architects' offices in London and later in Dorset, where he spent most of his life. He was twice married.

Hardy began writing by his mid-20s. His first published novel, *Desperate Remedies*, appeared when he was 31. Three years later came his first truly popular book, *Far from the Madding Crowd*. This was the first of his seven great novels, published between 1874 and 1895. The most moving tales are set in the old, brooding landscapes of Wessex. They tell of lonely individuals with human weaknesses struggling against a fate that always overcomes them. Two of these novels, *Tess of the D'Urbervilles* and *Jude the Obscure*, remind readers of the tragedies written by AESCHYLUS and SOPHOCLES. These ancient Greek playwrights wrote about royal families, but Hardy's heroes and heroines are ordinary people such as farmers, shepherds and dairymaids.

Despite the success of his novels, Hardy thought of himself as mainly a poet. At 58, he published *Wessex Poems*. By 68, he had also written *The Dynasts*, a long verse play about the Napoleonic Wars. In his 80s, Hardy was still writing lyric poems. Many make ordinary experiences seem rich and remarkable.

Publications
1871 Desperate Remedies
1874 Far from the Madding Crowd
1878 The Return of the Native
1880 The Trumpet-Major
1886 The Mayor of Casterbridge
1891 Tess of the D'Urbervilles
1895 Jude the Obscure
1898 Wessex Poems
1903–08 The Dynasts

HARPER, Frances E.W.

Frances E.W. Harper was the most important black woman poet of the 19th century. She was also an active antislavery campaigner.

Although her parents were free, Frances Ellen Watkins Harper was born in Baltimore, Maryland, which was then a slave state. She became an orphan at three and was raised by relatives. After an early education in her uncle's school, Harper got a job in a bookshop and read widely.

When she was 25, Harper moved to Ohio to teach domestic science. By the mid-1850s, she had become an activist in the antislavery movement and a highly popular public speaker for the cause. She used her poetry in many of her speeches, and when she was 29, she published *Poems on Miscellaneous Subjects*, which sold more than 10,000 copies. Slavery features in some of the poems, but many are about religious themes (Harper was a devout Christian), equality and individual responsibility. At age 34, she published "The Two Offers," which is thought to be the first short story published by an African-American woman in the US.

When she was 67, Harper published what became her best-known work, the novel *Iola Leroy*. It is about fair-skinned African Americans who reject the option of passing themselves off as white and stay with their oppressed communities. This was one of the first novels published in the US by a black woman and the first to reach a wide audience. Recently three of Harper's novels were rediscovered and published together in 1995.

American poet and novelist

Born Sep. 24, 1825
Died Feb. 22, 1911
Age at death 85

Publications
1854 Poems on Miscellaneous Subjects
1859 "The Two Offers"
1869 Moses
1872 Sketches of Southern Life
1890 The Sparrow's Fall
1892 Iola Leroy
1894 The Martyr of Alabama

Published after she died
1995 Minnie's Sacrifice, Sowing and Reaping, Trial and Triumph

HARRIS, Joel Chandler

American children's writer

Born Dec. 9, 1848
Died Jul. 3, 1908
Age at death 59

Joel Chandler Harris is famous for his collections of "Uncle Remus" tales.

Born in Eatonton, Georgia, Harris went to work when he was 13 as a printer for the *Countryman*, a newspaper published on a plantation near his home. There he became familiar with the customs, legends, and dialects of local slaves. From 1866 to 1876, Harris worked on various newspapers in Georgia and Louisiana. When he was 28, he joined the staff of the *Atlanta Constitution*, where he remained for 24 years.

Harris began publishing his "Uncle Remus" stories in the *Constitution*. They were so popular that he collected them in a book entitled *Uncle Remus: His Songs and His Sayings*, which was published when he was 32. The stories center on the character of the beloved family servant, Uncle Remus, an aging former slave. To entertain the family's young son, Uncle Remus tells him stories about animals who act and talk like humans, such as Brer (Brother) Fox and Brer Rabbit. In many of the tales, the rabbit outwits the fox, who is always trying to catch and eat him. The stories, based on African-American tales Harris learned on the plantation, are told in Southern African-American dialects. The book was an immediate success. Readers enjoyed its humor and critics praised its use of dialect, calling it an important record of African-American folklore. Its popularity led Harris to publish five other collections of "Uncle Remus" stories.

Harris also wrote stories depicting Southern life during and after the American Civil War.

Publications

1880	*Uncle Remus: His Songs and His Sayings*
1883	*Nights with Uncle Remus*
1884	*Mingo and Other Sketches in Black and White*
1892	*Uncle Remus and His Friends*
1904	*The Tar-Baby and Other Rhymes by Uncle Remus*
1905	*Told by Uncle Remus*

HARRIS, Thomas

American crime writer

Born c. 1940

Thomas Harris is one of today's most influential crime writers. He is the first and probably best writer to confront our fears about a new bogeyman in modern society, the serial killer.

Born in Mississippi, Missouri, Harris moved to New York, where he worked as a journalist for the Associated Press. His first novel, *Black Sunday*, written when he was about 35, is a story about a terrorist attack on the Super Bowl. But it was his second novel, *Red Dragon*, that made his name. In it he introduced Hannibal Lecter, a man who commits brutal murders apparently for pleasure. Not only is Lecter violent, he is also clever; and it is this combination that makes Harris's portrait of Lecter so terrifying.

Red Dragon is also frightening because Harris shows that we all have a capacity for evil within us. In the novel FBI agent Will Graham is only able to solve the crime by understanding how the murderer feels, almost to the point of feeling equally violent himself.

In *The Silence of the Lambs,* Harris introduces a female detective, Clarice Starling. Once again, he shows how murders are solved by understanding the culprits' motives. Harris bases this idea on the real FBI practice of "profiling" – that is, trying to build up a picture of the murderer's mental and emotional state in order to track his or her actions.

All three of Harris's books have been filmed (*Red Dragon* as *Manhunter*). But although his books are now famous, Harris himself remains a man of mystery, avoiding publicity and refusing to be interviewed.

Publications

1975 Black Sunday
1981 Red Dragon
1988 The Silence of the Lambs

HARRISON, Jim

American novelist, poet and screenwriter

Born Dec. 11, 1937

Jim Harrison is an established poet of the natural world, a novelist and a screenwriter. Perhaps his most famous work is *Legends of the Fall*, which was made into a 1993 blockbuster film.

Harrison was born in Grayling, Michigan. His father was a county agricultural agent, and from an early age Harrison enjoyed hunting and fishing. A childhood accident left him blind in his left eye, and for comfort he turned even more to nature. Both his parents were great readers, and they introduced him to the works of a wide range of writers. By the time he was 16, Harrison was sure that he was going to be a writer, and he studied English at Michigan State University. After graduating at the age of 23, he stayed on to get another degree. *Plain Song*, his first volume of poems, came out when he was 28 and still a university student. His first poetry collections were well received but earned little money. For years he worked on building sites to support his family.

Harrison's poetry explores the natural world, often in new and unusual ways or in unexpected verse forms. His first novel, *Wolf*, was written while he was recovering from a hunting accident. This story of a man leaving the city to search for meaning in the wilds of Michigan showed promise, but *Legends of the Fall* was his first commercial success. This collection of three short historical novels explores the themes of revenge, obsession and violence. *Dalva*, unlike his earlier work, centers on a woman. Part Sioux, she searches for the child she gave up when she was young. In *Julip* three different stories show three different ways of getting through life.

Publications

1965 Plain Song
1968 Locations
1969 Walking
1971 Outlyer and Ghazals
1971 Wolf
1975 Farmer
1979 Legends of the Fall
1988 Dalva
1990 The Woman Lit by Fireflies
1994 Julip

HARTE, Bret

American short-story writer and poet

Born Aug. 25, 1836
Died May 5, 1902
Age at death 65

Bret Harte is best known for his short stories about the American West in the Gold Rush days.

Harte was born in Albany, New York, and spent an unsettled childhood traveling from place to place with his family. His father died when Harte was only nine. Harte left school at 13 and went to work in an office. When he was 18, his mother remarried, and he went to live with his mother and stepfather in California. After unsuccessfully panning for gold and working for a short time with the stagecoach company Wells Fargo, Harte became a printer and journalist in San Francisco.

When in his 30s, Harte began to write a series of stories and sketches about life in the Wild West Gold Rush towns for a local newspaper. A collection of his stories was published in *The Luck of Roaring Camp* and brought 33-year-old Harte instant success across the country. His work was especially popular in the East, where readers loved his colorful, humorous tales of cowboys, drunks, prostitutes, gamblers, and fortunes won and lost.

On the strength of this popularity Harte visited the East in 1871. He was offered $10,000 by the *Atlantic Monthly* to contribute 12 poems or sketches over the next year. This was an enormous amount of money in those days, and Harte accepted the contract and moved to Boston. But by leaving California, Harte cut himself off from his main source of inspiration, and the quality of his writing quickly declined; his reputation rests almost solely on the stories from his San Francisco days. Harte spent the last years of his life in England, where he was very popular.

Publications

1860 M'liss
1869 The Luck of Roaring Camp
1870 The Heathen Chinee
1873 Mrs. Skagg's Husbands
1875 Tales of the Argonauts
1878 An Heiress of Red Dog
1891 A Sappho of Green Springs

HARTLEY, L.P.

English novelist and short-story writer

Born Dec. 30, 1895
Died Dec. 13, 1972
Age at death 76

L.P. Hartley is best remembered for his stylish, sometimes humorous novels set in England at the beginning of the 20th century. They are about the uneasiness of relationships between younger people and older people.

Born in Whittlesea in the east of England, Leslie Poles Hartley was raised in a big country house. His lawyer father became chairman of the family brickwork business and enjoyed a luxurious and privileged life, like many of the characters in Hartley's novels. Hartley went to the famous private school, Harrow ,aged 15 and to Oxford University at 20. During World War I, he served in the army, although he never saw any fighting. He returned to Oxford to study history. Supported by a private income, he started writing and was influenced by the works of HENRY JAMES and NATHANIEL HAWTHORNE.

Hartley published some short stories and a short novel in his 30s and then nothing more for almost 20 years. He reviewed books for newspapers and magazines and divided his time between England and Venice. When he was 49, he published *The Shrimp and the Anenome,* the first of three novels about young Eustace, who daydreams and depends on his elder sister Hilda. All three novels were highly praised, and the third, *Eustace and Hilda*, won an important award. He also wrote from the viewpoint of an adolescent in his most popular book, *The Go-Between*, in which an elderly man remembers a hot summer during his youth. It, too, received a prize and became a successful film.

Publications

1924 Night Fears and Other Stories
1944 The Shrimp and the Anenome
1946 The Sixth Heaven
1947 Eustace and Hilda
1949 The Boat
1953 The Go-Between
1957 The Hireling
1966 The Betrayal

HASEK, Jaroslav

Czech novelist and satirist

Born Apr. 24, 1883
Died Jan. 3, 1923
Age at death 39

Although he wrote many short stories, as well as poems and essays, Jaroslav Hasek is best known for his highly successful long novel and satire on military life, *The Good Soldier Schweik*. The "hero" Schweik is a totally undisciplined liar, drunkard and apparently stupid man, who seemingly blunders along but who actually outwits the army and medical establishments.

Hasek was born in Prague, now in the Czech Republic, the son of a schoolmaster who died from drink when Hasek was only three. Hasek went to a commercial college and then got a job in a bank. A practical joker, he was quite unsuited to banking and was soon sacked. He then became a freelance journalist, did time in jail for assaulting a policeman, and got a job editing a natural history magazine. The last was to prove to his girlfriend that he could be serious. He was, however, unable to resist inventing entirely fictitious animals and was again dismissed. He married in 1910, but suffered mental problems, and his wife went back to live with her parents.

During World War I, Hasek was drafted into the army but was captured by the Russians. While in Russia, he enjoyed enough freedom to become a member of the Communist Party.

At age 37, Hasek returned to Prague and set about completing the first three volumes of *The Good Soldier Schweik*. Schweik had already appeared in stories Hasek had been writing from the age of 29. No publisher dared to produce the book, so Hasek published it at his own expense. It has been internationally popular ever since. Hasek died before he could finish the fourth volume.

Publications

c. 1901 From the Old Pharmacy
1903 Cries of May
1912 The Good Soldier Schweik and Other Strange Stories
1913 The Tourist Guide: Twenty-Six Stories
1915 My Trade With Dogs
1917 The Good Soldier Schweik in Captivity
1920–23 The Good Soldier Schweik (4 vols.)

HAUPTMANN, Gerhart

German playwright, novelist and poet

Born Nov. 15, 1862
Died Jun. 6, 1946
Age at death 83

The German writer Gerhart Hauptmann was awarded the Nobel Prize for Literature in 1912.

Hauptmann was born in Obersalzbrunn, a fashionable resort in eastern Germany. He was educated in the city of Breslau and at 16 began working for his uncle as a farmhand. However, in 1880, he enrolled in Breslau Academy of Art, hoping to become a sculptor. After two years of study, he moved to Italy, but ill health forced him to return home the following year.

When Hauptmann was 23, he married Marie Thienemann, and her wealth gave him the freedom to choose his own career. He had already begun writing and now became involved with a literary movement called "Naturalism." Naturalists attempted to accurately portray everyday life and all the unpleasantness they saw in it. Inspired by them, Hauptmann wrote his first play, *Before Dawn*. It made him famous almost overnight.

When he was 31, Hauptmann wrote his best-known play, *The Weavers*, which is about a group of downtrodden weavers who take on their employers. The play shows great sympathy for ordinary people struggling against the pressures of an uncaring world.

The struggle often present in Hauptmann's plays, however, began to be echoed in his private life. After periods of separation from his wife and two sons, he was divorced in 1904. He remarried the same year.

In later years, Hauptmann's works rarely showed the sparks of greatness that were present in his best writing. Despite this, he is still acknowledged today as one of the finest exponents of Naturalist literature.

Publications

1889 Before Dawn
1891 Lonely Lives
1892 Lineman Thiel and Other Tales
1892 Colleague Crampton
1893 The Beaver Coat
1893 The Weavers
1911 The Rats
1926 Dorothea Angermann
1927 Till Eulenspiegel

HAVEL, Vaclav

Czech playwright, poet and essayist

Born Oct. 5, 1936

Vaclav Havel, president of the Czech Republic, is also a noted playwright. His plays, examples of theater of the absurd, use dramatic techniques to make situations or characters seem ridiculous.

Havel was born in Prague and educated at the local technical college. At 23, he began working at the Balustrade Theater, eventually graduating to resident playwright. During this time, he continued his education at the Prague Academy of Art.

When Havel was 25, he collaborated with the theater's artistic director on his first play, *The Hitchhike*. By the late 1960s, Havel was already considered one of the great Czech playwrights of his generation. His works, which satirize the behavior of government officials, often deal with the power of language to interfere with clear thought.

In *The Garden Party* the main character speaks in absurd slogans, while in *The Memorandum* characters use an entirely artificial language.

After the Russian invasion of Czechoslovakia in 1968, Havel's work, considered "antigovernment," was banned. Despite periods of imprisonment, he continued writing and became the focus of a strong anticommunist movement. His plays, performed abroad, did much to bring world attention to the Czechoslovakian struggle.

Following the collapse of communism in Eastern Europe, Havel was elected Czechoslovakian president in 1989. He became president of the Czech Republic in 1993. Of theater, he has said: "As soon as my homeland does not need me . . . I will with great appetite devote myself to my original profession."

Publications

1961 *The Hitchhike* (with Ivan Vyskocil)
1963 *The Garden Party*
1965 *The Memorandum*
1974 *The Conspirators*
1976 *Preview to an Exhibit*
1976 *An Audience*
1976 *The Beggar's Opera*
1984 *Largo Desolato*
1985 *Temptation*
1991 *Open Letters: Selected Writings*

HAWTHORNE, Nathaniel

American novelist and short-story writer

Born Jul. 4, 1804
Died May 19, 1864
Age at death 59

Nathaniel Hawthorne was a major American novelist and short-story writer. He was one of the first American writers to explore the hidden motivations of his characters and of humans in general. He also wrote some popular books for children.

Born in Salem, Massachusetts, Hawthorne graduated from Bowdoin College, where he knew HENRY WADSWORTH LONGFELLOW and future president, Franklin Pierce. Between the ages of 21 and 35 Hawthorne lived in seclusion, writing short stories. But he was unable to earn a living as a writer and, during the 1840s, he worked in customhouses. In 1842, he moved to Concord, Massachusetts, where he met RALPH WALDO EMERSON and HENRY DAVID THOREAU.

When he was 46, Hawthorne published his masterpiece, *The Scarlet Letter*. This allegorical novel, set in 17th-century Puritan Boston, tells the story of Hester Prynne, her husband Roger Chillingworth and her lover, Arthur Dimmesdale, who was the father of her child. In the work, Hawthorne explores the effect of guilt, anxiety and sorrow on the minds and characters of the three individuals.

The next year, Hawthorne published *The House of the Seven Gables*, the story of a family cursed by one of the victims of the 17th-century Salem witchcraft trials. In 1853, President Pierce made Hawthorne consul in Liverpool. The post permitted him to travel in Italy, the setting of his last book *The Marble Faun*, a novel about the conflict between innocence and guilt.

Publications

1828 *Fanshawe*
1837 *Twice-Told Tales*
1846 *Mosses from an Old Manse*
1850 *The Scarlet Letter*
1851 *The House of the Seven Gables*
1851 *A Wonder Book for Girls and Boys*
1853 *Tanglewood Tales for Girls and Boys*
1860 *The Marble Faun*

HAYASHI, Fumiko

Japanese novelist, poet and short-story writer

Born Dec. 31,1904
Died Jun. 28, 1951
Age at death 46

Hayashi Fumiko was the most distinguished Japanese woman writer of her time, best known for her novel *Floating Clouds*. Her life was short, but she wrote 25 novels, 20 books of short stories, 2 collections of poetry and many children's tales.

Hayashi was the daughter of an unmarried geisha, a woman trained to provide company for men. Her childhood was very deprived. She was raised by wandering peddlers and was often hungry and homeless. This left her with an intense feeling of insecurity.

When she was 12, Hayashi settled in Onomichi, central Japan, and went to secondary school, from which she graduated when she was 19. Reading helped her to overcome her loneliness, and while still a child she wrote stories and poems. The hardship of her early life gave her a great desire to work hard for success. When it finally arrived, she entered the lively world of writers and the theater in Tokyo. Hayashi knew from experience the hardships of the Tokyo poor and wrote about them with stark realism and without sentimentality.

The first two parts of Hayashi's first novel, *Journal of a Vagabond*, were published when she was 26. They were based on her childhood and were very successful. Later, they were followed by a series of autobiographical, diary-form books. *Floating Clouds* is about the tragic life of a quiet Japanese girl in Southeast Asia, of her development from timid child to sophisticated adult, and of her search for her former lover in war-torn Tokyo.

Hayashi is said to have died from overwork.

Publications

1929 I Saw a Pale Horse
1930–47 Journal of a Vagabond
1931 A Life of Poverty
1935 "Oyster"
1935 Lightning
1948 "Late Chrysanthemum"
1949 Downtown
1949 "Bones"
1949–51 Floating Clouds

HAYDEN, Robert

American poet

Born Aug. 4, 1913
Died Feb. 25, 1980
Age at death 66

Robert Hayden overcame immense personal and social difficulties to become one of America's finest modern poets. In 1976, he became the first African-American poetry consultant to the Library of Congress.

Hayden was born Asa Bundy Sheffey in Detroit. When he was a baby, he was abandoned by his parents. Neighbors took him in as part of their family and renamed him Robert Hayden. Although he suffered from poor eyesight, Hayden worked hard at school and studied at Detroit City College.

When he was 23, Hayden became a researcher for the Federal Writers' Project. He was particularly concerned with African-American folklore and the pre-Civil War antislavery movement. The influence of what he learned, together with his feelings about his own upbringing and experience in contemporary America, formed the essence of Hayden's first collection of poems, *Heart-Shape in the Dust*, which came out when he was 27. From 1941 to 1944, Hayden was a full-time student at the University of Michigan, where one of his tutors was the poet W.H. AUDEN. In 1946, he became a professor.

Although much of his work is concerned with racial subjects, its broad view of human experience lifts his poetry to a more universal level. The publication of his *Selected Poems* when he was 53 confirmed his stature as one of America's leading modern poets. One of his best-known poems is "Middle Passage," a collection of images and impressions of the Atlantic slave ships.

Publications

1940 Heart-Shape in the Dust
1955 Figure of Time
1962 A Ballad of Remembrance
1966 Selected Poems
1966 "Middle Passage"
1970 "El-Hajj Malik El-Shabazz"
1970 Words in the Mourning Time
1978 American Journal

Published after he died

1985 Collected Poems

HAZLITT, William

English essayist, critic, and biographer

Born Apr. 10, 1778
Died Sep. 18, 1830
Age at death 52

William Hazlitt was one of the greatest English writers of essays.

Hazlitt was born in a small town in southern England, the son of a minister. The family went to America but returned and settled in the village of Wem in the north of England. At an early age Hazlitt showed talent as a writer. His first essay was written when he was just 14. At age 15, he went to university in London to study religion but soon decided to take up art. He spent a number of years painting portraits before turning to literature.

When Hazlitt was 20, he met the poet SAMUEL TAYLOR COLERIDGE and became a part of London's busy literary scene. He later described this time in "My First Acquaintance with the Poets," which some regard as one of his best essays. Between the ages of 39 and 48 Hazlitt wrote essays on everything from philosophy to drama. Many of these are enthusiastic examinations of literature, which he obviously enjoyed. Hazlitt was a passionate man with strong opinions. His attacks on fellow writers in works such as *Table Talk* cost him many friendships. He was friendly with writers of the Romantic movement, and in *The Spirit of the Age* he set out his belief that reason and emotion can be in harmony. Hazlitt's lively and personal writing style means that his essays are highly readable and entertaining to this day.

Later, Hazlitt devoted his time to writing a four-volume biography of the French emperor Napoleon, whom he greatly admired. Hazlitt was a strong critic of social conditions in England and supported the aims of the French Revolution.

Publications

1798 "My First Acquaintance with the Poets"
1817 Characters of Shakespeare's Plays
1818 English Poets
1818–21 A View of the English Stage
1819 English Comic Writers
1819 Political Essays
1821–22 Table Talk
1825 The Spirit of the Age
1828–30 Life of Napoleon (4 vols.)

HAZZARD, Shirley

Australian-born American novelist and short-story writer

Born Jan. 30, 1931

Love, travel and chance are themes central to Shirley Hazzard's fiction. Like HENRY JAMES, to whom she has been compared, she writes of women traveling in Europe and usually falling in love.

Hazzard became widely traveled at a young age. She was born in Sydney, Australia, and when she was 16, she moved to Hong Kong, where her father, a government official, had been given a job. She worked for the British government in Hong Kong, then moved to New Zealand to work for the British High Commission. By the time she was 20, she was working for the United Nations in New York City.

In 1957, Hazzard spent a year in Italy, and since then she has nurtured a love for that country which is reflected in two of her novels, *The Evening of the Holiday* and *The Bay of Noon*. After working for the UN for ten years, Hazzard became increasingly disappointed with the bureaucracy of that organization; she used her experiences there as a basis for a collection of sharply funny short stories, *People in Glass Houses*, and a nonfiction work, *Defeat of an Ideal*. By the age of 31, she had "retired" and was able to devote all her time to writing.

Hazzard had already published several short stories in the *New Yorker* magazine, many based on her travels. A year after leaving the UN, she published a collection of ten stories, *Cliffs of Fall*, all involving relationships between men and women, which received positive reviews. At age 49, she published her masterpiece, *The Transit of Venus*, which established her reputation and for which she won the National Book Critics' Circle Award.

Publications

1963 Cliffs of Fall
1966 The Evening of the Holiday
1967 People in Glass Houses
1970 The Bay of Noon
1972 Defeat of an Ideal
1980 The Transit of Venus
1990 Countenance of Truth

HEAD, Bessie

South African-born Botswanan novelist

Born Jul. 6, 1937
Died Apr. 17, 1986
Age at death 48

Bessie Head was one of Africa's greatest women writers. She was born in a mental hospital in Natal, South Africa. Her mother, who came from a rich white family, was placed there when it was discovered that she was carrying a child fathered by a black man who worked in the family's stables. At that time interracial relationships were illegal in South Africa. Abandoned, Head grew up with a foster family. At the age of 13, she was placed in an orphanage where she was brutally informed, bit by bit, about the little that was known of her "shameful" past.

Head left the orphanage and went straight into an unhappy marriage. In an attempt to find peace of mind, she left her husband, her job as a journalist and her country, and moved with her young son to neighboring Botswana in 1964. There she lived in an experimental, self-supporting farming community. Unable to return to South Africa, Head was a refugee in Botswana until 15 years later, when she became a citizen. Her first novel, *When Rain Clouds Gather*, published when she was 31, grew out of this experience. Its hero, also a refugee, chooses a quiet and peaceful life over fame and status.

The rejection and racism Head experienced as a child influenced her writing. Her major novels all have outcasts at their heart. *Maru* explores racism between different African peoples. It reflects a concern of Head's that black cruelty could simply replace white cruelty in Africa. *A Question of Power* could almost be about Head's real mother – it is the story of a woman driven mad by an evil society. Head died at an early age from liver disease.

Publications

1968 When Rain Clouds Gather
1971 Maru
1974 A Question of Power
1977 The Collector of Treasures
1981 Serowe
1984 A Bewitched Crossroad: An African Saga

Published after she died

1990 A Woman Alone: Autobiographical Writings

HEANEY, Seamus

Irish poet

Born Apr. 13, 1939

Seamus Heaney is the foremost poet in Ireland in the late 20th century.

Heaney was born in County Derry, Northern Ireland. He was the eldest in a Catholic family of nine children whose father was a cattle farmer. On leaving St. Columb's College, Derry, he studied at Queen's University, Belfast. At age 27 he published his first collection of poetry, *Death of a Naturalist*. Heaney taught poetry at Queen's University until he was 33, when he moved to the Irish Republic.

Heaney was in Belfast at the outbreak, in 1969, of what has become known as "The Troubles." The Catholic minority in Northern Ireland had been discriminated against since the establishment of the country nearly 70 years earlier. Prompted by television pictures of civil rights protests elsewhere in Europe and in the United States, Catholic students led a civil rights campaign that rapidly developed into armed conflict against British rule.

Heaney left Belfast at the height of this conflict, but his work reflects his experiences of that time. His early poetry, with its reflections on his childhood in rural Ireland, gives way to darker commentaries on the social and political problems in Northern Ireland. In *The Government of the Tongue*, examining the role of poetry in a modern society, Heaney seems to question its validity.

Since the late 1980s, Heaney has taught at both Harvard University and Oxford University and, in 1995, he was awarded the Nobel Prize for Literature.

Publications

1966 Death of a Naturalist
1972 Wintering Out
1975 Bog Poems
1975 North
1980 Poems: 1965–75
1987 The Haw Lantern
1988 The Government of the Tongue
1991 Seeing Things
1995 The Redress of Poetry
1996 Spirit Level
1998 Opened Ground: Poems, 1966-96

HEATH, Roy A.K.

Guyanese novelist and short-story writer

Born Aug. 13, 1926

Roy A.K. Heath is probably Guyana's most famous modern author.

Roy Aubrey Kelvin Heath was born in Georgetown, the capital of Guyana in South America. At that time, Guyana was a British colony. Both his parents were teachers, but his father died while Heath was still a baby. As a result he was raised in poverty by his mother. He went to local schools before traveling to England when he was 25 to study modern languages at London University. Since graduating, Heath has taught German and French at schools in London. He qualified as a lawyer in 1964, but has never practiced.

Heath published his first novel, *A Man Come Home*, when he was 48. It is the story of a lazy man who suddenly becomes successful after a trip. Rumors spread that he has made a pact with the Fair Maid, a river spirit like ones worshiped in Africa. Like all of Heath's novels, *A Man Come Home* is set in Guyana. It has been praised for its realistic portrayal of daily life in Georgetown. Although Heath has lived in London since 1951, he regularly returns to Guyana and has kept his homeland fresh in his mind.

Heath's largest work is a set of three books (*From the Heat of the Day*, *One Generation* and *Genetha*) called the Georgetown Trilogy. Partly based on his own life, it traces the story of one family from the 1920s to the '50s. Heath grew up in a society of Creoles descended from Europeans, Indians and Africans, and this is reflected in his study of social and racial prejudices in the trilogy. His recent work *Shadows Round the Moon* tells of his upbringing in British-ruled Guyana.

Publications

1974 A Man Come Home
1978 The Murderer
1979 From the Heat of the Day
1980 One Generation
1981 Genetha
1982 Kwaku
1984 Orealla
1988 The Shadow Bride
1990 Shadows Round the Moon
1994 The Armstrong Trilogy

HEINE, Heinrich

German poet and critic

Born Dec. 13, 1797
Died Feb. 17, 1856
Age at death 58

The great German poet Heinrich Heine was a complex character who lived at a time of major social and political changes. The upsets of the French Revolution and the Napoleonic Wars are reflected in Heine's personality and writing. His poetry is amusing, thoughtful and very readable, ranging from simple romantic lyrics to political satire.

Heine was born in Dusseldorf, Germany. He was Jewish but converted to Christianity and changed his name from Harry to Heinrich. His first poetry collection, *Book of Songs*, was published when he was 30.

Throughout his life Heine had a love-hate relationship with German Romanticism. He was a master of the genre, producing examples of the purest quality. But he was also a strong critic of politics and art, using satire in a wickedly effective manner. For years he was more highly regarded in France, England and America than in his native Germany.

In his prose writing, Heine attacked German politics and personalities and was considered unpatriotic. He became less popular, and with anti-Jewish feelings growing in Germany, he was driven into exile. In 1831, he moved to Paris, where he remained until he died.

The trouble Heine stirred up persisted long after his death. In the late 19th and early 20th centuries proposals to erect his statue in various German cities sparked off riots. Later, the Nazis insisted that Heine's songs should be marked "author unknown" in poetry collections.

Publications

1826–31	*Travel Pictures* (4 vols.)
1827	*Book of Songs*
1833	*French Affairs*
1835	*Philosophy and Literature in Germany*
1836	*The Romantic School*
1844	*Germany: A Winter's Tale*
1844	*New Poems*
1847	*Atta Troll and Other Poems*
1854	*Various Writings*

HEINLEIN, Robert

American science fiction writer

Born Jul. 7, 1907
Died May 8, 1988
Age at death 80

Robert Heinlein was one of the most influential and popular writers of American science fiction.

Heinlein was born in Butler, Missouri, and later the family moved to Kansas City, where he attended secondary school and university. When he was 18, he enrolled in the Naval Academy at Annapolis. He served in the navy but suffered from seasickness. His health was weakened, and eventually he became ill with a serious infection of the lungs. Aged only 27, he retired from the navy and was given a small pension.

Heinlein tried working in engineering, in real estate, and as an artist, photographer and sculptor. But it was only when he turned to writing that he found what he wanted to do. The magazine *Astounding Science Fiction* published his story "Life-Line" when he was 32. Over the next 40 years, he wrote many more short stories for magazines and novels.

At first Heinlein wrote for young readers about the conquest of space, in books such as *Rocket Ship Galileo*. Later novels, such as the prizewinning *Starship Troopers*, had more adult themes. His best-known adult novel is *Stranger in a Strange Land*, about a human child raised by Martians who returns to Earth.

Heinlein extended the scope of science fiction and its readership. In his collection *The Past through Tomorrow*, he presented a series of connected stories that predict the future of human civilization. The prediction is that in the year 2000 there will be three revolutions: in the US, in Antarctica and on Venus. After that, society will be run by priests, and there will be little progress for many years.

Publications

1947	*Rocket Ship Galileo*
1949	*Sixth Column*
1956	*Double Star*
1958	*Have Space Suit – Will Travel*
1959	*Starship Troopers*
1961	*Stranger in a Strange Land*
1966	*The Moon Is a Harsh Mistress*
1967	*The Past through Tomorrow*
1973	*Time Enough for Love*

HELLER, Joseph

American novelist and playwright

Born May 1, 1923
Died Dec. 12, 1999
Age at death 76

Joseph Heller found success with his first and most famous novel, *Catch-22*. Like other writers before him, he drew on his own experiences in World War II.

Heller was born in Brooklyn, New York City. After graduating from Abraham Lincoln High School, he joined the US Air Force. As a wing bombardier stationed on the Mediterranean island of Corsica, he flew 60 missions. After the war, he attended the University of Southern California for a year before transferring to New York University. He received a Master's degree from Columbia University.

While writing *Catch-22*, Heller worked for a number of magazines such as *Time*, *Look* and *McCall's*. He left *McCall's* at age 38 to teach fiction and dramatic writing at Yale University and the University of Pennsylvania. *Catch-22* was published that year but did not immediately catch on. The novel, a satire on war, had a steady sale in the US but only began to sell well after its publication and enthusiastic reception in England. By 1975, it had sold over six million copies.

The main character in *Catch-22* is a fighter-pilot called Yossarian who is determined not to be killed. However hard he tries to leave the Air Force, he is always foiled by "catch-22," which says that "they (the army authorities) have a right to do anything we can't stop them from doing."

After recovering from a sudden paralytic illness, Heller wrote other works of fiction, including a sequel to *Catch-22* called *Closing Time*. His later books have not, however, received the same praise as *Catch-22*, nor have they sold in the same numbers.

Publications

1961 Catch-22
1967 We Bombed in New Haven
1973 Clevinger's Trial
1974 Something Happened
1979 Good as Gold
1984 God Knows
1986 No Laughing Matter (with Speed Vogel)
1988 Picture This
1994 Closing Time
1998 Now and Then: Memoir from Coney Island to Here

HELLMAN, Lillian

American playwright

Born Jun. 20, 1905
Died Jun. 30, 1984
Age at death 79

Lillian Hellman was a leading voice in American theater despite writing only 12 plays in her lifetime. Her plays often carry a message that is easy to understand, like "telling lies can hurt people" and "being greedy is wrong."

Born to a Jewish family in New Orleans, Hellman was an only child who spent half of every year in New York City and the other half back in Louisiana at a boarding house run by her aunts. Many of the characters in her work, such as those in *Toys in the Attic*, are based on family members.

With the encouragement of crime novelist DASHIELL HAMMETT, Hellman wrote her first and one of her most successful plays, *The Children's Hour*, in which girls at a boarding school spread gossip about their teachers. It opened when Hellman was 29 and ran on Broadway for nearly 700 performances.

In 1937, Hellman went to Paris and met ERNEST HEMINGWAY and other American writers who were living there. Nazi leader Adolf Hitler had risen to power in Germany, and Hellman helped smuggle $50,000 over the border for a group who wanted to oust him; she hid the money in a large box of candy!

By 1952, America had become very worried about the spread of communism. Hellman, along with many other creative people, was called before a government committee and asked if she was a communist during the McCarthy Era. She denied it but admitted she sympathized with some of their beliefs. She later wrote about this experience in *Scoundrel Time*. After 1960, Hellman wrote her memoirs in four books, beginning with *An Unfinished Woman*.

Publications

1934 The Children's Hour
1939 The Little Foxes
1941 Watch on the Rhine
1944 The Searching Wind
1946 Another Part of the Forest
1951 The Autumn Garden
1960 Toys in the Attic
1969 An Unfinished Woman
1973 Pentimento
1976 Scoundrel Time

HEMINGWAY, Ernest

American novelist and short-story writer

Born Jul. 21, 1899
Died Jul. 2, 1961
Age at death 61

Ernest Hemingway was one of the most influential American writers of the 20th century. His rough, adventurous life added a ring of truth to his novels and short stories. In 1953, he was awarded the Pulitzer Prize for his famous book *The Old Man and the Sea*; the following year he won the Nobel Prize for Literature.

Hemingway was born in Oak Park, Illinois, the second of six children. At the age of 19 he was badly wounded while serving as a Red Cross ambulance driver in Italy during World War I. After the war, he went to Paris, where he became part of a group of writers and artists later known as the "lost generation." He first gained recognition as a writer with the publication of his short-story collection *In Our Time* when he was 26.

In the 1920s and '30s, Hemingway spent much time pursuing his interest in hunting and dangerous sports in Africa, Spain, and Florida. During the Spanish Civil War, he went to Spain as a reporter. One of his greatest novels, *For Whom the Bell Tolls,* is about this war. He also reported on World War II, following American troops as they invaded France and liberated Paris from the Germans.

Hemingway's books are famous for their macho heroes and brutal stories. Hemingway himself was drawn to adventure and danger and was notorious for his hard-drinking macho lifestyle. He wrote in short, simple sentences that make the scenes he describes seem all the more harsh and unforgiving. His style of writing had a strong influence on the many writers who admired his work.

Publications

1925 In Our Time
1926 The Sun Also Rises
1927 Men Without Women
1929 A Farewell to Arms
1932 Death in the Afternoon
1935 Green Hills of Africa
1940 For Whom the Bell Tolls
1952 The Old Man and the Sea

Published after he died

1964 A Moveable Feast

HENLEY, Beth

American playwright

Born May 8, 1952

Beth Henley shot to fame with her Pulitzer Prize-winning play *Crimes of the Heart*. Written when she was only 27, it was her second play.

Henley was born in Jackson, Mississippi, one of four daughters of a lawyer father and an actor mother. The South features in all her writings, and she set her best-known work in her father's hometown of Hazlehurst, also in Mississippi. As a child, she was withdrawn and felt isolated from her own age-group, partly because of her severe asthma. Her first play,, a one-act comedy called *Am I Blue*, was produced when she was 21 and studying at Southern Methodist University in Dallas. She graduated from there in 1974, having studied drama.

When she was 24, Henley went to Los Angeles, hoping to establish a career in Hollywood as a writer of screenplays. But she was disappointed, and she decided she would have a better chance of having her work produced if she wrote for the theater.

The result was *Crimes of the Heart*, which tells the story of three sisters who are brought together by family tragedy: their grandfather's impending death and the shooting by one sister of her husband. In spite of the painful events in the sisters' lives, the play is a comedy, and the characters are endearingly bizarre. The play toured the country and eventually opened on Broadway in 1981. That year, Henley received the Pulitzer Prize for drama, the first woman to do so in more than 20 years. She also eventually got a chance to write a screenplay that was produced – for the film of *Crimes of the Heart*.

Publications

1973 Am I Blue
1979 Crimes of the Heart
1980 The Miss Firecracker Contest
1982 The Wake of Jamey Foster
1985 The Debutante Ball
1986 The Lucky Spot
1991 Monologues for Women
1991 The Debutante Ball

HENRY, O.

American short-story writer

Born Sep. 11, 1862
Died Jun. 5, 1910
Age at death 47

O. Henry was a short-story writer famous for his surprise endings. Although some critics rubbished his work, the public loved it, and in recognition of his talent an award was set up in 1918 in his name. The O. Henry Award is given each year to the author of the best story printed in an American magazine.

O. Henry was the pen name of William Sidney Porter. He was born in Greensboro, North Carolina. Poorly educated, he drifted from job to job. After moving to Austin, Texas, in 1882, he married and worked in a bank while editing a weekly comic paper, *The Rolling Stone*. It was at this time that he began the heavy drinking that was to undermine his health. In 1894, cash was found to have gone missing from the bank and although, he was not charged, O. Henry fled to Honduras when it became clear that a federal bank examiner was preparing to press charges. He returned to Austin the next year because his wife was dying and, in 1898, he was tried and convicted of stealing the bank's money.

O. Henry's five-year prison sentence served in Columbus, Ohio, allowed him to focus on his short-story writing. He published his first short story in a national magazine during the first year of his sentence. He was 36 at the time. By the time he was released (early) in 1901 and had moved to New York, his stories were already popular. He wrote prolifically: between 1904 and 1905, he produced a story each week. He published numerous collections, such as *The Four Million*, which includes "The Gift of the Magi" and "Mammon and the Archer" – stories typical of his style and love of surprise endings.

Publications

1904 Cabbages and Kings
1906 The Four Million
1907 The Trimmed Lamp
1907 The Heart of the West
1908 The Voice of the City
1908 The Gentle Grafter
1909 Roads of Destiny
1909 Options
1910 Strictly Business
1910 Whirligigs

HERBERT, Frank

American science fiction writer

Born Oct. 8, 1920
Died Feb. 11, 1986
Age at death 65

Frank Herbert is a popular science fiction writer best known for his series of novels set on the planet Dune.

Herbert was born and raised in Tacoma, Washington. As a young man he began his career as a journalist and then served in the US Navy during World War II. After the war, he wrote newspaper features, speeches for politicians and science fiction stories for magazines.

Herbert's first novel, *The Dragon in the Sea*, appeared when he was 36. It tells the story of America in the 21st century at war with other countries over scarce oil supplies. Remarkably, it predicted the worldwide conflicts over oil consumption and production that took place decades after it was published.

Herbert's second novel, *Dune*, also predicted another global problem: the destruction of the environment. The story concerns the adventures of Paul Atreides on a desert planet called Dune, or Arrakis. It describes the imaginary world of Dune in great detail, including its religions, politics, ecology and the dangerous giant sandworms that inhabit the desert. The book proved enormously popular and sold millions of copies. It later became a major film.

Herbert went on to write several sequels to *Dune*, as well as a number of other thought-provoking novels, such as *The White Plague* – about a madman who creates a disease that kills only women. Many of Herbert's novels tell the story of human beings in a hostile environment who have to use their instincts as well as their intelligence to survive. A common theme in his work is that our actions as human beings often have unforeseen effects on our environment.

Publications

1956 The Dragon in the Sea
1965 Dune
1968 The Santaroga Barrier
1969 Dune Messiah
1973 Hellstrom's Hive
1976 Children of Dune
1981 God-Emperor of Dune
1982 The White Plague
1984 Heretics of Dune
1985 Chapterhouse: Dune

HERBERT, James

English horror writer

Born Apr. 8, 1943

James Herbert is Britain's bestselling writer of horror fiction.

Herbert was born in London's East End, a poor area of the city that had been bombed during World War II, creating patches of wasteland where rats scavenged. Herbert later drew on his memory of this landscape for his early horror novels.

Herbert's first ambition was to be an artist. He attended art school in London and went on to work in an advertising agency. It was during long, boring meetings at work that he let his imagination wander, thinking up ideas for stories. When he was 31, his first novel, *The Rats*, was published.

The Rats was the first in a sequence of novels, including *Domain* and *Lair*, which are set in a decaying London and tell the story of a war between human beings and rats that are being controlled by a single, giant mutant rat somewhere beneath the city. These novels remain among Herbert's most popular work. A later series of novels, including *Haunted* and *The Ghosts of Sleath*, concern the adventures of an occult detective – or "ghostbuster" – called David Ash, who investigates strange events and supernatural happenings. The plots of these novels have many twists and turns, so the endings are always a complete surprise.

Herbert also wrote other novels, dealing with a variety of subjects from ancient folklore to life after death. He is a Roman Catholic, and the themes of many of his books are the conflict between good and evil and the ways in which sinners can redeem themselves and find forgiveness.

Publications

1974 The Rats
1975 The Fog
1976 The Survivor
1978 The Spear
1979 Lair
1983 Shrine
1985 Domain
1986 The Magic Cottage
1988 Haunted
1994 The Ghosts of Sleath

HERRIOT, James

English novelist

Born Oct. 3, 1916
Died Feb. 23, 1995
Age at death 78

James Herriot is best known for his humorous autobiographical novels about the life of an English veterinarian.

Herriot was born in Sunderland; his real name was James Alfred Wight. His father was a shipyard worker, but Herriot decided when he was 13 that he wanted to be a vet. He studied at Glasgow Veterinary College and wanted to specialize in looking after pets, but the only job available after he graduated was in a farming community in Yorkshire in the north of England. He grew to love the area, and his books are set there and filled with the characters he came into contact with in his work. Herriot worked happily in the area for 25 years (apart from service in the Royal Air Force during World War II) without doing any writing, but he was urged by his wife Joan

Publications

1970 If Only They Could Talk

to write down the many strange and amusing stories he told her about his work. His first attempts at plays and short stories were rejected by publishers, but his memoirs, *If Only They Could Talk*, published when he was 54, were instantly successful. He published under a pen name because he did not want to be accused of using his writing to advertise for veterinary work.

Herriot wrote 19 more books that have sold over 60 million copies worldwide. The three most successful titles are *If Only They Could Talk*, *All Things Bright and Beautiful* and *All Creatures Great and Small*. A much-loved TV series based on his books ran for 13 years.

Herriot continued to live in Yorkshire and practice as a vet until 1990. He said that his veterinary work had been the greatest satisfaction in his life.

1972 It Should Happen to a Vet
1972 All Creatures Great and Small
1973 Let Sleeping Vets Lie
1974 All Things Bright and Beautiful
1976 Vets in Harness
1976 Vets Might Fly
1977 All Things Wise and Wonderful
1981 The Lord God Made Them All
1992 Every Living Thing

HERSEY, John

American novelist and journalist

Born Jun. 17, 1914
Died Mar. 23, 1993
Age at death 78

John Hersey is an important writer whose works comment on issues such as freedom, racism, greed and political corruption. In 1945, he won the Pulitzer Prize for his first novel, *A Bell for Adano*.

Hersey was born and raised in China, where his parents were missionaries. When he was ten, the family returned to New York. He attended Hotchkiss Academy and then Yale University, graduating at age 22. His first job was with *Time* magazine. During World War II, he reported from battlefronts in the South Pacific, Italy and Moscow. After the war, he wrote for *Life* magazine and the *New Yorker*. For 18 years, he was a professor of writing at Yale and at the Massachusetts Institute of Technology.

Hersey's first book, *Men on Bataan*, published when he was 28, was an account of his wartime experiences. In *A Bell for Adano* he explores the conflict in wartime Italy between the ideal of democracy and the occupying American forces' desire to control the people. His next work, *Hiroshima*, a sort of nonfiction novel, retells the horrifying personal stories of six survivors of the atomic bomb dropped on that Japanese city. The book had an enormous impact in the US and was even recorded and broadcast nationwide on radio. In *The Wall* Hersey writes the fictional diary of a Jewish man living in Poland's Warsaw Ghetto as it is destroyed by the Nazis in 1944. *The Child Buyer* shows a corporation trying to "buy" a child genius and turn him into a human computer for the defense industry. Hersey's later books, however, are shorter and include more fanciful themes, as in *Antonietta*, which is about a violin.

Publications

1942 Men on Bataan
1944 A Bell for Adano
1946 Hiroshima
1950 The Wall
1959 The War Lover
1960 The Child Buyer
1974 My Petition for More Space
1985 The Call
1990 Fling and Other Stories
1991 Antonietta

HESIOD

Greek poet

Lived 8th century BC

Hesiod is one of the earliest known European writers. He was an ancient Greek poet who probably lived sometime during the 8th century BC, about 300 years before the height of Greek civilization. He was regarded by the Greeks of that time as a near legendary figure; his writings were treated like holy books, and poets aspired to match the beauty and skill of his language. Hesiod was the first to write didactic poetry, which means it was meant to teach rather than just entertain. Historians believe Hesiod may have been alive at the same time as another early poet, HOMER.

Everything that is known about Hesiod's life comes from his poems, particularly *Works and Days*. His father owned a small farm and was very poor. When he died, Hesiod and his brother Perses inherited the farm, but Perses illegally seized his brother's half of the property, and Hesiod moved away in disgust.

Hesiod's poem *Works and Days* is rooted in his experience as a poor farmer. It is an instructive handbook on farming written in the form of a long, beautiful poem. Hesiod mixes advice on how and when to plant crops with moral stories about the virtues of hard work and respect for the Greek gods. Many of these stories are directed at his cheating brother, Perses.

A second book, *Theogony*, is also thought to have been written by Hesiod. It is the first attempt to write down all the myths about the Greek gods and heroes. In *Theogony* Hesiod tried to make all the stories fit together and to trace the complicated relationships linking all the characters.

Publications

c. 8th century BC

Works and Days

Theogony

HESSE, Hermann

German novelist and poet

Born Jul. 2, 1877

Died Aug. 9, 1962

Age at death 85

The German novelist and poet Hermann Hesse is best known for works that explore the quest for a spiritual self. In 1946, he was awarded the Nobel Prize for Literature.

As a youth Hesse worked in a bookshop for three years and, in 1911, he moved permanently to Switzerland. He was a quiet, withdrawn, thoughtful loner who preferred books to people, but he was a close friend of a few writers such as T.S. ELIOT in Britain and THOMAS MANN in Germany. For several years in the mid-1910s, Hesse underwent psychoanalysis under Gustav Jung and his assistant J.B. Lang, who became a close friend. This experience was later reflected in his novel *Demian*.

Hesse hated the cultural values of the European establishment.

He was especially disgusted with the educational system, and he ran away from school on this account. His first novel, *Peter Camenzind*, features a wandering, searching outsider determined to break away from the restraints of society in the search of wisdom and peace. This period of his writing is identified with German Romanticism. During World War I, Hesse vigorously expressed his pacifist viewpoint, calling on the warring nations to work for an end to the horrors of war. He also promoted the interests of prisoners of war.

Some readers are attracted to Hesse's beautiful, poetic language. For others the appeal is his study of individuals' efforts to overcome obstacles to achieving a harmonious self. Hesse became very popular in the US in the late 1960s, when some of his work was adopted by the free-living hippies as a kind of gospel.

Publications

1904 Peter Camenzind
1906 Under the Wheel
1914 Rosshalde
1915 Knulp
1919 Demian
1922 Siddhartha
1927 Steppenwolf
1930 Death and the Lover
1943 The Glass Bead Game

HEYSE, Paul

German writer

Born Mar. 15, 1830
Died Apr. 2, 1914
Age at death 84

Paul Heyse was the first German to win the Nobel Prize for Literature.

Born in Berlin, Paul Johann Ludwig von Heyse studied classical and modern languages. He was awarded a research grant that allowed him to travel in Italy for a year, where he learned a lot about Italian literature.

At the age of 24, having completed his formal studies, he was invited by the king of Bavaria, Maximilian II, to settle in his capital, Munich, and take up a position as court poet. There he became the leader of a group of writers whose aim was to produce works in the traditional Romantic style and to oppose the growing trend toward realism. The fashionable writers of the time were concerned with new and radical ideas and ideals of wealth and pleasure rather than spiritual values. In contrast, Heyse's group produced more traditional writing that was sometimes negatively labeled "beautiful" by those who were critical of their aims.

Heyse's chief skill was as a writer of novellas – short novels – of which he became a master. These carefully written stories display excellent humor and a graceful style. *L'Arrabbiata*, considered his masterpiece, is probably among the best novellas ever written in Germany.

Heyse was a writer who tried to pretend that there is no dark side to life. History has proved him wrong. By the time he had received the Nobel Prize in 1910, his popularity had declined, and he is now regarded as a minor figure in literature.

Publications

1855 L'Arrabbiata
1855 Four Phases of Love
1858 The Maiden of Treppi
1859 Andrea Delfin
1873 Children of the World
1875 In Paradise
1875 Two Prisoners
1883 The Book of Friendship

HIGHSMITH, Patricia

American thriller writer

Born Jan. 19, 1921
Died Feb. 5, 1995
Age at death 74

Patricia Highsmith is the queen of the modern psychological thriller. In her books the object of investigation is the mystery of the human mind rather than the puzzle of a crime.

Highsmith was born in Fort Worth, Texas, and moved with her parents to New York when she was six. As a girl, she read books on psychiatry and became particularly interested in abnormal psychology. She edited a magazine at school and, at the age of 16, decided to become a writer.

Strangers on a Train, Highsmith's first novel, was published when she was 29 and was an instant success. It was filmed by Alfred Hitchcock with a script written by RAYMOND CHANDLER. As well as a complex plot there are many strong themes in the book, especially concerning guilt and responsibility, and the connection between rational thinking and madness.

Highsmith returned to these themes in her later books. Her characters are often apparently ordinary, sensible people who are nevertheless driven to commit murder. Her most famous character, Tom Ripley, is on the surface a pleasant, intelligent man who quite reasonably wants to be rich and have a good life. However, it turns out that in order to achieve these goals, he is prepared to dabble first in forgery and then in murder.

Highsmith never achieved great popularity in the US, but she has a very strong reputation in Europe, where she lived after 1963. Few crime writers can match her dark vision of humanity and its ever-present potential for evil.

Publications

1950 Strangers on a Train
1954 The Blunderer
1955 The Talented Mr. Ripley
1957 Deep Water
1960 This Sweet Sickness
1969 The Tremor of Forgery
1974 Ripley's Game
1975 The Animal-Lover's Book of Beastly Murder
1987 Found in the Street

HIJUELOS, Oscar

American novelist and short-story writer

Born Aug. 24, 1951

Oscar Hijuelos writes about the experiences of immigrants in America with compassion and accuracy. His novels untangle the mixed hopes and fears of immigrants who long to be accepted into American society but also fear losing their own culture.

Hijuelos's parents emigrated from Cuba to New York City before he was born. He earned a Bachelor's degree when he was 24 and his Master's a year later in English and writing, both from the City University of New York. Until he was 33, he worked for an advertising firm, after which he left to become a full-time writer. He traveled in Europe, Turkey and Africa before accepting a post at Hofstra University in 1989. He now lives in New York City.

Hijuelos's first novel, *Our House in the Last World*, was published when he was 32. It traces the life of a poor but ambitious Cuban couple who move to Spanish Harlem in New York City in 1943. Unlike their fellow immigrant friends, they do not achieve the American Dream. The novel chronicles each family member's response to failure: the bitter mother, the father and his addiction to alcohol, one son's rebelliousness, and the other's withdrawal.

Hijuelos's second novel, *The Mambo Kings Play Songs of Love*, integrates real events and fictional characters to tell the story of two Cuban musician brothers in 1950s New York. They achieve brief success only to sink back into obscurity. It won the Pulitzer Prize in 1990 and was made into a popular film. In *The Fourteen Sisters of Emilio Montez O'Brien* an Irishman takes his Cuban bride to Pennsylvania, where they have 14 daughters and finally, miraculously, a son.

Publications

1983	*Our House in the Last World*
1989	*The Mambo Kings Play Songs of Love*
1993	*The Fourteen Sisters of Emilio Montez O'Brien*
1995	*Mr. Ives's Christmas*

HILLERMAN, Tony

American crime writer

Born May 27, 1925

Tony Hillerman is best known for his crime novels set on the Navajo reservations of Arizona and New Mexico.

Hillerman was born into a poor white family in a small farming community in Oklahoma. Most of the family's neighbors were Potawatomies and Seminoles, and Hillerman attended a Native American girls' school. This experience gave him a lifelong fascination with Native American culture.

As a young man, Hillerman joined the US Army. He fought and was wounded in Europe during World War II. Later he went to journalism school and became a police reporter. He went on to work as a political journalist and a newspaper editor.

Hillerman's first novel, *The Blessing Way*, was published when he was 45. It introduced a minor character called Joe Leaphorn, a Navajo policeman. Leaphorn is a middle-aged man married to a white woman who is skeptical about the religion of his people. Hillerman's editor suggested he should give this character a bigger role, so in later novels Joe Leaphorn became the central figure.

In the 1980s, Hillerman introduced another main character, Jim Chee. Chee is also a Navajo policeman, but unlike Leaphorn he is young, idealistic and committed to Navajo traditions.

Hillerman's novels explore the clash between Native American cultures and the "American way." In his stories he tries to show that there is no such thing as racial difference, but that conflicts between white and Native American people arise out of what he sees as an unfair economic and political system.

Publications

1970	*The Blessing Way*
1971	*Fly on the Wall*
1973	*Dance Hall of the Dead*
1980	*People of Darkness*
1982	*The Dark Wind*
1986	*Skinwalkers*
1989	*Talking God*
1990	*Coyote Waits*
1993	*Sacred Clowns*
1995	*Finding Moon*
1998	*Fallen Man*
1999	*First Eagle*

HILLYER, Robert

American poet

Born Jun. 3, 1895
Died Dec. 24, 1961
Age at death 66

Robert Hillyer was an American poet best known for championing traditional poetic styles.

Born in East Orange, New Jersey, Hillyer was extremely proud of his English heritage and particularly of English literary traditions. While a student at Harvard, he began writing poetry, which became his lifelong passion. Following graduation in 1917, he served in the army during World War I. Hillyer returned to Harvard in 1919 and taught there until he retired in 1945.

When he was 21, Hillyer published his first poem, "To a Scarlatti Passepied," in the *New Republic*. The following year he and several friends, including JOHN DOS PASSOS and E.E. CUMMINGS, published a collection entitled *Eight Harvard Poets*. Hillyer produced his first collection of poetry, *Sonnets and Other Lyrics*, in the same year. During his career he published many books of verse, including *Collected Verse*, for which he won the 1934 Pulitzer Prize. He became a skillful craftsman of traditional poetic forms, particularly the sonnet and lyric, and he frequently used New England and sailing as subjects. His poems have a sophisticated tone, yet they are gentle and relaxed, with a self-mocking sense of humor.

A strong supporter of conventional poetic forms, Hillyer bitterly opposed the experimental poetry of T.S. ELIOT and EZRA POUND. In the late 1940s he attacked Pound, who had just received the first Bollingen Prize for Poetry, for his anti-Jewish and anti-American behavior during World War II. Controversy raged in the literary world, making Hillyer very unpopular.

Publications

1916	"To a Scarlatti Passepied"
1917	*Sonnets and Other Lyrics*
1920	*The Five Books of Youth*
1925	*The Halt in the Garden*
1928	*The Seventh Hill*
1933	*Collected Verse*
1940	*Pattern of a Day*
1947	*Poems for Music*
1949	*The Death of Captain Nemo*
1961	*Collected Poems*

HIMES, Chester

American crime writer

Born Jul. 19, 1909
Died Nov. 12, 1984
Age at death 75

Chester Himes was the first important crime writer to deal with the experience of African Americans. Most of his books are set in Harlem, New York City, and show the violence and poverty of life in the ghetto.

Born in Jefferson City, Missouri, Himes grew up in Cleveland and briefly attended Ohio State University. He withdrew because of his experience of racism on campus. In the following years, he became a petty criminal, and finally, at age 19, he was sentenced to 7 years for armed robbery in Ohio. When he was released, he worked for a writers' project in Ohio and then on the *Cleveland Daily News*. From 1941, he lived in California, working in the shipyards there. After 1953, he lived as a writer in Europe.

Himes started by writing serious novels about the experience of black people in America. When he was 48, a French publisher suggested Himes write a detective story. He had read DASHIELL HAMMETT and set out to write something similar. His first detective novel, *For Love of Imabelle*, later filmed as *A Rage in Harlem*, was a great success and won him an important French literary prize.

Himes was always taken more seriously as a writer in France than he was in the US. In America, his books were marketed as commercial "sex and violence" stories. However, they have a serious purpose, which is to show the conditions of life in the ghetto for many black Americans. He created two memorable characters: Grave Digger Jones and Coffin Ed Johnson, two Harlem policemen who fight for justice in an increasingly brutal world.

Publications

1945	*If He Hollers Let Him Go*
1957	*For Love of Imabelle*
1958	*The Real Cool Killers*
1959	*The Crazy Kill*
1959	*Run Man Run*
1959	*The Big Gold Dream*
1960	*All Shot Up*
1961	*The Heat's On*
1964	*Cotton Comes to Harlem*
1969	*Blind Man with a Pistol*

HINTON, S.E.

American young-adults' writer

Born Jul. 22, 1948

S.E. Hinton has been called the "grand dame" of young-adult fiction. She was one of the first authors to write books for young people that deal with violence and street life in a realistic way.

Susan Eloise Hinton was born in Tulsa, Oklahoma, where she has since lived most of her life. Her father died when she was young, but she still had a happy childhood. She went to local schools and the University of Tulsa.

Hinton always knew that she wanted to be a writer. As a teenager she could not find any books that dealt with life in a way that she could relate to. So she wrote *The Outsiders*, which was published when she was only 19. It is about the often violent conflict between two gangs, one poor (the "greasers") and one rich (the "socs"). The greasers, the outsiders of the book title, form their own family – their real parents are either dead, absent or uninterested. Since the story is narrated by a male character, many thought that Hinton was a man. In fact, most of her novels are told by male characters. Hinton says that this is because most of her teenage friends were boys.

Hinton followed her first novel with *That Was Then, This Is Now* – the story of two friends who slowly drift apart; one turns to crime, and the other turns him in. The next two novels, *Rumble Fish* and *Tex*, deal with the relationship between brothers. Hinton then spent most of the 1980s raising a family and advising on the film versions of her books. She has since returned to writing young-adults' books and has also written *Big David, Little David* for small children.

Publications

1967	*The Outsiders*
1971	*That Was Then, This Is Now*
1975	*Rumble Fish*
1979	*Tex*
1988	*Taming the Star Runner*
1994	*Big David, Little David*
1995	*The Puppy Sister*

HODGSON, William Hope

English horror/fantasy writer

Born Nov. 15, 1877
Died Apr. 17, 1918
Age at death 40

Publications
1907 The Boats of the Glen Carrig
1908 The House on the Borderland
1909 The Ghost Pirates
1912 The Night Land
1913 Carnacki, the Ghost Finder
1914 Men of the Deep Waters
1916 The Luck of the Strong

Published after he died
1920 The Calling of the Sea

William Hope Hodgson is best known for his stories of mystery and terror at sea.

Hodgson was born in southeast England, the son of a clergyman. He had 11 brothers and sisters. When he was 13, he ran away to be a sailor, but his parents found him and brought him home. However, a year later they allowed him to join the merchant navy as a cabin boy. He proved to be a brave sailor, once rescuing a drowning shipmate in shark-infested waters. Over a decade later, he left the navy, tired of the hard work and bad conditions of the sailor's life. He had also developed a horror of the sea. Instead, he became a bodybuilder and a photographer, also trying his hand at writing fiction.

Hodgson's first published story appeared when he was 28. He went on to write many more stories and novels, most of them strange tales of the sea. He wrote about supernatural, monstrous terrors from the deep, but his stories also had a realistic aspect that came from his years of experience as a sailor. Hodgson created a "ghostbuster" detective, Carnacki, who has many adventures at sea. Carnacki's role is to show that evidence of ghosts and other supernatural elements usually has a rational explanation. Unlike his other novels, *The House on the Borderland* is set in a ruined house in Ireland; the visitor to the house has strange visions of other worlds and other times.

When World War I broke out in 1914, Hodgson joined the army. He was sent to the front in Belgium and was killed by a shell at Ypres.

HOFFMANN, E.T.A.

German novelist and short-story writer

Born Jan. 24, 1776
Died Jun. 25, 1822
Age at death 46

The writer and composer E.T.A. Hoffmann was one of Germany's most important Romantic authors. The portrayal of him as the dreamy central character in Offenbach's brilliant comic opera *The Tales of Hoffmann* made him very famous. The real Hoffmann was a man of many talents: civil servant, composer, music critic, musical director, writer and judge.

All his life, Ernst Theodor Amadeus Hoffmann's principal interest was music. He wrote nine operas, several works for chorus and orchestra, chamber and piano music, and one symphony. Most of his music is now forgotten, but his opera *The Water Sprite* is still occasionally performed. It was one of the first German Romantic operas.

Hoffmann recognized that he would never be a great composer, so he turned to writing. His tastes were for sinister gothic horrors and wild fantasy enlivened by an absurd sense of humor. His stories – full of ghosts, vampires and drug-induced visions – show a genius close to madness. Most of his tales also reveal his serious and thoughtful nature. Typical of his style are the short stories collected in his famous *Nighttime Tales*, published when he was 41.

His work, although highly popular in its time, also had a major influence on later writers. This is recognizable in the work of world-class figures such as EDGAR ALLAN POE, FRANZ KAFKA, NATHANIEL HAWTHORNE, NIKOLAI GOGOL, and FYODOR DOSTOEVSKY. It also greatly influenced famous composers who used his tales in their ballets and operas. Delibes's *Coppelia* and Tchaikovsky's *Nutcracker Suite*, for example, derive from Hoffmann's writings.

Publications

1814	*The Golden Pot*
1814–15	*Fantasies*
1815–16	*The Devil's Elixir*
1817	*Nighttime Tales*
1818	*Strange Sufferings of a Theater Director*
1819–21	*Opinions of the Tomcat Murr*
1819	*Little Sachs, called Cinnaber*
1819–21	*The Serapion Brothers*

HOLMES, Oliver Wendell

American poet and essayist

Born Aug. 29, 1809
Died Oct. 7, 1894
Age at death 85

Oliver Wendell Holmes was a prominent doctor who won literary fame for his poems and witty essays.

Holmes was born in Cambridge, Massachusetts, where his father was a well-known Congregationalist minister. He graduated from Harvard Medical School in 1836 and practised medicine for ten years. In 1847, he became a professor of anatomy at Harvard. Holmes was a popular professor known for his humor and enthusiasm. He wrote many outstanding medical articles, the most important of which advocated using sterile conditions to prevent spreading disease. When he was only 21, Holmes gained national prominence for one of his first poems "Old Ironsides." In it he passionately protests the navy's decision to destroy the *Constitution*, a fighting ship from the War of 1812. His poem helped save the vessel.

Although he never gave up medicine, Holmes became known as a popular speaker and as the author of witty essays and amusing poems for special occasions. Holmes's best-known book, published when he was 49, was *The Autocrat of the Breakfast-Table*. It consists of 12 essays that he had submitted to the *Atlantic Monthly*, a journal which he had cofounded. Written like witty conversations, they are a mixture of stories, sermons, unconnected thoughts, and poems; they gave Holmes the opportunity to express his views about science, manners, nature and religion. The book was so popular that he produced four similar works.

Publications

1830	"Old Ironsides"
1833	"The Last Leaf"
1858	*The Autocrat of the Breakfast-Table*
1858	"The Chambered Nautilus"
1858	"The Deacon's Masterpiece"
1860	*The Professor of the Breakfast-Table*
1872	*The Poet of the Breakfast-Table*

HOMER

Greek poet

Lived 8th or 9th century BC

Of all the poets of ancient Greece Homer is the most mysterious and the most extraordinary. He is known as the author of the two earliest works of European literature, the *Iliad* and the *Odyssey*. Nothing at all is known for certain about his life, and many scholars have argued that he never even existed.

The *Iliad* and the *Odyssey* describe events during and soon after the Trojan War, a conflict between ancient Greeks and the citizens of a city called Troy around 1250 BC. The works were probably composed several hundred years after this time. If Homer was a real person, he may have lived during the 8th or 9th century BC. Those who argue that Homer is a myth say that the poems are the work of several generations of poets combined into one long text at a much later date.

Whatever the truth, the name of Homer was revered in ancient Rome and Greece. The *Iliad* and the *Odyssey* were regarded in much the same way as the Christian Bible was later regarded in medieval Europe – they were the basic educational texts of the time, and quotations from them were used to settle disputes and resolve moral problems.

Both the *Iliad* and the *Odyssey* are epic poems. They tell the stories of heroes and their incredible deeds in a mythical past when gods and goddesses interfered directly in the lives of mortals. Characters and events from the *Iliad* and the *Odyssey* were often used by later Greek writers and are still referred to in European literature today. JAMES JOYCE's novel *Ulysses*, written around 3,000 years later, is based on the adventures of Odysseus, hero of the *Odyssey*.

Publications

c. 9th–8th centuries BC

Iliad

Odyssey

HOPKINS, Gerard Manley

English poet

Born Jul. 28, 1844

Died Jun. 8, 1889

Age at death 44

Gerard Manley Hopkins was a 19th-century poet ahead of his time. None of the work for which he is known today was published until after his death.

Hopkins was born in Stratford near London. From his well-to-do middle-class parents came strict, conservative beliefs and an interest in the arts. He won a poetry prize at school, and at Oxford University he wrote poems and converted to Roman Catholicism.

From 1868 to 1877, Hopkins trained to become a Jesuit priest. For most of these years he wrote no poetry until encouraged by his Jesuit superior. When he was 31, a shipwreck in which five nuns died inspired him to write "The Wreck of the *Deutschland.*" This long, complex poem made lively use of what Hopkins called "sprung rhythm," based on the natural rhythms in which people speak. The same rhythm is apparent in his other fine poems, such as "The Windhover" and "Pied Beauty."

Ordained a priest in 1877, Hopkins preached and taught in England and Scotland. In 1884, he became Professor of Greek Literature at University College, Dublin. Later he died there of typhoid. The so-called "terrible sonnets" of his last years show him torn between love of the world and obligation to God.

Much of Hopkins's strange, abrupt verse is about God's relationship to humanity. His ideas and style owed debts to earlier thinkers and poets, including JOHN DONNE. Hopkins's poems influenced W.H. AUDEN, T.S. ELIOT and many other 20th-century poets.

Published after he died

1918	*Poems of Gerard Manley Hopkins*
1935	*Letters of Gerard Manley Hopkins to Robert Bridges; The Correspondence of Gerard Manley Hopkins and Richard Watson-Dixon*
1937	*Notebooks and Papers*
1938	*Further Letters*

HOPKINS, Pauline Elizabeth

Pauline Elizabeth Hopkins aimed to inspire pride among African Americans through her plays, novels and short stories. She created strong, educated, thoughtful characters who fought against racial prejudice, and she used the popular form of the traditional love story to convey her message.

Hopkins was born in Portland, Maine. Her mother's family had founded the Baptist Church in Boston, and Hopkins grew up in that city. She began writing as a child and, at 15, she won first prize in an essay contest.

Hopkins's first career was on the stage. By age 20, she had written a play about the Underground Railroad, which had helped slaves escape from the South before the Civil War. It was produced by the Hopkins's Colored Troubadours, an acting group that included the young Hopkins and several members of her family. For more than a decade she acted with the group. Then, in her 30s, she decided to concentrate on her writing.

In 1900, Hopkins helped found the *Colored American*, a literary magazine featuring writing by African Americans. As editor she helped promote the work of new writers. She also published several of her own stories and three novels in the magazine. Her first novel, *Contending Forces*, published when she was 41, uses elements of romance fiction – a hero and heroine falling in love and threatened by villains – but its theme is the history of the African-American experience from slavery to voting rights.

American novelist, playwright and short-story writer

Born 1859
Died Aug. 13, 1930
Age at death c. 71

Publications

1880	*Slaves' Escape: or the Underground Railroad*
1900	*Contending Forces*
1900	"The Mystery within Us"
1900	"Talma Gordon"
1901	"A Dash for Liberty"
1901–02	*Hagar's Daughter*
1902	*Winona*
1902–03	*Of One Blood*
1916	"Topsy Templeton"

HORACE

Roman poet and satirist

Born Dec. 8, 65 BC
Died Nov. 27, 8 BC
Age at death 56

Horace was one of the greatest ancient Roman poets, and even today his lyrical *Odes* remain popular.

He was born in the southern Italian town of Venusia. His father, who had originally been a slave, saved money and moved his family to the capital city, Rome, so that Horace could get a better education. Later, Horace went to study at the Academy, a famous and ancient school in the Greek city of Athens.

In 44 BC, while Horace was still at the Academy, the dictator Julius Caesar was assassinated, and the Roman world was plunged into chaos and civil war. Horace joined the army organized by Brutus, one of the conspirators who had killed Caesar. Two years later, Brutus was defeated by the future emperor Augustus and his ally Mark Antony.

Horace returned to Italy, sad and disillusioned. His father had died, and his property had been seized by the victorious new rulers. He took a job as a minor public employee and began to write in his spare time to earn extra money. The great poet VIRGIL noticed Horace's work and introduced him to a wealthy politician called Maecenas, who liked to help and encourage young writers.

Horace published his first book of poetry, *Satires*, when he was about 30. He followed this five years later with a second book of *Satires* and a collection of poems called *Epodes*. Maecenas recognized a great talent and gave Horace a small farm in the countryside so that he could escape the bustle of Rome whenever he wanted. Horace devoted the rest of his life to poetry, producing his greatest work, a collection of 88 poems called *Odes*, by the time he was 42.

Publications

35 BC *Satires* (Book I)
30 BC *Satires* (Book II)
30 BC *Epodes*
23 BC *Odes* (Books I, II, and III)
20 BC *Epistles* (Book I)
c. 14 BC *Epistles* (Book II)
c. 14 BC *Odes* (Book IV)
c. 8 BC *Ars poetica (Art of Poetry)*

HOUSMAN, A.E.

English poet

Born Mar. 26, 1859
Died Apr. 30, 1936
Age at death 77

A.E. Housman was a popular and much praised English poet. He was also one of the greatest classical scholars of his time.

Alfred Edward Housman grew up near Birmingham in the Midlands, within sight of the Shropshire Hills. A frail and timid child, he did not get on well with his father but had a deep affection for his mother, who died when Housman was 12. He won a place to study classics at Oxford University but failed his exams after showing great promise. In 1882, he became a lowly civil servant in London, writing poetry and studying classical literature in his free time. Ten years later, with more than 20 published scholarly articles to his name, he became Greek and Latin professor at University College, London. He moved to Cambridge University in 1911.

Housman's first collection, *A Shropshire Lad*, was published at his own expense when he was 37. This flood of creativity was a response to the loss of his beloved friend, Moses Jackson, who had moved to India and married, and the death of his hated father. Housman's clear and simple poems celebrate the virtues of the British soldier and country people, and the beauties of nature, but are overshadowed by thoughts of the shortness of life, lost youth and, above all, of death. *A Shropshire Lad* became a bestseller. He published only one other book of poems in his lifetime, *Last Poems*. After Housman's death, his poetry about his love for Jackson was finally published. He had seen Oscar Wilde jailed for homosexuality and had always kept this part of his life hidden.

Publications

1896 A Shropshire Lad
1922 Last Poems

Published after he died

1936 More Poems
1955 Manuscript Poems

HOWARD, Richard

American poet, critic, and translator

Born Oct. 13, 1929

Richard Howard writes poetry in the form of spoken conversations or speeches that explore the ideas, lives and works of historical figures. His third volume of poetry, *Untitled Subjects*, won the Pulitzer Prize in 1970.

Howard was born in Cleveland, Ohio. He could read before he was three and knew he wanted to write poetry by the time he was four. He attended Shaker Heights High School and earned both a Bachelor's and a Master's degree from Columbia University in New York City. His interest in French literature led him to study at the Sorbonne in Paris for a year. He then returned to the US, working until 1957 on the making of dictionaries in Cleveland and New York.

Quantities, Howard's first volume of poetry, was published when he was 33. The conversational structure and word rhythms show the influence of W.H. Auden. In each poem of *Untitled Subjects,* such famous figures from the worlds of 19th-century art, literature, music and politics as Alfred Tennyson and Sir Walter Scott speak in their own distinctive voices about their life and works. Howard's thorough research and attention to detail show his deep interest in literature and give a 20th-century view of earlier times. In later volumes, such as *Two-Part Inventions* and *Misgivings*, the voices carry on conversations about subjects that are sometimes more personal, including love, loss and isolation.

Howard is also one of the most important scholars of 20th-century French literature. He has translated into English many works by Simone de Beauvoir, Albert Camus and André Gide.

Publications

1962 Quantities
1967 The Damages
1969 Alone with America
1969 Untitled Subjects
1974 Two-Part Inventions
1976 Fellow Feelings
1979 Misgivings
1984 Lining Up
1989 No Traveler
1994 Like Most Revelations

HOWARD, Robert E.

American fantasy/ horror writer

Born Jan. 22, 1906
Died Jun. 11, 1936
Age at death 30

Robert E(rvin) Howard is one of the originators of "sword-and-sorcery" fiction, a style that combines historical adventure stories with tales of the supernatural. He is best known for creating the barbarian hero, Conan the Cimmerian.

Howard was born in Peaster, Texas, and later lived in Cross Plains. As a child he heard horror stories about the swamps of Louisiana from the family's African-American cook, and his grandmother told him tales from Celtic folklore. In his teenage years, he developed a passionate interest in the supernatural and began to write horror stories; "Spear and Fang" was published in a magazine called *Weird Tales* when he was 19. Howard went on to make his living writing for *Weird Tales* and other cheap, popular, fiction magazines known as "pulp" magazines. He wrote horror and fantasy tales and also Westerns and detective stories. In an effort to widen his market he came up with the idea of Conan, a barbarian warrior from a prehistoric world full of evil magical beings. Conan himself has no supernatural powers but is able to conquer these evil spirits through his immense strength and courage.

At the age of 30, Howard committed suicide. Toward the end of his life, he had switched to writing Westerns, largely because *Weird Tales* owed him over $1,000 for his Conan stories. He also wrote poems, but it is his adventure stories featuring superheroes like Conan, King Kull, Solomon Kane and Black Turlough that are remembered today. The two films of Conan, starring Arnold Schwarzenegger, have proved very popular.

Published after he died

1946 Skull-Face and Others
1950 Conan the Conqueror
1954 Conan the Barbarian
1955 Tales of Conan
1967 King Kull
1968 Red Shadows
1968 Wolfshead
1969 Black Canaan
1979 The Gods of Bal-Sagoth

HOWARD, Sidney

American playwright and screenwriter

Born Jun. 26, 1891
Died Aug. 23, 1939
Age at death 48

Sidney Howard was one of the most popular 20th-century playwrights. He wrote many realistic plays about American social values and manners but is perhaps best known for his screenplay of MARGARET MITCHELL's novel *Gone with the Wind*, which became an Academy Award-winning film.

Born in Oakland, California, Howard was struck by tuberculosis at the age of 19 and spent a year at a Swiss hospital. He then attended the University of California at Berkeley, where he started acting and writing. In World War I, Howard enlisted in the US Army and gained awards for gallantry in action. His experiences and hostility to war and the army appear in two of his plays, *Paths of Glory* and *The Ghost of Yankee Doodle*.

Howard's first play to attract wide attention was *They Knew What They Wanted*, which won a Pulitzer Prize in 1925. It tells the story of a winemaker from the Napa Valley who obtains a mail-order wife by sending her a photograph of his handsome foreman. Amy, the bride in the story, is a typical Howard female character: honest, brave and strong.

In 1927, films were made with sound for the first time. Howard's reputation as a playwright meant that he was soon approached by Samuel Goldwyn, a major producer, to write three screenplays. The first of these was *Bulldog Drummond*, which was a great success, largely due to Howard's witty dialogue and fast-paced plot. During his life, Howard wrote 27 plays, some of which were adapted for the theater by other writers, and more than a dozen film scripts.

Publications

1921 *Swords*
1924 *They Knew What They Wanted*
1929 *Bulldog Drummond*
1932 *The Greeks Had a Word for Them*
1932 *The Late Christopher Bean*
1935 *Paths of Glory*
1937 *The Ghost of Yankee Doodle*
1939 *Gone with the Wind*

HOWE, Julia Ward

American poet and essayist

Born May 27, 1819
Died Oct. 17, 1910
Age at death 91

It is not recorded whether Julia Ward Howe gave any hint when she was a girl that she would one day find herself in an army tent writing the words to one of America's most stirring patriotic songs, "The Battle Hymn of the Republic."

It was not really the sort of thing that was expected of the child of a wealthy banker, born in New York City and educated privately at home. Rejecting "a life of cultured leisure," Howe married a doctor who was involved in the antislavery movement and moved to Boston, where together they edited an antislavery newspaper. Whenever possible, Howe took time out to write and travel, although her first work, a book of poems called *Passion Flowers*, wasn't published until she was 35.

When the American Civil War broke out, campaigners like Howe hoped it would put an end, at last, to slavery in the South. Invited to visit the military camps of the Union Army, Howe heard the soldiers singing the popular song "John Brown's Body" as they marched to war. She became convinced that a more inspiring song would help them win. In her tent that night, Howe composed new words to the familiar "John Brown" tune and called it "The Battle Hymn of the Republic." It was first published when Howe was in her 43rd year, and it became not only the song that helped free America's slaves but was later taken up by the women campaigning for the vote and, later still, by the civil rights movement in the 1960s. Shortly before she died, Howe became the first woman elected to the American Academy of Arts and Letters.

Publications

1854 *Passion Flowers*
1857 *Words for the Hour*
1860 *A Trip to Cuba*
1862 "The Battle Hymn of the Republic"
1866 *Later Lyrics*
1881 *Modern Society*
1895 *Is Polite Society Polite?*
1899 *Reminiscences*

HOWELLS, William Dean

American novelist, playwright and critic

Born Mar. 1, 1837
Died May 11, 1920
Age at death 83

William Dean Howells played a major role in bringing realism to American literature. Following the example of European writers, he was one of the first to talk about real social problems in his books.

Born in Martin's Ferry, Ohio, the son of a printer, Howells was largely self-educated. At age 23, he wrote a biography of President Abraham Lincoln and was rewarded with an appointment as US consul in Venice, Italy. He described his experience there in *Venetian Life*, published when he was 29. The same year he became an editor of the literary magazine *Atlantic Monthly*. He remained there until, at age 44, he resigned to devote himself to writing.

Howells's first novels are comedies of manners that contrast different cultures and characters. Then, influenced by the novelists ÉMILE ZOLA and LEO TOLSTOY, he began to write about realistic characters facing realistic social problems, including the subject of divorce in *A Modern Instance*. His most famous work, *The Rise of Silas Lapham*, is about the rise and fall of a self-made businessman in a society where most wealthy people have inherited their money. Although Silas Lapham goes bankrupt and loses his smart home, he gains in moral character.

Later, Howells became concerned about the problems caused by industrialization. Aged 53, he published *A Hazard of New Fortunes*, a powerful novel describing the newly rich, the problems of industrialization, and the growth of labor unions and socialism in New York City.

Publications

1866 Venetian Life
1872 Their Wedding Journey
1875 A Foregone Conclusion
1882 A Modern Instance
1885 The Rise of Silas Lapham
1886 Indian Summer
1890 A Hazard of New Fortunes
1894 A Traveler from Altruria
1910 My Mark Twain
1916 The Leatherwood God

HUGHES, Langston

American poet, essayist and novelist

Born Feb. 1, 1902
Died May 22, 1967
Age at death 65

Langston Hughes was a poet and novelist who realistically depicted African-American life in the first half of the 20th century. He was a leading author of the Harlem Renaissance. This 1920s artistic and literary movement was concerned with developing black pride. It produced the first large collection of work in the US by African Americans, including Hughes, COUNTEE CULLEN and ARNA BONTEMPS.

Hughes was born in Joplin, Missouri, but educated at Cleveland Central High School and later at Columbia University and Lincoln University in Pennsylvania. He published his first collection of poetry, *The Weary Blues*, at age 24. After many travels, he served as a newspaper correspondent in the Spanish Civil War. Some of his sea trips are recorded in *I Wonder As I Wander*.

Publications

1926 The Weary Blues
1927 Fine Clothes to the Jew

Growing up in the United States at the beginning of the century, Hughes was influenced by leading thinkers such as W.E.B. Du Bois, who emphasized the importance of African culture to black Americans. Hughes shared Du Bois's belief that renewal could only come from an understanding of African roots. His writing often reflects these concerns, as in the collection of poems *Lament for Dark People*. He is remembered especially for the creation of Jesse B. Simple, a character who appears in several books, including *Simple Speaks His Mind*.

Hughes's autobiography, *The Big Sea*, describes the period of the Harlem Renaissance. Although the movement faded away during the Great Depression, its influence is to be found in the writings of later authors, such as James Baldwin.

1934 The Ways of White Folks
1940 The Big Sea
1944 Lament for Dark People
1951 Simple Speaks His Mind
1956 I Wonder As I Wander

Published after he died
1967 The Panther and the Lash
1974 Good Morning Revolution

HUGHES, Ted

English poet

Born Aug. 17, 1930
Died Oct. 28, 1998
Age at death 68

Ted Hughes is an English poet famous for his poems about the relationship between people and nature. He was made England's Poet Laureate in 1984.

Hughes was born and raised in a small town in the north of England where his parents owned a local store. The harsh landscape of the Yorkshire moors that surround his home were to have a strong influence on his poetry. He attended the local school, where he first began to write, and then studied at Cambridge University. After university he worked as a gardener and a zookeeper among other jobs.

In 1956, Hughes married the American poet Sylvia Plath, whom he had met at Cambridge. The following year, when Hughes was 27, his first collection of poems, *The Hawk in the Rain*, was published. It contains poems that are still regarded as among his best, including "The Thought-Fox" and the title poem, "The Hawk in the Rain." Like much of his work these poems are about the human struggle to survive in a world where natural forces do not care if we live or die.

In 1963, Hughes's and Plath's marriage broke down, and Plath committed suicide. Hughes was deeply affected by her death and wrote little while he spent three years editing and publishing Plath's poems. One of his first important works after this period was the children's book, *The Iron Giant*.

When he was 40, Hughes produced his most famous work, *Crow* – a series of story-poems told in the imagined voice of a crow. Since then he has become one of England's most popular poets.

Publications
1957 The Hawk in the Rain
1960 Lupercal
1967 Wodwo
1968 The Iron Giant
1970 Crow
1975 Cave Birds
1983 River
1987 Flowers and Insects
1989 Wolf Watching
1992 A Dancer to God
1997 Tales from Ovid
1998 Birthday Letters

HUGHES, Thomas

English children's writer and novelist

Born Oct. 20, 1822
Died Mar. 22, 1896
Age at death 73

Thomas Hughes is remembered as the author of the classic book for young boys, *Tom Brown's School Days*.

Hughes was born in Berkshire, west of London. He studied at private schools before being sent to Rugby at the age of 11. Rugby is an old and famous English private school. Many of its pupils became leaders of Britain and the British Empire. When Hughes was a pupil, Rugby's headmaster was Dr. Arnold, who became famous as an educational reformer. He tried to make his students ready to bear the responsibilities of their future roles as well as the power and status of these roles. Although Hughes was more interested in sports than scholarly pursuits, he was deeply affected by his headmaster's high ideals and principles. After Rugby, Hughes studied at Oxford University, became a lawyer in 1848, then a Liberal member of Parliament, and eventually a judge in 1882. He was a lifelong liberal and a devout Christian.

Tom Brown's School Days came out when Hughes was 35. His son was about to go off to school for the first time, and Hughes wanted to help him learn from his own experiences, so he wrote this story. Set in Rugby, it shows how the naughty schoolboy Tom Brown is set on the right path by Dr. Arnold. It was the first work of fiction about the realities of English private school life and established a new genre – the private school novel. The novel was an instant success in both England and America. Hughes wrote three novels in all, but none as good as his first.

Publications

1857 Tom Brown's School Days
1858 The Scouring of the White Horse
1859–61 Tom Brown at Oxford
1871 Alfred the Great
1879 The Manliness of Christ
1889 David Livingstone

HUGO, Victor

French novelist, poet and playwright

Born Feb. 26, 1802
Died May 22, 1885
Age at death 83

Victor Hugo was the most important of the French Romantic school of writers. He is known today – by people of all ages, worldwide – as the author of *The Hunchback of Notre Dame* and *Les Misérables*.

Hugo was born in Besançon, France, the third son of a soldier in the army of the great French leader, Napoleon. He was raised and educated by his mother. At the age of 14, he showed talent as a poet. Inspired by the example of the statesman and author FRANÇOIS RENÉ CHATEAUBRIAND, he published poetry, plays and novels that showed a strong sense of social responsibility. His novel *The Hunchback of Notre Dame*, published when he was 29, made him famous.

Tragedy struck Hugo at an early age. On his wedding day, his brother, Eugene, went insane, and for the rest of his life Hugo felt responsible for his brother's condition. Later, his favorite daughter died in an accident, after which he stopped writing for ten years.

In his later life Hugo became involved in politics as a supporter of the republican form of government. Following the overthrow of the Second French Republic in 1851 by Napoleon III, he went into exile on the Channel Islands. During his exile he wrote his greatest works, including *The Legend of the Centuries*, published when he was 57, and *Les Misérables*, published three years later. *Les Misérables*, an epic story about social injustice set against the background of the French Revolution, has become one of the most popular modern musicals.

After Napoleon III fell from power in 1870, Hugo returned to France. When he died more than two million people attended his state funeral in Paris.

Publications

1826	*Odes and Ballads*
1829	*Les Orientales*
1830	*Hernani*
1831	*The Hunchback of Notre Dame*
1859	*The Legend of the Centuries*
1862	*Les Misérables*
1869	*By Order of the King*
1872	*The Terrible Year*
1874	*Ninety-Three*

HULME, Keri

New Zealander novelist, poet and short-story writer

Born Mar. 9, 1947

Keri Hulme is probably New Zealand's most famous author. Her first novel, *The Bone People*, took the world by storm, becoming a bestseller both in New Zealand and abroad. It rocketed her from obscurity to fame, winning many awards on the way.

Hulme was born in Christchurch, New Zealand. Her mother was Maori – the Maori are the original inhabitants of New Zealand – and Maori culture and language inform a lot of Hulme's work. After university and various jobs such as letter carrier, mill worker and cook, she took up writing full time in 1972 and settled in Okarito, a tiny settlement on the west coast of the South Island. Ten years later, her first published work, a collection of poetry called *The Silences Between*, came out when she was 35.

The Bone People took Hulme 12 years to write. The central character, Kerewin Holmes, is heavily based on the author. Hulme, who is a very private person, has since said that had she known the book would be so widely read, she would have made Kerewin more different from herself. Both are solitary, clever, part-Maori women who live quietly in self-built homes in remote coastal villages, pursuing their favorite pastimes of fishing, drinking and writing.

The Bone People tells of Kerewin's mental and spiritual journey to greater wholeness. This involves her in a difficult relationship with a man called Joe and his adopted son, Simon, who cannot speak. Simon is beaten by Joe and loses his hearing as a result. All the main characters suffer personal crises but reach a greater understanding or acceptance of themselves by the end of the book.

Publications

1982	*The Silences Between*
1984	*The Bone People*
1985	*Lost Possessions*
1986	*Te Kaihau/The Windeater*
1988	*Strands*
1989	*Homeplaces*

HURSTON, Zora Neale

American novelist and short-story writer

Born Jan. 7, 1901
Died Jan. 28, 1960
Age at death 59

Zora Neale Hurston described herself as a "cultural worker." She loved African-American folklore, and her stories and novels preserve the language and the storytelling of that culture.

Hurston was born in Eatonville, Florida. She was one of eight children whose happy childhood was disrupted when their mother died in 1904. Hurston was sent to boarding school, and later she went from job to job, staying in relatives' homes and finishing secondary school in Maryland. She graduated from Howard University and then studied anthropology at Barnard College in New York. In her autobiography she describes herself as an obstinate, intelligent child.

In the early and mid-1920s, Hurston wrote plays and several short stories, including "Spunk" and "Sweat." She wrote musicals and worked with fellow Harlem Renaissance writer LANGSTON HUGHES on a play, *Mule Bone*. She also received a fellowship to study African-American folklore, and her research resulted in *Mules and Men* and *Tell My Horse*, two collections of folklore. Her best-known work, the novel *Their Eyes Were Watching God*, was published when she was 36. Set in Eatonville, her hometown, it tells the story of a black woman who searches for fulfillment.

Despite having achieved widespread recognition in the literary world, Hurston found it increasingly difficult to get her work published. In the late 1950s, she returned to Florida, where she died in poverty. She was buried in an unmarked grave. In the 1970s, her work was rediscovered by, among others, writer ALICE WALKER, who edited a collection of Hurston's writings.

Publications

1931 *Mule Bone* (with Langston Hughes)
1932 *The Great Day*
1934 *Jonah's Gourd Vine*
1934 *Singing Steel*
1935 *Mules and Men*
1937 *Their Eyes Were Watching God*
1938 *Tell My Horse*
1939 *Moses, Man of the Mountain*
1942 *Dust Tracks on a Road*
1948 *Seraph on the Suwanee*

HUXLEY, Aldous

English novelist, essayist and poet

Born Jul. 26, 1894
Died Nov. 22, 1963
Age at death 69

Aldous Huxley was a major British writer of the period just after World War I. He is best known for his novel *Brave New World*.

Huxley was born into a rich and famous family. His grandfather, Thomas Huxley, was a biologist who helped develop the theory of evolution. Huxley received a traditional British upper-class education at Eton College and Oxford University. Sadly, at the age of 16 an eye disease left him nearly blind. Unable to pursue his chosen career as a scientist or fight in World War I, he turned to writing poetry and fiction. His first novel, *Crome Yellow*, a witty criticism of society, was published when he was 27. His next four novels, including *Brave New World*, established him as an important voice in the world of literature and social criticism.

Brave New World is a vision of a well-ordered, highly-technological society of the future. A drug, "soma," has been developed to ensure citizens are always happy, and scientists are able to produce babies who will fit their future job roles exactly. Yet the society is a soulless one, in which people are deprived of ordinary emotions. The novel questions the values of Western civilization with its ever-increasing reliance on technology.

After living in France and Italy, Huxley moved to America and became a Hollywood screenwriter. For the rest of his life he lived in California, continuing to write novels as well as essays on philosophy, science and politics. In his later years, he became interested in the effects of mind-altering drugs and wrote two books about his experiments.

Publications

1921 Crome Yellow
1923 Antic Hay
1928 Point Counter Point
1932 Brave New World
1936 Eyeless in Gaza
1939 After Many a Summer
1944 Time Must Have a Stop
1948 Ape and Essence
1958 Brave New World Revsited
1962 Island

IBSEN, Henrik

Norwegian playwright and poet

Born Mar. 20, 1828
Died May 23, 1906
Age at death 78

Henrik Ibsen is often called the father of modern drama because his plays moved away from the Romantic style of theater popular in the 19th century toward realism.

Ibsen was born in Skien, Norway. His father was bankrupt and effectively a social outcast. This gave Ibsen a strong distrust of society, which much of his work reflects. At age 16, Ibsen became an apprentice pharmacist. Money was scarce, but he was determined to improve his situation and studied in the evenings. In 1848, revolution swept Europe and, at age 22, Ibsen, captivated by the new democratic ideas, wrote his first play, *Catiline*, which deals with personal freedom, but it was never performed.

At age 22, Ibsen went to college in Oslo. He hoped to become a physician and supported himself by writing. A year later, however, he was offered the job of writer-manager of the Norwegian Theater in Bergen – a position he held for 11 years. At 30, he married Suzannah Thoresen. Their son, Sigurd, was born a year later.

The turning point in Ibsen's career was *Brand*, published when he was 38. With its emphasis on the individual pitted against society, the play became popular with young liberals. A series of plays dealing with real-life issues followed. *A Doll's House*, about a woman who refuses to obey her husband, caused a sensation and toured Europe and America.

During his life Ibsen's work was much admired. In 1891, fellow playwright GEORGE BERNARD SHAW, in a lecture entitled *The Quintessence of Ibsenism*, called him the greatest living dramatist.

Publications

1866 Brand
1867 Peer Gynt
1879 A Doll's House
1881 Ghosts
1882 An Enemy of the People
1884 The Wild Duck
1890 Hedda Gabler
1892 The Master Builder
1894 Little Eyolf
1899 When We Dead Awaken

INGE, William

American playwright and screenwriter

Born May 3, 1913
Died Jun. 10, 1973
Age at death 60

William Inge was one of America's most successful playwrights in the 1950s. All the plays that he wrote in this decade were also made into popular films – the film version of *Bus Stop* starred Marilyn Monroe. He won the 1953 Pulitzer Prize for his play *Picnic*, which is still performed today, and an Academy Award for his screenplay *Splendor in the Grass*.

Inge was born in Independence, Kansas. His father, a traveling salesman, was often away, and Inge grew up to be very close to his mother. He studied at the University of Kansas and then at George Peabody College in Nashville, Tennessee. He had planned to become an actor but was put off by the uncertainty of success, so he turned to teaching instead. Inge regretted this decision, however, and, struggling with his inability to accept his homosexuality, he began drinking heavily.

Inge has been called Broadway's first truly midwestern playwright. His first successful play, *Come Back, Little Sheba*, was staged on Broadway when he was 37. Like most of his work, it is set in midwestern America and deals with lonely characters struggling to find happiness and love, and coming to terms with reality. *Picnic* describes a group of lonely women and how they are affected by the arrival of a handsome drifter. *Bus Stop* is a romantic comedy about characters stranded at a bus stop. His last really successful play was *The Dark at the Top of the Stairs*. After this, he moved to Hollywood and began writing films.

None of Inge's later plays was successful, and his depression and drinking grew worse until he committed suicide.

Publications

1947 Farther Off from Heaven
1950 Come Back, Little Sheba
1953 Picnic
1955 Bus Stop
1957 The Dark at the Top of the Stairs
1961 Splendor in the Grass
1963 Natural Affection
1966 Where"s Daddy?
1971 My Son Is a Splendid Driver

IONESCO, Eugène

Romanian-born French playwright

Born Nov. 13, 1909
Died Mar. 28, 1994
Age at death 84

Eugène Ionesco is best known for his experimental plays, which pioneered the development of a drama movement known as the theater of the absurd.

Born in Slatina, Romania, Ionesco was brought up in Paris, France, until he was a teenager. When his parents divorced, he returned to Romania with his father. He finished his schooling there and studied French literature at the University of Bucharest. He then taught French in Bucharest for two years. During World War II, he lived in Marseilles, France, and moved to Paris after its liberation from the Germans in 1944. After a spell as a proofreader, he started to write full time when in his late 30s.

Ionesco's first play, *The Bald Soprano*, was produced when he was 41. It was hailed as an important new work by established writers like JEAN ANOUILH, who helped make it a success. His style, expressed clearly in *The Chairs*, produced two years later, was a new kind of theater, sharing elements with the work of JEAN GENET, who was writing in France at the same time. Ionesco rejected realism, presenting characters who seem like robots, and he set out to show the absurdity of human life and human actions.

Although his plays deal with suffering, fear, and destruction, their dark humor makes them "tragicomic" rather than simply tragic. His characters can attain freedom, as in *Amédée* (in which a couple sense a corpse in their apartment), or at least maintain their integrity amid desolation, as in *Rhinoceros*. Ionesco also wrote short stories, a novel and several volumes of autobiography. In his later years, he devoted himself to painting.

Publications

1950 The Bald Soprano
1951 The Lesson
1952 The Chairs
1953 Victims of Duty
1954 Amédée
1958 The Killer
1960 Rhinoceros
1964 Hunger and Thirst
1972 Macbett
1981 Journey among the Dead

IRVING, John

American novelist

Born Mar. 2, 1942

John Irving is a gifted novelist with an extremely fertile imagination whose most famous work *The World According to Garp* became a bestseller.

Irving was born and raised in Exeter, New Hampshire. From an early age he had a passion for wrestling and writing. When at the University of Pittsburgh in 1961, he realized he did not have the ability to be a first-class wrestler, he decided to write full time. After a year-long stay in Vienna, Austria, Irving made Vienna the setting for his first novel *Setting Free the Bears*, which came out when he was 27. Irving's next two novels were not great successes financially. He then changed publisher and, aged 36, produced the classic *The World According to Garp*.

As with most of Irving's novels, *The World According to Garp* portrays a society where violence and deformity play a central role. Assassination, suicide and theft are among some of the features, but despite these horrific scenes the novel is full of comic episodes. Garp, a basically ordinary man, and the other characters have to find their way through this world and survive the obstacles thrown in their way. The book was made into a successful movie starring Robin Williams and Glenn Close.

Typical Irving trademarks include: a fascination with bears, Vienna, wrestling, and sports; humor, even when dealing with tragic subjects; and a great deal of interest in human characters and bizarre relationships. A good example of his style is *The Hotel New Hampshire*, which explores issues such as incest, suicide and rape in a darkly comic fashion.

Publications

1969 Setting Free the Bears
1972 The Water-Method Man
1974 The 158-Pound Marriage
1978 The World According to Garp
1981 The Hotel New Hampshire
1985 The Cider House Rules
1989 A Prayer for Owen Meany
1993 Trying to Save Piggy Sneed
1994 A Son of the Circus
1998 A Widow for One Year

IRVING, Washington

American short-story writer

Born Apr. 3, 1783
Died Nov. 28, 1859
Age at death 76

Publications

- *1809 A History of New York from the Beginning of the World to the End of the Dutch Dynasty*
- *1819–20 The Sketch Book*
- *1822 Bracebridge Hall*
- *1824 Tales of a Traveller*
- *1828 History of the Life and Voyages of Christopher Columbus*
- *1835 The Crayon Miscellany*
- *1855–59 George Washington* (5 vols.)

Washington Irving was one of the first American authors to achieve international recognition. He became famous for his humorous writings and helped establish the short story in American literature.

Irving, the son of a wealthy merchant, was born in New York City. He studied law privately but practised only briefly. When he was 26, he published *A History of New York from the Beginning of the World to the End of the Dutch Dynasty*. Irving wrote the book under the name Diedrich Knickerbocker, who was supposed to be an eccentric Dutch-American scholar. The book was a comic account of the early years of Dutch settlement in Manhattan, and it became part of New York folklore. Eventually the word Knickerbocker was used to describe any New Yorker who could trace his family to the original Dutch settlers.

When he was 37, he published his most successful book, *The Sketch Book*. Full of gentle humor, it is a collection of essays and sketches on English folk customs, Native Americans, and the Dutch in New York. It contains two of his most famous stories: "Rip Van Winkle," about a man who falls asleep for 20 years, and "The Legend of Sleepy Hollow," in which the schoolmaster Ichabod Crane meets with a headless horseman.

With the success of *The Sketch Book* Irving became a professional writer and returned to New York in 1832 a literary hero. In his later years, he expanded his writings to include history and biography.

ISHERWOOD, Christopher

Anglo-American novelist and playwright

Born Aug. 26, 1904
Died Jan. 4, 1986
Age at death 81

Christopher Isherwood was an English-born novelist whose gently humorous stories were often based on his own experiences.

The son of an army captain who was killed in World War I, Isherwood was born in northern England and went to school with the poet W.H. AUDEN, with whom he had a lifelong friendship. Isherwood left Cambridge University without a degree, studied medicine for a time, and then went to visit Auden in the German capital, Berlin.

Isherwood lived and worked in Berlin for four years. While in his early to mid-30s he wrote about his experiences of this exciting, culturally-mixed city in *The Last of Mr. Norris*, a comedy about a charming conman, and in *Goodbye to Berlin*. These stories were later adapted into the musical *Cabaret*, which was made into a famous movie.

When the Nazis came to power in Germany in 1933, Isherwood returned to England and then settled in California, becoming a US citizen in 1946. In America, he continued to write about incidents from his own life. Many of his famous literary friends appear in his books under different names, including Auden, STEPHEN SPENDER and VIRGINIA WOOLF.

Isherwood became interested in Hindu teachings and also became an outspoken campaigner for an end to discrimination against homosexuals. He discussed his own homosexuality in his book *Christopher and His Kind* and wrote *A Single Man*, a moving novel about a gay man whose partner dies.

Publications

1928 *All the Conspirators*
1932 *The Memorial*
1935 *The Last of Mr. Norris*
1938 *Lions and Shadows*
1939 *Goodbye to Berlin*
1962 *Down There on a Visit*
1964 *A Single Man*
1971 *Kathleen and Frank*
1976 *Christopher and His Kind*

ISHIGURO, Kazuo

Japanese-born British novelist

Born Nov. 8, 1954

After the publication of only four highly respected books, Kazuo Ishiguro has emerged as one of the foremost British novelists of his generation. His writing is known for its spare and precise story-telling and its power to evoke a distinctive setting.

Born in Nagasaki, Japan, Ishiguro went with his parents to live in London when he was six. His life has been spent in an environment where Japanese and British cultures are freely mixed, with Japanese spoken at home and English learned at school and by talking with friends. He completed a combined English and philosophy degree at the University of Kent, then attended the influential Master's course in creative writing at the University of East Anglia.

Ishiguro was employed as a community worker in Scotland at the end of the 1970s. At age 26, his first short stories were published in magazines and his first novel, *A Pale View of Hills*, two years later. The novel's narrator is a Japanese woman living in England who, on returning to Japan, turns from the role of the traditional housewife toward the kind of freedom she discovered in the West. Ishiguro's second novel, *An Artist of the Floating World*, is also set in Japan. His most successful book to date, *The Remains of the Day*, is set in an English country mansion recently purchased by an American. The aging butler, who is a study in emotional restraint, looks back over his life, regretting missed opportunities. The novel won an important British literary award and was made into a popular film in 1993.

Publications

1982 *A Pale View of Hills*
1986 *An Artist of the Floating World*
1989 *The Remains of the Day*
1995 *The Unconsoled*

JACKSON, Helen Hunt

American novelist, poet and children's writer

Born Oct. 15, 1830
Died Aug. 12, 1885
Age at death 54

Publications

1872	*Bits of Travel*
1874	*Saxe Holm's Stories*
1874	*Verses*
1876	*Mercy Philbrook's Choice*
1878	*Nelly's Silver Mine*
1881	*Mammy Tittleback and Her family*
1883	*A Century of Dishonour*
1884	*Ramona*
1884	*Easter Bells*

Although she was most famous in her lifetime for writing poems and children's stories, Helen Hunt Jackson is remembered today for her romantic novel *Ramona*, the story of a doomed love affair between two Native Americans.

Jackson was born in Amherst, Massachusetts. Both her parents died when she was a teenager. When she was 22, she married an army officer. They had two sons – the first-born died as a baby, and later her husband and other son died within two years of each other.

Alone and unhappy at the age of 35, Jackson was encouraged to write by friends, including her old schoolfriend the poet Emily Dickinson. She began by writing poems, essays, book reviews and children's stories. A great deal of her work was published. At that time, however, female writers were often not taken seriously, since many people thought they should concentrate on more "womanly" jobs such as raising children. For this reason, Jackson used various pen names, such as Rip Van Winkle, Saxe Holm, H.H. or simply "No Name."

In 1879, Jackson went to a talk given by a Native American chief and became aware of how badly the US government had treated Native Americans. After months of research, she published *A Century of Dishonor*, which chronicles the injustices dealt to seven ethnic groups by the government. It had little effect, so she wrote *Ramona* in an attempt to stir up public opinion. Sadly, Jackson did not live to see any great improvements made as a result of her writing.

JACKSON, Shirley

American horror writer

Born Dec. 14, 1919
Died Aug. 8, 1965
Age at death 45

Shirley Jackson is famous for her original stories about lonely or mentally disturbed people who appear to experience supernatural events.

Jackson was born in San Francisco and was brought up by a strict mother. She began writing stories as a teenager and had her first published at age 18. She married a literary critic and college lecturer, Edgar Hyman, and moved to a village in Vermont. From then on Jackson spent most of her time raising four children and writing. However, she found rural life difficult and suffered from depression.

When Jackson was 29, the *New Yorker* magazine published her story "The Lottery," which provoked a storm of protest. In it she describes an annual ritual of stoning a victim to death as though this was a form of entertainment like a baseball game. The story made her famous, and she went on to write other disturbing stories and novels.

Jackson was fascinated by black magic and once joked that she was "the only practising witch in New England." But it was never clear whether she believed in the existence of supernatural beings; there was always a sly wit and humor in her work. As a horror writer she showed how isolated, lonely individuals can come to see the outside world as unnaturally hostile and deeply evil. *The Haunting of Hill House* is about a woman who believes ghosts are more caring than the people she knows. In *The Sundial* a family awaits what they believe will be the end of the world. *We Have Always Lived in the Castle*, probably her best novel, explores the attempts of two sisters, one a murderess, to shut the real world out of their lives.

Publications

1948 "The Lottery"
1954 *The Bird's Nest*
1957 *Raising Demons*
1958 *The Sundial*
1959 *The Haunting of Hill House*
1962 *We Have Always Lived in the Castle*

Published after she died

1966 *The Magic of Shirley Jackson*

JAMES, Henry

American novelist, short-story writer and critic

Born Apr. 15, 1843
Died Feb. 28, 1916
Age at death 72

One of America's greatest writers, Henry James is best known for the way he creates very detailed and complex characters in his novels.

James was born in New York City into a wealthy and prominent family. The family moved frequently, and James lived in France, Germany, England, and Switzerland. At age 19, he enrolled in the Harvard Law School but preferred reading literature to studying law. He published his first story, "A Passionate Pilgrim," two years later and became a regular reviewer and contributor for literary journals. Although only in his 20s, he was considered to be one of the country's finest short-story writers.

In 1875, James settled in Europe. During his first years there he wrote novels that portrayed Americans living abroad in Europe; he was concerned with exploring the relationship between European and American cultures. *The Portrait of a Lady*, one of his best stories from this period, is about a young American woman who visits England and Italy with her aunt. In the 1880s, he began analyzing social ills in novels such as *The Bostonians* and *Princess Casamassima*. Then, the final stage of James's writing was devoted to combining the previous two themes by analyzing moral questions through the experiences of individuals. It was in this period that James published his greatest novels: *The Wings of the Dove*, *The Ambassadors* and *The Golden Bowl*.

In 1915, James became a British citizen in protest against the US's refusal to enter World War I. He died in 1916, having written 20 novels, 112 stories, 12 plays and thousands of pages of literary criticism.

Publications

1875 *Roderick Hudson*
1877 *The American*
1880 *Washington Square*
1881 *The Portrait of a Lady*
1886 *The Bostonians*
1886 *Princess Casamassima*
1890 *The Tragic Muse*
1902 *The Wings of the Dove*
1903 *The Ambassadors*
1904 *The Golden Bowl*

JAMES, M.R.

English horror writer

Born Aug. 1, 1862
Died Jun. 12, 1936
Age at death 73

M.R. James is best known for his clever, frightening and unforgettable ghost stories.

Montague Rhodes James was the youngest son of an English clergyman. He was educated at Eton, where he read ghost stories by the Irish writer J. SHERIDAN LE FANU, whom he admired all his life. James attended Cambridge University. A brilliant history scholar, he specialized in the study of ancient manuscripts. He became head of a college at Cambridge University and at Eton, his old school. He lived his whole life in the company of men and remained a bachelor.

Although James was a friendly, pleasant man, he had a nervous nature and was often disturbed by vivid nightmares. As a child, he had seen a toy Punch-and-Judy set with puppets cut out of cardboard. One of these figures was The Ghost. It was this image that haunted his dreams and later appeared in his stories.

James began to write ghost stories as a Christmas treat for his family and friends. Every Christmas Eve, he would prepare and read aloud a story, usually involving the adventures of a middle-aged scholar who unearths an ancient object and with it some horrific ghost. The stories were told in a matter-of-fact style that added to their spooky atmosphere. His first collection of stories, published when he was 42, established his reputation as a masterful teller of ghostly tales. It includes "Canon Alberic's Scrapbook," about a scholar who is shown a satanic manuscript, and "Oh, Whistle, and I'll Come to You, My Lad," in which a professor blows on an ancient whistle and is chased by a strange, menacing apparition.

Publications

1904 Ghost Stories of an Antiquary
1911 More Ghost Stories of an Antiquary
1919 A Thin Ghost and Others
1922 The Five Jars
1922 Twelve Medieval Ghost Stories
1926 A Warning to the Curious
1931 Collected Ghost Stories

JAMES, P.D.

English crime writer

Born Aug. 3, 1920

P.D. James is the most successful contemporary crime writer working in the tradition of AGATHA CHRISTIE. James takes the classic English "whodunit" story – in which the reader has to puzzle out from clues how a murder happened – and tries to give it more depth. As well as action and intrigue, James is interested in what motivates characters, and she includes serious themes in her books.

She was born Phyllis Dorothy James in Oxford, and educated at a girls' school in Cambridge. She came from the same type of middle-class English background as did Christie, but her work experience – as a theater stage manager, a hospital administrator and in a government police department – gave her more varied settings for her stories. Although she had long dreamed of being a writer, James was 42 before she published her first novel, *Cover Her Face.*

James's two central characters are Adam Dalgliesh, a middle-aged police detective and poet, and Cordelia Gray, a young private detective. She is particularly interested in describing the subtle relationships between people at work in social groups. Among the settings for her stories are, for example, a hospital, a psychiatric clinic, a science laboratory and a nuclear power station.

James's approach to her characters is mostly unemotional; there are few love stories in her books. She prefers to tackle general themes, whether political debates about the problems posed to society by technology, or more philosophical questions, such as the nature of human mortality.

Publications

1962	*Cover Her Face*
1972	*An Unsuitable Job for a Woman*
1975	*The Black Tower*
1977	*Death of an Expert Witness*
1980	*Innocent Blood*
1982	*The Skull Beneath the Skin*
1986	*A Taste for Death*
1989	*Devices and Desires*
1992	*The Children of Men*
1997	*A Certain Justice*

JARRELL, Randall

As well as being a famous critic, Randall Jarrell is one of America's most popular modern poets.

Jarrell was born in Nashville, Tennessee, but spent most of his childhood in California. He studied at Vanderbilt University under the writer ROBERT PENN WARREN. After leaving Vanderbilt, Jarrell taught briefly before joining the US Air Force to serve in World War II.

Jarrell spent most of the war in America as an instructor, and he wrote about the conflict in a series of poems published throughout the 1940s that brought him national attention. His first collection, *Blood for a Stranger*, came out when he was 28. The best-known poems of this period include "Lines," "Absent with Official Leave" and, possibly his most famous poem, *The Death of the Ball-Turret Gunner*. Jarrell uses a specific event or situation as the basis of each poem, but underneath the practical details is a strong message about the terrible effects of war.

After the war, Jarrell returned to his academic career. He published three more collections of poetry, *The Seven League Crutches*, *The Woman at the Washington Zoo* (winner of the 1960 National Book Award), and *The Lost World*, the title poem of which is regarded as an American classic. In spite of his professional success and happy second marriage, Jarrell seems to have been fundamentally a deeply depressed man. In 1965, he suffered a nervous breakdown. Later that year, he was hit and killed by an automobile; the question of whether or not he deliberately ran into the path of the vehicle has never been resolved.

American poet and critic

Born May 6, 1914
Died Oct. 14, 1965
Age at death 51

Publications

1942	*Blood for a Stranger*
1945	*Little Friend, Little Friend*
1951	*The Seven League Crutches*
1960	*The Woman at the Washington Zoo*
1963	*The Gingerbread Rabbit*
1965	*The Lost World*

Published after he died

1969	*The Complete Poems*
1969	*The Death of the Ball-Turret Gunner*

JEFFERS, Robinson

American poet and playwright

Born Jan. 10, 1887
Died Jan. 20, 1962
Age at death 75

Robinson Jeffers is a widely read poet best known for his descriptive poems about human suffering in a beautiful universe.

Born in Pittsburgh, Pennsylvania, Jeffers attended schools in Pittsburgh, Switzerland and Germany, learning French, German, Latin, and Greek. He entered the University of Pittsburgh aged 15 and later transferred to universities in California, where he studied a huge range of subjects from economics to ancient Greek literature.

As a boy, Jeffers had tried to fly with homemade wings, and many of his poems describe birds. Published when he was 25, his first book, *Flagons and Apples*, is a collection of simple love poems. Jeffers lived in the coastal town of Carmel, California. He described its people and magnificent scenery in his second book, *Californians*. Many other volumes had a similar setting. His poems tell a story, often of violence, murder, punishment and tragedy. He often adapted ancient Greek and other stories into modern versions; his *Medea*, derived from EURIPIDES's play, was a successful Broadway play, and the poems "Dear Judas" and "Tamar" are based on biblical stories.

Jeffers's early influences were the English writers WILLIAM WORDSWORTH and THOMAS HARDY but, after the horrors of World War I, Jeffers found his own voice and achieved success. By 1921, he had begun to express his view that humankind can help overcome its misery by looking beyond its own selfishness and corruption to the permanent and beautiful universe. In his last years, Jeffers won several awards, including the Shelley Memorial Award.

Publications

1912 Flagons and Apples
1916 Californians
1925 Roan Stallion, Tamar, and Other Poems
1927 The Women at Point Sur
1929 Dear Judas and Other Poems
1938 The Selected Poetry of Robinson Jeffers
1946 Medea
1948 The Double Axe and Other Poems

JEROME, Jerome K.

English novelist and playwright

Born May 21, 1859
Died Jun. 14, 1927
Age at death 68

Jerome K(lapka) Jerome is remembered as the author of *Three Men in a Boat*, a humorous book about three friends and their upriver boating vacation. It is now a classic of English literature.

Jerome was born in Walsall, a small town in the Midlands, but he grew up in London. After leaving Marylebone Grammar School at 14, he worked in various jobs such as railroad clerk, schoolmaster, actor and journalist. At age 26, he produced his first work, *On the Stage and Off*, a book about his adventures with touring theatrical companies. Four years later, he began writing full time and brought out his funniest and most famous book, *Three Men in a Boat*. It is a hilarious tale of the misadventures of George, Harris, Jerome and their dog as they row a boat up the River Thames. Modern readers find its serious passages too sentimental, but the comic episodes are still very funny. At 41, Jerome also wrote *Three Men on the Bummel*. This sequel to *Three Men in a Boat* tells of the same friends on a cycling holiday in Germany.

Jerome wrote or edited many more works. At 33, he cofounded *The Idler*, a magazine that had contributions from writers including BRET HARTE, ROBERT LOUIS STEVENSON and MARK TWAIN. The next year he started a weekly magazine called *To-Day*. Among his later books is *Paul Kelver*, a serious novel that is largely based on his own life. He also wrote successful plays. His best-known drama is *The Passing of the Third Floor Back*, about the effect a Christlike man has on a group of shady people.

Publications

1885 On the Stage and Off
1886 Idle Thoughts of an Idle Fellow
1889 Three Men in a Boat
1900 Three Men on the Bummel
1902 Paul Kelver
1907 The Passing of the Third Floor Back
1926 My Life and Times

JEWETT, Sarah Orne

American novelist and short-story writer

Born Sep. 3, 1849
Died Jun. 24, 1909
Age at death 59

Sarah Orne Jewett is best remembered as the author of *The Country of the Pointed Firs* and many short stories that describe the rural life of New England in the 19th century. She has been called one of the best writers of local-color fiction, which serves to portray accurately the people and landscape of a particular region of America.

Jewett was born in South Berwick, Maine. Her father, to whom she was very close, was a wealthy country doctor. Jewett felt she learned more by accompanying her father on his rounds than by attending school. After graduating from Berwick Academy in 1866, she thought about becoming a doctor herself but finally decided against it. She embarked on a busy social life, visiting friends and relatives and going to the theater. Jewett never married, though she had a close 30-year relationship with another woman, Annie Fields. She spent most of her life in Maine but often traveled to Europe and elsewhere in America.

Jewett began writing as a child. Her first published story was "Jenny Garrow's Lovers." She was 19 at the time. She continued to write short stories for many of the leading magazines of the day, and her reputation slowly grew. She did not publish her masterpiece, *The Country of the Pointed Firs*, until she was 47. It is narrated by a city woman who goes to stay in Dunnett Landing, a small coastal village in Maine. There is little plot but a series of descriptions of the people she meets and the places she visits. The novel has been called the finest example of regional literature published in the 1800s.

Publications

1877 Deephaven
1884 A Country Doctor
1885 A Marsh Island
1886 A White Heron and Other Stories
1895 The Life of Nancy
1896 The Country of the Pointed Firs

Published after she died

1925 The Best Stories of Sarah Orne Jewett

JHABVALA, Ruth Prawer

German-born American novelist and screen-writer

Born May 7, 1927

A respected novelist – author of the prizewinning *Heat and Dust* – Ruth Prawer Jhabvala is perhaps more widely known in America for her screenplay adaptations of classics of English literature. Among the novels that she has helped turn into highly successful movies are E.M. FORSTER'S *Howard's End* and KAZUO ISHIGURO'S *The Remains of the Day*.

Jhabvala was born in Cologne, Germany. Her Polish parents were refugees from Nazi Germany who fled to England, where Jhabvala grew up and was educated. At 21, she became a British citizen. Three years later she married a visiting Indian architect, C.S.H. Jhabvala, and returned with him to India. She lived in Delhi for the next 24 years.

Jhabvala began writing seriously while in India, and she published her first novel, *Amrita*, when she was 29. Most of her novels from this time concern Indian matters written from the point of view of an outsider. She was much concerned with middle-class Indian life and with Europeans living in India. In *Heat and Dust*, published when she was 48, she describes a British woman's journey through India. The novel was praised for its wit and passion, and it won Jhabvala a prestigious British literary award, the Booker Prize. Jhabvala wrote the screenplay for the 1983 film.

Jhabvala is now a US citizen, and in recent novels she has moved away from the theme of India. *Poet and Dancer*, set in New York City, and *Shards of Memory* both explore the theme of family history. Her partnership with film director James Ivory and producer Ismail Merchant has resulted in several award-winning films for which she wrote screenplays.

Publications

1956 Amrita
1958 Esmond in India
1960 The Householder
1965 A Backward Place
1968 A Stronger Climate
1975 Heat and Dust
1986 Out of India: Selected Stories
1987 Three Continents
1993 Poet and Dancer
1995 Shards of Memory

JIMÉNEZ, Juan Ramón

Spanish poet

Born Dec. 24, 1881
Died May 29, 1958
Age at death 76

Juan Ramón Jiménez was a Spanish poet who has been called "the poet's poet" because his work set a standard to which others aspire. In 1956 he was awarded the Nobel Prize for Literature.

Jiménez was born in Moguer, southern Spain, an area of exceptional beauty that features in many of his poems. He began writing at age 15. By 19, he had moved to the capital city, Madrid, in an attempt to further his writing career. It was there that he met the Nicaraguan poet RUBÉN DARÍO, who became his lifelong friend.

While in Madrid, Jiménez published two volumes of poetry that explore ideas about God, beauty and love. These themes feature in most of his work. Following the death of his father, Jiménez had a breakdown and returned to Moguer. Highly sensitive and emotional, he suffered bouts of illness and depression throughout his life.

Between the ages of 24 and 31, Jiménez published nine volumes of poetry. This time of frantic creativity marked a turning point in Jiménez's career. His work became more confident, using freer and less structured verse. During this time he wrote his most popular work, *Platero and I*.

With the outbreak of the Spanish Civil War Jiménez left Spain. After some years in Puerto Rico and Cuba he and his wife moved to the US, where they lived and taught in Miami and Washington, DC. They then settled in Puerto Rico. In 1956, the same year he won the Nobel Prize, his wife died, plunging Jiménez into a depression from which he never recovered before his death just over a year later.

Publications

1900	*Violet Souls*
1900	*Water Lilies*
1902	*Rhymes*
1903	*Sad Airs*
1914	*Platero and I*
1942	*Spaniards of Three Worlds*
1946	*The Total Season*
1948	*Coral Gables Ballads*
1949	*Animal of Depth*
1957	*Third Poetic Anthology*

JOHNSON, Dr.

English writer

Born Sep. 18, 1709
Died Dec. 13, 1784
Age at death 75

Dr. Johnson was probably the most important literary figure in 18th-century England. As a literary critic, poet, translator and the author of the first English dictionary, he has left his mark on literature.

Samuel Johnson was born in Lichfield in the Midlands. His father ran a failing bookstore, where Johnson spent many hours reading. He did well at the local school and excelled as a student at Oxford University. But because of poverty he did not finish his degree. Nervous and with odd manners, his hearing and sight damaged by childhood illnesses, and often depressed, Johnson found it hard to find work.

When Johnson was 28, he moved to London. For nearly two decades he worked as a journalist, writing articles and essays. He also wrote poetry and biographies and translated other poets. He was often poor until the government gave him a pension for services to literature when he was 53. His friend and biographer James Boswell made sure this remarkable man is known in detail today.

Johnson's first major published poem, *London* – an imitation of the Roman writer Juvenal's *Third Satire* – came out when he was 29. It was not as good or successful as his second imitation of a Juvenal satire, *The Vanity of Human Wishes*. This poem shows how people can be betrayed by their desires. Johnson's good judgment and polished writing are best seen in his book *Lives of the English Poets*. Seven years of work went into his *Dictionary of the English Language*. The first of its kind, it defines over 40,000 words and became a classic.

Publications

1738	*London*
1744	*An Account of the Life of Mr. Richard Savage*
1749	*The Vanity of Human Wishes*
1755	*Dictionary of the English Language*
1759	*Rasselas, Prince of Abyssinia*
1779–81	*Lives of the English Poets*

JOHNSON, Eyvind

Swedish novelist and short-story writer

Born Jul. 29, 1900
Died Aug. 25, 1976
Age at death 76

Eyvind Johnson is notable for having won the Nobel Prize for Literature in 1974.

Johnson was born to a poor working-class family near Boden in northern Sweden near the freezing Arctic Circle, where he suffered great hardship. He had almost no schooling and as a youth was engaged mainly in manual labor, especially as a lumberjack. At age 20, he traveled south into a Europe devastated by World War I and spent most of the 1920s in Berlin and Paris, working at various jobs. On his return visits to Sweden he was distressed by its sense of isolation from the rest of Europe.

Johnson's early novels betray the influence of some of the most famous writers of the time – JAMES JOYCE, MARCEL PROUST and ANDRÉ GIDE – and have the common theme of human frustration. *Bobinack*, published when Johnson was 32, is an attack on modern capitalist values. *Rain at Dawn* is concerned with the damaging effects on people of boring office jobs. His first important work, published when he was in his mid-30s, was the four-volume *Story of Olof.* Regarded as a classic in Sweden, this autobiographical novel, based on Johnson's experiences as a logger, follows the life of a Swedish boy growing up during World War I.

During World War II Johnson became involved in anti-Nazi activities; the *Krilon* series and other novels reflect his hatred of dictatorship and concern for human welfare. At age 46, he began to write historical novels, starting with *Return to Ithaca* – a modern version of the ancient Greek Odysseus myth from HOMER's *Odyssey*.

Publications

1927 City in Darkness
1928 City in Light
1932 Bobinack
1933 Rain at Dawn
1934–37 Story of Olof
1938 Night Maneuvers
1941–43 Krilon series
1946 Return to Ithaca
1949 Dreams of Roses and Fire
1960 The Days of His Grace

JOHNSON, Georgia Douglas

American poet and playwright

Born Sep. 10, 1886
Died May 14, 1966
Age at death 79

Georgia Douglas Johnson was one of the most influential African-American writers of her time.

Born in Atlanta, Georgia, Johnson began writing in secondary school, and her first poem appeared in print when she was 19. She then went to university and music school before marrying a lawyer. She had two children and continued to write while working for the government in Washington, DC. Published when she was 32, her first poems in *The Heart of a Woman* are gentle expressions of love and other emotions and are lyrical in style. Her second volume of poetry, *Bronze*, is much stronger in tone and was widely read. By then she had become part of a group of black writers, artists, and intellectuals who wanted to use their creativity to protest against racism and to celebrate their African heritage. Some of Johnson's new poems were about the horrors of slavery, particularly for women. After her husband died, however, she returned to the theme of love for her third collection, *An Autumn Love Cycle*.

During the Great Depression Johnson wrote plays about lynching and slavery that she submitted to the Federal Theater Project. They were rejected because it was felt she had exaggerated the horrors of slavery.

Johnson – who in later years was never seen without a pencil and notebook, which she tied on a ribbon around her neck in case an idea came to her – continued to write poetry for journals until her death. Her importance as one of the first modern black female poets has gradually gained acceptance.

Publications

1918	*The Heart of a Woman and Other Poems*
1922	*Bronze*
1927	*Plumes*
1928	*An Autumn Love Cycle*
1962	*Share My World*

JOHNSON, James Weldon

American poet and novelist

Born Jun. 17, 1871
Died Jun. 26, 1938
Age at death 67

James Weldon Johnson was an outstanding man with many abilities: he wrote poetry and novels, was the first African-American lawyer in Florida, and was also a songwriter, school headmaster and diplomat.

Johnson was born in Jacksonville, Florida, into a cultured family that gave him an all-round education. He attended Atlanta University, graduating at age 22, toured with a singing quartet, and then returned to Jacksonville as headmaster of his old school, Stanton. In 1895, Jackson started a newspaper for the black community that promoted civil rights. He then studied to be a lawyer and eventually moved to New York City, where his songwriting career took off.

After four years in New York Johnson's career changed direction again – he was appointed US consul to Venezuela. His new job gave him plenty of time for writing, and he began work on his first novel. *The Autobiography of an Ex-Colored Man* was published when Johnson was 41 and serving as consul in Nicaragua. It is about a light-skinned black man who rejects his origins and lives as a white man. Although not based on Johnson's own life, it reflects the way he had always rejected the restrictions placed on him because of his color.

With little hope of promotion, Johnson left the diplomatic service and returned to *New York Age*, a black newspaper. At age 46 he published *Fifty Years and Other Poems*, his first collection of poetry. The title poem commemorates the 50th anniversary of the end of slavery.

Publications

1912	*The Autobiography of an Ex-Coloured Man*
1917	*Fifty Years and Other Poems*
1922	*The Book of American Negro Poetry*
1925	*The Book of American Negro Spirituals*
1927	*God's Trombones; Seven Negro Sermons in Verse*
1933	*Along This Way*
1934	*Negro Americans, What Now?*

JONES, Gayl

American novelist, poet and playwright

Born Nov. 23, 1949

Novelist Gayl Jones credits her mother and her grandmother with giving her the love of storytelling that is the hallmark of her work.

Jones was born in Lexington, Kentucky, where her father was a cook, and her grandmother wrote plays that were performed in church. Her mother also wrote, and the stories she made up and read to her children stayed with the young Jones. By age eight, Jones was writing stories, and by the time she had graduated from Connecticut College she had earned several awards for her writing. She later went to Brown University, where she received a Master's degree.

Jones's work explores the legacy of slavery and the oppression of black women. At age 24, she produced her first play, *Chile Woman*. Her first novel, *Corregidora*, was edited by TONI MORRISON and published when Jones was 26. It is about a woman – a descendant of a Portuguese slave trader – who is abused by her husband, just as her mother and the women before her were abused by their husbands. The heroine becomes a blues singer as a way to express her pain and grief. The character in Jones's second novel, *Eva's Man*, is also the victim of sexual violence, but ends up in a psychiatric prison.

Although her native Kentucky is referred to in her work, Jones has set many of her stories in Brazil, including two book-length poems, *Song for Anninho* and *Xarque*. In addition to writing fiction, Jones has been a professor of English at the University of Michigan, and she has published a scholarly work on African-American oral traditions.

Publications

1973 Chile Woman
1975 Corregidora
1976 Eva's Man
1977 White Rat and Other Short Stories
1981 Song for Anninho
1983 The Hermit-Woman
1985 Xarque
1991 Liberating Voices

JONES, James

American novelist

Born Nov. 6, 1921
Died May 9, 1977
Age at death 55

James Jones is best known for his first novel, *From Here to Eternity*.

Born in Robinson, Illinois, Jones graduated from secondary school in Illinois and later took some courses at the University of Hawaii and at New York University. He was a welterweight boxer in the Golden Gloves and later in the army; his boxing experiences were the basis for the fight scenes in *From Here to Eternity*.

Jones served in the army throughout World War II and received the Bronze Star and a Purple Heart. After the war, he settled in Marshall, Illinois, and spent six years writing *From Here to Eternity*. He used his own war experiences as background for the story. The novel, published when he was 30, is about life on an army base in Hawaii. Its main character is Private Robert E. Lee Prewitt, a brave and honorable man who loves the army but who will not give in to the army system. Prewitt is also a boxer who refuses to fight because he once blinded a man. The novel became a bestseller and won the National Book Award in 1951.

Jones's second novel, *Some Came Running*, was not so successful. In 1958, he and his new wife moved to Paris, where their house became a meeting place for writers and artists. There he wrote *The Pistol* and *The Thin Red Line*, the second in the trilogy of war novels he had begun with *From Here to Eternity*. The series was completed with *Whistle,* which although not finished, was published in 1974. It was later finished by his friend Willie Morris. In 1974, Jones returned to the US to teach writing at Florida International University in Miami.

Publications

1951	*From Here to Eternity*
1957	*Some Came Running*
1959	*The Pistol*
1962	*The Thin Red Line*
1967	*Go to the Widow-Maker*
1968	*The Ice-Cream Headache*
1971	*The Merry Month of May*
1973	*A Touch of Danger*
1978	*Whistle* (finished version published after he died)

JONG, Erica

American novelist and poet

Born Mar. 26, 1942

Erica Jong's best-known novel, *Fear of Flying*, was daring in its frank depiction of a woman gaining control over her own sexuality. Although not her first work, it made her instantly famous, becoming one of the ten bestselling novels of the 1970s.

Jong was born in New York, one of three daughters in an artistic and intellectual Jewish family. She graduated from Barnard College in 1963, then received a Master's degree from Columbia University in 1965. More recently she has taught English in a number of universities. In 1966, she married; that marriage ended in divorce, and she has since remarried twice. She has one daughter, Molly.

The poetry collection *Fruits & Vegetables*, Jong's first book, was published when she was 29. It contains poems that express her anger at the way women poets are often relegated to the sidelines. She has said that she considers it her duty to challenge the presumption that "the noun 'poet' [is] of the male gender." A strong feminist, she often uses humor to criticize the constraints society places on women.

Jong shocked the nation with her novel *Fear of Flying*, in which her heroine, Isadora Wing, literally flies off in search of freedom on a sexual spree. It was a powerful statement at a time when the women's movement was still emerging. Jong, still just in her 30s, followed up this bestseller with a sequel, *How to Save Your Own Life*. One of her more recent works is *Inventing Memory*, which looks at the events of the 20th century through the lives of four generations of women in a Jewish-American family.

Publications

1971	*Fruits & Vegetables*
1973	*Fear of Flying*
1977	*How to Save Your Own Life*
1980	*Fanny*
1981	*Witches*
1983	*Ordinary Miracles*
1987	*Serenissima*
1990	*Any Woman's Blues*
1994	*Fear of Fifty*
1997	*Inventing Memory*

JONSON, Ben

English playwright and poet

Born Jun. 11, 1572
Died Aug. 6, 1637
Age at death 65

Ben Jonson was one of the most influential English playwrights of the 17th century.

Jonson was born in London just after his father died. A family friend paid for him to be educated at Westminster School, where he developed a love of literature that would last all his life.

When he was 17, Jonson was apprenticed to his stepfather's trade, bricklaying. He hated it, however, and joined the army instead. After fighting in Holland and winning fame for defeating an enemy in single combat, he returned to London, married, and started a career in the theater – first as an actor and then as a playwright. When he was 25, he coauthored *The Isle of Dogs*, a satire that got him sent to jail and the theater shut down. This was the first of Jonson's many encounters with the law. In 1598, he narrowly escaped execution for killing a fellow actor in a duel.

That same year 26-year-old Jonson had his first real success as a playwright with *Every Man in His Humor*, in which WILLIAM SHAKESPEARE was a principal actor. Every character in this satirical comedy has a particular "humor," such as jealousy, that Jonson uses to make fun of London life. *Every Man out of His Humor*, in which Jonson satirized his fellow playwrights, followed a year later.

In later life, wealthy patrons paid Jonson to write "masques" – combinations of dance, music and drama. Although Jonson's plays declined in popularity, he remained influential in literary circles and inspired a group of writers called the Sons of Ben. In 1616, he became the first playwright to publish a collection of plays in book form.

Publications

1597 *The Isle of Dogs* (with Thomas Nash)
1598 *Every Man in His Humor*
1599 *Every Man out of His Humor*
1601 *The Poetaster*
1606 *Volpone*
1609 *The Masque of Queens*
1609 *The Silent Woman*
1610 *The Alchemist*
1614 *Bartholomew Fair*
1616 *The Devil Is an Ass*

JORDAN, June

American poet, essayist, and children's writer

Born Jul. 9, 1936

Politics and black self-identity are at the heart of feminist and political activist June Jordan's work.

Jordan was born in Harlem, New York City, and grew up in Brooklyn. She was the only child of Jamaican immigrants. Her mother was a nurse and often worked nights; her father, a postal clerk, wanted her to become a doctor. But the young Jordan was more interested in writing poetry. She was the only black student at a school in Brooklyn and later attended a prep school in Massachusetts. At age 17, she enrolled at Barnard College in New York. Two years later she married. She never graduated from university but chose to pursue her career as a poet instead.

In 1966, Jordan began teaching. She has since been on the faculty at a number of universities, including the University of California at Berkeley, where she is now a professor of African-American studies.

Jordan first became known for two books for children. *Who Look At Me*, published when she was 33, explores black self-identity and recognition through paintings of African Americans. Jordan wrote the poems in Black English, in part to appeal to teenagers. Two years later, she published *His Own Where*, a novel for young adults. Although nominated for a National Book Award, the book was banned from some school libraries by parents who worried that it encouraged the use of Black English rather than standard English. Jordan argued that African Americans should know both.

Her poetry for adults includes *Some Changes* and *Things That I Do in the Dark*. She has also written plays, two of which were directed by NTOZAKE SHANGE.

Publications

1969	*Who Look At Me*
1971	*Some Changes*
1971	*His Own Where*
1974	*New Days*
1977	*Things That I Do in the Dark*
1981	*Kimako's Story*
1981	*Civil Wars*
1989	*Moving Toward Home: Political Essays*
1994	*The Haruko/Love Poetry*

JOYCE, James

Irish novelist, poet and short-story writer

Born Feb. 2, 1882
Died Jan. 13, 1941
Age at death 58

James Joyce is perhaps the most important author of the 20th century. He invented a new kind of storytelling and experimented with language to create a kind of writing unlike anything that had been seen before.

Joyce was born the youngest of ten children in the Irish city of Dublin. He was educated at strict Catholic schools that were intended to prepare him for a life as a priest. As a young man Joyce rejected this idea – the spiritual struggle he went through to reach this decision became a central theme of his writing in later life.

While studying at universities in Dublin and Paris, Joyce began to write. His first book, *Chamber Music* – published when he was 25 – is a collection of poems, but it wasn't until he began writing novels that Joyce's genius became clear. His first novel, *A Portrait of the Artist as a Young Man*, is based on his own early life. In it, Joyce used the stream-of-consciousness technique to tell the story through the thoughts and feelings of the main character – a sensitive young man who rejects religion and decides to become a great writer.

Joyce wrote his masterpiece, *Ulysses*, while living in Italy and Switzerland. It returns to the central character of his first novel – now a struggling writer living in Dublin. The events in the book take place in just one day in Dublin, but Joyce describes the thoughts of his characters so completely that many people claimed he had summed up the whole of human life in one book. *Ulysses* had a huge influence on many writers of the 20th century.

Publications

1907	*Chamber Music*
1914	*Dubliners*
1916	*A Portrait of the Artist as a Young Man*
1918	*Exiles*
1922	*Ulysses*
1927	*Pomes Penyeach*
1936	*Collected Poems*
1939	*Finnegans Wake*

JUANA INÉS de la CRUZ

Mexican poet, playwright and essayist

Born Nov. 12, 1651
Died Apr. 17, 1695
Age at death 43

Juana Inés de la Cruz was Mexico's leading poet of the 17th century. She was also an early feminist who argued that women must be allowed to become scholars. She is often known as Sor (Sister) Juana Inés de la Cruz since she spent most of her life as a nun.

Juana was born to a poor family, and her parents were probably not married. At the time this meant it was unlikely she would marry, which was the only future then for a woman. Her real name was Juana de Asbaje y Ramirez de Santillana, but she is known by her pen name.

From an early age Juana loved learning. She began to read at age three, and at seven she wanted to dress up as a man so she could go to university, which her parents wouldn't allow. By the time she was a teenager, however, Juana was mixing with the intellectuals of the day in Mexico City. Although she impressed everyone she met with her knowledge and intelligence, she knew that the only way she could become a scholar was to enter a convent. At age 18, she became a nun. She continued to write – love poetry, plays and essays – and her library of 4,000 books was the largest in the country. By the time she was 35, she had published several volumes of poetry.

Juana was outspoken about her belief that women should not be forbidden from studying and teaching. Her bishop criticized these views, and after much pressure she gave up writing. She died while tending to fellow nuns during a plague epidemic.

Publications

1683 The Obligations of a House
1690 Carta Atenagórica
1691 Response of the Poetess to the Very Illustrious Sor Filotea de la Cruz
First Dream (date unknown)

JÜNGER, Ernst

German novelist and essayist

Born Mar. 29, 1895
Died Feb 18, 1998
Age at Death 103

Ernst Jünger has published numerous works – novels, and essays and books on war, travel and history – over the course of much of the 20th century.

Jünger, who celebrated his 100th birthday in 1995, was born in Heidelberg, Germany. At the age of 17, he ran away from home to join the French Foreign Legion, where he survived the harsh discipline and served in North Africa. At 19, he enlisted in the German army in World War I, showed great bravery, and was wounded on the Western Front in France. He was awarded high military honors. Jünger turned to writing militaristic novels that, while not glorifying war, suggested that it was necessary. His early novels, such as *Storm of Steel*, published when he was 25, helped to keep alive the military spirit in Germany by arguing that Germany's suffering in the war was a prelude to great developments for the German people.

The rise of the Nazis in the 1930s, however, made him change his mind. He was strongly critical of them in the allegorical novel *On the Marble Cliffs*, and he rejected offers of friendship from the Nazi leader, Hitler. Fortunately, his reputation in Germany was so high that the Nazis could not touch him.

In World War II, Jünger was again fighting in the front line as a captain, but his ideas about war had radically changed. He now hated it and regarded it as a blind, brutal force. This may have been partly because his son had died fighting in Italy. Jünger now became a strong supporter of European unity and a promoter of individual dignity and human rights. His later writings continued to earn him many German and international awards.

Publications

1920 *Storm of Steel*
1925 *Copse 125*
1936 *African Diversions*
1939 *On the Marble Cliffs*
1945 *The Peace*
1949 *Heliopolis*
1957 *The Glass Bees*
1977 *Eumeswil*
1983 *Aladdin's Problem*
1985 *A Dangerous Encounter*

JUSTICE, Donald

American poet, short-story writer and essayist

Born Aug. 12, 1925

Donald Justice won a Pulitzer Prize for *Selected Poems* in 1980. He is admired for his quiet, precise and carefully crafted poems that accurately capture the loneliness and isolation of 20th-century life.

Justice's father was a carpenter and his mother a cook in Miami, Florida, then a quiet Southern city. As a child he studied piano and taught himself how to compose music. He earned his Bachelor's degree from the University of Miami when he was 20 and his Master's from the University of North Carolina in 1947. He married Jean Ross, a short-story writer, the same year. Since 1982, Justice has been professor of English at the University of Florida.

Justice uses many different forms for writing poetry, including old verse forms and sonnets, for which there are strict rules about the number of lines for each verse and the use of words. He has also written ballads and free verse. A keen gambler, he has even written poems resulting from the chance dealing out of word-cards. His poems center on the importance and unstable nature of memory and how poetry helps remembrance and reconsideration of memories.

Justice's first book of poetry, *The Summer Anniversaries*, was published when he was 35. It contains unsentimental yet haunting poems about his childhood during the Great Depression and about illness and madness. The works that followed also deal with loss, loneliness and the shortness of human life. *Night Light* is witty and gentle and is about ordinary situations and events that seem to be unimportant but are a vital part of life.

Publications

1960 *The Summer Anniversaries*
1967 *Night Light*
1970 *Sixteen Poems*
1971 *From a Notebook*
1973 *Departures*
1979 *Selected Poems*
1984 *Platonic Scripts*
1984 *Tremayne*
1987 *The Sunset Maker*
1995 *New and Selected Poems*

JUVENAL

Roman satirist

Born c. 65
Died c. 140
Age at death c. 75

Juvenal was a Roman writer. He is remembered for his brilliantly witty satires about life in ancient Rome.

Like many writers of his time, Juvenal came from a fairly wealthy background and benefited from a good education. Scholars think that he was born in a southern Italian town called Aquinum and that he first went to the capital city, Rome, to earn a living as a teacher of public speaking. He may also have served in the Roman army for a short time.

During Juvenal's early life, Rome was ruled by the emperors Nero and Domitian. They were both cruel and harsh rulers who neglected government and committed terrible crimes against their people. At some time during Domitian's reign, Juvenal was punished for an unknown crime. Possibly he offended the emperor by criticizing him in a public speech. This unfair punishment, and the corruption he saw in government, made Juvenal very angry. He felt that the traditional values of Roman society were being ignored and that the wealthy ruling classes had become interested only in luxurious living rather than looking after the people.

It wasn't until several years after Domitian's death that Juvenal dared to publish his satires. The first of his five books was published around the year 110, when he was about 55. Over the next 20 years Juvenal produced 16 satires that attacked everything from the lifestyles of rich, upper-class Roman women to the management of the army. But his most savage writing was directed against Domitian and the people who had supported his rule.

Publications

c. 110	*Book I* (Satires 1–5)
c. 116	*Book II* (Satire 6)
c. 120	*Book III* (Satires 7–9)
c. 125	*Book IV* (Satires 10–12)
c. 127	*Book V* (Satires 13–16)

KAFKA, Franz

Czech novelist and short-story writer

Born Jul. 3, 1883
Died Jun. 3, 1924
Age at death 40

Franz Kafka's strange and disturbing tales have had a great influence on 20th-century literature.

Kafka was born in Prague (now in the Czech Republic, but then part of Austria). The son of German-speaking Jewish parents, he was a shy and sensitive man who lived with his parents for most of his short life. He studied law at the German University in Prague and then got a job writing reports on industrial accidents and health hazards. The only time he had for creative writing was in the evenings.

Some of Kafka's early stories were published in 1909 when he was 26. In the summer of 1912, he wrote the two short stories, "The Judgment" and "The Metamorphosis," that established his importance as a writer. "The Metamorphosis," which was to become Kafka's most famous story, is about a man who wakes to find that he has been transformed overnight into a giant insect. Both stories feature a theme common to all his work: a lonely victim who suffers persecution for a crime he does not understand. This theme is carried further in Kafka's most famous novel, *The Trial*. In this book the hero, Joseph K., is unaware of the offense for which he is persecuted and finally executed. This idea has been described as an allegory for the bewilderment felt by many people in the modern world.

Kafka refused to allow any of his three novels to be published during his lifetime and left instructions to his friend Max Brod that all his manuscripts should be burned after his death. Fortunately for literature, Brod decided to publish the manuscripts.

Publications

1913 "The Boilerman"
1913 "Meditations"
1913 "The Judgment"
1915 "The Metamorphosis"
1919 "In the Penal Colony"
1919 *The Country Doctor*

Published after he died

1925 *The Trial*
1926 *The Castle*
1927 *America*

KALIDASA

Indian poet and playwright

Lived c. AD *400–500*

Kalidasa is widely considered to be the greatest Indian poet and dramatist of all time. He wrote in the ancient Sanskrit language. He has been called the WILLIAM SHAKESPEARE of India for the quality and beauty of his work and for the influence he has had on generations of Indian writers.

Very little is known of Kalidasa's life. He could have lived any time from the 2nd century BC to the 7th century AD. It is most likely that he lived during the reign of the kings Chandragupta II (c. 375–415) and his son Kumaragupta (c. 415–55). Chandragupta's empire controlled most of northern India and what are now Pakistan and Bangladesh. According to tradition, Kalidasa was the greatest of the "Nine Jewels" at Chandragupta's court. These poets were responsible for the flowering of literature during the famous Golden Age of the Guptas.

There are only seven works that were almost certainly written by Kalidasa: two epic poems, two shorter poems, and three plays. Much of his work celebrates mythical rulers of the past and Indian gods, probably both to praise the Guptas and remind them that great rulers do not forget the interests of their citizens. Kalidasa often stressed that people should balance enjoyment of life with responsibility.

Perhaps Kalidasa's best-known work is the play *Sakuntala*. Based on an Indian legend, it tells of the separation of a king and his wife, Sakuntala, and their reunion in Heaven. His finest poem is *Cloud Messenger*, in which an exiled demigod asks a cloud to take a message to his lover. The poem beautifully describes the cities, rivers and mountains the cloud passes.

Publications

Dates unknown
Birth of Kumara
Cloud Messenger
Cluster of Seasons
Dynasty of Raghu
Malavika and Agnimitra
Sakuntala
Uhvarshi Won by Valour

KANTOR, MacKinlay

American novelist, short-story writer and journalist

Born Feb. 4, 1904
Died Oct. 11, 1977
Age at death 73

MacKinlay Kantor is best known for his historical novels, especially *Andersonville*, which won a Pulitzer Prize in 1956.

Kantor was born in Webster City, Iowa. His parents had a disastrous marriage, with his father spending time in jail and eventually abandoning the family. His mother, a newspaper editor, encouraged Kantor's literary interests and got him a job as a reporter.

After marrying at 22, Kantor produced his first novel, *Diversey*, about Chicago gang wars in the 1920s. During World War II, he served as a war correspondent and published *Glory for Me*, a novel about the war; the 1946 movie version, *The Best Years of Our Lives*, won 13 Academy Awards.

Kantor's first historical novel *Long Remember*, about a single battle during the American Civil War, was followed by *The Voice of Bugle Ann*. This very successful book is about the relationship between a hound dog and her master. Kantor's most critically acclaimed novel, *Andersonville*, depicts a Confederate prison for Union prisoners in Georgia and was praised for showing how terrible the Civil War was and how so many suffered. The main character is Ira Claffey, who owns the land on which the prison is built. Through his eyes the reader understands both the bullying prison chief and the tragic prisoners.

Kantor also enjoyed writing stories about historical figures such as George Washington and Abraham Lincoln. The stories have simple plots but are historically accurate and entertaining, often with surprise endings.

Publications

1928 Diversey
1934 Long Remember
1935 The Voice of Bugle Ann
1937 The Romance of Rosy Ridge
1945 Glory for Me
1955 Andersonville
1961 Spirit Lake
1972 I Love You, Irene
1973 The Children Sing
1975 Valley Forge

KARLFELDT, Erik Axel

Swedish poet

Born Jul. 20, 1864
Died Apr. 8, 1931
Age at death 66

Swedish poet Erik Axel Karlfeldt was offered the Nobel Prize for Literature in 1918 but refused it, possibly because he was, for many years, on the Nobel Prize committee. He was awarded the honor in 1931, however, shortly after he died. Some of his poetry, inspired by rural life, has been described as difficult, but the collections that feature his bachelor-poet Fridolin were extremely popular with the public in Sweden. Fridolin, although a simple peasant, displays deep learning.

Karlfeldt was born at Folkärna in the rural province of Dalarna, Sweden. His carefree early poetry was influenced by his friend Gustaf Fröding and the popular 1890s movement in Sweden to return to a simple life in the countryside. However, the mood darkened in his later work, which expresses a very personal view of the countryside tinged with profound sadness and fear of death.

Karfeldt's first volume of poetry, *Songs of Wilderness and Love*, came out when he was 31. Fridolin first appeared three years later in *Fridolin's Songs*. The Fridolin poems reflect the old peasant customs that Karlfeldt had seen in Dalarna. The poem *Flora and Bellona*, which was written during World War I, contrasts the peacefulness of rural life with the horrors of a distant war, the effect of which was to change the traditional way of life permanently. The darkening mood of his later work attracted criticism and lost him popularity with his public. Some critics felt that he had wasted his talents on a dying culture. Karlfeldt left the countryside and went to live in Stockholm, where he died.

Publications

1895	*Songs of Wilderness and Love*
1898	*Fridolin's Songs*
1901	*Fridolin's Pleasure Garden*
1906	*Flora and Pomona*
1918	*Flora and Bellona*
1927	*The Horn of Autumn*

KÄSTNER, Erich

German children's writer, novelist and poet

Born Feb. 23, 1899
Died Jul. 29, 1974
Age at death 75

Erich Kästner is best known for his humorous stories for children.

Kästner was born in Dresden, Germany, and studied in several German cities, including Berlin. He set out to be a teacher but turned to writing and became a freelance writer at 28. Like many German writers of the 1920s, he developed a light yet sharp way with words. He was 29 when his most famous novel appeared. Apart from a tale by MARK TWAIN, *Emil and the Detectives* was the first story where children play the part of detectives. It is about a ten-year-old boy whose money is stolen on his way to Berlin and the comic adventures that follow as Emil and his gang attempt to recover the money. The book portrays city boys in a humorous and sympathetic manner, and its charm and witty style led to its being translated into 24 languages; it was also turned into a play and a movie.

During the 1930s, Germany's Nazi government so disliked Kästner's satirical writings that they had his books burned. After this he had his new books printed in Switzerland. But Kästner stayed on in Germany through World War II. He claimed that "a writer must experience how the nation to which he belongs bears its fate during troubled times and one day give evidence."

Kästner went on to write more stories. *The Animals' Conference*, a sharp but funny satire on humankind's inability to secure peace, was published when he was 50. In the same year came *Lisa and Lottie*, later made into a Walt Disney movie, *The Parent Trap*.

Publications

1928	*Emil and the Detectives*
1932	*Fabian: The Story of a Moralist*
1934	*Three Men in the Snow*
1935	*The Missing Miniature*
1935	*Emil and the Three Twins*
1949	*The Animals' Conference*
1949	*Lisa and Lottie*
1956	*The School of Dictators*
1957	*When I Was a Boy*
1966	*The Little Man*

KAUFMAN, George S.

American playwright and critic

Born Nov. 16, 1889
Died Jun. 2, 1961
Age at death 71

Publications

1921	*Dulcy* (with Marc Connelly)
1922	*Merton of the Movies* (with Marc Connelly)
1930	*Once in a Lifetime* (with Moss Hart)
1932	*Of Thee I Sing* (with Morris Ryskind)
1932	*Dinner at Eight* (with Edna Ferber)
1936	*You Can't Take It with You* (with Moss Hart)

George S(imon) Kaufman wrote over 40 plays, more than half of which were popular hits, and he won Pulitzer Prizes for two of them. All but one of his plays was co-written. With MARC CONNELLY he wrote lighthearted comic satires that made fun of businessmen, politicians and Hollywood; with EDNA FERBER he wrote more dramatic, moralizing plays; with Morris Ryskind he wrote musical comedies, some of which launched the careers of the comedy team of the Marx Brothers; and with Moss Hart he wrote comedies. To all his plays Kaufman brought his wit and talent for writing funny lines.

Kaufman was born in Pittsburgh, Pennsylvania. His brother died at an early age, and Kaufman's mother was very protective of her remaining son. As a result he grew up with particular eating habits and great fears about failure and death. After graduating from secondary school, Kaufman held a variety of jobs before settling into a career as a journalist. He got his own column when he was 23, but was fired when his boss discovered he was Jewish.

After this Kaufman moved to New York City, where he became a drama critic. It was there that he met Connelly. Together they wrote a series of successful comedies. *Dulcy*, the tale of a meddling businessman's wife, and *Merton of the Movies*, a satire that mocked Hollywood, were the most popular. With Ryskind he wrote *Of Thee I Sing*, a pointed satire of presidential politics and the first musical comedy to win the Pulitzer Prize for drama. *You Can't Take It with You*, written with Hart, a madcap comedy about a wacky family, won Kaufman his second Pulitzer.

KAWABATA Yasunari

Japanese novelist and short-story writer

Born Jun. 11, 1899
Died Apr. 16, 1972
Age at death 72

Kawabata Yasunari is regarded by many as the greatest Japanese novelist of the 20th century. In 1968, he became the first Japanese to be awarded the Nobel Prize for Literature.

Kawabata was born in Osaka, Japan. Orphaned at the age of three, he was left totally without family at 16. He was educated at Tokyo Imperial University, where he studied English and Japanese literature. His first literary efforts were short stories published in the monthly magazine *The Artistic Age*, a journal that encouraged young writers and which he had helped found.

Kawabata's first important novel, *The Izu Dancer*, was published when he was 26. It is autobiographical and recounts his youthful infatuation with a dancer. His early writing was influenced by

European surrealism, especially in its strange images and in the close association of the beautiful and the revolting. This book also set the pattern for his later work with its focus on sexual themes. Many of his books explore the place of sex in peoples lives. There is a sadness in Kawabata's writing, and it is often difficult for Westerners who know little about Japanese culture to understand. *Snow Country*, which took him more than 14 years to write, explores the relationship of people to nature. *The House of the Sleeping Beauties* deals with his characteristic themes: loneliness, love, guilt, old age and death.

Four years after Kawabata was awarded the Nobel Prize and soon after the death of his friend YUKIO MISHIMA, he committed suicide.

Publications

1925	*The Izu Dancer*
1937	*Snow Country*
1952	*Thousand Cranes*
1952	*The Sound of the Mountain*
1954	*The Master of Go*
1961	*The Lake*
1962	*The Old Capital*
1965	*Beauty and Sadness*
1969	*The House of the Sleeping Beauties*

KAZANTZAKIS, Nikos

Greek novelist, poet and playwright

Born Feb. 18, 1883
Died Oct. 26, 1957
Age at death 74

Kazantzakis is best known for his novels *Zorba the Greek*, which was made into a popular and highly successful movie, and the controversial *The Last Temptation of Christ*, which was also filmed. He produced a wide variety of work and made an important contribution to modern Greek literature.

Kazantzakis was born in Heraklion on the island of Crete, was raised among peasants, and studied law at the University of Athens and philosophy in Paris. He then spent several years traveling in Europe, Russia, the Middle East and Japan. His jobs included that of a minister in the Greek government and an official in the United Nations agency UNESCO. In 1948, he settled in Antibes, southern France.

His first novel, *Toda-Raba*, was published in French when he was 51, but he was relatively unknown as a novelist until he published the autobiographical story *Zorba the Greek* at age 63 and *The Last Temptation of Christ*, a fictional biography of Christ, at age 72. He was an immensely hard-working man who translated a large number of ancient Greek classics and other great works of literature into modern Greek, including the *Divine Comedy* of Dante, Charles Darwin's *Origin of Species*, and JOHANN WOLFGANG VON GOETHE'S *Faust*. He also wrote travel books and poetry. Taking up where HOMER left off, he produced his own enormous epic poem, *The Odyssey: A Modern Sequel*.

Kazantzakis came within one vote of winning the Nobel Prize for Literature in 1957, but lost to the French writer ALBERT CAMUS. A month later he died of leukemia in Germany.

Publications

1934	*Toda-Raba*
1936	*The Rock Garden*
1937	*Spain*
1938	*The Odyssey: A Modern Sequel*
1946	*Zorba the Greek*
1953	*Freedom or Death*
1954	*The Greek Passion*
1955	*The Last Temptation of Christ*
1956	*St. Francis: A Novel*

KEATS, John

English poet

Born Oct. 31, 1795
Died Feb. 23, 1821
Age at death 25

Publications
1816 "O Solitude"
1817 *Poems*
1818 *Endymion*
1820 *Lamia, Isabella, The Eve of St. Agnes, and Other Poems*

Published after he died
1888 "The Beautiful Woman Without Mercy"

John Keats was one of the finest poets of the Romantic school of writing. Most of his best work appeared in one year.

Keats was born in London, the eldest of five children. His father kept horses for hire but died when Keats was only eight. Keats grew up in his grandmother's home at Edmonton, near London. At school he read widely, won prizes and learned to love poetry. From 1811 to 1816, he studied medicine at Edmonton and at Guy's Hospital, London. Meanwhile he was composing verses and meeting writers, including the poet PERCY BYSSHE SHELLEY.

In 1816, Keats gave up medicine to write, living poorly off a little money left by his grandmother. His first published poem, "O Solitude," appeared in a magazine when he was 21. At age 23, his first long poem, *Endymion*, was published. It tells in 4,000 lines of the love of the moon goddess, Cynthia, for the young shepherd Endymion. Then, in 1819, Keats produced the epic poems "Hyperion" and "The Fall of Hyperion." In the same year, he wrote his famous "Ode to a Nightingale," "To Autumn," "Ode on a Grecian Urn" and most of his other best pieces. These poems use vivid word pictures to praise the world's beautiful things. They are tinged with sadness because Keats knew we cannot enjoy beauty forever.

Keats felt sad for good reasons. He was too poor to marry Fanny Brawne, the woman he loved. His mother and brother Tom had died of tuberculosis. And by age 24, Keats also had the disease. He moved to Italy to escape England's cold winter but died there early the next year.

KELLY, George

American playwright

Born Jan. 16, 1887
Died Jun. 18, 1974
Age at death 87

George Kelly was a playwright most famous for his comedy *The Show-Off*, which is still popular today.

Born in Schuylkill Falls, Pennsylvania, Kelly was the second youngest of ten children. His brother, John, was an Olympic rower and father of the actress, Grace Kelly. He was educated privately and became an actor at the age of 25 with a national touring company. After appearing in vaudeville productions, he started writing.

Kelly's first play, *The Torchbearers*, was produced when he was 35. His third, *Craig's Wife*, written three years later, won the 1926 Pulitzer Prize. Together with *The Show-Off* these plays established Kelly's reputation as a popular writer.

One of Kelly's favorite themes was marriage and, later, infidelity in marriage. He also liked to write about people's flaws, such as vanity and greed. *The Torchbearers* tells the story of a sweet, simple wife, Paula Ritter, who takes to the stage encouraged by a hopeless but enthusiastic director, Mrs. Pampinelli. Mr. Ritter pleads with his wife to stop making a fool of herself. She agrees, and the play ends happily. There is little plot, but the strength lies in the colorful characterization. The main character in *The Show-Off* is Aubrey Piper, a windbag who lies to impress others and starts to believe his own lies. In *Craig's Wife,* Walter Craig's wife becomes obsessed with gaining control over their beautifully furnished house but ends up alone with an empty home.

Kelly's next four plays were less successful, so he left for Hollywood. He contributed to one film and had three more plays produced.

Publications

1922	*The Torchbearers*
1924	*The Show-Off*
1925	*Craig's Wife*
1926	*Daisy Mayme*
1927	*Behold the Bridegroom*
1929	*Maggie, the Magnificent*
1931	*Philip Goes Forth*
1936	*Reflected Glory*
1946	*The Deep Mrs. Sykes*
1946	*The Fatal Weakness*

KENEALLY, Thomas

Australian novelist, playwright and short-story writer

Born Oct. 7, 1935

Thomas Keneally is a leading Australian novelist whose works are often based on historical figures. They are about characters, not necessarily heroic, who must make tough moral choices.

Keneally, of Irish Catholic descent, was born in Sydney, Australia, and educated at St. Patrick's College. He studied for the priesthood but left before being ordained; two of his early novels are based on that period. His first important novel, *Bring Larks and Heroes*, was published when he was 32. It is about Irish prisoners exiled to Australia in the 18th century. *The Chant of Jimmy Blacksmith* is based on the true story of a half-Aboriginal man who killed several white women and was in turn murdered by white Australians. *The Cut-Rate Kingdom* is about Australia's uncomfortable relationship with the US during World War II.

Not all Keneally's novels focus on his native land. In *Confederates* he wrote about the American Civil War and received critical praise for his accurate depiction of the American South. *Blood Red, Sister Rose* is based on the life of French heroine Joan of Arc.

Keneally's most famous novel is *Schindler's List*, based on the true story of a rich German industrialist who saves Jews from the Nazi gas chambers during World War II. This novel won an important literary prize and was later made into a very successful film.

Keneally has held university teaching posts in both Australia and the US and continues to write about Australia and other subjects, including autobiographical memoirs and children's stories.

Publications

1967	*Bring Larks and Heroes*
1972	*The Chant of Jimmy Blacksmith*
1974	*Blood Red, Sister Rose*
1975	*Gossip from the Forest*
1979	*Confederates*
1980	*The Cut-Rate Kingdom*
1982	*Schindler's List*
1985	*A Family Madness*
1995	*A River Town*
1996	*Homebush Boy: A Memoir*
1998	*The Great Shame*

KENNEDY, William

American novelist, journalist and screenwriter

Born Jan. 16, 1928

Despite early lack of success, William Kennedy persisted in his writing; his fourth novel, *Ironweed*, after many rejections, was finally published to great acclaim in 1983. It won both the National Book Critics' Award and the 1984 Pulitzer Prize and established him as a major American novelist.

Kennedy was born to Irish-American parents in Albany, New York, and raised in a predominantly Irish-Catholic neighborhood. He attended a local school and the Christian Brothers' Academy, where he worked on his secondary school newspaper. He went to Siena College and, after being drafted in 1950, served as an Army journalist in Europe. Between 1956 and 1963, he was a journalist in Puerto Rico and Florida. While in Puerto Rico he married and enrolled in a writing course run by the American novelist SAUL BELLOW, who later helped get *Ironweed* published.

On his return to Albany in 1963, Kennedy embarked on a series of essays and loosely connected novels set in 1920s and '30s Albany. His first novel, *The Ink Truck*, published when he was 41, was about a newspaper union's strike. The hero, Bailey, remains the sole striker after everyone else has been bought off by management. *Legs* is based on the life of John T. Diamond, a famous 1920s Albany gangster. *Ironweed* is the fourth of his Albany sagas, continuing the story of one member of the Phelan family who returns 20 years after accidentally killing his infant son. Kennedy also wrote the screenplay for the film of this novel.

Publications

1969 The Ink Truck
1976 Legs
1978 Billy Phelan's Greatest Game
1983 Ironweed
1983 O Albany!
1988 Quinn's Book
1992 Very Old Bones
1993 Riding the Yellow Trolley Car
1996 The Flaming Corsage

KEROUAC, Jack

American novelist

Born Mar. 12, 1922
Died Oct. 21, 1969
Age at death 47

Jack Kerouac first coined the phrase "the beat generation," source of the word "beatnik." The "beats" rebelled against the conformity of 1950s "square" society and valued artistic and personal freedom of expression. Kerouac's novel *On the Road*, the first beat novel, was based on his wild adventures while traveling across America with his friend Neal Cassady. It is a defining text of beat culture.

Kerouac was born in Lowell, Massachusetts, to French-Canadian parents. His real name was Jean-Louis Lebris de Kerouac, and he spoke only French until he was six. When he was four, his beloved older brother Gerard died, and for much of his life Kerouac believed that his brother was his guardian angel. At Columbia University in New York City, he met WILLIAM S. BURROUGHS and ALLEN GINSBERG, cofounders of the beat movement, but Kerouac left a year later. After briefly serving in the merchant marine in World War II, he traveled through the US, Mexico and Europe, taking odd jobs and writing about his experiences.

Kerouac wrote his first novel, *The Town and the City*, when he was 28. He believed that creative writing was similar to a spontaneous, almost theatrical, performance: *On the Road* was written over a period of just 20 days on a single roll of telegraph paper. It made him a cult figure, but other works were not as successful. In his search for spiritual liberation, he experimented with drugs and sex and studied Zen Buddhism. Later in life, he found his role as a spokesman for the beat generation something of a burden and settled with his third wife in Florida. In 1969, he died of an alcohol-related illness.

Publications

1950	*The Town and the City*
1957	*On the Road*
1958	*The Dharma Bums*
1958	*The Subterraneans*
1959	*Mexico City Blues*
1959	*Doctor Sax*
1962	*Big Sur*
1963	*Lonesome Traveler*
1965	*Desolation Angels*
1968	*Vanity of Duluoz*

KERR, M.E.

American young-adults' writer

Born May 27, 1927

M.E. Kerr is the pen name that Marijane Meaker uses when she writes fiction for young adults. Since publishing her first young-adult novel, the still famous *Dinky Hocker Shoots Smack!*, Kerr has become one of America's top writers for young adults.

Kerr was born in Auburn, New York, into a reasonably well-off family; her father owned a company that made mayonnaise. She went to the local secondary school before being sent to a boarding school as a teenager. Kerr graduated from the University of Missouri in 1949 with a degree in English. In the same year she moved to New York City, planning to become a writer. She took menial jobs and was often fired because she was writing when she should have been working.

When Kerr was 25, she published her first novel, *Spring Fire*, which was written for adults. This and the 20 suspense novels that followed were written under the pen name Vin Packer.

In the 1970s, Kerr was inspired by the growing body of young-adult fiction to try writing for that age group herself. After reading PAUL ZINDEL's *The Pigman*, she realized that young-adult fiction could be as challenging as any writing. When she was 45, she published *Dinky Hocker Shoots Smack!*, which is about a young girl who, in order to get her parents' attention, spreads a rumor that she is a drug addict. In this and other books Kerr deals with issues such as drug abuse, physical disability, racism and AIDS in a realistic and often humorous way. In *Gentlehands,* a young boy discovers his charming grandfather was a brutal Nazi during World War II.

Publications

1952	*Spring Fire*
1972	*Dinky Hocker Shoots Smack!*
1975	*Is That You, Miss Blue?*
1978	*Gentlehands*
1981	*Little Little*
1983	*Me, Me, Me, Me, Me: Not a Novel*
1986	*Night Kites*
1994	*Deliver Us from Evie*

KESEY, Ken

American novelist

Born Sep. 17, 1935

Ken Kesey is best known for his first novel, *One Flew Over the Cuckoo's Nest*. A major figure of the West Coast culture of the 1960s, he has been identified as the man who changed the beat generation into the hippie movement.

Kesey was born in La Junta, Colorado. He attended local schools in Springfield, Oregon, graduated from the University of Oregon, and married his high school sweetheart, Faye Haxby, in 1956. In 1960, after doing graduate work in creative writing at Stanford University, he signed up as a paid volunteer for government drug experiments being held at the Veteran's Hospital in Menlo Park, California; he then took a job as an aide in the hospital. It was his experiences both with the drugs and the hospital work that provided him with the background for *One Flew Over the Cuckoo's Nest*, which was published when Kesey was 27.

The novel is set in a mental hospital and shows what happens when McMurphy, a small-time hustler, arrives and disrupts hospital life. The story is told by another patient, a large Native American called Bromden, who pretends to be dumb because he cannot adapt to modern life. McMurphy, with his energy and ability to make other patients laugh, encourages them to rebel against the strict rules of the hospital and restores their belief in themselves.

In 1965, Kesey was arrested for possession of marijuana. He fled to Mexico to avoid prosecution but returned to serve five months in jail. When he was released, he moved to a farm where he turned away from drugs and began to write again.

Publications

1962 One Flew Over the Cuckoo's Nest
1964 Sometimes a Great Notion
1973 Kesey's Garage Sale
1986 Demon Box
1988 Little Trickler the Squirrel Meets Big Double the Bear
1990 The Further Inquiry
1992 Sailor Song
1994 Last Go Round

KEY, Francis Scott

American poet

Born Aug. 1, 1779
Died Jan. 11, 1843
Age at death 63

Francis Scott Key was a well-known 19th-century American lawyer and poet. He is best known for writing the words to America's national anthem, "The Star-Spangled Banner."

Born in Frederick (now Carroll) County, Maryland, Key attended St. John's College, Annapolis, Maryland. He studied law privately and, in 1801, opened a practice in Frederick with Roger B. Taney, who would later become chief justice of the United States. Key moved to Georgetown (now part of Washington, DC) in 1805.

During the War of 1812 Key was asked to negotiate the release of a hostage taken by the British after they burned Washington. The mission was successful, but the British held Key until after a planned attack on Baltimore. Key watched the bombardment of Fort

McHenry in Baltimore harbor from a British warship. He was so inspired by the sight of the American flag still flying over the fort at dawn after the attack that he wrote a poem, "The Star-Spangled Banner," to express his emotions.

Key was 35 when the poem was first published in the Baltimore *American* as "The Defense of Fort McHenry." Soon after, it was set to the music of "To Anacreon in Heaven," a popular tune of the time.

Key later became a prominent lawyer in Washington, DC, and served as US Attorney for the District of Columbia from 1833 to 1841. The United States formally adopted "The Star-Spangled Banner" as its national anthem in 1931.

Publications

1814 "The Star-Spangled Banner"

1834 *The Power of Literature and its Connection with Religion*

Published after he died

1857 *Poems*

KILMER, Joyce

American poet and essayist

Born Dec. 6, 1886

Died Jul. 30, 1918

Age at death 31

Joyce Kilmer was a poet and journalist who became internationally famous for his short poem "Trees."

Kilmer was born in New Brunswick, New Jersey. His father was a scientist, and his mother was a writer. Kilmer married soon after graduating from Columbia University; his wife, Aline Kilmer, also became a respected poet.

Kilmer's first job was teaching secondary school in New Jersey. He later joined the staff of *Standard Dictionary*, for which he wrote word definitions. When he was 25, Kilmer's first collection of poems, *Summer of Love*, was published. Strongly influenced by the romantic poetry of the Irish writer W.B. YEATS, the collection was not a great success.

When he was 26, Kilmer started working for a magazine published by the Episcopal Church, of which he was then a member. The following year his poem "Trees" appeared in *Poetry* magazine and became almost instantly famous. Although the poem is very simple and has no complicated message, the public loved it. Kilmer made it the title poem of his next collection, *Trees and Other Poems*, which sold much better than his first.

When World War I broke out, Kilmer was eager for America to get involved. He wrote a poem, "The White Ships and the Red," about the sinking of the British passenger liner *Lusitania* by German submarines – an event that helped bring America into the war. Kilmer joined the army and was sent to France. He was killed in action during the last year of the war.

Publications

1911 *Summer of Love*

1914 *Trees and Other Poems*

1916 *The Circus and Other Essays*

1917 *Literature in the Making*

1917 *Main Street*

1918 "Rouge Bouquet"

KINCAID, Jamaica

Antiguan-born American novelist, short-story writer and journalist

Born May 25, 1949

Jamaica Kincaid is best known for her widely acclaimed first novel, *Annie John*. In all her work she uses beautiful, poetic language to explore connections to place and to family.

Kincaid was born Elaine Potter Richardson in St. John's, Antigua, in the Caribbean. After finishing school she became a seamstress apprentice, but at age 17, she decided to move to the United States to study and work. She changed her name to Jamaica Kincaid in 1973 when, as she describes it, she began her "real writing." She regularly contributed to the *New Yorker* in the mid-1970s and later became a staff writer.

Many of Kincaid's stories in that magazine went into her first book, *At the Bottom of the River*, published when she was 34. *Annie John*, which was published two years later, tells the story of a young girl who struggles against the constricting love of her family and who leaves her home in Antigua to work in England as a nurse. Like Kincaid herself, Annie John experiences a wrenching separation from her mother and her homeland. In 1988, Kincaid wrote a passionate book about Antigua, *A Small Place*. Full of rage, it argues that foreign rule in the past and tourism in the present have helped to exploit and destroy Antigua. *Lucy*, a novel, features a young Caribbean woman living in the United States and explores the character's relationship with her mother. Kincaid's *Autobiography of My Mother* was well received by critics, some of whom compared her to TONI MORRISON and V.S. NAIPAUL.

Kincaid lives in Vermont with her husband and two children and teaches part time at Harvard University.

Publications

1983	*At the Bottom of the River*
1985	*Annie John*
1988	*A Small Place*
1989	*Annie, Gwen, Lilly, Pam, and Tulip*
1990	*Lucy*
1996	*Autobiography of My Mother*

KING, Stephen

American horror writer

Born Sep. 21, 1947

Stephen King is the world's most successful horror writer. Many of his novels have been made into films.

King was born in Portland, Maine. His father left home when he was a young child: the story goes that one day his father went out to buy a packet of cigarettes and never returned. From then on Stephen and his elder brother were raised by their mother. King attended secondary school in Durham, Maine, and then studied English at the University of Maine. While he was a student, he wrote a column for the local college paper and also began to write horror stories. He had his first professional story published in a magazine when he was 19 years old.

After graduating, King worked at an industrial laundry. He later became a secondary school teacher and wrote in his spare time. His first novel, *Carrie*, about a girl whose thoughts can destroy, was published when he was 27 and was a huge success, enabling him to write full time.

King's novels are full of the traditional figures of horror stories – shapeshifters, vampires, werewolves and innocent people with destructive psychic power. In *The Shining* an old hotel destroys a family, and in *Firestarter* an eight-year-old girl is able to set fire to things by the power of her mind. King's originality lies in the way he updates these figures by introducing them into the lives of ordinary people today. For example, in *Salem's Lot* a small village in Maine is taken over by vampires, and in *Christine* a haunted Plymouth Fury seizes control of a teenage boy. King is skilled at making our ancient fears of the supernatural believable in today's world.

Publications

1974 Carrie
1975 Salem's Lot
1977 The Shining
1978 The Stand
1980 Firestarter
1983 Christine
1986 It
1987 Misery
1994 Insomnia
1996 Desperation
1996 The Green Mile
1998 Bag of Bones
2000 Riding the Bullet

KINGSLEY, Charles

English novelist and children's writer

Born Jun. 12, 1819
Died Jan. 23, 1875
Age at death 55

In his own time, during the Victorian period in England, Charles Kingsley was a radical and controversial figure. Today he is remembered for his novel *Westward Ho!* and the children's book *The Water-Babies*.

At school Kingsley was taught by the son of the great English poet SAMUEL TAYLOR COLERIDGE. He developed a passion for literature and the study of living things, which he continued at Cambridge University.

Like his father, Kingsley became a priest. He was shocked by the poverty and ignorance he found among the rural people of his local church parish and became interested in social reform. He wrote many books and articles attacking the government's policies on social welfare and the attitude of the church, which he felt did not care for the poor as well as it should.

At age 29, Kingsley published his first novel, *Yeast*. Two years later he published *Alton Locke*. Both books were about social reform. Neither was a success, and Kingsley turned to writing historical adventure stories. He finished *Westward Ho!* when he was 36. The book was immediately popular. Its story of an English sailor's adventures in a war against the Spanish caught the public mood of patriotism at the time. People also loved the action-packed, bloodthirsty plot.

Kingsley wrote his books for children later in his life. *The Water-Babies* became a favorite in Victorian households, and Queen Victoria herself read it to her children. The story successfully combined Kingsley's love and knowledge of underwater wildlife, a wild and vividly imagined story, and a moral.

Publications

1848 Yeast
1850 Alton Locke
1853 Hypatia
1855 Westward Ho!
1856 The Heroes
1857 Two Years Ago
1863 The Water-Babies
1866 Hereward the Wake

KINGSTON, Maxine Hong

American writer

Born Oct. 27, 1940

Maxine Hong Kingston's writing – part fiction, part autobiography – explores the experience of Chinese Americans using myths and legends. With the publication of *The Woman Warrior* she became one of the first famous Chinese-American writers.

Kingston, the daughter of Chinese immigrants, grew up in Stockton, California. Her mother had been a midwife in China and her father a poet and scholar. In California, however, the only work they could get was running a laundry and a gambling house. Kingston was the eldest of six children, and she and her sisters and brothers sometimes had to help in the family's laundry. They spoke Chinese at home, and Kingston went to both American and Chinese schools.

After secondary school Kingston won several scholarships and studied at the University of California in Berkeley. In 1962, she graduated, and that year she married. She taught secondary school until she and her husband moved to Hawaii in 1967.

At age 36, Kingston – who had been writing since she was nine – published her first book. *The Woman Warrior* retells the myths and stories of her female relatives and combines them with elements of her own life. It was well received and won a National Book Critics' Circle Award for nonfiction. Her second book, *China Men*, looks at the history of North America through the lives of men who immigrated from China.

Publications

1976 The Woman Warrior
1980 China Men
1987 Hawaii One Summer
1989 Tripmaster Monkey

KINNELL, Galway

American poet

Born Feb. 1, 1927

Galway Kinnell is a major American poet often compared to WALT WHITMAN.

Born in Providence, Rhode Island, Kinnell began writing poetry at Princeton University, where he became friends with the poet W.S. MERWIN. After serving in the US Navy, he graduated from Princeton at age 21. He taught in many American and European colleges and universities, while keeping a home in Vermont.

Kinnell's first published collection of poems, *What a Kingdom It Was*, came out when he was 33 and is written in traditional forms, unlike his later poetry, which is in free verse. The poems focus on death, loss, guilt, and on healing. To emphasize intense experiences he uses images of fire and darkness in this volume as well as in his third collection, *Body Rags*. A famous poem in *Body Rags* is "The Bear," about an Eskimo hunter who wounds a bear and tracks it across frozen land for days. When the bear finally dies, the hunter cuts it open, climbs inside, and dreams he has become a bear: he identifies with the bear through dreaming about its suffering and death.

Kinnell's poetry has been criticized for being bleak and obsessed with violence, death and suffering. For the poet, however, death is the thing that gives life meaning. He tries to show how humanity is related to the natural world and how we should not try to ignore death. In his more recent poems, especially since the birth of his children, Kinnell seems to feel less despairing about life. He has won many awards, including the 1983 Pulitzer Prize for *Selected Poems*, which included his best work.

Publications

1960 What a Kingdom It Was
1968 Body Rags
1971 The Book of Nightmares
1974 The Avenue: Poems 1946–64
1980 Mortal Acts, Mortal Words
1982 Selected Poems
1985 The Past
1990 When One Has Lived a Long Time Alone
1994 Imperfect Thirst

KINSELLA, W.P.

Canadian novelist and short-story writer

Born May 25, 1935

W.P. Kinsella is best known for his popular short stories and his novel *Shoeless Joe*.

William Patrick Kinsella was born in Edmonton, a town on the North Saskatchewan River in Canada, and he attended the University of Victoria and the University of Iowa. After graduating, he worked in a shop, in a restaurant and as a cab driver. When he was 42, his first collection of short stories, *Dance Me Outside*, was published. He then joined the staff of the English department of the University of Calgary in Alberta, working there for five years until 1983.

While at Calgary, Kinsella wrote two further collections of short stories, *Born Indian* and *The Moccasin Telegraph*. They are about the growth and development of a young Native American boy and his passage through the various stages of childhood. Kinsella's first novel, *Shoeless Joe*, was published when he was 47. Later, it was made into a movie called *Field of Dreams*. Like many of his short stories it is about baseball. Kinsella believes that baseball can become like magic to those who love the game – it can help unite people who are separated by death, distance, or bad feelings. Kinsella's work has been influenced by J.D. SALINGER's famous novel *Catcher in the Rye*.

Kinsella left his college teaching job to become a full-time writer and has produced other collections of short stories, the novel *The Iowa Baseball Confederacy*, and various nonfiction books.

Publications

1977 Dance Me Outside
1981 Born Indian
1982 Shoeless Joe
1983 The Moccasin Telegraph
1984 The Thrill of the Grass
1986 The Iowa Baseball Confederacy
1988 The Further Adventures of Slugger McBatt
1997 Diamonds Forever

KIPLING, Rudyard

English children's writer

Born Dec. 30, 1865
Died Jan. 18, 1936
Age at death 70

Rudyard Kipling is one of England's most popular writers. He is the author of world famous children's stories, including *The Jungle Book* and the *Just So Stories*. In 1907, he was awarded the Nobel Prize for Literature, becoming the first English writer to win the prize.

Kipling was born to English parents in India, which was then ruled by the British. He was educated in England between the ages of 5 and 17, and then returned to India to work as a journalist. He began writing short stories and poems about India, a place he loved for its ancient and sophisticated culture. Aged 24, Kipling set off on a voyage to sell his work in America and England. Eventually some of his poems were printed in England, and his literary fame began to spread.

While living in America, he wrote *The Jungle Book* when he was 29, based on stories he told to his daughter. This book about a boy growing up among the animals was to become his best-known work. After his daughter's death in 1899, the family returned to England, and Kipling wrote his great novel *Kim* – an adventure set in India. The *Just So Stories* – a humorous collection of tales about how animals came to be the way they are today – was published when he was 37.

Readers loved Kipling's animal stories and romantic tales about the adventures of Englishmen in strange and distant parts of the world, and he became very famous. During World War I, Kipling's 18-year-old son was killed, and Kipling's later poems have a darker and less hopeful mood.

Publications

1888 *Soldiers Three*
1888 "Baa, Baa, Black Sheep"
1890 *Wee Willie Winkie*
1892 *Barrack-Room Ballads*
1894 *The Jungle Book*
1895 *The Second Jungle Book*
1899 *Stalky & Co*
1901 *Kim*
1902 *Just So Stories*
1906 *Puck of Pook's Hill*

KIZER, Carolyn

American poet and translator

Born Dec. 10, 1925

Carolyn Kizer is one of America's most prominent contemporary poets and a translator of ancient Chinese poetry. She was awarded a Pulitzer Prize for her book *Yin* in 1985.

Kizer was born in Spokane, Washington, where her mother was a scientist and her father a prominent lawyer. She began writing poetry at age eight – writing for her mother, she says – and had her first poem published at 17 in the *New Yorker* magazine. After graduating from Sarah Lawrence College, Kizer married; she and her husband had three children but divorced after six years. When she was 34, she published her first volume of poetry and founded a magazine, *Poetry Northwest*.

Kizer served as the editor of *Poetry Northwest* for several years.

She left in 1965 and studied Urdu poetry while spending a year in Pakistan working for the US State Department. Talented with languages, she collected her translations from a number of languages, including Urdu, Yiddish and Chinese, in *Carrying Over*. One of her books, *Knock upon Silence*, contains translations from Du Fu, a Chinese poet of the 8th century.

Observations on nature, children, animals, and relations between men and women are important in Kizer's work. She also writes on feminist themes such as sexual violence and society's expectations of women. In the mid-1980s she produced two companion volumes – *Mermaids in the Basement: Poems for Women* and *The Nearness of You: Poems for Men* – which together explore and celebrate the differences between the sexes.

Publications

- *1959 Poems*
- *1965 Knock upon Silence*
- *1971 Midnight Was My Cry: New and Selected Poems*
- *1984 Yin*
- *1984 Mermaids in the Basement: Poems for Women*
- *1986 The Nearness of You: Poems for Men*
- *1988 Carrying Over*

KOGAWA, Joy

Canadian poet and novelist

Born Jun. 6, 1935

Joy Kogawa is best known for her haunting, poetic novel *Obasan*, which is about Canada's imprisonment of its Japanese residents during World War II.

Born Joy Nakayama in Vancouver, on Canada's west coast, Kogawa grew up in detention centers in British Columbia and Alberta. During World War II all Canadians of Japanese descent were forced to live in these centers (called internment camps) away from Canada's west coast because they were thought to be potential spies for the Japanese war effort. It was this experience that formed the basis of her famous novel.

After attending colleges in Alberta and Saskatchewan, Kogawa settled in Toronto and married in 1957; she and her husband had two children but later divorced. Her first book, the poetry collection *The Splintered Moon*, was published when she was 32. Later, she visited Japan, and in the poems included in *A Choice of Dreams* she tells of this visit and of how as a child she longed to be "white." Throughout her poetry she writes of her experience as a "Nisei," the name used for children of Japanese ancestry. *Obasan* (which means "aunt" in Japanese) is a look at the past through the eyes of a young "Nisei" woman who learns from her aunt's writing about the internment and the dropping of the atomic bombs in Japan. A revised version of the novel for children was published as *Naomi's Road*.

Kogawa was involved in the efforts to force the Canadian government to compensate Japanese-Canadian families for what they had suffered, and she wrote about these efforts in *Itsuka*, the sequel to *Obasan*.

Publications

- *1967 The Splintered Moon*
- *1974 A Choice of Dreams*
- *1977 Jericho Road*
- *1981 Obasan*
- *1985 Woman in the Woods*
- *1986 Naomi's Road*
- *1992 Itsuka*

KOONTZ, Dean R.

American horror writer

Born Jul. 9, 1945

Dean R. Koontz is one of the most successful horror writers in America today. Many of Koontz's books have been made into major feature films.

Dean Ray Koontz was born and raised in Pennsylvania. His father was violent and addicted to alcohol, and the family was often short of money. As a child Koontz wrote stories, bound them with masking tape, and tried to sell them to his relatives. At university he won a fiction competition run by *Atlantic Monthly* magazine. After graduating, he took a job working with underprivileged children in the Appalachian Poverty Program. In his spare time he wrote science fiction. He then became an English teacher, until his wife Gerda offered to support him for five years so that he could try to become a professional writer. For the first six months he earned nothing at all, but by the end of the five years Koontz was a successful writer, and Gerda was running his business affairs.

Koontz has written science fiction, suspense, and horror stories and novels under a variety of pen names. His novel *Night Chills*, published under his own name when he was 31, became a bestseller. Koontz's books deal with many themes: for example, *Night Chills* is about mind control, and *Phantoms* was inspired by Koontz's fascination with bizarre, unexplained disappearances throughout history. Koontz's novels also draw on his own experiences; for example, *Whispers* is about characters who have been abused as children. His one constant aim is to grip his readers' imaginations and to scare them witless.

Publications

1973 Demon Seed
1976 Night Chills
1980 Whispers
1983 Phantoms
1989 Midnight
1992 Hideaway
1993 Mr. Murder
1993 Winter Moon
1995 Intensity
1996 Tick-Tock

KOSINSKI, Jerzy

Polish-born American novelist and essayist

Born Jun. 14, 1933
Died May 3, 1991
Age at death 57

Jerzy Kosinski is best known for his first novel, *The Painted Bird*, which is based on his own terrible experiences as a child during World War II.

Born in Poland of Russian parents, Kosinski was separated from his family at the beginning of World War II. From the age of six until age twelve he wandered lost around Eastern Europe. Because the Nazis suspected him of being either a Jew or a gypsy, he was brutally ill-treated. After the war he was reunited with his parents, but his experiences made him lose the power of speech for five years. While studying at the University of Lodz, he engineered his escape from communist Poland.

Kosinski arrived in the US when he was 24. His childhood experiences provided the main themes for all his novels: his characters find themselves in situations they are totally unprepared for. Published when he was 32, *The Painted Bird* tells of a child hiding in Nazi-occupied Eastern Europe. Its sequel, *Steps*, won the 1969 National Book Award. In Kosinski's novels, people find that familiar surroundings have suddenly become strange and dangerous. He shows that when laws, family and culture are suddenly removed, there is nothing to stop people from resorting to violence.

Because of his experiences Kosinski was obsessively secretive all his life, so much so that he used a pen name for his first nonfiction books, which are about communism. Perhaps feeling that he had accomplished in his writing all that it was possible for him to say about his life and his view of the world, he committed suicide in 1991.

Publications

1960 The Future Is Ours, Comrade (as Joseph Novak)
1965 The Painted Bird
1968 Steps
1971 Being There
1973 The Devil Tree
1975 Cockpit
1978 Blind Date
1979 Passion Play
1982 Pinball

KUMIN, Maxine

American poet, novelist and children's writer

Born Jun. 6, 1925

Maxine Kumin, like many women poets of her generation, began writing from a recognition of the pain and loneliness of women's traditional role. She says that feminism came to her slowly, "as social conditions changed and as I dared to develop a sense of my own worth."

Kumin grew up in Philadelphia, where her father was a successful pawnbroker. Although Jewish, she attended the local convent school. Status and possessions were important in the household, and she was relieved to concentrate on intellectual and political concerns when she went away to Radcliffe College. At 21, after graduating from university, she married; she had her first child at the same time as earning her Master's degree.

Kumin says that she had been "a closet poet since the age of eight," but she didn't begin writing seriously until she was pregnant with her third child. She started by writing light verse and gradually developed her style. Her autobiographical first novel, *Through Dooms of Love*, was written soon after the death of her father; it explores a young girl's troubled relationship with her father. In 1973, she was awarded the Pulitzer Prize for poetry for *Up Country*. Kumin's poetry expresses her concerns with personal relationships, childhood and motherhood, and interaction of people with nature.

Kumin has also written almost two dozen children's books, which she began as a way to earn money. She was friends with the poet Anne Sexton; they read one another's work and wrote two books for children together. She now lives on a farm in New Hampshire.

Publications

1961 Halfway
1965 The Privilege
1965 Through Dooms of Love
1970 The Nightmare Factory
1972 Up Country
1974 The Designated Heir
1975 House, Bridge, Fountain, Gate
1987 In Deep: Country Essays
1989 Nurture
1992 Looking for Luck

KUNDERA, Milan

Czech-French novelist, short-story writer and poet

Born Apr. 1, 1929

Milan Kundera is regarded as one of the major novelists of the late 20th century. His novel *The Unbearable Lightness of Being* – set in Czechoslovakia during the Russian invasion of 1968 – was made into a successful movie and brought his works to the attention of a wide audience.

Born in Brno, Czechoslovakia (now the Czech Republic), Kundera was the son of a distinguished concert pianist. Educated at college and at the Film Faculty of the Academy of Music and Dramatic Arts in Prague, he worked as a jazz musician before becoming a professor of film studies. At the age of 24, he published his first volume of poetry. Two further volumes appeared in the next four years. These were followed by collections of short stories and a highly successful play, *The Owners of the Keys*.

Kundera's first novel, *The Joke*, was published when he was 38. It is a satirical attack on communism and the opportunists who thrived under it. Some critics consider it to be his best novel. At the time, however, it and his earlier works earned him disapproval from the authorities. After the Russians invaded Czechoslovakia in 1968, his works were banned, and he was dismissed from his job. In 1975, Kundera was allowed to leave Czechoslovakia and settle in France, where he got a job teaching literature. In 1979, the Czech government deprived him of his citizenship, so he became a French citizen. From then on, his books commanded increasing respect and popularity, but they were not available in his homeland until the fall of communism in Eastern Europe.

Publications

1953 Man: A Broad Garden
1962 The Owners of the Keys
1967 The Joke
1970 Laughable Loves
1973 Life Is Elsewhere
1976 The Farewell Party
1984 The Unbearable Lightness of Being
1991 Immortality
1996 Slowness
1998 Identity

KUNITZ, Stanley

American poet, critic and translator

Born Jul. 29, 1905

Stanley Kunitz is one of the most renowned poets of his time; according to one critic, he writes "truthfully about what matters most." He won the Pulitzer Prize in 1959 for his *Selected Poems, 1928–58*.

Kunitz was born in Worcester, Massachusetts; his father committed suicide before his birth, and his stepfather died when Kunitz was 14. The figure of the lost father often appears in Kunitz's poetry.

Kunitz was an outstanding pupil at Worcester Classical High School and won a scholarship to Harvard, earning a Master's degree in English at age 22. He worked for a publishing house in New York City and edited, over many years, nine collections of literary biographies. He has held many university teaching posts and, as editor of the Yale Younger Poets series, has helped many poets.

Intellectual Things, published when Kunitz was 25, was his first collection. Unlike many poets of the time, who took on other identities in their poems, Kunitz wrote in his own voice about intense moments of self-knowledge. After serving in World War II, Kunitz produced *Passport to the War*. This collection contains one of his most famous poems, "Father and Son," which explores a son's grief at the loss of his father. Until the end of the 1960s, Kunitz wrote in a formal, ordered way about "disorderly" emotional events. *The Testing-Tree*, his 1971 volume, has a looser style. In the frightening poem "Illumination" from this collection, Kunitz recalls the nightmare of a lifetime's mistakes.

Kunitz visited the Soviet Union in 1967 and was inspired to translate the poems of ANNA AKHMATOVA and ANDREI VOZNESENSKY.

Publications

1930	*Intellectual Things*
1944	*Passport to the War*
1958	*Selected Poems, 1928–58*
1971	*The Testing-Tree*
1979	*The Poems of Stanley Kunitz, 1928–78*
1983	*The Wellfleet Whale and Companion Poems*
1985	*Next-to-Last Things*
1995	*Passing Through*

KUSHNER, Tony

American playwright

Born Jul. 16, 1956

Tony Kushner's *Angels in America* was the first Broadway play to focus on the effects of AIDS on American society. It is now considered an important 20th-century play.

Kushner was born in New York City, the second of three children whose parents were both musicians. The family moved to Louisiana after Kushner's father inherited a lumber business there. Kushner returned to New York to attend Columbia University, then New York University for postgraduate work.

Kushner's first full-length play, *A Bright Room Called Day*, was produced when he was 29. It criticized President Reagan's economic policy, the effects of which Kushner compared to those of Nazi Germany. This comparison angered many critics, but it led to a commission for his next major work.

Angels in America was based on a poem Kushner wrote in the mid-1980s. By the early 1990s, the AIDS crisis was in full swing. Homosexual himself, Kushner subtitled his play "A Gay Fantasia on National Themes." It features a gay couple, a Mormon man, and Roy Cohn, a real-life gay lawyer who nevertheless was fiercely anti-homosexual and right wing and who had died of AIDS in the mid-1980s. The Broadway establishment was wary of producing such a controversial work, so it was staged first in San Francisco, then London, before arriving in New York in 1993. The epic – divided into two sections, *Millennium Approaches* and *Perestroika*, which together run for nearly seven hours – was a huge success. It won several prestigious drama awards and the Pulitzer Prize in 1993.

Publications

1985	*A Bright Room Called Day*
1985	*Yes, Yes, No, No*
1987	*Stella*
1987	*Hydriotaphia*
1988	*The Illusion*
1991	*Angels in America*
1991	*Widows*
1994	*Slavs!*
1995	*Thinking about the Long-Standing Problems of Virtue and Happiness*

KYD, Thomas

English playwright

Born Nov. 6, 1558
Died c. Dec. 1594
Age at death c. 36

The Spanish Tragedy is the only play certainly written by Thomas Kyd to have survived, yet it has secured his reputation as an important English playwright.

Kyd was born in London, the son of a professional copier of texts. He was educated at Merchant Taylor's School, where one of his schoolmates was the future poet EDMUND SPENSER, and then took up his father's trade. Little is known about Kyd's life except that he soon decided to become an actor and also began writing plays.

When Kyd was 34, his great play *The Spanish Tragedy* was produced. It is regarded by scholars as one of the most influential plays of the time because it established a genre known as the revenge-tragedy, which strongly influenced the plays of WILLIAM SHAKESPEARE and JOHN WEBSTER. Revenge-tragedies always feature ghosts, murderers, terrible crimes and madness, and were very popular at the time.

In 1593, Kyd was suddenly arrested and accused of owning documents that showed he was anti-Christian. Nobody knows why Kyd was really arrested; the story about the documents was probably just a cover for some other political motive. At that time politics and literature were closely connected. Poets and playwrights often got in trouble with the authorities for exploring new political ideas or for attacking important figures in their writings – Kyd's friend, the playwright CHRISTOPHER MARLOWE, was assassinated because of his involvement in politics! Little is known about Kyd's life after his release.

Publications

1592	*The Spanish Tragedy*
c. 1592	*Soliman and Perseda*
1594	*Cornelia*

LACLOS, Pierre

French writer

Born Oct. 19, 1741
Died Nov. 5, 1803
Age at death 62

Pierre Laclos's reputation as a writer rests on the success of his novel *Dangerous Liaisons*.

Born in Amiens, France, Laclos was the son of a minor nobleman. Little is known about his early life. At 18, he entered military service, reaching the rank of captain when he was 37.

Laclos published his first and only novel, *Dangerous Liaisons*, when he was 41. Written as a series of letters between the immoral seducer Valmont and his female accomplice, it describes the suffering of the innocent young women whose reputations are ruined by his attentions. The novel was considered very shocking at the time, although this didn't stop it being widely read. It was important in the development of modern literature because it was one of the first novels to concentrate on the inner thoughts and feelings of its characters. Laclos's masterpiece was influenced by the English novel *Clarissa*, written by SAMUEL RICHARDSON.

Laclos also wrote *On the Education of Women*, an essay about women's position in society. In 1786, he wrote a public letter criticizing what he saw as outdated methods in the army and was stripped of his rank. He became involved in politics and played a minor role in the French Revolution on the side of the republicans, only narrowly escaping being executed by guillotine during the bloodiest year of the struggle. When the emperor Napoleon came to power, Laclos joined his army, fought in many important battles, and eventually became a general.

Publications

1782 Dangerous Liaisons

1785 On the Education of Women

1786 Letter to the Gentlemen of the French Academy in Praise of the Marshal of Vauban

La FARGE, Oliver

American novelist and short-story writer

Born Dec. 19, 1901

Died Aug. 2, 1963

Age at death 61

Oliver La Farge was a writer of novels and short stories and also an expert on Native American life and culture.

La Farge was born to wealthy parents in New York City; he attended Saint Bernard's School and later Groton School in Lowell, Massachusetts. At Harvard he read anthropology – the study of human culture and customs. Although he started out as a scientific investigator, it was his interest in writing that would come to dominate his life.

During his third year at Harvard La Farge took part in an archeological field trip to northern Arizona, where he saw ancient Navajo ruins for the first time. This was the beginning of a lifelong fascination with the experiences of people caught between their traditional world and the modern world. His first novel, *Laughing Boy*, published when he was 28, received the Pulitzer Prize for fiction in 1930. It is the tragic story of a young Navajo named Laughing Boy who falls in love with a Navajo girl who has been living away from her people among the temptations of modern American society. With the help of Laughing Boy, she manages to return to the Navajo world, only to be killed by a jealous rival.

La Farge's archeological trips to countries like Mexico and Guatemala provided him with much of the background material for his fiction. In addition to 12 works of fiction, he wrote scientific and social history works; he also published short stories in the *New Yorker* magazine and *Esquire*.

Publications

1929 Laughing Boy

1931 Sparks Fly Upward

1933 The Long Pennant

1937 The Enemy Gods

1942 The Copper Pot

1946 Raw Material

1956 Behind the Mountains

Published after he died

1965 The Door in the Wall

1966 The Man with the Calabash Pipe

La FAYETTE, Madame de

French novelist

Born Mar. 16, 1634
Died May 25, 1693
Age at death 59

Madame de La Fayette did more than any other author to influence the form of the early novel.

La Fayette was born in Paris, and raised in a convent. When she was 21, she married an army officer who was 18 years older than her. They had two sons but later led separate lives. In 1659, she returned to Paris from her husband's estate in the south of France. There she became the center of a literary group that included some of the great writers of the day. She was also involved in politics and diplomacy and became such an important and popular figure in Parisian society that she was the first person to be given a guided tour around the new palace of Versailles by King Louis XIV.

It was then the fashion for members of literary circles to collaborate in writing a novel. It is likely that other authors helped La Fayette write a series of historical novels, starting with *The Princess of Montpensier*, published under the name Ségrais when she was 28. Her most important novel, *The Princess of Clèves*, is the story of a virtuous wife who falls in love with a nobleman.

La Fayette's novels have simple, fast-moving plots and focus on the inner thoughts of the main characters – the first time this had been done in a work of fiction. Her stories were so realistic and relevant to the concerns of men and women of the time that her readers often wrote to her about the fictional characters in the novels as if they were real people.

Publications

1662	*The Princess of Montpensier*
1670	*Zaydé*
1678	*The Princess of Clèves*

Published after she died

1724	*The Countess of Tende*

La FONTAINE, Jean de

French poet

Born Jul. 8, 1621
Died Apr. 13, 1695
Age at death 73

Jean de La Fontaine is best known for his fables, which have been read and appreciated by generations of children and writers in many languages.

La Fontaine was born in Château-Thierry, central France, the son of a government official. He studied at a Catholic Jesuit college and qualified as a lawyer. He held a number of government posts, including inspector of waters and forests, but they did not pay much money. At the age of 26, he married an heiress, but they separated in 1658. He then had to depend on wealthy patrons to help finance his writing.

La Fontaine had his first success with *Short Tales*, published when he was 43. These amusing stories about love affairs were based on the works of Italian authors, such as Giovanni Boccaccio. They went through four editions during La Fontaine's lifetime, but the last edition was banned by the authorities because it was considered obscene. In later life, La Fontaine regretted having written them.

The first volume of La Fontaine's *Fables* was published when he was 47. Based on the fables of the ancient Greek Aesop, they are simple, humorous tales with talking animals as the main characters. Each tale has a moral – a little instruction about how life should be lived. La Fontaine's versions of the stories were longer and more complex than Aesop's. In the second volume of his *Fables*, La Fontaine based his tales on stories from Asia and other places. Again he gave his versions more rounded characters and better dialogue than the originals. In 1683, he was elected to the French Academy in recognition of his contribution to French literature.

Publications

1664 Short Tales
1668 Fables (vol. 1)
1679–94 Fables (vol. 2)

LAGERKVIST, Pär

Swedish novelist, poet and playwright

Born May 23, 1891
Died Jul. 11, 1974
Age at death 83

Pär Lagerkvist was a major Swedish novelist, playwright, and poet. He was the first to bring to Sweden the new ideas about literature that were developing in Europe during the first part of the 20th century. In 1951, he was awarded the Nobel Prize for Literature.

Lagerkvist was born in Växjö, southern Sweden, and educated at the University of Uppsala. His first success came with the publication when he was 21 of a short novel, *People*. The next year he visited Paris, where he was inspired by the new ideas in art, writing, and politics that he encountered. He brought out several books of experimental poetry based on these new ideas and established his reputation as Sweden's leading poet. His 1916 collection, *Anguish*, demonstrates his negative view of human society. The poems explore how a person can find a meaningful life in a world where a war can kill millions for very little reason.

When he was 28, Lagerkvist turned to drama. In the 1930s, with fascists coming to power all over Europe, Lagerkvist's work developed in a new direction as he saw humanity trapped in conflict with evil forces. For example, his play *The Hangman* has a clear anti-Nazi theme, and the highly acclaimed novel *The Dwarf*, which became his first bestseller, is about a character who only enjoys death and destruction.

Lagerkvist received international recognition with the novel *Barabbas*, which was also turned into a play. Set during Roman times, it is the story of the man who was freed instead of Jesus.

Publications

1912 People
1916 Anguish
1919 The Secret of Heaven
1933 The Hangman
1941 Midsummer Night in the Workhouse
1944 The Dwarf
1949 Let Man Live
1950 Barabbas
1953 Evening Land
1964 Pilgrim at Sea

LAGERLÖF, Selma

Swedish novelist and short-story writer

Born Nov. 20, 1858
Died Mar. 16, 1940
Age at death 81

Selma Lagerlöf is notable for being the first woman, and the first Swedish writer, to win the Nobel Prize for Literature, which she was awarded in 1909.

Born at Mårbacka in southeastern Sweden, Lagerlöf was educated at home. After teacher training in Stockholm she became a schoolmistress and taught at a girls' secondary school for ten years. During that time she began to write. Her first novel, *The Story of Gösta Berling*, published when she was 33, is a historical tale about a less-than-perfect priest set in her native Värmland. It became very popular and helped to promote a revival of Romanticism in Sweden in the 1890s. This book was followed by a collection of stories.

In 1895, she was awarded a traveling scholarship and gave up teaching. A visit to Palestine inspired her to write the two-volume novel *Jerusalem*, which won her international recognition. Many other books and collections of stories followed and two imaginative geography schoolbooks for children, *The Wonderful Adventures of Nils* and *Further Adventures of Nils,* which describe a boy's flying journey over Sweden.

The tragedy of World War I almost stopped Lagerlöf writing altogether, but in the 1930s she published autobiographical volumes called *Memories of My Childhood* and *The Diary of Selma Lagerlöf*. She then returned to writing historical novels and produced several fine works. The award of the Nobel Prize for Literature enabled her to buy back the beloved manor house in which she had been born and that had been sold after her father's death. She lived there for the rest of her life.

Publications

1891 The Story of Gösta Berling
1897 The Miracles of Antichrist
1901–02 Jerusalem (2 vols.)
1906–07 The Wonderful Adventures of Nils
1911 Further Adventures of Nils
1925–28 The Ring of the Löwenskölds (3 vols.)
1930 Memories of my Childhood
1932 The Diary of Selma Lagerlöf

LAMB, Charles

English essayist and poet

Born Feb. 10, 1775
Died Dec. 27, 1834
Age at death 59

Charles Lamb was a 19th-century English writer whose retellings of the classic works of literature are still popular today. He is best known for his essays.

Lamb was born in London and educated at a school called Christ's Hospital. It was there that he met the future poet SAMUEL TAYLOR COLERIDGE, who became a lifelong friend.

After leaving school at 14, Lamb joined the East India Company as a shipping clerk and worked there until his retirement at 50. When he was 21, Coleridge invited Lamb to contribute to a book called *Poems on Various Subjects*. This was the beginning of Lamb's writing career.

In 1796, something happened that changed the course of Lamb's

Publications

1798 Blank Verse

life. During a period of temporary insanity his sister Mary murdered their mother. She was committed to an asylum but later released. Lamb devoted the rest of his life to caring for her.

Despite these pressures, Lamb continued writing and contributed to a number of well-respected newspapers. His growing reputation resulted in a commission to write a children's book. Written with his sister, *Tales from Shakespeare* was published when he was 32. These simple retellings of WILLIAM SHAKESPEARE's plays were very popular and have never been out of print. Charles and Mary wrote several other books for children, including *The Adventures of Ulysses*, *Mrs. Leicester's School* and *Poetry for Children*.

Lamb's most famous works are his essays. Originally published in newspapers, they were collected in two volumes: *Essays of Elia*, published when he was 48, and *The Last Essays of Elia*, which came out ten years later.

1798	*A Tale of Rosamund Gray*
1807	*Tales from Shakespeare*
1808	*The Adventures of Ulysses*
1809	*Mrs. Leicester's School*
1809	*Poetry for Children*
1811	*Prince Dorus*
1818	*The Works of Charles Lamb*
1823	*Essays of Elia*
1833	*The Last Essays of Elia*

L'AMOUR, Louis

American novelist

Born Mar. 2, 1908
Died Jun. 10, 1988
Age at death 80

Louis L'Amour was one of America's bestselling authors of all time. He is most famous for his adventure stories set in the Wild West.

Born in Jamestown, North Dakota, L'Amour was raised hearing stories of pioneers and Native Americans. At 15, he left school to work at various odd jobs. He was even an elephant handler for a while. During the 1930s he became a successful boxer and traveled in Asia. He was an officer in the tank corps during World War II.

After the war, L'Amour started writing detective stories and others set in Asia, but he soon turned to writing Westerns. At 42, he published his first novel, *Westward the Tide*, and the following year his first Western, *Hopalong Cassidy and the Riders of High Rock*, using the pen name Tex Burns. One of his most popular books, *Hondo*, was the first he wrote under his own name.

L'Amour was a busy writer, publishing about three books every year. In the mid-1970s, he began writing a series of books about three families – the Sacketts, Talons and Chantrys. The Sackett series includes *The Lonely Men* and *To the Far Blue Mountains*.

L'Amour's novels are fast-paced action stories featuring tough, romantic heroes but little violence. They are noted for their accurate descriptions of the American frontier and its people in the 1860s and '70s. Critics never supported his books, but they became extremely popular. They have been translated into dozens of languages and made into 30 films. At his death it was estimated that L'Amour's novels had sold over 180 million copies.

Publications

1950	*Westward the Tide*
1951	*Hopalong Cassidy and the Riders of High Rock*
1953	*Hondo*
1954	*Heller with a Gun*
1962	*Shalako*
1963	*How the West Was Won*
1969	*The Lonely Men*
1976	*To the Far Blue Mountains*
1987	*The Haunted Mesa*

LAMPEDUSA, Giuseppe di

Italian novelist

Born Dec. 23, 1896
Died Jul. 26, 1957
Age at death 60

Giuseppe di Lampedusa's one great work, *The Leopard*, is considered one of the finest Italian novels of the 20th century. A sweeping historical saga, it has been compared to work by Marcel Proust.

Lampedusa was born in Palermo on the Italian island of Sicily. His father was the duke of Parma, and his grandfather was the prince of Lampedusa, so he was well connected socially. The family had once been very rich, but they had become rather poor. Giuseppe was a wild youth, and only his dominating mother could keep him under control.

The family did not approve of books and writers and were not pleased when, as a young man, Lampedusa began to show an unexpected passion for literature. Heads were shaken when, day after day, he remained in the family library reading books of all kinds in several languages. The influence of Lampedusa's mother effectively prevented him from writing while she was alive but could not stop his scholarly activities. After she died, however, he was free to write what was to be his masterpiece, *The Leopard*. Lampedusa was 59 when he began work on it. He submitted the manuscript anonymously and died before the book was even ready to print.

Published after he died

1958 The Leopard
1961 Two Stories and a Memory

This melodramatic historical novel about 19th-century Sicily was published under the title *Il Gattopardo* and made a sensation. It has been praised for its superb characterization, particularly of the main character, Don Fabrizio, prince of Salina. In 1963, *The Leopard* was made into a film.

LANGLAND, William

English poet

Born c. 1332
Died c. 1400
Age at death c. 68

William Langland is believed to be the author of one of the earliest pieces of English literature, a 14th-century poem entitled *The Vision of William Concerning Piers the Plowman* (usually known as *Piers Plowman*).

Almost nothing is known for certain about Langland's life. Historians believe that he was born in a small country town called Ledbury, the son of a man named Eustace de la Rokayle, who may have been a farmer or a minor priest.

Late in his life Langland joined the Church as a low-ranking priest and moved to London. By this time he was married and had a daughter. He earned a living in London from his work as a priest and as a copier of legal documents for the law courts.

During his life Langland wrote three versions of *Piers Plowman*. The poem is set in the hills near Langland's hometown, suggesting that he began writing it while he still lived there. Later versions of the poem have the same setting but contain new ideas added by the author as his thoughts and opinions changed. *Piers Plowman* is an allegory. It describes a series of dreams or visions in which aspects of society are represented by good and evil characters. The poem is a fascinating insight into life in medieval England. At the time it was written the system known as feudalism – in which peasants worked land given to their masters by lords in return for military and other services – was beginning to break down as big towns and commerce developed. Langland shows these changes and his fears about what they would bring. The central character, Piers Plowman, is a simple farmer who is revealed to be the savior of humanity.

Publications

The Vision of William Concerning Piers the Plowman (14th century)

LARDNER, Ring

American short-story writer and journalist

Born Mar. 6, 1885
Died Sep. 25, 1933
Age at death 48

Ring Lardner was an outstanding writer of satirical short stories.

Lardner was born in Niles, Michigan, one of nine children of a prosperous, middle-class family. He tried various jobs after leaving school but finally settled on a career as a sportswriter. While working for the *Chicago Tribune* in his late 20s, Lardner began to specialize in baseball reporting, joining the Chicago White Sox in the dugout. These experiences formed the basis for his stories about a rookie baseball player, Jack Keefe, that appeared weekly in the *Tribune*. They proved to be so popular that a collection was published as a book when Lardner was 31. The title, *You Know Me, Al*, soon became a popular catchphrase. Two more successful collections of stories about Jack Keefe followed, but Lardner lost his enthusiasm after the 1919 Black Sox scandal involving the "fixing" of the World Series.

In 1921, Lardner moved to Great Neck, Long Island, where his neighbor was the writer F. Scott Fitzgerald. Fitzgerald encouraged Lardner to continue with his short stories, and Lardner began to write about the everyday lives of ordinary Americans: salesmen, actresses, stockbrokers, hairdressers, songwriters, and shopkeepers. Characterized by their humor and sharp insight into the absurdities of human nature, Lardner's stories were both popular and highly praised by serious writers like Virginia Woolf. Lardner died at the fairly young age of 48 from tuberculosis, made worse by his lifelong heavy drinking.

Publications

1916 You Know Me, Al
1917 Gullible's Travels
1918 Treat 'Em Rough
1919 The Real Dope
1919 Own Your Own Home
1919 Regular Fellows I Have Met
1921 The Big Town
1924 How to Write Short Stories
1926 The Love Nest
1929 Round-Up

LARKIN, Philip

English poet

Born Aug. 9, 1922
Died Dec. 2, 1985
Age at death 63

Philip Larkin is one of the most popular and widely read British poets. He is best known for three books: *The Less Deceived*, *The Whitsun Weddings* and *High Windows*. Larkin used traditional verse forms and disliked modern poetry. His poems are direct, use everyday language, and are easily understood. In 1981, an interviewer asked him why he had become a poet. He replied: "I didn't choose poetry – poetry chose me."

Larkin was born in Coventry, and educated at King Henry VIII School, where he wrote for the school magazine. At age 18, he went to Oxford University to study English. There, he met KINGSLEY AMIS, who became a lifelong friend. In 1943, Larkin graduated and began work as a librarian. He continued to write and published his first book, *The North Ship*, at his own expense at age 23. He also wrote two novels in his 20s, *Jill* and *A Girl in Winter*.

The turning point in Larkin's career came when he was 33. He became the librarian at the University of Hull, a post he held for the rest of his life. Also, *The Less Deceived* was published and brought him acclaim as a poet.

Larkin was a solitary man. He never married, though he was involved for most of his life with Monica Jones, whom he met when he was 24. The death of Larkin's mother in 1977 was a blow that ended his own writing career. After her death he wrote only 11 poems, although he produced a book of essays in 1983. He turned down the post of Poet Laureate in 1984, partly because he felt that he could no longer produce good poetry.

Publications

1945	*The North Ship*
1946	*Jill*
1947	*A Girl in Winter*
1951	*XX Poems*
1955	*The Less Deceived*
1964	*The Whitsun Weddings*
1970	*All What Jazz*
1974	*High Windows*
1983	*Required Writing*

LARSEN, Nella

American novelist

Born Apr. 13, 1891
Died Mar. 30, 1964
Age at death 72

Nella Larsen completed only two novels in her lifetime and, apparently, didn't publish anything at all during the last 20 years of her life. Nevertheless, she is considered to be an important African-American novelist.

Larsen was born in Chicago; her mother was Danish and white, her father was a black West Indian. After finishing secondary school, Larsen spent two years in Denmark before returning to America and New York City, where she trained first as a nurse and later as a librarian. During this time she got caught up in the excitement of the Harlem Renaissance, when black artists and writers were flocking to Harlem in New York City from all over the United States.

Larsen only had a few short stories published before her first novel came out when she was 37. *Quicksand* was based on Larsen's own life; it tells the story of a young woman of mixed race who is rejected by her white relatives in America but who also feels uncomfortable in black communities, even though they welcome her. The following year Larsen's second novel, *Passing*, was published. It centers on the lives of two young black women who have light skin and pretend to be white. Both novels were a success, and Larsen was expected to produce even better writing in the future. However, although she began work on three more novels, none was ever published.

After 1937, Larsen began to distance herself from her literary life, and following the death of her husband in 1941, she returned to nursing.

Publications

1928 Quicksand

1929 Passing

LAURENCE, Margaret

Canadian writer

Born Jul. 18, 1926

Died Jan. 5, 1987

Age at death 60

Margaret Laurence is probably Canada's most famous fiction writer. She is particularly well known for creating strong female characters.

Laurence was born in the small prairie town of Neepawa, Manitoba. Both her parents died when she was young, and she was raised by her aunt. After graduating in 1947 from United College, Winnipeg, she worked as a reporter. Later in the same year she married. Her husband was a civil engineer, and between 1950 and 1957 his job took them to Africa, where they lived in Somalia (East Africa) and then in Ghana (West Africa). Both these countries were British colonies at the time.

They returned to Canada in 1957. Laurence left her husband five years later and lived in England before returning to Canada in the 1970s to teach in various universities. She finally settled in Lakefield, Ontario, where she lived until her death.

Laurence's first novel, *This Side Jordan*, published when she was 34, is set in Ghana. It is about the struggle for independence that nations and individual people have to go through. She wrote about her time in Somalia in *New Wind in a Dry Land*. Her most famous books, however, are set in the imaginary small Canadian prairie town of Manawaka. *A Jest of God* (made into a film called *Rachel, Rachel*) and *The Fire-Dwellers* trace the journeys of two sisters toward personal freedom. *The Diviners*, Laurence's most complex book, was the last to be set in Manawaka. It describes a novelist coming to terms with herself. Laurence also wrote several children's books.

Publications

1960 This Side Jordan

1963 New Wind in a Dry Land

1963 The Tomorrow-Tamer

1964 The Stone Angel

1966 A Jest of God

1969 The Fire-Dwellers

1970 A Bird in the House

1974 The Diviners

Published after she died

1989 Dance on the Earth

LAWRENCE, D.H.

English novelist, short-story writer and poet

Born Sep. 11, 1885
Died Mar. 2, 1930
Age at death 44

D.H. Lawrence, one of the 20th century's most important authors, wrote books whose frankness in describing sexual relations between men and women upset a great many people. For years some of his books could be published only with passages cut out.

David Herbert Lawrence was born in a village in central England. His father was a coal miner and his mother a former schoolteacher. His parents were poor and quarreled all the time, and he was often ill. Lawrence's early years formed the basis for his first major work, *Sons and Lovers*, which was published when he was 28. Lawrence trained to be a teacher at Nottingham University and later ran off with Frieda Weekley, the aristocratic German wife of a professor there. They married in 1914. His next novel, *The Rainbow,* was seized by the police because it used swearwords and talked openly about sex. The book is about two sisters growing up in the north of England; the story continues in the sequel *Women in Love*.

The Lawrences spent many years traveling, to Italy, Sri Lanka, Australia and North America. They finally settled in Italy after Lawrence was told he was dying from tuberculosis. There he wrote his last novel, *Lady Chatterley's Lover*, which caused a bigger storm than any of his other books. At first privately printed in Italy, the book tells of the affair between a wealthy, married woman and a man who works on her husband's estate. The first uncut version was not published in England until 30 years after Lawrence's death. The publishers were accused of publishing obscene material. They were acquitted after a sensational trial.

Publications

1913 Sons and Lovers
1915 The Rainbow
1920 Women in Love
1920 The Lost Girl
1922 Aaron's Rod
1923 Kangaroo
1923 Birds, Beasts, and Flowers
1926 The Plumed Serpent
1927 Mornings in Mexico
1928 Lady Chatterley's Lover

LAWRENCE, T.E.

English writer

Born Aug. 15, 1888
Died May 19, 1935
Age at death 46

T(homas) E(dward) Lawrence was better known in his lifetime as "Lawrence of Arabia" because of the part he played in helping Arabs in the Middle East revolt against the Turks during World War I. His account of the campaign is one of the greatest war books written as well as a work of literature.

After graduating from Oxford University when he was 22, Lawrence began his career as an archeologist in Syria and Egypt. When World War I began in 1914, he joined the British Army. By late 1916 ,he was organizing a revolt by the Arabs of Arabia and leading a guerrilla force against the Turkish Empire. He was wounded several times and captured by the Turks and tortured, but he escaped.

Lawrence wanted the Arabs to have independence, but the victorious Allies at the Peace Conference at the end of the war would not agree. Disgusted, he resigned from all public duties, refused honors, and in 1922 enlisted in the Royal Air Force under a false name. His identity was revealed, and he soon joined the army as a private soldier, changing his name to T.E. Shaw. In 1925, he returned to the RAF and served for 10 years, retiring at age 46. A few weeks after his retirement he died in a motorcycle crash.

Lawrence's epic book about the desert campaign, the Arabs and his life among them first appeared as a limited edition called *The Seven Pillars of Wisdom* when he was 38, and then later as a shorter, popular version, *Revolt in the Desert*. The full-length version was published again the year he died. *The Mint*, published after his death, is about his life in the RAF.

Publications

- *1915 The Wilderness of Zin* (with Leonard Woolley)
- *1926 The Seven Pillars of Wisdom*
- *1927 Revolt in the Desert*
- *1929 Oriental Assembly*

Published after he died

- *1936 Crusader Castles*
- *1937 The Diary of T.E. Lawrence*
- *1938 The Letters of T.E. Lawrence*
- *1955 The Mint*

LAXNESS, Halldór K.

Icelandic novelist, playwright and essayist

Born Apr. 23, 1902
Died Feb. 8, 1998
Age at death 95

Halldór K. Laxness is noted for his contribution to Icelandic literature – in particular for the stream of brilliant novels that won him the Nobel Prize for Literature in 1955.

Laxness was born Halldór Kiljan Gudjónsson and grew up on a farm in Laxness near Reykjavik, the capital of Iceland. His family had enough money to allow him to travel freely and, after World War I, he took full advantage of this to gain experience for writing by studying in Europe and America.

Laxness was eager for experience. In an early book published when he was 25, he describes his conversion to Catholicism; two years later he published an enthusiastic essay on communism. In his late 20s, he returned to settle in Iceland and began to produce the series of epic novels that made him famous. Initially, these were concerned with the social life of Iceland and especially with the hardships of the working fishermen and farmers. Between 1937 and 1940, he produced the four volumes of his great novel, *World Light,* about the struggles of a poor peasant poet. As was to be expected, they prompted much controversy because they were critical of Iceland's political situation.

The trilogy, *Iceland's Bell*, published when Laxness was in his early 40s, made him famous, and from then on he was widely acknowledged as Iceland's greatest writer. His later books were more concerned with philosophy and personal problems. He also produced two volumes of memoirs and several plays, and he adapted some of his novels for the stage.

Publications

- *1927 The Great Weaver from Kashmir*
- *1931 Salka Valka*
- *1934–35 Independent People*
- *1937–40 World Light* (4 vols.)
- *1943–46 Iceland's Bell* (3 vols.)
- *1957 The Fish Can Sing*
- *1960 Paradise Reclaimed*
- *1968 Christianity at the Glacier*
- *1987 Days with Monks*

LAYE, Camara

Guinean novelist and short-story writer

Born Jan. 1, 1928
Died Feb. 4, 1980
Age at death 52

Camara Laye was one of the first black African writers to achieve international fame. He was born in the ancient city of Kouroussa in the West African country of Guinea, which was then a French colony. He went to local schools before studying at a technical college in Conakry, the capital city. He then traveled to France to study engineering in Paris.

While still a poor student in France Laye spent his evenings writing *The Dark Child*. Based on his own childhood growing up in Guinea, it tells of an Africa before European rule. Well received in Europe, the book shot Laye to fame at the age of 25. His next novel, *The Radiance of the King*, sometimes referred to as his best work, describes a white man's search for an African king. The story has been given many different meanings, but a popular interpretation is that it reflects Laye's belief that white and black people can learn from each other.

On returning to Guinea in 1956, Laye worked as an engineer before getting a job with the Ministry of Information. In 1965, he was forced to leave Guinea after criticizing the president, Sékou Touré. He fled to the neighboring Ivory Coast before settling in Senegal (also in West Africa), where he worked in the capital city at the University of Dakar. In Senegal, he wrote *A Dream of Africa*, a sequel to *The Dark Child*. Again based on Laye's experiences, the hero returns to Africa after six years in Paris to find that his country has been destroyed by political violence. Sékou Touré appears thinly disguised as the "Big Brute." The book was banned in Guinea. Laye died in Senegal at an early age after years of ill health.

Publications

1953 The Dark Child
1954 The Radiance of the King
1966 A Dream of Africa
1978 The Guardian of the Word

LAZARUS, Emma

American poet and translator

Born Jul. 22, 1849
Died Nov. 19, 1887
Age at death 38

Emma Lazarus earned a permanent place in American social and literary history when she wrote the sonnet "The New Colossus." Its lines – including "Give me your tired, your poor, / Your huddled masses yearning to breathe free" – were carved onto the base of the Statue of Liberty and became symbolic of America's welcome to immigrants in the 19th century.

Lazarus was born and raised in New York City, where her wealthy family was part of fashionable society. From an early age she loved languages and poetry and, by age 18, she had published a collection of translations of well-known writers, including Victor Hugo. She met the writer Ralph Waldo Emerson, to whom she dedicated her second book, the poetry collection *Admetus, and Other Poems*.

In the late 1900s, waves of immigrants were coming to the United States, many of them Jewish refugees escaping persecution in Russia. Lazarus, herself Jewish, was moved by their plight and produced a collection of poems and translations, *Songs of a Semite*, in support. She also began to write essays calling for the establishment of a Jewish homeland.

Lazarus's most famous poem was also an effort to show her support for immigrants to America. "The New Colossus" was written to help raise money for a base so that the Statue of Liberty, a gift to the US from France, could be set up in New York Harbor. The project, which involved Lazarus and other writers, raised $100,000. In 1903, after Lazarus's death from cancer, the base was inscribed with her famous lines, ensuring her place in American history.

Publications

1871 Admetus, and Other Poems
1874 Alide: An Episode of Goethe's Life
1876 The Spagnoletto
1881 Poems and Ballads of Heinrich Heine
1882 Songs of a Semite
1883 "The New Colossus"
1887 By the Waters of Babylon

Published after she died

1889 The Poems of Emma Lazarus

LEAR, Edward

English children's writer

Born May 12, 1812
Died Jan. 29, 1888
Age at death 75

Edward Lear is best remembered for his limericks and his nonsense poetry, which includes such well-known verses as "The Owl and the Pussycat" and "The Jumblies."

Lear was born in London. He was his parents' 20th child, and many of his brothers and sisters did not survive. Although he lived to the age of 75, he suffered from poor health and epilepsy.

Lear showed an early talent for drawing and began working as an illustrator from the age of 15. When he was 20, a book of his drawings of birds attracted the attention of a wealthy aristocrat, the Earl of Derby, who wanted an artist to draw his collection of rare animals. Lear lived on the earl's estate for five years, and while he was there he made up amusing nonsense poems for the earl's children. Under the pen name Derry down Derry these were published, along with his own cartoon illustrations, in *A Book of Nonsense*. It became extremely popular with children and adults.

Lear's poor health had forced him to leave England for the warmer climate of Italy when he was 25. For the rest of his life, he traveled restlessly around Europe. He wanted to be a serious painter and did not publish any more of his nonsense verse for 14 years. Surprised at the popularity of his new verses, he then published longer poems in *Nonsense Songs*, including "The Owl and the Pussycat" and "The Jumblies." His last collection of verse, *Laughable Lyrics*, includes poems such as "The Dong with the Luminous Nose," which hints at the loneliness of his wandering life.

Publications

1846 A Book of Nonsense
1870 Nonsense Songs
1872 More Nonsense
1877 Laughable Lyrics

LE CARRÉ, John

English thriller writer

Born Oct. 19, 1931

John Le Carré is one of the most important writers to use the genre of the spy thriller to deal with the politics of the Cold War.

John Le Carré is the pen name of David Cornwell, who was born in Dorset in the south of England. After a traditional, upper-class British education he worked in the British Foreign Service. His experiences there helped him write his novels about the world of British and Russian spies.

During the 1950s, the British and Russian governments employed secret service agents, or spies, to try to get information (especially about weapons) from the other side. Sometimes spies had to lie, cheat and even commit murder to do this. This situation gave rise to a dilemma: was it right for governments to be involved in lying and killing to protect the long-term interests of their countries? This was the question Le Carré asked in his first successful novel, *The Spy Who Came in from the Cold*, which he wrote when he was 32. It was later filmed with actor, Richard Burton.

Unlike previous spy novelists, Le Carré illustrates the world of espionage in a realistic way. His spies operate not as romantic loners like James Bond, the famous character in IAN FLEMING's novels, but as part of a bureaucratic government department – what he calls "the Circus." However, he focuses on the individual in one of his finest novels, *A Perfect Spy*, examining what makes a man turn to a life of deception. In recent novels like *The Russia House* and *Our Game,* Le Carré has turned his attention to the new role of the spy now that the Cold War is over.

Publications

1960 Call for the Dead
1963 The Spy Who Came in from the Cold
1974 Tinker, Tailor, Soldier, Spy
1977 The Honorable Schoolboy
1980 Smiley's People
1983 The Little Drummer Girl
1986 A Perfect Spy
1989 The Russia House
1995 Our Game
1999 Single and Single

LEE, Harper

American novelist

Born Apr. 28, 1926

Harper Lee's only published work, *To Kill a Mockingbird*, has become a classic of American literature and has established its author as a leading American writer.

Lee was born and raised in Monroeville, Alabama, and grew up during the Great Depression. Her family is descended from the American Civil War general Robert E. Lee. After state schooling in Alabama, she followed in the footsteps of her father, a local lawyer, and went to law school. But the young Lee had been writing since she was 7 and, at age 29, she left law school and went to New York City to pursue her writing career.

While in New York, Lee supported herself by working for an airline company, taking reservations. She spent more than two years rewriting her novel after it had been accepted by a publisher. *To Kill a Mockingbird* was finally published when Lee was 34, and it was an immediate success.

The story is told through the eyes of a young girl nicknamed Scout whose father is a lawyer in a small Alabama town. He unsuccessfully defends a young black man accused of raping a white woman, and in the process he and his family are threatened by racists. The novel explores the themes of justice and prejudice, and it suggests that children's natural sense of justice is damaged by society's racism.

In 1961, Lee was awarded the Pulitzer Prize for her novel. A year later the book was made into a film starring Gregory Peck. Lee has continued to write but has not yet published another book.

Publications

1960 To Kill a Mockingbird

LEE, Laurie

English poet and writer

Born Jun. 26, 1914
Died May 13, 1997
Age at death 82

Laurie Lee is famous for his book *Cider with Rosie*, which is about his childhood in a traditional rural English village. He is also remembered for his lyrical poems.

Lee was born and raised in the village of Stroud in the west of England. The youngest in a family of 12 children, he was educated at the village school. At age 19, Lee set out from his country home with a knapsack and a violin to walk to London. There he joined the Communist Party and worked as a builder's laborer. Seeking adventure, he went to Spain but was sent home when the Spanish Civil War broke out in 1936. He returned to Spain to write about the war and was nearly shot as a spy. In 1950, he married a girl whom he met on his first journey to Spain.

Lee's success with *Cider with Rosie* came when he was 46. Later, he wrote two more autobiographical books: *As I Walked Out One Midsummer Morning*, which describes his departure from home, his walk to London, and his time in Spain before the war; and *A Moment of War*, which recalls memories of his months with the Republican forces in Spain.

The poems by Lee are collected in the volumes *The Sun My Monument*, *The Bloom of Candles*, and *My Many-Coated Man*. They are mainly concerned with childhood and nature. During World War II, he worked for the British government, writing film scripts for the Ministry of Information. He also wrote several travel books and a collection of beautifully written prose, *I Can't Stay Long*.

Publications

1944 The Sun My Monument
1947 The Bloom of Candles
1948 The Voyage of Magellan
1955 My Many-Coated Man
1960 Cider with Rosie
1969 As I Walked Out One Midsummer Morning
1975 I Can't Stay Long
1983 Selected Poems
1991 A Moment of War

Le FANU, J. Sheridan

Irish horror writer

Born Aug. 28, 1814
Died Feb. 7, 1873
Age at death 58

Publications

1838 "The Ghost and the Bonesetter"
1847 *Torlogh O'Brien*
1851 *Ghost Stories and Tales of Mystery*
1863 *The House by the Churchyard*
1864 *Wylder's Hand*
1864 *Uncle Silas*
1871 *Chronicles of Golden Friars*
1872 *In a Glass Darkly*

Published after he died

1923 *Madam Crowl's Ghost*

J. Sheridan Le Fanu was one of the most important writers of gothic ghost stories in the 19th century.

Born into a wealthy family in Dublin, Joseph Sheridan Le Fanu attended Trinity College, University of Dublin. After graduating, he became editor of the college magazine, where many of his own early ghost stories first appeared. He married aged 29 and lived happily with his wife until her sudden death 15 years later left him lonely and depressed. He became a recluse, hardly ever leaving his house and working on his horror stories from midnight to dawn.

Le Fanu published his first short story, "The Ghost and the Bonesetter," when he was 24. *The House by the Churchyard* was his first murder mystery novel. It is about the chance discovery of a battered skull as a grave is being dug and the mystery of who it belonged to. Le Fanu's best-known novel is *Uncle Silas*. A man is discovered with his throat cut in a locked room with the key on the inside. With great skill Le Fanu keeps the reader guessing how it was done.

Le Fanu was one of the first horror writers to set his stories in everyday situations. It is often not clear, however, whether his characters really do experience supernatural events or whether they are suffering from a mental illness. For example, in the story "Green Tea" doctors offer many explanations as to why their patient can see a monkey when no one else is able to.

Le Fanu's ghost stories were republished in the 1920s by another writer of ghost stories, M.R. JAMES.

Le GUIN, Ursula K.

American fantasy and science fiction writer

Born Oct. 21, 1929

Ursula K(roeber) Le Guin is one of the most thought-provoking contemporary writers of fantasy and science fiction stories.

Le Guin was born Ursula Kroeber in Berkeley, California. Her father was an anthropologist, and her mother wrote children's books. When she was a child, Le Guin's parents taught her about myths and legends from around the world. She graduated with a Master's degree from Columbia University and won a Fulbright scholarship to study in France. There she met her future husband, Charles Le Guin, and returned with him to Macon, Georgia, where she worked as a lecturer and began to write fiction.

Le Guin published her first story when she was 33. "April in Paris" is a tale of time travel in which figures from different historical periods travel to 15th-century Paris to meet and marry. More short stories followed. Her first two novels, *Rocannon's World* and *Planet of Exile*, appeared when she was 37. They were part of a sequence of novels about an imaginary race called the Hain who populate the Universe and evolve into different types of beings. Among the forms of life they give rise to are human beings on Earth.

Le Guin went on to write many more novels, including her *Earthsea* and *Orsinia* sequences. Her novels have always interested scholars and academics because they raise serious questions about how we can understand and communicate with people different from ourselves, whether they are just of the opposite sex or from a different cultural background.

Publications

1966 Rocannon's World
1966 Planet of Exile
1968 A Wizard of Earthsea
1969 The Left Hand of Darkness
1974 The Dispossessed
1979 Malafrena
1985 Always Coming Home
1990 Tehanu: The Last Book of Earthsea
1996 Unlocking the Air

LEIBER, Fritz

American science fiction/fantasy/horror writer

Born Dec. 24, 1910
Died Sep. 5, 1992
Age at death 81

Fritz Leiber is best known for his "sword and sorcery" stories, which mix elements of science fiction, fantasy and historical romance.

Leiber was born in Chicago. His father was a well-known actor who starred in silent films and had his own touring theater company. As a young man Leiber briefly acted with the company. He decided instead to be a writer and, at 29, he published his first story, "Two Sought Adventure." It features two characters he had invented with a college friend: "Fafhrd," a tall intelligent man from a northern country, and "the Gray Mouser," a more outgoing, playful figure. He returned to these characters throughout his writing career.

Leiber's first two novels, *Gather, Darkness!* and *Conjure Wife*, were both initially published in magazines when he was in his early 30s. *Gather, Darkness!* is the story of a state that tries to control its people by making them afraid of supernatural events. *Conjure Wife* puts forward the idea that all women are secretly witches and was the subject of much debate. Later novels introduce the idea of cats and other animals as supernatural beings.

Leiber went on to write more than 40 books, in spite of periods when he had to stop work because of his alcoholism. His most popular work continues to be his Swords series, featuring the adventures of Fafhrd and the Gray Mouser. This has influenced younger writers such as MICHAEL MOORCOCK and ROGER ZELAZNY.

Publications

1943 Gather, Darkness!
1943 Conjure Wife
1958 The Big Time
1964 The Wanderer
1968 The Swords of Lankhmar
1969 A Spectre Is Haunting Texas
1970 Swords Against Death
1977 Swords and Ice Magic
1988 The Knight and Knave of Swords
1990 The Leiber Chronicles

LEM, Stanislaw

Polish science fiction writer

Born Sep. 12, 1921

Stanislaw Lem is one of the few writers of science fiction who is regarded as a great literary figure.

Lem was born in the city of Lvov, then in Poland and now in the Ukraine. At the beginning of World War II, when Lem was 18 and studying to become a doctor like his father, Poland was occupied by the Germans. Lem worked as a mechanic during the war and joined the resistance fighting against the Germans. Toward the end of the war, Poland was occupied by Russian forces; it was closely controlled by Russia for the next 50 years.

Lem gave up his medical studies and decided to become a writer instead. The communist Polish government would not tolerate criticism of their policies, and Lem found that the only way he could express himself with any freedom was by writing science fiction, which the authorities regarded as unimportant fantasy. His first sci-fi novel, *The Astronauts*, was published when he was 30, but it was with the publication of his novel *Solaris* 10 years later that he began to establish an international reputation as an important and thought-provoking writer. In *Solaris,* human scientists probe the mysteries of a planet where the only living thing is an intelligent ocean that covers the whole surface. The ocean creates ghosts from the scientists' pasts, forcing them to explore their own minds.

As well as novels, Lem has written many comic short stories about the adventures of an astronaut character called Ijon Tichy. In these stories, Lem satirizes politics and shows just how silly some commonly accepted ideas really are.

Publications

1951 The Astronauts
1955 The Magellan Nebula
1957 The Star Diaries
1959 Eden
1961 Solaris
1965 The Cyberiad
1968 His Master's Voice
1973 Imaginary Magnitude
1976 The Chain of Chance
1987 Fiasco

LEONARD, Elmore

American crime writer

Born Oct. 11, 1925

Elmore Leonard is generally recognized as one of the most important crime writers in America today. During the 1970s and '80s, he revitalized the hard-boiled style of crime writing, giving it back the popularity it had in the 1920s and '30s.

Leonard was born in New Orleans but moved to Detroit and graduated from university there in 1950. Many of his novels are set in Detroit, and he writes about the different levels of society in the city, from the suburbs to the ghetto. After military service in the American navy during World War II, Leonard began a career as an advertising copywriter, and he formed his own company when he was 38. Since 1967, he has been a full-time writer.

During the 1950s and '60s, Leonard wrote Westerns for the

paperback market, several of which were made into films. He published his first novel, *The Bounty Hunters*, when he was 28. In the 1970s, he turned to crime fiction, drawing inspiration from the novels of DASHIELL HAMMETT and RAYMOND CHANDLER. Like them he wrote realistic stories about life on the city streets of Miami and Detroit, full of action, violence, criminals and policemen. He was one of the first white crime novelists to create realistic African-American and Hispanic characters.

At age 52, he divorced his first wife and stopped drinking. His novel *Touch* deals with the religious faith that helped him to quit. In recent years he has inspired a new generation of crime writers and filmmakers. His popular novel, *Get Shorty,* was successfully filmed with John Travolta.

Publications

1953 The Bounty Hunters
1961 Hombre
1969 The Big Bounce
1976 Swag
1977 Unknown Man No. 89
1983 Stick
1983 La Brava
1987 Touch
1990 Get Shorty
1995 Riding the Rap
1998 Cuba Libre
1999 Be Cool

LERMONTOV, Mikhail

Russian poet and novelist

Born Oct. 3, 1814
Died Jul. 15, 1841
Age at death 26

Mikhail Lermontov was one of Russia's finest poets. He also wrote an exceptional novel. His work is about freedom and finding beauty in nature.

Lermontov was born in Moscow. His mother died when he was three, so he was brought up by his grandm other. He went to a boarding school, where he had begun to write poetry by the age of 14. These early poems were Romantic and much influenced by the work of the English poet LORD BYRON.

Lermontov's first published poem, *Spring*, was written when he was 16, the year he entered Moscow University. After only two years he left and joined a military school. On graduation in 1834, he was stationed in St. Petersburg. There he observed and often criticized the social life of the wealthy.

Upset by the death in a duel of ALEKSANDR PUSHKIN, Lermontov wrote about it in his poem *The Death of a Poet*, denouncing the killer and blaming the evil lifestyle of the aristocracy. He was arrested and banished to a remote region of Russia. Returning a year later, he published his influential novel *A Hero of Our Time*. It reveals the thoughts of a young officer who has an adventurous yet tragic life. This was followed by his best-known poem, "The Demon," about an angel who falls in love with a mortal.

After a duel with the son of the French ambassador, Lermontov was again banished to a dangerous border region. In 1840, pretending to be ill, he returned to the town of Pyatigorsk, near Moscow. He joined in the social life of the town, but some of his biting comments to a fellow officer caused a challenge to yet another duel; this time he was killed.

Publications

1830 Spring
1831 A Strange Man
1835 The Masquerade
1837 The Death of a Poet
1837 Song of the Merchant Kalashnikov
1839 Sashka
1840 The Novice
1840 A Hero of Our Time
1841 The Demon

LESSING, Doris

English novelist and short-story writer

Born Oct. 22, 1919

Doris Lessing is a popular author best known for her novels that examine the individual's search for freedom in society.

Lessing was born to English parents in what was then Persia – a part of the British Empire – and is now Iran. Later, the family moved to the British colony of Rhodesia (now Zimbabwe) in southern Africa. Much of her education was gained through reading at home on the family farm. From the age of 18, she worked at the Rhodesian parliament and helped start a nonracist left-wing party in the country. She married twice and had three children.

When her second marriage ended in 1949, Lessing went to London, where her first novel, *The Grass Is Singing*, was published when she was 31. This critical examination of European rule in Africa was well received, and she developed the theme in a collection of short stories, *This Was the Old Chief's Country*. In her 30s and 40s, she wrote a 5-volume work called *The Children of Violence*, which follows the adventures of a character called Martha Quest as she searches for happiness in a world torn apart by violence. Lessing based Martha Quest's character and life on her own.

The Golden Notebook, considered to be Lessing's greatest novel, was published when she was 43. It is about the mental breakdown and recovery of a woman writer and is also closely based on Lessing's own experiences. In 1979, she began a series of science fiction books called *Canopus in Argos: Archives* in which she writes about the fate of the human race.

Publications

1950 The Grass Is Singing

1951 This Was the Old Chief's Country

1952–1969 The Children of Violence (5 vols.)

1962 The Golden Notebook

1979–1983 Canopus in Argos: Archives (5 vols.)

1988 The Fifth Child

1996 Love Again

LESSING, Gotthold

German playwright and critic

Born Jan. 22, 1729

Died Feb. 15, 1781

Age at death 52

Gotthold Lessing, who has been described as the true founder of modern German literature, was born in the German town of Kamenz, where his father was a pastor. In early childhood, he showed a great enthusiasm for reading. At the University of Leipzig he studied to become a pastor but soon, to the distress of his family, he began to take an interest in writing for the stage.

Before Lessing was 20, two of his plays were performed at the Leipzig Theater. His father was horrified and threatened to cut off his allowance. Lessing dropped out of university and went to seek his fortune in the great German city of Berlin. Soon he had a newspaper job as a drama critic and then as editor of a theatrical journal.

Lessing became established as a playwright at age 26 with his successful drama, *Miss Sara Samson*. It was Germany's first modern domestic tragedy. The play's English style and setting showed Lessing's determination to break from the French style that dominated German drama at that time.

Lessing's career had its ups and downs. He became Germany's greatest dramatic critic, but VOLTAIRE denounced him to Frederick the Great, ruler of Prussia (now part of Germany), and he left Berlin to take up a minor post in Hamburg. While there he wrote some of his finest criticism. His publications, however, caused a bitter dispute with the Church authorities, and he was officially forbidden to engage in such activities. It was then that he wrote *Nathan the Wise*, a play in verse that pleads for religious tolerance. Many people consider it to be his finest work.

Publications

1747	*The Young Scholar*
1749	*The Jews*
1755	*Miss Sara Sampson*
1766	*Laocoon, or, The Limits of Poetry and Painting*
1767	*Minna von Barnhelm*
1772	*Emilia Galotti*
1777	*The Education of the Human Race*
1779	*Nathan the Wise*

LEVERTOV, Denise

English-born American poet and essayist

Born Oct. 24, 1923
Died Dec. 20, 1997
Age at death 74

Denise Levertov's writing career covers more than four decades of poetry and began when she published her first volume at age 23.

Born in Ilford, Essex, Levertov's background is a mix of cultures and religions; her father, a Russian Jew, became an Anglican minister, and her mother was descended from a Welsh mystic. As a child Levertov was surrounded by artists and intellectuals, and during World War II her parents welcomed Jews who were escaping the horrors of Nazism.

Until she was 13, she was taught at home by her mother, who encouraged her curiosity and love of books. Levertov says that in childhood she had "time and solitude" to pursue poetry, and she was never in doubt about being a poet. She worked as a nurse for some years, but after she was fired from the British Hospital in Paris, at age 24, she set off traveling around Europe. In Switzerland, she met an American soldier and aspiring writer, and soon afterward they married and moved to the US. In 1949, she had a son, and in 1955 she became an American citizen.

Levertov's first volume of poetry, *The Double Image*, appeared in England in 1946. In the US, influenced by the poet WILLIAM CARLOS WILLIAMS, she published several collections during the 1950s and '60s. In the decade after that she became active in the movement protesting the Vietnam War, and many of her poems from this time – especially in the collection *To Stay Alive* – reflect her commitment to pacifism. In her later works she explores the themes of travel and spirituality.

Publications

1946	*The Double Image*
1957	*Here and Now*
1959	*With Eyes at the Back of Our Heads*
1961	*The Jacob's Ladder*
1970	*Relearning the Alphabet*
1971	*To Stay Alive*
1975	*The Freeing of the Dust*
1978	*Life in the Forest*
1987	*Breathing the Water*

LEVI, Primo

Italian writer

Born Jul. 31, 1919
Died Apr. 11, 1987
Age at death 67

Primo Levi was an Italian-Jewish writer who is remembered for his accounts of life in the Nazi concentration camps of World War II.

Levi was born in the Italian city of Turin. He studied chemistry at the University of Turin and graduated first in his class in 1941, the year after Italy had entered World War II as an ally of Nazi Germany. Italy at this time was ruled by the fascist leader Mussolini. Both the Italian fascists and their allies the German Nazis discriminated against Jews, and the Nazis planned to exterminate all the Jews in Europe.

By 1943, Levi felt he had to do something to fight the fascists, and he tried to join a resistance group in the north of Italy. Before he could make contact, Levi was captured and sent to a prison camp at Auschwitz, in Poland, where the Nazis were forcing thousands of Jews and other prisoners to work as slaves.

Levi survived his years at Auschwitz, although millions of other Jews were executed or died of neglect there. After the war, he returned to Turin and began to write about what he had seen. Two years after the end of the war he published *If This Is a Man*, based on his experiences at Auschwitz. The book was widely read and is regarded as one of the most powerful accounts of its kind. Part of what makes the book so powerful is the way Levi describes terrible events with the detached voice of an observing scientist.

Levi wrote several more books based on his experiences of the war. At the age of 67, perhaps feeling he had nothing more to say, he killed himself.

Publications

1947 If This Is a Man
1965 The Reawakening
1967 Natural Histories
1976 Shema: Collected Poems
1978 The Monkey's Wrench
1981 Moments of Reprieve
1982 If Not Now, When?
1984 The Periodic Table
1986 The Drowned and the Saved

LEVINE, Philip

American poet

Born Jan. 10, 1928

Philip Levine writes poems about the harsh lives led by working-class, city-dwelling people. For his collection of poems *The Simple Truth* he was awarded the 1995 Pulitzer Prize for poetry.

Levine's parents were Russian Jews who had immigrated to Detroit. His poems draw on childhood memories of Detroit during the years of the Great Depression and World War II. He became politically aware as a teenager, listening to debates about political movements like communism and anarchism. His family had experienced some aggression from local anti-Jewish fascists, and many of his poems are about people and governments driven by prejudice and the brave few who resist them.

After graduating from Wayne State University in 1950, Levine worked in a number of menial factory jobs. His experience of factory life is vividly portrayed in such poems as "Coming Home, Detroit" from the collection *They Feed They Lion*. In 1954, he married Frances Artley and left Detroit. He earned a Master's degree from the University of Iowa in 1957 and joined the faculty at Fresno State College, California, in 1958.

Levine's first poetry collection, *On the Edge*, was published when he was 33. His early poems were formal. Over the years, his style has become less rigid and more lyrical; the subject matter, however, has remained focused on ordinary people's struggles and achievements. *They Feed They Lion* and *The Simple Truth* have established his reputation as a poet who writes of loss, love and the strength of the human spirit.

Publications

1961 On the Edge
1968 Not This Pig
1972 They Feed They Lion
1974 1933
1976 The Names of the Lost
1979 Ashes: Poems New and Old
1988 A Walk with Tom Jefferson
1991 New Selected Poems
1991 What Work Is
1994 The Simple Truth

LEWIS, C.S.

Irish children's writer and novelist

Born Nov. 29, 1898
Died Nov. 22, 1963
Age at death 64

C.S. Lewis was a 20th-century British novelist and scholar. He created one of the best-loved series of books for children in English literature, *The Chronicles of Narnia*.

Clive Staples Lewis was born in Belfast. When he was nine years old, his mother died, and Lewis was sent away to boarding school. His great unhappiness at losing his mother and being separated from his family was made worse by the harsh treatment he received at the school.

During World War I, Lewis was drafted into the army. He was injured in the fighting and spent months recovering before going to study at Oxford University in 1918. He was to spend the next 35 years living and working there.

Lewis was a brilliant scholar, and in 1925, aged only 27, he became a teacher at the university. In his 30s, he became a Christian and began to write stories that expressed his religious beliefs. In 1938, he published *Out of the Silent Planet*, the first of a trilogy of books that put his Christian beliefs in the setting of a science fiction story.

It was not until Lewis was in his early 50s that he began to write the series of seven books known as the *The Chronicles of Narnia*. Beginning with *The Lion, the Witch, and the Wardrobe*, published when he was 52, the series describes the adventures of a group of children in a magical land inhabited by talking animals. Lewis included many ideas from the Bible in his *Narnia* stories.

Publications

1926 Dymer
1938 Out of the Silent Planet
1942 The Screwtape Letters
1943 Perelandra
1945 That Hideous Strength
1950 The Lion, the Witch, and the Wardrobe
1954 The Horse and His Boy
1955 The Magician's Nephew
1956 The Last Battle

LEWIS, Sinclair

American novelist

Born Feb. 7, 1885
Died Jan. 10, 1951
Age at death 65

In 1930 Sinclair Lewis became the first American to win the Nobel Prize for Literature.

Lewis was born in Sauk Center, Minnesota, the third son of a country doctor. He was a high-spirited and imaginative child, and he ran away from home when he was 13 to become a drummer boy in the Spanish-American War. His father caught up with him at the railroad station, however, and brought him home.

Lewis graduated from Yale University and spent the next few years struggling to make a living as a newspaper reporter, freelance writer and book editor. By the time he was 30, Lewis had become a full-time writer, but it was not until his sixth novel, *Main Street*, was published when he was 35 that he achieved major success. This vivid satire on life in a small, conservative town in the Midwest caught the public imagination and became an immediate bestseller. Lewis followed *Main Street* with *Babbitt*, about a small-town businessman. It has become a classic satire of American middle-class life, highlighting the dangers of conforming – trying to be like everyone else.

For his next novel, *Arrowsmith*, Lewis was awarded a Pulitzer Prize in 1926, which he rejected. He explained that because the award was meant for books that celebrate American wholesomeness, his novels – which criticize American lifestyles – should not be awarded the prize.

The award of the Nobel Prize marked the height of Lewis's achievement. He continued to write but never again achieved the success of his novels of the 1920s.

Publications

1920 Main Street
1922 Babbitt
1925 Arrowsmith
1926 Mantrap
1927 Elmer Gantry
1929 Dodsworth
1935 It Can't Happen Here
1943 Gideon Planish
1947 Kingsblood Royal
1951 World So Wide

LEWIS, Wyndham

British novelist and critic

Born Nov. 18, 1882
Died Mar. 7, 1957
Age at death 74

Wyndham Lewis was a British writer and painter. He also published the magazine *Blast*, which although short-lived presented work by many of the finest writers and artists of the period.

Lewis was born on a yacht off Nova Scotia, Canada, and moved to England with his family when he was six. He studied art in London and then continued his studies in Paris. On returning to England at the age of 27, he exhibited his paintings and began to write. He brought out the first edition of *Blast* when he was 32.

During World War I, Lewis served in the army, first as an artillery officer and then as a war artist. His first novel, *Tarr*, about the future of the artist in modern society, came out at the end of the war when he was 36. Then, after reading widely on art, literature and politics, he stunned literary London with *The Apes of God*, a novel in which he attacked writers like VIRGINIA WOOLF and her contemporaries in the Bloomsbury Group.

In the 1930s, Lewis produced some fine paintings and books, including the novel *The Revenge for Love*, but made very little money. In 1939, he went to America, hoping to make a profitable lecture tour. The outbreak of World War II made this impossible, as did his writings championing fascism and the Nazi party leader Adolf Hitler. He described his North American stay in the novel *Self Condemned*.

On his return to England Lewis worked as an art critic until he became blind in 1951. He continued work on a four-part fantasy, *The Human Age*, but had finished only three parts before he died.

Publications

1918 Tarr
1926 The Art of Being Ruled
1930 The Apes of God
1934 Men without Art
1937 Blasting and Bombardiering
1937 The Revenge for Love
1950 Rude Assignment
1951 Rotting Hill
1954 Self Condemned
1955–56 The Human Age

LINDGREN, Astrid

Swedish children's writer

Born Nov. 14, 1907

Astrid Lindgren created one of the most unique and popular characters in children's literature – Pippi Longstocking, an amazing nine-year-old girl who is incredibly strong and who lives alone with a monkey and a horse. She fulfills every child's dream of freedom and power.

Lindgren was born Astrid Ericsson in Vimmerby, Sweden, where she grew up on her parents' farm. When she was 19, she moved to Stockholm, the capital, and started work as a secretary in an office. Within a few years she married, becoming Astrid Lindgren, and started a family.

As her two children were growing up, Lindgren told them stories that she recalled from her childhood. In her mid-30s she created Pippi Longstocking; her daughter made up the name. Lindgren made up many stories about Pippi, but at first she had no intentions of writing them down. When she was 37, however, she found herself stuck in bed for two weeks after a fall. To pass the time she began to write down the Pippi stories. One year later, when Lindgren was 38, *Pippi Longstocking* came out. Some were shocked by Pippi's behavior: she tells tall stories, is untidy, and has no parents around, but she was (and still is) hugely popular with children in many countries.

Lindgren has since produced over 100 works for children, including plays, poems, novels, short stories, fairy tales and screenplays based on her work. She wrote many other Pippi stories as well as three series of books about a detective called Bill Bergson, a five-year-old boy called Emil, and the Bullerby children.

Publications

1945 Pippi Longstocking
1946 Bill Bergsen, Master Detective
1946 Pippi Goes Aboard
1947 The Six Bullerby Children
1948 Pippi in the South Seas
1950 Kati in America
1961 The Children of Noisy Village
1963 Emil in the Soup Tureen

LISPECTOR, Clarice

Russian-born Brazilian writer

Born Dec. 12, 1925
Died Dec. 9, 1977
Age at death 51

Clarice Lispector is regarded as the leading Brazilian short-story writer. Her simple, clear style and ability to combine the witty and the thoughtful brought her worldwide acclaim, although only after her early death.

Lispector was born in Russia. Her parents moved to Brazil when she was still a baby, and she was brought up in the tropical northeastern port of Recife, before moving, at the age of 12, to Rio de Janeiro. She studied law in Rio but, on graduating, decided to pursue a career in journalism. She was soon famous for a column in which she mixed everyday conversations with musings on domestic life and profiles of the famous. It became a stream-of-consciousness style chronicle. Her first novel, *Near to the Wild Heart*, was published when she was 19.

Lispector married a diplomat and traveled the world with him, living in various European cities before staying in New York City for eight years. Her marriage ended in divorce, and she returned to Brazil with her children, living in the capital city, Brasília.

Family Ties, Lispector's first short-story collection, came out when she was 35. It explores a common theme in her writing – the idea that a life guided by basic instincts and simple routines can lead to greater happiness than a life yearning after love, freedom and success. One of her best novels, *The Apple in the Dark*, describes how, through simple living on a farm, a man becomes more aware of himself and able to face up to a crime he has committed.

Publications

1944 Near to the Wild Heart
c. 1949 The Besieged City
1960 Family Ties
1961 The Apple in the Dark
1964 The Passion According to G.H.
1969 An Apprenticeship
1973 The Stream of Life
1977 The Hour of the Star

Published after she died

1989 Soulstorm: Stories

LLEWELLYN, Richard

Welsh novelist

Born Dec. 8, 1906
Died Nov. 30, 1983
Age at death 76

Richard Llewellyn, a Welsh writer, is best remembered for his novel *How Green Was My Valley*.

Born into a mining family in St. David's, Wales, Llewellyn spoke only Welsh until he was six. Then the family moved to London, and he attended various schools in London and Wales. He worked briefly in the hotel business in London, Venice, Florence and Rome before enlisting in the British Army for 6 years when he was 17.

After service in India and Hong Kong, Llewellyn began to work in filmmaking. At age 33, he published his first novel, *How Green Was My Valley*, which he had started 12 years before. It is the story of the Morgan family and describes in detail the lifestyle of a Welsh valley community. A huge success in the US, it was released as a film in

1941. His next novel, *None But the Lonely Heart*, was also filmed. Drawing from his experiences of London in the 1930s, it tells the story of a London boy who becomes a criminal.

After World War II, when he served in the Welsh Guards, Llewellyn lived in the US, then went to Patagonia (in Argentina) for five years. He wrote about his experiences in *Up into the Singing Mountain*, which is a sequel to *How Green Was my Valley*.

A confirmed traveler, Llewellyn lived in Brazil, Paraguay, Uruguay and Chile, then went to East Africa and lived with the Masai people. In Europe once more, he traveled through Italy, France and Switzerland, writing spy novels, before settling for a while in Israel. Although he wrote more than 60 books, some for children, none matched the critical or popular acclaim of the first.

Publications

1939 How Green Was My Valley
1943 None But the Lonely Heart
1960 Up into the Singing Mountain
1961 A Man in a Mirror
1966 Down Where the Moon Is Small
1973 Bride of Israel, My Love
1975 Green, Green My Valley Now

LOFTING, Hugh

English-born American children's writer

Born Jan. 14, 1886
Died Sep. 26, 1947
Age at death 61

Hugh Lofting is famous for creating Dr. Dolittle – a gentlemanly 19th-century physician who gives up his career treating people to look after animals instead. His parrot, Polynesia, teaches him to speak the animal language, and his household includes a duck, Dab Dab, who is his housekeeper.

Lofting was born in Maidenhead, Berkshire, to an Irish father and an English mother. As a child he spent ten years at an isolated boarding school. He trained to be an engineer in Boston, Massachusetts, and in London. Once he qualified, his work took him to many different parts of the world, including Africa, the Caribbean, and Canada. During World War I he served in the Irish Guards. While in the trenches he wrote his children letters in which he created Dr. Dolittle. He left the army in 1917 after being injured and moved to New York with his family, eventually becoming a US citizen. His wife convinced him to turn his wartime letters into a book, and *The Story of Dr. Dolittle* came out when Lofting was 34. After writing seven more Dr. Dolittle books, he tried to stop writing about the doctor (by sending him to the Moon), but demand was so great that he had to continue.

Lofting's original stories included Native-American and African characters that were offensively portrayed as fools and clowns. Revised editions of Lofting's stories came out in the 1980s, after his death, with these racist parts removed. This has much improved the stories, leaving only Lofting's imaginative, lively writing style and unforgettable animal characters such as the two-headed Pushmi-Pullyu.

Publications

1920 The Story of Dr. Dolittle
1922 The Voyages of Dr. Dolittle
1923 Dr. Dolittle's Post Office
1923 The Story of Mrs. Tubbs
1924 Dr. Dolittle's Circus
1925 Dr. Dolittle's Zoo
1926 Dr. Dolittle's Caravan
1927 Dr. Dolittle's Garden
1928 Dr. Dolittle in the Moon
1933 Dr. Dolittle's Return

LOMONOSOV, Mikhail

Russian writer

Born Nov. 19, 1711
Died Apr. 15, 1765
Age at death 53

Mikhail Lomonosov was an 18th-century Russian genius. As well as being a noted poet, he made important scientific discoveries and pioneered the use of the Russian language for Literature.

Lomonosov was born in the far north of Russia, the son of a fisherman. As a boy, Lomonosov followed his father's trade, but he was desperate to educate himself. When he was 19, he left his native village and traveled, penniless and on foot, to Moscow. He disguised his humble origins and studied at prestigious academies. His tutors recognized his brilliance, and at age 25 he was sent to study in Germany, where he began to write poetry. In 1745, he became professor of chemistry at the Academy of St. Petersburg. He founded Russia's first chemistry laboratory and carried out experiments on heat, gases and electricity that were years ahead of his time.

Lomonosov loved Russia; his lifelong aim was to promote Russian science and culture. At the time French was considered the language of great literature, and Lomonosov set out to promote Russian as an alternative. He was the first to attempt to standardize the Russian language from all the many different versions that existed, and he laid the basis for Russian literature by developing three different styles of writing that could be used for the many different types of literature – epics, tragedies, comedies, fables and so on. Lomonosov himself wrote most of his scientific papers as well as his poems in Russian.

Publications

1743 Morning Meditation
1743 Evening Meditation on the Majesty of God
1750 Tamira and Selim
1752 Demofont
1756 Hymn to the Beard

LONDON, Jack

American novelist and short-story writer

Born Jan. 12, 1876
Died Nov. 22, 1916
Age at death 40

Jack London's novels portray the heroic struggle of men and animals against a hostile, amoral environment – in Alaska and other isolated places. London was a "rugged individualist" who believed strongly that only the fittest should survive and that white people are superior to other races.

Although born in San Francisco, London was raised in Oakland, California. His mother was not married, and his father deserted them. London's short life was fast paced and fascinating and directly inspired the 50 books he wrote. For example, he drew on the experiences of working in the Oakland dockland gangs and running away to sea at 17 when writing *Cruise of the Dazzler* and other early adventure stories. He even lived as a hobo. However, the humiliation of frequently being jailed made him determined to better himself. By taking jobs in canneries and laundries around Oakland, he worked his way through secondary school. At age 24, he published his first book, a collection of short stories called *The Son of the Wolf*.

London went to northwest Canada during the Gold Rush of 1897–98, and his description of the struggle for survival in the Klondike against a hostile environment produced the classic novels *Call of the Wild* and *White Fang*. Although London may have believed that only the strongest deserve to survive, he wrote eloquently about the plight of the poor in *People of the Abyss*. His description of social outcasts in *The Road* inspired later writers like JOHN STEINBECK and JACK KEROUAC. His own horrific experiences at sea formed the basis for his fine novel *Sea Wolf*.

Publications

1900	*The Son of the Wolf*
1902	*Cruise of the Dazzler*
1903	*Call of the Wild*
1903	*People of the Abyss*
1904	*Sea Wolf*
1906	*White Fang*
1907	*The Road*
1908	*Iron Heel*
1909	*Martin Eden*
1910	*Burning Daylight*

LONGFELLOW, Henry Wadsworth

American poet

Born Feb. 27, 1807
Died Mar. 24, 1882
Age at death 75

Henry Wadsworth Longfellow wrote some of the most well-known poems in American literature, including "Paul Revere's Ride." He was the first American to be honored with a bust in the Poets' Corner of Westminster Abbey.

Born in Portland, Maine, Longfellow traced his family back to the Plymouth Pilgrims. He graduated in 1825 from Bowdoin College, where NATHANIEL HAWTHORNE had been his classmate. Longfellow spent his early career teaching foreign languages, first at Bowdoin and later at Harvard. Thereafter he concentrated on poetry. He was one of the few American poets who was so popular that he could support himself by writing. Longfellow's private life was filled with sadness. His first wife died shortly after they were married, and his second wife was killed in a fire. This sadness is reflected in many of his poems.

At age 32, he published his first book of verse, *Voices of the Night*, which brought him wide public recognition. Two years later he published *Ballads*, which contains some of his most famous poems, including "The Village Blacksmith." Longfellow had a gift for romantic storytelling. He became known for his long poems that use simple ideas and language to tell stories based on American history and mythology. These include *The Song of Hiawatha*, a tale from Native-American legends; *Evangeline*, the story of the French exiles of France's colonies in North America; and *The Courtship of Miles Standish*, a romance set in the early days of the Pilgrim Fathers.

Publications

1839	*Voices of the Night*
1841	*Ballads*
1847	*Evangeline*
1849	*The Seaside and the Fireside*
1855	*The Song of Hiawatha*
1858	*The Courtship of Miles Standish*
1863	*Tales of a Wayside Inn* (including "Paul Revere's Ride")
1880	*Ultima Thule*

LOOS, Anita

American novelist, playwright and screenwriter

Born Apr. 26, 1893
Died Aug. 18, 1981
Age at death 88

Although she wrote many successful Hollywood screenplays, Anita Loos is remembered today for *Gentlemen Prefer Blondes*, considered to be one of the best American comic novels.

Loos was born in Sisson, California. As a child she acted in her father's theatrical company and, by age 19, she had sold her first script to the silent movies. After a marriage that lasted one day when she was 22, Loos married again – this time to a movie director.

At age 32, Loos published her famous novel *Gentlemen Prefer Blondes*. It is a sharply written satire, making fun of sex and of Americans' desire for wealth – in short, the wild excesses that characterized America in the 1920s. The main character, Lorelei Lee, is a beautiful, diamond-loving, but unsophisticated American traveling in Europe, moving from man to man and acquiring diamond-studded jewelry as she goes. It was an immediate success, attracting praise from the writers Edith Wharton and James Joyce and also a popular audience. It was adapted into plays, musicals and films, including one starring Marilyn Monroe.

After "talking movies" were invented, Loos's scriptwriting career became even more successful. By 1931, she was earning an incredible $3,500 a week, at a time when millions of Americans were out of work and lining up for free bread and soup. During the late 1930s, while at MGM Studios in Hollywood, Loos wrote lines for the superstars of the 1930s and '40s, including Clark Gable, Jean Harlow and Joan Crawford. She also wrote plays based on writings by Colette, including *Gigi* and *Chéri.*

Publications

1925	*Gentlemen Prefer Blondes*
1928	*But Gentlemen Marry Brunettes*
1951	*A Mouse is Born*
1951	*Gigi*
1959	*Chéri*
1961	*No Mother to Guide Her*
1966	*A Girl Like I*
1974	*Kiss Hollywood Good-by*
1977	*Cast of Thousands*
1978	*The Talmadge Girls*

LOPE de VEGA

Spanish playwright and poet

Born Nov. 25, 1562
Died Aug. 27, 1635
Age at death 72

Lope de Vega, one of Spain's most popular playwrights ever, is regarded as the father of Spanish national theater or "comedia." He popularized this dramatic form – three-act plays in verse – which broke all the classical rules and appealed to a wide audience. As well as over 1,500 plays (of which nearly 500 survive), Lope wrote many fine poems.

Born in Madrid, Lope attended a Jesuit school. After studying at the University of Alcala, he took part in the Spanish campaign against Portugal in 1580 and the Spanish Armada against England in 1588. He had already written many poems, stories and plays before his first work, *Dragoneta*, was published when he was 36. *Dragoneta* is an epic attacking Sir Francis Drake, the English hero who defeated the Spanish Armada.

Lope began to write for the stage in his 30s. His plays were very popular because they were realistic and full of excitement. Some were based on occurrences in Lope's own life, for example *Dorothy* drew heavily on his own chaotic love life. He had many affairs, married twice, and fathered at least six children, only three of them with his wives. Although he became a priest in 1614, he continued to have affairs.

Other plays by Lope were based on historical events. One of his most famous works, *Fuente Ovejuna*, depicts a peasant uprising and has been dramatized to great acclaim in the 1990s.

In 1634, Lope was grief-stricken when his daughter disappeared; he repented for his sins and left his great wealth to charity. His state funeral lasted for nine days.

Publications

1598 Arcadia
1598 Dragoneta
1602 Angelica
1604 Rimas
1604 The Pilgrim of Casteel
1611–18 Fuente Ovejuna
1621 Filomena
1624 Circe
1627 Tragic Crown
1632 Dorothy

LORDE, Audre

American poet and essayist

Born Feb. 18, 1934
Died Nov. 17, 1992
Age at death 58

Poet Audre Lorde described herself as a black lesbian feminist, and all her life she fought against the divisions that split the African-American community along lines of gender and sexuality.

Lorde was born in Harlem during the Great Depression. Her parents were from Grenada in the Caribbean. As a child she felt isolated and unable to express herself, and she didn't speak until she was five. By the age of 12, however, she was writing poetry, and she had her first poem published at 15. She graduated from Hunter College in 1959, and received a Master's degree from Columbia University. In 1962, she married and later had two children. She was professor of English at Hunter College from 1981.

At age 34, Lorde published her first book of poetry, *The First Cities*. It brought her widespread recognition as a poet. Encouraged by her success, she ventured for the first time into the American South, where she taught poetry to black students. This experience confirmed for her that she wanted to be both a writer and a teacher.

Lorde's work is about feelings and relationships and explores the oppression of women within the African-American community and the racism of the mainly white feminist movement. Her 1973 poetry collection, *From a Land Where Other People Live*, was nominated for a National Book Award.

In addition to several volumes of poetry, Lorde wrote two autobiographical works, *Zami: A New Spelling of My Name*, describing her life up to 1960, and *The Cancer Journals,* which tells of her experience with breast cancer.

Publications

1968 The First Cities
1973 From a Land Where Other People Live
1974 The New York Head Shop and Museum
1976 Coal
1978 The Black Unicorn
1980 The Cancer Journals
1982 Zami: A New Spelling of My Name
1992 Undersong

LOVECRAFT, H.P.

American horror writer

Born Aug. 20, 1890
Died Mar. 15, 1937
Age at death 46

H.P. Lovecraft's strange stories have a unique place in American horror writing.

Howard Phillips Lovecraft was born in Providence, Rhode Island. His father was a traveling salesman who had a nervous breakdown, became ill, and died when his son was five. Lovecraft himself then began to suffer nervous illnesses and was often kept away from school by his overprotective mother. At home, he loved reading and listening to the horror stories his grandfather told him.

Lovecraft was a highly intelligent child who was fascinated by science as well as literature. However, because of his fragile mental state he failed to leave secondary school with a diploma and did not go to university.

By the age of 16, he was writing on astronomy for local newspapers. In his 20s, he began to write stories for publication in science fiction magazines and was eventually offered the job of editor at the magazine *Weird Tales.* He turned the job down and continued to live on very little money.

In his stories Lovecraft wrote about an imaginary town, Arkham, which was based on his home town of Providence. He described a race that once ruled the world but now lies sleeping under the Earth's seas. His stories are full of horror and slimy monsters rising from the deep.

Lovecraft died of cancer at 46. His stories were scattered in many magazines, but only one of his books was published while he was alive. His friends set up a publishing house for his work, Arkham House, and his books have remained in print ever since.

Publications

1936 The Shadow Over Innsmouth

Published after he died

1939 The Outsider and Others
1943 Beyond the Wall of Sleep
1945 The Dunwich Horror
1964 At the Mountains of Madness
1965 Dagon and Other Macabre Tales

LOWELL, Amy

American poet

Born Feb. 9, 1874
Died May 12, 1925
Age at death 51

Amy Lowell is remembered today as an original poet who pioneered modern American poetry in the early 20th century.

Born into a very wealthy Bostonian family, Lowell was educated at home by governesses before going to public schools. She finished school at 17, after which she studied alone in the family library of over 7,000 books. Unhappy with her family's plans for her to become a wife, Lowell suffered years of depression in her 20s. Although she often traveled abroad, Lowell lived at the family home all her life.

Lowell was encouraged to write from an early age; when she was 13, Lowell, her mother, and her sister privately published a collection of stories called *Dream Drops*. When she was 28, Lowell began to focus on becoming a poet. Eight years later her first poem, "Fixed Idea," was published. Soon after this her first collection, *A Dome of Many-Colored Glass*, appeared. It showed promise but was not a great success.

Lowell read the work of the American poet HILDA DOOLITTLE and was inspired by her experimental style. She traveled to London to meet Doolittle and another leading American poet, EZRA POUND, in 1913. Strongly influenced by the ideas she was introduced to in London, Lowell began experimenting with new forms of poetry in her next collection, *Sword Blades and Poppy Seeds*. She attacked the restrictions placed on art and life by meaningless traditions in her famous poem "Patterns," which appeared in her third collection, *Men, Women, and Ghosts*. Lowell's final collection, *What's O'Clock*, was awarded the Pulitzer Prize a year after her death.

Publications

1887	*Dream Drops*
1912	*A Dome of Many-Colored Glass*
1914	*Sword Blades and Poppy Seeds*
1915	*Six French Poets*
1916	*Men, Women, and Ghosts*
1919	*Pictures of the Floating World*
1921	*Legends*
1925	*What's O'Clock*

LOWELL, James Russell

American poet, satirist and essayist

Born Feb. 22, 1819
Died Aug. 12, 1891
Age at death 72

James Russell Lowell was one of America's finest 19th-century poets, known for his images of New England and humorous satires on social problems. Lowell's gifts for literature and poetry, coupled with his interests in politics and social issues, allowed him to influence the cultural life of his times.

Born into a New England family, Lowell attended Harvard University. After graduating from Harvard Law School at age 21, he quickly abandoned law and turned to poetry, publishing his first collection, *A Year's Life*, when he was 22. By the time he was 26, Lowell had become interested in literary criticism and published *Conversations on Some of the Old Poets*.

Lowell reached the peak of his literary achievement at age 29 when he published three books: his popular story-poem *The Vision of Sir Launfal*, *A Fable for Critics* and *The Biglow Papers*. The last is a satire in Yankee dialect about the Mexican-American War of 1846. It was one of America's first political satires.

When he was 37, Lowell replaced HENRY WADSWORTH LONGFELLOW as the modern languages professor at Harvard, beginning a new era of literary activity in his life. From 1857 to 1861 Lowell was the first editor of the *Atlantic Monthly*, an important literary journal. Later, he published a second series of *The Biglow Papers*, focusing on the American Civil War and his antislavery views. At age 51 he published one of the most important religious poems of the century, *The Cathedral*.

Lowell left Harvard in 1875 and began a career as a diplomat. Between 1877 and 1885 he was ambassador to Spain and then Great Britain.

Publications

1841	*A Year's Life*
1845	*Conversations on Some of the Old Poets*
1848	*A Fable for Critics*
1848	*The Vision of Sir Launfal*
1848	*The Biglow Papers* (first series)
1867	*The Biglow Papers* (second series)
1870	*The Cathedral*
1871	*My Study Windows*

LOWELL, Robert

American poet and playwright

Born Mar. 1, 1917
Died Sep. 12, 1977
Age at death 60

Publications

1946	*Lord Weary's Castle*
1951	*The Mills of the Kavanaughs*
1959	*Life Studies*
1964	*For the Union Dead*
1965	*Selected Poems*
1967	*Near the Ocean*
1973	*For Lizzie and Harriet*
1973	*The Dolphin*
1973	*History*
1976	*Selected Poems*

Robert Lowell is one of the best known of a generation of American poets who became important just after World War II.

Lowell was a member of a distinguished, intellectual Boston family whose members included the poet and critic JAMES RUSSELL LOWELL and the poet AMY LOWELL. Robert was a complex child with a violent temper. He was nicknamed Cal after the Roman emperor Caligula, who was notoriously cruel, and this nickname stayed with him his whole life.

Lowell studied at Harvard and at Kenyon College. After graduating at age 23, he married the writer JEAN STAFFORD and converted to Roman Catholicism. During World War II he refused army service, and his antiwar beliefs resulted in a six-month prison sentence. After leaving prison, Lowell became a teacher. One of his first collections of poetry, *Lord Weary's Castle*, was published when he was 29, and it won a Pulitzer Prize in 1947. The best-known poem in this collection is "The Quaker Graveyard at Nantucket."

Lowell's turbulent personal life (he married three times) and his recurring problems with depression and heavy drinking resulted in periods of mental instability. He used his poetry to try to come to terms with these experiences. In *For Lizzie and Harriet*, for example, the poet talks about his feelings for his second wife – the writer ELIZABETH HARDWICK – and their daughter after the failure of the marriage. In the title poem of *The Dolphin* Lowell celebrates his love for his third wife. This book won him a second Pulitzer Prize in 1974.

LOWRY, Malcolm

English novelist

Born Jul. 28, 1909
Died Jun. 27, 1957
Age at death 47

Malcolm Lowry is famous for *Under the Volcano*, an autobiographical novel that reflects his own tragic life.

Lowry was born near Liverpool, the son of a wealthy businessman. Like his three brothers, he attended public boarding schools. When he was 17, he enlisted as a deckhand on a ship bound for Japan, an experience used in his first novel, *Ultramarine*, which was written during his time as a student at Cambridge University and published when he was 24. It received very mixed reviews.

Lowry traveled to Spain with CONRAD AIKEN, whose work had considerable influence on his writing. There he met the American writer Jan Gabrial and married her in 1934. Their stormy relationship features in some of his short stories

A heavy drinker since his teenage years, Lowry spent some time in the psychiatric ward of Bellevue Hospital in New York City. Immediately following his release he wrote about his experiences in a short novel, which was published as *Lunar Caustic* after he died.

Under the Volcano is based on Lowry's time in Mexico and is the story of the last 12 hours of a man drinking himself to death. Lowry said that it was about the guilt of a man and his doom. Despite its gloomy subject matter, it is written in a lyrical style and is full of humor. He revised the book several times while living in a cabin by the ocean in Canada with his second wife. It was a popular success and is now regarded as one of the great works of the 20th century. Lowry left several incomplete works when he died from an overdose of sleeping tablets.

Publications

1933 Ultramarine

1947 Under the Volcano

Published after he died

1961 Hear Us O Lord from Heaven Thy Dwelling Place

1963 Selected Poems

1968 Lunar Caustic

LUCIAN

Greek writer

Born c. 120

Died c. 200

Age at death c. 80

Lucian was a Greek satirical writer of the Roman period. He was born in a part of the Roman Empire that was then called Syria and which is now part of modern-day Turkey. In one of his books he tells us that he was apprenticed to a sculptor when he was young, but that he broke an expensive slab of marble and was beaten for it. This experience persuaded him to become a writer instead.

As a young man Lucian made a living as a public speaker. He traveled all over the Roman Empire, giving entertaining speeches for money. A number of these speeches have survived as written texts. When he was about 40, he gave up this wandering life and settled in the Greek city of Athens to study philosophy. It was here that his literary career really began.

Lucian invented a new kind of literature, known today as the humorous dialogue. He lived at a time when the traditional religious beliefs of the ancient Greek and Roman worlds were being taken less and less seriously, and his writings made fun of people who clung to old-fashioned ways of thinking. He hated superstition, and portrayed the mythical gods and heroes as absurd characters.

Lucian also wrote humorous fantasy stories that satirized the travel stories of earlier writers such as the Greek historian Herodotus. Lucian's book *The True History* begins with the sentence "Every word of this is a lie, and my readers should put no trust in it at all!" It tells the story of an incredible voyage in which the heroes visit the Moon and are swallowed by a giant whale more than 100-miles long!

Publications

2nd century

The True History

Dialogues of the Dead

Dialogues of the Gods

Dialogues of the Courtesans

Charon

Descent into Hades

Menippus

The Cock

How to Write History

LUCRETIUS

Roman poet and philosopher

Born c. 94 BC
Died c. 55 BC
Age at death c. 39

Lucretius was a Roman poet and philosopher. He is remembered for his one surviving work, a long poem in six books called *On the Nature of Things*.

Almost nothing is known about his life. The fact that he was obviously highly educated suggests that he came from a wealthy family, and historians believe he may have been born in, or near, the city of Rome.

Other classical writers who lived after Lucretius tell a story about his life that says that he became mad after drinking a love-potion and wrote his poetry in brief periods of sanity. It seems unlikely that this story is true; Lucretius's book *On the Nature of Things* is too carefully thought out to have been written by a man who was mad. The story may have been invented by enemies of Lucretius who disagreed with his ideas.

On the Nature of Things is a philosophical poem. It describes the universe and everything in it according to the theories of an ancient Greek philosopher called Epicurus, who lived almost 200 years before Lucretius. The main argument of the poem is that the universe is made up of nothing more than tiny particles of matter called atoms. Lucretius also argued that people do not really have souls and that there is no afterlife. Considering that he lived more than 2,000 years ago, it is remarkable how similar his beliefs are to modern ideas.

Lucretius was the first Roman author to write a philosophical work in verse. To make his ideas understood, he had to invent new words and give new meanings to old words. In this way, he did a lot to develop Latin, the Roman language.

Publications

On the Nature of Things (1st century BC)

LUDLUM, Robert

American crime writer

Born May 25, 1927

Robert Ludlum is known for his fast-paced, entertaining thrillers, which have sold more than 200 million copies worldwide.

Ludlum was born in New York City and educated in Connecticut. After military service in the US Marine Corps he became a stage and television actor. He went on to work as a theater producer in New Jersey. At age 42, he became a full-time writer.

Ludlum's experience with producing plays gives his novels a strong sense of drama and an emphasis on action. His plots are often complex, but the message he delivers is usually very straightforward: that it is the responsibility of ordinary individuals to uphold moral standards and preserve the American way of life. The theme of the little man who pits his wits against the might of large and corrupt organizations appears frequently in Ludlum's work.

Ludlum's hero is usually an unremarkable middle-aged man who becomes involved in a struggle against evil. For example, in *The Osterman Weekend,* the hero is a news director who is recruited by a man from the CIA. The newsman's help is needed to undermine a Russian scheme that will bring economic chaos to the US. After intrigues, abductions and murders the newsman is finally left to deal with the situation alone. A similar theme recurs in a later novel, *The Matlock Paper*. Here the hero is a professor called on by the Justice Department to investigate a network of vice – gambling, drugs and prostitution – on university campuses.

More recently Ludlum's novels have dealt with issues such as arms dealing and terrorism and have been set in many different countries.

Publications

1971	*The Scarlatti Inheritance*
1972	*The Osterman Weekend*
1973	*The Matlock Paper*
1980	*The Bourne Identity*
1982	*The Parsifal Mosaic*
1984	*The Aquitaine Progression*
1988	*The Icarus Agenda*
1990	*The Bourne Ultimatum*
1993	*The Scorpio Illusion*
1995	*The Apocalypse Watch*

LURIE, Alison

American novelist and children's writer

Born Sep. 3, 1926

Alison Lurie's novels are full of entertaining observations on the lives and manners of middle-class Americans. With her sharp eye for detail and use of comedy she has been compared to the 19th-century English novelist JANE AUSTEN.

Lurie was born in Chicago but grew up in New York. Her father was a social worker, her mother a former journalist, and Lurie had a privileged upbringing that included expensive public schools. She graduated from Radcliffe College, and the following year she married and settled in Cambridge, Massachusetts.

Although Lurie had already published some stories and poems in magazines while raising three children and working at odd jobs, she could not get anything published for several years. As a result she virtually stopped writing. Then, in her 30s, she was "discovered" by a publisher who had seen some of her work. She sent him her novel *Love and Friendship*, and it was accepted.

All of Lurie's early novels – *Love and Friendship*, *The Nowhere City*, and *The War between the Tates* – are set in New England college towns. She creates portraits of college life, especially troubled marriages and family relationships, set against a background of real events. *The War between the Tates*, for example, takes place during the Vietnam War, a period of great social change and unrest. It was made into a movie in 1976.

Lurie won the Pulitzer Prize in 1985 for *Foreign Affairs*, a novel about American academics visiting London. An expert on children's literature, which she taught at Cornell University for several years, she has written a number of books for children.

Publications

1962	*Love and Friendship*
1965	*The Nowhere City*
1967	*Imaginary Friends*
1969	*Real People*
1974	*The War between the Tates*
1979	*Only Children*
1984	*Foreign Affairs*
1988	*The Truth about Lorin Jones*
1990	*Don't Tell the Grown-ups*
1994	*Women and Ghosts*
1998	*Last Resort*

MACAULAY, Rose

English novelist and critic

Born Aug. 1, 1881
Died Oct. 30, 1958
Age at death 77

Rose Macaulay wrote travel books, literary criticism and poetry but is best remembered for her novels, which are mostly witty satires on the life of the English and their travels abroad. The prizewinning *The Towers of Trebizond*, about religion, travel, love and adventure, and the sadder *The World My Wilderness*, set in London after World War II, were her most successful books.

The daughter of a lecturer in classical literature at Cambridge University, Macaulay herself studied at Oxford University. Her first success was at age 39 with the novel *The Lee Shore*, which won a literary prize. *Potterism*, published the same year, was the first in a series of satires on the society of her day and established her as a leading novelist.

Macaulay wrote fewer novels after 1930, and none at all for about ten years, during which time she had an unhappy love affair. While the affair lasted, she lapsed from her religious beliefs. She regained her faith thanks to help from a cousin who was a priest. Macaulay began writing again and produced some of her best novels in the 1950s. Her elegant style of prose and sense of comedy appealed to many readers.

Macaulay's most important critical works include her books about the poets JOHN MILTON and Robert Herrick and *Some Religious Elements in English Literature*. Her travel books include *Fabled Shore*, about an automobile trip to Spain, and the outstanding *The Pleasure of Ruins*, which describes the romantic remains of abandoned cities from Central America to the Middle East.

Publications

1920 The Lee Shore
1920 Potterism
1921 Dangerous Ages
1931 Some Religious Elements in English Literature
1934 Going Abroad
1949 Fabled Shore
1950 The World My Wilderness
1953 The Pleasure of Ruins
1956 The Towers of Trebizond

MacDIARMID, Hugh

Scottish poet

Born Aug. 11, 1892
Died Sep. 9, 1978
Age at death 86

Hugh MacDiarmid was a leading Scottish writer in the early 20th century. His work inspired a flowering of Scottish literature in that period.

Born in Langholm in the Scottish border country, MacDiarmid was the son of a rural postman. The family lived close to the town library, where the young MacDiarmid spent many hours reading. He was educated at Langholm Academy, then was a teacher at Broughton Higher Grade School in Edinburgh before becoming a journalist. During World War I, he served in the army medical corps. He then married and set up home in Montrose, Scotland.

In 1922, aged 30, MacDiarmid founded *The Scottish Chapbook*, a journal that published poetry and encouraged a revival of Scottish literature. His own early collections of lyrical verse, *Sangschaw* and *Penny Wheep*, were followed by the long poem *A Drunk Man Looks at the Thistle*. Published when he was 34, it established him as a leader of a Scottish literary revival and has remained his most popular poem. It examines Scottish political problems without allowing the politics to overwhelm the poetry, as it does in some of his later works.

MacDiarmid often wrote in a mixture of English and Scottish known as Lallans. This meant that his work could be understood by English readers, but other Scottish writers criticized him for not using the Scottish language only. In 1928, MacDiarmid became a founding member of the Scottish National Party, which aims to achieve independence for Scotland.

Publications

1925 Sangschaw
1926 Penny Wheep
1926 A Drunk Man Looks at the Thistle
1930 To Circumjack Cencrastus
1930 Hymn to Lenin
1932 Scots Unbound
1934 Stony Limits
1947 A Kist o' Whistles
1955 In Memoriam James Joyce

MacDONALD, John D.

American crime writer

Born Jul. 24, 1916
Died Dec. 28, 1986
Age at death 70

John D. MacDonald is best known for his series of novels featuring private investigator Travis McGee.

John Dann MacDonald was born in Sharon, Pennsylvania. When he was 12 years old, he became ill with scarlet fever and had to stay in bed for a year. It was during this time that he turned to reading adventure stories and novels.

After attending Harvard, MacDonald joined the US Army. He was posted to Delhi, the capital of India, and instead of writing letters home to his wife, Dorothy, he sent her short stories that she in turn submitted to the magazines of the day. When MacDonald left the army, he continued to write stories. Although initially he had many rejections, he finally became one of the most popular "pulp" writers of the time. His stories were printed in the cheap "pulp" magazines that were popular in the 1940s and '50s.

In the mid-1950s, paperback novels took over from the pulp magazines as the main type of popular fiction. MacDonald became a successful paperback writer with a series of crime novels set in Florida and featuring Travis McGee – a modern-day Robin Hood who first appeared in *The Deep Blue Goodbye*, published when MacDonald was 48. McGee calls himself a "salvage expert," meaning that he tries to recover stolen property or goods for his clients.

In his novel, *Cape Fear,* MacDonald introduced one of the first psychopaths into crime fiction, Max Cody. A dangerously disturbed man, Cody was played in a famous 1960 movie version by Robert Mitchum and again in 1990 by Robert de Niro.

Publications

1950 The Brass Cupcake
1952 The Damned
1958 Cape Fear
1964 The Deep Blue Goodbye
1968 Pale Gray for Guilt
1970 The Long Lavender Look
1975 The Dreadful Lemon Sky
1977 Condominium
1982 Cinnamon Skin
1986 Barrier Island

MACDONALD, Ross

American crime writer

Born Dec. 13, 1915
Died Jul. 11, 1983
Age at death 67

Ross Macdonald ranks with DASHIELL HAMMETT and RAYMOND CHANDLER as one of the great writers of American crime fiction.

Ross Macdonald is the pen name of Kenneth Millar. He was born in Los Gatos, California, but raised and educated in Canada. He later taught English and history at universities in Canada and America. When he was 23, he married Margaret Sturm, who also became a crime writer. During World War II, he served in the US Naval Reserve in the Pacific.

Macdonald was influenced by the writing of Hammett and Chandler. Like them he wrote novels that explore the social world of crime. His novels, usually set in California, feature a private detective as the main character. Lew Archer is a low-key figure who observes the action from the sidelines; he was later played by Paul Newman in the film version of *The Moving Target*.

In *The Doomsters*, a family saga published when he was 43, Macdonald moved away from Hammett and Chandler influences to create his own style. From then on he wrote stories that explore the minds of his characters as well as their social world.

The ideas of the founder of psychoanalysis, Sigmund Freud, were then making a big impact in America. Freud believed that many problems of adult behavior have their roots in childhood experiences, and in Macdonald's novels people often commit a crime because of events in their family history. His exploration of the motives behind crimes has influenced many crime writers today.

Publications

1947 Blue City
1949 The Moving Target
1950 The Drowning Pool
1952 The Ivory Grin
1958 The Doomsters
1959 The Galton Case
1962 The Zebra-Striped Hearse
1965 The Far Side of the Dollar
1971 The Underground Man
1976 The Blue Hammer

MACHADO de ASSIS, Joaquim Maria

Brazilian poet, novelist and short-story writer

Born Jun. 21, 1839
Died Sep. 29, 1908
Age at death 69

Joaquim Maria Machado de Assis is best known for his realist novels about urban life in 19th-century Brazil. These stories, which explore the psychology of human beings, are deeply pessimistic but full of ironic wit.

Machado was born in Rio de Janeiro, then the capital of Brazil. His father was an African-American house painter, and his mother was Portuguese. Machado had epilepsy and was in poor general health. At 17, he was apprenticed to a printer and began to take an interest in literature. By the time he was 30, he was well established as a writer and was making rapid progress toward becoming a high-ranking official in the Brazilian civil service. Unfortunately, ill health forced him to give up his career in administration.

When he was 42, Machado published a remarkably original novel called *Epitaph of a Small Winner*. It uses many techniques of the modern novel that were then highly innovative, including shifts in time and point of view. Machado's masterpiece, *Dom Casmurro*, published when he was 60, is a frightening study of a mind warped by jealousy. His work is full of bitterness about human failings, but this is disguised by his humor.

In spite of his illnesses, Machado founded the Brazilian Academy of Letters in 1896 and became its first president, an appointment he held until his death.

Publications

1881 Epitaph of a Small Winner
1891 Philosopher or Dog?
1899 Dom Casmurro
1904 Esau and Jacob
1908 Counselor Ayres's Memorial

Published after he died

1963 The Psychiatrist and Other Stories
1977 The Devil's Church and Other Stories

MACHEN, Arthur

Welsh horror writer

Born Mar. 3, 1863
Died Dec. 12, 1947
Age at death 84

Arthur Machen is famous for his classic horror stories, which reflect his interest in witchcraft, folklore, religions and the study of demons. He was a master at creating sinister atmospheres.

Machen, the son of a clergyman, was born in a Welsh village, Caerleon-on-Usk, set among hills and woodland. His first work, a poem called *Eleusinia*, was published when he was 18. Before he was 20, he had moved to London, hoping to become a writer. He had no friends and very little money and spent most of his time wandering around the streets of London. Later, he set many of his horror stories in the city.

Machen began to earn a living by teaching and translating books. He then joined a company of actors and toured the country. After eight years, he returned to London to become a journalist. He also began to write horror stories for magazines. Though he worked hard, he earned very little money.

When Machen was 31, one of his horror stories, "The Great God Pan" (published in *The Great God Pan and the Inmost Light*), caused a sensation. It is the story of a scientist who operates on a girl's brain, causing her to see the cruel reality of the primitive natural world. She is so terrified by what she sees that she goes mad. Machen went on to write many more stories, often returning to the same theme: that ancient magic and folklore are more powerful forces than modern science.

When Machen was 80, he was rescued from poverty by a group of admirers in Britain and the US who raised some money for him so that he could live more comfortably. He died four years later.

Publications

1881 Eleusinia
1894 The Great God Pan and the Inmost Light
1895 The Three Impostors
1906 The House of Souls
1907 The Hill of Dreams
1917 The Terror
1923 The Shining Pyramid
1936 The Children of the Pool
1936 The Cosy Room

MACHIAVELLI, Niccolò

Italian philosopher and playwright

Born May 3, 1469
Died Jun. 26, 1527
Age at death 58

Niccolò Machiavelli was an important political thinker in early 16th-century Italy. The work for which he is best known, *The Prince*, is often seen as promoting ruthlessness in political leaders; it has been called "a handbook for tyrants."

Machiavelli was born into a scholarly family of lawyers in Florence, Italy, and was educated at home. At the age of 29, he got a government job in what was then the Republic of Florence. He was sent on a number of diplomatic missions to foreign courts, where he wasted no opportunity to study their politics. During this time, he was an energetic opponent of the tyrannical Medici family, who had formerly been in power and was plotting to return.

In 1512, the Medici succeeded in overthrowing the republic. Machiavelli was suspected of being involved in a major conspiracy against them and was arrested, but nothing could be proved. He was released and allowed to retire to the country, where, in 1513, he wrote his most celebrated work, *The Prince*. Originally titled *On Principalities*, the book contains advice to an imagined ruler, including recommendations that the ruler discourage political protest by the masses and preserve power by using violence when necessary.

Twelve years later, the Medici invited Machiavelli to return to the court and to write a history of Florence.

Today Machiavelli's name is used to describe cynical and crafty tactics, but this is not entirely fair. He strongly supported the view that individuals should lead moral lives, and it was only in political matters that he thought that efficiency of government might take priority over morality.

Publications

1513 The Prince
1513–21 The Discourses
1521 The Art of War
1524 The Mandrake
1525 The Clizia

Published after he died

1532 History of Florence

MacLACHLAN, Patricia

American children's writer

Born Mar. 3, 1938

Patricia MacLachlan is considered to be one of America's best children's authors. She is famous for writing about family relationships in a sensitive way.

MacLachlan was born Patricia Pritzkau in Cheyenne, Wyoming. She was raised in Wyoming and Minnesota. Both her parents were teachers, and they encouraged her to read from an early age. She had an active imagination and liked to act out scenes from her favorite books. An only child, she had an imaginary friend called Mary who sometimes got her into trouble. After attending local schools, she moved to the East Coast and attended the University of Connecticut. She graduated in 1962, and got married almost immediately, becoming Patricia MacLachlan. For most of the next two decades she taught English at a nearby secondary school while raising her three children. She also worked part time as a social worker, which involved working with foster mothers.

MacLachlan did not begin writing until she was in her 30s. Her children had become more independent, and she felt the need to do something new. As a mother she had become interested in children's literature, and she realized that she wanted to write. She read over 30 children's books a week and joined a writing class. Her first book, *The Sick Day*, came out when she was 41. Her most famous book is probably *Sarah, Plain and Tall.* It is the story of a "mail-order bride" who goes to Kansas to become the wife of a farmer and mother to his children. Sensitively and masterfully told, the story was a great success. MacLachlan also wrote the popular televised version, which was watched by 50 million viewers.

Publications

1979 The Sick Day
1980 Through Grandpa's Eyes
1980 Arthur, for the Very First Time
1982 Mama One, Mama Two
1984 Unclaimed Treasures
1985 Sarah, Plain and Tall
1988 The Facts and Fictions of Minna Pratt
1994 Skylark

MacLEAN, Alistair

Scottish thriller writer

Born Apr. 28, 1922
Died Feb. 2, 1987
Age at death 64

Alistair MacLean found fame and fortune as an author of adventure stories. Many of his novels were made into successful films for which he wrote the screenplays.

MacLean was born in Glasgow, the son of a minister. The family spoke the Scottish language, Gaelic, and English was MacLean's second language. Shortly after his birth the family moved north to Daviot, near Inverness. When he was 14, his father died suddenly, and MacLean returned to Glasgow with his mother. He left school at 17 and, after a short time working in an office, joined the navy. His years in service during World War II were eventful and provided material for his novels; he was captured by the Japanese and tortured. In 1946, he returned home, studied English at Glasgow University, and later became a teacher.

MacLean's writing career began at age 32 when he entered a short-story competition in the *Glasgow Herald* newspaper. The story won and led to a suggestion from a publisher that he should write a novel. The result was *HMS Ulysses*, which was based on MacLean's experiences on a navy ship escorting merchant vessels in the Arctic Ocean. It sold a quarter of a million copies in six months. His next novel, *The Guns of Navarone*, was even more successful, and MacLean gave up teaching and moved to Sweden. Although he became a prolific writer, producing on average one book a year, MacLean researched his novels thoroughly, making sure that they were technically correct.

Publications

1955 HMS Ulysses
1957 The Guns of Navarone
1961 Fear Is the Key
1962 The Golden Rendezvous
1963 Ice Station Zebra
1966 When Eight Bells Toll
1967 Where Eagles Dare
1968 Force 10 from Navarone
1970 Caravan to Vaccares
1974 Breakheart Pass

MacLEISH, Archibald

American poet and playwright

Born May 7, 1892
Died Apr. 20, 1982
Age at death 89

Publications

1924	*The Happy Marriage*
1925	*The Pot of Earth*
1926	*Streets in the Moon*
1928	*The Hamlet of A. MacLeish*
1932	*Conquistador*
1936	*Public Speech*
1952	*Collected Poems 1917–52*
1958	*J.B.*
1976	*New and Collected Poems 1917–76*

Archibald MacLeish, "the Poet Laureate of the New Deal," believed that poetry could be harnessed to serve the public good. The New Deal policies were adopted by President Franklin D. Roosevelt in the 1930s to improve social welfare and promote economic recovery.

Born in Glencoe, Illinois, MacLeish attended both Yale and Harvard universities. He taught at Harvard before practicing law in Boston. In 1923, MacLeish moved with his wife and family to France. His early poetry – such as his first book, *Towers of Ivory*, published when he was 25 – reflects the influences of EZRA POUND and T.S. ELIOT.

MacLeish returned to the United States at age 36. The poetry he wrote afterward highlighted his increasing awareness of social and economic problems. *Conquistador*, a narrative poem about the 15th-century Spanish conquest of Mexico, won him a Pulitzer Prize. MacLeish was awarded a second Pulitzer for *Collected Poems 1917–52*, and a third for his verse play *J.B.*

MacLeish's later works are perhaps more impersonal and patriotic than the earlier poems, but they broadly reflect his belief that it is possible to combine public service and private art. He was appointed librarian of Congress by Roosevelt in 1939 and kept this post until 1944. His other numerous public offices included chairman of the US delegation to the European conferences of 1945 and 1946 that established UNESCO. MacLeish also had a distinguished academic career; he held a professorship at Harvard from 1949 to 1962.

MacNEICE, Louis

Irish poet, novelist and playwright

Born Sep. 12, 1907
Died Sep. 3, 1963
Age at death 55

Louis MacNeice is best remembered for individual poems such as "Bagpipe Music" and "Autumn Journal," and also for *Letters from Iceland*, one of the most entertaining – and oddest – travel books of the 20th century.

MacNeice was born in Belfast. After his mother died, he was sent to be educated in England. His first collection of poems, *Blind Fireworks*, was published when he was 22 and still an undergraduate at Oxford University.

Two important things happened to MacNeice when he was 28. The publication of a collection of work entitled *Poems* established him as one of the brightest new talents of the 1930s, and his beloved wife suddenly left him. It took MacNeice a long time to recover from the loss, although this period did see the beginning of more and better poetry than he had written when he was happily married. It was also during this time that he and W.H. AUDEN wrote *Letters from Iceland*; the book, a mixture of prose and poetry, is an oddity because it says more about the inner life of its authors than it does about Iceland.

MacNeice's poetry is memorable more for its strong rhythms than for the boldness of its images. The high promise he showed in the 1930s was never quite fulfilled, although his last two volumes show that he was again approaching his best work.

MacNeice also taught in England and briefly the US and, from 1941 until his death, he worked for the BBC as a scriptwriter and producer of radio drama in verse.

Publications

1929 Blind Fireworks
1935 Poems
1937 Letters from Iceland
1938 Modern Poetry
1940 The Last Ditch
1941 Plant and Phantom
1948 Holes in the Sky, Poems 1944–47
1957 Visitations
1961 Solstices

MAETERLINCK, Maurice

Belgian playwright and poet

Born Aug. 29, 1862
Died May 6, 1949
Age at death 86

Maurice Maeterlinck was a Belgian playwright and poet best known for his involvement with the French literary movement called symbolism, which uses symbols to represent ideas and emotions. He was awarded the Nobel Prize for Literature in 1911.

Maeterlinck was born in Ghent, Belgium. He studied law at the University of Ghent and published his first poem, "The Rushes," when he was a 21-year-old university student. After graduating, Maeterlinck moved to Paris, gave up law and became closely involved with the symbolist movement. He was 27 when his first book of poetry, *Hot Houses*, came out.

In the same year, Maeterlinck wrote his first play, *The Princess Maleine* but, although printed, it was never performed. At 30, he wrote one of his best-known plays, *Pelléas and Mélisande*, which has a dreamlike quality and uses dark stage sets and haunting sound effects to create an emotional response from the audience. It was later made into an opera by the French composer Claude Debussy.

By 1896, Maeterlinck had moved away from his symbolist-inspired writing into a more realistic approach. Many works were written for his companion, the actress Georgette Leblanc. After their affair was over, he married Renée Dahon. In his later years, Maeterlinck became interested in philosophy and mysticism. He also wrote another well-known play, *The Blue Bird*, in which children search for a bird that represents happiness. This play recaptures the fairy-tale, dreamlike quality of *Pelléas and Mélisande*.

Publications

1883 "The Rushes"
1889 Hot Houses
1889 The Princess Maleine
1891 The Blind
1892 Pelléas and Mélisande
1896 Aglavaine and Selysette
1901 Ariadne and Bluebeard
1902 Sister Beatrice
1908 The Blue Bird
1918 The Burgomaster of Stilmonde

MAHFOUZ, Naguib

Egyptian novelist, short-story writer and playwright

Born Dec. 11, 1911

Publications

- *1943 Radobis*
- *1949 The Beginning and the End*
- *1956–57 The Cairo Trilogy*
- *1962 The Thief and the Dogs*
- *1965 The Beggar*
- *1967 Miramar*
- *1967 Children of Gebelawi*
- *1977 The Harafish*
- *1988 Qushtumor*
- *1997 Echoes of an Autobiography*

In 1988, Naguib Mahfouz became the first Arab to win the Nobel Prize for Literature. He has written some 40 novels and short-story collections, 30 screenplays, and many plays and is now one of the most widely read and translated Arabic authors in the world.

Mahfouz was born in Cairo, the capital of Egypt in North Africa. His father was a civil servant, and Mahfouz eventually followed in his footsteps. After graduating from Cairo University at the age of 23, he joined the Egyptian civil service, where he worked until retiring in 1971.

When he was a child, his mother often took him to museums to see the glories of ancient Egypt, and Egyptian history later became a major theme in many of his books. His most important work – a set of three novels published when Mahfouz was in his 40s and known as *The Cairo Trilogy* – deals with a period of great change in 20th-century Egypt. It follows the lives of its characters from World War I to after the 1952 military overthrow of the Egyptian king, Farouk. The trilogy is set in the parts of Cairo where Mahfouz grew up and still lives today.

Religion is often a theme in Mahfouz's books. *Children of Gebelawi*, one of his most controversial works, was banned in much of the Arab world for its portrayal of average Egyptians living the lives of Muhammad, Moses and Jesus. Mahfouz's work is still unavailable in many Arab countries because of his support of Egypt's 1979 Camp David peace treaty with Israel. In 1995, two Egyptians were sentenced to death for attempting to kill Mahfouz.

MAILER, Norman

American novelist and essayist

Born Jan. 31, 1923

Publications

- *1948 The Naked and the Dead*
- *1955 The Deer Park*

Norman Mailer, an American novelist and essayist, has written about American society and morals of the past 50 years. His work is often seen as controversial, since he explores the hidden motivations behind the behavior of individuals, groups, corporations and governments.

Born in Long Branch, New Jersey, Mailer was raised in Brooklyn, New York; at the age of nine, he wrote a 250-page story in notebooks, called "Invasion From Mars." He studied engineering at Harvard and was determined to be a writer, setting himself the goal of writing 3,000 words every day.

His first novel exploded onto the bestseller list in 1948. *The Naked and the Dead*, published when he was just 25, is an antiwar novel and draws upon his own battle experiences in the Pacific during World War II. *The Deer Park* – published seven years later – is about the corruption of values in Hollywood. During the 1960s, Mailer became a prominent campaigner and protestor. His work explored American consciousness and morals in this turbulent decade of the civil rights movement, political assassinations and other upheavals. Two of his books focus on American involvement in the Vietnam War: *The Armies of the Night*, which won the Pulitzer Prize for non-fiction in 1969, and *Why Are We in Vietnam?*

Mailer is a practitioner of the style known as "New Journalism," which applies the techniques of novel writing to depict real events and people. In 1980, he won a second Pulitzer Prize for *The Executioner's Song*, a portrait of a real-life prisoner on Death Row who insisted on his own execution.

1959 Advertisements for Myself
1965 An American Dream
1967 Why Are We in Vietnam?
1968 The Armies of the Night
1979 The Executioner's Song
1983 Ancient Evenings
1984 Tough Guys Don't Dance
1997 Gospel According to the Son

MALAMUD, Bernard

American novelist and short-story writer

Born Apr. 26, 1914
Died Mar. 18, 1986
Age at death 71

In his novels and short stories Bernard Malamud created characters who embody the often difficult relationship between Old World (usually Jewish) culture and the New World's striving for success at any price. He often wrote humorous but moral stories about the suffering of humankind.

Malamud was born in Brooklyn, New York City, to Russian-Jewish immigrants who ran a corner grocery store, a setting that later appeared in *The Assistant*, his novel set in the era of the Great Depression. His stories first appeared in his secondary school's literary magazine. In 1942, he received his Master's degree from Columbia University in New York. At the age of 32, he married Italian-American Ann de Chiara, who gave him an appreciation of Italian culture.

For some years Malamud taught English at Oregon State College. From 1961, to his death he taught at Bennington College in Vermont, dividing his time between Vermont, New York and Europe, especially Italy. From 1979 to 1981, he presided over the American chapter of PEN, a group that campaigns worldwide against the political repression of writers.

Malamud's first novel, *The Natural*, is the story of a baseball player who sacrifices his friends to further his career. In later novels and short stories, he portrays his (mostly Jewish) heroes as ordinary men trying to find a satisfactory life in a harsh world, thus using the image of the Jew as a symbol of all those who learn through suffering and struggle. In 1967, *The Fixer*, about a Jew accused of ritual murder in Russia just before the Russian Revolution, won both the Pulitzer Prize and the National Book Award.

Publications
1952 The Natural
1957 The Assistant
1958 The Magic Barrel
1961 A New Life
1963 Idiots First
1966 The Fixer
1971 The Tenants
1979 Dubin's Lives
1982 God's Grace
1983 The Stories of Bernard Malamud

MALLARMÉ, Stéphane

French poet

Born Mar. 18, 1842
Died Sep. 9, 1898
Age at death 56

Stéphane Mallarmé was one of the most influential French poets of the 19th century.

Born in Paris into a comfortable family in which careers in the French civil service were traditional, Mallarmé was expected to follow his father and grandfather into the same profession. At school he did not do well but became fascinated by the study of languages. It was also while still at school that he read and fell in love with the work of the great French poet CHARLES BAUDELAIRE. As a teenager he wrote poems in the style of his literary hero.

After leaving school Mallarmé, aged 21, visited England so that he could continue his study of English. While in London he also got married. On returning to France, he began a career as a schoolteacher, which forced him to move from one area of France to another far more often than he wished.

Mallarmé's first important poem, "L'Azur," was published when he was 24. He was fascinated by the power of language all his life and spent a very long time on each of his poems, making them as perfect as possible. He believed that the point of a poem was the beauty of the language and preferred to hint at meanings rather than state them clearly. The best examples of his carefully worked poetry are *Hérodiade*, "The Afternoon of the Faun," and his masterpiece, "A Throw of the Dice Will Never Abolish the Hazard." His work had a great influence on French literature in the 20th century.

Publications

1866	"L'Azur"
1869	*Hérodiade*
1876	"The Afternoon of a Faun"
1897	"A Throw of the Dice Will Never Abolish the Hazard"

MALORY, Sir Thomas

English writer

Born Unknown
Died Mar. 14, 1471
Age at death Unknown

Sir Thomas Malory was a mediaval English writer. His only book, *The Death of Arthur* (also known as *Morte d'Arthur*), has become the best-known version of the legend of King Arthur and his knights of the Round Table. It has inspired generations of writers all over the world.

Historians believe that Malory owned an estate called Newbold Revell roughly in the center of England and that he inherited this land from his father in 1433 or 1434. The date of Malory's birth is unknown, but he was probably still a young man when his father died.

In medieval England, a man who owned land had a duty to serve as a knight for a local ruler of a higher rank. Malory fought in France during the Hundred Years' War and then in the Wars of the Roses, a civil war that divided England in the late 15th century.

For much of his life Malory was in constant trouble with the law. This led him into adventures that could have come straight from a story about King Arthur himself. Malory was charged with theft, cattle rustling, attempted murder and breaking into a monastery. On one occasion, he fought his way out of a castle prison and escaped by swimming the moat. Many of the charges against him were probably made up by his enemies. This was common in war-torn England of the time.

Whether the charges against him were true or false, Malory spent many years of his life in prison. *The Death of Arthur* was written while he was in prison and published 14 years after his death.

Published after he died

1485 The Death of Arthur

MALRAUX, André

André Malraux was a major 20th-century novelist who was also an archeologist interested in art. His novels are based on his experiences of war, revolution and struggles for political freedom.

Malraux was born in Paris, France, into a wealthy family and studied Asian cultures at college. At age 21, he traveled to the French colony of Indochina in Southeast Asia to look for a temple and then went to China, where he was involved in a communist revolution. His first novel, *The Conquerors*, published when he was 27, and his next two novels are based on his experiences in Asia. *Man's Fate* is about politically oppressed people and how heroic actions and loyalty can help overcome human suffering; it won the Prix Goncourt, the most important French literary prize.

In 1936, Malraux was a pilot on the Republican side in the Spanish Civil War. In his novel *Man's Hope* he shows his commitment to the cause of democracy in Spain. During World War II, Germany invaded France, and Malraux was captured. Later he escaped and led a resistance unit against the German occupation. After the war, he served briefly as a government minister.

In the 1940s and '50s, Malraux gave up novel writing and turned to the history of art. In *The Voices of Silence* he wrote that works of art could help mankind be noble and overcome tragic fate.

Malraux was a friend of Charles de Gaulle, the postwar president of France, and one of his last books, *Felled Oaks*, reports their final conversations.

French novelist and essayist

Born Nov. 3, 1901

Died Nov. 23, 1976

Age at death 75

Publications

1928 The Conquerors

1930 The Royal Way

1933 Man's Fate

1935 Days of Wrath

1937 Man's Hope

1943 The Walnut Trees of Altenburg

1947–49 The Psychology of Art

1951 The Voices of Silence

1967 Anti-Memoirs

1971 Felled Oaks

MAMET, David

American playwright and screenwriter

Born Nov. 30, 1947

David Mamet has written many plays and is known especially for *Glengarry Glen Ross*, which won the Pulitzer Prize in 1984.

Mamet was born in the Jewish section of Chicago's South Side and attended public school before going on to Goddard College in Vermont. In the 1970s, he returned there as artist-in-residence. Mamet was strongly influenced by his experiences at Goddard and with the Neighborhood Playhouse School of Theater in New York City. In his writing he imitates acting exercises, encouraging performers to develop characters by constant repetition. The resulting dialogues consist of half-spoken thoughts and quickly changing moods. His work usually involves a few characters in a limited space and conversations and arguments in sharp, everyday language, often slang. A main theme is the disappointment of Americans in the American Dream – their sense that life has not come up to expectations.

Mamet's first plays, *Sexual Perversity in Chicago*, about the progress and failure of relationships between young people, and *Duck Variations*, the conversations of two old men on a park bench, were staged in small theaters off-Broadway when Mamet was 25. These plays marked him as a writer of new realism. Set in a Chicago junk store, *American Buffalo* is a shocking attack on American big business, with its grim outlook and antisocial bias. *Glengarry Glen Ross* is about real estate agents who will do anything to make a sale. Mamet has also written successful screenplays, nonfiction, and a novel, *The Village*.

Publications

1972 Sexual Perversity in Chicago
1972 Duck Variations
1975 American Buffalo
1983 Glengarry Glen Ross
1987 Writing in Restaurants
1988 Speed-the-Plow
1993 Oleanna
1994 The Village
1995 The Cryptogram
1997 The Old Neighborhood

MANDELSTAM, Osip

Russian poet and essayist

Born Jan. 15, 1891
Died Dec. 27, 1938
Age at death 47

Osip Mandelstam is regarded as one of Russia's finest 20th-century poets.

Born into a Jewish, middle-class family in Warsaw, Poland, Mandelstam was raised in St. Petersburg, Russia, where at that time only privileged Jews were permitted to live. He spent several years traveling in western Europe before returning to study philosophy at St. Petersburg University.

Mandelstam was recognized as an important new poet with the publication of his first volume of poems, *Stone*, when he was 22. The poems in this collection are full of vivid details and range in subject matter from music to human culture. Along with Anna Akhmatova, he founded a literary movement known as acmeism, which revolutionized Russian poetry. It promoted the use of very clear and direct language to describe real people's thoughts and feelings.

In 1922, Mandelstam married Nadezhda Khazina, who accompanied him throughout his years of exile and imprisonment. Mandelstam was not politically active, but in 1934, after writing a short poem ridiculing the communist leader Joseph Stalin, he was exiled to Siberia for three years. He and Nadezhda then returned to Moscow in 1937, where they lived in poverty until he was again arrested for "counterrevolutionary" activities and sentenced to five years' hard labor. He died at the labor camp. His later poems, collected in five notebooks, were published after his death. They are mainly concerned with the survival of Russia's artistic and moral heritage at a time when the future for many people in Soviet Russia looked bleak.

Publications

1913 Stone
1922 Tristia
1925 The Noise of Time
1928 The Egyptian Stamp
1928 Poems 1921–25
1933 Journey to Armenia
c. 1933 Conversations about Dante

Published after he died

1973 The Complete Poetry of Osip Mandelstam

MANN, Thomas

German novelist

Born Jun. 6, 1875
Died Aug. 12, 1955
Age at death 80

At age 25 Thomas Mann became one of the leading novelists of 20th-century Germany.

Mann came from a wealthy, middle-class family. In his early 20s he worked in business but wanted to be a writer. A change in his family's fortunes inspired him to write a long, detailed family novel, *Buddenbrooks*, which was an immediate success and made his reputation. For such a young man this was a remarkably mature work.

During the next 20 years or so, Mann concentrated on short novels, or novellas. But at age 49 he published his second long novel, *The Magic Mountain*. This book, set in a hospital for patients recovering from tuberculosis, had started as a short story but grew into a long and serious novel. It earned Mann the 1929 Nobel Prize for Literature and established him as a novelist of international fame.

Mann then embarked on his most ambitious work, a modern version of the biblical story of Joseph and his brothers. Published in four volumes between 1933 and 1943, and together known as *Joseph and His Brothers*, the work concerns the conflict between personal freedom and political tyranny. During the writing he was forced, as a free and outspoken spirit, to leave Germany, which was then under the control of the Nazis. He went to the United States, where he produced his final great work, *Doctor Faustus*. It is a version of a German legend in which a man, Faust, makes a deal with the devil. In *Doctor Faustus,* Mann was probably making a comment on the destructive course of Nazi Germany.

Publications

1901 Buddenbrooks
1903 Tonio Kröger
1903 Tristan
1909 Royal Highness
1912 Death in Venice
1924 The Magic Mountain
1933–43 Joseph and His Brothers
1939 Lotte in Weimar
1947 Doctor Faustus
1954 Felix Krull, Confidence Man

MANSFIELD, Katherine

New Zealand short-story writer

Born Oct. 14, 1888
Died Jan. 9, 1923
Age at death 34

Katherine Mansfield is one of New Zealand's most famous writers. Her short stories, noted for their use of stream of conciousness, are about everyday events in the lives of ordinary women.

Mansfield was born Katherine Beauchamp to a middle-class family in Wellington, New Zealand. She lived for six years in the rural village of Karori. As a teenager she attended Queen's College, London, to study music. In 1906, aged 18, she returned to New Zealand, her father having denied her the opportunity to become a professional cello player. She decided instead to become a writer. Her lifelong friend, Ida Baker, persuaded Mansfield's father to allow Katherine to return once more to England in 1908. She was never to see New Zealand again.

In London, Mansfield led an unconventional life, attracted to both women and men. Initially, she contributed work to the British literary magazine *New Age* and went on to have stories published in various journals. During her life only three volumes of her short stories were published. Her first volume, *In a German Pension*, came out when she was 23 and includes mainly satirical sketches of German characters.

The shock of her brother's death during World War I led Mansfield to write stories drawing on her childhood in New Zealand, published as *Bliss and Other Stories*. This collection includes some of her best writing and is characterized by sharp, realistic descriptions of places and people. Mansfield's second marriage was to critic and editor John Middleton Murry, after a long romantic and writing relationship.

Publications

1911	*In a German Pension*
1920	*Bliss and Other Stories*
1922	*The Garden Party and Other Stories*

Published after she died

1923	*The Dove's Nest*
1923	*Poems*
1927	*The Journal*
1928	*The Letters*

MANZONI, Alessandro

Italian novelist and poet

Born Mar. 7, 1785
Died May 22, 1873
Age at death 88

Alessandro Manzoni's reputation as the greatest novelist in Italian literature is based on his only novel, *The Betrothed*, a compassionate portrayal of 17th-century Italy.

Manzoni was born in Milan, Italy, the son of a noble family. His parents separated when he was a boy, and at age 20 he went to Paris in France to live with his mother. The following year, he published his first book of poems. In Paris, he became aware of literary developments in Europe and recovered his religious faith. Reconciled to Roman Catholicism, he was restored to a deep faith that he expressed in strongly religious poetry with titles such as "The Resurrection," "The Passion" and "Pentecost."

Manzoni turned to drama and wrote two verse tragedies modeled on WILLIAM SHAKESPEARE's plays. Then, inspired by the work of SIR WALTER SCOTT, he produced *I promessi sposi*, known in English as *The Betrothed*, when he was 42. His only novel, it was an immense success and made Manzoni famous all over Europe. It is now widely regarded as one of the greatest works of Italian literature. Although on the surface an adventure story set in the plague-ridden Milan of the 17th century, *The Betrothed* deals with some deeply important matters. It contains brilliant characterization and an entirely convincing portrayal of human virtue and the triumph of good over evil.

In 1860, Manzoni became a senator in a unified Italy. The composer Giuseppe Verdi was so impressed by Manzoni that in 1874 he dedicated his *Requiem Mass* as a memorial to him.

Publications

1815–22 Sacred Hymns
1820 Il Conte di Carmagnola
1821 The Fifth of May
1822 Adelchi
1827 The Betrothed

MARINETTI, Filippo Tommaso

Italian writer

Born Dec. 22, 1876
Died Dec. 2, 1944
Age at death 67

Marinetti is remembered as the founder of the Futurism movement, which insisted that all links with the past should be broken and artists and writers should practice total freedom of expression.

Although Italian, he was born in Alexandria, Egypt, and studied in both France and Italy. Such early volumes of poetry as *Destruction*, written in French, were ignored, but he was later to stir up interest with his outspoken "Futurist Manifesto," which he published in the Paris daily paper *Le Figaro* when he was 33. This was the start of Futurism. The manifesto glorified war, speed, violence and modern technology.

Marinetti became even better known when he published an experimental novel, *Mafarka the Futurist*, and followed this up with a series of lectures and demonstrations insisting that in politics, literature, music, art and architecture, all traditional forms should be abandoned. To set an example, Marinetti began to write poems and plays without commas, full stops and descriptive words, and with unusual sentence structures. The result was unclear and difficult to read, and his ideas had a more lasting influence than his writings.

Marinetti welcomed World War I with enthusiasm. His support of the fascist leader, Benito Mussolini, led to Marinetti's nomination to the Royal National Academy in 1929. Eight years later, Marinetti was appointed president of the academy. He died on Lake Como in north Italy.

Publications

1904 Destruction
1910 Mafarka the Futurist
1911 Futurism
1914 Zang Tumb Tumb: The Siege of Adrianople
1915 War the Only Hygiene of the World
1916 Synthetic Futurist Theater
1920 Manifesto of Futurism
1924 Futurism and Fascism

MARLOWE, Christopher

English poet and playwright

Born Feb. 1564
Died May 30, 1593
Age at death 29

Christopher Marlowe was the first great dramatist of the English theater and the most important writer of tragedy before WILLIAM SHAKESPEARE.

Marlowe was the son of a shoemaker in the city of Canterbury and attended the King's School there. At 17, he went to Cambridge University on a scholarship. He graduated after three years and then stayed on to study for a higher degree. This was nearly refused because he had been away too much from his studies, but the university relented when an official letter arrived saying he had been on government business. Historians believe that he had been abroad, working as a spy.

In London, Marlowe made important friends, including Sir Walter Raleigh, who had started the first colony in Virginia. In 1589, Marlowe was imprisoned after a brawl in which a man was killed. He was involved in another street fight in 1592, and in 1593 he was murdered in a dockside tavern. The official story was that he had been stabbed in the eye during an argument over the bill, but a week earlier a warrant had been issued for Marlowe's arrest, and his former roommate, THOMAS KYD had been tortured to make him give information about Marlowe. Many people think that Marlowe was deliberately silenced to stop him exposing secrets about powerful people.

Marlowe first began to write poems and plays at university. It is not known exactly when his tragedies were written. Both parts of his greatest tragedy, *Tamburlaine the Great*, had been performed by the time he was 23. Marlowe wrote his dramas in blank verse.

Publications

c. 1587 *Tamburlaine the Great* (in two parts)
c. 1588 *Doctor Faustus*
c. 1589 *The Jew of Malta*
1592 *The Massacre at Paris*
c. 1592 *Edward II*

Published after he died

1594 *Dido, Queen of Carthage*
1598 *Hero and Leander*
1599 *The Passionate Shepherd*

MARQUAND, John P.

American novelist and short-story writer

Born Nov. 10, 1893
Died Jul. 16, 1960
Age at death 66

John P. Marquand was one of the most popular and successful novelists writing in mid-20th-century America. His affectionate but satirical portraits of upper-class Bostonians are drawn from his own life experience.

John Phillips Marquand was born in Wilmington, Delaware, and brought up in New York, Boston and Newburyport, Massachusetts, from where his prominent upper-class family originated. He attended public schools until his father left to work in Panama after going bankrupt in 1907; Marquand was left in the care of his aunts. He then attended Newburyport High School, where he felt socially out of place. This insecurity increased when he became a scholarship student at Harvard in 1911; many of the characters in his writing would later reflect the sense of social and financial inadequacy he had felt. He graduated in 1914 and worked as a reporter until 1917, when he joined the army and saw heavy fighting in France during World War I.

After the war, Marquand wrote many stories for popular magazines such as the *Saturday Evening Post*. His first novel, *The Unspeakable Gentleman*, was published when he was 29. By the mid-1930s, he had devoted himself to novel writing, including the popular Mr. Moto series about a Japanese detective. His most famous novel, *The Late George Apley*, won the Pulitzer Prize in 1938. This and two subsequent novels, *Wickford Point* and *H.M. Pulham, Esquire*, provide a telling portrait of Boston society and those who unsuccessfully challenge class and custom.

Publications

1922	*The Unspeakable Gentleman*
1937	*The Late George Apley*
1939	*Wickford Point*
1941	*H.M. Pulham, Esquire*
1943	*So Little Time*
1945	*Repent in Haste*
1949	*Point of No Return*
1951	*Melville Goodwin, USA*
1955	*Sincerely, Willis Wayde*
1958	*Women and Thomas Harrow*

MARSH, Ngaio

New Zealand crime writer

Born Apr. 23, 1899
Died Feb. 18, 1982
Age at death 82

Ngaio Marsh is remembered as one of the great writers of popular mystery novels or "whodunits" – entertaining stories in which the reader has to figure out from clues in the text which character is guilty of murder.

Marsh was born and educated in Christchurch, New Zealand. She attended art school and initially wanted to become a painter but soon became attracted to the theater. She became an actress and theatrical producer in New Zealand but then decided to move to England when she was 33. In London, she supported herself by writing travel articles for a New Zealand newspaper. During this time she also tried her hand at writing novels and plays.

When World War II broke out, Marsh returned to New Zealand and drove a hospital bus. After the war she set up a theater company to teach young actors and stayed involved with the project for many years.

Marsh's first novel, *A Man Lay Dead*, was published when she was 35. In it, she introduced Inspector Roderick Alleyn, a forgetful but intelligent detective. His assistant is the reliable Inspector Fox. In their conversations together they often quote from William Shakespeare. Alleyn and Fox appear in a whole series of novels. Marsh's early stories are set in the country houses of the English upper classes in the traditional style of British mystery writers like Agatha Christie. She also used her experiences of travel and the theater in many of her novels. Her later books are set in New Zealand. In 1966, Marsh was given the honorary title Dame of the British Empire.

Publications

1934	*A Man Lay Dead*
1936	*Death in Ecstacy*
1938	*Death in a White Tie*
1941	*Death and the Dancing Footman*
1947	*Final Curtain*
1951	*Night at the Vulcan*
1959	*False Scent*
1970	*When in Rome*
1972	*Tied Up in Tinsel*
1980	*Photo-Finish*

MARSHALL, Paule

American novelist and short-story writer

Born Apr. 9, 1929

Paule Marshall's fiction powerfully conveys the experience of being a young African-American woman caught between two worlds: her native New York and the Caribbean community of her family.

Marshall was born in Brooklyn, but her parents were immigrants from Barbados, and she grew up surrounded by West Indian influences. She was writing poetry by age nine, after having visited Barbados. The country made a strong impression on her and features in her later work.

At age 21, Marshall married. She and her husband had one son but divorced in 1963. She later remarried. After graduating with honors from Brooklyn College, Marshall worked as a researcher for *Our World*, a small black journal in New York. Her first novel, *Brown Girl, Brownstones*, was published when she was 30. It describes the experiences of a young girl growing up in the Barbadian community in Brooklyn who feels isolated from both the white and black communities. The girl longs to be white, but as she matures, she learns that her community is part of her; she cannot reject it. This story of a young girl's coming of age is now a classic of African-American literature.

Marshall's story "To Da-duh, in Memoriam" (published in the collection *Reena and Other Stories*) retells a young girl's visit to Barbados to stay with her grandmother, just as the young Marshall had. The grandmother, Da-duh, represents the heritage that Marshall wanted to reclaim, and the story shows the way the young girl comes to terms with the conflicts in this heritage: the warmth of Barbados, on the one hand, and the cold concrete of New York.

Publications

1959	*Brown Girl, Brownstones*
1961	*Soul Clap Hands and Sing*
1969	*The Chosen Place, the Timeless People*
1983	*Praisesong for the Widow*
1983	*Merle, a Novella and Other Stories*
1984	*Reena and Other Stories*
1991	*Daughters*

MARTÍ, José

Cuban writer

Born Jan. 28, 1853
Died May 19, 1895
Age at death 42

José Martí is remembered for both his literary talent and his political leadership. He is the principal symbol of Cuba's fight for independence from Spain.

Born in Havana, Cuba, the son of a Spanish army sergeant, Martí had published a number of poems by the age of 15. When he was 16, he started a newspaper called *The Free Fatherland* to promote the cause of Cuban independence. He was soon arrested and sentenced to six months' imprisonment with hard labor. At the age of 18, he was deported to Spain, where he continued his studies and earned a law degree.

For a few years Martí lived in France, Mexico and Guatemala, working as a teacher and writing on politics. He returned to Cuba when he was 25, but his political activities again angered the authorities, and he was again exiled to Spain. After more traveling he returned to New York City, where he lived the rest of his life, writing newspaper articles, poems and essays on political freedom. He also founded the Cuban Revolutionary Party. These activities made him a hero throughout Latin America. In January 1895, Martí set off for Santo Domingo to take part in a revolutionary invasion of Cuba that he had organized. The invasion began in April, and the following month Martí was killed in battle.

Martí wrote poems, stories and a novel. With its vivid imagery and simple language his work signalled the start of modern Latin American literature. His best-known poem is "Guantanamera," which has been set to music and is a favorite of Cubans even today.

Publications

1882 Ismaelillo
1885 Ill-Omened Friendship
1891 Simple Verses
1891 Our America

Published after he died

1898 The Golden Age
1936–53 Complete Works
1978 Writings on Latin America and the Cuban Struggle for Independence

MARTIN du GARD, Roger

French novelist and dramatist

Born Mar. 23, 1881
Died Aug. 28, 1958
Age at death 77

Roger Martin du Gard's literary reputation rests on his eight-part novel *Les Thibault* (also known as *The World of the Thibaults*). He was awarded the Nobel Prize for Literature in 1937.

Martin du Gard was born in the Paris suburb of Neuilly-sur-Seine, France. He studied history and then qualified as a librarian and as an expert in old handwriting and manuscripts.

At the age of 27, he published a novel, *Becoming!*, and decided to be a writer. *Jean Barois*, published five years later, brought him to the attention of the writer André Gide, who became his lifelong friend. It is the story of a man's mental struggle between the Roman Catholic faith he was brought up with and his adult desire for wealth. It also deals in detail with the Dreyfus affair – a famous French court case in 1893 in which Alfred Dreyfus, a Jewish army officer, was wrongly jailed for spying.

After military service in the French Army during World War I, Martin du Gard became a recluse and devoted himself to writing. His saga about the Thibault family was published in eight parts between 1922 and 1940. It is about how members of the family react to the moral, religious and social problems facing the French middle class between the beginning of the century and World War I. This was the period of the rise and spread of communism. The novel shows how the family relationships are affected by the changing beliefs and loyalties of its members and by the war.

Publications

1908 Becoming!
1913 Jean Barois
1914 Old Leleu's Will
1922–40 Les Thibault (Parts 1–8)
1931 A Silent Man
1931 African Confidence
1933 The Postman
1951 Notes on André Gide

MARVELL, Andrew

English poet, essayist and satirist

Born Mar. 31, 1621
Died Aug. 18, 1678
Age at death 57

Andrew Marvell was a famous 17th-century English political writer and satirist. It was not until the 20th century that he was also recognized as a great poet. His writing is dominated by the themes of political unrest that rocked England in his lifetime.

Marvell was born in the north of England. After studying at Cambridge University, he spent four years traveling around Europe. While he was away, civil war broke out in England as Oliver Cromwell fought to overthrow the king (English Civil War). The king was defeated and executed, and England became a republic ruled by Cromwell. Marvell was convinced that the republican cause was right, and at age 29 he wrote his most famous poem, *An Horatian Ode upon Cromwell's Return from Ireland*, in praise of its hero. It is perhaps the best political poem written in English. For a time Marvell worked as a tutor for the daughter of a powerful lord. He wrote many beautiful verses about rural and legendary subjects during this happy period of his life. A famous example is the romantic poem "To His Coy Mistress."

Marvell was recommended to Cromwell by his friend, the great poet John Milton. In 1654 he became the unofficial "court" poet to Cromwell. A year before the restoration of the monarchy Marvell, aged 39, was elected to parliament as representative for the northern city of Hull. He kept this job until his death, and he continued to write savage satires that mocked the new king and his government, often putting himself in danger of imprisonment.

Publications

1650 An Horatian Ode upon Cromwell's Return from Ireland
1677 Account of the Growth of Popery and Arbitrary Government

Published after he died

1681 Miscellaneous Poems
1689–97 Poems on Affairs of State

MASEFIELD, John

English poet, novelist and playwright

Born Jun. 1, 1878
Died May 12, 1967
Age at death 88

John Masefield was a popular English poet and novelist known for his tales of life at sea. In 1930, he became Poet Laureate, a post he held until his death nearly 40 years later.

Masefield was born in a small English rural town. His mother died when he was six, and he was brought up by relatives. At the age of 13, Masefield began training for the merchant navy and, at 16, he made his first voyage aboard a sailing ship to Chile.

After only his second voyage, Masefield abandoned his ship in America and spent two years taking any job he could in and around New York City. Although he had not enjoyed serving in the merchant navy, the sea had left a deep impression on him. Returning to England, he worked as a newspaper journalist and began writing poems and stories about his experiences. His first book, *Salt-Water Ballads*, was published when he was 24. It includes one of his most famous poems, "Sea Fever," which is about the compulsion a sailor feels to return to the sea.

Two more collections of sea-inspired verses followed before Masefield wrote *The Everlasting Mercy*, a long story-poem about the religious conversion of a rough street criminal. Masefield went on to write almost 50 volumes of poetry, including several more story-poems. One of these, *Reynard the Fox*, is based on his childhood experience of rural life.

Masefield's poetry was very popular in his time. He also wrote 8 plays, more than 20 novels, and several children's stories.

Publications

1902 Salt-Water Ballads
1910 Ballads and Poems
1911 The Everlasting Mercy
1919 Reynard the Fox
1924 Sard Harker
1926 Odtaa
1927 The Midnight Folk
1941 In the Mill
1952 So Long to Learn
1966 Grace Before Plowing

MASTERS, Edgar Lee

American poet
Born Aug. 23, 1868
Died Mar. 5, 1950
Age at death 81

Edgar Lee Masters was one of the most important early 20th-century American poets. His first major work was hugely successful, but nothing he produced after it was as well received.

Born in Garnett, Kansas, Masters grew up in Lewistown and Petersburg, Illinois, near the Spoon River. These villages were the models for the fictional village where he set the poems in his first major collection, *Spoon River Anthology*, which was published when he was 47. In these poems past inhabitants of the village tell their stories from beyond the grave. The idea came from Masters's mother, with whom he discussed people they used to know in the villages.

At age 47, Masters, who was also a successful lawyer for 30 years, contracted pneumonia through overwork. His legal clients were decreasing partly due to the notoriety of his poems. One critic said they were full of "seductions, liaisons and perversions"; many did not like the way he wrote openly about sex and broke poetry's rules.

Masters's later work was never as well received as *Spoon River Anthology*, and his marriage was in trouble. He became angry and frustrated. This came through in his writing, and he was criticized for blaming others and not being objective.

There were other successes, however – when he was 56, Masters brought out *The New Spoon River*, another collection of poetry and his second most important work. He also wrote biographies of MARK TWAIN, Abraham Lincoln, and the American poet, Vachel Lindsay.

Publications

1910 Songs and Sonnets
1912 Songs and Sonnets: Second Series
1915 Spoon River Anthology
1924 The New Spoon River
1931 Lincoln: The Man
1935 Vachel Lindsay
1936 Across Spoon River: An Autobiography
1938 Mark Twain: A Portrait

MATHESON, Richard

American horror/ science fiction writer

Born Feb. 20, 1926

Richard Matheson is best known for his work as a writer on the TV series *The Twilight Zone*.

Matheson was born and grew up in Allendale, New Jersey. His writing was first published in a local newspaper when he was nine years old. After attending university, he began to sell his stories to magazines. At 24, he published his first story, "Born of Man and Woman," a tale told from the point of view of a mutant child who is ill-treated by his parents and who secretly plots his revenge on them. The story shocked many of the magazine's readers. It later became the title story of Matheson's first collection of short stories.

Matheson went on to write many memorable stories that combine elements of science fiction, horror and fantasy in a new way and emphasize his characters' sense of being outsiders in an alien, hostile world.

When he was 30, Matheson wrote a science fiction novel called *The Shrinking Man*, which was later made into a film. Several of his other works, including an early novel about vampires, *I Am Legend*, have also been adapted for film.

Matheson's involvement with the movie studio that produced the film of *The Shrinking Man* gave him the opportunity to break into screenwriting. He became a writer for detective, Western and science fiction television series. His stories for *The Twilight Zone* were particularly inventive. They explored the boundaries between normal life and the supernatural, raising the question of whether strange events really happen or whether they merely exist in the minds of frightened human beings.

Publications

1954 I Am Legend
1954 Born of Man and Woman
1956 The Shrinking Man
1957 The Shores of Space
1958 A Stir of Echoes
1959 Ride the Nightmare
1961 Shock
1971 Hell House
1975 Bid Time Return
1978 What Dreams May Come

MATTHIESSEN, Peter

American writer

Born May 22, 1927

Novelist and nature writer Peter Matthiesson explores the relationship between humans and their environment, describing the damage that "civilized" societies have done to nature and native cultures.

Matthiessen was born in New York City. After graduating from Yale University, he went to Paris and, at age 25, founded a literary magazine, *Paris Review*. Two years later came his first novel. *Race Rock* is the story of four middle-class young people, longtime friends, who cannot take control of their lives and so remain in destructive relationships with one another. Matthiessen's criticism of the educated middle classes, and particularly of the men among them, is a theme of his other two early novels, *Partisans* and *Raditzer*.

Matthiessen returned to the US in 1954 and worked as a commercial fisherman on Long Island. From the mid-1960s, when Matthiessen embarked on natural history expeditions to South America, Africa, New Guinea and the Northwest Territories, his fiction began to explore the conflicts between unspoiled nature, native cultures and the invading forces of "civilization," with its technology and destructive power. *At Play in the Fields of the Lord* (later made into a movie) is about the clash between missionaries and the Amazon Indian culture they try to tame. His travel and nature writings, which are as well known as his novels, describe the cultures and natural landscape of South America, New Guinea and other places. His award-winning book *The Snow Leopard* is an account of his search for this rare great cat in Tibet and of his own spiritual journey.

Publications

1954	*Race Rock*
1955	*Partisans*
1961	*Raditzer*
1961	*The Cloud Forest*
1965	*At Play in the Fields of the Lord*
1978	*The Snow Leopard*
1983	*In the Spirit of Crazy Horse*
1990	*Killing Mister Watson*
1991	*African Silences*
1997	*Lost Man's River*

MAUGHAM, W. Somerset

English playwright, short-story writer and novelist

Born Jan. 25, 1874
Died Dec. 16, 1965
Age at death 91

W(illiam) Somerset Maugham wrote with humor and often satire, sometimes basing his stories on the lives of real people. In his novels and short stories, he had a plain style but invariably told a story well.

Maugham was orphaned at the age of ten and was brought up by an aunt and uncle. After qualifying as a doctor, he gave up medicine to become a full-time writer. In his first novel, *Liza of Lambeth*, published when he was 23, he drew on his experiences of attending women in childbirth. Success came when he turned to the stage. At age 34, he had four plays running in London theaters.

During World War I Maugham served as a secret agent for the government. He then set off with a friend on a series of travels to eastern Asia, the Pacific Islands and Mexico. He eventually settled in the south of France.

Most of Maugham's early plays now seem dated. Some of his later work, notably *Our Betters*, about Americans in Europe, is on serious themes. *The Constant Wife* is about a wife who takes revenge on her unfaithful husband. A few of his many novels are outstanding. *Of Human Bondage* is based on his own life. *The Moon and Sixpence* was inspired by the life of the painter Paul Gauguin. *Cakes and Ale*, a happy book about the wife of a famous novelist, is probably based on THOMAS HARDY's life. In *The Razor's Edge,* a young American veteran seeks relief in India from the horrors of war. His stories include "Rain," which has been made into a play and movies.

Publications

1897	*Liza of Lambeth*
1915	*Of Human Bondage*
1917	*Our Betters*
1919	*The Moon and Sixpence*
1921	*The Circle*
1921	*The Trembling of a Leaf* (including "Rain")
1926	*The Constant Wife*
1930	*Cakes and Ale*
1944	*The Razor's Edge*

MAUPASSANT, Guy de

French short-story writer and novelist

Born Aug. 5, 1850
Died Jul. 6, 1893
Age at death 42

Guy de Maupassant is regarded as one of the world's finest short-story writers. His style is characterized by simplicity, directness, irony and sometimes sheer comedy. He excelled at revealing the hidden sides of people in his fiction.

Maupassant was born in Normandy in northern France. His parents separated when he was 11 years old. This led him to fear marriage and to be concerned about loneliness and persecution. He was expelled from school and went to study law in Paris. In 1870, the Franco-Prussian War began between France and what is now Germany. Maupassant's studies were interrupted, and, aged 20, he became a soldier. After the war, he joined the civil service and, under the influence of his mother's friend GUSTAVE FLAUBERT, started to write short stories. His first success, and one of his best short stories, "Ball of Fat" – about the defeat of France in the Franco-Prussian War – was published when he was 30.

Over the next ten years Maupassant published around 300 short stories, as well as novels, travel books and poems. Much of his work reflects his interest in the emotional problems of all classes and his passion for women. His best novels include *Pierre and Jean* and *Bel-Ami*. The latter was thought to be immoral because the hero succeeds by doing "bad" deeds.

Maupassant was a popular author in France and other countries and made a lot of money. He lived a hectic life and caught syphilis, a sexually transmitted disease, from one of his lovers. This led to his insanity, and he died in a mental asylum at the age of 42.

Publications

1880	"Ball of Fat"
1881	*The House of Madame Tellier*
1882	*Mademoiselle Fifi*
1883	*A Woman's Life*
1884	*Miss Harriet*
1885	*Bel-Ami*
1888	*Pierre and Jean*

MAURIAC, François

French novelist, poet and playwright

Born Oct. 11, 1885
Died Sep. 1, 1970
Age at death 84

François Mauriac, one of France's greatest 20th-century writers, won the Nobel Prize for Literature in 1952. He was also elected, in 1933, to the French Academy – a group of top scholars and writers.

Mauriac was born into a middle-class family in the southwestern town of Bordeaux. He studied first at the University of Bordeaux and then in Paris, but writing became more important to him, and he left without completing his degree. His first publication, a book of poems called *Joined Hands*, came out when he was 24. It was with his novels, however, that he made his name. *Young Man in Chains*, published when he was 28, is the first of many that draw on his experience of middle-class life in Bordeaux.

In the 1930s, Mauriac began writing essays for a French newspaper called *Le Figaro*. At that time, fascism was becoming a powerful force in many European countries, and Mauriac often attacked its extreme ideas in his essays. During World War II, Mauriac worked for the French Resistance, which fought against German occupation.

His novels often explore relationships that lack love. An example is *Thérèse*, in which a wife is driven to murder her husband. Mauriac's belief in Roman Catholicism was a major influence on his work. He saw a problem in writing about the evil side of people without making it seem attractive and tempting to the reader. *God and Mammon* is a nonfiction work in which he tried to solve this problem.

When he was 53, Mauriac began to write plays. He also published journals, memoirs and a biography of the French president Charles de Gaulle.

Publications

1909	*Joined Hands*
1913	*Young Man in Chains*
1922	*The Kiss to the Leper*
1925	*The Desert of Love*
1928	*Thérèse*
1929	*God and Mammon*
1932	*Viper's Tangle*
1934–51	*Journals*
1938	*Asmodée*
1959–67	*Memoirs*

MAYAKOVSKY, Vladimir

Russian poet and playwright

Born Jul. 19, 1893
Died Apr. 14, 1930
Age at death 36

Vladimir Mayakovsky is best known for his revolutionary poems.

Mayakovsky was born in Georgia, Russia. After his father's death he moved with his family to Moscow, where they lived in poverty. When he was 15, Mayakovsky joined a communist group. He was arrested many times and began writing poetry while in prison. He helped found the Russian Futurists, a group of revolutionary poets who wanted to find new ways of writing. Two major poems from his early 20s include "A Cloud in Trousers" and "The Backbone Flute." They describe unhappy love affairs and Mayakovsky's discontent with Russian society.

Mayakovsky wholeheartedly supported the Russian Revolution of 1917 and celebrated it in poems such as "Ode to Revolution" and "Left March." When he was 25, he produced his most important work, a verse play called *Mystery Bouffe*. It describes a struggle between two groups, the "Unclean" working class and the "Clean" upper class. The "Unclean" defeat the "Clean" and create a workers' paradise on Earth. The play was extremely popular, and for a few years Mayakovsky was the chief poet of the revolution. When Lenin, the communist leader, died in 1924, Mayakovsky wrote a 3,000-line poem in his honor.

In his final years, Mayakovsky became critical of some of the changes in Russia. He wrote two satirical plays, *The Bedbug* and *The Bathhouse*, that attacked Soviet officials. The banning of his work and an unhappy love affair both contributed to his suicide.

Publications

1915	"A Cloud in Trousers"
1916	"The Backbone Flute"
1917	*War and Peace*
1918	"Ode to Revolution"
1918	*Mystery Bouffe*
1919	"Left March"
1922	*I Love*
1928	*The Bedbug*
1929	*The Bathhouse*
1929–30	*At the Top of My Voice*

McBAIN, Ed

American crime writer

Born Oct. 15, 1926

Ed McBain is best known as the crime writer who perfected the "police procedural" – that is, a story about the work of a whole police department in solving a crime, rather than the work of just one detective.

Ed McBain is the pen name of Salvatore Lombino. He also wrote under other pen names, most famously as Evan Hunter for the book *The Blackboard Jungle*. This book highlights the problem of bad behavior and crime in America's schools and was made into a well-known film.

McBain was born and educated in New York City. After completing his military service, he taught in secondary schools and worked for a literary agency. In 1956, aged 30, he introduced a series of books about crime in the 87th Precinct of an imaginary city called Isola, which is obviously modeled on New York. The fictional 87th Precinct McBain describes ranges from rich suburbs to poor tenements.

The books became very popular and were made into a television series called *87th Precinct*. These stories set the standard for later TV police series such as *Hill Street Blues*, *NYPD Blue* and *Homicide*. McBain was part of a new generation of crime writers whose work was influenced by television as much as by film. He is an extremely versatile author who has also written for TV and film, including the screenplay for Alfred Hitchcock's famous thriller *The Birds*.

As well as producing more than 35 crime books, McBain has continued to write novels and short stories on other themes under the name Evan Hunter.

Publications

1954 The Blackboard Jungle
1956 Cop Hater
1958 Lady Killer
1960 Give the Boys a Great Big Hand
1965 Doll
1972 Sadie When She Died
1983 Ice
1989 Lullaby
1995 Romance

McCAFFREY, Anne

American science fiction/fantasy writer

Born Apr. 1, 1926

Anne McCaffrey is best known for her series of novels set on the imaginary planet Pern, which have made her one of America's most popular writers today.

McCaffrey was born in Cambridge, Massachusetts, the daughter of an army officer and a real estate agent. After leaving secondary school, she studied at Radcliffe College, graduating with honors. Against her family's advice she then became an actor and stage director for musicals and opera.

McCaffrey began to write fiction seriously after she had married and her children were in school. Her first novel, *Restoree*, was published when she was 41. It concerns a woman who goes adventuring in space and was written as a protest against the unrealistic women characters she had found in science fiction stories of the time.

Her next novel, *Dragonflight*, was the first in a series of novels about a lost planet, Pern, where human beings ride a race of great dragons. The dragons can breathe fire and are able to communicate by telepathy (mind reading) and travel through time.

The Pern series of novels captured the imagination of many readers and became extremely popular. Today many fans play Pern games on the Internet. The novels are often regarded as pure fantasy, although McCaffrey argues that her stories are based on common sense as well as science and thus are closer to science fiction.

Recently, McCaffrey has written a number of books with coauthors. She now lives in Ireland in a house she designed herself called Dragonhold.

Publications

1967 Restoree
1968 Dragonflight
1969 The Ship Who Sang
1971 Dragonquest
1976 Dragonsong
1979 Dragondrums
1985 Killashandra
1989 The Renegades of Pern
1991 All the Weyrs of Pern
1997 Dragonseye

McCARTHY, Cormac

American novelist

Born Jul. 20, 1933

Cormac McCarthy is best known for *All the Pretty Horses* and *The Crossing*, the first two novels in a series of three about Texas called *The Border Trilogy*.

McCarthy was born in Providence, Rhode Island, but moved with his parents to Knoxville, Tennessee, at an early age. He attended the Roman Catholic secondary school in Knoxville and later the University of Tennessee, where his studies were interrupted by four years' service in the US Air Force.

Many of McCarthy's earlier novels are set in his native eastern Tennessee. The characters in these novels are often social outcasts, people who are scorned by their communities, who do not have a job, a family or a home. His plots are sometimes violent, and the actions of the characters often shocking. In his first novel, *The Orchard Keeper*, published when he was 32, he describes the gruesome and tragic effect a murder has on the three main characters in the book. It is evidence of McCarthy's skill that the reader comes to understand and even to sympathize with the damaged people he writes about.

All the Pretty Horses, published when McCarthy was 59, is the story of a young boy – the last survivor of generations of Texas ranchers – who sets out to find the old American West that his parents and grandparents knew. Like *The Crossing*, published two years later, it is a classic coming-of-age adventure with two young men learning survival skills, facing danger and finding romance in late 1940s Mexico.

McCarthy lives in El Paso, Texas.

Publications

1965 The Orchard Keeper
1968 Outer Dark
1974 Child of God
1977 The Gardener's Son
1979 Suttree
1985 Blood Meridian
1992 All the Pretty Horses
1994 The Crossing
1994 The Stonemason
1998 Cities of the Plain

McCARTHY, Mary

American novelist and short-story writer

Born Jun. 21, 1912
Died Oct. 25, 1989
Age at death 77

Politics and the social pretenses of liberal intellectuals are at the heart of Mary McCarthy's work, which includes seven novels, many short stories and essays.

McCarthy was born in Seattle. Her parents both died of flu when she was six, and she was raised by relatives in a strict Catholic environment. This upbringing is the subject of one of her novels, the autobiographical *Memories of a Catholic Girlhood*. After attending public school she went to Vassar College, where she met the poets ELIZABETH BISHOP and MURIEL RUKEYSER.

McCarthy graduated with honors at age 21, and soon afterward she married the first of her four husbands and moved to New York City. There she mixed with writers and other intellectuals, and in 1942, at age 30, she published her first novel. *The Company She Keeps* is a satire about New York intellectuals. She often used her friends, and even herself, as models for her characters. *The Group*, her bestselling novel, focuses on a group of graduates and their experiences after university. It is a comic exploration of the values and lifestyles of university-educated, middle-class women, following the group of friends through first sexual experiences, marriage and domestic duties. The book was made into a movie in 1966.

In later works McCarthy explored political themes, including the Vietnam War, the Watergate scandal (in *The Mask of State*), and terrorism (in *Cannibals and Missionaries*). Most of her work, both fiction and nonfiction, is about the response of intellectuals to political and moral problems.

Publications

1942 The Company She Keeps
1949 The Oasis
1955 A Charmed Life
1957 Memories of a Catholic Girlhood
1961 On the Contrary
1963 The Group
1971 Birds of America
1974 The Mask of State
1979 Cannibals and Missionaries
1987 How I Grew

McCULLERS, Carson

American novelist

Born Feb. 19, 1917
Died Sep. 29, 1967
Age at death 50

Carson McCullers was one of the greatest novelists of the American South. Her best-known novels were completed by the time she was 34. She wrote about feelings that are common to a lot of us; about people who think they're different and don't fit in and who feel sad and lonely as a result.

McCullers was born Lula Carson Smith in Columbus, Georgia, and like her characters she didn't fit in too well when she was growing up. Encouraged by her mother, she spent a lot of time on her own, playing the piano and writing plays. At the age of 17, she moved to New York City, where she took a series of odd jobs and studied writing part time. At 20, she married Reeves McCullers, eventually divorcing and remarrying him.

Publications

1940 The Heart Is a Lonely Hunter

McCullers's first novel, *The Heart Is a Lonely Hunter*, was published when she was only 23. It tells the story of a deaf-mute man and the troubled people who confide in him. Critics praised the book and were astounded that it had been written by someone so young. Six years later her most successful novel, *The Member of the Wedding*, was published. Like McCullers's first book, it is set in the American South and centers on a group of characters troubled by feelings of loneliness and inner turmoil. One critic called it the work of "a genius." She later adapted the novel as a successful play.

A short novel, *The Ballad of the Sad Cafe*, and a collection of stories followed. Only a few years later McCullers, who had been sick on and off since childhood, was struck down by a series of terrible illnesses from which she never fully recovered.

1941 Reflections in a Golden Eye
1946 The Member of the Wedding
1951 The Ballad of the Sad Cafe
1958 The Square Root of Wonderful
1961 Clock without Hands
1964 Sweet as a Pickle and Clean as a Pig

Published after she died
1971 The Mortgaged Heart

McEWAN, Ian

English novelist, short-story writer and screenwriter

Born Jun. 21, 1948

Some critics think that Ian McEwan could become one of the greatest British writers of his generation. Others find his work deliberately shocking, with little literary merit. Most do agree, however, that he writes elegantly and carefully in an icy-clear and at times unnervingly funny style. McEwan has been dubbed "Ian Macabre" for his fascination with vice, child abuse and violence.

McEwan was born in the army town of Aldershot, southern England. His father was in the army, and McEwan grew up in distant parts of what was then the British Empire, including Singapore and North Africa. After attending more than seven different schools, McEwan was sent to a boarding school in England, which he hated. He then studied English at the universities of Sussex and East Anglia.

McEwan's first publication was a collection of short stories called *First Love, Last Rites*, which he wrote for his course at East Anglia. Although written by a 27-year-old university student, the book won a major British award and was widely reviewed in the US and Britain. The stories deal with a variety of sexual fantasies and perversions, and McEwan has since said the collection was like an outpouring after years of repression that stemmed from his childhood.

The Cement Garden, McEwan's first novel, also created a stir. Four children attempt to conceal the deaths of their parents, and the elder two take to playing "Mummy and Daddy" too seriously. Three of his novels (*The Innocent*, *The Comfort of Strangers* and *The Cement Garden*) have been made into films, and McEwan has also written screenplays and plays.

Publications
1975 First Love, Last Rites
1978 The Cement Garden
1978 In Between the Sheets and Other Stories
1981 The Imitation Game
1981 The Comfort of Strangers
1987 The Child in Time
1990 The Innocent
1992 Black Dogs
1997 Enduring Love
1998 Amsterdam

McGINLEY, Phyllis

American poet and children's writer

Born Mar. 21, 1905
Died Feb. 22, 1978
Age at death 72

Phyllis McGinley's humorous poetry commenting on the details of middle-class lives was widely popular in her time and earned her a Pulitzer Prize. She has been called the best American woman writer of light verse.

McGinley was born in Ontario, Oregon, where she grew up in a Roman Catholic family. As a child, she began writing poetry. After graduating from university (she had attended the University of Southern California and the University of Utah), she continued to write and to publish poems in literary magazines while supporting herself by teaching and doing odd jobs. She eventually settled in New York City, where she began to publish in the *New Yorker* magazine.

McGinley published her first collection of poems, *On the Contrary*, when she was 29. Over the next decades she published a number of collections, including *Love Letters*, which earned her the EDNA ST. VINCENT MILLAY Memorial Award. Her collection *Times Three* won the Pulitzer Prize in 1961, the first book of light verse to do so. It contained an introduction by the great English poet W.H. AUDEN, who praised her work highly.

McGinley wrote about relationships and domestic life, including many funny observations of children and marriage. These themes are reflected in some of her book titles, for example, *Husbands Are Difficult*. She was a skillful satirist, poking fun at the attitudes and lifestyles of the middle class, her primary audience. McGinley also wrote 17 children's books and a book on saints.

Publications

1934 On the Contrary
1937 One More Manhattan
1940 A Pocketful of Wry
1941 Husbands Are Difficult
1954 Love Letters
1959 Province of the Heart
1960 Times Three
1962 Boys Are Awful
1964 Sixpence in Her Shoe
1969 Saint-Watching

McGONAGALL, William

Scottish poet

Born 1830
Died 1902
Age at death c. 72

William McGonagall was a 19th-century Scottish writer who is often described as the worst poet in the world.

McGonagall was born in Scotland, the son of an immigrant Irish cloth weaver. After spending some time in the remote Scottish islands, the McGonagall family settled in the city of Dundee. William learned his father's trade and became a weaver.

McGonagall married when he was 16. He lived a quiet life, occasionally acting in plays at the theater in Dundee. His literary career was slow to begin; his first book of verse, *Poetic Gems*, was published when he was 52. Soon he had a dedicated group of fans who found his work funny and refreshingly simple.

After his first poems began to appear in newspapers and magazines, McGonagall made a series of tours in Scotland and gave public readings of his verses. In the city of Edinburgh crowds of college students turned up to hear him read. His fame quickly spread. In 1880, he visited London and, in 1887, gave readings in New York City.

Most people did not think that McGonagall's poetry was good, but many people found it extremely funny. McGonagall himself did not intend his poems to be comic. He wrote about Scotland, people he met, and events in the news. One of his most famous poems, "The Tay Bridge Disaster," describes the destruction of a bridge and the train on it by a violent storm.

Publications
1890 Poetic Gems

McKAY, Claude

Jamaican-born American poet and novelist

Born Sep. 15, 1889
Died May 22, 1948
Age at death 58

Claude McKay was a leading figure of the Harlem Renaissance – an explosion of African-American literary and artistic talent in 1920s New York.

McKay, the youngest of 11 children, was born in Jamaica, then a British colony. An older brother, a schoolteacher, introduced him to literature, science and politics, encouraging him to question authority and think for himself. McKay's first poetry book, *Constab Ballads*, was published when he was 23, and it won a literary prize. He used the prize money to travel to America, where he settled in New York City.

McKay had been taught to be proud of his heritage, so he was shocked to encounter racism for the first time in America. At age 30, he published his best-known poem, "If We Must Die." It expresses both McKay's love for America and his hatred of racism and was written in response to the racial violence that erupted in America in 1919. Aged 33, McKay published *Harlem Shadows*, his most famous collection. These are angry poems based on McKay's experience of the constant degradation endured by the African-American community. Scholars have described the book as the inspiration for the Harlem Renaissance. After the publication of *Harlem Shadows* McKay went to Marseilles, in France, where he lived for ten years, and where he wrote *Home to Harlem*, his most highly regarded novel.

McKay had a major influence on black America's search for identity. His books were widely read at the height of the civil rights movement in the 1960s. He remained dedicated throughout his life to the fight against racism and injustice.

Publications
1912 Constab Ballads
1919 "If We Must Die"
1922 Harlem Shadows
1928 Home to Harlem
1929 Banjo
1933 Banana Bottom
1937 A Long Way from Home
1940 Harlem: Negro Metropolis

Published after he died
1953 Selected Poems

McMILLAN, Terry

American novelist

Born Oct. 18, 1951

Publications

1987 Mama
1989 Disappearing Acts
1990 Breaking Ice: An Anthology of Contemporary African-American Fiction (editor)
1992 Waiting to Exhale
1996 How Stella Got Her Groove Back

With her novel *Waiting to Exhale* novelist Terry McMillan shot to fame and became the voice of young, professional African-American women.

McMillan was born in Port Huron, Michigan, where she and her sisters and brothers were raised by their mother; Terry's father died when she was 16. In 1979, she graduated from the University of California in Berkeley, then studied film and earned a Master's degree at Columbia University in New York. She worked at word processing to support herself and her son while she wrote.

McMillan's big break came when she was 32 and was accepted at a writers' colony where she began *Mama*, her first novel. When it was published, her publishers wanted to market it to a white audience, believing that black readers do not buy books. McMillan promoted the book herself, and she found hundreds of fans, many of them black. Her second novel, *Disappearing Acts*, is about star-crossed lovers, and her third, *Waiting to Exhale*, became a *New York Times* bestseller. In it, McMillan focuses on the problem of male–female relationships among African-American professional women who are both cynical and romantic. She created characters that young black women could identify with, and her fresh voice and humor made her popular with both white and black readers. McMillan also wrote the screenplay for *Waiting to Exhale*, which was made into a movie starring Whitney Houston.

In 1996, McMillan published her fourth novel, *How Stella Got Her Groove Back*. She is also an academic and has received a number of grants and honors.

McMURTRY, Larry

American novelist

Born Jun. 3, 1936

Larry McMurtry was born, raised and educated in Texas; his work is closely identified with the scenery and people there.

Born in Wichita Falls, Texas, McMurtry graduated from North Texas State University and earned a further degree from Rice. After being "starved for books" on his family's ranch, he started writing at university and produced a critically acclaimed first novel, *Horseman, Pass By*, at age 25. This was made into the film *Hud*, starring Paul Newman, and deals with life as seen through the eyes of a 17-year-old boy whose grandfather is forced to slaughter his diseased cattle herd.

McMurtry's next two novels, including the well-known *The Last Picture Show*, are also set in Texas and describe the frustrations of small-town life there. McMurtry then explored the way people cope with the move from country to city life in *Moving On* and *Terms of Endearment*. In these and other works, ordinary characters seem to drift aimlessly around scenes of old-style Texas. McMurtry also likes to write about the way that reality does not always live up to people's expectations. Many of his novels, including *Terms of Endearment* and *The Last Picture Show*, have been made into successful Hollywood films.

Perhaps McMurtry's most famous work is *Lonesome Dove*, which won the Pulitzer Prize in 1986. It is about Texas rangers on their last trail drive. This was made into a hugely popular TV miniseries first shown in 1988.

These days McMurtry runs rare bookstores in Dallas and Washington, DC, and continues to write.

Publications

1961 Horseman, Pass By
1966 The Last Picture Show
1970 Moving On
1975 Terms of Endearment
1982 Cadillac Jack
1983 The Desert Rose
1985 Lonesome Dove
1988 Anything for Billy
1992 Evening Star
1993 Streets of Laredo
1997 Commanche Moon
1999 Crazy Horse

McPHERSON, James Alan

American short-story writer and novelist

Born Sep. 16, 1943

James Alan McPherson is a gifted writer of short stories and novels, whose second book, *Elbow Room*, won him the 1978 Pulitzer Prize.

McPherson was born in Savannah, Georgia, and grew up at the height of the civil rights movement. He attended a segregated school but also experienced the end of segregation in schools, housing and public places. A federal loan enabled him to attend Morris Brown College in Atlanta, Georgia, from which he graduated, aged 22. In the same year his short story "Gold Coast" was awarded first prize by *Atlantic Monthly*, and McPherson was offered a place at Harvard Law School. He received his law degree in 1968.

Atlantic Monthly continued to publish McPherson's work and helped fund the publication of his first collection of short stories, *Hue and Cry*, when he was 26. He was appointed contributing editor to the magazine in 1969.

McPherson's ideas are different from those of many other black writers of the 1960s. He believes all cultures are connected and, in an advertisement for *Hue and Cry*, stated that he hoped his stories would be read by all kinds of people: the old, the young, the lonely, the confused and the wronged. He does not write about people because of their race and tries to keep the question of color in the background. His sympathies lie with every person who is trying to make their way in the vastness of America and who suffers injustice.

Publications

1965 "Gold Coast"
1969 Hue and Cry
1977 Elbow Room
1987 A World Unsuspected
1988 The Prevailing South

MELVILLE, Herman

American novelist

Born Aug. 1, 1819
Died Sep. 28, 1891
Age at death 72

Herman Melville is one of the most important figures in American literature. His reputation is based largely on one classic novel, *Moby-Dick*.

Melville, the son of a wealthy merchant, was born in New York City. His father died when Melville was 13, leaving the family in poverty. He left school to support his family, working at various jobs until he was 22, when he became a seaman on a whaling ship bound for the Pacific. Melville deserted the ship on the Marquesas Islands and lived with the islanders until another ship rescued him and took him to Tahiti. He eventually landed in what is now Hawaii and enlisted in the US Navy.

After he left the navy at age 25, Melville wrote novels based on his experiences. The books made him extremely popular. He soon gained a reputation as an author of exotic adventure stories. At age 31, Melville moved to Pittsfield, Massachusetts, where he became a close friend of NATHANIEL HAWTHORNE. Melville had almost completed *Moby-Dick* when Hawthorne encouraged him to change it from a simple book about whaling to an allegorical and philosophical novel. On one level *Moby-Dick* is the story of Captain Ahab's search for the fierce white whale known as Moby-Dick. It is full of details about whaling and a whaler's life. On another level it is a story of a man's search for meaning in his life and a tale of good versus evil.

Moby-Dick, published when Melville was 32, was not a popular success. It was only recognized as a masterpiece 30 years after Melville's death.

Publications

1846	*Typee: A Peep at Polynesian Life*
1847	*Omoo: A Narrative of Adventures in the South Seas*
1849	*Mardi*
1851	*Moby-Dick*
1856	*The Piazza Tales*
1857	*The Confidence-Man*

Published after he died

1924	*Billy Budd*

MENANDER

Greek playwright

Born c. 342 BC
Died c. 292 BC
Age at death c. 50

Menander was an ancient Greek writer of comedy drama. He was born in the city of Athens into a wealthy family. Scholars think that his father was a general and a prominent politician. Menander probably got his enthusiasm for the theater from his uncle, Alexis, who was a friend of several playwrights and may have been a writer himself.

Not much is known about Menander's life, and very little of his writing has survived. He is remembered because other writers, particularly the Roman comic playwrights TERENCE and Plautus, based many of their plays on his. For centuries after his death, Menander was the most popular of ancient Greek writers.

Drama had been an important part of Greek society for hundreds of years before Menander was born. Regular competitions were held to find the best play, and almost everybody attended drama festivals to see the entrants. The earliest dramas were tragedies. Later, comedy became more popular, and writers such as ARISTOPHANES wrote plays in a style known as Old Attic Comedy ("Attic" because they came from a region of Greece called Attica). Menander became the leading representative of a more sophisticated style known as New Attic Comedy.

Although he wrote over 100 plays, Menander won the drama prize only 8 times. His comedy was much more subtle and clever than audiences were used to and was not very popular with the ordinary public. Through the work of later imitators, however, Menander became the inspiration for a style of European drama called comedy of manners, which has been popular since the 17th century.

Publications

Only one of Menander's plays survives in a complete form: *The Bad-Tempered Man*, performed about 317 BC. The date it was written is not known. Fragments of other plays have been found. Their titles include *Anger*, *Afraid of Noises*, *The Unpopular Man* and *The Girl with Her Hair Cut Short*.

MEREDITH, George

English novelist and poet

Born Feb. 12, 1828
Died May 18, 1909
Age at death 81

A poetic style of writing gives the novels of George Meredith a character all of their own. Most of them are romantic comedies, full of wit.

Meredith was born in Portsmouth, in southern England. He was the son of a tailor and claimed to be descended from Welsh princes. His mother's family had set aside money to pay for his education. For part of the time he was at a school in Germany run by the Moravian Church, a Protestant group.

Meredith began his career as an apprentice to a lawyer but soon gave up law to write poems and articles. His first published prose, the short work *The Shaving of Shagpat*, came out when he was 27. It is a fantastic tale in imitation of *The Arabian Nights*. His first full-length novel was *The Ordeal of Richard Feverel*, a romantic comedy with a sad ending. Its treatment of sex made it controversial, and for a time it was banned. About this time his first wife left him. He wrote about the breakdown of his marriage in *Modern Love*, a book of sonnets.

Meredith could not make enough money from his novels and poems, so he took a job as a reader of manuscripts for a book publisher. For a time he also wrote for a small local newspaper. In his late 30s, he served briefly as a war correspondent in a conflict between Prussia (now northern Germany) and Austria. He finally achieved success and financial independence in the 1870s with several novels that sold well. *The Egoist*, considered by many to be his masterpiece, explores every aspect of self-centeredness, the part of human nature Meredith believed to be the most evil.

Publications

1855 The Shaving of Shagpat
1859 The Ordeal of Richard Feverel
1862 Modern Love
1871 The Adventures of Harry Richmond
1876 Beauchamp's Career
1879 The Egoist
1885 Diana of the Crossways
1890 One of Our Conquerors
1895 The Amazing Marriage

MEREDITH, William

American poet

Born Jan. 9, 1919

William Meredith is most famous for the war poems contained in his first volume of poetry, *Love Letter from an Impossible Land*.

Meredith was born in New York City and received his degree from Princeton University in 1940. He was to keep up his relationship with the university for some years after his graduation; during the late 1940s and mid-1960s, he served three terms as a teacher of creative writing there.

During World War II, Meredith served in the US Army Air Force and in the US Navy – much of his earlier poetry reflects what he experienced during this time. In common with many other poets and writers, he was both horrified and fascinated by the world conflict. The 12 war poems in *Love Letter from an Impossible Land*, published when he was 25, describe how he felt as a young man: on the brink of a promising life but facing the possibility of death.

Ships and Other Figures, Meredith's second collection, and *The Wreck of the Thresher*, about the loss of an American submarine, were based on his experiences in the navy. Some critics say that Meredith's later poems are not as intense and do not move the reader as much as his war poems. He is, however, a clever, positive and honest poet whose work has earned him much praise. *Love Letter from an Impossible Land* won the Yale Series of Younger Poets competition in 1944, and *Partial Accounts: New and Selected Poems* won the 1988 Pulitzer Prize for poetry.

As well as writing his own poetry, Meredith has translated some of the work of the French surrealist poet GUILLAUME APOLLINAIRE.

Publications

- *1944 Love Letter from an Impossible Land*
- *1948 Ships and Other Figures*
- *1964 The Wreck of the Thresher and Other Poems*
- *1970 Earth Walk: New and Selected Poems*
- *1975 Hazard, the Painter*
- *1987 Partial Accounts: New and Selected Poems*

MERRILL, James

American poet

Born Mar. 3, 1926

Died Feb. 7, 1995

Age at death 68

James Merrill is one of the most highly regarded American poets of the late 20th century. Among the many awards he has received, he was given the Pulitzer Prize in 1977 for his poetry collection *Divine Comedies*.

Merrill was born in New York City to extremely wealthy parents. He was educated at home by private tutors until the age of 12, when his parents divorced, and he was sent to Lawrenceville School. When he was 16 and in his final year, his father privately printed his first collection of poems, *Jim's Book*. Army service during World War II interrupted his studies at Amherst College, but he returned after the war had ended and graduated in 1947.

Recognized from the first as a master of poetic form, Merrill at first wrote poems that reflected his traditional upbringing. Later collections, such as *Nights and Days*, deal in a more mature way with personal themes. *Nights and Days* won Merrill the first National Book Award and gave him a reputation as a writer of moving love poetry.

The Pulitzer Prize-winning *Divine Comedies* is a mystical poem featuring a ghost called Ephraim who instructs the poet with messages from beyond the grave. Two more books, *Mirabell's Books of Number* and *Scripts for the Pageant*, also feature the ghostly Ephraim. Later, all three were put together into a 560-page epic poem called *The Changing Light at Sandover*. This is considered to be Merrill's finest work and has been compared to the work of the great Irish poet W.B. YEATS.

Publications

1942	*Jim's Book*
1959	*The Country of a Thousand Years of Peace*
1966	*Nights and Days*
1977	*Divine Comedies*
1978	*Mirabell's Books of Number*
1980	*Scripts for the Pageant*
1982	*The Changing Light at Sandover*
1988	*The Inner Room*
1995	*A Scattering of Salts*

MERWIN, W.S.

American poet and translator

Born Sep. 30, 1927

W.S. Merwin is a major American poet and translator. He has won many prizes and awards, including the Pulitzer Prize in 1971 for his collection *The Carrier of Ladders.*

William Stanley Merwin was born in New York City and grew up in Union City, New Jersey, and Scranton, Pennsylvania. He studied English at Princeton University, followed by one year of graduate study in modern languages. From 1949 to 1956, he was in Europe, working first as a tutor, at one time for the son of the English poet ROBERT GRAVES, and then translating classic Spanish and French plays for the BBC in London.

Merwin's first book, published when he was 25, was *A Mask for Janus*. One of the major themes in his poetry is the idea that words give order to life and help us relate to the natural world about us – he feels strongly that we are abusing the environment because we have lost touch with it. Critics have described Merwin as a kind of negative WALT WHITMAN. While Whitman glorified humanity's connection to nature in the 19th century, Merwin talks about the tragedy of having lost that connection in the 20th century. This is the depressing message of *The Carrier of Ladders*.

Merwin has also published essays, partly autobiographical prose works, and translations of important writers such as the South American poet PABLO NERUDA and the Russian poet OSIP MANDELSTAM. His other translations range from ancient Greek to medieval Spanish plays and are highly acclaimed.

Publications

1952	*A Mask for Janus*
1954	*The Dancing Bears*
1956	*Green with Beasts*
1960	*The Drunk in the Furnace*
1967	*The Lice*
1970	*The Carrier of Ladders*
1977	*The Compass Flower*
1983	*Opening the Hand*
1993	*The Second Four Books of Poems*

MICHENER, James A.

American novelist and short-story writer

Born Feb. 3, 1907
Died Oct. 16, 1997
Age at death 90

James A. Michener was a bestselling author known for his long, complex historical novels that cover huge periods of time.

James Albert Michener was raised in Bucks County, Pennsylvania, and graduated from Swarthmore College when he was 22. He worked as a teacher and college professor until he was 35, after which he became an editor in New York City.

During World War II, Michener served in the US Navy and was stationed in the South Pacific. His wartime experiences provided him with material for his first novel, *Tales of the South Pacific*, which won the Pulitzer Prize when he was 41. It was made into a musical, *South Pacific*, in 1949 and a movie in 1958. These successes provided Michener with the freedom to write full time.

Michener's epic novels are characterized by broad time spans and carefully researched historical detail. *Hawaii*, for example, begins with the actual formation of the islands millions of years ago and ends in 1959, the year Hawaii became a US state. Michener interweaves the plot with information on physical geography, culture and history.

Michener's other novels are equally detailed. For example, in *The Source* he tells the 12,000-year story of Palestine against the backdrop of an archeological dig. In *Centennial,* he traces the history of Colorado. Similarly, he follows 500 years of South African history in *The Covenant*. Michener also published several nonfiction works, including *Literary Reflections* and *The World Is My Home*, his autobiography.

Publications

1947 Tales of the South Pacific
1953 The Bridges at Toko-Ri
1954 Sayonara
1959 Hawaii
1965 The Source
1974 Centennial
1978 Chesapeake
1980 The Covenant
1992 The World Is My Home
1993 Literary Reflections

MILLAY, Edna St. Vincent

American poet and playwright

Born Feb. 22, 1892
Died Oct. 19, 1950
Age at death 58

Poet Edna St. Vincent Millay (who also wrote under the pen name Nancy Boyd) used traditional forms of poetry writing – ballads and sonnets – but in her youth she lived a very unconventional life as a well-known Greenwich Village "bohemian" and feminist.

Millay was born in Rockland, Maine. She and her two sisters were raised by their divorced mother, a nurse. While studying at Vassar College, Millay published her first poem. After graduating, she moved to New York City, where she joined the artists and intellectuals who had gathered in Greenwich Village, then a center of creative activity.

At age 25, Millay published her first volume of poetry, *Renascence and Other Poems*. This was followed three years later by *A Few Figs from Thistles*, which captures the intensity of her life then. It contains the famous poem that begins "My candle burns at both ends; / It shall not last the night." This volume was expanded and published in 1922 as *The Harp-Weaver and Other Poems*, for which Millay received the Pulitzer Prize in 1923.

Although many of Millay's poems describe her active love life, she was also politically active. In the 1920s, she demonstrated against the death sentence given to Sacco and Vanzetti, two anarchists who were widely believed to have been wrongly convicted of murder and who were executed in 1927. She was also concerned about the rise of fascism in Europe. These issues are the subjects of some of her poems, but Millay is mostly remembered for her earlier work, which celebrates the pleasures to be had in life and love.

Publications

1917	*Renascence and Other Poems*
1920	*A Few Figs from Thistles*
1921	*The Lamp and the Bell*
1922	*The Harp-Weaver and Other Poems*
1928	*The Buck in the Snow*
1931	*The Fatal Interview*
1939	*Huntsman, What Quarry?*
1940	*Make Bright the Arrows: 1940 Notebook*

MILLER, Arthur

American playwright and screenwriter

Born Oct. 17, 1915

Arthur Miller is one of America's leading playwrights. He has written some of the most important and famous plays of the 20th century.

Miller was born in New York City. Just before the Great Depression his father's business closed, and the family was reduced to near poverty. This sudden change in fortune had a strong influence on Miller – in many of his plays families are destroyed because they live by the rules of a society that says money is the most important thing.

At school, Miller was more interested in sports than literature, but all that changed when he read *The Brothers Karamazov* by the Russian novelist FYODOR DOSTOEVSKY. Miller decided to become a writer and enrolled at the University of Michigan to study journalism.

Miller's first successful play, *All My Sons*, was performed when he was 32. About a factory owner who sells faulty aircraft parts during World War II, the play clearly shows Miller's belief that the desire for money in American society encourages people to act immorally. Two years later *Death of a Salesman*, probably Miller's greatest play, was produced. It is about a man who kills himself when he realizes he will never be considered a success. The play won Miller a Pulitzer Prize in 1949.

Miller's 1953 play, *The Crucible*, is based on the 17th-century Salem witch trials, but it is really an attack on the anticommunist trials held during the McCarthy Era. From 1956 to 1961, Miller was married to the famous actress Marilyn Monroe. He wrote the screenplay for her last movie, *The Misfits*.

Publications

1947	*All My Sons*
1949	*Death of a Salesman*
1953	*The Crucible*
1955	*A View from the Bridge*
1964	*Incident at Vichy*
1964	*After the Fall*
1980	*The American Clock*
1990	*The Last Yankee*
1994	*Broken Glass*
1995	*Plain Girl*

MILLER, Caroline

American novelist and short-story writer

Born Aug. 26, 1903
Died Jul. 12, 1992
Age at death 88

Caroline Miller won a Pulitzer Prize in 1934 for her first novel, *Lamb in His Bosom*.

Miller was born Caroline Pafford in Waycross, Georgia. Right after graduating from secondary school she married her former English teacher when she was just 17, and became Caroline Miller. In the happy early years of her marriage she spent time walking the Georgia countryside, meeting the swamp dwellers who later appeared in her first work.

While raising three sons, she took up writing to add to the family's finances. Her first attempts were short stories, but she could not get any published. One developed into a novel, *Lamb in His Bosom*, and with the help of Pulitzer Prize-winner JULIA PETERKIN it was published when Miller was 30. Set in Georgia in the 1840s, when the countryside was still frontier land, the book focuses on the life of Cean Carver and her journey of self-discovery. It is written in an unsentimental style and combines historical fact and fiction. *Lamb in His Bosom* also relates the stories of the whole Carver family. One of the central male characters is based on Miller's own great-grandfather, a minister who had settled in Waycross during the frontier period. Miller was praised for her realistic portrayal of frontier life, the detailing of daily life, and her descriptions of the Georgia countryside.

After Miller had divorced her first husband and remarried, she wrote *Lebanon*, 11 years after her first novel. Again it is set in frontier Georgia, but this novel is a romance and was not as well received.

Publications

1933 Lamb in His Bosom
1944 Lebanon

MILLER, Henry

American novelist

Born Dec. 26, 1891
Died Jun. 7, 1980
Age at death 88

Henry Miller is famous for the novels that chronicle his life in Paris between 1930 and 1940. Well known for describing sex with frankness, the novels focus on a penniless artist who struggles to survive in Paris as a creative "free spirit."

Miller was born in New York City, the only child of German-American working-class parents. His difficult relationship with his mother is reflected in his life (he married five times) and in his novels' characters. After secondary school, he drifted through various jobs in the US and Europe, settling in Paris, where he wrote and painted. At 40, he found his "writing voice"; after many drafts *Tropic of Cancer* was published in Paris in 1934, and it received praise from T.S. ELIOT.

Encouraged by Anaïs Nin, he wrote *Black Spring* and *Tropic of Capricorn*. These novels alternate between his Brooklyn childhood and his vagabond life in Paris. He wrote a study of the poet Arthur Rimbaud, identifying with Rimbaud as a rebellious figure and a sexual adventurer. For Miller, the human sexual drive was part of creative expression, and he made no moral judgments about sexuality. He used dream, symbols, fantasy, humor and personal experience in his writings.

After a brief time in Greece, depicted in *The Colossus of Maroussi*, he settled in California in the 1940s and continued to write. He became a hero of the beat generation. In 1961, *Tropic of Cancer* was banned in the US as obscene. Only after a long court battle during which he was publicly supported by many writers, was the ban lifted. The novel became a bestseller.

Publications

1934	*Tropic of Cancer*
1936	*Black Spring*
1939	*Tropic of Capricorn*
1941	*The Colossus of Maroussi*
1949	*Sexus*
1953	*Plexus*
1956	*Quiet Days in Clichy*
1956	*The Time of the Assassins: A Study of Rimbaud*
1960	*Nexus*

MILLER, Jason

American playwright

Born Apr. 22, 1939

Jason Miller's fame as a playwright rests solely on *That Championship Season*, the second of his two full-length plays.

Miller was born in Long Island, New York, but brought up in Scranton, Pennsylvania. He attended St. Patrick's High School, where he was encouraged by one of his teachers to study elocution because of his deep, strong voice. He went on to study theater and playwriting at the University of Scranton and then drama at the Catholic University of America in Washington, DC.

Miller's first full-length play, *Nobody Hears a Broken Drum*, was produced when he was 31; it was not, however, a success. For the next two years, while writing his second play, he took jobs as a bit-part actor, truck driver, messenger and waiter. *That Championship Season*, produced when he was 33, was to make him famous. The play is about the 20th annual reunion of four members of a secondary school championship basketball team and their coach. The surprising part is that the men, now middle-aged, have not changed much. As young men they won the championship game by cheating, and as adults they are still selfish and dishonest. Although they claim to be friends, they do not hesitate to betray each other. To them, winning is still everything.

The play won the New York Drama Critics' Circle Award in 1972 and the Tony Award for best play as well as the Pulitzer Prize in 1973. Since *That Championship Season* Miller has concentrated on his acting career. He was nominated for an Academy Award in 1974 for his role as the priest in *The Exorcist*.

Publications

1967	*It's a Sin to Tell a Lie*
1967	*Circus Lady*
1967	*Perfect Son*
1968	*Stone Step*
1970	*Lou Gehrig Did Not Die of Cancer*
1970	*Nobody Hears a Broken Drum*
1972	*That Championship Season*

MILNE, A.A.

English children's writer and playwright

Born Jan. 18, 1882
Died Jan. 31, 1956
Age at death 74

A.A. Milne was a popular and productive English writer. Although he wrote many different kinds of books, he will always be remembered as the author of the children's classic *Winnie-the-Pooh*.

Alan Alexander Milne was born in London. At school, one of his teachers was the science fiction writer H.G. WELLS. Milne studied math at Cambridge University and then, aged 24, went to work for a well-known satirical magazine called *Punch*.

In 1914, World War I broke out and Milne joined the army. The horrors he witnessed on the battlefields left him with a lifelong disgust of war and a longing for the innocence of childhood. In the army, Milne wrote plays to amuse his comrades, and when the war was over, he began a career as a comic playwright. He also began to write poetry for children.

Milne became famous when he was 42 with the publication of *When We Were Very Young*, a collection of poetry for children. He followed this two years later with *Winnie-the-Pooh*, which is based on stories he told to his own son Christopher Robin, which is also the name of the little boy whose animal friends are the main characters in the book.

Although Milne continued to write books for adults, it was always his work for children that brought him recognition. His second volume of poems for children, *Now We Are Six*, was just as popular as his first, and *The House at Pooh Corner*, which relates the further adventures of Pooh Bear and friends, was an instant success. Milne also wrote a popular stage version of the classic children's novel *The Wind in the Willows* by KENNETH GRAHAME.

Publications

1919	*Mr. Pim Passes By*
1921	*The Red House Mystery*
1921	*The Truth about Blayds*
1922	*The Dover Road*
1924	*When We Were Very Young*
1926	*Winnie-the-Pooh*
1927	*Now We Are Six*
1928	*The House at Pooh Corner*
1932	*The Perfect Alibi*
1939	*It's Too Late Now*

MILOSZ, Czeslaw

Polish-American poet, novelist and essayist

Born Jun. 30, 1911

Czeslaw Milosz is one of Poland's leading modern poets. In 1980, he was awarded the Nobel Prize for literature.

Born in Vilnius, Lithuania, which was then part of Poland, Milosz published his first book of poetry, *Poem of the Frozen Time*, when he was just 22.

Milosz studied at the University of Vilnius. There he became a socialist and headed up a group of poets who predicted an upcoming disaster. The disaster came in 1939 when Germany invaded Poland and World War II broke out. Milosz was an active member of the resistance movement in Warsaw.

At age 34, when the war ended, Milosz published a book of verse entitled *Salvage*, which so impressed the new communist rulers of

Publications

1933	*Poem of the Frozen Time*
1945	*Salvage*

Poland that they made him a junior diplomat. His first appointment was in Washington, DC. After a time in Paris, Milosz returned to the United States, where he took a teaching post at the University of California, Berkeley. Ten years later, he became a US citizen.

Milosz continued to write in Polish, his native language, but published many works in English, some of which he translated himself.

One of Milosz's most famous works is the essay collection *The Captive Mind*, which deals with the effects of communism on Polish writers. He later returned to this theme in an autobiographical novel, *The Seizure of Power*. This story about life in Warsaw after a change in power begins with the Russian occupation of the city at the end of World War II.

1953	*The Captive Mind*
1955	*The Seizure of Power*
1959	*Native Realm*
1988	*Collected Poems: 1931–87*
1991	*Provinces: Poems 1987–91*
1992	*Beginning with My Streets*
1994	*The Year of the Hunter*
1995	*Facing the River*

MILTON, John

John Milton was one of the greatest English poets. He was born in London and educated at Cambridge University. His father was a successful lawyer and composer who was wealthy enough to afford a second house in the country. Milton spent six years in private study there after finishing university in 1632. He had given up his original ambition to become a priest and decided to devote his life to God as a poet instead.

Milton began to write poetry while he was at college. He completed one of his first major works, *Lycidas*, perhaps the finest short poem in English, at age 29. Five years later in 1642, the English Civil War divided the country as Oliver Cromwell fought to overthrow the king. At the outbreak of war, Milton stopped composing poetry and threw himself into writing political essays supporting Cromwell's aims. In the same period, Milton also became aware that he was slowly going blind.

In 1660, the monarchy was restored, and Milton retired to devote himself to poetry. His ambition had always been to compose an epic poem to rival the works of ancient writers such as HOMER and VIRGIL. By then completely blind, he began dictating his great poem, *Paradise Lost*, to his wife and daughters. The work, published when he was 55, was immediately recognized as an outstanding achievement. It tells the story of how Satan was thrown out of Heaven and how he came to Earth to corrupt Adam and Eve. The themes of war and religious conflict it explores constantly remind the reader of the troubled times Milton lived through.

English poet and essayist

Born Dec. 9, 1608
Died Nov. 8, 1674
Age at death 65

Publications

1629	"On the Morning of Christ's Nativity"
c. 1631	"L'Allegro"
c. 1631	"Il Penseroso"
1634	*Comus*
1637	*Lycidas*
1645	*Poems*
1667	*Paradise Lost*
1671	*Paradise Regained*
1671	*Samson Agonistes*

MISHIMA, Yukio

Japanese novelist and playwright

Born Jan. 14, 1925
Died Nov. 25, 1970
Age at death 45

Publications

1949 Confessions of a Mask
1950 Thirst for Love
1954 The Sound of Waves
1956 The Temple of the Golden Pavilion
1960 After the Banquet
1963 The Sailor Who Fell from Grace with the Sea
1969–71 The Sea of Fertility (4 vols. – fourth volume published after he died)

Mishima Yukio was one of Japan's leading modern writers. He wrote about Japanese society and the changes it has gone through in the 20th century.

Mishima was born in Tokyo and attended Tokyo University, where he studied law. During World War II, he was rejected by the army because of his poor health. He later felt guilty that he had survived the war when so many others had been killed.

In 1948, when Mishima was 23, his first novel, *Confessions of a Mask*, was published. It was strongly based on Mishima's own life and shows how society forced him to hide his homosexuality behind a mask of "normality." This was the first time a Japanese writer had talked about homosexuality. It was translated into English and widely praised.

Another of Mishima's early novels, *The Temple of the Golden Pavilion*, was also highly praised. It is based on the true story of a young Buddhist monk who, angered at his own physical ugliness, comes to hate the beauty of the temple where he studies and destroys it. Mishima went on to write popular modern versions of traditional Japanese No plays.

All his life Mishima was fascinated by the traditions of the samurai warriors. He came to feel that Japan had become weak after its defeat in World War II and needed new leadership. In 1970, Mishima publicly committed ritual suicide in an attempt to bring about an angry uprising against the government. On the day of his death, he finished writing the fourth and final part of his greatest novel, *The Sea of Fertility* – a critical study of Japanese society in the 20th century.

MISTRAL, Gabriela

Chilean poet

Born Apr. 7, 1889
Died Jan. 10, 1957
Age at death 67

Gabriela Mistral combined a busy life – first as a teacher and then as a diplomat – with a gift for poetry that brought her the Nobel Prize for Literature in 1945. She was the first South American writer to win the prize.

Born in Vicuña, Chile, Mistral's real name was Lucila Godoy Alcayaga. She used the pen name Gabriela Mistral only for her poetry. A gifted teacher, she became an important figure in Chile's education system. She traveled in Mexico, the United States and Europe to study teaching methods and became a visiting professor at several universities, including the University of Puerto Rico.

Later in life Mistral became a diplomat, working in the world's capitals during some of the most turbulent years of the 20th century, including World War II and the beginning of the Cold War in Europe.

In contrast to the horrors of war, Mistral's poetry is personal, full of warmth and emotion. Her main themes are childhood, death, love, motherhood and religion. She began writing poetry in her 20s after the suicide of her fiancé. Her "Sonnets on Death" won a writing contest in Chile in 1914. In addition, Mistral wrote verses for children and fantasy stories.

Mistral wrote in her native tongue, Spanish. She became one of the most translated of all South American writers: her work has appeared in English, French, German, Italian and Swedish. American poet LANGSTON HUGHES translated a selection of her verses that was published just after she died. Mistral never married but adopted a child who later died.

Publications

1922 Desolation
1924 Tenderness
1936 Poems
1938 Felling

Published after she died

1957 Selected Poems of Gabriela Mistral
1967 Gabriela Mistral's Anthology
1972 Crickets and Frogs
1974 The Elephant and His Secret

MITCHELL, Margaret

American novelist

Born Nov. 8, 1900
Died Aug. 16, 1949
Age at death 48

Margaret Mitchell was the author of one of the most famous novels ever written, *Gone with the Wind*.

Mitchell was born in Atlanta, Georgia. Her father was president of the local historical society, and Mitchell grew up listening to stories about old Atlanta and the battles the Confederate Army had fought there during the American Civil War. Later, she used these tales as inspiration for *Gone with the Wind*.

At age 22, Mitchell began a career as a journalist, but an ankle injury forced her to retire. By that time she had married and started work on her novel, which took ten years to complete. When a traveling book editor visited Atlanta in search of new material, she reluctantly let him have a look at her manuscript. The novel was published when Mitchell was 36.

Gone with the Wind is the vividly drawn tale of Southern life during and after the Civil War told through the lives of two families, their slaves, friends and relatives, centering on Scarlett O'Hara and Rhett Butler. It has been praised as the first novel to tell the story of the Civil War from a Southern woman's point of view but criticized for glorifying a society that practiced slavery. A romantic epic, it is full of stirring events and has created a lasting image of the South for over 60 years. It won the Pulitzer Prize in 1937. Worldwide sales are enormous: about 250,000 copies are sold in paperback in the US alone each year, and the book has been translated into some 30 languages. The 1939 film version starring Clark Gable and Vivien Leigh is one of the most popular films ever made.

Mitchell never published another book during her lifetime and died after an automobile accident.

Publications

1936 Gone with the Wind

Published after she died

1976 Margaret Mitchell's "Gone with the Wind" Letters
1985 A Dynamo Going to Waste: Letters to Allen Edee 1919–21
1996 Lost Laysen

MITFORD, Nancy

English novelist and biographer

Born Nov. 28, 1904
Died Jun. 30, 1973
Age at death 68

Nancy Mitford became successful for her comic novels about upper-class English society and for her popular biographies.

The eldest of seven children of the second Baron Redesdale, an eccentric British nobleman, she and her five sisters were unconventionally raised and educated at home by a series of governesses.

Mitford left home as soon as she could and lived for a time with EVELYN WAUGH and his wife while she began writing for *Harper's Magazine* and *Vogue*. Her first novel, *Highland Fling*, was published when she was 27. Then she made her name with four highly amusing books, beginning with *The Pursuit of Love*. These recount the lively activities and gently irresponsible behavior of a large group of upper-class relatives, based loosely on her own remarkable family. In them, her father is satirized as "Uncle Matthew."

After an unsuccessful marriage of 15 years, Mitford moved in the 1940s to Paris, where she spent the rest of her life. There she wrote the sequels to *The Pursuit of Love* and then turned to writing biographies, including one of France's King Louis XIV.

Mitford was also an essayist, and in 1955 she coined the terms "U" and "non-U" – "U" standing for "upper-class" – to describe words with similar meanings that were or were not sociably acceptable in British aristocratic circles: "writing paper" was "U," "notepaper" was definitely "non-U." These terms show her keen observation of people, which also makes the characters in her novels and their dialogue believable.

Publications

1931	*Highland Fling*
1945	*The Pursuit of Love*
1949	*Love in a Cold Climate*
1951	*The Blessing*
1953	*Madame de Pompadour*
1957	*Voltaire in Love*
1960	*Don't Tell Alfred*
1962	*The Water Beetle*
1966	*The Sun King*
1970	*Frederick the Great*

MOFOLO, Thomas

Lesotho novelist

Born Aug. 2, 1875
Died Sep. 8, 1948
Age at death 73

Thomas Mofolo was the first African novelist. He was born in the British colony of Basutoland, now called Lesotho, which was surrounded by white-ruled South Africa. His parents were Christians, and Mofolo attended the local mission school when he could. Despite being very poor, he managed to earn a teacher's certificate when he was 22. He began working for a Christian printing press, but business was interrupted by the Boer War, fought between the British and the white South Africans. After the war, he studied carpentry and then began teaching and, in 1904, he returned to work at the printing press.

Mofolo was encouraged by his friends to begin writing. His first novel, *The Traveler of the East*, was serialized in a Lesotho newspaper when he was 31 and came out in book form the following year. This was the first novel written by an African and the first in an African language and is more important for historical than literary reasons. It is a very religious book about a Lesotho man's quest for wisdom. Mofolo's masterpiece, *Chaka*, was written around 1911. This story of the famous 19th-century Zulu king Shaka is a moral tale of his rise to power and increasingly cruel behavior. The printing press refused to publish the book until 1925, and by this time Mofolo had written about another great king, Moshoeshoe I – the founder of Lesotho – but had lost the manuscript in a fire. Disheartened, he gave up writing. Mofolo spent the rest of his life in various business ventures that were not always successful, and he died in poverty.

Publications

1907 The Traveler of the East
1910 Pitseng
1925 Chaka

MOLIÈRE

French playwright

Born Jan. 15, 1622
Died Feb. 17, 1673
Age at death 51

Molière was the pen name of Jean-Baptiste Poquelin, one of the greatest French comedy writers. The son of a wealthy upholsterer, Molière was born in Paris and had a strict upbringing at a Jesuit school. Despite qualifying as a lawyer, he never practiced law. His first love was the theater, and at the age of 21 he formed a theater company with a group of friends. They toured France for a number of years before coming to the attention of King Louis XIV, who gave them a permanent theater.

When he was 40, Molière had his first major success as a playwright with *The School for Wives*. The play poked fun at the limited education that was given to daughters of rich families, and it was the first of what are generally regarded as a series of masterpieces.

Molière's comedies range from broad slapstick comedy to subtle satire. He nearly always acted in the lead role himself. Molière firmly believed that there was "no comedy without truth, and no truth without comedy." He made fun of anyone he thought was dishonest, and because of this he often found himself in trouble – two of his plays, *The Imposter* and *Don Juan*, were banned.

Later in life Molière concentrated on writing musical comedies. In these plays the drama was interrupted by songs and dance or a combination of both. He was taken ill while performing in *The Imaginary Invalid* and died the same day. After his death, the theater group Comédie Française was formed to promote his works. They are still enjoyed by modern theatergoers throughout the world.

Publications

1662 The School for Wives
1664 The Imposter
1665 Don Juan
1666 The Misanthrope
1666 The Doctor in Spite of Himself
1668 The Miser
1668 George Dandin
1670 The Would-Be Gentleman
1672 The Learned Ladies
1673 The Imaginary Invalid

MOMADAY, N. Scott

American poet and novelist

Born Feb. 27, 1934

N. Scott Momaday's writings started a new wave of Native American literature. His ancestors include Kiowas, Cherokees and Anglo-Americans, and he writes mostly about his search for cultural identity.

Navarre Scott Momaday was born at the Kiowa Indian Hospital in Lawton, Oklahoma. His family settled at Jemez Pueblo, New Mexico, where his parents were teachers. Though they were accepted by the community, they were not allowed to participate in sacred ceremonies. At 18, he went to the University of New Mexico, then to the University of Virginia, where he was influenced by the work of WILLIAM FAULKNER.

Momaday began by writing poetry: his novel, *House Made of Dawn*, which won the 1969 Pulitzer Prize, began as a series of poems. It is about Abel, a Native American, who returns to his reservation after serving in World War II. Momaday explores relationships between races and the often complicated, violent encounters between different groups.

With powerful, sharply detailed writings Momaday recreates the lost landscape of his childhood and his people. In *The Way to Rainy Mountain*, which is illustrated by his father, Momaday uses poems, stories, myths and memoirs to illustrate the development and decline of Kiowa culture. *The Names* is a poetic memoir of his childhood. For Momaday, Native American myths are about another plane of reality: he is very influenced by the bear figure, which is prominent in Kiowa myth and in his own stories and paintings.

Publications

1968 House Made of Dawn
1969 The Way to Rainy Mountain
1973 Colorado, Summer/Fall/Winter/Spring
1974 Angle of Geese
1976 The Gourd Dancer
1976 The Names
1989 The Ancient Child
1992 In the Presence of the Sun: Stories and Poems 1961–91

MONTAIGNE, Michel de

French essayist

Born Feb. 28, 1533
Died Sep. 13, 1592
Age at death 59

Michel de Montaigne is famous as the writer who invented the essay – a short piece that discusses the author's personal thoughts about a particular subject.

Born at his family estate in southwest France, Montaigne benefited from his father's advanced views about education that he had formed while serving as a soldier in Italy – then the center of European culture. As a baby he was sent to live with a peasant family so that his earliest memories would be of humble surroundings. His father then hired tutors who brought him up speaking nothing but Latin, the ancient Roman language. At school, when all the other pupils were struggling to learn Latin, Montaigne spent his time reading the classics of Roman literature.

As a young man Montaigne studied in Paris and at the University of Bordeaux. He then returned to his home region to serve in the legal courts, a job he disliked but carried out with characteristic skill and devotion to duty. Aged 38, he "retired" to his family estate and devoted himself to writing.

Montaigne's first book of collected essays was published when he was 47. It covers a huge range of subjects, reflecting Montaigne's wide interests and learning. In one famous essay, "Of Cannibals," he wrote about the native peoples of the Americas, which were then just beginning to be explored by Europeans. He argued that the beliefs of different cultures should be respected, and he was always interested in new ideas and new discoveries.

Publications

1569	*Apologia for Raymond Sebond*
1580–88	*Essays*

Published after he died

1774	*Journal of Travels*

MONTALE, Eugenio

Italian poet, critic, and essayist

Born Oct. 12, 1896
Died Sep. 12, 1981
Age at death 84

Eugenio Montale is an important figure in modern Italian literature. He won the Nobel Prize for Literature in 1975.

Montale was born in the city of Genoa, a large and ancient seaport in northwest Italy, and spent his youth in a small village nearby on the shores of the Ligurian Sea. The harsh, dry landscape and rugged coastline of his homeland seem to have strongly influenced his poetry, which is difficult, private and full of a sense of loneliness. His first collection of poems, *The Bones of Cuttlefish*, was published when he was 29.

Like many European poets writing in the period after World War I, Montale felt there was little hope for the future. His style of writing was influenced by the work of the great poet T.S. ELIOT, whose famous poem *The Waste Land* Montale translated into Italian. He wanted to create a new kind of Italian poetry that could escape from the influence of the great literature of Italy's past. One of the ways he tried to do this was by writing about his own personal experience. Critics called Montale's poetry "hermetic" because, like a hermit, he concentrated only on himself.

When the fascists came to power in Italy before World War II, Montale opposed them despite the risk of being sent to jail. He became a newspaper editor and was well known for his literary criticism. After the war, he continued writing poetry, which gradually became less difficult to understand. *Xenia*, one of his last collections, is a series of moving love poems to his dead wife.

Publications

1925	*The Bones of Cuttlefish*
1939	*The Occasions*
1956	*The Storm and Other Poems*
1956	*The Butterfly of Dinard*
1963	*Satura: Five Poems*
1965	*Selected Poems*
1970	*Xenia*
1978	*Selected Essays*
1980	*It Depends: A Poet's Notebook*

MONTGOMERY, L.M.

Canadian children's writer

Born Nov. 30, 1874
Died Apr. 24, 1942
Age at death 67

L.M. Montgomery's classic novel *Anne of Green Gables* has become a favorite of young female readers around the world.

Lucy Maud Montgomery was born on Prince Edward Island, Canada. When she was two, her mother died, and her father remarried and moved away, leaving the young Montgomery to be raised by her cruel grandparents. At 15, she published her first poem in the local paper. She became a teacher and a reporter in Halifax, Nova Scotia then, at age 24, she returned to Prince Edward Island to care for her grandmother. There she wrote for magazines and began what was to become her classic.

Montgomery wrote and rewrote *Anne of Green Gables* and received several rejections from publishers before it was finally accepted when she was 34. It tells the story of Anne, a young orphan adopted by an elderly couple who were hoping for a boy. The novel captures the struggles and dreams of childhood and adolescence, and in many ways it reflects Montgomery's own experiences. It was instantly a success and was said to have been admired by MARK TWAIN. In response to its popularity Montgomery wrote seven "Anne" sequels, including *Anne of Avonlea* and *Rilla of Ingleside*, which follow the heroine through teaching, marriage and raising a family.

In 1911, after the death of her grandmother, Montgomery married a preacher and moved with him to Ontario. While raising a family, she managed to write a book every other year, producing more than 20 novels and short-story collections.

Publications

1908 Anne of Green Gables
1909 Anne of Avonlea
1911 The Story Girl
1915 Anne of the Island
1917 Anne's House of Dreams
1919 Rainbow Valley
1921 Rilla of Ingleside
1923 Emily of New Moon
1936 Anne of Windy Poplars
1939 Anne of Ingleside

MOORCOCK, Michael

English fantasy/science fiction writer

Born Dec. 18, 1939

Michael Moorcock is the most important British fantasy author of the 1960s and '70s.

Moorcock was born in London. As a child he read and was influenced by EDGAR RICE BURROUGHS. When he left school, he contributed stories to a magazine called *Tarzan Adventures* and then became editor there. He also worked as a blues singer in London nightclubs.

Moorcock's first novel, *Caribbean Crisis*, was written when he was 23, under the pen name Desmond Reid. Two years later he became editor of a science fiction magazine, *New Worlds*, where he began to publish experimental fiction by authors like J.G. BALLARD and BRIAN ALDISS. Although *New Worlds* became a very influential magazine, it did not make money. To make a living, Moorcock wrote commercial fantasy novels at great speed, sometimes in a matter of days. In 1971, *New Worlds* stopped publication, and Moorcock, then aged 32, turned to writing more serious fiction. He also continued his musical career, performing with the rock band Hawkwind and his own band, Deep Fix.

Starting with *The Sundered Worlds*, published when he was 26, most of Moorcock's novels form part of a series about the adventures of a central figure, the Eternal Champion. Instead of living in the universe, the Eternal Champion lives in a "multiverse" where there are different layers of reality. This allows him to become different characters, with names such as Jerry Cornelius, Elric of Melniboné and Dorian Hawkmoon, who all fight to balance the forces of order and chaos. Moorcock is also respected as a writer of serious modern fiction.

Publications

1962	*Caribbean Crisis*
1965	*The Sundered Worlds*
1965	*Stormbringer*
1968	*The Sword of the Dawn*
1972	*The English Assassin*
1981	*Byzantium Endures*
1984	*The Laughter of Carthage*
1988	*Mother London*
1992	*Jerusalem Commands*
1995	*Blood: A Southern Fantasy*

MOORE, Clement Clarke

American poet

Born Jul. 15, 1779
Died Jul. 10, 1863
Age at death 83

Clement Clarke Moore was an American scholar who is remembered today for one poem, "A Visit from St. Nicholas," with its famous first line, "T'was the night before Christmas."

The son of a bishop, Moore grew up in an extremely wealthy family in New York City. After graduating from Columbia College, he settled on his family's estate in Manhattan, devoting his time to the study of Hebrew, the language of the Bible, and ancient Greek. From 1821 to 1850, Moore was Professor of Asian and Greek literature at the Episcopal General Theological Seminary, built on land that he had donated. A political conservative, Moore opposed the expansion of democracy and the abolition of slavery.

When he was 43, Moore wrote the poem "A Visit from St. Nicholas" as a Christmas present to his children. It was published anonymously in the *Troy Sentinel* (NY) in 1823. This popular poem helped shape America's ideas of Christmas. In those days, Christmas was a time for crowds of rowdy young men to roam the streets and go from door to door demanding gifts in return for songs; the poem depicted Christmas as a celebration centered on the family and particularly the children. Its vivid descriptions changed the image of St. Nicholas from a dignified bishop of tradition to a plump, jolly old man, the origin of today's Santa Claus.

Moore produced a number of scholarly works, including a Hebrew dictionary and some political addresses. He also published a volume of other poetry and edited two volumes of his father's sermons.

Publications

1804	*Observations upon Certain Passages in Mr. Jefferson's Notes on Virginia*
1809	*A Compendious Lexicon of the Hebrew Language*
1844	*Poems*
1848	"A Visit from St. Nicholas"
1850	*George Castriot, Surnamed Scanderbeg, King of Albania*

MOORE, Marianne

American poet

Born Nov. 15, 1887
Died Feb. 5, 1972
Age at death 84

Marianne Moore was a renowned American poet whose work influenced generations of women. Her best-known poems feature animals and are written in precise, clear language.

Moore was born in Kirkwood, near St. Louis, but after her mentally ill father was institutionalized, her mother moved to Carlisle, Pennsylvania, where she supported the family by teaching. Moore was already writing poetry when she graduated from Bryn Mawr College at 22. For four years she taught typing and bookkeeping, and then, when she was 28, a journal in England accepted her poem on war called "To the Soul of Progress."

Moore then moved to New York City, where she lived with her mother in Greenwich Village and worked as a librarian. Her first poetry collection, *Poems*, was published in England when she was 34; *Observations* appeared in the US three years later. At age 37, she became editor of *Dial* magazine, where she helped publish such writers as T.S. ELIOT and EZRA POUND. When *Dial* closed in 1929, Moore supported herself by writing. Her *Selected Poems* was highly praised by Eliot. In 1952, Moore received the Pulitzer Prize and the National Book Award for her *Collected Poems*. She dedicated the book to her mother, crediting her as an important influence.

A lifelong baseball fan, Moore was honored in 1968 with the role of throwing out the first ball to open the season at Yankee Stadium.

In addition to several volumes of poetry, Moore wrote essays on contemporary writers and artists and a translation of fables by JEAN DE LA FONTAINE.

Publications

1921	*Poems*
1924	*Observations*
1935	*Selected Poems*
1941	*What Are Years*
1951	*Collected Poems*
1954	*The Fables of La Fontaine*
1955	*Predilections*
1961	*A Marianne Moore Reader*
1966	*Tell Me, Tell Me*
1969	*The Accented Syllable*

MORAVIA, Alberto

Italian novelist and short-story writer

Born Nov. 28, 1907
Died Sep. 26, 1990
Age at death 82

Alberto Moravia was the pen name of Alberto Pincherle. Moravia is best known for his antifascist novels and for his exploration of sexuality.

Moravia was born in Rome, Italy, into a middle-class family. As a boy he suffered from poor health and spent much of his enforced leisure reading. Later he became a journalist, traveled widely, and learned several languages.

Moravia's first novel, *Time of Indifference*, was published when he was 22. At that time the fascist dictator Benito Mussolini ruled Italy. Moravia's book caused a sensation for criticizing the ultraright-wing fascists, and it earned the disapproval of the authorities. This forced him to hide the true message of his stories by writing in an allegorical style. He was not quite successful in this, however, and his increasing involvement in politics led to his books being banned. Forced to disappear, he remained in hiding until Italy was liberated.

Several other popular novels followed toward the end of World War II, including his best-known, *The Woman of Rome*. Moravia was no brilliant stylist, but he could tell a good story and write excellent dialogue. His purpose was essentially serious. Some of his books, for example *The Woman of Rome*, include sympathetic portraits of prostitutes and other women, whom he generally regarded as being superior to men. Others attack right-wing politics, moralism and corruption. Much of his work is concerned with the important question of the relationship of love to sex. In Moravia's view sex is the enemy of love.

Publications

1929 Time of Indifference
1944 Two Adolescents
1947 The Woman of Rome
1949 Conjugal Love
1951 The Conformist
1954 Roman Tales
1957 Two Women
1960 The Empty Canvas
1978 Time of Desecration
1985 The Voyeur

MORRIS, William

English poet and novelist

Born Mar. 24, 1834
Died Oct. 3, 1896
Age at death 62

William Morris was one of the most popular poets of his time. Today he is remembered for founding the Arts and Crafts movement in England, which encouraged a return to handmade objects and away from industrialization. He is also known as a designer of furniture, fabrics and wallpaper, and as an artist.

Morris was born into a family with money. He originally planned to become a clergyman but turned to architecture instead. Friends persuaded him to switch to painting, and he became obsessed with mediaeval art. With his friends he started a company to design and make furniture, stained glass, and wallpaper. Later, he founded the Kelmscott Press, a publishing firm dedicated to producing beautiful books.

Morris's poems and other writings first appeared in a magazine. They were reprinted in *The Defense of Guenevere*, which he published when he was 24. Fame and success came with two long poems, *The Life and Death of Jason*, based on ancient Greek myths, and *The Earthly Paradise*, 24 tales from classical and medieval times. His greatest poetic book was *Sigurd the Volsung*, a retelling of ancient sagas from Iceland and Norway.

Most of Morris's later writings were in prose, and many were devoted to spreading his socialist views and ideas for a better future (for example, *News from Nowhere*). In 1887, he and GEORGE BERNARD SHAW led a political demonstration in London. He also wrote historical romances of times long past in northern Europe, including *The Roots of the Mountains* and *The Wood beyond the World*.

Publications

1858 The Defense of Guenevere
1867 The Life and Death of Jason
1868–70 The Earthly Paradise
1876 Sigurd the Volsung
1882 Hopes and Fears for Art
1888 A Dream of John Ball
1890 The Roots of the Mountains
1891 News from Nowhere
1894 The Wood beyond the World

MORRISON, Toni

American novelist

Born Feb. 18, 1931

Toni Morrison is one of the world's most notable contemporary writers and only the second American woman to have won the Nobel Prize for Literature.

Morrison was born Chloe Anthony Wofford in Lorain, Ohio. Her parents shared a love of African-American folklore and music with their children, and she was taught to read before she started school.

Morrison graduated from Howard University in 1953 (where she became known as "Toni") then received a Master's degree from Cornell University in 1955. She married and had two sons, whom she raised on her own after her divorce in 1964. She became a book editor and eventually became responsible for the work of a number of leading black women writers, including TONI CADE BAMBARA and GAYL JONES. While working as an editor by day and caring for her children on her own, she wrote her first novel, *The Bluest Eye*, which was published when she was 39. It describes the experiences of young black girls struggling to define themselves. Part of their struggle is against "white" standards of beauty that are adopted even within the black community.

While compiling a book on "black life" in America from slavery to the 1940s called *The Black Book*, Morrison read documents that describe the lives of ordinary African Americans. Her novel *Beloved* is based on a story she discovered among these documents of a woman who tried to kill her children rather than allowing them to be sent back into slavery. The book earned her the Pulitzer Prize for fiction. She won the Nobel Prize for Literature in 1993.

Publications

1970 The Bluest Eye
1973 Sula
1974 The Black Book
1977 Song of Solomon
1981 Tar Baby
1986 Dreaming Emmett
1987 Beloved
1992 Jazz
1998 Paradise

MOSLEY, Walter

American crime writer

Born 1952

Walter Mosley is the most well-known African-American crime writer in the US today. President Clinton has called him his favorite crime novelist.

The son of a black father and a white Jewish mother, Mosley grew up in the tough Watts area of Los Angeles. His father was a school janitor. Mosley later moved to New York, where he worked as a painter, a caterer and a computer programer before becoming a full-time writer. Today Mosley still lives in New York, but his novels are set in Los Angeles.

Mosley's first work of fiction, *Gone Fishin',* was not a crime novel. It failed to find a publisher, and Mosley turned to the more commercial thriller genre instead. He wrote his first crime novel, *Devil in a Blue Dress*, when he was 38. It was an immediate success and was made into a film starring Denzel Washington.

In the series of novels that follow, Mosley offers a history of black Los Angeles, starting in the 1940s just after World War II, when African Americans migrated from the Southern states to work in California. He then moves on to the 1950s, a period when American society was obsessed with the fear of communism. His later books are set in the 1960s against a background of social rebellion during the civil rights movement.

The main character in Mosley's novels is Easy Rawlins, a school janitor (like Mosley's father) and a reluctant private detective. His friend Mouse is loyal but extremely violent. Like the hard-boiled detectives before him – such as RAYMOND CHANDLER's Philip Marlowe – Easy struggles to build a decent life for himself but becomes increasingly cynical about human nature.

Publications

1990 Devil in a Blue Dress
1991 A Red Death
1992 White Butterfly
1994 Black Betty
1996 A Little Yellow Dog
1997 Always Outnumbered, Always Outgunned

MPHAHLELE, Es'kia

South African novelist, short-story writer and poet

Born Dec. 17, 1919

Es'kia (formerly Ezekiel) Mphahlele, one of Africa's leading writers in English, wrote the classic novel *Down Second Avenue*.

Mphahlele was born in the slums of Pretoria, one of South Africa's major cities. From the age of 12, he lived with his grandmother and aunt, who made sure that Mphahlele could finally start school at the age of 13. He went on to be a teacher but was banned from teaching in 1952 after criticizing the government's planned Bantu Education Act. At that time, the white South Africans controlled the government and all the major industries. Racist laws restricted where black people could live and what work they could do. While continuing his studies, Mphahlele took a variety of jobs instead of teaching.

Mphahlele began writing short stories, but his work was banned by the white government, so he left South Africa. For 20 years, he lived abroad in Nigeria, France, Kenya, the US and Zambia. He worked as a university teacher while writing novels, poems and essays. Based on his years growing up in Pretoria, the novel *Down Second Avenue* came out when Mphahlele was 40. It describes the harm caused by racist apartheid policies. *Chirundu* is based on his time in Zambia, telling of the ups and downs of life in a newly independent country. His prizewinning *The Wanderers* is based on his years of exile. Mphahlele returned to South Africa in 1977. Back home, he continued the story of his life in *Africa My Music* and became head of African literature at the University of Witwatersrand in Johannesburg.

Publications

1947 Man Must Live
1959 Down Second Avenue
1961 The Living and Dead
1967 In Corner B
1971 The Wanderers
1972 Voices in the Whirlwind
1980 Chirundu
1984 Africa My Music
1984 Father Come Home
1985 Let's Talk Writing

MQHAYI, Samuel

South African novelist, short-story writer and poet

Born Dec. 1, 1875
Died Jul. 29, 1945
Age at death 69

Samuel Mqhayi is the most famous South African writer in the Xhosa language.

Mqhayi was born in the British Cape Colony, South Africa. Descended from a chief and the son of a teacher, he belonged to a high-ranking Xhosa family. The Xhosa are one of South Africa's main ethnic groups. When he was nine, the Cape was hit by famine, so his family moved northeast to Transkei. They settled near one of Mqhayi's uncles, a Xhosa chief. Listening to the tales of Xhosa warriors and attending meetings at the local court made a great impression on the young Mqhayi. He later used these memories in his classic novel *The Case of the Twins*.

When he was 22, Mqhayi's poems appeared in the newspaper *The Voice of the People*. Like most of his poetry, they were based on Xhosa praise-poems sung in honor of others. Mqhayi continued to work on this newspaper in between teaching jobs. Then, when he was 39, *The Case of the Twins* was published and made him famous. About the conflict between twin sons to decide who was born first and could, therefore, claim their father's estate, this novel shows how well African justice systems worked before the introduction of European laws. During Mqhayi's lifetime he had seen white South Africans become increasingly powerful at the expense of the rights of black Africans. His novel *U-Don Jadu* looks toward a future without racism.

Mqhayi would recite poems at important events and came to be known as the praise-poet of the entire Xhosa nation. He also translated many books into Xhosa, recorded Xhosa praise-poems, and standardized Xhosa spelling and grammar.

Publications

1914 The Case of the Twins
c. 1920 The Heroes of the Mendi
1923 The Church of the People
1927 Songs of Exaltation
1929 U-Don Jadu
1937 Hintza the Great
1939 Mqhayi from the Mountain of Glory
1942 Reward

MUNRO, Alice

Canadian short-story writer

Born Jul. 10, 1931

Alice Munro is known for the way she captures the details of ordinary rural lives in her short stories.

Munro was born in the small town of Wingham in rural Ontario. She grew up on a farm with her sister and brother. Her mother had been a teacher, and her father raised foxes, then worked as a watchman, then farmed. Munro also was expected to farm when she grew up, but she had other plans; by age 12 she had decided to become a writer.

Munro attended the University of Western Ontario on a scholarship. In 1951, she married a fellow student and moved with him to Vancouver, where she found herself trying to combine writing with being a suburban wife and mother. She published a few stories in literary magazines, and in the 1960s she and her husband started a bookstore.

It was not until she was 37 that Munro published a book – a collection of 15 stories called *Dance of the Happy Shades*. It was highly praised and won her Canada's prestigious Governor General's Award. But it was *Lives of Girls and Women*, Munro's second collection, that earned her international attention. The linked stories describe the childhood of a young woman in rural Canada who wants to become a writer. The book was made into a TV movie starring Munro's daughter, Jenny.

Influenced by writers such as EUDORA WELTY and FLANNERY O'CONNOR, Munro writes about the peculiarities and customs of small-town life. However, the issues she addresses are broad and relevant to all of humanity.

Publications

1968 Dance of the Happy Shades
1971 Lives of Girls and Women
1974 Something I've Been Meaning to Tell You
1978 The Beggar Maid
1982 The Moons of Jupiter
1986 The Progress of Love
1990 Friend of My Youth
1994 Open Secrets
1998 Love of a Good Woman: Stories

MURASAKI Shikibu

Japanese poet and novelist

Born c. 978
Died c. 1026
Age at death c. 48

Murasaki Shikibu is the pen name of the author of *The Tale of Genji*, which has been described as the greatest work in the history of Japanese literature.

Little is known about Murasaki's life, not even her real name. She was born into a powerful aristocratic family and was educated along with her brothers in the arts of poetry. It was not uncommon for aristocratic women to be educated in literature at this time in Japan.

In 999 Murasaki was married to a man so much older than herself that he already had a son who was older than she was. Around this time she began to keep a diary detailing life at the court of a Japanese empress. Murasaki's husband died within two years. The empress came to hear of her talents as a poet and appointed her to the imperial court.

The Tale of Genji was based on Murasaki's experiences of court life. It is about the romances of Prince Genji and the lives of his descendants. Set in a world of complex social ritual, elegance and beauty, it is a very long and complicated tale that follows the intricate social lives and love affairs of its characters. Although there is no real central story, the skill with which the author describes the emotions and thoughts of the many characters, especially the women, was far ahead of any other writer of the period. For this reason many scholars describe *The Tale of Genji* as the first true novel.

The Tale of Genji became known in the West more than 900 years after it was written when an English poet published a translation in the 1920s.

Publications

c. 1010 The Tale of Genji

MURDOCH, Iris

Anglo-Irish novelist, philosopher and playwright

Born Jul. 15, 1919
Died Feb. 8, 1999
Age at death 79

Iris Murdoch is one of the most important writers of her generation. She has written many books on philosophy, and even her fiction has been described as "novels of ideas." In recognition of her work, she was made a Dame in 1987.

Murdoch was born in Dublin, Ireland, but was brought up in England. Her mother was Irish and her father English. After graduating from Oxford University, she worked for the United Nations as an administrative officer. From 1948 to 1963, she taught philosophy at Oxford.

Murdoch's first book was about philosophy. She began writing stories as a hobby, and her first novel, *Under the Net*, came out when she was 35. It was an instant success, and she has since followed it by over 20 others as well as more philosophical works.

The Bell, whose subject is an unofficial religious community, is regarded as one of her best novels. *A Severed Head*, first published as a novel, was turned into a play with the help of J.B. PRIESTLEY. She later wrote several more plays.

Murdoch's novels combine realistic characters with extraordinary situations, often bordering on the fantastic. Many of them have a religious or philosophical theme. For example, *The Time of the Angels* features a priest in an inner-city parish who goes in for devil worship. Some critics describe her novels as "psychological detective stories" because of the way in which they investigate in great detail the motives and consequences of the characters' behavior.

Publications

1954	*Under the Net*
1958	*The Bell*
1961	*A Severed Head*
1966	*The Time of the Angels*
1972	*The Two Arrows*
1974	*The Sacred and Profane Love Machine*
1978	*The Sea, the Sea*
1983	*The Philosopher's Pupil*
1995	*Jackson's Dilemma*

NABOKOV, Vladimir

Russian-born American novelist

Born Apr. 23, 1899
Died Jul. 2, 1977
Age at death 78

Vladimir Nabokov was an outstanding 20th-century writer. He is best known for his novel *Lolita*.

Nabokov was born in St. Petersburg, Russia, into an aristocratic family. An intelligent child, he learned to speak English and French as well as his native Russian. His first poems were published before he was 20.

Nabokov's family lost its wealth during the Russian Revolution and in 1919 moved abroad. Nabokov studied at Cambridge University, and from 1922 until 1940 lived first in Germany and then Paris, where he met the great novelist JAMES JOYCE and mixed with Russian refugees. During these years he published nine novels, writing in Russian under the pen name Vladimir Serin. His reputation as an inventive novelist grew, but he earned little money and survived by teaching.

In 1940, Nabokov, his wife and son moved to America, where he took citizenship in 1945. His first novel in English was *The Real Life of Sebastian Knight*, published when he was 42; from then on he wrote all his books in English. From 1948 to 1959, he taught at Cornell University, using this experience for his novel *Pnin*, a comic account of a Russian professor at an American university.

When he was in his mid-50s, Nabokov's masterpiece, *Lolita*, was published. It tells the story of a middle-aged man and his passion for his 12-year-old stepdaughter. The novel's subject matter shocked many people, but its humor and literary style were praised by critics. *Lolita* was an instant success; it shot Nabokov to fame and enabled him to devote himself to writing.

Publications

1926 Mary
1928 King, Queen, Knave
1932 Laughter in the Dark
1936 Despair
1937–38 The Gift
1938 Invitation to a Beheading
1941 The Real Life of Sebastian Knight
1947 Bend Sinister
1955 Lolita
1957 Pnin

NAIPAUL, V.S.

Trinidadian-born British novelist

Born Aug. 17, 1932

Many consider V.S. Naipaul to be one of the world's most gifted novelists. He has written about many different cultures and problems faced by ordinary people all over the world.

Vidiadhar Surajprasad Naipaul was born in Trinidad to Indian parents. He went to England to study at Oxford University and settled in that country.

Naipaul's first three books are lighthearted novels about Trinidadian life, starting with *The Mystic Masseur*, which came out when Naipaul was 25. He came to fame at the age of 29 with his fourth novel, *A House for Mr. Biswas*, also set in Trinidad. Its central character was based on his father, a mild-mannered journalist.

From then on, Naipaul moved the setting of his novels to other places. *Mr. Stone and the Knights Companion* is set in London. He returned to the Caribbean in *The Mimic Men*, in which the action takes place on a fictitious island, and in *Guerrillas*, which describes a violent uprising on yet another island.

Naipaul has become increasingly absorbed with the problems of less-developed countries. In *A Bend in the River* he traces, with the expectance of a bad outcome, the development of a West African state whose dictator-president tries to control events through periods of revolution and counterrevolution.

Besides his novels, Naipaul has written several books about travel and politics. Among them are three studies of India since independence, including *India: A Wounded Civilization* (1977) and *Among the Believers: An Islamic Journey* (1981).

Publications

1957 The Mystic Masseur
1958 The Suffrage of Elvira
1961 A House for Mr. Biswas
1963 Mr. Stone and the Knights Companion
1967 The Mimic Men
1971 In a Free State
1975 Guerrillas
1979 A Bend in the River
1994 A Way in the World
1998 Beyond Belief

NARAYAN, R.K.

Indian novelist, short-story writer and essayist

Born Oct. 10, 1906

Publications

1935	*Swami and Friends*
1937	*The Bachelor of Arts*
1938	*The Dark Room*
1945	*Grateful to Love and Death*
1949	*The Printer of Malgudi*
1958	*The Guide*
1961	*The Man-Eater of Malgudi*
1967	*The Vendor of Sweets*
1977	*The Painter of Signs*
1990	*The World of Nagaraj*

R.K. Narayan is an outstanding Indian novelist recognized as a writer of international importance.

Narayan was born Rasipuram Krishnaswami Narayanswami in Madras in the south of India and was raised by his grandmother. He was educated in Madras and at the Maharaja's College in Mysore. He worked as a teacher before becoming a full-time writer, choosing to write in English, the language of educated Indians.

Narayan's 11 novels are set in the imaginary town of Malgudi. The last seven of the series are works of the first rank, revealing his wisdom, sophistication and power. His style is simple, elegant, and has a delicate humor. As the greatest Hindu novelist who has written in English, he provides an insight into the values and traditions of Hinduism. His books deal with the realities of life, with moral questions, human relationships, and the conflict between traditional and modern urban life.

Narayan believes in the Hindu doctrine of reincarnation (being reborn after death), and this is an important theme in his later fiction. He is concerned with the process of human improvement – the characters that interest him most are those people who are "insane" because of their lack of knowledge about themselves.

Many critics regard *The Guide* as his best work. It is a part-comedy, part-tragedy about the conversion to holiness of a con man. Narayan has also written short stories, travel and children's books, essays and his memoirs.

NASH, Ogden

American poet

Born Aug. 19, 1902
Died May 19, 1971
Age at death 68

Ogden Nash was an original and funny poet whose work has often been imitated, but few other poets of light verse have been as popular. He used simple, oddly spelled, unusually rhymed verse to mock, surprise, or just raise a laugh. Some of his lines, such as "Candy is dandy, but liquor is quicker," have become established parts of American culture.

Nash was born in Rye, New York, to parents of Southern stock. He was raised in Savannah, Georgia, and several other cities because the family moved around with his father's business. Between 1917 and 1920, he attended St. George's School in Newport, Rhode Island, then Harvard University from 1920 to 1921, when he left to earn a living. He went back to St. George's to teach, then to Wall

Street to work as a bond salesman. He admits he sold only one bond, to his godmother, and wisely moved into advertising. Nash did well in advertising, having an original and clever sense of humor.

In his spare time he tried his hand at serious poetry. He wanted to write about beauty, truth, eternity and pain, like the poets he admired, such as JOHN KEATS and LORD BYRON. He decided later that he was better at humorous verse. His first published work, *The Cricket of Carador*, was a children's book. After a few years of scribbling down verses on office paper, Nash published his first book of humorous verse, *Hard Lines*, when he was 29. It was so successful that Nash soon quit his job in advertising and within four years was able to concentrate on his writing alone. Other well-known works include *Happy Days* and *The Bad Parents' Garden of Verse*.

Publications

1925 The Cricket of Carador
1931 Hard Lines
1931 Free Wheeling
1936 The Bad Parents' Garden of Verse
1938 I'm a Stranger Here Myself
1953 The Private Dining Room, and Other New Verses
1959 Verse from 1929 On
1959 Custard the Dragon

NAYLOR, Gloria

American novelist

Born Jan. 25, 1950

The strength of women working together to fight racism is one of the themes of Gloria Naylor's novels, which convey both the sufferings and the triumphs of African-American women. When she was 38, Naylor became one of the few African-American women writers to win a prestigious Guggenheim fellowship.

Although she was born in New York, the South had a big influence on Naylor. Her parents – a telephone operator and a transit worker – had worked as sharecroppers in Mississippi until just before she was born, and she grew up with stories of life there.

After secondary school, Naylor worked as a Jehovah's Witness missionary for seven years, then enrolled in Brooklyn College. While there she read TONI MORRISON's *The Bluest Eye*, which made a huge impression on her; it was the first time she saw her own experience as a black woman reflected in literature, and it made her want to write.

While in university Naylor supported herself as a telephone operator in New York hotels. After graduating in 1981, she went to Yale, where she received her Master's degree in 1983. She had also been working on her first novel, which she published when she was 32. In seven separate but interlocking stories *The Women of Brewster Place* tells of a community of women who live on a run-down street in a black ghetto. They struggle together to break down the walls of racism that keep them poor and oppressed. It won the National Book Award for best first novel and was made into a television movie starring Oprah Winfrey.

Publications

1982 The Women of Brewster Place
1985 Linden Hills
1988 Mama Day
1992 Bailey's Café

NELLIGAN, Emile

Canadian poet

Born Dec. 24, 1879
Died Nov. 18, 1941
Age at death 61

Emile Nelligan wrote all his poems in a period of three years between the ages of 17 and 20. He is famous not only for the brilliance of these poems but also for bringing French-Canadian poetry into the modern age.

Nelligan was born in Montreal, Quebec, where he and his two sisters attended school. Doted on by his French-Canadian mother, he enjoyed a blissfully happy childhood. At age 17, he quit school and joined the now famous L'École Littéraire de Montréal, a circle of young writers who met weekly to discuss the arts and to try to revive the French cultural life of Quebec. At the circle's meetings, he read his poems to great acclaim. In 1899, however, a minor French critic spoke harshly of his work. Nelligan was so devastated that he withdrew into his own private world and threatened to commit suicide. A year later he was diagnosed as suffering from mental illness and, at age 20, was admitted to a hospital, where he remained until his death 40 years later.

Nelligan's poems were considered modern because, unlike other French-Canadian poets of the time, he did not write about overused, impersonal subjects such as patriotism and the glories of old France. Instead, he explored the dark corners of his own tortured soul and turned to his dreams and his childhood memories for inspiration and escape from the difficulties of the world. His poems were first published four years after he was hospitalized. He made such an impact in his short creative life that more than 600 critical writings on his work have appeared in print.

Publications

1903 Emile Nelligan and His Work

Published after he died

1952 Complete Poems: 1896–99
1960 Selected Poems
1983 The Complete Poems of Emile Nelligan

NEMEROV, Howard

American poet, short-story writer and novelist

Born Mar. 1, 1920
Died Jul. 5, 1991
Age at death 71

Howard Nemerov is highly respected for his witty and often ironic poetry. He was also a successful novelist and short-story writer. His achievements both as a poet and an educator earned him many awards, including the post of Poet Laureate of America from 1988 to 1990.

Nemerov was born in New York City and educated at the Fieldston School. He graduated from Harvard in 1941 and, during World War II, served in both the Royal Canadian and US air forces. After the war, he taught at various universities and for two years was poetry consultant at the Library of Congress. He taught at Washington University, St. Louis, from 1969, and for the last 14 years of his life he was titled Distinguished Professor of English there.

Nemerov's first volume of poetry, *The Image and the Law*, was published when he was 27. His early poetry was influenced by the great Irish poet W.B. YEATS and by WALLACE STEVENS. Like them, Nemerov saw poetry as a shield from the chaos that is the natural world. The poems of Nemerov's collections *The Next Room of the Dream* and *The Blue Swallows* show a new clarity and directness and reflect the mood of rapid change in 1960s America. Nemerov himself identified influences of more radical poets, such as T.S. ELIOT.

The Collected Poems, published when Nemerov was 57, contained verse from all his previous books and caused a reevaluation of Nemerov's status. He was awarded the Pulitzer Prize the following year. *Trying Conclusions* was published in the year of his death and contained many new poems. It is the companion volume to *The Collected Poems*.

Publications

1947 The Image and the Law
1950 Guide to the Ruins
1957 The Homecoming Game
1960 New and Selected Poems
1962 The Next Room of the Dream
1967 The Blue Swallows
1973 Gnomes and Occasions
1977 The Collected Poems
1984 Inside the Onion
1991 Trying Conclusions

NERUDA, Pablo

Chilean poet

Born Jul. 12, 1904
Died Sep. 23, 1973
Age at death 69

Pablo Neruda was one of the greatest South American poets and is certainly the best known. His poems have been translated into many languages, and he was awarded the Nobel Prize for Literature in 1971.

Neruda was born in Chile, the son of a poor railway worker. He was named Naftalí Reyes, and he began writing poetry when he was ten years old. He did not use the name by which he is now known until he published his first poems in student magazines as a teenager.

In 1921, Neruda went to study at teachers' training college in Santiago, the capital city. Almost immediately he established himself as a powerful new voice in Chilean poetry. When he was 20, he published *Twenty Love Poems and a Song of Despair*, the collection that first brought him international fame.

At the age of only 23, Neruda was appointed by the Chilean government as a consul in Burma (now Myanmar). This was the start of a diplomatic career that took him all over Asia and South America and to Spain, where he became close friends with the poet FEDERICO GARCÍA LORCA. When García Lorca was executed soon after the outbreak of the Spanish Civil War, Neruda's poetry grew increasingly political, and he became a committed communist.

Soon after World War II, Neruda's politics almost cost him his life when the Chilean government was taken over by right-wing extremists. He escaped by crossing the Andes Mountains on horseback. Neruda returned to Chile in 1952 and lived there for the rest of his life, writing and campaigning.

Publications

1924 Twenty Love Poems and a Song of Despair
1933 Residence on Earth
1945 The Heights of Macchu Picchu
1950 Canto General
1954 Elementary Odes
1967 Twenty Poems
1972 Captain's Verses

Published after he died

1977 Memoirs

NESBIT, E.

English children's writer

Born Aug. 15, 1858
Died May 4, 1924
Age at death 65

Publications

1886	*Lays and Legends*
1899	*The Story of the Treasure Seekers*
1901	*Nine Unlikely Tales for Children*
1901	*The Wouldbegoods*
1902	*Five Children and It*
1904	*The Phoenix and the Carpet*
1904	*The New Treasure Seekers*
1906	*The Railway Children*

Published after she died

1928	*The Bastable Children*

E. Nesbit was an English writer who is remembered for her stories for children. Her most famous book is *The Railway Children*.

Edith Nesbit was born in London, the last of six children. Her father, a scientist, died when she was young, and she was sent to a boarding school for her education, which she hated. Memories of her early life as part of a large family later inspired Nesbit's writings for children.

When she was 22 and living back in London, Nesbit married. Soon after the wedding her husband was cheated in a business deal, and the couple found themselves with little money and a young son to support. Nesbit had already had a few poems published, and she turned to writing articles and stories to earn money for the family.

Nesbit had always wanted to be a poet, and her first collection of poems, *Lays and Legends*, was published when she was 28. Her poetry was never successful, and she did not become known until she began to write children's stories in her mid-30s.

Nesbit started writing a series of books about the adventures of six brothers and sisters called the Bastables. The first of these, *The Story of the Treasure Seekers*, was published when she was 41. The Bastable family was very like Nesbit's own, and their adventures were set in the real world. *The Railway Children* was another realistic adventure, based on Nesbit's memories of a childhood home that had a railway nearby. She also wrote fantasy stories, such as *Five Children and It* and *The Phoenix and the Carpet*, which are full of magic and mystery.

NETO, Agostinho

Angolan poet

Born Sep. 17, 1922
Died Sep. 10, 1979
Age at death 56

Agostinho Neto was Angola's leading poet as well as that country's first president.

Neto was born in a village near Luanda, the capital of Angola, which was then a Portuguese colony. He studied at local schools before becoming a nurse at the age of 22. For three years he saved money to study medicine, and during that time he helped set up a cultural association which became increasingly anticolonial. With his savings and extra help from his village and friends, he traveled to Portugal to study medicine in 1947.

Neto's studies in Portugal were interrupted three times by arrest and imprisonment. He became involved in various anticolonial political movements and began writing poetry that reflected his political views. His poems, some of which were published when he was 26, deal with freedom, and many were smuggled out of jail. His writings brought him much attention, and after being arrested for the third time, international outcry forced the Portuguese to release him. Neto finally returned to Angola as a doctor in 1958.

In 1959, Neto was made leader of the MPLA (Popular Movement for the Liberation of Angola). A year later he was arrested and held in prisons and under house arrest. He managed to escape in 1962 and lead the MPLA in the armed struggle against Portuguese rule. Angola finally became independent in 1975 with Neto as its first president. By that time, however, the struggle had turned into a civil war, and Neto was never to rule over a unified Angola; he died of cancer four years later.

Publications

1961 Collected Poems
1963 With Dry Eyes
1974 Sacred Hope
1979 Poems from Angola

NGUGI, wa Thiong'o

Kenyan novelist, short-story writer and playwright

Born Jan. 5, 1938

Ngugi wa Thiong'o (formerly known as James Ngugi) is East Africa's most important writer. He wrote the first major English language novel, *Weep Not, Child*, to be published by an East African author.

Ngugi was born near Nairobi, the capital of Kenya, which was then a British colony. His family was poor and belonged to Kenya's largest ethnic group, the Kikuyu. His mother managed to send him to school, and he attended university in Kampala, now the capital of neighboring Uganda. After graduating in 1964, Ngugi worked as a reporter before traveling to England to study at the University of Leeds.

Together, his three famous novels of the 1960s chart the history of Kenya from before British rule to independence. *The River Between* tells of a time when European missionaries, but not European rule, had come to East Africa. *Weep Not, Child* tells of the impact the anti-British Mau Mau rebellion during the mid-1950s had on a poor boy's family. *A Grain of Wheat* deals with the social, moral and racial issues in the struggle for independence and in the early days of independence.

Ngugi returned to Kenya at age 29 and became the head of the literature department at the University of Nairobi five years later. In 1977, he published *Petals of Blood* and co-wrote the play *I Will Marry When I Want*, both of which criticized the leaders of Kenya. For this he was imprisoned for nearly a year without trial and lost his job. He now writes full time but deplores the fact that most of the Kenyans about whom he writes cannot read his books. He has since tried to overcome this by writing only in Kikuyu.

Publications

1964 Weep Not, Child
1965 The River Between
1967 A Grain of Wheat
1974 Secret Lives
1977 Trial of Dedan Kimathi
1977 Petals of Blood
1977 I Will Marry When I Want
1980 Devil on the Cross
1981 Detained: A Writer's Prison Diary
1986 Matigari

NICHOLS, Grace

Guyanese-British poet and children's writer

Born Jan. 18, 1950

Publications

1980	*Trust You, Wriggly*
1983	*i Is a Long Memoried Woman*
1984	*Leslyn in London*
1984	*The Fat Black Woman's Poems*
1986	*Whole of a Morning Sky*
1988	*Come On into My Tropical Garden*
1989	*Lazy Thoughts of a Lazy Woman*
1994	*Give Yourself a Hug*

Grace Nichols is one of Britain's most respected and popular contemporary poets. She often uses the landscapes and language of her native Guyana in her work.

Nichols was born in Georgetown, the capital of Guyana in South America, where she attended the University of Guyana. At 17, she began working as a teacher, then as a journalist for several years. At age 27, she moved to Britain, where she became known initially for her writing for children. Her first book, the children's story collection *Trust You, Wriggly*, was published when she was 30, and four years later she published a children's novel, *Leslyn in London*.

It was when she was 33 that Nichols first came to the attention of adult readers with her poetry collection, *i Is a Long Memoried Woman*. The book won an important literary prize and launched Nichols's career as a "serious" writer. Since then she has written for both children and adults.

In much of her work, Nichols explores Guyanese life and issues of race and gender. In *The Fat Black Woman's Poems* she argues against the "jovial Jemima" image often used to stereotype black women, and her character celebrates her large body: "my thighs are twin seals / fat slick pups." At age 36, she wrote her first novel for adults, *Whole of a Morning Sky*, based on her childhood in Guyana.

Nichols uses humor in her work and language that reflects the way people speak rather than read. She is married to John Agard, another poet from Guyana, and they have one daughter. In 1994, she and Agard edited the poetry collection *A Black Dozen*.

NIETZSCHE, Friedrich

German philosopher and writer

Born Oct. 15, 1844
Died Aug. 25, 1900
Age at death 55

Publications

1872	*The Birth of Tragedy*
1873–76	*Untimely Meditations*

Friedrich Nietzsche was an important German philosopher whose work had a strong influence on politics and literature.

Nietzsche was born in a small German village. His father died when he was five, and he and his younger sister were brought up by their mother. At university in the German city of Bonn, he studied theology at first but soon switched to philosophy.

Nietzsche was a brilliant student, and at the age of just 24 became a professor at the University of Basel in Switzerland. At Basel he became a close friend of the great German composer Richard Wagner, who shared his views about politics and society – views Nietzsche made clear in his *Untimely Meditations*, which contains strong criticisms of German culture and institutions.

In famous books such as *Thus Spoke Zarathustra* and *Beyond Good and Evil* Nietzsche set out his radical ideas. He believed that Christianity no longer had a place in society, and individuals must create their own ideas about what is right and wrong, a view he summed up in his famous phrase "God is dead." Many writers have been both fascinated and horrified by Nietzsche's ideas. The ideal human being described by Nietzsche – a passionate person who controls his passion and puts it to creative use – became the hero of many late 19th-century novels and plays.

Nietzsche acquired a bad reputation when his ideas were taken up by German Nazis in the 1930s to justify their anti-Jewish policies, although this was never part of his philosophy.

1878–90 Human, All-Too-Human
1883–85 Thus Spoke Zarathustra
1886 Beyond Good and Evil
1887 On the Genealogy of Morals
1889 Twilight of the Idols

Published after he died
1901 The Will to Power
1908 Ecce Homo

NIN, Anaïs

French-born American writer

Born Feb. 21, 1903
Died Jan. 14, 1977
Age at death 73

Anaïs Nin is most famous for her eight-volume *Diary of Anaïs Nin*. Combining truth and fiction, the diaries relate her inner journey of self-discovery and also give a fascinating account of the era from 1914 to the 1970s. The diaries also made Nin a major figure in the 1970s women's movement.

Nin was born to artistic parents near Paris. After her father deserted the family when Nin was 11, they moved to New York City. She left school when she was 15, and taught herself in public libraries. Nin moved back to Paris in the 1920s and studied the workings of the mind with the famous doctor Otto Rank. In the 1930s, Nin, already a published author, became friends with a group of well-known writers and artists, including HENRY MILLER. Lifelong friends, Nin and Miller both influenced each other in their work. When World War II broke out, she returned to New York and set up the Gemor Press to print her own books. Nin had been writing lyrical books about women for over 30 years before becoming famous with the publication of the first volume of her diary when she was 63. She died 11 years later, at the height of her fame.

The *House of Incest* has been called Nin's best fiction. It combines prose and poetry to retell a woman's nightmare. One of her largest projects was the five-volume *Cities of the Interior*, which follows the lives of three women. After trying to find happiness through lovers, art and analysis, only one manages to reach acceptance of herself. The bestselling *Delta of Venus* collects sexually explicit stories that Nin wrote for a dollar a page while poor in the 1940s.

Publications
1936 House of Incest
1939 Winter of Artifice
1944 Under a Glass Bell
1946–61 Cities of the Interior (5 vols.)
1964 Collages
1966–80 Diary of Anaïs Nin (8 vols, some after she died)

Published after she died
1977 Delta of Venus

NIXON, Joan Lowery

American young-adults' writer

Born Feb. 3, 1927

Joan Lowery Nixon has been called the "grande dame" of young-adult mystery writers. She is the first author to have won the EDGAR ALLAN POE Award for the best mystery book of the year four times.

Nixon was born Joan Lowery in Los Angeles. She had a happy and creative childhood and published her first poem in the magazine *Children's Playmate* when she was just ten. She grew up in Hollywood and attended local state schools before studying journalism at the University of Southern California. After graduating in 1947, she found it difficult to find work as a journalist since she was a woman competing against men returning from World War II. She took a job teaching primary school and liked it so much that she trained to be teacher. In 1949 she married, becoming Joan Lowery Nixon, qualified as a teacher, and began teaching 8-year-olds. Over much of the next two decades Nixon was busy raising her four children and teaching.

The family often moved due to her husband's work. While they were living in Texas, Nixon went to a writers' conference, which inspired her to try writing fiction for children. Her daughters insisted that she include them in her book, which should be a mystery. Nixon had always enjoyed mystery books even as a child, and her first book, *The Mystery of Hurricane Castle*, came out when she was 37. She gave up teaching soon afterward and focused on writing. Nixon has since written over 100 books for children and young adults, mostly mysteries and historical fiction. She is known for well-written characters, fast-paced plots, and for mixing suspense with humor.

Publications

- *1964 The Mystery of Hurricane Castle*
- *1979 The Kidnapping of Christina Lattimore*
- *1980 The Seance*
- *1986 The Other Side of Dark*
- *1988 A Family Apart*
- *1989 In the Face of Danger*
- *1992 Land of Hope*
- *1993 The Name of the Game Was Murder*

NORMAN, Marsha

American playwright

Born Sep. 21, 1947

Marsha Norman won the 1983 Pulitzer Prize for her play *'Night Mother* and has been described as one of America's most promising new playwrights. Most of her plays focus on women and their search for identity. Several explore the relationship between mother and daughter.

Before becoming a playwright, Norman held a variety of jobs. After graduating from the University of Louisville, Kentucky, she taught emotionally disturbed children and worked as a writer for television and as a journalist.

Although from the South (she was born in Louisville, Kentucky), Norman insists that she is not a "Southern woman." She writes from a universally American point of view and makes sure that her plays are not obviously set in a particular region. *Getting Out*, first staged when Norman was 30, is now one of her most popular plays and has won several awards. It attacks the failure both of a daughter's relationship with her mother and of the prison system. Arlene, the main character, is released from prison supposedly reformed, yet it becomes clear that she has left one prison for another.

Among Norman's many plays, her most famous is *'Night Mother*. This powerful play has only two characters, a mother and her daughter. The daughter, Jessie, commits suicide, but this action is portrayed as an act of triumph. There was great controversy over this treatment of suicide when the play first appeared.

Norman has also written a musical, *The Secret Garden*, based on FRANCES HODGSON BURNETT's famous children's book, and a novel, *The Fortune Teller*.

Publications

1977 Getting Out

1978 Third and Oak: The Laundromat

1979 Circus Valentine

1980–83 The Holdup

1983 'Night Mother

1984 Traveler in the Dark

1987 The Fortune Teller

1988 Sarah and Abraham

1991 The Secret Garden

1992 D. Boone

NORRIS, Frank

American novelist

Born Mar. 5, 1870

Died Oct. 25, 1902

Age at death 32

Frank Norris has been called the first important naturalistic American novelist. He pioneered the literary style of realism in his books about social injustice.

Shortly after his birth in Chicago, Norris and his family moved to San Francisco, where he spent his early years. From 1887 to 1889, Norris studied art in Paris, France. Once back in the United States, he attended the University of California, where he was greatly influenced by the writings of French novelist ÉMILE ZOLA. He also studied at Harvard, where his professors encouraged him to write.

From 1895 to 1896, Norris covered the Boer War in South Africa for the *San Francisco Chronicle* and *Collier's* magazine. When he was 28, he moved to New York City to write for *McClure's Magazine* and was sent to Cuba to report on the Spanish-American War.

These experiences inspired Norris to develop a realistic literary style to portray the effects of modern technology on society. His first major novel was *McTeague*, which was published when he was 29. It is about a drunken dentist who murders his wife.

Toward the end of his life, Norris began to write a trilogy called *Epic of the Wheat*. The first volume, *The Octopus*, highlights the struggle between railway interests and wheat farmers in California. The second volume, *The Pit*, describes wheat speculation on the Chicago Board of Trade. Norris died of complications following an operation for appendicitis before he was able to begin the third volume, *The Wolf*, which was to be about wheat and food distribution.

Publications

1898 Moran of the Lady Letty

1899 McTeague

1899 Blix

1900 A Man's Woman

1901 The Octopus

Published after he died

1903 The Pit

1903 A Deal in Wheat

1909 The Third Circle

1914 Vandover and the Brute

NWAPA, Flora

Nigerian novelist and short-story writer

Born Jan. 18, 1931
Died Oct. 16, 1996
Age at death 65

Flora Nwapa has been called the mother of modern African literature. Her novel *Efuru*, the first published by a woman in Nigeria (West Africa), was one of the first works of African literature to concentrate on the experiences of women.

Nwapa was born in Oguta, eastern Nigeria, which was then a British colony. She was educated at various Nigerian schools before training to be a teacher at the University of Edinburgh. On her return to Nigeria, she worked as an education officer for women and as a teacher and was assistant registrar at the University of Lagos. After the Biafran War, a civil war in Nigeria in the late 1960s, Nwapa was employed by the Ministry of Health and Welfare in the war-torn eastern part of the country. Her tasks included finding homes for 2,000 war orphans. *Never Again*, her novel written in remembrance of the war, tells of the vital role that women played.

After five years, Nwapa retired from her work for the state government. Soon after this, however, she founded her own printing press and a publishing company. Her aims are to publish African-language books, to guide African children, and to educate non-Africans about Africa.

Many of Nwapa's books focus on the lives and roles of women. *Efuru*, *Idu* and *One Is Enough* are stories of women searching for fulfillment. Efuru and Idu want more than just to have children. Efuru loses two husbands and a child but eventually finds happiness as an independent, single woman and follower of the goddess Uhamiri, who gives her worshipers wealth and beauty but few children.

Publications

1966 Efuru
1970 Idu
1971 This Is Lagos and Other Stories
1975 Never Again
1979 Mammywater
1980 Wives at War and Other Stories
1981 One Is Enough
1986 Women Are Different

OATES, Joyce Carol

American novelist and short-story writer

Born Jun. 16, 1938

Joyce Carol Oates is one of America's most respected and prolific contemporary writers, having published more than 55 books since 1963.

Oates was born in Lockport, New York, and was raised a Catholic in an Irish-American, working-class family. Her primary school was a one-room schoolhouse. She began writing at age 14, after being given a typewriter. Oates received a scholarship to Syracuse University, and while there she wrote a novel each semester. She earned a Master's degree in 1961, and that year she married. She and her husband settled in Detroit. The city's social turmoil at that time had an enormous influence on her early career.

Oates published her first book, the short-story collection *By the*

North Gate, at age 25. For the next few years, in addition to teaching at a nearby university, she wrote two or three books a year, including the National Book Award-winning *Them*. Like much of her work it features violence, in particular men's violence against women.

In 1978, Oates and her husband moved to Princeton, New Jersey, where they founded a literary magazine, *The Ontario Review*. She teaches creative writing at Princeton University and continues to write. In addition to novels she writes short stories; one of her stories that often appears in short-story collections is "Where Are You Going, Where Have You Been." Her novels cover a range of literary genres, including gloomy gothic stories, romances and thrillers (the latter published under the pen name Rosamond Smith). She is also a boxing fan, an interest reflected in her collection of essays entitled *On Boxing* (1987).

Publications

1967	*A Garden of Earthly Delights*
1968	*Expensive People*
1969	*Them*
1973	*Do With Me What You Will*
1980	*Bellefleur*
1986	*Marya: A Life*
1992	*Black Water*
1993	*Foxfire: Confessions of a Girl Gang*
1997	*Man Crazy*

O'BRIAN, Patrick

Irish novelist and biographer

Born 1914
Died Jan 2, 2000
Age at death 88

Patrick O'Brian is celebrated for his exciting sea stories set during the Napoleonic Wars.

O'Brian was born in Ireland to Anglo-Irish parents. As a child he suffered ill-health. He also moved about a good deal and was partly self-taught. O'Brian learned French, Catalan and Spanish, and this knowledge helped his secret intelligence-gathering work during World War II. After the war, he lived in Wales with his wife Mary, and later they moved to a French village on the Mediterranean Sea, close to Spain.

From his home in France, O'Brian wrote short stories and reviews and translated some of the works of Simone de Beauvoir. His first novel, *Testimonies*, appeared when he was 38, but he earned little from writing until the first of his series of historical naval novels was published 18 years later. *Master and Commander* introduced readers to the adventures of Captain "Lucky" Jack Aubrey of the Royal Navy and his oddball friend Stephen Maturin, an Irish-Catalan doctor, naturalist and British government spy.

O'Brian's own background helped him invent believable sea stories set in the past. They are filled with unexpected incidents and lively details that show how sailors talked, thought, ate, slept, worked and fought two centuries ago.

By the age of 83, O'Brian had produced 18 Aubrey-Maturin stories set in various parts of the world. Some critics consider them among the finest of all historical novels. O'Brian's other works include his biography of the artist Pablo Picasso, who was a friend and neighbor in France.

Publications

1952	*Testimonies*
1970	*Master and Commander*
1972	*Post Captain*
1973	*HMS Surprise*
1977	*The Mauritius Command*
1981	*The Ionian Mission*
1984	*The Far Side of the World*
1989	*The Thirteen-Gun Salute*
1990	*The Letter of Marque*
1997	*The Yellow Admiral*
1998	*The Hundred Days*

O'BRIEN, Edna

Irish novelist, short-story writer, and playwright

Born Dec. 15, 1932

Edna O'Brien is best known for her stories of girls and women living in Ireland.

O'Brien was born a farmer's daughter, in Tuamgraney, a Catholic village in the west of Ireland. She received a strict Catholic education at a convent school in the town of Loughrea. At 16, she left to work in a Dublin pharmacy, studying at the Pharmaceutical College in her spare time. At 20, she married the novelist Ernest Gebler. The couple moved to London when O'Brien was 25, but divorced when she was in her early 30s. By then she had two sons.

O'Brien had written tales while a child but was 28 when she published her first novel. *The Country Girls* tells of two Irish girls: soft-hearted and trusting Caithleen and bolder and spiteful Baba. Like O'Brien herself, both are strictly brought up in a small, narrow-minded village community and excited when they become old enough to find work and romance in the city of Dublin. O'Brien's next books, *The Lonely Girl* and *Girls in Their Married Bliss*, take both grown-up girls to London, where they live after making unhappy marriages – as O'Brien herself did.

Many of O'Brien's stories attack the harsh way girls like her were brought up in Ireland or tell of a heroine's loneliness and sad love affairs. Her musical language conveys a strong feeling of what Ireland and the Irish are like.

A Fanatic Heart and other collections of short stories by O'Brien also deal with feelings of love, loss and guilt. She has written several plays and a book of fairy stories for children based on Irish folklore.

Publications

1960	*The Country Girls*
1962	*The Lonely Girl*
1964	*Girls in Their Married Bliss*
1968	*The Love Object*
1970	*A Pagan Place*
1972	*Night*
1982	*Returning*
1984	*A Fanatic Heart*
1986	*Tales for the Telling*
1994	*The House of Splendid Isolation*

O'BRIEN, Flann

Irish novelist and journalist

Born Oct. 5, 1911
Died Apr. 1, 1966
Age at death 54

Flann O'Brien was the pen name of Brian Ó Nualláin, who was best known for his remarkable experimental comic novel *At Swim-Two-Birds*.

O'Brien was born in Strabane, now in Northern Ireland, one of 12 children of a customs and excise officer. Although the family moved frequently, O'Brien spent most of his childhood in or near Dublin. He was educated by priests there and went to University College, Dublin, at the age of 18. He remained a student for six years, and during this time he also spent a year in Germany.

At age 24, O'Brien got a job as a civil servant. His first novel, which was influenced by the experimental novels of the great Irish author JAMES JOYCE, is a clever mix of fantasy, farce, legend, folklore, satire and poetry; it is about a man who is writing a novel about a man who is writing a novel. *At Swim-Two-Birds* (the title is a translation of an Irish place name) was published when O'Brien was 28, but was ignored until it was republished to great praise 21 years later.

O'Brien's next novel, *The Third Policeman*, was rejected by his publisher as too unusual but was published after he died. It is both serious and funny: one of the characters is concerned that the water he drinks is too strong and asks if it can be diluted!

For over 20 years from 1940, O'Brien wrote a successful column of comic and serious pieces in the *Irish Times* under the name Myles na Gopaleen. A selection was later published as *The Best of Myles*. One of O'Brien's other novels, *The Dalkey Archive*, was made into a successful play, *When the Saints Go Cycling In*.

Publications

1939 At Swim-Two-Birds
1941 The Poor Mouth
1943 Faustus Kelly
1961 The Hard Life
1964 The Dalkey Archive

Published after he died

1967 The Third Policeman
1968 The Best of Myles
1976 The Hair of the Dogma

O'CASEY, Sean

Sean O'Casey was an important Irish playwright. He is best known for his dramas about the political unrest in Ireland during the early years of the 20th century.

O'Casey was born in Dublin, the youngest of 13 children in a poor, working-class family. He received almost no education and taught himself to read and write. He also developed a love of the theater through attending amateur productions.

The early death of O'Casey's father left the family in poverty, and O'Casey had to work as a laborer from the age of 14. In 1913, he helped found the Irish Citizen Army, a radical organization dedicated to improving conditions for the poor and achieving independence from the British, who ruled all of Ireland at the time. He left the following year when it became clear that the other leaders were interested more in war than in social reform.

Between 1916 and 1921, Irish nationalists fought the British in a bitter war. O'Casey sympathized with the aims of the nationalists but was horrified by the effects of the fighting. Although Ireland achieved independence, a civil war followed that brought more bloodshed and sadness. His first successful play, *The Shadow of a Gunman*, produced when he was 43, shows the tragic consequences for poor families.

Because O'Casey's plays showed the negative side of the struggle for independence, he was very controversial. His play *The Plough and the Stars* caused several days of rioting. He left the country soon after to live in England, where he continued writing about Irish themes and the futility of war.

Irish playwright

Born Mar. 30, 1880
Died Sep. 18, 1964
Age at death 84

Publications

1923 The Shadow of a Gunman
1924 Juno and the Paycock
1926 The Plough and the Stars
1928 The Silver Tassie
1933 Within the Gates
1940 The Star Turns Red
1940 Purple Dust
1955 The Bishop's Bonfire
1956 Mirror in My House
1958 The Drums of Father Ned

O'CONNOR, Flannery

American novelist and short-story writer

Born Mar. 25, 1925
Died Aug. 3, 1964
Age at death 39

Publications

1952	*Wise Blood*
1955	*A Good Man Is Hard to Find*
1960	*The Violent Bear It Away*

Published after she died

1965	*Everything That Rises Must Converge*
1969	*Mystery and Manners*
1971	*Complete Stories*
1979	*The Habit of Being*

Flannery O'Connor is best known for part tragic, part comic stories that combine a cartoonlike quality with serious criticisms of Southern society. She once wrote that "all comic novels that are any good must be about matters of life and death."

O'Connor was born in Savannah, Georgia, the only child of Southern Catholic parents. When her father was diagnosed with lupus, a rare disease, the family moved to a town called Milledgeville.

O'Connor began writing at a young age, and she had her first story published when she was 21, a year after graduating from Georgia State College for Women. In 1947, she attended the Writers' Workshop at the University of Iowa, where she earned a Master's degree. Her first novel, *Wise Blood*, arose from her work while at Iowa.

At age 25, O'Connor was also diagnosed with lupus, and she became an invalid in her 30s. She returned to Milledgeville, where she lived with her mother and raised peacocks. She continued to write until her early death at age 39.

O'Connor's Southern background and her Catholicism both influenced her writing. Themes in her stories include religion in general and the piety of religious individuals. Her characters are exaggerated in their awfulness, demonstrating the dangers of pride. She uses the same characters to expose prejudice in society, as in her two novels *Wise Blood* and *The Violent Bear It Away*. In 1959, O'Connor received a Ford Foundation grant to help her to continue writing. Her *Complete Stories* received the National Book Award in 1972.

O'DELL, Scott

American young-adults' writer

Born May 23, 1898
Died Oct. 15, 1989
Age at death 91

Scott O'Dell is one of America's best-known writers of historical fiction for young adults. He won every major award in children's literature and sold millions of copies of books. The yearly Scott O'Dell Award for historical fiction is his legacy to children's literature.

O'Dell was born near Los Angeles. His father's job with the railway meant that the family often had to move, and he grew up all over southern California. Between 1919 and 1921, he studied at various universities so that he could see the country but never completed a degree. He then moved to Hollywood, where he worked as a cameraman. O'Dell traveled to Italy to help film the 1925 silent classic *Ben Hur* and studied at the University of Rome. He then returned to California and worked as a book reviewer and book editor.

O'Dell had planned to become a writer while still a university student. He wrote his first book when he was in Italy, but it was never published. His first published work, *Woman of Spain*, a novel for adults, came out when he was 36. His first historical novel for young adults was not published until 26 years later, when he was 62. *Island of the Blue Dolphins* was a great success and is still one of his most popular books. It is based on the true story of a Native American woman who survives for 18 years alone on an island. It is written in simple sentences as if told by the woman herself – a style that became O'Dell's trademark. He followed this success with many other stories based on actual events, most often from American history, and some with more modern settings. He was still writing at the age of 91.

Publications

1934 Woman of Spain
1960 Island of the Blue Dolphins
1966 The King's Fifth
1967 The Black Pearl
1968 The Dark Canoe
1969 Journey to Jericho
1970 Sing Down the Moon
1974 Child of Fire
1980 Sarah Bishop
1983 The Amethyst Ring

ODETS, Clifford

American playwright and screenwriter

Born Jul. 18, 1906
Died Aug. 14, 1963
Age at death 57

Clifford Odets's best-known plays, *Waiting for Lefty* and *Awake and Sing!*, are about the suffering of those who have to fight to make a living.

Raised in a middle-class family in New York City, Odets left school when he was 15 to become an actor. At age 24, he joined the Group Theater, which later put on many of his plays.

Waiting for Lefty, produced when Odets was 29, won him national fame. About a cab drivers' strike, it focuses on the struggles of the working class. His next play, *Awake and Sing!*, is the story of a poor Jewish family. These and others of Odets's early plays were written during the Great Depression. They are about people who try to keep their sense of identity in an often hostile world. Their social concerns reflect Odets's belief in the family and in the dignity of human beings.

Odets moved to Hollywood in 1935 to write screenplays. Rejecting the love for money and corruption he found there, he returned to New York City and continued to write plays on social themes. *Golden Boy* and *Clash by Night* concern the frustration felt by those who have no financial security. *Golden Boy*, his greatest commercial success, is about a man who gives up a career as a violinist to become a boxer and realizes too late how much he has sacrificed for success. Odets's later plays were less well received, except for *The Country Girl*, which tells the story of a wife's support of her alcoholic husband.

During the 1940s and '50s Odets returned to Hollywood and wrote screenplays for such movies as *The Sweet Smell of Success.*

Publications

1935 Waiting for Lefty
1935 Awake and Sing!
1935 Till the Day I Die
1935 Paradise Lost
1937 Golden Boy
1941 Clash by Night
1949 The Big Knife
1950 The Country Girl
1954 The Flowering Peach
1957 The Sweet Smell of Success

OE, Kenzaburo

Japanese novelist and short-story writer

Born Jan. 31, 1935

Publications

1958	"Prize Stock"
1958	*Nip the Buds, Shoot the Kids*
1964	*A Personal Matter*
1967	*The Silent Cry*
1973	*The Deluge Flooded into My Soul*
1977	*Teach Us to Outgrow Our Madness*
1984	*The Crazy Iris and Other Stories of the Atomic Aftermath*
1994	*A Flaming Tree*
1996	*Healing Family*

Oe Kenzaburo writes novels about the conflict between Japanese traditions and modern Western culture and ideas. He was awarded the Nobel Prize for Literature in 1994.

Oe was born in a mountain village on Shikoku, smallest of the four main Japanese islands. He graduated from the University of Tokyo in 1959, having published a number of award-winning short stories. His final-year thesis was on the French writer JEAN-PAUL SARTRE, and he has been deeply influenced by Western literature, especially the work of ALBERT CAMUS and NORMAN MAILER.

In his early writings, Oe focused on young people who use sex and violence to numb feelings of rootlessness and despair in the insecure world of post-World War II Japan. By the 1960s, his stories were challenging the policies of the Japanese government. He still campaigns against nuclear weapons and the censorship of writers.

In 1963, Oe's first son, Hikari, was born severely brain damaged. Doctors advised Oe and his wife to let Hikari die, but after speaking with someone who had treated the victims of the atomic bombing of Hiroshima, Oe rejected their advice. His seventh novel (the first to be published in English), *A Personal Matter*, is a fictional account of his life with Hikari; much of his later writing centers around the relationships between disabled and nondisabled people.

After receiving the Nobel Prize, Oe announced that his novel *A Flaming Tree* would be his last, but he has continued to write.

O'FAOLAIN, Sean

Irish short-story writer and novelist

Born Feb. 22, 1900
Died Apr. 20, 1991
Age at death 91

Sean O'Faolain is one of Ireland's most celebrated writers. He is known particularly for his short stories, which realistically portray the lives and struggles of ordinary Irish people.

O'Faolain was born in Cork, southern Ireland, which was then under British rule. His name at birth was John Whelan, but he later changed this to its Irish equivalent. O'Faolain was educated at University College, Cork, where he joined the Irish nationalist movement that later became the Irish Republican Army (IRA). When British rule ended, Ireland was divided into Northern Ireland and the Irish Free State and civil war broke out. O'Faolain served with the IRA, but the republicans were defeated.

Disillusioned, O'Faolain studied English literature at Harvard

(1926–29). While there he married a former IRA comrade, Eileen Gould. He then taught literature in the US and England for a few years, planning to earn enough to return home.

O'Faolain's first published book, *Midsummer Night Madness and Other Stories*, came out when he was 32. Its success allowed him to write full time and return to Ireland. His work reflects his political concerns, drawing initially on his youthful revolutionary activities and, later, on his views about the new Irish state. As well as fiction, he wrote an analysis of the Irish national character and biographies of important Irish figures. He founded a literary magazine, *The Bell*, and used it to encourage young writers to comment on social conditions and to campaign against Ireland's strict censorship laws.

Publications

1932	*Midsummer Night Madness and Other Stories*
1933	*A Nest of Simple Folk*
1936	*Bird Alone*
1940	*Come Back to Erin*
1947	*The Irish*
1964	*Vive Moi!*
1976	*Foreign Affairs and Other Stories*
1980	*Collected Stories*

OGOT, Grace

Kenyan novelist and short-story writer

Born May 15, 1930

Grace Ogot is Kenya's most famous female writer. With the publication of her first novel, *The Promised Land*, she became one of the founders of modern African women's literature.

Ogot was born in Kenya's central Nyana region at a time when the country was a British colony. She went to local schools before studying to be a nurse in neighboring Uganda and then England in the late 1950s. While studying in London, she began writing short stories after a friend commented on her well-written letters. She was also inspired by the lack of East African work at the 1962 African Writers' conference in Uganda.

Ogot's work often explores the conflicts brought about by British rule in Kenya. She has written several books in Luo – her mother tongue – to preserve the language and make her work readable to her own people. *The Promised Land*, published when Ogot was 36, is set in the colonial period and centers on the experience of a new bride, her feelings of isolation in her husband's village, and the couple's migration to a new region.

In 1975, the Kenyan president appointed Ogot to Kenya's seat at the United Nations. She was made a member of the Kenyan parliament in 1983 but resigned two years later to fight for her seat in elections. She won and later became assistant minister of culture. Similar to Ogot's experiences, her novel *The Graduate* tells of a female politician's fight to be judged on her ability, not on her sex. In the 1992, elections Ogot lost her seat, and she now owns two clothing stores in Nairobi, the Kenyan capital.

Publications

1966	*The Promised Land*
1968	*Land without Thunder*
1976	*The Other Woman*
1980	*The Graduate*
1980	*The Island of Tears*
1983	*Miaha*
1989	*The Strange Bride*

O'HARA, John

American novelist and short-story writer

Born Jan. 31, 1905
Died Apr. 11, 1970
Age at death 65

John O'Hara was a popular author best known for writing about the morals, prejudices and anxieties of upper-middle-class Americans. By his death 20 million copies of his books had been sold.

O'Hara was born in Pottsville, Pennsylvania. His school career was a disaster: he was "honorably dismissed" from Fordham Preparatory School in New York and expelled from the Keystone State Normal School near Pottsville. When his father, a physician, died suddenly, leaving the family poor, O'Hara worked for several newspapers and magazines; because he drank too much, the jobs did not last long. His unstable behavior was also responsible for the breakup of his first marriage. Finally, he isolated himself in a Manhattan hotel, determined to write and make something of his life.

O'Hara's first novel, *Appointment in Samarra*, was published when he was 29 and was an instant success. It covers the last three days in the life of the main character. The themes of this novel became familiar in all O'Hara's later work: the power of certain social classes to exclude people they consider "outsiders"; the power of lust over love in human relationships; and the failures of parents.

Although O'Hara's fiction was hugely popular, critics never rated him highly. He claimed to be the hardest working author in the US, turning out some 37 books, most of them after he gave up drinking in 1949; he even conquered Broadway when he helped produce the musical adaptation of his *Pal Joey* stories. In 1956, he won the National Book Award for *Ten North Frederick*.

Publications

1934	*Appointment in Samarra*
1935	*Butterfield 8*
1938	*Hope of Heaven*
1940	*Pal Joey*
1949	*A Rage to Live*
1955	*Ten North Frederick*
1958	*From the Terrace*
1960	*Sermons and Soda Water*
1963	*The Hat on the Bed*
1967	*Waiting for Winter*

OKIGBO, Christopher

Nigerian poet

Born Aug. 16, 1932
Died Aug. 1967
Age at death c. 35

Christopher Okigbo was one of Nigeria's best poets. Written in English, his work can be difficult but has inspired many African writers.

Okigbo was born near Onitsha in eastern Nigeria (West Africa), which at the time was a British colony. His family was Christian but still followed the Igbo religion. Okigbo's grandfather had been a priest of the river god Idoto, and Okigbo, who was believed to be his grandfather reborn, took over this role at the same time he decided to become a poet. Okigbo studied Greek and Latin at the University of Ibadan, Nigeria, and then took a variety of jobs, including civil servant, Latin teacher and librarian. Soon, however, he decided that he could not be anything but a poet. Every job Okigbo held he viewed simply as a way to earn money to support his family.

Okigbo's first volume of poetry, *Heavensgate*, was published when he was 30. He was influenced by both European literature and his African upbringing. Having been educated when Nigeria was a colony, he felt he belonged to both the European and African worlds and tried to unite the two in his work.

In 1966, Okigbo won the poetry prize at the Festival of Negro Arts in Dakar, Senegal (West Africa). He refused the prize because he felt that his work and not his race should be judged. Okigbo's work slowly became more political. *Silences* mourns the troubles of newly independent Nigeria, and *Path of Thunder* predicted the Biafran War that split Nigeria. In July 1967, Okigbo joined the forces fighting for the independence of Biafra – the Igbo region of eastern Nigeria. He was killed in action one month later.

Publications

1962 Heavensgate
1964 Limits
1964 Distances
1965 Silences

Published after he died

1968 Path of Thunder
1971 Labyrinths
1986 Collected Poems

OKRI, Ben

Nigerian novelist, poet and short-story writer

Born Mar. 15, 1959

Ben Okri is one of Nigeria's most famous younger writers. In 1991, his novel *The Famished Road* won the Booker Prize, which is given each year to the best book published in Britain.

Okri was born in Nigeria (West Africa) just before the country became independent from British rule. As a child he read widely, anything from English literature to African myths and folklore. His father brought many books back from his time in England, where he had studied law, and his mother told him many African stories.

As early as the age of 17, Okri knew that he wanted to be a writer. At first he wrote articles on social and political issues, most of which he could not get published. When he wrote short stories based on these articles, however, he found that they were well received. These first short stories appeared in Nigerian journals and newspapers. Okri's first novel, *Flowers and Shadows*, published when he was only 21, grew out of one of these short stories. It is about a successful businessman whose jealous relatives try to destroy him. Okri moved to southern England when he was 19 to study at the University of Essex. He has since settled in London.

Okri's most famous book, *The Famished Road*, is set in Nigeria. It is the story of Azaro, a spirit child, who is supposed to die soon after being born. On this occasion, however, Azaro decides to remain in the real world, while keeping one foot in the spirit world. Like much of Okri's work it combines magic, fantasy and reality. The story continues in the sequel *Songs of Enchantment*.

Publications

1980 Flowers and Shadows
1981 The Landscapes Within
1986 Incidents at the Shrine
1988 Stars of the New Curfew
1991 The Famished Road
1992 An African Elegy
1993 Songs of Enchantment
1995 Astonishing the Gods
1996 Dangerous Love
1998 Infinite Riches

OLIVER, Mary

American poet

Born Sep. 10, 1935

Mary Oliver is famous for her powerful poetry that often describes natural forces and wildlife but also deals with important human concerns that affect everyone. In 1984, she won the Pulitzer Prize for her collection of poetry called *American Primitive*.

The daughter of a teacher, Oliver was born in Cleveland, Ohio, and raised in the countryside. She studied at Ohio State University for one year and for a further year at Vassar College, New York. Her first collection of poetry, *No Voyage*, came out when she was 28. It was first published in England and was highly praised by critics. Despite the title, the poems are set in various parts of the world, including Ohio, New England, England and Scotland. The title poem won an award from the Poetry Society of America in 1963, and since then Oliver has regularly won prizes for her work. These prizes, awards, and fellowships have allowed her to support herself by writing.

In 1980, Oliver took her first college teaching job – as visiting professor at the Case Western Reserve University in Cleveland. Since 1991, she has been writer-in-residence at Sweet Briar College, Virginia.

Oliver's early poems focus on nature. She is passionate about the natural world and uses images drawn from it to explore human experience. She often compares humans to animals in a way that makes her poetry more than simply descriptive. Her work has gradually come to include more references to herself, her relatives and her life. This has added to the depth and power of her verse.

Publications

1963 No Voyage
1972 The River Styx, Ohio, and Other Poems
1978 The Night Traveler
1978 Twelve Moons
1979 Sleeping in the Forest
1983 American Primitive
1986 Dream Work
1990 Provincetown
1992 New and Selected Poems

OLSEN, Tillie

American novelist, essayist and short-story writer

Born Jan. 14, 1913

Although she has published relatively little, Tillie Olsen has had a huge impact on women's writing in America through her fiction, essays and teaching. Her first novel, *Yonnondio*, has been described as one of the best novels to come out of the 1930s.

The second of seven children, Olsen was born Tillie Lerner in Wahoo, Nebraska. Her parents were poor Russian-Jewish immigrants. Olsen inherited her father's socialist beliefs and from a young age was politically active. After being forced to leave school early, she held a variety of low-paid jobs. This did not stop her from fighting to improve workers' lives, and she twice spent time in jail for her union activities.

While Olsen was still in her 20s, she managed to publish two poems and several political essays and begin writing *Yonnondio*. In 1936, she married and started a family, which prevented her from writing for the next two decades. She began writing again in her late 40s after winning a grant for a creative-writing course. In this time she wrote the short stories that later appeared in *Tell Me a Riddle* but had to return to work in 1957 when the money ran out. After this book was published a few years later, Olsen won various grants and teaching jobs.

Yonnondio was finally published when she was 61. About the fortunes of a working-class family during the Great Depression, it shows how women suffered even more than their unemployed husbands. Olsen has since worked to rediscover the voices of writers silenced by their race, class or gender, as hers was for so many years.

Publications

1934 There Is a Reason
1934 I Want You Women up North to Know
1961 Tell Me a Riddle
1974 Yonnondio
1978 Silences
1981 I Stand Here Ironing

OMAR KHAYYAM

Persian poet

Born May 18, 1048
Died Dec. 4, 1131
Age at death 83

The Rubaiyat of Omar Khayyam is one of the world's most famous poetic works. Its author, Omar Khayyam, was a great scholar in the ancient Muslim kingdom of Persia almost a thousand years ago.

Omar Khayyam was born in Nishapur, Persia (now Iran). At that time Persian civilization was far more advanced than that of Europe, and as a young man Omar Khayyam learned about astronomy, mathematics, philosophy and medicine.

When one of Omar Khayyam's student friends became an important official at the court of a powerful ruler, Omar Khayyam traveled there and was allowed to live and study at the court. Between the years 1074 and 1079 he worked on a project to reform the Islamic calendar according to highly accurate astronomical observations. He also wrote an important book on the branch of math known as algebra.

It is not known when Omar Khayyam wrote the 200 or so four-line verses for which he has become famous. They were probably composed at different stages of his life. His work became known outside the Muslim world when the English poet Edward Fitzgerald published a translation of his collected poems as *The Rubaiyat of Omar Khayyam* more than 700 years after his death. The book became extremely popular – readers loved its descriptions of luxury and pleasure and its sense of ancient wisdom. The images it conjured up of beautiful gardens and mysterious veiled women became the stereotyped Western idea of Muslim culture. *The Rubaiyat* has since been translated into most of the world's languages.

Published after he died

1859 The Rubaiyat of Omar Khayyam

ONDAATJE, Michael

Sri Lankan-born Canadian novelist and poet

Born Sep. 12, 1943

Michael Ondaatje is a Canadian writer who uses poetic, sensual language in experimental ways; the results are well received by both literary critics and readers.

Born in Sri Lanka, where his grandfather owned a tea plantation, Ondaatje's parents divorced, and he went to England with his mother when he was nine. Unhappy with the British higher education system, he emigrated to Canada in 1962, where he studied at Bishop's, Toronto, and Queen's universities before gaining a teaching position at York University, Toronto in 1971.

Ondaatje married in 1964, and his family inspired many poems for his first volume, *The Dainty Monsters*, which came out when he was 24. It depicts domestic life peppered with bizarre occurrences – cars chewing up bushes and dragons in the backyard. He also wrote a study of LEONARD COHEN, who has been a major influence on his writing.

He won two major Canadian awards for subsequent volumes, one of which was based on the life of Billy the Kid. Poems, prose, and illustrations combine Billy's experiences with Ondaatje's to produce a work of art. He repeats this process in *Coming Through Slaughter*, drawn from the life of a New Orleans jazz musician who went mad. *Running in the Family*, written after a return to Sri Lanka, explores the links between the island's past under British rule and his own family history. The novel *The English Patient* depicts four characters in an abandoned World War II Italian hospital surrounded by unexploded mines. It was made into an Academy Award-winning film.

Publications

1967	*The Dainty Monsters*
1970	*The Collected Works of Billy the Kid: Left-Handed Poems*
1970	*Leonard Cohen*
1973	*Rat Jelly*
1976	*Coming Through Slaughter*
1982	*Running in the Family*
1987	*In the Skin of a Lion*
1991	*The Cinnamon Peeler*
1992	*The English Patient*
1998	*Handwriting*

O'NEILL, Eugene

American playwright and poet

Born Oct. 16, 1888
Died Nov. 27, 1953
Age at death 65

Eugene O'Neill was a leading American playwright. His drama is famous for its realism and for its depressing stories of people who have no hope of controlling their destinies. He was awarded the Nobel Prize for Literature in 1936.

O'Neill was born in New York City, the son of an actor, and his early childhood was spent touring with his father. He was educated at a Catholic boarding school in Connecticut and spent a year at Princeton University before leaving to begin traveling.

O'Neill was a passionate man prone to depression, and he spent much of his youth drifting from job to job and living in poverty. His experiences during this period, particularly his time spent at sea, form the basis for much of his later work. Returning to America in

1912, he was admitted to a hospital, suffering from tuberculosis. During this period of enforced rest he started writing. The following year, when he was 25, he wrote his first play, *The Web*. By 1920, O'Neill was already becoming recognized as a serious playwright, winning his first Pulitzer Prize for *Beyond the Horizon*. He went on to win three more Pulitzers: one in 1922, for *Anna Christie*; another in 1928 for *Strange Interlude*; and the last was awarded in 1957, after he had died, for *Long Day's Journey into Night*.

O'Neill's plays often deal with characters looking for a meaning to life. His most famous work, *The Iceman Cometh*, performed when he was 58, is set in a dockside bar where characters discuss their hopeless lives. Altogether he wrote 45 plays, which range in style from satire to tragedy.

Publications

1920 Beyond the Horizon
1920 The Emperor Jones
1921 Anna Christie
1922 The Hairy Ape
1924 Desire under the Elms
1928 Strange Interlude
1931 Mourning Becomes Electra
1946 The Iceman Cometh

Published after he died

1956 Long Day's Journey into Night

ONETTI, Juan Carlos

Uruguayan novelist and short-story writer

Born Jul. 1, 1909
Died May 30, 1994
Age at death 84

Juan Carlos Onetti, one of Latin America's finest writers, is notable for a series of brilliant novels that describe the breakdown of modern town life. Although often pessimistic and complex, his stories are rich in creativity and imagination.

Onetti was born in Montevideo, Uruguay, where his schooling was brief, and he then survived on various low-paid jobs. Later, he studied at the university in Buenos Aires, Argentina.

In Montevideo, at the age of 30, Onetti got a job on the important weekly journal *Marcha*. He then moved to Buenos Aires, where he worked as a journalist for 12 years. Returning to Montevideo in 1957, he was appointed director of the city's municipal libraries.

Onetti's first novel, *The Pit*, was published when he was 30. It is a study of aimlessness, isolation and the failure of human communication. A succession of remarkable novels followed, including *The Shipyard*, about a worker who attempts to improve his social position by courting the shipyard owner's daughter but doesn't realize that the society he aspires to has disintegrated. Onetti's best-known novel, *A Brief Life*, was published when he was 41 and describes a man who copes with a series of tragedies by disappearing into a fantasy world.

In 1974, Onetti left Uruguay for Spain after being imprisoned for publishing a young writer's story that had upset the military government. He died in Madrid.

Publications

1939 The Pit
1941 No Man's Land
1950 A Brief Life
1951 A Dream Fulfilled
1961 The Shipyard
1964 Body Snatcher
1974 Complete Stories 1933–50
1990 Goodbye and Stories

Published after he died

1996 Let the Wind Speak

OPPEN, George

American poet

Born Apr. 24, 1908
Died Jul. 7, 1984
Age at death 76

George Oppen is a respected figure in 20th-century American literature. His career as a poet was unusual, and he only received recognition late in life, winning the Pulitzer Prize for his collection *Of Being Numerous* when he was 61.

Oppen was born in New Rochelle, New York, and grew up in San Francisco, California. He briefly attended Oregon State University, where he met his wife. In 1929, two years after their marriage, they moved to France, where many young American artists and writers lived at that time. In France they started their own publishing company and published other American poets such as EZRA POUND and WILLIAM CARLOS WILLIAMS.

When they returned to New York in 1933, Oppen, then 25, published his first book, *Discrete Series*. The poems in this collection have been described as "objectivist" because they are strictly concerned with real objects and make no mention of emotion or human involvement. He then decided to put his own writing aside and work with the Communist Party. During World War II, Oppen served in the army and was badly wounded and, after the war, like many other artists in the McCarthy Era, he was forced to flee to Mexico because of FBI harassment over his political activities. He only began to write again when he returned to the United States eight years later.

Oppen's second collection of poems, *The Materials*, came out when he was 54, almost 30 years after his first book. These poems are more connected to his own life and emotions.

Publications

1934	*Discrete Series*
1962	*The Materials*
1965	*This in Which*
1968	*Of Being Numerous*
1969	*Alpine: Poems*
1970	*Communion*
1972	*Seascape: Needle's Eye*
1975	*The Collected Poems of George Oppen*
1978	*Primitive*

ORTON, Joe

English playwright

Born Jan. 1, 1933
Died Aug. 9, 1967
Age at death 34

Joe Orton is remembered for his plays, which capture the changing mood of Britain in the 1960s and which provide cruel yet hilarious attacks on "normal" or conventional society. Often in deliberately bad taste, Orton's bizarre and violent comedies shocked many people.

Orton came from a working-class family in the industrial city of Leicester. He was educated at Clark's College but did not do well. His family life was not happy, and he dreamed of escaping into an acting career. When Orton was 18, he moved to London to study at the famous Royal Academy of Dramatic Art (RADA). Shortly after his arrival he met Kenneth Halliwell, an older student, and began a homosexual relationship with him.

Orton's acting career failed, and he and Halliwell turned to writing. This was also unsuccessful, and they lived in poverty for several years. When Orton was 29, he was sent to prison for 6 months for defacing library books. Prison was a turning point for Orton; it convinced him that society was rotten and helped to focus his writing. His first play, *The Ruffian on the Stair*, was performed on the radio when Orton was 31. *Entertaining Mr. Sloane* became a success soon afterwards. With typical Orton black humor, the play depicts a middle-aged brother and sister who protect their father's killer because they are attracted to him.

As Orton's fame grew, Halliwell became increasingly depressed. He felt neglected and was afraid that Orton was going to leave him. Finally, unable to stand any more, Halliwell murdered Orton and then killed himself.

Publications

1964 *The Ruffian on the Stair*
1964 *Entertaining Mr. Sloane*
1966 *Loot*
1966 *The Erpingham Camp*

Published after he died

1969 *What the Butler Saw*

ORWELL, George

English novelist, poet and essayist

Born Jun. 23, 1903
Died Jan. 21, 1950
Age at death 46

George Orwell was the pen name of Eric Arthur Blair. Two of his books, *Nineteen Eighty-Four* and *Animal Farm* – which contains the memorable phrase "All animals are equal, but some are more equal than others" – have become classics of political satire.

Orwell was born in India to English parents and was taken to England as a child. After studying at Eton College, he served in the Imperial Police in Burma from 1922 to 1927. Returning to Europe, he took a series of poorly paid jobs, while trying to get his writing published. He described this period of his life in his first book, *Down and Out in Paris and London*, published when he was 30. His novel *The Road to Wigan Pier* highlights the grinding poverty of the working classes in Britain at that time.

Orwell fought on the left-wing Republican side in the Spanish Civil War and was wounded. Despite his left-wing views, his experiences made him dislike the communists, who backed the Republicans, and he attacked them in *Homage to Catalonia*. He was unfit for military service in World War II and worked for the BBC. Toward the end of the war he wrote *Animal Farm*. It depicts the betrayal of a revolution. The farm animals overthrow their human rulers, but eventually the pigs take over the former role of the humans. Orwell died from tuberculosis soon after the publication of *Nineteen Eighty-Four*. In this book he describes a nightmare life under the dictatorship of a party leader, known as "Big Brother," whose people are constantly warned: "Big Brother is watching you."

Publications

1933 *Down and Out in Paris and London*
1934 *Burmese Days*
1935 *A Clergyman's Daughter*
1936 *Keep the Aspidistra Flying*
1937 *The Road to Wigan Pier*
1938 *Homage to Catalonia*
1939 *Coming up for Air*
1945 *Animal Farm*
1949 *Nineteen Eighty-Four*

OSBORNE, John

English playwright and novelist

Born Dec. 12, 1929
Died Dec. 24, 1994
Age at death 65

Publications

1956 Look Back in Anger
1957 Epitaph for George Dillon
1957 The Entertainer
1961 Luther
1964 Inadmissible Evidence
1965 A Patriot for Me
1971 West of Suez
1972 A Sense of Detachment
1981 A Better Class of Person
1991 Almost a Gentleman

John Osborne was one of the English writers known in the 1950s as the Angry Young Men. They wrote about ordinary, often working-class characters who feel they do not belong to society.

Osborne was born in London, England, to a family of "misfits" – not working class but not middle class. This gave Osborne a strong sense of not belonging that lasted all his life. Desperately unhappy at school, Osborne left at age 16 and drifted in and out of jobs before becoming an actor and appearing on stage, television and in films. It is as a playwright, however, that he is remembered.

When he was 27, Osborne wrote the play *Look Back in Anger*, which features the original "angry young man," Jimmy Porter. Working with others, Osborne had already written plays, but these had not been memorable. *Look Back in Anger* caused a sensation, expressing a frustration with society felt by many; great sacrifices had been made during World War II, but life for the ordinary person in Britain had changed very little once the war was over.

Osborne's next big success was *The Entertainer* – an allegory for the decline of postwar Britain. It follows the fading career of a bitter and frustrated third-rate actor. By the late 1950s, Osborne was increasingly working in film and television. Four of his plays were adapted for the movies, and in 1963 he won an Academy Award for best screenplay for *Tom Jones*, based on HENRY FIELDING's novel. In 1991, Osborne published the final volume of his autobiography, *Almost a Gentleman*. It reveals an obsession with class and society formed in early life.

OVID

Roman poet

Born Mar. 20, 43 BC
Died c. AD 17
Age at death c. 60

The ancient Roman poet Ovid is remembered for his witty poems about love and his retelling of ancient myths. He was born in Sulmona, a town in central Italy, into a wealthy, landowning family. His father encouraged him to become a lawyer and sent him to study in Rome, but Ovid found that he loved poetry more than legal argument and soon settled into a life of luxurious living and literature. By age 30, he was the most popular poet in Rome.

Ovid lived during the reign of Augustus, the first emperor of Rome. The old Roman Republic, a system of government that had ruled Rome for centuries, had become corrupt and collapsed after years of bitter civil war. The new emperor was determined to reform Roman society and return it to the old values and strict morals of the early republic. One of Ovid's most popular poems, *the Art of Love*, provoked the anger of Augustus. It was a witty, sophisticated work about how to seduce a lover. Augustus thought the book was immoral and banished Ovid to a desolate town by the Black Sea. He also had all of Ovid's works removed from public libraries.

Before leaving Rome, Ovid had finished his greatest work, the long poem *Metamorphoses*. Its vivid and beautiful retelling of ancient Greek and Roman myths remained loved and widely read for centuries after his death. In exile, Ovid continued to write. He hated being so far from the life he had enjoyed in Rome and wrote poems begging the emperor to let him return. Augustus, and his successor Tiberius, never relented, and Ovid died far from home.

Publications

Between 16 BC and AD 2
Amores
Heroides
The Art of Love
The Cures of Love
Medea

Between AD 2 and 17
Fasti
Metamorphoses
Tristia

OWEN, Wilfred

English poet

Born Mar. 18, 1893
Died Nov. 4, 1918
Age at death 25

Wilfred Owen was an English poet who fought and died in World War I. One of the most admired of the so-called war poets, he is remembered for his angry poems about the waste and pointlessness of war.

Born in Shropshire, western England, Owen was the son of a railway station master. After school he began work as a teacher, hoping to study at London University, but there was no money to pay for his courses. He had already begun to write poetry, at first in the style of JOHN KEATS. In 1913, he went to France to teach English. War broke out the following year and, in 1915, he returned to England to enlist in the army, aged 22. He soon became an officer.

In 1917, Owen was invalided home, suffering from concussion and fever. While recovering in a military hospital near Edinburgh, he met the older war poet SIEGFRIED SASSOON, who had also been sent home due to ill health. Sassoon encouraged Owen to write about his experiences in the trenches.

Friends tried to find Owen a "safe" post away from the front, but in August 1918 he was sent back to the trenches to command a company. His courage won him a medal, but three months later he was killed – just one week before the end of the war.

Owen wrote most of his famous war poems in the year before he died. Only a few were published in his lifetime. Many of his poems were published by Sassoon two years after Owen's death. Those written after 1917 reflect the horror of life in the war, especially his well-known sonnet "Anthem for Doomed Youth."

Published after he died

1920 Poems
1931 The Poems of Wilfred Owen
1963 Collected Poems

OYONO, Ferdinand

Cameroonian novelist and short-story writer

Born Sep. 14, 1929

Ferdinand Oyono is one of the most important African authors writing in French. His novels are considered classics of African literature.

Oyono was born near Ebolowa in southwest Cameroon (West Africa), which was then a French colony. His father was an important chief who had more than one wife. His mother, a Catholic, refused to share her husband and left him while Oyono was still young. She supported herself and her children by working as a seamstress. Oyono helped by working as a priest's personal servant (or "boy"), and later he wrote about this experience in his novel *Boy!*

Oyono went to local schools and then studied law and administration in Paris, France. Lonely and poor in a foreign country, he began to write his first novel, *Boy!*, and then a second, *The Old Man and the Medal*. Like all of Oyono's books, these describe life in Cameroon under French rule. They use humor and satire to make fun of the idea that French rule in Africa was of benefit to Africans. *The Old Man and the Medal* is the story of an African given a medal for his loyalty to France. This "loyalty" involves the death of two of his sons in European wars and the loss of his land to a Catholic mission. Oyono's books received little attention at first, though Oyono himself became quite successful as a theater and television actor in Paris.

Cameroon became independent when Oyono was 31. Since then he has worked for his country's government in Europe and Africa, as Cameroon's United Nations delegate, and as minister for foreign affairs.

Publications

1956	*Boy!*
1956	*The Old Man and the Medal*
1958	*Men without Shoulders*
1960	*The Road to Europe*
1971	*The Big Confusion*

OZ, Amos

Israeli novelist, short-story writer and essayist

Born May 4, 1939

Amos Oz is one of Israel's greatest modern writers. He writes about the problems faced by people of Israel today and about the long and complex history of the Jews.

Oz was born Amos Klausner in Jerusalem, Israel, and as a teenager lived for a time on a kibbutz (a communal farm) where he taught in the school. He was educated at the Hebrew University in Jerusalem and at Oxford University, and was required to serve in the Israeli army during various times of trouble, including the Six Day War of 1967.

Oz belongs to a generation that views the ideals of the founders of modern Israel with suspicion. But unlike many of his contemporaries, he has been content to spend his life on a kibbutz. This attitude, and his perception of the realities of modern Israeli life, is reflected in his work. He expresses the conflicts between the ideals of Israel's founders and the longing of a later generation for a more sophisticated way of life.

Written in the ancient Jewish language Hebrew, Oz's novels have been more widely read than those of any other Israeli writers and have been translated into many languages. They are brilliant works, concerned with guilt, persecution, demonic forces and the inevitability of fate. In some of his later work there are elements of fantasy. Oz's intelligence and great gifts as a writer always prevent his stories from becoming predictable.

Oz is also noted for his political essays, in which he sometimes expresses highly controversial views.

Publications

1965	*Where the Jackals Howl and Other Stories*
1966	*Elsewhere, Perhaps*
1968	*My Michael*
1973	*Touch the Water, Touch the Wind*
1973	*The Hill of Evil Counsel*
1982	*A Perfect Peace*
1987	*Black Box*
1991	*The Third State*

PAGE, P.K.

English-born Canadian poet and novelist

Born Nov. 23, 1916

Although she is best known as a poet, P.K. Page is also an accomplished painter.

Patricia Kathleen Page was born in England but emigrated to Canada with her parents at an early age. After graduating from St. Hilda's School in Calgary, she moved to Montreal, which was at the time the most important center of English-language poetry in Canada. In Montreal, she met other poets and artists for the first time; it quickly became apparent that she was a new and important talent. She was 30 when her first volume of poetry, *As Ten as Twenty*, appeared. That same year, while working as a scriptwriter for the National Film Board of Ottawa, she met her future husband, William Irwin.

When Irwin became a diplomat, Page lived abroad with him for ten years; during this time she suffered a writing block that put an end to her poetry. Unable to write, she turned to painting to express herself. As P.K. Irwin she is now a highly respected painter, and her work hangs in Canada's National Gallery. Critics have said that her paintings are so closely related to her poetry that they seem like poems.

Page began writing poetry again when she returned to Canada. Her seventh book, *Evening Dance of the Grey Flies*, was her first entirely new collection of poems for 27 years. From the 1950s, Page has kept a daily diary, including the time when she stayed in Brazil from 1957 to 1959. This autobiographical work was published as *Brazilian Journal* almost 30 years after it was started. It is a remarkable prose work telling not only of her struggles to complete her poems but of the diplomatic life she and her husband shared.

Publications

1944	*The Sun and the Moon*
1946	*As Ten as Twenty*
1954	*The Metal and the Flower*
1974	*Poems (1942–73): Selected and New*
1981	*Evening Dance of the Grey Flies*
1984	*The Traveling Musicians*
1985	*The Glass Air*
1987	*Brazilian Journal*
1989	*A Flask of Sea Water*

PAINE, Thomas

English-born American writer

Born Jan. 29, 1737
Died Jun. 8, 1809
Age at death 72

Thomas Paine was one of the most influential and controversial writers of the American Revolution.

Born in Thetford, England, to a very religious family, Paine received a basic but moral education. He grew up influenced by the work of the scientist Isaac Newton and the philosopher John Locke, both leading thinkers of the 17th century.

By the age of 36, Paine had married twice and been fired from his job as a customs officer for publishing an argument in favor of higher wages. That year Paine met Benjamin Franklin, who offered to find him a job in America. He also helped him become the editor of *Pennsylvania Magazine*, where Paine wrote about subjects ahead of his time, including women's rights and freedom for slaves.

Paine left the magazine and joined George Washington's army in its retreat across New Jersey in 1776. There he published two series of pamphlets called *Common Sense* and *The American Crisis*, both stirring, patriotic works that made him a leading spokesman for the independence cause.

In 1787, Paine traveled to France, a country in political turmoil just before the French Revolution. There he wrote his great defense of revolution, *The Rights of Man*; he also helped draft a constitution for the new republic and was imprisoned for writing against the execution of the French king. His last book was *The Age of Reason*, an analysis of the Bible that caused offense because it seemed to be denying the existence of God. At 65, he returned to America, poor, shunned and in bad health, and he died seven years later.

Publications

1776 Common Sense
1776–77 The American Crisis
1791–92 The Rights of Man
1794–95 The Age of Reason
1796 Letter to George Washington

PALEY, Grace

American short-story writer and poet

Born Dec. 11, 1922

Although she has published only a few collections of short stories, Grace Paley is considered to be one of America's best short-story writers.

Paley was born in New York's Bronx. Her parents were Russian-Jewish immigrants who had both spent time in exile. Paley grew up very aware of politics and the different cultures of New York City. After secondary school she went to university but did not complete a degree. At the age of 19, she married, and she spent most of the next 20 years raising two children. Since the 1950s, Paley has become increasingly active in various political causes. She campaigned against the Vietnam War, delivering leaflets and speeches, and has long been an active campaigner for the women's movement. Paley has been arrested on several occasions for her activities and has even spent time in jail. On her release she successfully campaigned for improvements in prison conditions.

In the 1950s, Paley began writing short stories. After many rejections her first collection, *The Little Disturbances of Man*, was published when she was 37. Paley's political activities meant that she did not get around to finishing her second collection, *Enormous Changes at the Last Minute*, until 15 years later. This book and her more recent collection, *Later the Same Day*, established her fame as a master storyteller. All of Paley's stories are set in New York City and use both sympathy and humor to create believable working-class characters. Her fiction is unusual in that talking rather than plot reveals the characters' personalities, and the stories are often brief. In recent years she has published collections of poetry.

Publications

1959	*The Little Disturbances of Man*
1974	*Enormous Changes at the Last Minute*
1985	*Leaning Forward*
1985	*Later the Same Day*
1991	*Long Walks and Intimate Stories*
1992	*New and Collected Poems*

PARETSKY, Sara

American crime writer

Born Jun. 8, 1947

Sara Paretsky is one of America's leading feminist crime writers.

Paretsky was born in Ames, Iowa. Her father was a scientist and her mother a librarian. She attended the University of Kansas during the 1960s and became involved in the civil rights movement. During the 1970s, Paretsky earned a Ph.D. in history and a Master's degree in business administration. In 1977, she started working at a Chicago-based insurance company where she remained for the next nine years. Her experiences there gave Paretsky the idea of creating a fictional woman heroine battling to hold her own in a man's world. It also gave her background information on how big institutions operate.

Paretsky's first novel, *Indemnity Only*, appeared when she was 35. The book introduced her heroine, private detective V.I. Warshawski – a tough streetwise investigator from Chicago and one of the first female private detectives in crime fiction. A series of V.I. Warshawski books have since followed, and her character's success allowed Paretsky to become a full-time writer at age 38. In 1991, a movie, *V.I. Warshawski*, based on Paretsky's heroine and starring Kathleen Turner, appeared.

V.I. Warshawski is committed to fighting for equality and fairness in society. She champions the rights of women and minorities who come into conflict with large organizations of all kinds – big businesses, unions, the police, the Church or the medical profession. Unlike most male detectives, Warshawski has a large group of family and friends around her who give her support and help her solve crimes.

Publications

1982	*Indemnity Only*
1984	*Deadlock*
1985	*Killing Orders*
1987	*Bitter Medicine*
1988	*Blood Shot*
1990	*Burn Marks*
1991	*Guardian Angel*
1994	*Tunnel Vision*

PARKER, Dorothy

American critic, short-story writer and poet

Born Aug. 22, 1893
Died Jun. 7, 1967
Age at death 73

Dorothy Parker became famous in the 1920s for her cruel humor. Many of the things she said and wrote are still repeated today, including the rhyme "Boys don't make passes / At girls who wear glasses."

Parker was born in New Jersey, and her mother died when she was a baby. Following her education at public schools, Parker moved to New York City. She wrote during the day and earned money at night playing the piano in a dancing school. *Vogue* magazine liked her poems and, when she was 23, gave her a job writing captions for fashion drawings.

Two years later Parker became drama critic for another magazine and began meeting with other writers at the Algonquin Hotel. Their lunches at a special round table soon became famous. Members of this select group – including RING LARDNER and JAMES THURBER – entertained each other by making funny but cruel remarks about people they felt superior to. Parker was usually the only woman in the group, but her humor was often the nastiest, especially when it was directed at other women. During this time she published several collections of poems and short stories. Her stories are characterized by sharp dialogue and detail and by use of irony.

After working for the *New Yorker* and other magazines, she moved with her second husband to Hollywood, where they earned a good income writing screenplays for the movie studios.

Parker suffered from depression for most of her life, and as her view of the world became increasingly bleak, humor seemed to desert her. She died alone in the New York hotel that had become her final home.

Publications

1922 Men I'm Not Married To
1926 Enough Rope
1928 Sunset Gun
1930 Laments for the Living
1931 Death and Taxes
1933 After Such Pleasures
1936 Not So Deep As a Well
1939 Here Lies

Published after she died

1970 Constant Reader

PARKER, Robert B.

American crime writer

Born Sep. 17, 1932

Robert B(rown) Parker is a highly successful crime writer best known for reviving the tradition of private detective stories during the 1970s.

Parker was born in Springfield, Massachusetts, and after graduating from Boston University, he joined the US Army. He then worked in advertising until 1962, when he became a university teacher. At age 41, he published his first novel, *The Godwulf Manuscript*.

In the series of novels that followed, Parker showed his debt to RAYMOND CHANDLER, the great crime writer of the 1930s. Like Chandler, Parker writes in the hard-boiled tradition – that is, stories about the tough lives of people on the streets of America's big cities. Parker's hero, Spenser, is in many ways similar to Chandler's hero,

Marlowe: on the surface cynical and hard, but essentially a crusader in the cause of justice; streetwise and fond of sarcastic humor, but also well read and intellectual.

Parker also adds a number of features to update the Marlowe model. Instead of being a loner like Marlowe, Spenser has a long-term girlfriend, counselor Susan Silverman. In an attempt to address modern ideas about women's equality, Parker describes the development of the relationship between Spenser and Silverman in depth. He also introduces contemporary social issues, such as drug-taking in the sports world and child abuse.

In 1989, Parker completed an unfinished novel left by Raymond Chandler, *Poodle Springs*. He followed this in 1991 with *Perchance to Dream*, a sequel to Chandler's *The Big Sleep*. His Spenser novels inspired a TV series, *Spenser for Hire*, in the 1980s.

Publications

1973	*The Godwulf Manuscript*
1974	*God Save the Child*
1976	*Promised Land*
1978	*The Judas Goat*
1981	*Early Autumn*
1984	*Valediction*
1989	*Poodle Springs*
1991	*Perchance to Dream*
1991	*Pastime*
1996	*Chance*
1998	*Night Passage*
1999	*Trouble in Paradise*

PASTERNAK, Boris

Russian poet and novelist

Born Feb. 10, 1890
Died May 30, 1960
Age at death 70

Boris Pasternak was one of Russia's greatest 20th-century poets, but he is best known for his novel *Doctor Zhivago*.

Pasternak was born in Moscow and grew up in a cultured, artistic home. His mother was a concert pianist, his father a celebrated painter. Pasternak studied music and philosophy, and in 1914, aged 24, published a collection of verse, *A Twin in the Clouds*. *My Sister, Life*, his third book, established him as an important new poet.

Pasternak had supported the Russian Revolution but was disappointed by the brutality of the new communist government. His writings were more concerned with individuals and emotions than political issues, and during the 1930s he fell out of favor with the communist authorities for failing to write about socialist themes. None of his work could be published.

In 1956, Pasternak completed his great masterpiece, *Doctor Zhivago*. The novel describes in moving detail the Russian Revolution and its effects on the lives of Zhivago, a doctor and poet based on Pasternak, and his love Lara, who was modeled on Pasternak's companion, Olga Ivinskaya. The authorities refused publication, seeing the novel as anticommunist, but the manuscript was smuggled into Italy, where it was published in 1957 to worldwide acclaim. In 1958, Pasternak was awarded the Nobel Prize for Literature. The Russian government was outraged, Ivinskaya was arrested, and Pasternak was forced to refuse the prize. He was persecuted and spent his last years in exile. *Doctor Zhivago* was finally published in Russia in 1988.

Publications

1914	*A Twin in the Clouds*
1917	*Above the Barriers*
1923	*My Sister, Life*
1923	*Themes and Variations*
1926	*The Year 1905*
1927	*Lieutenant Schmidt*
1931	*Spektorsky*
1932	*Second Birth*
1925	*Aerial Ways*
1957	*Doctor Zhivago*

PATON, Alan

South African novelist and short-story writer

Born Jan. 11, 1903
Died Apr. 12, 1988
Age at death 85

Publications

1948	*Cry, the Beloved Country*
1953	*Too Late the Phalarope*
1958	*Hope for South Africa*
1967	*Tales from a Troubled Land*
1967	*The Long View*
1980	*Towards the Mountain*
1981	*Ah, But Your Land Is Beautiful*

Alan Paton was one of South Africa's most important white writers. He is best known for the novel *Cry, the Beloved Country*, which has been made into a film.

Paton was born in Pietermaritzburg in the east of South Africa. Despite the black majority, white South Africans controlled the government and major industries at that time. During Paton's lifetime, he witnessed the increase of white power at the expense of the rights of black people. Laws were introduced that dictated where black people could live and what work they could do.

Paton attended the University of Natal and then became a teacher. In 1935, he took over a reform school for African boys near Johannesburg in the northeast. He made many changes that improved the lives of his pupils. Then, aged 43, he wrote *Cry, the Beloved Country* while touring prisons in Europe and the US. The book tells of an elderly black minister's grief when he discovers his sister is a prostitute and that his son has killed a white man. It highlights the injustices of the racist apartheid system and brought worldwide attention to South Africa.

Following the success of *Cry, the Beloved Country,* Paton began writing full time; he also became more active in politics. He campaigned for a nonracial solution to apartheid and was unpopular with the white government. His second novel, *Too Late the Phalarope*, which was banned, is about a white man who is destroyed because of his affair with a black girl. His short stories *Tales from a Troubled Land* and the novel *Ah, But Your Land Is Beautiful* are on the same racial theme.

PAZ, Octavio

Mexican poet, critic and essayist

Born Mar. 31, 1914
Died Apr. 19, 1998
Age at death 84

Octavio Paz is one of the greatest Latin American poets. In 1990, he became the first Mexican to win the Nobel Prize for Literature.

Paz was born in Mexico City, into a family of mostly Spanish but part-Indian descent. His novelist grandfather had a large library, and through his teenage years Paz read widely. He was educated at a Roman Catholic school, then at the University of Mexico. However, he refused to take his degree and set off suddenly to found a secondary school in Yucatán, where he researched Mexican history.

At the outbreak of the Spanish Civil War, Paz went to Spain to fight for the antifascist republicans but was appalled by the horrors of war he experienced. Returning to Mexico, he started several literary magazines and, at age 29, was awarded a Guggenheim fellowship that enabled him to study and travel in the US. At 31, he entered the Mexican diplomatic service. His first posting overseas was to Paris, where he met many leading French writers. Paz resigned as ambassador to India in 1968 in protest against his government's suppression of student riots in Mexico.

Paz's writing career began when he was only 19 with the publication of his first book of poems, *Forest Moon*. *Eagle or Sun?*, published when Paz was 37, contains a series of poems that together provide a haunting picture of Mexico's past and future. Paz's most important poem, *Sun Stone*, came out when he was 43 and is about the planet Venus, a symbol of sun and water in Aztec folklore. The poem's 584 lines reflect the structure of the Aztec calendar.

Publications

1933	*Forest Moon*
1937	*Beneath Your Clear Shadow and Other Poems*
1950	*The Labyrinth of Solitude*
1951	*Eagle or Sun?*
1957	*Sun Stone*
1974	*The Monkey Grammarian*
1985	*One Earth, Four or Five Worlds*
1995	*The Double Flame: Love and Eroticism*

P'BITEK, Okot

Ugandan poet and novelist

Born 1931

Died Jul. 19, 1982

Age at death c. 51

Okot p'Bitek was one of Africa's best 20th-century poets and most original writers.

P'Bitek was born into a family of the Luo people in Gulu, northern Uganda, which was then a British colony. His mother was a gifted singer and composer, and p'Bitek grew up listening to her recount the tales, proverbs and songs of Luo folklore. He went to local schools and colleges before joining the national soccer team. After touring Britain as a soccer player, he stayed there to study.

At age 33, p'Bitek returned home to teach at Makerere University College in Kampala, the capital city. He founded the Festival of African Arts in Gulu and then became director of the National Cultural Center in Kampala. After criticizing the Ugandan government, he left for a neighboring country, Kenya. In 1971, he became a senior academic at the Institute of African Studies in Nairobi, the Kenyan capital, and he spent his remaining years teaching in universities in Nigeria and the US.

P'Bitek was a champion of African values and culture at a time when the influence of Europeans through their colonies dominated much of African life. He wrote in Luo and in English, adopting a fresh, humorous style to explore the clash of European and African cultures. In his most famous poem, *Song of Lawino*, he introduced a style that became known as "comic singing." Like his other long poems, it is written as a story told by one person, in this case Lawino, lamenting her husband's Western ways. *Song of Ocol* is her husband's response.

Publications

1953	*White Teeth*
1966	*Song of Lawino*
1970	*Song of Ocol*
1971	*Song of a Prisoner*
1971	*Two Songs: Song of a Prisoner; Song of a Prostitute*
1974	*Horn of My Love*
1978	*Hare and Hornbill*

PEPYS, Samuel

English writer

Born Feb. 23, 1633
Died May 26, 1703
Age at death 70

Samuel Pepys was the author of probably the most famous diary written in English.

Pepys was born into a large family in the heart of London, England. He went to a good private school and then to Cambridge University, from which he graduated in 1654.

Through an influential cousin Pepys was appointed in 1660 to an important job with the navy, which at the time was very badly organized. He introduced many reforms and turned it into a professional and efficient fighting force. He also served in parliament several times. After he lost his job with the navy in 1688, he wrote his memoirs of his time in the navy, of the war with the Netherlands, and of the restoration of Charles II to the throne in 1660.

Pepys's diary was not published until after his death. He wrote in shorthand, so that no one could read it while he was alive; but when he died, he left it with his other papers to his old college. It covers the years from 1660 to 1669 in great detail. As well as providing eyewitness accounts of some major historical events – such as the 1666 Great Fire of London, in which much of the city burned down, and the Great Plague – Pepys's diary gives a fascinating insight into his own character, his loves, his work and the gossip he heard. It is a very personal account, telling as it does of his stormy marriage and various affairs. Some of the sexually explicit parts were not published until this century. The conflict between his need to be busy and industrious at work and his love of pleasure, beautiful women and the theater provides many comic moments.

Publications

1690 Memoirs of the Royal Navy 1679–88

Published after he died

1825 Memoirs of Samuel Pepys
1893 The Diary of Samuel Pepys
1970–83 The Diary of Samuel Pepys: a New and Complete Transcription

PERCY, Walker

American novelist and essayist

Born May 28, 1916
Died May 10, 1990
Age at death 73

Walker Percy is best known for his comic novels that depict the effects of living in a world transformed by science.

Percy was born in Birmingham, Alabama. After the suicide of his father and the death of his mother in an automobile accident, 15-year-old Percy and his two brothers were adopted by their father's cousin and taken to live in Greenville, Mississippi.

Percy's first love was science, not literature. He received a degree in chemistry from the University of North Carolina in 1937 and a medical degree from Columbia four years later. He turned to writing only when his plans for a career in medicine ended after he caught tuberculosis, which forced him to rest for long periods of time.

After years of writing nonfiction, Percy's first novel, *The Moviegoer*, was published when he was 45 and won the National Book Award. The main character uses movie-going as an escape from everyday life. In Percy's satirical masterpiece *Love in the Ruins* a doctor has discovered the cure for modern despair and tries to save humankind from itself.

A general theme running through Percy's books is the individual's battle against the boring but necessary day-to-day routines of life. His main characters are usually people of great sensitivity who are tormented by the despair of the modern age; like pilgrims, they look for answers to what they see as the pointlessness of their humdrum lives. Whether or not their search for the cause of their despair is successful, the characters learn how to cope with the ordinariness of their lives.

Publications

1961	The Moviegoer
1966	The Last Gentleman
1971	Love in the Ruins
1975	The Message in the Bottle
1977	Lancelot
1980	The Second Coming
1983	Lost in the Cosmos
1987	The Thanatos Syndrome

PERELMAN, S.J.

American writer

Born Feb. 1, 1904
Died Oct. 17, 1979
Age at death 75

S. J. Perelman was an American writer who used humor to criticize popular culture.

Born in Brooklyn, New York City, Sidney Joseph Perelman was raised in Rhode Island. After graduating in 1925 from Brown University, where he was a cartoonist for the student magazine the *Brown Jug*, he spent the next four years as a cartoonist and humorist for the magazine *Judge*. He then wrote for another magazine, *College Humor*, where he developed a style of humor based on imitating the work of famous writers such as JAMES JOYCE. These early pieces were collected in *Dawn Ginsbergh's Revenge*, published when he was 25. Five years later Perelman began writing for the *New Yorker*. Most of his work was to appear in this magazine.

Perelman's clever use of language led the Marx Brothers to hire him to write the screenplays for the films *Monkey Business* and *Horse Feathers* in the 1930s. Other screenplays followed, most notably *Around the World in Eighty Days*, which won him an Academy Award and the New York Film Critics Award when he was 52. He also wrote Broadway plays, including *One Touch of Venus* with OGDEN NASH.

Over 400 of Perelman's humorous essays have been collected in several books, including *The Dream Department*, which satirizes advertising and shoddy workmanship, and *Acres and Pains*, about the foolishness of city folk who move to the country. Two other volumes, *Westward Ha!* and *Eastward Ha!*, explore the human condition through travel stories. Perelman's later pieces lost some of their comic edge.

Publications

1929	Dawn Ginsbergh's Revenge
1937	Strictly from Hunger
1943	One Touch of Venus (with Ogden Nash)
1943	The Dream Department
1948	Westward Ha!
1961	The Rising Gorge
1966	Chicken Inspector No. 23
1970	Baby, It's Cold Inside
1977	Eastward Ha!

PERRAULT, Charles

French writer and poet

Born Jan. 12, 1628
Died May 15, 1703
Age at death 75

Charles Perrault was a 17th-century French scholar and poet who is remembered today for the collection of fairy tales he published late in his life, *Tales of Mother Goose*.

Perrault was born in Paris into a wealthy middle-class family. He trained as a lawyer and became a government official responsible for the care of royal buildings. He had begun writing poetry in his 20s, and by the time he was in his early 30s, had become a respected poet. On several occasions he wrote poems for the French royal family to celebrate special events, such as the birth of an heir to the throne in 1661.

At age 42, Perrault was made a member of the French Academy – an official group of leading scholars and writers. He became the center of a fierce debate among Academy members when at age 59 he published his poem *The Century of Louis the Great*, in which he argued that French writers of his own century were better than writers of ancient Greece or Rome. The argument between Perrault and other Academy members, who said that ancient writers were the best, became famous.

Perrault's collection of fairy tales, *Tales of Mother Goose*, was published when he was 69. It includes such famous stories as "Cinderella," "Little Red Riding Hood" and "Sleeping Beauty." These stories probably started out as folklore, and many other writers before and since have published versions of them. Although he regarded them as his least important work, Perrault's versions are remembered because of the skill with which he told them.

Publications

1687 The Century of Louis the Great
1688–97 Parallels between the Ancients and the Moderns
1697 Tales of Mother Goose

PERSE, Saint-John

French poet

Born May 31, 1887
Died Sep. 20, 1975
Age at death 88

Saint-John Perse was a major poet who has been described as the embodiment of the French national spirit. He was awarded the Nobel Prize for Literature in 1960.

Perse is the pen name of Marie-Réné-Auguste-Alexis Saint-Léger Léger. He was born on Saint-Léger-les-Feuilles, a small coral island his family owned in the then French Caribbean colony of Guadeloupe. After completing his studies at the universities of Bordeaux and Paris, he joined the French diplomatic service at age 27. He served in many countries, rising to the post of ambassador. In 1940, he was removed from office for opposing the French government's policy of cooperating with the Nazis during World War II. Perse went first to England and then to the US, where he became poetry consultant to the Library of Congress. He returned to France in 1957.

Throughout his life Perse had been writing his poetry in secret. His first collection, *Eulogies*, was published when he was 24. His next work, the long epic song of a conqueror, *Anabasis*, was translated into English by the great poet T.S. Eliot. Between 1924 and 1940, although Perse wrote many poems, none was published. The manuscripts were left behind in Paris when he went to England in 1940, and they were seized and destroyed by the Nazi secret police.

Two years later, Perse published *Exile, and Other Poems*, the title poem of which has been described as one of the greatest works inspired by World War II. His distinctive writing style centers on the themes of solitude and exile.

Publications

1911 Eulogies
1924 Anabasis
1942 Exile, and Other Poems
1946 Winds
1957 Seamarks
1960 Chronique
1961 On Poetry
1962 Birds
1972 Complete Poems
1975 Song for an Equinox

PESSOA, Fernando

Fernando Pessoa is regarded as Portugal's greatest poet of the 20th century, although he was virtually unknown during his lifetime.

Pessoa was born in Lisbon, but when he was seven, the family moved to Durban, South Africa, where his stepfather was the Portuguese consul. Educated in the English language, he developed an early love for such authors as William Shakespeare and John Milton, whose work he later imitated. When he was 17, Pessoa returned to Portugal. He attended the University of Lisbon and, after graduating, he spent the rest of his life working as a business advisor and translator.

Aged 30, Pessoa published his first volume of poetry, *35 Sonnets*, followed soon after by *English Poems*. He also began to write in Portuguese; but although his work showed great skill and invention, success did not come his way.

Pessoa became frustrated with the literary fashions in Portugal and wanted his poetry to change direction. He started to write under different names, creating fictional life stories for his entirely invented authors. In total Pessoa made up eight "alter egos" that he called "heteronyms." Each of them represented a different aspect of his personality. For example, the poetry of "Alvaro de Campos" is highly emotional, the poetry of "Alberto Caeiro" is realistic, while that of "Ricardo Reis" imitates the literature of ancient Greece and Rome.

Increasingly depressed and drinking heavily, Pessoa nevertheless continued writing until his death. It is only recently that his work has received the acclaim he was denied in his life.

Portuguese poet and essayist

Born Jun. 13, 1888
Died Nov. 30, 1935
Age at death 47

Publications

1918 35 Sonnets
1921 English Poems
1934 Message

Published after he died

1971 Selected Poems
1971 60 Portuguese Poems
1975 The Tobacconist (Alvaro de Campos)
1976 The Keeper of Flocks (Alberto Caeiro)

PETERKIN, Julia

American novelist and short-story writer

Born Oct. 31, 1880
Died Aug. 10, 1961
Age at death 80

Publications

1924	*Green Thursday*
1927	*Black April*
1928	*Scarlet Sister Mary*
1932	*Bright Skin*
1933	*Roll, Jordan, Roll*
1934	*A Plantation Christmas*

Published after she died

1970	*The Collected Short Stories of Julia Peterkin*

Julia Peterkin was a white woman, well educated and well off, who wrote about the African-American Gullah people of rural South Carolina. The heroine of *Scarlet Sister Mary*, for which Peterkin won the Pulitzer Prize in 1929, is a Gullah woman whose strong sense of self and connections to the land guide her through life.

Peterkin was born in Laurens County, South Carolina. Her mother died soon after her birth, and she and her brothers and sisters were raised by their grandparents. After earning her undergraduate and Master's degrees, she taught school. Then at age 23, she married a plantation owner. Later, she managed the plantation herself.

Slavery had ended in the previous century, but the tradition of plantation stories – sentimental tales written by whites describing stereotyped black workers and their lives – continued. Although Peterkin's work is seen as part of this tradition, she is recognized as having brought to it a new sense of realism, doing away with sentimentality and unrealistic scenes.

Peterkin began writing in her 40s, when her son was old enough to look after the plantation. Her earliest works were short stories showing the Gullah way of life and written in the Gullah language, with its special speech patterns and elements of African languages, which Peterkin had learned as a child from her African-American nursemaid. Her first book, *Green Thursday*, published when she was 44, is a collection of related stories focusing on a particular family, and her first novel, *Black April*, published three years later, gives a fuller picture of the Gullah community.

PETRARCH

Italian poet

Born Jul. 20, 1304
Died Jul. 19, 1374
Age at death 69

Petrarch was one of the greatest writers of lyrical poetry. His sonnets became the model for love poetry in Europe, influencing writers for many centuries.

Francesco Petrarca (he is known as Petrarch in English) was born in Arezzo, Italy, but soon moved with his family to Avignon, France. When he was 23, an event occurred that was to color his whole life. He met and fell desperately in love with a young woman whom he called Laura. She was already married, but Petrarch immediately wrote a remarkable series of love poems inspired by her. These were an instant success.

Soon Petrarch was as well known for his scholarship and humanism as he was for his literary abilities. He traveled widely in Europe, where he visited royal courts and impressed all with his knowledge and skills. He was able to find classical manuscripts and to inspire a revival of interest in ancient Greek literature. During this time he continued to write sonnets and songs in praise of Laura as well as brilliant imitations of classical writers such as VIRGIL and HORACE. Petrarch also wrote a series of biographies of famous men, some religious works, and many letters to his close friend GIOVANNI BOCCACCIO that have been preserved. When he was 37, he was crowned Poet Laureate of Naples. His work typified the Renaissance – freedom from medieval prejudice, love of sensuality and the flowering of Italian thought and language.

Laura died in 1348, but Petrarch continued to write poems about her. He was offered high appointments but refused to accept them and retired to a village, where he continued to study until he died.

Publications

1338–41 Africa
1342 Canzoniere
1344 Triumphs
1346 The Life of Solitude
1353–58 Secret
1354–66 Remedies against Fortune
1363–66 Letters

Published after he died

1544 Complete Works

PETRY, Ann

American novelist and short-story writer

Born Oct. 12, 1911
Died Apr. 28, 1997
Age at death 85

Ann Petry's fiction, including her best-known novel *The Street*, realistically describes urban life. Petry was one of the first successful female African-American writers.

Petry grew up in the mostly white New England town of Old Saybrook, Connecticut, where her family had lived for four generations. Her father was a pharmacist who owned the local drugstore, and her mother was a licensed foot doctor. In spite of her family's middle-class status, the young Petry experienced racial harassment from an early age, and this fueled her desire to write about the damaging effects of racism. But Petry was also surrounded by wonderful role models, especially women – an aunt was the first black pharmacist in the state.

After graduating from university, Petry worked as a pharmacist in her father's drugstore until 1938, when she married writer George Petry and moved to New York. There she worked as a reporter for a black newspaper, the *People's Voice*, and wrote short stories. She first published a story at age 32 under the pen name Arnold Petry. When she was 35, her novel *The Street* was published. Set in Harlem, it tells of a young black woman who tries to improve her situation but is defeated by the harsh environment in which she lives. It was a major seller and established Petry's literary reputation. That year, Petry also graduated from Columbia University with a degree in creative writing.

Petry's other novels, *Country Place* and *The Narrows*, are set in her native Connecticut, where she and her husband and daughter returned to live in 1948.

Publications

1946 The Street
1947 Country Place
1949 The Drugstore Cat
1953 The Narrows
1955 Harriet Tubman, Conductor on the Underground Railroad
1964 Tituba of Salem Village
1970 Legends of Saints
1971 Miss Muriel and Other Stories

PIERCY, Marge

American poet and novelist

Born Mar. 31, 1936

Marge Piercy is one of America's foremost feminist writers. Her work takes a political stance even when referring to personal concerns, because for her the two are closely connected.

Piercy was born and raised in a working-class area of Detroit. Her mother was Jewish, and her father was part Welsh and part English. The young Piercy was greatly influenced by her mother and grandmother, who spoke the Jewish language of Yiddish and told stories of her large Jewish family. Piercy was the first in her family to go to university: she won a scholarship to the University of Michigan, from which she graduated in 1957, then went to Northwestern University for her Master's degree.

During the 1950s and '60s, she lived in Chicago, doing what she describes as "dreary" part-time jobs, and was a political activist, protesting in particular against the Vietnam War. She did not begin to earn a living as a writer until she was 32, when her first book of poems, *Breaking Camp*, was published. In the 1970s, the women's movement brought increased interest in her work, and many of her early novels – especially *Woman on the Edge of Time* – are now used as texts in women's studies courses. Later work, in particular *The Twelve-Spoked Wheel Flashing*, focuses on love, relationships and country life.

Piercy writes full time and has taught at a number of writers' workshops and universities. She now lives with her third husband, Ira Wood, on Cape Cod, Massachusetts. She and Wood, who have collaborated on a play, have worked together on a novel called *Storm Tide*.

Publications

1968 Breaking Camp
1969 Going Down Fast
1973 Small Changes
1976 Woman on the Edge of Time
1978 The Twelve-Spoked Wheel Flashing
1983 Stone, Paper, Knife
1989 Summer People
1994 The Longings of Women

PINDAR

Greek poet

Born c. 518 BC
Died c. 438 BC
Age at death c. 80

Pindar was the greatest poet of ancient Greece. He was admired all over the Greek world during his own lifetime and for hundreds of years after his death.

Pindar was born near the city of Thebes. He was from an ancient aristocratic family that traced its roots back to the earliest, partly mythical days of Greek history. In his youth, he studied music in Athens, and there is an ancient story that he was defeated in a poetry competition by a Theban woman called Corinna, who may have been his teacher.

In Pindar's time, poetry was sung by individual performers who also played the stringed instrument called a lyre, or by groups of young people called choruses. Pindar mainly wrote poems for choruses (these poems are known as "odes," from the Greek word meaning "to sing"). His first known poem was composed when he was about 20.

One of the most important parts of ancient Greek society was the four athletic championships known as the Olympian, Pythian, Isthmian, and Nemean games. The modern Olympic games are based on these contests, which were open to competitors from all over the Greek world. Pindar's poems known as the *Triumphal Odes* were written in honor of victorious athletes at these games.

Later in Pindar's life, when his fame had spread to every part of the Greek world, many powerful kings and important families asked him to write poems glorifying them. He traveled widely to fulfill these commissions, and wherever he went people gathered to hear him recite his poetry.

Publications

Complete works (5th century BC)

Triumphal Odes (44 in total)

Surviving fragments (5th century BC)

Hymns

Paeans

Choral Dithyrambs

Processional Songs

Choral Songs for Maidens

Choral Dance Songs

Laudatory Odes

PINTER, Harold

English playwright

Born Oct. 10, 1930

Harold Pinter is an English playwright famous for his "comedies of menace." In his works Pinter uses silences to increase tension and to suggest that unknown truths are being avoided.

Born in London to a Jewish family, Pinter was evacuated out of the war-torn city when he was 9, and returned only when he was 14. This, combined with growing up in a time of anti-Jewish sentiment, gave him a feeling of being out of place and under threat, which is seen in many of his works.

In school, Pinter developed a love of literature, particularly the works of FRANZ KAFKA and ERNEST HEMINGWAY. He later studied at the famous Royal Academy of Dramatic Arts but left before the end of the first year.

After narrowly avoiding jail for refusing to do National Service, Pinter returned to drama school, determined to become an actor. It was during a period of unemployment that he wrote his first play, *The Room*. This was followed by *The Birthday Party*, written when he was 28 and still probably his most famous work. The play deals with an apparently ordinary man who is threatened by strangers for an unknown reason.

During the 1960s, Pinter began to split his time among stage, television and film – showing equal talent and winning awards in all three areas. In 1989, he wrote the screenplay for the film *The Trial*, based on Kafka's novel. Recently Pinter has focused his attention on politics, becoming a strong opponent of censorship.

Publications

1958 The Birthday Party

1960 The Caretaker

1960 The Dumb Waiter

1965 The Homecoming

1968 Landscape

1971 Old Times

1975 No Man's Land

1978 Betrayal

1993 Moonlight

1995 Ashes to Ashes

PIRANDELLO, Luigi

Italian playwright, novelist and poet

Born Jun. 28, 1867
Died Dec. 10, 1936
Age at death 69

Luigi Pirandello is regarded as one of the leading and most influential playwrights of the 20th century. His plays are often seen as forerunners for the experimental drama movement known as theater of the absurd. He was awarded the Nobel Prize for Literature in 1934.

Pirandello was born in Girgenti, on the southern coast of the Italian island of Sicily, an area that was to be the inspiration for most of his writing. After studying at universities in Palermo, Rome and Bonn (Germany), Pirandello finally settled in Rome. While in college, he published two volumes of poetry and began to write short stories. His work shows great creativity, with believable characters, inventive plots and unexpected endings.

In 1903, the Pirandello family business collapsed, and Luigi supported himself by teaching. This was a difficult time for Pirandello, who struggled to write, work and care for his wife, who was mentally ill.

By the outbreak of World War I, Pirandello had turned his attention to theater. His first stage success was with *Right You Are If You Think You Are*, produced when he was 50. About a woman whose identity remains hidden and who could be one of two very different people, the play is typical of Pirandello's interest in how fiction mixes with reality and how people see things in very different ways. In Pirandello's most famous play, *Six Characters in Search of an Author*, produced when he was 54, the six characters of the title are called into existence by a writer, but they get left in limbo when he then refuses to finish the play for which they were created.

Publications

1917	*The Jar*
1917	*Right You Are If You Think You Are*
1917	*The Pleasure of Honesty*
1918	*The Rules of the Game*
1921	*Six Characters in Search of an Author*
1922	*To Clothe the Naked*
1922	*Henry IV*
1924	*Each in His Own Way*
1930	*Tonight We Improvise*

PLAATJE, Sol T.

South African writer

Born Oct. 9, 1876
Died Jun. 19, 1932
Age at death 55

As a writer, journalist, diarist, editor, translator, language specialist and political activist Sol T. Plaatje dedicated his life to improving the lot of South Africans living under the harsh and brutal rule of the white minority.

Solomon Tshekisho Plaatje was born in the Orange Free State, which was then a Boer republic, in southern Africa. (The Boers, or Afrikaners, originally came from Holland.) Although he had little schooling, Plaatje learned German, Dutch and English at an early age. By the time he became interpreter and signalman at the town of Mafeking in 1899, he had mastered many African languages other than his own Tswana. During the Boer War, at age 23, he wrote the *Boer War Diary*, about his experience of the siege of Mafeking.

In 1901, Plaatje set up the first Tswana newspaper. Nine years later, after the creation of the white-ruled Union of South Africa, he cofounded the South African Native National Congress, which became the African National Congress. He then traveled to Europe, Canada, and the US, trying to win support for South Africans dispossessed of their land and civil rights by the whites. This was also his aim in writing *Native Life in South Africa* and his only novel, *Mhudi*. Set in the 1830s, *Mhudi* tells African history from an African point of view and celebrates the values of African culture. Plaatje wrote *Mhudi* before 1920, making it probably the first English novel written by a black African, but he could not get it published until 1930. His *Boer War Diary* was discovered and published 43 years later.

Publications

1916 Native Life in South Africa

1930 Mhudi

Published after he died

1973 Boer War Diary

PLATH, Sylvia

American poet and novelist

Born Oct. 27, 1932

Died Feb. 11, 1963

Age at death 30

Sylvia Plath was a renowned American poet whose promising career was cut short by her tragic suicide. In 1982, nearly 20 years after her death, she was awarded the Pulitzer Prize for her *Collected Poems*.

Plath was born near Boston. Her father, a German immigrant, died when she was eight; her mother was a secondary school teacher. From an early age, Plath had a drive to achieve, and she did. By the time she was 18, she had published poetry, stories and art in national magazines, and had won a scholarship to Smith College.

While still at Smith she had a mental breakdown, which became the subject of her partly autobiographical novel, *The Bell Jar*. She returned to Smith to graduate with honors and then went to Cambridge University. While at Cambridge, she married an English poet, TED HUGHES. At age 28, she gave birth to a daughter and also published her poetry collection, *The Colossus*. She had a son two years later. Separated from Hughes, feeling isolated, and struggling with the difficulties of trying to write and raise two small children, she killed herself the following year.

Plath's poems focus on the themes of women's creativity and madness. The pressures on her to conform as a middle-class woman and the conflict between being a "good" wife and mother and being a poet contributed to her breakdown and suicide. *Ariel*, published after her death, was the collection through which she became well known. It was also very controversial, linking women's oppression with racial oppression (including the Holocaust) and describing negative aspects of motherhood.

Publications

1960 The Colossus

1962 Three Women

1963 The Bell Jar

Published after she died

1965 Ariel

1971 Crossing the Water

1971 Winter Trees

1981 Collected Poems

1983 The Journals of Sylvia Plath

1985 Selected Poems

POE, Edgar Allan

American horror writer

Born Jan. 19, 1809
Died Oct. 7, 1849
Age at death 40

Publications

1833 "Manuscript Found in a Bottle"
1839 "The Fall of the House of Usher"
1840 *Tales of the Grotesque and Arabesque*
1841 "The Murders in the Rue Morgue"
1843 "The Gold Bug"
1845 *The Raven and Other Poems*
1845 "The Pit and the Pendulum"
1845 *Tales*
1849 *Annabel Lee*

Edgar Allan Poe was an influential 19th-century American writer. He is famous for his horror stories and his eerie poetry.

Both of Poe's parents died before he was three years old, and he was adopted by a wealthy tobacco merchant from Richmond, Virginia. Poe never felt settled in his new family, and his bad behavior often brought him into conflict with his adopted father, who also disapproved of him spending more time writing poetry than studying. In 1827, Poe had to leave the University of Virginia, where he had got into debt through gambling and, in 1831, he was expelled from West Point Military Academy. His adopted father disowned him, and Poe went to live with an aunt in Baltimore.

At the age of 24, Poe had his first literary success when his short story "Manuscript Found in a Bottle" won a cash prize. He began working for magazines, but his unpredictable behavior and heavy drinking often got him fired. The stories and poems he produced, however, began to make him famous and were published in the collection *Tales of the Grotesque and Arabesque* when he was 31. In the same year, Poe went to work for *Graham's Magazine*, which published his famous story "The Murders in the Rue Morgue." Many scholars have called this the world's first modern detective story.

Poe was obsessed with death, fear and the supernatural. The modern genres of horror, mystery and crime writing were all pioneered by Poe, and his work influenced many later writers.

POOLE, Ernest

American novelist and journalist

Born Jan. 23, 1880
Died Jan. 10, 1950
Age at death 69

Ernest Poole is best known for his second novel, *The Harbor*, and also for his crusading journalism, which brought about important changes in the laws of the United States. His third novel, *His Family*, won the first ever Pulitzer Prize for fiction in 1918.

Poole was born in Chicago, where he received his early education. After graduating with honors from Princeton University, he went to live among the poor at the University Settlement House in New York City. He was determined to write fiction, but after several unsuccessful attempts at short-story writing he turned to journalism. He was a socialist and wrote about the hardships and poor living conditions of the people around him. As a result of his articles, better health care was provided, and the incidence of tuberculosis was reduced; the terrible conditions of the tenements were also improved, and the laws governing child labor were changed.

Poole published his first novel, *The Voice of the Street*, when he was 26; but it was his second novel, *The Harbor*, published nine years later, that brought him fame. This novel, although set in the harbor area of New York, is based on Poole's own experiences and knowledge of the 1904 Chicago stockyard strike. All Poole's novels promote the ideas of socialism – sometimes at the expense of a convincing plot and characters. However, his best fiction, like his journalism, is powerful and sincere. Although his later books were not as well received or as popular, Poole left his mark – particularly with *The Harbor* – on the written history of American socialism.

Publications

1906 The Voice of the Street
1915 The Harbor
1917 His Family
1918 The Dark People
1919 The Village
1927 Silent Storms
1934 One of Us
1940 The Bridge
1943 Giants Gone
1949 The Nancy Flyer

POPE, Alexander

English poet, satirist and critic

Born May 21, 1688
Died May 30, 1744
Age at death 56

Alexander Pope was the leading English poet of the early 18th century. He was also a major critic and satirist. So respected was he in the 1700s that this era was once known as the "Age of Pope."

Pope was born into a Roman Catholic family in London. At that time, Roman Catholics were not able to live where they wished, practise their religion openly, or attend certain schools. As a result Pope's formal education was often interrupted and of poor quality, but despite this he learned Latin, Greek, French and Italian by teaching himself. At a young age, Pope was struck by an infection of the spine that left him humpbacked and stunted his growth, permanently affecting his health. The effect of his poor health was to make him concentrate on his studies and on writing poetry.

Pope began to write as a teenager, which is when he started his remarkable, witty poem *An Essay on Criticism*. Published just before he became 23, it includes such famous lines as "A little learning is a dangerous thing." Some of the critics and writers that it made fun of responded by cruelly attacking Pope's physical deformities, calling him a "hunchbacked toad." His mock epic poem *The Rape of the Lock* was published the following year. It tells of a suitor who steals a lock of hair from a young woman. Pope wrote the poem to mock the habits of fashionable people.

Between 1715 and 1726, Pope translated classical texts such as HOMER's *Iliad*. He then went on to write many satirical poems, including *The Dunciad*, which ridicules bad writers, scientists and critics.

Publications

1711 An Essay on Criticism
1712 The Rape of the Lock
1728–43 The Dunciad
1731–35 Moral Essays
1733–34 An Essay on Man
1733–38 Imitations of Horace
1735 Of the Characters of Women

PORTER, Katherine Anne

American short-story writer and novelist

Born May 15, 1890
Died Sep. 18, 1980
Age at death 90

Katherine Anne Porter is remembered as one of America's most distinguished short-story writers.

Porter was born on a small farm in Texas, and her mother died when she was two. She left school at 14 and supported herself by giving elocution lessons. A month after her 16th birthday, she married the first of her three husbands, but she left him in 1914 to become an actress. A year later, Porter contracted tuberculosis, and it was during her recovery that she decided she wanted to be a writer. After working as a journalist for a while, she set out on a series of journeys that took her across America and abroad. She made detailed notes of all the places she saw and the people she met, using her experiences as material for her writing.

Porter's first book of short stories, *Flowering Judas*, published when she was 40, was based on her friendships with Mexican revolutionaries. For other stories she drew on her Texas farm life and on conversations she had overheard. Porter's only full-length novel, *Ship of Fools*, made her rich and famous. Set aboard a German liner traveling from America to Germany at the time the Nazis were rising to power, the book is an allegory that explores the roots of evil in ordinary people. Published when she was 72, it topped the American bestseller list for 45 weeks and was made into a movie. But it was *The Collected Stories of Katherine Anne Porter* that won her a Pulitzer Prize and the National Book Award in 1966.

Porter owed both awards to the craftsmanship of her writing. She was at her best in short stories and had to struggle to complete *Ship of Fools*.

Publications

1930 Flowering Judas
1939 Pale Horse, Pale Rider
1944 The Leaning Tower and Other Stories
1952 The Days Before
1962 Ship of Fools
1965 The Collected Stories of Katherine Anne Porter

POTOK, Chaim

American novelist

Born Feb. 17, 1929

Chaim Potok is best known for his novels exploring the Jewish experience in modern America.

Born in New York City, Potok was educated in Orthodox Jewish schools. He graduated from Yeshiva University, an Orthodox college in New York City, and then studied at the Jewish Theological Seminary. He was ordained a rabbi when he was 25. Potok taught at several seminaries before becoming the managing editor of the magazine *Conservative Judaism* in 1964. The following year, he joined the editorial staff of the Jewish Publication Society in Philadelphia, where he remained while pursuing a writing career.

When he was 38, Potok published his first and most important novel, *The Chosen*. It is the story of the friendship between a progressive Orthodox Jewish scholar and a young Hasid – a member of a very traditional Jewish group. He uses the story of the growing friendship between these two young men to explore the tensions within the modern Jewish community. Potok wrote a sequel to *The Chosen* entitled *The Promise* two years later.

All Potok's novels explore the theme of how Judaism relates to the modern world. His main characters, most of whom are men, struggle with their attempts to fit their Jewish heritage into the 20th century. In each of his books, he develops a confrontation between Judaism and some aspect of modern society. In *My Name Is Asher Lev,* the confrontation is with Western art. In *In the Beginning,* it is with modern criticism of the Bible. In *The Book of Lights,* it is with atomic weapons.

Publications

1967 The Chosen
1969 The Promise
1972 My Name Is Asher Lev
1975 In the Beginning
1978 Wanderings
1981 The Book of Lights
1985 Davita's Harp
1990 The Gift of Asher Lev
1992 I Am the Clay

POTTER, Beatrix

English children's writer

Born Jul. 28, 1866
Died Dec. 22, 1943
Age at death 77

Beatrix Potter was an English writer and illustrator who created some of the best-known characters in children's literature, including Peter Rabbit, Squirrel Nutkin and Jemima Puddle-Duck.

Potter was born into a wealthy London family. She was educated at home by governesses rather than being sent away to school. Her parents hardly ever allowed her to go out, and her only brother was at boarding school. She was very lonely and spent hours drawing and painting. During holidays in the Lake District, a beautiful part of the English countryside, she would draw animals and plants from nature. Back in London, she longed to escape to the freedom of the woods and the fields.

When Potter grew up she kept in touch with one of her old governesses, Annie Moore, and in a letter to Moore's son in 1893 she included the first version of *The Tale of Peter Rabbit*. It wasn't until Potter was in her mid-30s that she thought to publish the story as a book. She paid for the printing of *The Tale of Peter Rabbit* and her next book, *The Tailor of Gloucester,* with her own money. Both were beautifully illustrated with watercolor paintings by Potter herself of the animal characters dressed like people. A publisher noticed Potter's books and offered to buy more. She had her first big success with *The Tale of Squirrel Nutkin*, which appeared when Potter was 37.

Later Potter fulfilled a childhood dream and bought a farm in the Lake District. She lived there for the rest of her life, writing and illustrating the funny, simple tales that have since been loved by generations of children and their parents.

Publications

1901 The Tale of Peter Rabbit
1902 The Tailor of Gloucester
1903 The Tale of Squirrel Nutkin
1904 The Tale of Benjamin Bunny
1904 The Tale of Two Bad Mice
1905 The Tale of Mrs. Tiggy-Winkle
1907 The Tale of Tom Kitten
1908 The Tale of Jemima Puddle-Duck
1912 The Tale of Mr. Tod

POUND, Ezra

American poet, translator and critic

Born Oct. 30, 1885
Died Nov. 1, 1972
Age at death 87

Ezra Pound was an American poet who had a great influence on the development of poetry in the 20th century. Not only did he write poems that were admired for their originality, he also encouraged the early careers of other innovative authors, including T.S. ELIOT, JAMES JOYCE and ERNEST HEMINGWAY.

Born in Hailey, Idaho, Pound went to the University of Pennsylvania at age 16 then studied at Hamilton College, Indiana. After a short stay in Venice, Italy, where he had his first collection of poems, *A Lume Spento*, published, he moved to London and quickly established himself as a champion of experimental literature. He used his contacts to get the work of T.S. Eliot and James Joyce published for the first time.

In 1920, aged 35, Pound moved to Paris. He had already begun his masterpiece, the sequence of 30 poems known as *The Cantos*. This long, complex work, which occupied Pound for much of his life, is extremely difficult to understand. It makes references to a vast range of characters, events and books from the past. Pound wanted *The Cantos* to be an epic for his time, like the works of the great writers HOMER and DANTE.

By 1925, Pound had settled in Italy, a country whose history and literature he had always loved. He stayed in Italy when World War II began and made a series of radio broadcasts that blamed the Jewish people for causing the war. After the war, Pound was arrested by the US Army because of his involvement with the fascist Italian government. He spent 12 years in an American mental hospital, where he continued to write great poetry before returning to live in Italy.

Publications

1908 A Lume Spento
1912 Ripostes
1915 Cathay
1917 Homage to Sextus Propertius
1917–68 The Cantos (unfinished)
1920 Hugh Selwyn Mauberley
1926 Personae
1948 "If This Be Treason..."
1948 The Pisan Cantos

POWELL, Anthony

English novelist and playwright

Born Dec. 21, 1905
Died Mar. 28 2000
Age at death 95

Anthony Powell is best known for his 12-volume novel *A Dance to the Music of Time*, which chronicles life in Britain between 1914 and the late '60s.

Powell was born in London into a wealthy family. He was educated at Eton and at Oxford University. This privileged upbringing among the English aristocracy was to provide Powell with the material for his writing.

After graduating, Powell worked for a large publishing firm in London and began writing. His first novel, *Afternoon Men*, published when he was 26, is set among the wealthy, party-going upper class that he knew so well. It is a satire on the aimless and lazy existence of a group of people who live only for the next party invitation.

Publications

1931 Afternoon Men
1932 Venusburg

Powell finished four more novels with similar themes before the outbreak of World War II, during which he served in the intelligence corps. Six years after the end of the war, when Powell was 46, *A Question of Upbringing* was published. This first volume of *A Dance to the Music of Time* sets the scene for the 11 volumes that were to follow over the next 25 years.

A Dance to the Music of Time follows the fortunes of a range of upper-class characters through a time of great change in British society – from the beginning of World War I, through World War II, and into the radical changes of the 1960s. Powell shows how British society is shaken apart by the stresses of two terrible wars and how the aristocracy has to adapt to new conditions in order to survive.

1939 What's Become of Waring?
1948 John Aubrey and His Friends
1951 A Question of Upbringing
1951–75 A Dance to the Music of Time (12 vols.)
1975 Hearing Secret Harmonies
1976–82 To Keep the Ball Rolling
1986 The Fisher King

PRATCHETT, Terry

English fantasy writer

Born Apr. 28, 1948

Terry Pratchett is a highly successful writer of comic fantasy novels.

Pratchett was born in the town of Beaconsfield near London. At age 13 he wrote a short story, "The Hades Business," for his school magazine. The story was then published in the magazine *Science Fantasy*, and with the money he earned, Pratchett bought a typewriter and began to write seriously.

After finishing his education, Pratchett became a journalist and then worked as a press officer for British nuclear power stations. In his spare time he continued to write. His first novel, *The Carpet People*, was published when he was 23. It is a children's fantasy story set in a world of tiny creatures who live in the weave of a carpet and who are too small and fast to be seen by humans.

Pratchett's early work got good reviews, but it was when he published a series of comic novels set in an imaginary world called Discworld that he found fame. Discworld is an absurd, imaginary flat world supported by four elephants standing on a huge turtle swimming through space. In the series Pratchett pokes fun at some of the conventions of fantasy fiction: the brave heroes, the witches and wizards, and the magic spells.

In 1989, Pratchett began a new fantasy series called *Bromeliad*, this time for children. It tells of the adventures of the "nomes," four-inch-high people from another planet who have crashed on Earth and made a new world for themselves under the floorboards of a department store.

Publications
1971 The Carpet People
1976 The Dark Side of the Sun
1983 The Color of Magic
1986 The Light Fantastic
1987 Mort
1989 Eric
1992 Small Gods
1994 Interesting Times
1996 Hogfather
1997 Jingo
1998 Last Continent
1998 Carpe Jugulum

PRELUTSKY, Jack

American children's poet

Born Sep. 8, 1940

Jack Prelutsky is one of America's best authors of poems for children – his *Ride a Purple Pelican* very soon became a classic. Probably one of Prelutsky's greatest achievements is that he lets children know that poetry can be fun.

Prelutsky was born into a poor but happy family in the Bronx, New York. He hated the local schools that he went to, but as a teenager he was sent to the High School of Music and Art, which he loved. He studied singing, and after he graduated in 1958, he continued to sing with opera companies and at coffeehouses in New York. He held many jobs – cab driver, salesman, busboy, actor and potter, to name a few – before becoming a writer. He wrote his first poems when he was 24 to go with some pictures of strange animals he had drawn. His first collection, *A Gopher in the Garden and Other Animal Poems*, came out when he was 27.

Prelutsky's verse lends itself well to being read out loud or even sung; Prelutsky himself often sings his poems when he visits schools and libraries. The poems deal humorously with topics that most children can relate to, such as bullies, homework, school and being afraid of the dark. He has also created a whole range of monstrous imaginary beasts as well as cleverly describing real creatures. Some of Prelutsky's work has even been banned from libraries for being too scary. In his *Nightmares: Poems to Trouble Your Sleep* and *The Headless Horseman Rides Tonight* bogeymen, ghouls, ghosts and other assorted monsters can be found. He also often writes nonsense verse, which intrigues the listener or reader with its rhythms and interesting sounds.

Publications

1967	*A Gopher in the Garden and Other Animal Poems*
1969	*The Terrible Tiger*
1976	*Nightmares: Poems to Trouble Your Sleep*
1980	*The Headless Horseman Rides Tonight*
1986	*Ride a Purple Pelican*
1993	*The Dragons Are Singing Tonight*

PRIESTLEY, J.B.

English playwright, novelist and journalist

Born Sep. 13, 1894
Died Aug. 14, 1984
Age at death 89

J.B. Priestley became famous in two roles: as a writer and during World War II and after as a patriotic radio broadcaster. For his achievements he was made a member of the prestigious Order of Merit. He was also offered the honorary titles of "Sir" and "Lord" but turned them down.

John Boynton Priestley was born in the north of England in Yorkshire. After army service during World War I, he graduated from Cambridge University and became a critic and journalist in London. He achieved his first success, aged 35, with *The Good Companions*, a light-hearted novel about a traveling theater group. His next book, *Angel Pavement*, was a more somber picture of life in London.

Altogether Priestley published over 100 books, including volumes of essays, such as *The English Novel*; travel books, such as *English Journey* and *Journey Down a Rainbow*, based on a journey in New Mexico and which he wrote with his third wife, the archeologist Jacquetta Hawkes; and collections of his wartime broadcasts, including *Britain Speaks*.

As a playwright he wrote comedies, such as *When We Are Married*, and a successful mystery play, *An Inspector Calls*. Altogether he wrote about 50 plays. In several, he explores our understanding of time by changing the normal order of events. These include *Dangerous Corner* and *Time and the Conways*.

In much of his work, and especially in his radio talks, Priestley served as a common-sense spokesman for the ordinary man-in-the-street.

Publications

1927	*The English Novel*
1929	*The Good Companions*
1930	*Angel Pavement*
1932	*Dangerous Corner*
1934	*English Journey*
1937	*Time and the Conways*
1938	*When We Are Married*
1940	*Britain Speaks*
1947	*An Inspector Calls*
1955	*Journey Down a Rainbow*

PROPERTIUS, Sextus

Roman poet

Born c. 50 BC
Died c. 16 BC
Age at death c. 34

Sextus Propertius was a leading Roman poet best known for his elegies (a style of Latin verse) describing passionate love.

He was born in the town of Assisi, Italy, into a wealthy family and received an excellent education. His early life was made difficult by his father's death and the state's seizure of his family's lands after a civil war, which left him relatively poor.

Moving to Rome with his mother when he was about 16, Propertius intended to become a lawyer but soon found that poetry suited him better. A few years later, he began a love affair with an older woman whom he called Cynthia (her real name was Hostia).

The poetry Propertius wrote about Cynthia is some of the greatest love poetry in history. At the age of about 25, he published his first book of poetry, which was dedicated to Cynthia. By writing about his personal feelings, he followed the example of CATULLUS, an earlier Roman poet who had introduced this kind of poetry to Roman literature.

Propertius was quickly recognized as a talented young poet and was looked after by a powerful Roman politician called Maecenas, who took an interest in many leading poets of the day, including VIRGIL, HORACE and OVID. Maecenas introduced Propertius to these great literary figures and the circle of wealthy and powerful aristocrats with whom they socialized.

Almost nothing is known about Propertius's life after his affair with Cynthia ended. He stopped writing poetry for six or seven years and might have been married. His last poems were published not long before he died.

Publications

c. 28 BC	*Book I*
25 BC	*Book II*
22 BC	*Book III*
c. 16 BC	*Book IV*

PROULX, E. Annie

American novelist

Born Aug. 22, 1935

E. Annie Proulx is best known for her Pulitzer Prize-winning novel *The Shipping News*, set in bleak Newfoundland on the northeastern coast of Canada.

Edna Annie Proulx was born in Norwich, Connecticut. Not much is known about her life; she is said to be a recluse who avoids publicity. Struggling to bring up three sons, she spent many years working as a freelance journalist and writing "how-to" books. She published her first fiction book, the collection *Heart Songs and Other Stories*, at age 53. Proulx set these stories in rural New England, where the characters hunt for survival. Her love for "the great outdoors" – even at its most harsh – is evident in this collection, as in most of her work.

Proulx's second book and first novel, *Postcards*, was published when she was 57 and earned her the prestigious PEN/Faulkner Award: she was the first woman to win this. In the book, Proulx returns to the theme of the individual's connection to the land and follows one character, Loyal Blood, as he journeys across the United States and sends postcards home.

Proulx shot to fame with her second novel, *The Shipping News*, which was published when she was 58. It won the National Book Award in 1993 and in 1994 a Pulitzer Prize. Set in Newfoundland, the novel tells the story of Quoyle, a journalist who settles on the remote Canadian island – the land of his ancestors – with his aunt and two daughters, determined to leave his troubled past behind. The novel was hugely popular and became an international best-seller.

Publications

- *1988 Heart Songs and Other Stories*
- *1992 Postcards*
- *1993 The Shipping News*
- *1996 Accordion Crimes*
- *1999 Close Range: Wyoming Stories*

PROUST, Marcel

French novelist, short-story writer and critic

Born Jul. 10, 1871

Died Nov. 18, 1922

Age at death 51

Marcel Proust is known for writing the novel *Remembrance of Things Past*, which many regard as one of the most profound and most perfect achievements of world literature.

Proust was born in Anteuil, near Paris in France, the son of an eminent doctor and a wealthy Jewish mother. He suffered with asthma from an early age, but this did not prevent him from attending secondary school, doing his military service, and studying law and literature at the famous Sorbonne in Paris.

While at school Proust started writing in magazines, and when he was 25, he published a collection of profound and stylish short stories entitled *Pleasures and Days*. Gradually Proust withdrew from his high-society social life. His health was deteriorating, and his support for Captain Dreyfus, the Jewish army officer who was wrongly accused of betraying French secrets to the Germans, lost Proust some of his aristocratic friends. The death of his father and beloved mother caused him to withdraw still further, and he became a virtual recluse.

Proust became financially independent when he was 34, following the death of his parents, and was free to start on his great novel, *Remembrance of Things Past*. Influenced by the autobiographies of JOHANN WOLFGANG VON GOETHE and FRANÇOIS RENÉ CHATEAUBRIAND, he set out to tell the story of a search for truth based on the events of his own life. The main character, Marcel, discovers that as an artist he can reveal truths about life by the careful expression of his own memories. The novel was originally published in seven parts between 1913 and 1927.

Publications

Remembrance of Things Past (in the following 7 parts)

1913 Swann's Way

1919 Within a Budding Grove

1920–21 The Guermantes Way

1921–22 Cities of the Plain

Published after he died

1923 The Captive

1925 The Sweet Cheat Gone

1927 The Past Recaptured

PUSHKIN, Aleksandr

Russian poet, novelist and short-story writer

Born Jun. 6, 1799

Died Feb. 10, 1837

Age at death 37

Aleksandr Pushkin is generally considered to be Russia's greatest poet. He was the first to use everyday speech in his poetry instead of the formal style of language used in Russian literature up until then. He also introduced new themes from Russian history and folklore.

Pushkin was born in Moscow into a cultured but poor aristocratic family. He studied in the town of Tsarskoye Selo, now renamed Pushkin in his honor. After graduating in 1817, he was appointed to a government position in St. Petersburg and lived a dazzling social life. He had been writing poetry from an early age; his first published poem, "To a Poet Friend," was written when he was only 14. His first major work, the verse fairy tale *Ruslan and Lyudmila*, came out when he was 21.

In spite of his rich lifestyle, Pushkin was deeply committed to social reform. His poem "Ode to Liberty" so angered the Russian emperor that Pushkin was banished from St. Petersburg for six years. During this time, he wrote some of his finest work, including *The Prisoner of the Caucasus* and *The Gypsies.* He also began his masterpiece, *Eugene Onegin*, a novel in verse that satirized Russian society. Pushkin enjoyed writing about Russian heroes, and in *The Bronze Horseman* he depicts the legendary Russian emperor Peter the Great.

Pushkin was pardoned by the emperor in 1826 and returned to St. Petersburg. He married Natalia Goncharova in 1831, but her social ambitions drove him into debt. To defend her reputation he was forced to fight a duel and was killed.

Publications

1820 Ruslan and Lyudmila

1822 The Prisoner of the Caucasus

1823–31 Eugene Onegin

1827 The Gypsies

1827 The Robber Brothers

1831 Boris Godunov

1834 The Queen of Spades

Published after he died

1837 The Bronze Horseman

1843 The Captain's Daughter

PUZO, Mario

American novelist

Born Oct. 15, 1920
Died July 2, 1999
Age at death 78

Mario Puzo is an American writer best known as the author of *The Godfather*, the tale of the Italian-American Corleone family of Mafia gangsters.

Puzo was born in the area known as "Hell's Kitchen" in Manhattan, New York City, the son of a railway trackman. He lived with his six brothers and sisters above the railway yards. Crime was common in the area, but Puzo's stable family life, regular holidays with a boys' charity, and the discovery of public libraries helped form his character and point him in the direction of writing.

After serving in the army during World War II, Puzo attended New York's New School for Social Research and then Columbia University. His first novel, *The Dark Arena*, a story set in Germany just after the war, came out when he was 35. Next came *The Fortunate Pilgrim,* which, like most of his later novels, features Italians living in America. Common themes are also the importance of money and power, and the resourcefulness of immigrants in making a living.

Neither of Puzo's first two books was a financial success, though both received good reviews. It was only when Puzo, in debt to his family for $20,000 and with six children, decided "to write a best-seller" that he really made his mark on the American public with *The Godfather*, which was the number one bestseller in the US for 67 weeks. Three screenplays were made for the hugely successful movies *Godfather I*, *II* and *III*, earning him two Academy Awards. This helped Puzo achieve his dream of worldwide success.

Publications

1955	*The Dark Arena*
1964	*The Fortunate Pilgrim*
1969	*The Godfather*
1978	*Fools Die*
1984	*The Sicilian*
1991	*The Fourth K*
1996	*The Last Don*

PYNCHON, Thomas

American novelist

Born May 8, 1937

Thomas Pynchon is a highly regarded modern American novelist. Popular culture, scientific theories and historical facts are intertwined with large casts of characters in his novels.

Although Pynchon's work is very influential, little is known about his life. He was born in Glen Cove, New York City, and attended Cornell University, where he started to study engineering but finally graduated in English. One of his teachers at Cornell was Russian-born novelist VLADIMIR NABOKOV. Pynchon's studies were interrupted for two years by service in the US Navy.

After leaving Cornell, Pynchon worked as a technical writer for the Boeing Aircraft Corporation, leaving after two years to devote his time to writing. He published his first book, *V*, when he was 26. It is a puzzling story that describes with absurd humor the search of a middle-aged Englishman for an adventuress known only by the initial "V."

A search is also the subject of Pynchon's next novel, *The Crying of Lot 49* – this time a woman searches for the meaning of a strange symbol. *Gravity's Rainbow* carries on the quest theme. Like much of his writing it is about the way industry, the media and military interests have come to dominate 20th-century American society. The plot is very complicated and full of bizarre images and ideas. The novel won the National Book Award.

Pynchon's fourth novel, *Vineland*, appeared after a break of 17 years in his literary output, during which all he published was a collection of short stories called *Slow Learner* that he had written earlier.

Publications

1963 V
1966 The Crying of Lot 49
1973 Gravity's Rainbow
1984 Slow Learner
1990 Vineland
1997 Mason & Dixon

QUASIMODO, Salvatore

Italian poet and translator

Born Aug. 20, 1901
Died Jun. 14, 1968
Age at death 66

Salvatore Quasimodo was an important Italian poet who won the 1959 Nobel Prize for Literature.

He was born in Modica, on the island of Sicily at the toe of Italy. At age 17, he moved to Rome in northern Italy to study engineering. But he was never really interested in technology, and he turned to poetry, becoming Professor of Literature at the Milan Conservatory of Music in 1941.

Quasimodo's earliest poems appeared in magazines and were published as a collection called *Waters and Lands* when he was 29. These poems, while full of fine imagery, are remote in tone and reveal an underlying fear about loneliness and about life in general. Quasimodo's very personal poetry of the 1930s is described as "hermetic" because, like a hermit, he concentrated only on himself.

World War II had a great effect on Quasimodo's mind and changed the direction of his poetry. In his *New Poems,* he reacted with grief to the loss and destruction caused by war. And in *Day after Day,* his work expresses his deep disillusionment and horror at Italy's conduct in the war.

Thereafter his concern as a poet was to seek a solution to the problem of human suffering. His ideas tended toward communism and against Christianity. The lecturing tone of some of this poetry attracted criticism but did not prevent him from being awarded the Nobel Prize. Quasimodo also wrote many essays on literature and translated the work of writers such as WILLIAM SHAKESPEARE.

Publications

1930 Waters and Lands
1933 Scent of Eucalyptus
1942 And Suddenly It Is Evening
1942 New Poems
1947 Day after Day
1949 Life Is Not a Dream
1956 The False and the True Green
1958 The Incomparable Land

QUEEN, Ellery

American crime writers

Frederic Dannay

Born Jan. 11, 1905
Died Sep. 3, 1982
Age at death 77

Manfred B. Lee

Born Oct. 20, 1905
Died Apr. 3, 1971
Age at death 65

Publications

1929 The Roman Hat Mystery
1932 The Greek Coffin Mystery
1932 The Egyptian Cross Mystery
1938 The Four of Hearts
1942 Calamity Town
1948 Ten Days' Wonder
1951 The Origin of Evil
1958 The Finishing Stroke
1964 And On the Eighth Day
1971 A Fine and Private Place

The novels of Ellery Queen are classic works in the best American tradition of crime and mystery writing.

Ellery Queen is the pen name adopted by two cousins, Frederic Dannay and Manfred B(ennington) Lee. Both men were born in Brooklyn, New York, and attended secondary school together there. They both became commercial writers in New York: Dannay worked as a copywriter in advertising, while Lee was a publicity writer for film companies. In 1928, a competition for a detective novel was announced, offering a prize of $7,500; the cousins entered, and their novel, *The Roman Hat Mystery*, won the prize (it was later published when they were both aged 24). From then until 1971, they went on to publish dozens more mystery stories.

The hero of the duo's stories is a detective also named Ellery Queen. In the stories, Ellery Queen is a professional mystery writer who is occasionally called in to help his father, a police inspector, solve a particularly puzzling murder. The books are typical "whodunits" – that is, stories in which the reader has to pick up clues in a murder puzzle and try to solve the mystery. With their backgrounds in commercial writing the cousins produced sophisticated, fast-moving stories full of twists and turns, and Ellery Queen soon became one of the most popular mystery heroes of the day. The stories also became a radio series, *The Adventures of Ellery Queen*, which ran between 1939 and 1948. In 1941, Frederic Dannay became editor of *Ellery Queen's Mystery Magazine*, a job he continued to do until his death.

QUIROGA, Horacio

Uruguayan short-story writer and novelist

Born Dec. 31, 1878
Died Feb. 19, 1937
Age at death 58

The most famous Uruguayan writer of his time, Quiroga wrote of his obsessions – the jungle, madness, horror, death and his passionate love life. His life was dominated by an extraordinary mixture of adventure, tragedy, poverty and violence (his father was killed when he was a baby, and his stepfather committed suicide). He wrote over 200 short stories, and into these he poured the drama of his life.

Quiroga was born in Salto, Uruguay. When he was 13, his family moved to the capital, Montevideo. He visited Europe in his early 20s and in Paris met the important South American author Rubén Darío. On returning to Uruguay, Quiroga became the center of a group of young writers and at the age of 23 published his first collection of prose and poetry, *Coral Reefs*.

In 1906, Quiroga bought a plot of virgin jungle in the state of Misiones in the Uruguayan interior and went to live there. Life in the jungle was very harsh, and his young wife committed suicide. Alone with his two children, Quiroga wrote a tender and funny collection of children's stories, *South American Jungle Tales*, and two more adult collections of short stories. Many of these are about his admiration for the jungle and his love for animals. In *Anaconda,* the animals are the characters. Some of his more horrific stories were influenced by the work of EDGAR ALLAN POE.

For many years Quiroga lived in Buenos Aires, Argentina, but he returned for some time to Misiones and remarried.

Publications

1901	*Coral Reefs*
1917	*Stories of Love, Madness, and Death*
1918	*South American Jungle Tales*
1921	*Anaconda*
1924	*The Wilderness*
1925	*The Decapitated Chicken*
1926	*The Exiles*
1929	*Bygone Love*

RABÉARIVELO, Jean-Joseph

Madagascan poet

Born Mar. 4, 1901
Died Jun. 22, 1937
Age at death 36

Jean-Joseph Rabéarivelo, one of Africa's most important French-language poets, has been called the father of modern Madagascan literature. He led the first wave of modern literature writing that swept Madagascar in the 1920s and '30s.

Rabéarivelo was born in Antananarivo, the capital of Madagascar, a large island off the southeast coast of Africa. At the time, Madagascar was a French colony. His mother, an aristocrat, had married a tailor, and the family was very poor. After only eight years of schooling, Rabéarivelo left school and began work as a publisher's clerk, moving from one low-paid job to another.

In spite of the family's poverty, Rabéarivelo was encouraged by his mother to write. His first poems were published in a journal when he was only 20. He went on to produce hundreds of poems, mostly in French. The collections *Nearly Dreams* and *Translations of the Night* are considered his best works.

Rabéarivelo's poems create a mythical world shadowed by visions of death and disaster offset by glimpses of hope. His early poetry was influenced by 19th-century French poets and written in his own unique version of imperfect French. His final volume, *Old Songs of the Merina Country*, is based on Madagascan love poems and was published two years after Rabéarivelo committed suicide. Various reasons have been given for his taking his own life, including addiction to drugs, depression, lack of money and failure to fulfill his ambition of traveling to France.

Publications

1924	*The Blow of Cinders*
1931	*Children of Orpheus*
1934	*Nearly Dreams*
1935	*Translations of the Night*
1937	*Songs for Abéone*

Published after he died

1939	*Old Songs of the Merina Country*
1959	*Some Forgotten Positions*
1962	*24 Poems*

RABELAIS, François

French writer

Born c. 1494
Died Apr. 9, 1553
Age at death c. 59

François Rabelais wrote *Gargantua and Pantagruel*, a hilarious classic of French literature and one of the greatest books ever written.

Rabelais was born near the town of Chinon in western France, the son of a lawyer. By the age of 15, he had joined a monastery – the Church was the only place where most people could hope to receive an education at the time. This was the period known as the Renaissance, when scholars in monasteries were beginning to study ancient Greek and Roman texts that had been ignored for centuries and were rediscovering knowledge that had been forgotten. Rabelais became a leading scholar in the study of ancient Greek books and particularly in the study of medical works.

In 1527, Rabelais left his monastery without permission and enrolled as a medical student at the University of Montpellier in the south of France. A few years later, at about age 38, he became the physician at the general hospital in Lyon. In the same year, the first part of his famous comedy, *Gargantua and Pantagruel*, was published under the pen name Alcofribas Nasier (an anagram of the author's real name). It was an instant success, and Rabelais wrote three more volumes in the years that followed.

Rabelais's books are satires on French society of the time. Gargantua and Pantagruel, the two main characters, are simple-minded giants living in a world populated by idiots, greedy aristocrats and corrupt monks. They are renowned even today for being extremely rude and very funny.

Publications

1532–52 Gargantua and Pantagruel
1533 Pantagrueline Prognostication

RACINE, Jean

French playwright, poet and essayist

Born c. Dec. 1639
Died Apr. 21, 1699
Age at death 59

Jean Racine is one of the greatest figures in French literature. He wrote tragic plays strongly influenced by the drama of ancient Greece, and his poetry ranks among the best written in French.

Racine was born near Paris. An orphan by the age of three, he was raised by his grandmother and educated at the Catholic school at Port-Royal, which remained an important influence on him throughout his life.

When he was 19, Racine moved to Paris, where he became friends with a group of writers, including the playwright MOLIÉRE and JEAN DE LA FONTAINE. Two years later, he wrote his first play, *Amasie*, which has since been lost. Racine then found himself in conflict with his family and supporters at Port-Royal. At the time, theater was considered immoral, and Racine was pressured to leave Paris and become a priest. Unable to secure a living with the Church, however, he returned to Paris and the theater in 1663.

When he was 25, Racine met the actress Mademoiselle du Parc. Inspired by her, he wrote his most successful play, *Andromaque*, in which she played the lead. In the ten years after this play was finished, he wrote all of his greatest plays.

When he was 38, and at the peak of his fame after the success of his play *Phèdre*, Racine was invited to become royal historian. Never happy at the distress that his theatrical career caused his family, he gave up writing plays to concentrate on his new post. In the same year, he married Cathérine de Romanet. They had two sons and five daughters. He wrote only two more plays, both at the request of the king's wife.

Publications

1667	*Andromaque*
1668	*The Litigants*
1669	*Britannicus*
1670	*Bérénice*
1672	*Bajazet*
1673	*Mithridate*
1674	*Iphigénie*
1677	*Phèdre*
1689	*Esther*
1691	*Athalie*

RADCLIFFE, Ann

English novelist

Born Jul. 9, 1764
Died Feb. 7, 1823
Age at death 58

Ann Radcliffe was a famous writer of sinister gothic novels set in creepy castles and ancient monasteries. She was one of the first to write this kind of fiction.

Radcliffe was born in London. At 23, she married a law student who later owned and edited a newspaper. As a young woman she had read HORACE WALPOLE'S *The Castle of Otranto*, the first gothic novel published. She also read books about old buildings and became fascinated by Italian paintings of wild, forested mountain scenery. Soon she began writing her own gothic novels.

The Castles of Athlin and Dunbayne, Radcliffe's first novel, was published when she was 25. She set the story in the wild Scottish countryside, later books were also set in remote parts of Europe. At 30, she became England's most popular novelist with *The Mysteries of Udolpho*. In this story wicked relatives imprison orphaned Emily St. Aubert in the gloomy Italian mountain castle of Udolpho. She is terrified by what seem to be supernatural events, but she manages to escape and discover that they actually have harmless explanations.

Although Radcliffe described scenes in France, Spain and Italy, she left Britain only once – for a visit to Holland and Germany when she was 30. Her vivid descriptions of castles and wild landscapes set the scene for other writers of the Romantic movement such as SIR WALTER SCOTT. Her use of suspense and terror influenced such writers of horror stories as MARY SHELLEY and EDGAR ALLAN POE.

Publications

1789	*The Castles of Athlin and Dunbayne*
1790	*A Sicilian Romance*
1791	*The Romance of the Forest*
1794	*The Mysteries of Udolpho*
1795	*A Journey Made in the Summer of 1794*
1797	*The Italian*

Published after she died

1826	*Gaston de Blondeville*

RAND, Ayn

Russian-born American novelist and essayist

Born Feb. 2, 1905
Died Mar. 5, 1982
Age at death 77

Publications

1936	*We the Living*
1938	*Anthem*
1943	*The Fountainhead*
1957	*Atlas Shrugged*
1961	*For the New Intellectual*
1965	*The Virtue of Selfishness*
1969	*The Romantic Manifesto*
1971	*The New Left: The Anti-Industrial Revolution*
1982	*Philosophy: Who Needs It*

Ayn Rand's novels, especially *The Fountainhead*, were influential during the 1950s and '60s, when their theme of individual self-reliance was popular among young readers. Although briefly popular again during the politically conservative years of President Reagan, today her work is not highly regarded.

Rand was born in St. Petersburg, Russia. When she was 12, the Russian Revolution overturned the rule of the czar (emperor) and established a communist government. Although Rand attended university in Russia, studying history at the University of St. Petersburg, she left her native country at the age of 18, unable to accept communist rule. In 1931, she became a US citizen, and for several years she worked as a Hollywood screenwriter.

Once in the United States, Rand became a strong supporter of capitalism and a critic of communism. She believed in individualism: that people should do what is in their own interests and live for themselves rather than others.

Rand wrote four novels based on these beliefs. Her first, *We the Living*, was published when she was 31. Like her other books, this features a hero whose individual desires triumph over the desires of a community. *The Fountainhead*, her third novel, defended the individualism of an architect and was made into a film starring Gary Cooper. Rand's novels were popular with university students, many of whom saw her as encouraging them to behave selfishly.

RANSOME, Arthur

English children's writer and journalist

Born Jan.18, 1884
Died Jun. 3, 1967
Age at death 83

Arthur Ransome is best known as the author of *Swallows and Amazons*, the first in a series of 12 books for children about the imaginative Walker and Blackett children on vacation. This classic, written in fine prose style, tells of the children's camping and sailing adventures and reflects Ransome's love of sailing, fishing and the countryside.

Ransome was born in Leeds in the north of England. His father, a history professor and a keen fisherman, died when his son was still a young boy. They had spent several memorable vacations together in the beautiful countryside of the English Lake District. Ransome studied at Rugby, but was a poor student. After university he decided he wanted to write and moved to London to pursue this career.

He worked as an office boy in a publishing company for several years, graduating to reviewing books and writing short stories.

Ransome became a journalist, covering World War I and the 1917 Russian Revolution. He learned to speak Russian, published a collection of Russian folktales, and married the secretary of Leon Trotsky, the famous Russian revolutionary.

It was not until he was middle aged that Ransome turned to writing children's books. By the time *Swallows and Amazons* came out, he was 46 and already a published author. He wrote the book for the grandchildren of a childhood friend he had met while vacationing in the Lake District. *Swallowdale*, its sequel, and the novels that followed have been enjoyed by generations of children and also by adults.

Publications

1916	*Old Peter's Russian Tales*
1930	*Swallows and Amazons*
1931	*Swallowdale*
1932	*Peter Duck*
1933	*Winter Holiday*
1937	*We Didn't Mean to Go to Sea*
1940	*The Big Six*
1941	*Missee Lee*
1943	*The Picts and the Martyrs*
1947	*Great Northern?*

RATTIGAN, Terence

English playwright and screenwriter

Born Jun. 10, 1911
Died Nov. 30, 1977
Age at death 66

Terence Rattigan was a popular English playwright. He was born in London, the son of a diplomat. During Rattigan's early years his parents spent much of their time abroad, and he was raised by his grandmother, Lady Rattigan, whom he hated. Educated at Harrow and Oxford University, he decided early in life to become a writer.

When Rattigan was 22, he wrote his first play, *First Episode*, with a university friend. The play was a surprise success, and when Rattigan left Oxford, he was in no doubt over his choice of career. However, he soon discovered that his contract for *First Episode* gave him virtually no money, and he was forced to move in with his parents. His father gave him an allowance and two years in which to prove himself as a writer.

Rattigan's first major success came when he was 25 with the play *French without Tears*, which was influenced by the work of the Russian playwright Anton Chekhov. Like many of his plays, it was based on an event from his own life; in this case a visit to France he made as a student.

As his career progressed, Rattigan ensured that his plays remained popular by adapting his style to suit the tastes of his audience. He claimed to write for a fictional Aunt Edna – "a nice, respectable, middle-class, middle-aged maiden lady." Unlike some authors', Rattigan's works deal with people rather than ideas.

In later life, he began to write for TV and movies, adapting many of his own works as screenplays. He was given the honorary title "Sir" in 1971.

Publications

1936	*French without Tears*
1942	*Flare Path*
1944	*Love in Idleness*
1946	*The Winslow Boy*
1948	*The Browning Version*
1952	*The Deep Blue Sea*
1954	*Separate Tables*
1958	*Variations on a Theme*
1970	*A Bequest to the Nation*
1977	*Cause Célèbre*

RATUSHINSKAYA, Irina

Russian poet

Born Mar. 4, 1954

Irina Ratushinskaya is best known for her poems attacking the old communist government of Russia, which led to her persecution and exile.

Ratushinskaya was born in the city of Odessa (now in the Ukranian Republic), into a Polish family. She studied physics and mathematics, then worked as a teacher, while writing poems critical of the Russian communist system.

In 1979, Ratushinskaya married Igor Gerashzenko, a physicist and human rights activist. In 1982, they were both arrested for demonstrating on behalf of the physicist and political activist Andrei Sakharov. Ratushinskaya was accused of anti-Soviet activity and in 1983 was sentenced to seven years' hard labor and four years' internal exile. Conditions in prison were dreadful, but Ratushinskaya continued writing. Sitting in freezing cells, she scratched some 250 poems onto bars of soap with a matchstick, memorized them, and then washed them away. The poems describe her experience of surviving in the prison camp.

Western writers campaigned for Ratushinskaya's release. Her work was banned in Russia, but her poems were smuggled out and published as *Beyond the Limit* and *No, I'm Not Afraid*. In 1986, she and her husband were released temporarily for medical treatment in England. Ratushinskaya remained in the West. She eventually settled in the United States.

Ratushinskaya has traveled widely, speaking for political prisoners. She has also published two autobiographical volumes: *Grey Is the Color of Hope*, named after the gray uniform worn by prisoners, and *In the Beginning*.

Publications

c. 1984 Poems
1985 Beyond the Limit
1986 No, I'm Not Afraid
1988 Pencil Letter
1988 Grey Is the Color of Hope
1991 In the Beginning
1992 Dance with a Shadow
1996 The Odessans

RAWLINGS, Marjorie Kinnan

American novelist and short-story writer

Born Aug. 8, 1896
Died Dec. 14, 1953
Age at death 57

Marjorie Kinnan Rawlings is best remembered today as the author of the Pulitzer Prize-winning novel *The Yearling*. She also wrote many successful short stories and novels that detail the life of "Crackers" – poor white people living in the Florida backwoods.

Rawlings was born Marjorie Kinnan in Washington, DC, where she lived until the death of her father when she was 17. The family then moved to Madison, Wisconsin, where Rawlings studied at the University of Wisconsin. In 1919, one year after graduating, she married the writer Charles A. Rawlings.

Rawlings began writing as a child. At age six, she was writing for the children's pages of newspapers, and she had won prizes by the time she was 15. As an adult, though, she found it difficult to get her stories published, and for much of the 1920s she worked as a journalist. 1928 was a turning point, however. She moved to Cross Creek, Florida, and bought a farm. There she began to write about the "invisible" side of Florida – the undeveloped areas little visited by tourists where poor white families known as "Crackers" lived. Three years later, at age 35, she published her first story, *Cracker Chidlings*. She continued to explore the lives of Crackers, even living with families for months at a time to do research. *The Yearling* was published when she was 42. Written for young adults, it is the story of a boy's coming-of-age in the Florida backwoods. It won the Pulitzer Prize in 1939. In the 1940s, Rawlings left Florida and wrote her final novel, *The Sojourner*, in New York.

Publications

1931 Cracker Chidlings
1931 Jacob's Ladder
1933 South Moon Under
1935 Golden Apples
1938 The Yearling
1940 When the Whippoorwill
1942 Cross Creek
1953 The Sojourner

Published after she died

1955 The Secret River

REED, Ishmael

American novelist, poet and essayist

Born Feb. 22, 1938

Ishmael Reed is best known for writing novels that explore the mystical and legendary past of African Americans and which attempt to restore to them the folklore of their African roots.

Reed was born in Chattanooga, Tennessee, but at the age of four moved with his mother to Buffalo, New York, where he lived until moving to New York City. He began writing while attending the State University of New York.

Reed's first novel, *The Free-Lance Pallbearers*, published when he was 29, is a humorous look at the identity crisis and search for selfhood that was typical of the "black" novel of the 1960s. *Mumbo Jumbo* is about a voodoo detective and the spread of Jes Grew, an involuntary dance that makes its victims unable to function in American society.

Reed does not use the writing technique employed by other major black writers such as James Baldwin; instead of writing in the first person – like the autobiographical "slave narratives" of the 19th century – he tries to avoid negative attitudes by concentrating on the positive aspects of African Americans' past. He uses satire to mock, among other things, the main Western religions, Western science and technology, and the black revolutionary organizations that sprang up in the 1960s. In his fiction, Reed sets out to encourage his readers to appreciate the myths and cults surrounding some of the ancient Egyptians gods and the voodoo religion. In the process he rewrites history so that it celebrates what he calls "hoodooism" – all that is culturally spontaneous and joyful.

Publications

1967 The Free-Lance Pallbearers
1969 Yellow Back Radio Broke-Down
1970 Catechism of D NeoAmerican Hoodoo Church
1972 Conjure
1972 Mumbo Jumbo
1973 Chattanooga
1974 The Last Days of Louisiana Red
1976 Flight to Canada
1982 The Terrible Twos

REID BANKS, Lynne

English children's writer, playwright and novelist

Born Jul. 31, 1929

Although she writes successful adult novels, Lynne Reid Banks is best known as a children's author.

Reid Banks was born in London, England. Her father was a doctor and her mother an actress. When she was ten, she and her mother went to live in Canada for five years to escape World War II. Reid Banks knew at an early age that she wanted to act. After the war, she went to famous acting schools in London before working in local theaters until 1954.

Finding it difficult to make a living as an actress, she became one of the first female television reporters in England. She got fed up with her job, however, and turned to writing plays and novels for adults. Some of her plays were staged, but she first became famous for her novel *The L-Shaped Room*, which came out when she was 31. About a young pregnant woman who defies society by deciding to raise her baby unwed and alone, it captured the mood of the rebellious 1960s. The success of this book allowed Reid Banks to quit her job and travel to Israel. There she married and spent the next ten years living on a kibbutz (a farm where everyone works together) and raising three children. She returned to England with her family in 1972 and began her career as a children's writer.

Reid Banks's most famous children's book is *The Indian in the Cupboard*, which is about a young boy who discovers that toys come to life when they are left in a magic cupboard. It sold over five million copies, but some people have criticized it for reinforcing stereotypes about Native Americans. The popular 1995 movie version created a more realistic "Indian."

Publications

1960 The L-Shaped Room
1968 Children at the Gate
1973 One More River
1976 The Farthest-Away Mountain
1978 I, Houdini
1980 The Indian in the Cupboard
1986 The Return of the Indian
1988 The Secret of the Indian
1993 The Magic Hare
1994 The Broken Bridge

REMARQUE, Erich Maria

German novelist

Born Jun. 22, 1898
Died Sep. 25, 1970
Age at death 72

Erich Maria Remarque is best known for his antiwar novel set during World War I, *All Quiet on the Western Front*.

Remarque had French ancestors but was born in the northwest German city of Osnabruck. He studied at the University of Münster but at 18 had to enlist in the German Army. During World War I, he fought on the Western Front and was wounded on several occasions. After the war he worked at various times as a teacher, racing driver and sportswriter. He also began to write his first novel.

All Quiet on the Western Front was published when Remarque was 31. Based on his own wartime experiences, it tells in a matter-of-fact way the horrors of a soldier's daily life in the trenches, where shells and machine guns killed millions. No other book had given such a realistic yet pitying account of the terrible conflict.

At 33, Remarque brought out a sequel. *The Road Back* deals with the collapse of the German Army after World War I. Germany's new Nazi government declared such novels unpatriotic and accused Remarque of pacifism. He was declared no longer a German citizen, and stores were ordered to stop selling his books. Remarque felt forced to leave Germany. He moved to Switzerland, then to the United States. He became a US citizen at 41 and married the movie star Paulette Goddard.

Altogether Remarque wrote ten antiwar novels, but his first one remained the most popular.

Publications

1929	*All Quiet on the Western Front*
1931	*The Road Back*
1937	*Three Comrades*
1941	*Flotsam*
1945	*Arch of Triumph*
1952	*Spark of Life*
1956	*The Black Obelisk*
1963	*The Night in Lisbon*

Published after he died

1972	*Shadows in Paradise*

RENAULT, Mary

English-South African novelist

Born Sep. 4, 1905
Died Dec. 13, 1983
Age at death 78

Mary Renault is the pen name of Mary Challons. She is famous for her carefully researched and atmospheric historical novels.

Born in London, the daughter of a doctor, Renault escaped from her parents' arguments into an imaginary world of cowboys and knights about whom she wrote verses. At boarding school she found an excellent library and had read all the works of the ancient Greek philosopher Plato by the time she went to Oxford University to study English. She continued to write poetry after she graduated.

At age 28, Renault went back to Oxford to train as a nurse and met another nurse, Julie Mullard, who was to become her lifelong companion. Her first novel, based on her hospital experiences and called *The Purposes of Love*, was published when she was 34. During World War II, she and Mullard worked as nurses in Bristol and Oxford, but Renault continued to write. In 1947, *Return to Night* won the MGM Award, a $150,000 prize, and she decided to leave the harsh life of postwar Britain and emigrate to South Africa.

Fascinated since youth by Greek myths and history, Renault immersed herself through research in the ideas and attitudes of the past. She traveled to Greece and gained inspiration for her most successful book, *The King Must Die*, which is about Theseus and the minotaur. She later wrote about another Greek hero, Alexander the Great. One of the first novelists to write about homosexual love directly and positively, Renault was also an expert in many areas of classical scholarship.

Publications

1947	*Return to Night*
1953	*The Charioteer*
1956	*The Last of the Wine*
1958	*The King Must Die*
1962	*The Bull from the Sea*
1966	*The Mask of Apollo*
1970	*Fire from Heaven*
1972	*The Persian Boy*
1978	*The Praise Singer*
1981	*Funeral Games*

RENDELL, Ruth

English crime writer

Born Feb. 17, 1930

Publications

1964	*From Doon with Death*
1965	*To Fear a Painted Devil*
1970	*A Guilty Thing Surprised*
1977	*A Judgment in Stone*
1980	*The Lake of Darkness*
1983	*The Speaker of Mandarin*
1984	*The Killing Doll*
1985	*A Dark-Adapted Eye* (as Barbara Vine)
1995	*Simisola*
1996	*Keys to the Street*
1997	*Road Rage*
1998	*Sight for Sore Eyes*

Ruth Rendell is one of Britain's most popular and imaginative crime novelists.

Born in London, Rendell grew up near the city. After leaving school, she began a career in journalism, working as a reporter and a subeditor. Her background as a journalist has helped her write a wide variety of crime novels.

Rendell's first novel, *From Doon with Death*, was published when she was 34. It is set in the imaginary small town of Kingsmarkham and features an intelligent policeman, Chief Inspector Wexford, together with his reliable but unimaginative assistant, Mike Burden. The close and, at times, difficult relationship between these two characters is a major attraction of the story. The novel was the first in a popular series that continues to this day.

The Wexford books are written in the British tradition of "whodunits" – novels in which the reader has to figure out which character in the story is reponsible for the crime. But Rendell also writes more realistic novels that could be described as "whydunits" – stories that look at the reasons why people commit crimes. These stories are often set in the seedy atmosphere of London's suburbs and describe what happens when ordinary people come into contact with dangerously disturbed individuals.

Rendell also writes under the pen name Barbara Vine. Her novels under this name are character studies rather than stories full of action and suspense. In recent books Rendell has become concerned with political and environmental issues and, in 1997, she was given the honorary title of "Lady."

REYMONT, Wladyslaw S.

Polish novelist

Born May 6, 1868
Died Dec. 5, 1925
Age at death 57

Wladyslaw S. Reymont is best known for his epic four-part novel *The Peasants*, which has been widely translated and led to his being awarded the Nobel Prize for Literature in 1924.

Reymont was born in a small village in Poland, the son of a village organist. He failed at school and left early to take up one job after another, including wandering actor, tailor, railway official and monk. Having benefited financially from a railway accident, he then settled in Warsaw determined to be a writer.

The Comedienne, his novel set in the theatrical world, was published when he was 28. This was successful, and he followed it up three years later with *The Promised Land*, a story of the cruel effect of industrialization on textile mill owners in the Polish town of Lodz.

Then came his massive four-part work *The Peasants*. It is a complete and moving study of peasant life, with each part corresponding to a season of the year. Reymont was writing about a subject he understood well, and he was at the height of his creative power. The result was his finest work, and it brought him international recognition.

Reymont's interests then widened, but his imagination was nearly exhausted. His later books deal with religious, philosophical and historical subjects. His last important work, *The Year 1794*, is a long historical trilogy based on Polish social and political life at the close of the 18th century.

Publications

1893 The Death
1895 Justice
1895 A Pilgrimage to Jasna Gora
1896 The Comedienne
1897 Ferments
1899 The Promised Land
1902–09 The Peasants (4 vols.)
1913–18 The Year 1794 (3 vols.)
1914 The Vampire
1915 The Mother

RHYS, Jean

Dominican-born British novelist and short-story writer

Born Aug. 24, 1894
Died May 14, 1979
Age at death 84

Jean Rhys has come to be recognized as one of the finest British writers of recent times. She was born on the island of Dominica. Her father was a Welsh doctor, and her mother was a native Creole islander. As a child, she loved literature and longed to visit England and the other places she read about.

At the age of 16, her father sent her to London so that she could study acting at the Royal Academy of Dramatic Arts. His death the same year meant that she had to leave before completing the course and get a job with a touring theater company to support herself. In 1919, she moved to Paris and married the first of her three husbands.

Between 1927 and 1939, Rhys produced a series of successful short stories and novels about life in Paris and London. Her first book, a collection of short stories called *The Left Bank*, was published when she was 33. Almost all of her stories from this period are about women who have been mistreated or had unlucky lives.

For almost 30 years after the publication of her novel *Good Morning, Midnight* in 1939, Rhys wrote nothing more. She lived quietly in Cornwall, and her books were almost completely forgotten. Then, at the age of 72, Rhys finished her most admired novel, *Wide Sargasso Sea*. This highly original book set in Dominica tells the early life story of Mrs. Rochester – the mysterious mad wife of Mr. Rochester, hero of CHARLOTTE BRONTË's classic novel *Jane Eyre*. It was an immediate success and brought about a revival of interest in Rhys's earlier books.

Publications

1927 The Left Bank
1928 Quartet
1930 After Leaving Mr. Mackenzie
1934 Voyage in the Dark
1939 Good Morning, Midnight
1966 Wide Sargasso Sea
1968 Tigers Are Better-Looking
1976 Sleep it Off, Lady

Published after she died

1979 Smile, Please

RIBAS, Oscar

Angolan novelist and short-story writer

Born Aug. 17, 1909

Oscar Ribas is one of Angola's most important writers and one of the most distinguished writers from the former colonies of Portuguese Africa.

Ribas was born in Luanda, the capital of Angola (west-central Africa), which was then a Portuguese colony. His father was Portuguese and his mother Angolan. Ribas went to school in Luanda before working as a civil servant.

Although he published most of his work at his own expense, Ribas has achieved an international reputation. Written in Portuguese, his early books were romances in the style of Portuguese novelists of the 1800s. *Passing Clouds*, his first novel, was published when he was only 18. When he was 21, his eyesight began to fail, and he soon went completely blind. This brought his writing career to an end for nearly two decades. During this time, he devoted himself to researching and recording Angolan folklore. Members of his family took down his notes. Before he learned to type, he even continued to write for a while. He would fold the paper into pleats so that his writing would not go all over the page. He has since become the world expert on the religion and culture of the Kimbundu people of Angola.

In his late 30s, Ribas began to write again, this time on African themes. *Enchantment*, published when he was 42, follows the marriage of an African couple. *Echoes of My Land* is a collection of short stories. Both of these books draw on Angolan stories. His autobiography, *All of This Happened*, describes his wish to live in an Angola in which black and white people live peacefully together.

Publications

1927 Passing Clouds
1929 Attonement
1948 Flowers and Thorns
1951 Enchantment
1952 Echoes of My Land
1955 Angolan Divinations and Rites
1961 Tales
1967 Story-time
1973 Pastime
1975 All of This Happened

RICE, Anne

American horror writer

Born Oct. 4, 1941

Anne Rice has become one of America's most popular writers since the publication of her Vampire Chronicles, beginning with *Interview with the Vampire.*

Rice was born Howard O'Brien in the Irish Catholic quarter of New Orleans. She was named after her father but hated her name. By the time she entered first grade, she was calling herself Anne. One of four sisters, she attended a Catholic school. Her father worked for the post office; her mother, who died when Rice was 14, was addicted to alcohol. By the time Rice was 18, she had rejected Catholicism, unable to accept the Church's teachings on sex and death. At age 20, she married Stan Rice. The couple moved to California, both attending San Francisco State University. Rice stud-

Publications

1976 Interview with the Vampire

ied creative writing there and at the University of California.

In 1972, Rice's daughter Michele died of leukemia just before her sixth birthday. Feeling she had nothing to lose, Rice took to writing full time. The result was *Interview with the Vampire*, which was published when she was 35. Reflecting her lifelong interest in the supernatural, it is a dark, painfully personal tale. Louis, a sensitive and philosophical vampire, tells his life story to a reporter. It involves a six-year-old girl whom he saves from mortal death by turning her into a vampire. The book was made into a film starring Tom Cruise and Brad Pitt.

Rice has since written further Vampire Chronicles, which together have updated and popularized the ancient vampire myth. She has also written a series of novels about the Mayfairs – a family of New Orleans witches.

1985 The Vampire Lestat
1988 The Queen of the Damned
1989 The Mummy
1990 The Witching Hour
1992 The Tale of the Body Thief
1993 Lasher
1994 Taltos
1995 Memnoch the Devil
1996 Servant of the Bones
1998 Pandora
1998 Vampire Armand
1999 Vittorio the Vampire

RICE, Elmer

American playwright and novelist

Born Sep. 28, 1892
Died May 8, 1967
Age at death 74

Elmer Rice was a prolific American playwright known for supporting personal freedom and championing the poor.

Born Elmer Leopold Riezenstein, Rice grew up in New York City and graduated from New York Law School at age 20. He abandoned the law two years later for a career as a playwright when his first play, a murder mystery entitled *On Trial*, became a hit. It was the first American play to use "flashbacks," in this case to present scenes that are being described by trial witnesses.

During his career Rice frequently experimented with different kinds of plays to tell stories about the way people live in society, especially those who are poor. In his second success, *The Adding Machine*, he used distorted settings and nonrealistic acting to produce a satire on how modern machines seem to make people less human and more like robots. He used honest realism to explore crowded slum life in a New York City apartment block in *Street Scene*. This won the 1929 Pulitzer Prize for drama and was made into an opera by the composer Kurt Weill in 1947.

Many of Rice's plays deal with contemporary events. The Great Depression, the rise of the Nazis, and Russia under Joesph Stalin's rule are central to *We, the People*, *Judgment Day*, *Two on an Island*, and *Flight to the West*. During the Great Depression, Rice was regional director of the Federal TheaterProject.

Rice also wrote several novels, including *The Show Must Go On*, as well as his autobiography, *Minority Report*.

Publications

1914 On Trial
1923 The Adding Machine
1929 Street Scene
1933 We, the People
1934 Judgment Day
1940 Flight to the West
1940 Two on an Island
1945 Dream Girl
1949 The Show Must Go On
1954 Minority Report

RICH, Adrienne

American poet

Born May 6, 1929

Adrienne Rich is one of America's most highly regarded feminist poets.

Born in Baltimore, Maryland, Rich grew up in a house full of books. Until the fourth, grade she was taught at home by her parents, particularly by her mother, who was a composer and pianist. Rich went on to graduate from Radcliffe College at age 22; in the same year, she published her first collection of poems, *A Change of World*.

Rich lived in Boston with her husband and had three sons. In 1966, she and her husband separated, and she left Boston to take up teaching jobs in New York state. She also taught in California for some time before settling in western Massachusetts.

During the late 1960s, Rich became involved with the civil rights movement and began to turn to more political themes in her poetry, particularly to feminism and to her experience as a woman. Her *Snapshots of a Daughter-in-Law* focuses on women's lives and how difficult it can be for women to maintain their identity. In 1974, she was awarded the National Book Award for *Diving into the Wreck*, which contains some of her best-known poems. She accepted the award with fellow feminist writers AUDRE LORDE and ALICE WALKER.

As well as poetry, Rich has written a number of influential works of feminist theory, including her book *Of Woman Born*, which challenges the idea that motherhood is "natural." In 1986, Rich won the Ruth Lilly Poetry Prize – then the richest poetry prize in the United States. In 1991, she won the Commonwealth Poetry Prize.

Publications

1951 A Change of World
1963 Snapshots of a Daughter-in-Law
1969 Leaflets
1973 Diving into the Wreck
1976 Of Woman Born
1978 The Dream of a Common Language
1981 A Wild Patience Has Taken Me This Far
1991 An Atlas of the Difficult World

RICHARDSON, Samuel

English novelist

Born c. Aug. 1689
Died Jul. 4, 1761
Age at death 71

Samuel Richardson was one of the pioneers of novel writing. His books were written in the form of a series of letters. The first of them, *Pamela: or, Virtue Rewarded*, is often described as the first true English novel.

Richardson was the son of a woodworker. The exact date of his birth is not known, but he was baptized on August 19, 1689. He began his career as apprentice to a printer and set up in business on his own when he was 32. Like many printers at that time, he was also a bookseller and publisher. He worked hard and became prosperous.

In the 1730s, Richardson began writing pamphlets and, when he was 52, published his first book, *Letters to and for Particular*

Friends (often called *Familiar Letters*). It was intended to help uneducated people write their own letters, and it gave advice on social behavior. He then expanded the idea into his first novel, *Pamela: or, Virtue Rewarded*, which was also published when he was 52. It is the story of a servant girl who falls in love with a man who tries to seduce her. She preserves her virtue and eventually marries him. The book was immensely popular, and to prevent other writers continuing the story, he immediately wrote *Pamela in Her Exalted Condition*. Not everyone liked the character of Pamela, and Richardson's friend HENRY FIELDING wrote a comic version of the novel, called *Shamela*, that made fun of her virtuousness. Richardson never forgave him.

Richardson's third novel, *Clarissa: or, The History of a Young Lady*, was also written as a series of letters. It influenced the French author PIERRE LACLOS in the writing of his novel *Dangerous Liaisons*.

Publications

1741 Letters to and for Particular Friends
1741 Pamela: or, Virtue Rewarded
1742 Pamela in her Exalted Condition
1747–48 Clarissa: or, the History of a Young Lady
1753–54 The History of Sir Charles Grandison

RICHLER, Mordecai

Canadian novelist and screenwriter

Born Jan. 27, 1931

Mordecai Richler's novels draw deeply on his Jewish childhood in Montreal, Canada. He has received many awards for his novels and an Academy Award nomination for his screenplays.

Richler was born in Montreal and had a strict Jewish upbringing. He attended Sir George Williams University for two years only. Feeling creatively stifled, he left for Europe in 1954, having completed his first novel. He lived in Paris and then in England before returning to Montreal in 1972. He has been criticized for rejecting Canadian and Jewish society. However, Richler insists that he feels forever rooted in Montreal, and his targets in his writing are not Canada and Jews but hypocrisy and greed in general.

Richler's first novel, *The Acrobats*, was published when he was 23, but it was his second novel, *The Apprenticeship of Duddy Kravitz*, published five years later, that signaled his arrival as a mature writer. Duddy Kravitz is a complicated character who scrapes and schemes to become a wealthy landowner, only to lose his soul in the process.

After this success, Richler became involved in writing for television and film, returning to novel writing with *The Incomparable Atuk*. This is about an Eskimo poet who takes advantage of the fact that he is seen as an innocent representative of a primitive culture and makes lots of money. Richler's latest novel, *Barney's Version*, is set in Montreal and Europe and is written as a memoir. It is a humorous tale about the outrageous exploits of a colorful character called Barney Panofsky.

Publications

1954 The Acrobats
1959 The Apprenticeship of Duddy Kravitz
1963 The Incomparable Atuk
1968 Cocksure
1971 St. Urbain's Horseman
1972 Shovelling Trouble
1980 Joshua Then and Now
1989 Solomon Gursky Was Here
1997 Barney's Version

RICHTER, Conrad

American novelist and short-story writer

Born Oct. 13, 1890
Died Oct. 30, 1968
Age at death 78

Conrad Richter is best known for his trilogy of novels *The Awakening Land*, describing life on the American frontier. The final book of the series, *The Town*, won the 1951 Pulitzer Prize.

Richter was born in Pine Grove, Pennsylvania, where his family had settled after emigrating from Germany. His father, grandfather and uncles were all churchmen, but Richter, an eager reader, craved a different kind of life. At age 16, he left school, and for the next few years he worked as a bank teller, farm worker, lumberjack and salesman. He became a journalist and also began to write fiction.

Disappointed to receive only $25 for a highly praised story, he nevertheless continued to write in his spare time, and when he was 34, he published his first collection of short stories, *Brothers of No Kin*.

Several years later he and his wife moved to New Mexico. The landscape, people, and history of the region inspired him to write full time. His first novel, *The Sea of Grass* – about a feud between farmers and cattle ranchers in 19th-century New Mexico – is considered one of his best works.

At age 50, Richter published *The Trees*, the first in his famous trilogy. It begins in the 18th century and follows the life of Sayward Luckett, a pioneer woman, and her family. Richter frequently had a strong woman as the central character in his fiction.

Richter's writing career spanned half a century – he published *The Waters of Kronos*, which won a National Book Award, when he was 70. Six of his novels were made into movies.

Publications

1924 Brothers of No Kin
1936 Early Americana
1937 The Sea of Grass
1940–50 The Awakening Land (including *The Trees, The Fields* and *The Town*)
1942 Tacey Cromwell
1957 The Lady
1960 The Waters of Kronos
1962 A Simply Honorable Man

RILKE, Rainer Maria

German poet and writer

Born Dec. 4, 1875
Died Dec. 29, 1926
Age at death 51

Rainer Maria Rilke, one of the most important figures in modern German literature, was an outstanding lyric poet whose verse reveals his deepest thoughts and feelings. He was part of a group of writers known as symbolists, who used striking images to stand for the way a person felt or thought.

Rilke was born in Prague, then part of the Austrian Empire and now the capital of the Czech Republic. He was sent to a military academy, but this proved to be not to his taste, and he left to study art history in Germany. He was a shy, complicated man and did not make friends easily. His response to social difficulties was to move away.

Rilke became a constant wanderer through Europe. He made two journeys to Russia, where he met LEO TOLSTOY and was deeply impressed by what he learned of Russian religion. In Paris, he became secretary to the sculptor Auguste Rodin and, in 1901, he married one of Rodin's pupils.

Rilke's first book of poems, *Life and Songs*, was published when he was 19. His earliest poems were about nature, folklore, and traditional religion. Later, these simple themes were left behind as his poems became increasingly mystical. Between the ages of 30 and 40, he produced some of his finest poetry and the important prose work *The Tale of the Love and Death of Cornet Christopher Rilke*. During this period he wrote the book *Journal of My Other Self*, which is the story of an imaginary poet. Rilke's two masterpieces, *Sonnets to Orpheus* and *Duino Elegies*, were written shortly before his premature death from blood poisoning.

Publications

1894 Life and Songs
1900 Stories of God
1905 The Tale of the Love and Death of Cornet Christopher Rilke
1910 Journal of My Other Self
1923 Sonnets to Orpheus
1923 Duino Elegies

Published after he died

1978 Where Silence Reigns

RIMBAUD, Arthur

French poet

Born Oct. 20, 1854
Died Nov. 10, 1891
Age at death 37

Arthur Rimbaud is best known for the power and faultless technique of his poetry and for his eventful but short life.

Rimbaud was born in Charleville, northeast France, and he was raised by his strict mother, who had been abandoned by her husband. He was a brilliant student, but at the age of 16 he ran away to Paris, where he met the older poet PAUL VERLAINE. Just before his 17th birthday, Rimbaud published *The Drunken Boat*. In this poem he sends a toy boat on a remarkable journey that is an allegory for a spiritual quest.

Verlaine and Rimbaud soon began a love affair. In 1873, Rimbaud tried to break off the relationship, and Verlaine shot and wounded him. Verlaine was tried for attempted murder and imprisoned. The same year Rimbaud's book *A Season in Hell* was published and condemned by the critics. Deeply hurt, Rimbaud burned all his manuscripts, gave up writing, and, aged 19, wandered around Europe for several years before traveling to Africa, where he lived as a gun runner and possibly a slave dealer.

In 1886, Verlaine, believing his former lover to be dead, published Rimbaud's book of poems *The Illuminations*. This remarkable work contains the best of Rimbaud and reveals his longing for spiritual values in a world concerned with possessions. It created a sensation and established Rimbaud's reputation as a major poet. But by then he was indifferent to fame and to art and ignored the public's enthusiasm. He died aged 37 after having had his leg amputated.

Publications

1871 The Drunken Boat
1873 A Season in Hell
1886 The Illuminations

RINEHART, Mary Roberts

American crime writer

Born 1876
Died Sep. 22, 1958
Age at death c. 82

Mary Roberts Rinehart was a popular American crime writer in the first half of the 20th century. She also wrote plays and romantic novels.

Rinehart was born into a poor family in Pittsburgh, Pennsylvania. Her father, a failed inventor, committed suicide as Mary was finishing training to be a nurse. Aged 20, she married a doctor and had three sons within five years.

In the early years of her marriage some unsuccessful stock market investments left her husband in debt, and Rinehart began writing to help with the family finances. She sold more than 40 short stories to magazines in her first year, one of which, a crime story called *The Circular Staircase*, was published as a book when she was 32.

Rinehart's stories became very popular, and she went on to publish many novels. Her main characters are usually innocent young women who get caught up in murder and mystery. One of her most popular characters is Nurse Adams, a young nurse who gets involved in mysteries so often that the police nickname her Miss Pinkerton, after the famous private detective agency. Another of her characters, Letitia Carberry, gets involved in danger mostly because she is a bit dumb. As well as the main elements of crime and mystery, Rinehart's stories contain much romance and humor.

In 1920, Rinehart rewrote *The Circular Staircase* as a hugely successful play called *The Bat*. This became the basis for a number of film versions.

Publications

1908 The Circular Staircase
1909 The Man in Lower Ten
1914 The After House
1920 The Truce of God
1925 The Red Lamp
1932 Miss Pinkerton
1933 The Album
1938 The Wall
1940 The Great Mistake
1945 The Yellow Room

RINGGOLD, Faith

American children's writer

Born Oct. 8, 1930

Faith Ringgold is an award-winning artist and writer whose work deals with her experience as an African-American woman. Her writing and art are enjoyed by both children and adults.

Ringgold was born Faith Jones in New York City. She grew up in Harlem, which was then a cultural center for black people. With her mother she would regularly visit museums and go to jazz concerts. Ringgold suffered from asthma and often had to miss school. While recovering at home, she would paint, and by the time she graduated from secondary school in 1948, she knew that she wanted to study art.

At the City College of New York, she was taught to copy the paintings of European masters – her efforts to create art that reflected her heritage were discouraged. While still a university student, Ringgold married and had two children. Four years later she left her husband, who was a drug addict, and returned to college, finishing her degree in fine arts and then qualifying as a teacher. For nearly 20 years, she worked as an art teacher at state schools in New York, while pursuing her career as an artist.

In 1983, Ringgold made the first of her famous story quilts – works of art that use painted canvas, fabric, and stories written on fabric. In 1988, an editor saw one of her quilts on display in a museum. He asked Ringgold to turn it into a book. The result, *Tar Beach*, was published when she was 61. It is the story of an eight-year-old girl living in 1930s Harlem and was an instant success. Ringgold has since written several other successful books that introduce the lives of famous African Americans to her readers.

Publications

1991 Tar Beach
1992 Aunt Harriet's Underground Railroad in the Sky
1993 Dinner at Aunt Connie's House
1995 My Dream of Martin Luther King
1995 We Flew over the Bridge: The Memoirs of Faith Ringgold
1996 Bonjour, Lonnie

ROA BASTOS, Augusto

Paraguayan novelist, short-story writer and poet

Born Jun. 13, 1917

Augusto Roa Bastos is perhaps Paraguay's greatest literary figure, although he spent more than 40 years living in exile from his homeland.

Roa Bastos was born in a small, rural village in Paraguay. At the age of eight he was sent to a military academy in the capital city Asunción, where his uncle was an important member of the Catholic Church. It was in his uncle's huge library that Roa Bastos first discovered literature.

Before he was 20, Roa Bastos fought in a war with the neighboring country, Bolivia. He decided not to follow a military career, however, and later worked as a journalist in rural areas of the country. His first published work, *The Nightingale of Dawn* – a collection of poems – came out when he was 25. At age 27, he won an award to study journalism in England, where he witnessed and reported on the final months of World War II. From England, Roa Bastos traveled to France and Africa before returning to Paraguay in 1946 to find his country in the grip of a bloody civil war.

Like many other writers and intellectuals, Roa Bastos was forced to leave Paraguay because of the political violence. He spent the next 42 years living as an exile in Argentina and France while Paraguay was ruled by a series of oppressive dictators. His greatest novel, *I the Supreme*, is a study of the nature of dictatorship government. It shows how absolute power corrupts and makes a leader mad enough to believe he can do anything, even change history.

Roa Bastos returned to a freer Paraguay aged 72, where he was hailed as a great writer.

Publications

1942 The Nightingale of Dawn
1953 Thunder among the Leaves
1960 The Burning Orange Grove
1960 Son of Man
1966 The Empty Field
1967 The Feet on the Water
1967 Burnt Madeira
1969 Slaughter
1974 I the Supreme
1980 Personal Anthology

ROBERT, Shaaban

Tanzanian poet and novelist

Born Jan. 1, 1909
Died Jun. 20, 1962
Age at death 53

Shaaban Robert has come to be known as the SHAKESPEARE of East Africa because of the huge influence he has had on literature.

Robert was born in Tanzania (East Africa), which became the British colony of Tanganyika in 1918. He was brought up to be a Muslim – a follower of the Islamic religion. The British did not allow Muslims to be fully educated unless they became Christians, but Robert would not convert, so he left school early and worked as a government clerk.

Robert began writing verse at the age of 26. He wrote in the East African Swahili language, then an important trade language; but Swahili literature, which was written with the Arabic alphabet, was read by only a minority. Robert introduced new ideas, such as using the Roman alphabet, and helped update Swahili, making it the common language in East Africa. His work saved Swahili literature from being wiped out during the colonial era and made it accessible to more people. For this he is called the father of modern Swahili literature.

Robert's early work has been described as hard-to-understand fairy tales. His writing became more political, however, as he tired of being treated as a third-class citizen (whites and Asians were the "upper" classes). The poetic novels *Kufikirika* and *Kusadikika*, for example, are anticolonial novels about imaginary countries. Robert set up his own publishing company to produce his work, but the business failed because the British did not allow criticism of their rule in Africa. Robert died from tuberculosis one year after Tanganyika gained independence.

Publications

1947 Kufikirika
1951 Kusadikika
1952 Adili and His Brothers
1959–69 Diwani ya Shaaban
1960 African Diamonds

Published after he died

1967 Epic of the War for Freedom: 1939–45
1968 The Day of Reckoning
1968 Utubora the Farmer

ROBINSON, Edwin Arlington

American poet

Born Dec. 22, 1869
Died Apr. 6, 1935
Age at death 65

One of America's most important modern poets, Edwin Arlington Robinson is best remembered for his insightful studies of characters from "Tilbury Town," which appeared in many of his collections. Robinson won three Pulitzer Prizes – one in 1922 for his *Collected Poems*, one in 1925 for *The Man Who Died Twice*, and the third in 1928 for his long, popular poem *Tristram*.

Born in Head Tide, Maine, Robinson spent much of his childhood in Gardiner, Maine – the model for his imaginary Tilbury Town. Difficult circumstances meant that Robinson could only spend two years at Harvard. His father lost much of his fortune in 1893. One brother, a physician, became a drug addict, and the other, a businessman, became an alcoholic.

Publications

1896 The Torrent and the Night Before

Robinson returned to Gardiner and attempted to become a professional poet. However, he survived only by relying on friends and patrons. He published his first poetry collection, *The Torrent and the Night Before* at his own expense when he was 27. At age 30, he moved to New York City, where his work began to attract more attention; it was favorably reviewed by President Theodore Roosevelt in 1905. By the time he won his first Pulitzer Prize (at last gaining some financial security) Robinson was in his 50s.

Robinson was attracted to the tragic vision of the British novelist THOMAS HARDY, and his best poems are about impoverished or wasted lives. *The Children of the Night* is a collection of verse that describes the pain of leading an isolated existence.

1897	*The Children of the Night*
1902	*Captain Craig*
1910	*The Town Down the River*
1916	*The Man Against the Sky*
1917	*Merlin*
1920	*Lancelot*
1921	*Collected Poems*
1924	*The Man Who Died Twice*
1927	*Tristram*

RODGERS, Carolyn M.

American poet

Born Dec. 14, 1945

Carolyn M. Rodgers is an African-American poet who emerged during the 1960s in what was known as the Black Arts Movement.

Carolyn Marie Rodgers was born in Chicago; her parents had just arrived there after migrating north from Little Rock, Arkansas. At school she was involved in drama and sang in the choir; although she was already writing poetry (secretly, she says), she wanted to become a singer. While at Chicago's Roosevelt University she met the poet GWENDOLYN BROOKS at a reception, and after building her nerve, she sent Brooks some of her poems. The encouragement she received from the older poet inspired her to submit her poems to journals.

After graduating in 1965, Rodgers went to work with young people at the YMCA for several years. But she continued her writing, and at age 22 she published her first volume of poetry, *Paper Soul*. It was well received and led to many invitations to give readings around the country. Her early work, such as the poems in *Paper Soul*, *Songs of a Blackbird* and *Love Raps*, explores the revolutionary feelings among African-American youth during the 1960s civil rights movement. Often she used Black English and nonstandard spellings to convey the urgency of her themes.

In the 1970s, Rodgers turned toward more personal themes, including her complex feelings for her mother and the Christian faith in which she was raised. Her 1975 collection, *How I Got Ovah*, was nominated for a National Book Award.

Publications

1968	*Paper Soul*
1969	*Love Raps*
1969	*Songs of a Blackbird*
1975	*How I Got Ovah*
1978	*The Heart As Ever Green*
1980	*Translation*
1983	*Eden and Other Poems*

ROETHKE, Theodore

American poet

Born May 25, 1908
Died Aug. 1, 1963
Age at death 55

Theodore Roethke wrote visionary, deeply personal poetry in which the imagery is grounded in his experience of nature.

Roethke was born in Saginaw, Michigan, where his family had a successful gardening business. A shy, sickly child, Roethke spent much of his time in the greenhouses and gardens that later became central images in two volumes of his poetry: *The Lost Son* and *Praise to the End!* When Roethke was 14, his father died after a prolonged illness. Though he had clashed often with his perfectionist father, Roethke also loved him, and his sense of deep loss appears in later poems.

At secondary school, Roethke decided he wanted to be a writer. In 1925, he enrolled in the University of Michigan at Ann Arbor and secretly began to write poetry. After a brief stint at Harvard University he took his first position as teacher and tennis coach at Lafayette College, Pennsylvania.

Roethke's well-received first volume, *Open House*, was published when he was 33. His fourth, *The Waking*, won a Pulitzer Prize in 1954. In its poems, a female spirit leads the poet to human love through the love of nature. In 1947, Roethke moved to the University of Washington, Seattle. Although he was well liked as a teacher, his life was scarred by mental breakdowns and overwork.

His early formal poetic style gradually became freer and more experimental, reflecting his own self-discovery through exploration of the most basic elements of the natural world.

Publications

1941 Open House
1948 The Lost Son
1951 Praise to the End!
1953 The Waking
1957 Words for the Wind
1963 Party at the Zoo

Published after he died

1964 The Far Field
1975 Collected Poems

ROLLAND, Romain

French novelist, biographer and playwright

Born Jan. 29, 1866
Died Dec. 30, 1944
Age at death 78

Romain Rolland, winner of the 1915 Nobel Prize for Literature, was a celebrated biographer and novelist. His novels were among the first to follow the main character from the cradle to the grave.

Rolland was born in Clamecy, France, into a financially comfortable family. He studied in Paris and Rome, earning his Ph.D. in 1895. At the age of 29 he became Professor of Art History at the École Normale in Paris, and eight years later he took up the same appointment at the famous Sorbonne college.

While still a teacher Rolland began his literary career writing plays. A series of dramas about the French Revolution brought him a degree of success in his mid-30s. At age 38, he published the first part of his multivolume masterpiece *Jean-Christophe*. It is the detailed life story of a fictional musical genius whom Rolland portrays as a heroic figure trying to live a moral life. The novel was popular with both readers and critics. Around the same time Rolland began writing biographies, starting with one of Beethoven.

Thanks to his controversial antiwar writings, collected in *Above the Battle*, Rolland became a figurehead for pacifism during World War I. *Above the Battle* caused a storm of protest in France. After the war Rolland wrote another multivolume novel, *The Enchanted Soul*. It reflects his increasing interest in communism, and the main character, a free-spirited woman, becomes disenchanted with material possessions.

During the rise and dominance of the Nazi Party in Germany and during World War II, Rolland was a courageous opponent of fascism.

Publications

- *1900 Danton*
- *1902 The Fourteenth of July*
- *1902 Life of Beethoven*
- *1904 Life of Michelangelo*
- *1904–12 Jean-Christophe* (10 vols.)
- *1911 Life of Tolstoy*
- *1914–19 Journal of the War Years*
- *1915 Above the Battle*
- *1922–33 The Enchanted Soul* (6 vols.)
- *1924 Mahatma Gandhi*

ROSSETTI, Christina

English poet

Born Dec. 5, 1830
Died Dec. 29, 1894
Age at death 64

Christina Rossetti was a leading Victorian poet. She is remembered mainly for her simple but effective ballads, carols and sonnets.

Rossetti was born in London, one of four children of talented Italian parents. One of her brothers was the poet and painter Dante Gabriel Rossetti. Educated at home, from early on she shared her parents' interest in poetry and respect for religion. Even as a young girl she wrote verse in English and Italian, and her childhood efforts were privately printed before she was 17. Three years later, she contributed verses to *The Germ*, a short-lived magazine started by her brother William with some friends.

Rossetti was 31 when her first volume of poems appeared. *Goblin Market* brought together verses already published in various magazines. This collection shows her songlike way with words, love of fantasy, and fascination with sadness. Similar traits figure in later collections such as *The Prince's Progress*.

Two of her favorite themes – death and giving up earthly love – sprang partly from her own devout religious feelings. Her gloominess also owed something to her own ill health, which might have been imagined at first. Despite two offers of marriage Rossetti lived at home as a semi-invalid with her mother and sister. She became even more of a recluse after the age of 40, when she developed a disease of the thyroid gland. However, that did not stop her producing *Sing-Song*, a book of delightful children's nursery rhymes. Most of her later works, though, deal with somber religious feelings.

Publications

- *1861* "Up-Hill"
- *1861* "A Birthday"
- *1862 Goblin Market*
- *1866 The Prince's Progress*
- *1872 Sing-Song*
- *1874 Annus Domini*
- *1879 Seek and Find*
- *1881 A Pageant*
- *1885 Time Flies*
- *1893 Verses*

ROSSETTI, Dante Gabriel

English poet

Born May 12, 1828
Died Apr. 9, 1882
Age at death 53

Dante Gabriel Rossetti was a Victorian poet and painter inspired by early Italian artists and writers. He helped found the British Pre-Raphaelite school of art.

Rossetti was born in London, the son of a scholar forced to leave Italy because of his political views. CHRISTINA ROSSETTI was his younger sister. Rossetti attended King's College School and two schools of art. He admired the works of early Italian poets such as DANTE and the simple style of early Italian artists. In 1848, Rossetti and like-minded young artists founded the Pre-Raphaelite Brotherhood, so called because the group was inspired by artists who worked before the great Italian painter Raphael. Its aim was to create pure, rich art influenced by medieval works of art.

Rossetti was writing poetry by his teens. When he was 22, "The Blessed Damozel" and ten other poems appeared in the Pre-Raphaelites' magazine *The Germ*.

Much of Rossetti's painting and poetry was inspired by Elizabeth Siddal, the beautiful young woman he married in 1860. When she died in 1862, her grieving husband buried his unpublished poems beside her. Later, though, he had the buried verses dug up, and in 1870 they were published as *Poems*. This book included most of his best verse and established his reputation as a poet. *Ballads and Sonnets* includes the 102 love sonnets that Rossetti called "The House of Life." They tell of the poet's deep feelings stirred by his love for Elizabeth and sadness over her death.

Publications

1850	"My Sister's Sleep"
1850	"Hand and Soul"
1850	"The Blessed Damozel"
1861	*The Early Italian Poets*
1870	*Poems*
1881	*Ballads and Sonnets*
1881	*Poems*

ROSSNER, Judith

American novelist

Born Mar. 31, 1935

Judith Rossner found fame with her fourth novel, *Looking for Mr. Goodbar*, which brilliantly portrays the moral and sexual confusion of many Americans after the "free-love" era of the 1960s.

Rossner was born and raised in New York City, where she sets most of her novels. She attended New York City state schools, including the City College of New York, but dropped out when she was 19 to get married. During the next 20 years she wrote only three novels. Although they all had weaknesses, such as unpredictable and unsympathetic characters, they were quite favorably reviewed. After her divorce in 1973, and while working as a secretary, she produced her best and most original book.

Looking for Mr. Goodbar has none of the flaws of the earlier novels. Its main character, Theresa Dunn, is a split personality: by day she teaches little children, and at night she goes to singles bars to satisfy her overdeveloped sex drive. Two of the men she meets expose the different halves of her personality: one is a violent, macho hoodlum, the other a well-behaved, sensitive young lawyer. Unable to reconcile her two personalities, Theresa's life leads to self-destruction, and she ends up being murdered by a stranger she picks up in a bar.

Theresa's murder occurs as a result of her double life. In deciding this particular fate for her heroine, the author is suggesting that the 1960s dream of complete sexual freedom is ultimately an impossible one; although traditional values may limit our freedom, they at least allow us to survive in the world.

Publications

1966 To the Precipice
1969 Nine Months in the Life of an Old Maid
1972 Any Minute I Can Split
1975 Looking for Mr. Goodbar
1977 Attachments
1983 August
1990 His Little Women
1994 Olivia or the Weight of the Past

ROTH, Philip

American novelist

Born Mar. 19, 1933

Philip Roth is one of the leading satirists of modern American life. He is also one of the major voices of Jewish-American literature of the past 30 years.

Born in Newark, New Jersey, to lower-middle-class Jewish parents, Roth had a suburban upbringing. The suburbs and its people have served as a subject for many of his novels, which he began writing after graduating from the University of Chicago. At age 26, Roth published his first book, a collection of short stories called *Goodbye, Columbus*. In this he wrote, often negatively, about the habits and manners of suburban Jewish life and traditions. Many critics praised his work of satire, but many readers were offended by what they saw as criticism of the Jewish community.

His next novels, *Letting Go* and *When She Was Good*, gained much attention but not as much controversy. When he was 36, however, Roth produced a bestseller: *Portnoy's Complaint*, about a young man trying to escape the guilt of his youth and his domineering mother. Roth said that in writing this book he dealt with many of his own feelings of guilt about his youth.

Roth's most artistically successful novel is *The Ghost Writer*, the first of a series of novels featuring a writer named Nathan Zuckerman. Some of Zuckerman's experiences mirror Roth's own life, including coming up against censorship.

Roth's greatest gifts are describing the details of ordinary life and producing great dialogue and satiric comic touches.

Publications

1959 Goodbye, Columbus
1962 Letting Go
1967 When She Was Good
1969 Portnoy's Complaint
1977 The Professor of Desire
1979 The Ghost Writer
1981 Zuckerman Unbound
1986 The Counterlife
1995 Sabbath's Theater
1997 American Pastoral
1998 I Married a Communist

ROUSSEAU, Jean Jacques

Swiss-born French philosopher and novelist

Born Jun. 28, 1712
Died Jul. 2, 1778
Age at death 66

Jean Jacques Rousseau is one of the outstanding figures of French literature and philosophy.

Rousseau was born in Geneva, Switzerland, the son of a watchmaker. His mother died at his birth, and his father left his upbringing to anyone who would take him. At age 16, Rousseau ran away from Geneva and wandered around Europe until his late 20s.

In 1741, he settled in Paris, where he had five children by a woman named Thérèse Levasseur, whom he never married. These children were abandoned to an orphanage. Rousseau had great charm and he got to know the leading writers of the time. Through one of them he received work writing for an important encyclopedia that began to appear in 1751. Rousseau's first great work, *Julie, or the New Heloise*, a novel promoting the value of the family, was published when he was 49. It made him famous and was to have a great influence on European fiction. Soon after this he published *The Social Contract*, which starts with the famous sentence: "Man is born free and everywhere he is in chains." This major work of political philosophy, with its catchphrase "Liberté, Égalité, Fraternité," inspired the French Revolution.

Rousseau produced a wide range of writings, including moralistic novels such as *Émile, or a New System of Education*, operettas, articles on art, music and science, books on politics and religion, and a celebrated autobiography called *Confessions*, which, although highly entertaining, is not a true account of his life.

Publications

1750 Discourse on the Sciences and Arts
1753 Discourse on the Origin of Inequality
1761 Julie, or the New Heloise
1762 Émile, or a New System of Education
1762 The Social Contract

Published after he died

1782 Confessions

ROWSON, Susanna

English-born American novelist and playwright

Born 1762
Died Mar. 2, 1824
Age at death c. 62

A playwright, actress, novelist and teacher, Susanna Rowson wrote the first bestselling American novel, *Charlotte Temple*.

Rowson was born in Portsmouth, England. Her mother died in childbirth, and when she was five, Rowson went to America with her father, an officer in the British navy. They settled in Massachusetts, but during the American Revolution they were treated as loyalists, faithful to the English crown, and sent back to England, where Rowson eventually became a governess and began to write.

Rowson's first novel, *Victoria*, was published when she was 24. The same year she married a musician, and after two more novels she wrote *Charlotte Temple*. It was first published in England when she was 29, but it received little notice. A few years later, it was published in the United States, however, and became an instant best-seller. By this time, Rowson and her husband had moved to America. They settled in Boston and became successful stage performers. During this period Rowson wrote songs, musicals and plays. She then opened a drama school for young women, pioneering the education of girls over the next 25 years.

Many of Rowson's novels, including *Charlotte Temple*, feature young women who, through innocence or misplaced trust, meet with disaster. The plots are sentimental and highlight the pitfalls that young women face from men who seduce and abandon them. But they also display early feminist ideas by criticizing the way society and its double standards put women in danger.

Publications

1786 Victoria
1788 A Trip to Parnassus
1789 The Test of Honor
1791 Charlotte Temple
1792 The Fille de Chambre
1794 Slaves in Algiers
1795 Trials of the Human Heart
1813 Sarah, or the Exemplary Wife

Published after she died

1828 Charlotte's Daughter

ROY, Gabrielle

Canadian novelist and short-story writer

Born Mar. 22, 1909
Died Jul. 13, 1983
Age at death 74

Gabrielle Roy is one of Canada's most widely read authors. Her first novel, *The Tin Flute*, became the first French-Canadian novel to win a major literary prize in France. It also won Canada's prestigious literary prize, the Governor General's Award.

Roy was born in St. Boniface, Manitoba – the western province of Canada to which her French-Canadian parents had moved from Quebec. She was the youngest of 11 children, and she grew up speaking both French and English. After attending convent school, she began teaching; then, in her late 20s she traveled in Europe, where she studied drama.

When World War II broke out, Roy returned to Canada, settling in Montreal. A Montreal slum was the setting for her famous novel *The Tin Flute*. Published when she was 36, it is a realistic portrayal of a poor family and a woman who struggles to overcome the constraints of the society in which she lives.

In 1947, at age 38, Roy became the first woman to be admitted to the Royal Society of Canada, a prestigious group of scholars and writers. Although by now living in Quebec City, Roy set many of her later novels in Manitoba, describing in straightforward style the simple lives of remote communities in that "prairie province." She also set some of her short stories in the Canadian Arctic, where she explored the conflicts between the way of life of the Inuit people and the changes being brought by white settlers.

In *Children of My Heart* she used her experiences as a teacher in rural schools as the basis for sketches depicting the lives of children in Manitoba. This won her another Governor General's Award.

Publications

1945 The Tin Flute
1950 Where Nests the Water Hen
1954 The Cashier
1955 Street of Riches
1963 The Hidden Mountain
1966 The Road Past the Altamonte
1975 Garden in the Wind
1976 Enchanted Summer
1977 Children of My Heart
1978 Fragile Lights of Earth

RUKEYSER, Muriel

American poet, essayist and playwright

Born Dec. 15, 1913
Died Feb. 12, 1980
Age at death 66

Although known chiefly as a poet, Muriel Rukeyser published an extraordinary range of work, including plays, screenplays, children's books, essays and translations. She was also an activist who saw poetry as a way to create social change.

Rukeyser was born into a wealthy Jewish family in New York City, where she grew up. As an undergraduate at Vassar College she became friends with fellow writers ELIZABETH BISHOP and MARY MCCARTHY; later she went to Columbia University. At age 22, she published her first book of poetry, *Theory of Flight*, which won the Yale Series of Younger Poets competition in 1935.

Rukeyser was strongly opposed to the Vietnam War, and in the 1960s she was imprisoned because of her involvement in the protests. A single mother, she used the contrast between maternal feelings and the destruction of war to describe what she saw. She also used poetry to protest the treatment of Sacco and Vanzetti, two anarchists whose trial and execution in 1927 had been the focus of much controversy.

Experience and sensation are major features of Rukeyser's work. Whether it be the pleasure of a caress or the pain of injustice, she celebrates the importance of feeling for its own sake.

Science and scientific processes were another interest of Rukeyser's. For nearly 15 years, she was vice-president of the House of Photography in New York. She also translated work by Mexican poet OCTAVIO PAZ and wrote three major biographies in addition to her 14 volumes of poetry. Her *Collected Poems* was published just two years before she died.

Publications

1935 Theory of Flight
1938 US One
1944 Beast in View
1949 The Life of Poetry
1958 Body of Waking
1962 Waterlily Fire
1965 The Orgy
1967 The Outer Banks
1968 The Speed of Darkness
1978 Collected Poems

RULFO, Juan

Mexican novelist and short-story writer

Born May 16, 1918
Died Jan. 7, 1986
Age at death 67

Juan Rulfo is noted for his sympathetic descriptions of the poverty and difficulties of life in rural Mexico. He has been described by the Mexican poet OCTAVIO PAZ as "the only Mexican novelist to have provided us an image – rather than a mere description – of our physical surroundings."

Rulfo was born in the province of Jalisco, Mexico, which during his youth was going through a period of political unrest. His father and two uncles were murdered in the troubles, and when his mother died, Rulfo was sent to an orphanage. He completed his education in Guadalajara and attended the national university in Mexico City for a short time. Rulfo then worked as an immigration agent.

Rulfo loved to read and was influenced by the work of the

Scandinavian writers KNUT HAMSUN and HALLDOR K. LAXNESS, and the American novelist WILLIAM FAULKNER. When he was 35, Rulfo published his first collection of short stories, *The Burning Plain and Other Stories*. These stories show his identification with the harsh plight of the rural Mexican peasants and also draw on memories of his own early life, when death and violence were commonplace during years of civil war. Two years later he published his major work *Pedro Páramo*. This novel – which he had been planning for ten years – is a complex mixture of reality and fantasy. Halfway through the book, for example, the reader discovers that all the characters are already dead and that the narrator is the son of the main character. It is a perfectly told story of a greedy, cruel man who always operates from behind the scenes, never in public.

Publications

1953	*The Burning Plain and Other Stories*
1955	*Pedro Páramo*
1980	*Inframundo: The Mexico of Juan Rulfo*
1980	*The Golden Cock*

RUNYON, Damon

American journalist and short-story writer

Born Oct. 4, 1884
Died Dec. 10, 1946
Age at death 62

Damon Runyon wrote popular short stories about unsavory characters with tender hearts.

Runyon was born in Manhattan, Kansas. While he was still a young child, Runyon's family moved to Pueblo, Colorado. His mother died soon after, and Runyon was left on his own. He earned his living as a messenger boy. By age 15, he was a full-time writer with the Pueblo *Evening Press*. During the Spanish-American War, Runyon wrote for the *Manila Freedom* and *Soldier's Letter* in the Philippines.

In 1905, Runyon became a sportswriter for the *Denver Post*, where he created vivid and imaginative descriptions of his subjects. In 1908, he began to publish short stories in *Collier's* and *McClure's* magazines based on his earlier experiences. In 1910, he went to New York City as a sportswriter for the *New York American* and soon became the paper's humorist. To get material for his column, "The Mornin's Mornin," he spent time with the unsavory characters of Broadway.

Runyon's stories feature characters with colorful names from New York's underworld; often they are hardened gangsters with tender hearts. In "Little Miss Marker" he writes about a man who gives his young daughter a two dollar "marker" for a bet. Most of these "Broadway Stories" appeared when Runyon was in his 40s and 50s. They were also published in collections, such as *Guys and Dolls*, his first, and *Blue Plate Special*. Some of these stories were combined to create the musical *Guys and Dolls*.

Runyon died in Manhattan, New York City, and his ashes were scattered on Broadway from an airplane.

Publications

1931	*Guys and Dolls*
1932	"Little Miss Marker"
1934	*Blue Plate Special*
1935	*Money from Home*
1938	*Take It Easy*
1938	*The Best of Damon Runyon*
1939	*My Wife Ethel*
1939	*My Old Man*
1946	*Three Wise Guys and Other Stories*

RUSHDIE, Salman

British novelist

Born Jun. 19, 1947

Salman Rushdie is one of the most distinguished and controversial of contemporary novelists.

Born in Bombay, India, into a wealthy Muslim family, Rushdie was brought up speaking both English and Urdu. He has lived in England since he was a young man. His time at school there was unhappy – he did not make friends and was the target of racist comments. After school, Rushdie studied history at Cambridge University. He graduated in 1968, spent a year as an actor, and then worked in advertising in London while writing.

Rushdie's first novel, *Grimus*, was unsuccessful, but *Midnight's Children*, published when he was 34, won a major British prize and established him as an important novelist. Using fantasy and magic, *Midnight's Children* tells the story of India through the eyes of Saleem Sinai, who is born at midnight on the eve of India's independence from British rule.

The publication of *The Satanic Verses* seven years later turned Rushdie's world upside down. The novel contains references to the Prophet Muhammad and to the Islamic holy book, the Koran, that many Muslims saw as an attack on their religion. It was banned in several countries after protests. In 1988, Iran's leader, the Ayatollah Khomeini, issued a fatwa (legal ruling) in which he called on Muslims to execute Rushdie. Rushdie and his family immediately went into hiding. He continued to write and even to make occasional public appearances while the fatwa was in place. Eventually, diplomatic efforts between Britain and Iran paid off when the fatwa was lifted, after more than ten years. Nevertheless, many people feel that he is unlikely ever to be completely free of the death threat.

Publications

1975 Grimus
1981 Midnight's Children
1983 Shame
1987 The Jaguar Smile: A Nicaraguan Journey
1988 The Satanic Verses
1990 Haroun and the Sea of Stories
1994 East, West
1995 The Moor's Last Sigh
1999 Ground Beneath Her Feet

RUSKIN, John

English writer and critic

Born Feb. 8, 1819
Died Jan. 20, 1900
Age at death 80

John Ruskin was a writer who deeply influenced art and thought in 19th-century Britain.

Ruskin was born in London, the only child of a wealthy middle-class couple. He was taught by a private tutor and then studied at Oxford University, where he won a poetry prize. His parents encouraged his early interest in art, and family vacations to the Alps fired Ruskin with enthusiasm for natural scenery.

At 24, Ruskin brought out the first of five volumes called *Modern Painters* – a study of the work of painters that Ruskin admired, such as J.M.W. Turner and the Victorian Pre-Raphaelite painters.

Ruskin also studied and wrote about building design. In *The Stones of Venice* and *The Seven Lamps of Architecture* he admired and praised medieval architecture. Ruskin believed artists and craftsmen inspired by religious faith had created the greatest works of art ever in Europe's medieval cathedrals.

Ruskin blamed the ugly cities of his own time on the mass production and bad working and living conditions of the industrial age. In later life, this led him to become interested in social reform. In *Unto This Last*, *Fors Clavigera* and other books he urged better workers' pay and other improvements. Like his ideas on art, Ruskin's writings about social reform helped change the way people thought in England at the time.

At 50, Ruskin became professor of fine art at Oxford University, but his personal life was unhappy. His marriage had collapsed in his mid-30s, and in his last years he suffered from depression.

Publications

1843–60 Modern Painters (5 vols.)
1849 The Seven Lamps of Architecture
1851–53 The Stones of Venice
1862 Unto This Last
1865 Sesame and Lilies
1871–84 Fors Clavigera
1872 Munera Pulveris
1880 A Joy for Ever
1885–89 Praeterita (unfinished)

RUSSELL, George William

Irish poet and essayist

Born Apr. 10, 1867
Died Jul. 17, 1935
Age at death 68

George William Russell, who often used the pen name AE, is best known as a poet and as one of the key figures in the rebirth of Irish literature in the late 19th and early 20th centuries.

Russell was born in Lurgan, County Armagh, Ireland. When he was ten, his family moved to Dublin, where Russell studied painting at the Metropolitan School of Art and met the great Irish poet W.B. YEATS. Yeats introduced him to theosophy, a set of mystical beliefs about the nature of God. Russell, who was already interested in mysticism, decided to give up painting as a career, but his interest in theosophy remained for the rest of his life.

Russell worked briefly at a brewery and then for ten years as a clerk in a drapery store. In 1905, he was appointed editor of the magazine *Irish Homestead*, which later became *Irish Statesman*, and worked there for 25 years.

At the age of 27, Russell published his first poetry collection, *Homeward: Songs by the Way*. It brought him instant recognition as an important figure on the Irish literary scene. Russell was one of the cofounders of the Irish National Theater, later the famous Abbey Theater in Dublin. His only play, *Deirdre*, was produced there when he was 35. As well as many other books of poems, he wrote about farming and about his mystical religious beliefs (in *The Candle of Vision*). He is nowadays remembered not so much for his poetry but as an important figure in the Irish literary revival.

Publications

1894 Homeward: Songs by the Way
1903 The Divine Vision, and Other Poems
1907 Deirdre
1913 Collected Poems
1918 The Candle of Vision
1925 Voices of the Stones
1929 Dark Weeping
1934 The House of the Titans and Other Poems

RYLANT, Cynthia

American children's and young-adults' writer

Born Jun. 6, 1954

Cynthia Rylant is the author of many award-winning novels, short stories and poems written for children and young adults. She is well known for her simple, poetic writing style and the sensitive and sympathetic ways she portrays characters.

Rylant was born in Hopewell, Virginia. She had a troubled childhood; her father was an alcoholic, and her mother left him when Rylant was four. She spent the next four years with her mother's parents in West Virginia, while her mother trained to be a nurse. Her grandfather was a coal miner, and they lived in a house with no running water or indoor toilets, but Rylant was happy there. After her mother qualified as a nurse, they moved to the nearby town of Beaver. Rylant enjoyed school and planned to become a nurse, but at university she became interested in literature instead.

After finishing a second degree in English literature in 1976, Rylant took a job in the children's section of a public library. For the first time she began to read children's literature. She knew instantly that she wanted to write children's books, and by the time she was 28 she had finished her first book, *When I Was Young in the Mountains*. This picture book lovingly recalls her early years living in the Appalachian mountains with her grandparents. Since then Rylant has written a wide range of books for young people of all ages, including the famous "Henry and Mudge" series about the exploits of Henry and his huge dog Mudge. Her most widely praised novel so far is *Missing May*, in which a 12-year-old orphan comes to terms with the death of her aunt.

Publications

1982 When I Was Young in the Mountains
1985 The Relatives Came
1985 A Blue-Eyed Daisy
1986 A Fine White Dust
1987 Henry and Mudge
1989 But I'll Be Back Again
1992 Missing May
1995 Henry and Mudge and the Best Day Ever

SAADAWI, Nawal el

Egyptian novelist and journalist

Born Oct. 27, 1931

Nawal el Saadawi is one of Egypt's leading writers. Her books about the position of women in Arab society have broken new ground for Arabic writers and earned her time in an Egyptian prison.

Saadawi was born in a rural village in northern Egypt. Although few Egyptian girls received a good education at that time, she qualified as a doctor at 25. She went on to become Egypt's director of public health, chief editor of a health journal, and assistant general secretary for Egypt's Medical Association. In 1972 Saadawi published her nonfiction book *Women and Sex*. By highlighting the position of women in Egypt, it angered many religious and political leaders, and she was dismissed from her jobs. Saadawi continued, however, to fight for women's social and political freedoms.

In 1974, as part of her research into women's mental health, Saadawi met Firdaus – a woman prisoner who was to be executed for killing a man. In *Woman at Point Zero,* Saadawi tells this proud woman's story and how her refusal to accept her inferior role in society led to her death. Saadawi's sensitive treatment of the relationships between men and women in this and other novels has earned her several literary prizes. From 1978 to 1980, she served as an advisor on women's issues to the United Nations. In 1981, she was imprisoned for a while by the government for "crimes against the state." Since her release Saadawi has focused on writing, journalism and speaking internationally on women's issues. She also founded the Arab Women's Solidarity Organization, which was banned in 1991.

Publications

1972 Women and Sex
1974 God Dies by the Nile
1975 Woman at Point Zero
1980 The Hidden Face of Eve: Women in the Arab World
1987 Death of an Ex-Minister
1988 Memoirs from the Women's Prison
1989 The Circling Song
1991 Searching

SACHS, Hans

German writer

Born Nov. 5, 1494
Died Jan. 19, 1576
Age at death 81

Hans Sachs, one of the 16th century's most prolific writers, claimed to have written 208 plays, 1,700 stories, and no fewer than 4,275 songs. These works provide a wonderful insight into his times and reveal him as a man of the finest qualities, with a kind heart and no trace of meanness. He would, however, be almost unknown today had it not been for the German composer Richard Wagner, who made him a main character in his opera *The Mastersingers of Nuremberg*.

As a youth, Sachs was apprenticed to a shoemaker. Before settling down in his home town of Nuremberg, he spent some time traveling throughout Germany and living by his trade. As well as being a good cobbler, Sachs wrote stories, plays and songs. He was a leading member of one of the "Mastersinger" guilds, which were organized to compose and perform poetry and music.

Sachs remained in Nuremberg for the rest of his life and became a master cobbler, repairing shoes and industriously writing words and music, much of which became extremely popular. He first became famous at the age of 29 with his poem *The Wittenberg Nightingale*. Many of the melodies he wrote for his poems survive to this day.

Sach's subjects include biblical, classical and medieval matters, his dialogue is lively and vivid, and his style realistic. Many of his characters are stereotypes of his day – the cunning peasant, the snake-oil merchant, the nagging wife and the military braggart. Happily, almost his complete literary output has been preserved.

Publications

1523 The Wittenberg Nightingale
1530 The Vagabond Student in Paradise

Published after he died

1870–1908 Complete Works
1923 Selections of Works (2 vols.)

SACHS, Nelly

German-Swedish poet and playwright

Born Dec. 10, 1891
Died May 12, 1970
Age at death 78

Nelly Sachs, a German-born poet, wrote about the Holocaust during World War II. She shared the 1966 Nobel Prize for Literature with the Jewish novelist S.Y. AGNON.

Sachs was born in Berlin, the only daughter of wealthy Jewish parents. She was educated privately, studied music and dance, but did not attend university. Her tutors encouraged her to read widely, and she enjoyed German Romantic writers.

In 1933, the Nazis came to power in Germany and began a campaign of violence against the Jews. Seven years later, with the help of her friend the Swedish novelist SELMA LAGERLÖF, Sachs and her mother escaped from the Nazis to Sweden. Other members of her family died in concentration camps. Wartime life in Sweden was hard, but Sachs taught herself Swedish and translated literary works into German.

Sachs's first publication, when she was 30, was a volume of short stories, *Tales and Legends*. She also wrote several volumes of lyrical, hymnlike poetry. When she got to Sweden, she continued to write, producing powerful and emotional poems about the suffering of the Jewish people. Much of her poetry of this period represents ideas as symbolic images – in her most famous collection, *O the Chimneys*, the Jewish nation is represented as smoke drifting from concentration camp chimneys.

In 1965, Sachs was awarded the Peace Prize of German publishers. Accepting the award, she said, "In spite of all the horrors of the past, I believe in you." Hope for a better future and forgiveness are the themes of much of Sachs's later work.

Publications

1921 Tales and Legends
1951 Eli: A Mystery Play of the Sufferings of Israel
1967 O the Chimneys
1968 Selected Poems

SACKVILLE-WEST, Vita

English novelist, poet and biographer

Born Mar. 9, 1892
Died Jun. 2, 1962
Age at death 70

Vita Sackville-West is best remembered today for her novels set among the English upper classes; her long poem *The Land* that describes the beauties and seasons of the English countryside; and for her love affair with the novelist VIRGINIA WOOLF, who wrote her famous novel *Orlando* as a tribute to Sackville-West.

Sackville-West was born into an old aristocratic English family. She grew up in the south of England at the ancestral family home, Knole House. She was educated at home by private tutors before attending a girls' school in London as a teenager. When she was 20, she married a diplomat whose job often took them abroad. At first Sackville-West played her role as dutiful wife. Then her husband admitted he had a male lover, and she began a long relationship with VIRGINIA

Woolf. Some say the marriage was strained by them both being unfaithful with members of the same sex; their son called the marriage happy and successful for the same reason.

Sackville-West began writing as a child. Her first collection of poetry, *Chatterton*, was published when she was 17. Her first novel, *Heritage*, came out ten years later. Her early novels were experimental, but her three bestselling novels – *The Edwardians*, *All Passion Spent* and *Family History* – were more traditional in their style. Based on the Sackville family history, they are excellent studies of English upper-class manners and life. An underlying theme is the role of women; Sackville-West believed in equal rights for women, including the right to have a career. She also became a respected expert on gardening, a subject on which she wrote some classic texts.

Publications

1909 Chatterton
1919 Heritage
1923 Challenge
1924 Seducers in Ecuador
1927 The Land
1930 The Edwardians
1931 All Passion Spent
1932 Family History
1933 Collected Poems
1946 The Garden

SADE, Marquis de

French writer

Born Jun. 2, 1740
Died Dec. 2, 1814
Age at death 74

The Marquis de Sade is the most infamous writer in the history of French literature. He wrote books about sex and cruelty that have been criticized, banned and even burned at various times.

De Sade was born near Paris into an aristocratic French family. After an expensive private education, he became an officer in the army at the age of only 14. After nine years he left the military and married the daughter of another wealthy aristocratic family.

Soon after his marriage, de Sade began having affairs and spending a lot of time with prostitutes. In 1768, there was a public scandal when he held a prostitute called Rose Keller captive and abused her. In the years that followed, de Sade was found guilty of all kinds of sexual crimes and was sent to jail many times. The word "sadism" – used to describe the enjoyment of cruelty – is derived from his name.

It was during one of de Sade's longer stays in jail that he began writing to overcome his boredom and frustration. He wrote plays, novels and other works full of sex scenes that horrified many readers. *Justine, or the Misfortunes of Virtue*, one of his most famous books, was published when he was 51. While de Sade was in prison, France was torn apart by the French Revolution, and the power of the aristocracy was overthrown. De Sade survived, although many other aristocrats were executed.

Although de Sade was regarded as a madman in his day, some 19th-century writers were inspired by his belief that people should act on their instincts, and his writings have influenced modern literature.

Publications

1791 Justine, or the Misfortunes of Virtue
1795 Philosophy of the Boudoir
1795 Aline and Valcour
1797 Juliette, or the Luxuries of Vice
1800 Crimes of Love

Published after he died

1904 One Hundred and Twenty Days of Sodom

SAGAN, Françoise

French novelist and playwright

Born Jun. 21, 1935

Françoise Sagan became an overnight sensation at the age of 19 when her first novel, *Bonjour Tristesse* (*Hello Sadness* in English), became an instant bestseller. Three years later it was made into a successful film.

Sagan was born in the village of Cajarc in southwestern France but, during World War II, she lived in Switzerland. She was educated at convent schools in Paris after the war ended and attended the University of the Sorbonne, Paris, but she failed her examinations and left determined to become a writer.

Bonjour Tristesse is the story of a spoiled teenager's attempt to prevent her father's remarriage. Her second novel, *A Certain Smile*, was also a success and tells of a student's love affair with a middle-aged father figure. Most of Sagan's books are about the way rich people can become bored with their lives and lead a rootless existence. Further novels include *Do You Like Brahms?* and *The Surrender*, both about love, marriage and the difficulties of personal relationships.

In the 1960s, Sagan turned from novels to writing plays. Several, including *Castle in Sweden*, *Sometimes, Violins* and *A Piano on the Grass*, were produced and well received by critics and public alike.

Sagan married twice, but both ended in divorce. In 1973, she announced her intention of going to live in Ireland but has continued to write. Her latest novels, which have not been too well received, are *The Painted Lady* and *The Still Storm*.

Publications

1954 Bonjour Tristesse
1956 A Certain Smile
1959 Do You Like Brahms?
1960 Castle in Sweden
1961 Sometimes, Violins
1965 The Surrender
1970 A Piano on the Grass
1977 The Unmade Bed
1981 The Painted Lady
1983 The Still Storm

SAINT-EXUPÉRY, Antoine de

French novelist and children's writer

Born Jun. 29, 1900
Died Jul. 31, 1944
Age at death 44

During his lifetime Antoine de Saint-Exupéry was famous for his books about the daring exploits of pilots in the early days of flying. He also wrote and illustrated a children's book, *The Little Prince*, about a boy from another planet who saves a pilot stranded in the desert. It is now a classic and Saint-Exupéry's best-known book.

Saint-Exupéry was born into a poor but aristocratic French family. Three years after his birth, the American Wright brothers made the world's first powered flight and began the era of air exploration that was to dominate Saint-Exupéry's life. He learned to fly while doing his military service at the age of 22. This was soon after the end of World War I, when airplanes had just begun to play an important part in warfare. After his military training, Saint-Exupéry went to

Africa and became involved in the job of pioneering air routes for mail across the continent. His first novel, *Southern Mail*, published when he was 29, was based on his and other pilots' experience of this dangerous life.

In *Southern Mail* and his next two novels, *Night Flight* and *Wind, Sand, and Stars*, Saint-Exupéry helped to establish the popular image of the pioneering pilot as a modern hero. He himself felt that the pilot, facing the unknown alone and without fear, was the greatest kind of human. During World War II, Saint-Exupéry again served as a military pilot – in North Africa. One day in 1944, he failed to return from a mission over the sea and was never seen again.

Publications

1929 Southern Mail
1931 Night Flight
1939 Wind, Sand, and Stars
1942 Flight to Arras
1943 The Little Prince

Published after he died

1952 The Wisdom of the Sands

SAKI

British short-story writer, novelist and journalist

Born Dec. 18, 1870
Died Nov. 14, 1916
Age at death 45

Saki was the pen name of Hector Hugh Munro, a British writer of satirical and humorous short stories and novels. He got the name from a character in the *Rubaiyat of Omar Khayyam*, an ancient Persian poem. His short stories have fantastic plots, often with surprise endings, and are full of witty sayings. One of the most frequently quoted is: "She was a good cook, as cooks go, and as cooks go she went."

Saki was born in British-ruled Burma (now Myanmar), the son of an officer in the Burma police. His mother died when he was two, and he and his brother and sister were sent to England to be brought up by two strict and eccentric aunts. After a short spell in the Burma police, from which he retired due to illness, Saki turned to journalism. He wrote political sketches for newspapers and later served as a foreign correspondent.

Saki's first book was a serious work, *The Rise of the Russian Empire*. It was followed by four books of short stories, beginning with *Reginald*, published when he was 34, and ending with *Beasts and Super-Beasts*. His two novels were *The Unbearable Bassington* and *When William Came*, in which he portrayed what might happen if the German emperor conquered England.

When World War I broke out in 1914, Saki enlisted as an ordinary soldier, although he was already 43 and officially over age. He was killed by a sniper while sheltering in a shell crater in France. Two more volumes of short stories and his three plays were published after his death.

Publications

1900 The Rise of the Russian Empire
1904 Reginald
1910 Reginald in Russia
1912 The Chronicles of Clovis
1912 The Unbearable Bassington
1914 When William Came
1914 Beasts and Super-Beasts

Published after he died

1919 The Toys of Peace
1924 The Square Egg

SALINGER, J.D.

American novelist and short-story writer

Born Jan. 1, 1919

J(erome) D(avid) Salinger is famous for his classic, *The Catcher in the Rye*, a novel about two days in the life of 16-year-old Holden Caulfield. Its masterful depiction of characters and original "hero" have made the book unique.

Born in New York City to a Jewish father who was a successful food importer and a Scotch-Irish mother, Salinger attended some good schools but achieved below average grades. In 1934, he was sent to the Valley Forge Military School, where he acted in school plays, edited the yearbook, and wrote the class song and several short stories. Many incidents in *The Catcher in the Rye* were based on events at the school.

After graduating in 1936, he drifted for a year then attended university at Columbia but didn't graduate. In 1939, he enrolled in a short-story class run by Whit Burnett, who edited *Story* magazine. Burnett encouraged him and published one of his short stories in *Story* when Salinger was 21. Heartened by this, Salinger sold several stories to other magazines, until he was drafted by the army in 1942 to fight in World War II. The experience of war influenced his work – there is a sense of boredom, frustration and anxiety in his later pieces.

Little happens in Salinger's stories; he is more concerned with what people say and the environment in which they live their lives. *Nine Stories* describes the Glass family, who are also in the rest of his later work, including *Franny and Zooey*. Salinger now lives a quiet and secretive life in New Hampshire, where rumor has it he still writes, although he has published nothing new for more than 30 years.

Publications

1951 The Catcher in the Rye

1953 Nine Stories

1961 Franny and Zooey

1963 Raise High the Roof Beam

1974 The Complete Uncollected Short Stories of J.D. Salinger

SANCHEZ, Sonia

American poet and playwright

Born Sep. 9, 1934

Sonia Sanchez is an award-winning poet whose work expresses the pain and anger of black and white relations in America since the 1960s.

Sanchez was born in Birmingham, Alabama. Her mother died when she was a baby, and the young Sanchez was raised by relatives. She graduated from Hunter College in New York City in 1955 and has taught at various colleges since 1965. She has been married (and divorced) and has three children. Always politically aware – as a child she wrote a poem about an aunt who, having been ordered off a bus, spat in the driver's face – Sanchez became a leading activist in the civil rights movement.

Homecoming, published when she was 35, was Sanchez's first book. Her *We A BaddDDD People* uses language in new ways and is said to have been influenced by the activist Malcolm X. She has also written more traditional forms of poetry, such as the ballads in her collection *Love Poems*. Sanchez often uses the speech of urban African Americans in her poetry. She addresses racism, sexism, poverty and crime and the struggles of the black community to overcome these challenges. She says about herself, "I write to tell the truth about the black condition as I see it. Therefore I write to offer a black woman's view of the world."

In 1984, Sanchez won the National Book Award for her prose-poetry collection *Homegirls & Handgrenades*. She has also written a number of plays, and among her many awards are a National Endowment for the Arts Award and an honorary Ph.D. from Wilberforce University.

Publications

1969 Homecoming
1970 We A BaddDDD People
1973 Love Poems
1973 A Blues Book for Blue Black Magical Women
1978 I've Been a Woman
1984 Homegirls & Handgrenades
1987 Under a Soprano Sky
1995 Wounded in the House of a Friend
1995 Does Your House Have Lions

SAND, George

French novelist and playwright

Born Jul. 1, 1804
Died Jun. 8, 1876
Age at death 71

George Sand, the most celebrated female French novelist of the 19th century, is also famous as an early feminist and for her many love affairs.

Sand was born Amandine-Aurore-Lucile Dupin, and she grew up on the family estate in Nohant, a small village in central France. She married when she was 18 but grew bored with her husband and at age 27 went to live in Paris with her two children. She started writing novels to make her living, taking her pen name from the writer Jules Sandeau, with whom she lived for a time. Other lovers included the poet Alfred de Musset and the Polish composer Frédéric Chopin. Her passionate way of life shocked Parisian society; she also smoked cigars and sometimes wore men's clothes – unheard of then for women.

Sand's first novel, *Indiana*, was published when she was 28. It was an immediate success. Sand used it, and her next works, to attack marriage and the Church and to argue for the right of women to lead independent lives. During the 1840s, she argued for equality and radical political ideas, and she supported an unsuccessful revolution in France in 1848. She returned to her home in Nohant, where she wrote successful novels about rural life. These were among the first to portray ordinary country people.

Sand also wrote many plays. Her first, *Cosima*, was performed when she was 36, and it was followed by many others. Her long autobiography, *The Story of My Life*, not only tells of her childhood but also reflects on the political events of her lifetime. Two of her last books, both called *Tales of a Grandmother*, are collections of stories for her grandchildren.

Publications

1832 Indiana
1833 Lélia
1840 Cosima
1842 Consuelo
1843 The Countess of Rudolstadt
1843 Jeanne
1848 The Haunted Marsh
1848 Little Fadette
1854–55 The Story of My Life
1872/1876 Tales of a Grandmother

SANDBURG, Carl

American poet and biographer

Born Jan. 6, 1878
Died Jul. 22, 1967
Age at death 89

Carl Sandburg is often called the successor to WALT WHITMAN because his writings celebrate the American spirit. In 1919, he won a Pulitzer Prize for poetry for *Corn Huskers*.

Sandburg, the son of a Swedish immigrant, was born in Galesburg, Illinois. He traveled around Kansas as a hobo, later joining a volunteer force serving in Puerto Rico during the Spanish-American War. After the war, he attended Lombard College in Galesburg. His first poems were published by his teacher while Sandburg was still in his 20s. In 1902, he left college and took a more active interest in politics.

In 1913, Sandburg moved with his wife, Lillian Steichen, to Chicago, where he became a journalist on the *Day Book* and the *Daily News* and contributed to the magazine *Poetry*. The Levinson Prize, awarded by *Poetry* in 1914 for his many contributions, established him as an important new voice in American literature. Shortly afterward his series of poetic volumes describing the Midwest (*Corn Huskers*) and particularly the people and city of Chicago (*Chicago Poems*) began to appear. Sandburg's championship of the working man combined with his use of nonrhyming free verse and everyday language at first shocked readers. His *Complete Poems* won a Pulitzer Prize in 1951.

Sandburg was also a biographer of note. His *Abraham Lincoln: the Prairie Years* and *Abraham Lincoln: the War Years* gained him the 1940 Pulitzer Prize for history. Sandburg's fame as a lecturer and folk singer gained him the nickname "the singing bard."

Publications

1916	*Chicago Poems*
1918	*Corn Huskers*
1922	*Slabs of the Sunburnt West*
1926	*Abraham Lincoln: the Prairie Years*
1928	*Good Morning, America*
1936	*The People, Yes*
1939	*Abraham Lincoln: the War Years*
1950	*Complete Poems*

SAPPHO

Greek poet

Born c. 610 BC
Died c. 580 BC
Age at death c. 30

Sappho was one of the greatest poets of ancient Greece and is perhaps the most famous female poet in the history of European literature. All that is known for certain about her life is that she was born on the Greek island of Lesbos, that she was married, and that she had a daughter named Cleïs.

Sappho's poetry was loved and admired by later Greek writers, and many legends grew up about her life. Some said that she was the lover of Alcaeus, another poet from the island of Lesbos. The ancient Roman poet OVID tells the story that she jumped to her death from a cliff because of her love for a boatman called Phaon. It is unlikely that either of these stories is true.

Only a few incomplete poems remain of the nine books of poetry that Sappho wrote in her lifetime. Most of Sappho's poems are about her friends and family. She was one of the first to write lyrical poems that expressed personal feelings. They are remarkable for their passionate descriptions of emotion and the simple beauty of their language.

The majority of Sappho's love poems are addressed to women; it seems that she had a circle of close female friends who were the audience for her poetry and with whom she may have performed religious rituals, worshiping the goddess Aphrodite. Because of her relationship to these women Sappho has often been described as a homosexual. The word "lesbian," which originally meant "a person from the island of Lesbos," has become the term for a female homosexual.

Publications

Sappho's poems were arranged in nine books but only fragments have survived. It is not known for sure when they were written.

SARO-WIWA, Ken

Nigerian novelist, playwright and poet

Born Oct. 10, 1941
Died Nov. 10, 1995
Age at death 54

Ken Saro-Wiwa was a popular Nigerian writer of satirical novels, children's tales and plays. He became internationally famous following his unjust imprisonment for inciting political violence.

Saro-Wiwa was born in Bori, Rivers State, Nigeria. After graduating from the University of Ibadan he began a career in teaching, taking a post at the University of Lagos from 1967 to 1973. At the age of 31, he received an award for his first widely heard work, a radio play entitled *The Transistor Radio*.

It was during the 1980s that Saro-Wiwa's career as a writer really took off. His first novel *Sozaboy* was published when he was 44. It was his first attempt to write a full length work in "pidgin" English – an English-based dialect spoken by many Nigerians. "Sozaboy" is a pidgin term meaning "soldier boy," and the novel is a bitter anti-war tale about a young man who serves as a soldier during the Biafran War. In contrast to his controversial novels, Saro-Wiwa also created an extremely popular series of comic novels for young people based around a character called Basi – a likable fellow whose eternal optimism is constantly leading to trouble.

Saro-Wiwa's third novel *Prisoners of Jebs*, published when he was 47, is a strong satire about government weakness and corruption. It was this hatred of injustice that led Saro-Wiwa to publicize the plight of the Ogoni people, an ethnic group within Nigeria who were being persecuted by the government. Saro-Wiwa was imprisoned twice for his efforts and eventually, despite an international outcry, he was executed.

Publications

1972 The Transistor Radio
1985 Sozaboy
1985 Songs in a Time of War
1986 A Forest of Flowers
1987 Basi and Company
1988 Prisoners of Jebs

Published after he died

1995 A Month and a Day: A Detention Diary

SAROYAN, William

American novelist, short-story writer and playwright

Born Aug. 31, 1908
Died May 18, 1981
Age at death 72

Publications

1934	*The Daring Young Man on the Flying Trapeze and Other Stories*
1936	*Inhale & Exhale*
1936	*Three Times Three*
1939	*My Heart's in the Highlands*
1939	*The Time of Your Life*
1940	*My Name Is Aram*
1943	*The Human Comedy*
1956	*The Whole Voyald*
1972	*Places Where I've Done Time*

William Saroyan is remembered for his short stories and plays that combine fantasy and reality with sympathetically depicted characters. In 1940 he refused the Pultizer Prize for his play *The Time of Your Life* because he believed that business should not fund art.

Saroyan was born in Fresno, California, of immigrant Armenian parents. After his father died suddenly, he spent four years in an orphanage in Oakland; he returned to Fresno with his mother in 1915. Fascinated by the footloose people who passed through the Fresno-San Francisco area, Saroyan quit secondary school and began to hang out with them in gambling parlors, bars and barbershops.

At age 21, as America plunged into the Great Depression, Saroyan abandoned his job and decided to become a writer. After four years of poverty and rejection, a magazine published his short story "The Daring Young Man on the Flying Trapeze." Later that same year a collection of his stories was published under the same title. The book was popular because it showed the lives of ordinary people trying to survive in the Depression; many of the characters are immigrants living on the breadline in rundown flats and feeling lost in the vastness of America.

Saroyan's work was most popular in the 1930s and early '40s. From the late 1940s onward, however, when he tried to write about global events such as World War II, he found that a harsher voice was demanded by his readership. Although he continued to write, his work was never as well received again.

SARTON, May

Belgian-born American writer

Born May 3, 1912
Died Jul. 16, 1995
Age at death 83

Novelist, poet and journal-keeper May Sarton was a prolific writer whose more than 40 books were both critically acclaimedand widely read. Her work explores the complicated emotions of life.

Sarton was born in Belgium, but her family fled to the United States during World War I when May was four. She was an only child, the daughter of a science historian and a painter. By age 17, she had published several poems, but she was most interested in the theater. She studied drama and founded the Apprentice Theater, but it closed in 1936, and from her mid-20s Sarton focused on writing. She was a regular visitor to Europe, where she met Virginia Woolf and the Anglo-Irish writer Elizabeth Bowen. Sarton's first collection of poems, *Encounter in April*, was published when she was 25.

Both friendship and solitude are explored in Sarton's work. She valued her time alone at her house in York, Maine, where she spent her later years, but she also treasured her many close friendships and enjoyed having visitors. Her memoirs and journals – including *Plant Dreaming Deep* and *Journal of a Solitude* – combine details of everyday domestic life with reflections that convey Sarton's wisdom. She focused on the lives of women – herself, her friends and her fictional characters – and explored themes such as women's friendships, lesbianism and women's creativity. She also explored aging and illness both in her novels and in her journals; she survived surgery to remove breast cancer as well as a stroke and wrote about her recovery.

Publications

1939	*Inner Landscape*
1955	*Faithful Are the Wounds*
1965	*Mrs. Stevens Hears the Mermaids Singing*
1968	*Plant Dreaming Deep*
1970	*Kinds of Love*
1973	*Journal of a Solitude*
1977	*The House by the Sea*
1985	*The Magnificent Spinster*
1988	*After the Stroke*

SARTRE, Jean-Paul

French philosopher, novelist and playwright

Born Jun. 21, 1905
Died Apr. 15, 1980
Age at death 74

Jean-Paul Sartre was one of the leading thinkers of the 20th century. As well as being a famous philosopher, he was also an important writer of fiction. He was awarded the Nobel Prize for Literature in 1964, but he refused to accept it.

Sartre was born and educated in Paris. He lived in the city for most of his life. While still a student he met SIMONE DE BEAUVOIR, who was to become one of the great feminist writers of the century, and they became lifelong partners. After graduating, Sartre taught philosophy in schools and began writing. When he was 33, he published his first novel, *Nausea*, in which he explored some of the ideas he made famous in his greatest philosophy book, *Being and Nothingness*.

During World War II, Sartre served in the French army, was captured by the Germans, and later escaped to fight in the Resistance. His experience of war led him to become involved in politics – he founded a radical left-wing party and wrote about communism in his philosophical works. Sartre also began to concentrate on writing plays rather than novels. One of his most famous plays, *No Exit*, was produced as the war was ending in France. It is about three characters trapped in a room who gradually come to realize that they are in hell.

In his best plays, Sartre combines an exciting and dramatic story with thought-provoking ideas about morality and politics. He remained committed to political action all his life, campaigning against the Vietnam War and French rule in Algeria, North Africa.

Publications

1938	*Nausea*
1939	*Intimacy*
1943	*The Flies*
1943	*Being and Nothingness*
1944	*No Exit*
1945	*The Age of Reason*
1945	*The Reprieve*
1948	*Dirty Hands*
1959	*The Condemned of Altona*
1960	*The Critique of Dialectical Materialism*

SASSOON, Siegfried

English poet and novelist

Born Sep. 8, 1886
Died Sep. 1, 1967
Age at death 80

Publications

1917	*The Old Huntsman*
1918	*Counterattack*
1919	*The War Poems of Siegfried Sassoon*
1935	*Vigils*
1937	*The Complete Memoirs of George Sherston*
1945	*Siegfried's Journey, 1916–20*
1961	*Collected Poems 1908–1956*

Siegfried Sassoon was one of the most famous of England's war poets. He wrote satirical antiwar poems about his experiences during World War I.

Sassoon was born to a wealthy family in the south of England. His father was Jewish and his mother Christian. He was educated privately and at Cambridge University.

In 1914, Sassoon joined the army. It was while he was a soldier that he wrote his most memorable poems. He was in his late 20s to early 30s at the time. England in those days would much rather embrace the patriotic and heroic verse of RUPERT BROOKE, however, than be forced to face the brutal realities of war described in Sassoon's work.

Following his first experience of combat, Sassoon was awarded the Military Cross for his bravery. He threw the medal away in protest against the war. During a period in hospital suffering from "shell-shock," he met WILFRED OWEN, whom he encouraged in his own antiwar poetry. In *The Old Huntsman* and *Counterattack* Sassoon continually highlights the possibilities of life in stark contrast to the senseless brutality of war. This theme was continued in a series of novels partly based on his own life that he published after the war, issued collectively as *The Complete Memoirs of George Sherston.* These award-winning novels earned praise for their depiction of rural life.

It was only after World War II, that Sassoon's war poetry began to be widely appreciated. In later years his work declined in importance and reflected his increasingly religious outlook.

SAYERS, Dorothy L.

English crime writer

Born Jun. 13, 1893
Died Dec. 17, 1957
Age at death 64

Publications

1923	*Whose Body?*
1926	*Clouds of Witness*

Dorothy L(eigh) Sayers is one of England's most famous writers of detective stories. She is best known for her aristocratic detective, Lord Peter Wimsey, but she also wrote religious plays. Sayers's detective stories are now considered classics of their kind.Well researched with clever plots and interesting backgrounds, her books also feature carefully portrayed characters.

Sayers was the daughter of a clergyman who was also a classical scholar. After graduating from Oxford University in 1915, she found few jobs open to women in which she could use her talents. At age 30, she took a job as a copywriter in an advertising agency, where she coined the slogan "It pays to advertise." Her first detective novel, *Whose Body?*, was published the year she joined the agency. A string of Wimsey novels followed, and by the time she was 38, Sayers had made enough money to give up her job. In 1936 she and a friend wrote a play about Wimsey called *Busman's Honeymoon*, which Sayers later turned into a novel.

Wimsey made Sayers rich enough to do as she liked, and she stopped writing detective novels in 1937. She then wrote several religious plays and a radio series, *The Man Born to Be King*, which attracted criticism because Jesus was one of the speaking characters. In 1926 she had married Captain Fleming, a soldier whose health had been shattered in World War I. She cared for him until he died in 1950. A fine scholar, she also translated part of DANTE's *Divine Comedy* from Italian into English in her later years.

1930 Strong Poison
1930 The Documents in the Case
1933 Murder Must Advertise
1934 The Nine Tailors
1935 Gaudy Night
1936 Busman's Honeymoon
1937 The Zeal of Thy House
1943 The Man Born to Be King

SCARRY, Richard

American children's writer

Born Jun. 5, 1919
Died Apr. 30, 1994
Age at death 74

Richard Scarry has created a whole world populated by animal characters. Lowly the Worm, Sergeant Murphy, Sam and Dudley, and Huckle Cat are just a few of his creations that have enchanted young children for many years.

Scarry was born in Boston. After graduating from secondary school, he studied at the Boston Museum School of Fine Arts from 1938 to 1941. During World War II, he served in the army and spent time in North Africa. As part of his job he drew maps and designed entertaining or informative pictures. Scarry left the army in 1946 and worked as a children's book illustrator in New York City. The first books he helped write were produced with his wife Patsy Murphy. The couple lived in Connecticut before moving to Switzerland in 1968.

Scarry's first big success was *Richard Scarry's Best Word Book Ever*, which came out when he was 44. It defines and illustrates over 1,400 objects within various stories and is still one of his most popular books. Equally well known is his Busy, Busy World series in which animals from all over the world get caught up in exciting, madcap adventures. Although they are all animals, Scarry's characters act like people – they wear clothes, live in houses and hold human jobs. Scarry's stories are told in pictures and words. His illustrations are detailed and easily catch the eye of small children. In the stories from *Busy, Busy World*, and the mysteries and picture dictionaries, Scarry's characters discover how things work, how they are made, and what people do at work in an educational and entertaining way.

Publications

1951 The Great Big Car and Truck Book
1960 Tinker and Tanker
1963 Richard Scarry's Best Word Book Ever
1965 Busy, Busy World
1968 What Do People Do All Day?
1969 The Great Pie Robbery
1987 Lowly Worm's Schoolbag
1991 Watch Your Step, Mr. Rabbit!

SCHILLER, Friedrich von

German playwright and poet

Born Nov. 10, 1759
Died May 9, 1805
Age at death 45

Friedrich von Schiller is one of the greatest writers in the history of German literature.

Schiller's father was an officer in the army of the small German state of Württemberg and insisted that his son attend the military academy. Schiller hated the academy and was eventually thrown out for writing a controversial essay on religion. At age 21, he was forced to join his father's regiment.

Despite his father's warnings Schiller continued to write. His first play, *The Robbers*, was performed when he was 22. It was popular with audiences, but Schiller was nearly arrested for neglecting his military duties and had to flee from Württemberg.

Freed from his duties he wrote plays that savagely attacked the corruption and bad rule he saw in many German states. He also wrote poetry; one of his best poems, "Ode to Joy," was later set to music by the famous German composer Beethoven.

While living in the city of Jena, Schiller became a close friend of the great German dramatist and poet JOHANN WOLFGANG VON GOETHE. The two men worked together on a number of plays, and through Goethe's influence Schiller was appointed Professor of History at the city's university. Schiller became fascinated with the study of history, philosophy and the theory of art. He began to explore complex philosophical ideas in his plays and poems.

Schiller's last plays are masterpieces of historical drama. They include *Maria Stuart*, about Queen Elizabeth I of England and Mary Queen of Scots; *The Maid of Orleans*, about Joan of Arc; and *William Tell*, about the Swiss hero of that name.

Publications

1781	*The Robbers*
1783	*Fiesco*
1784	*Intrigue and Love*
1787	*Don Carlos*
1798–99	*Wallenstein*
1799	*Song of the Bell*
1800	*Maria Stuart*
1801	*The Maid of Orleans*
1803	*The Bride of Messina*
1804	*William Tell*

SCHREINER, Olive

South African novelist

Born Mar. 24, 1855
Died Dec. 11, 1920
Age at death 65

Olive Schreiner is one of the most famous white African authors who wrote in English. Her book, *The Story of an African Farm*, has been described as the first great South African novel. It is considered a classic for its groundbreaking analysis of relationships between men and women and among different races.

Schreiner was born in the British-ruled Cape Colony, now part of South Africa. Her father was a German missionary, and she grew up in isolated rural communities. Largely self-educated, she earned her living from 1874 to 1881 working as a governess. During this time, she wrote *The Story of an African Farm*, partly based on her own life. It tells of a girl growing up and her struggle for independence. Her views on religion and marriage were to cause great controversy when Schreiner moved to England in 1881 and published it under the pen name Ralph Iron. It was widely read for its descriptions of African landscapes and anti-Christian and feminist views.

Schreiner returned to South Africa in 1889 and married the politician Samuel C. Cronwright, who took her name. Her next major work was *Trooper Peter Halket of Mashonaland*. It mocked the activities of British politician Cecil Rhodes, who was ruthlessly trying to extend British rule from the Cape to North Africa. Most of her later work was nonfiction. It focused on political and social issues such as the Boer War and women's rights. In fact, her book *Woman and Labor* became a "bible" for the early women's movement.

Publications

1883 The Story of an African Farm
1891 Dreams
1893 Dream Life and Real Life
1897 Trooper Peter Halket of Mashonaland
1911 Woman and Labor

Published after she died

1926 From Men to Men
1928 Undine

SCHWARTZ, Delmore

American poet and short-story writer

Born Dec. 8, 1913
Died Jul. 11, 1966
Age at death 52

Delmore Schwartz was one of the outstanding American poets of his time.

Schwartz's parents were Romanian-Jewish immigrants; he was born in Brooklyn and lived in Manhattan from the age of 14. His parents' marriage was unhappy, and his father left in 1923. Schwartz attended George Washington High School, in whose school magazine his poems were first published, and New York University. An exceptional student, he earned his degree in 1935 and then undertook postgraduate work at Harvard. Schwartz returned to New York in 1937, and contributed poems and prose to various magazines and journals.

Schwartz's first published collection, *In Dreams Begin Responsibilities*, appeared when he was 25. It gained immediate critical praise, and Schwartz was compared to W.H. AUDEN, the famous English poet of the 1930s who was well known in America. The title poem draws on Schwartz's emotions while growing up with his feuding parents. In the poem "The heavy bear who goes with me," Schwartz uses the image of the circus bear to represent the stumbling, fumbling human poet and his desire to achieve a less clumsy, spiritual existence.

Schwartz served as poetry editor of both the *Partisan Review* and the *New Republic* and, from 1943 onward, introduced many new poets to the American public. Sadly, his initial promise as a writer declined as his mental instability and drug dependency increased. His reputation as a brilliant poet rests on only a small body of work.

Publications

1938 In Dreams Begin Responsibilities
1941 Shenandoah
1943 Genesis: Book One
1948 The World Is a Wedding
1950 Vaudeville for a Princess
1959 Summer Knowledge
1961 Successful Love

Published after he died

1979 Last and Lost Poems of Delmore Schwartz

SCOTT, Duncan Campbell

Canadian poet and short-story writer

Born Aug. 2, 1862
Died Dec. 19, 1947
Age at death 85

Publications

1893 The Magic House
1896 In the Village of Viger
1898 Labor and the Angel
1905 New World Lyrics and Ballads
1906 Via Borealis
1916 Lundy's Lane and Other Poems
1921 Beauty and Life
1923 The Witching of Elspie
1935 The Green Cloister
1947 The Circle of Affection

Duncan Campbell Scott is remembered as one of Canada's favorite poets of the early 20th century, particularly for his "Indian poems," describing the lives of Native Americans in the north of Canada.

Scott was born in Ottawa. His father was a Methodist minister, and the family moved frequently for his work. After graduating from university in Quebec, Scott joined the civil service. There he remained until his retirement, working as a superintendent with the Canadian Department of Indian Affairs for 50 years. At age 32, he married a Boston violinist, Belle Botsford. He remarried after her death, when he was almost 70.

Although poetry was only a hobby for Scott, he published several successful volumes. The first, *The Magic House*, appeared when he was 31; it was followed by *Labor and the Angel* a few years later. But it was his book *New World Lyrics and Ballads* that made his reputation.

Scott's work with the Department of Indian Affairs – for which he made difficult journeys into northern Canada – brought him close to the issues affecting Canada's native population. He was sympathetic to the injustices suffered by Native Americans and described, in the so-called Indian poems in *New World Lyrics and Ballads*, how their culture suffered from being uprooted. He also described the clash between Native American culture and that of the settling communities in Canada.

Scott also published two collections of short stories and contributed to a weekly newspaper column.

SCOTT, Paul

English novelist

Born Mar. 25, 1920
Died Mar. 1, 1978
Age at death 57

Paul Scott is best known for his four novels – *The Jewel in the Crown*, *The Day of the Scorpion*, *The Towers of Silence* and *A Division of the Spoils* – that make up *The Raj Quartet*. The quartet paints a complex and vivid picture of India in the years leading up to independence from British rule.

Scott was born in London, the son of two commercial artists. His childhood was a happy one. His parents sent him to a nearby public school, Winchmore Hill Collegiate School, but he had to leave at 16 after his father's business failed. He had dreamed of becoming an artist or writer but instead found a job as an accountant.

During World War II, Scott joined the army. He got married the following year but had to leave his wife in 1943 to go to India as an air-supply officer. He was there for only three years, but the country and the strained relationship between the Indians and the British made a deep impression on him. His thoughts and feelings are recorded in some of the poems and plays he wrote during this period.

After the war, Scott and his family settled in London. He worked in publishing and then as a literary agent. When he was 32, his first novel, *Johnnie Sahib*, was published. Scott became a full-time writer eight years later. This had a bad effect on his family, since he would shut himself away for days in his study, working and drinking. Eventually, his wife left him.

Scott's final novel, *Staying On*, won a major British award. However, *The Raj Quartet*, which was less successful when it was published, is now recognized as his finest work.

Publications

1952	*Johnnie Sahib*
1953	*The Alien Sky*
1958	*The Mark of the Warrior*
1960	*The Chinese Love Pavilion*
1962	*The Birds of Paradise*
1966	*The Jewel in the Crown*
1968	*The Day of the Scorpion*
1971	*The Towers of Silence*
1975	*A Division of the Spoils*
1977	*Staying On*

SCOTT, Sir Walter

Scottish novelist and poet

Born Aug. 15, 1771
Died Sep. 21, 1832
Age at death 61

Sir Walter Scott wrote romantic adventure stories and poems of past times, often set in Scotland.They influenced the historical novels of JAMES FENIMORE COOPER, ALEXANDRE DUMAS, ALEKSANDR PUSHKIN and others.

Scott was born in Edinburgh, the son of a lawyer and a doctor's daughter. He attended Edinburgh University and trained as a lawyer. He was married at 26 and had five children.

In spare time from his legal work, Scott walked and rode around the countryside, collecting the old ballads people sang. These had fascinated him since his boyhood, which he spent near Scotland's border with England. Scott's ballads appeared in a three-volume collection called *Minstrelsy of the Scottish Border* when he was 31. Soon after came *The Lay of the Last Minstrel*, his own long poem about an old border country legend. By 40, Scott had written two more story-poems and was rich and famous. He bought a border country estate and began building a mansion beside the River Tweed.

Scott was 43 when he wrote *Waverley*, the first of his 27 novels. *Waverley* deals with the rebellion of 1745, which attempted to restore a Scottish family to the British throne. Like most of his later novels, this has a hero whose loyalty is split between two rulers or two ways of life.

Scott eventually worked himself into ill health trying to pay off a large debt left to him by his partners in a publishing firm.

Publications

1802–03	*Minstrelsy of the Scottish Border*
1805	*The Lay of the Last Minstrel*
1808	*Marmion*
1810	*The Lady of the Lake*
1814	*Waverley*
1815	*Guy Mannering*
1816	*Old Mortality*
1817	*Rob Roy*
1818	*The Heart of Midlothian*
1819	*Ivanhoe*

SEFERIS, George

Greek poet, essayist and critic

Born Mar. 13, 1900
Died Sep. 20, 1971
Age at death 71

In 1963, George Seferis became the first Greek to win the Nobel Prize.

Seferis was the son of a university professor; he was born in Smyrna (now Izmir), which was then Greek but became part of Turkey in 1922. Seferis – a man of high intelligence and great honesty – studied law in France and England and then entered the diplomatic service at the age of 26. Over the next 36 years, he lived in many different places while working as a diplomat. His political outlook was, however, colored by his hatred of the Turks.

Seferis's first published collection of poems, *Turning Point*, which appeared when he was 31, caused a sensation in his homeland. As the title suggests, it was a remarkable change from the work of other Greek poets and firmly set aside the depressing hopeless tone that had become characteristic of Greek poetry. Seferis's work is extremely stylish and sophisticated and shows influences of both T.S. ELIOT and EZRA POUND.

Myth-History, Seferis's second collection, is generally considered his masterpiece. Most of the characters are taken from the ancient Greek poet HOMER's *Odyssey* – the ordinary sailors and soldiers referred to only in passing in the original. In these poems Seferis manages to bridge the gap between ancient legends and the less heroic present. The refined, singing quality of his writing and his use of clear, direct language was like a new breath of life in Greek poetry. His work expressed his intense feeling for modern humanity in general and the tragic wartime situation of Greece in particular.

Publications

1931 Turning Point
1932 The Cistern
1935 Myth-History
1940 Logbook I
1944 Logbook II
1947 The Thrush
1955 Logbook III
1966 On the Greek Style
1966 Three Secret Poems
1969 Collected Poems

SEGHERS, Anna

German novelist and short-story writer

Born Nov. 19, 1900
Died Jun. 1, 1983
Age at death 82

Anna Seghers is best remembered for her novels about the persecution of Jews and other groups in Germany under the rule of the Nazis.

Anna Seghers is the pen name used by Netty Reiling. She was born into a wealthy Jewish family in Mainz, Germany. Her father was an art dealer, and Netty had a cultured upbringing. She studied at Heidelberg University, where she earned a Ph.D. at age 24. The following year Seghers married a political writer named Lászlo Radványi.

At age 28, Seghers joined the Communist Party. That year she won an important prize for her short novel *The Revolt of the Fishermen*, in which she described a revolt by fishermen against their employer. It sets out what became a key theme in Seghers's life and writing: that individuals need to work together to fight oppression.

When Adolf Hitler's Nazi party came to power in 1933, Seghers's writing was banned. She fled to Paris; then, in 1940, she and her family settled in Mexico, where she wrote her most famous work. *The Seventh Cross* describes an attempted escape by seven prisoners from a German concentration camp during World War II. All but one are killed by the Nazis; the seventh escapes and gives hope to other inmates. The novel was later made into a movie.

Seghers became involved in the cultural and political development of socialist East Germany after returning in 1947. Remaining an active member of the Communist Party, she inspired younger writers, including CHRISTA WOLF.

Publications

1928	*The Revolt of the Fishermen*
1933	*A Price on His Head*
1942	*The Seventh Cross*
1944	*Transit*
1946	*The Excursion of the Dead Girls*
1949	*The Dead Stay Young*
1959	*The Decision*
1965	*The Strength of the Weak*
1968	*The Confidence*
1971	*The Crossing*

SEIFERT, Jaroslav

Czech poet

Born Sep. 23, 1901
Died Jan. 10, 1986
Age at death 84

Jaroslav Seifert is an important Czech poet noted for having been awarded the Nobel Prize for Literature in 1984.

Seifert was born into a poor working-class family in a suburb of Prague, Czechoslovakia (now the Czech Republic), and grew up a dedicated socialist with great enthusiasm for the Russian Revolution of 1917. He joined the Communist Party and earned his living as a journalist.

Seifert's early poetry reflects his deep human sympathy and his approval of the caring aspects of socialism. His first published work, a poetry collection entitled *The City in Tears*, is an angry protest at the human waste of World War I and a call for a workers' revolution. As is often the case with intellectuals, Seifert became more critical of socialism as he grew older, and his passion for socialist causes weakened. His later poetry was lyrical, more personal, and less concerned with politics.

When he was 22, Seifert moved to France and settled in Paris and, in 1929, he was expelled from the Communist Party. Politics again came to the fore in his work when Adolf Hitler took over part of Czechoslovakia at the beginning of World War II. The 1945 Prague uprising, in which the Czech people rose in resistance against the Nazi forces, prompted his grieving response in *The Helmet of Clay*. In 1966, his country recognized his merits by naming him Poet of the Nation, but two years later he was again in trouble when he condemned the Soviet invasion of Czechoslovakia.

Publications

1921	*The City in Tears*
1923	*Nothing But Love*
1925	*On Radio Waves*
1936	*The Hands of Venus*
1938	*Put Out the Lights*
1940	*Dressed in Light*
1945	*The Helmet of Clay*
1977	*The Prague Column*
1981	*All the Beauties of the World*
1986	*The Selected Poetry of Jaroslav Seifert*

SEMBÈNE Ousmane

Senegalese novelist, screenwriter and short-story writer

Born Jan. 8, 1923

Sembène Ousmane is most famous as Africa's leading filmmaker, but he is also an important writer of novels and short stories.

Sembène was born in southern Senegal (West Africa), which was then a French colony. His father was a fisherman, and after just a couple of years at school Sembène became a fisherman too. As a teenager, Sembène moved to the capital, Dakar, where he held various low-paid jobs such as bricklayer and mechanic. When World War II broke out, 19-year-old Sembène was drafted into the French Army. He served in Europe, returning to Senegal in 1947 at the beginning of the bitter strike by African railway workers. The strike caught Sembène's attention, and he got involved in trade union activities. Sembène returned to France in 1948 as a stowaway aboard a ship, and for the next ten years he worked as a docker in the southern port of Marseilles, eventually becoming a trade union leader for African workers.

Sembène began to write when he was in Marseilles. He decided to write in French to reach a wider audience. *The Black Docker*, his autobiographical novel, came out when he was 33. It was moderately successful, and when Sembène was unable to continue manual work after injuring his back, he returned to Dakar to write full time. His third novel, *God's Bits of Wood*, firmly established his reputation. It described the 1947–48 rail strike – a major event in the fight against French rule.

In the late 1960s, Sembène turned to making films, again to reach a wider audience. Many are based on his own novels or short stories.

Publications

1956	*The Black Docker*
1957	*O My Country, My Beautiful People*
1960	*God's Bits of Wood*
1961	"Black Girl"
1962	*Tribal Scars*
1965	*The Money-Order, with White Genesis*
1971	*Emitai*
1973	*Impotence*
1981	*The Last of the Empire*

SENDAK, Maurice

American children's writer

Born Jun. 10, 1928

American writer and illustrator Maurice Sendak is internationally famous for his children's books.

Born in Brooklyn, New York City, to poor Jewish-Polish immigrants, Sendak hated school, preferring comics, movies and the bedtime folklore stories told by his father.

Sendak began his working life as a window dresser and toymaker by day while attending art school at night. He began illustrating books when he was 19, and wrote and illustrated his first book, *Kenny's Window*, when he was 28. He achieved his great success with *Where the Wild Things Are*, in which he created a unique fantasy world. He wrote two other books in the same series, *In the Night Kitchen* and *Outside Over There*. The wild things of the first title were modeled on childhood memories, and in the second book he used the experience of getting lost at the New York World's Fair.

Some critics consider *Where the Wild Things Are* too frightening, but children love it. The book won the American Library Association's Caldecott Medal, sold more than 2.5 million copies, and was adapted as an opera, for which Sendak designed the sets and costumes. He went on to design for other operas, such as Mozart's *The Magic Flute* and an opera based on his story *Higglety Pigglety Pop!*

Sendak developed the illustrated children's book into a new form, where words and text are closely linked. He was awarded the HANS CHRISTIAN ANDERSEN International Medal in 1970, the first American to win it, and the LAURA INGALLS WILDER Award in 1983.

Publications

1956	*Kenny's Window*
1960	*The Sign on Rosie's Door*
1962	*Nutshell Library*
1963	*Where the Wild Things Are*
1967	*Higglety Pigglety Pop!*
1970	*In the Night Kitchen*
1977	*Seven Little Monsters*
1981	*Outside Over There*
1993	*We Are All in the Dumps with Jack and Guy*

SENGHOR, Léopold Sédar

Senegalese poet

Born Oct. 9, 1906

Léopold Sédar Senghor has been described as the greatest of the African poets to write in a European language. He was born in Senegal, which was then part of the French West Africa colony. His family was Christian, and he was sent to a missionary school to become a priest. At the age of 20, he abandoned this career and switched schools.

In 1928, Senghor went to Paris, France, to study at the Sorbonne university. He was one of the group of African and Caribbean students based there who founded the literary and philosophical movement called Negritude ("Blackness") in the 1930s. It began as a protest against French rule in Africa. Negritude celebrated African history and the positive values of African culture. Senghor became one of the movement's leading thinkers. He wrote verse in French and edited a collection of Negritude poetry. The movement reached its height in the 1930s and '40s, and inspired many modern African writers.

World War II in Europe broke out in 1939, and Senghor joined the French Army. He was captured in 1940, and held for two years in a Nazi concentration camp where he wrote some of his finest poems. In 1946 Senghor was elected to the French National Assembly as a deputy for Senegal. The following year he helped establish *Présence Africaine*, which became the most important literary journal in the black world. Senegal became independent in 1960 with Senghor as president. He remained president for the next 20 years.

Publications

1945	*Songs of Shadow*
1948	*Black Offerings*
1956	*Ethiopics*
1961	*Nocturnes*
1964	*Selected Poems*
1964	*On African Socialism*
1975	*Negritude and Humanism*
1979	*Major Elegies*

SERLING, Rod

American television playwright and screenwriter

Born Dec. 25, 1924
Died Jun. 28, 1975
Age at death 50

Publications

1955	Patterns
1956	Requiem for a Heavyweight
1957	The Comedian
1960	Stories from the Twilight Zone
1961	More Stories from the Twilight Zone
1965	New Stories from the Twilight Zone
1967	The Season to Be Wary
1971	Night Gallery
1972	Night Gallery 2

Rod Serling was an American television and movie writer best known as the creator of the television series *The Twilight Zone*.

Serling, the son of a butcher, was born and raised in upstate New York. Following service as a paratrooper in World War II, he attended Antioch College, Ohio, where he began writing television scripts. He was rejected 40 times before he sold his first television play at age 26.

During the 1950s, Serling was a freelance script writer of live television dramas. His early works often dealt with social issues and emphasized character analysis. Among his most important teleplays are *Patterns*, about the pressures of big business; *Requiem for a Heavyweight*, about a lonely, confused boxer at the end of his career; and *The Comedian*, about a man who exploits others to further his career. Serling won Emmy Awards for all these works.

Battles with television networks over censorship led Serling to develop his own TV series. Created when he was 35, *The Twilight Zone* ran from 1959 to 1964. Serling wrote many of the stories that appeared in the series, and he used them to explore social issues that the networks would not have accepted in more realistic settings. A major theme was that there are forces in the universe which people cannot control.

Serling's success as a television writer led him to work on screenplays. His best include *Seven Days in May*, about an attempted military takeover of America, and *Planet of the Apes*, about a space traveler who returns to find that his planet has been taken over by apes.

SEUSS, Dr.

American children's writer

Born Mar. 2, 1904
Died Sep. 24, 1991
Age at death 87

Publications

1937	And to Think That I Saw It on Mulberry Street

Dr. Seuss was the creator of many well-loved children's books. His real name was Theodor Seuss Geisel.

Seuss was born in Springfield, Massachusetts, into a German-American family. His father owned a brewery, and Seuss had a comfortable, happy childhood. He studied English literature at Dartmouth College, where he was editor of the college humor magazine, then went to Oxford University, where he met an American student, Helen Palmer. They married in 1927. Seuss had spent his time learning to draw, rather than studying, while at Oxford and earned a living as a cartoonist. In 1936, on board a ship returning to the US, he wrote and illustrated his first children's book, *And to Think That I Saw It on Mulberry Street* – a humorous book with rhyming text.

Although rejected by 27 publishers, it was finally published a year later when Seuss was 33, and it was immediately popular. He knew how to appeal to children, even though he never had any of his own.

During World War II, Seuss wrote films for the war effort but returned to children's books afterward with *McElligot's Pool* and wrote and illustrated over 40 more, working for much of the time with his wife as editor. Particularly successful were *How the Grinch Stole Christmas*, *The Cat in the Hat* (a revolutionary primary one reader), and *Green Eggs and Ham*, all in his zany nonsense style. He won an Academy Award for his animated cartoon character Gerald McBoing-Boing and in 1984 was given a special Pulitzer Prize for his lifetime contribution to children's literature.

1947 McElligot's Pool
1954 Horton Hears a Who
1957 How the Grinch Stole Christmas
1957 The Cat in the Hat
1958 Yertle the Turtle
1960 Green Eggs and Ham
1960 Fox in Socks
1971 The Lorax

Published after he died
1998 Hooray for Diffendoofer Day

SEWELL, Anna

English author Anna Sewell wrote one of the most famous children's stories of all time, *Black Beauty*.

Born in a coastal town, daughter of Quaker parents Mary and Isaac Sewell, Anna moved with her family to London, where Isaac opened a clothing shop. The neighborhood was busy, noisy and dirty, and Mary Sewell liked to take the children to spend summers on a relative's farm in the country.

Both Anna and her brother Phillip were taught at home by their mother – natural history, as well as moral behavior. Anna went to school for the first time when she was 12. Running home one day, she fell and injured her foot and never fully recovered her health.

The family moved frequently, sometimes living in the country and sometimes in towns. Anna learned to drive a pony and cart, which helped her get around when walking was difficult. She never married.

In 1867, Anna and Mary Sewell settled near the family farm. When she was 50, Sewell began to write a book about the life of a horse, which became the novel *Black Beauty*. Now an invalid, lying down most of the day, she wrote short pieces at a time, which her mother copied out. The completed work was sold to a London publisher for a relatively small amount. The book was an immediate bestseller; in the US alone it sold a million copies within two years. Based on observations of places, people and horses she had known, Sewell's book is a plea for kindness to animals and for the moral values taught by her mother – the evils of alcohol and the virtues of hard work and responsible behavior. Unfortunately, Sewell did not live to see its enormous success.

English children's writer

Born Mar. 30, 1820
Died Apr. 25, 1878
Age at death 58

Publications
1877 Black Beauty

Published after she died
1907 Autobiography

SEXTON, Anne

American poet

Born Nov. 9, 1928
Died Oct. 4, 1974
Age at death 45

Anne Sexton was a Pulitzer Prize-winning poet whose work was often criticized for speaking out about women's most private experiences, including menstruation, abortion and abuse. She suffered from depression for much of her life and committed suicide at age 45.

Sexton had a privileged background, growing up in a well-to-do family in Massachusetts. But she was rebellious and felt unloved by her parents, and she left home at age 19 to marry. She worked as a model and then began writing poetry when she was 28 – as a form of therapy after her first suicide attempt. By the early 1960s, people were beginning to recognize her as an important new poet.

Like SYLVIA PLATH – with whom she was friends – Sexton explored the mixed emotions of motherhood; she also had two children, and their needs often conflicted with her own depression and need for psychiatric care. Her first poetry collection, *To Bedlam and Part Way Back*, came out when she was 32. It is about the guilt associated with her depression and describes the helplessness felt by mental patients. Although her subject matter was often controversial – she was labeled a "confessional" poet for writing so openly about her own emotions – she was also critically acclaimed. *Live or Die* won the Pulitzer Prize for poetry in 1967, and Sexton was awarded a number of fellowships and other honors. In *Transformations* she retold the fairy tales of the BROTHERS GRIMM, and she worked with fellow poet MAXINE KUMIN on a number of children's books.

Publications

1960 To Bedlam and Part Way Back
1962 All My Pretty Ones
1966 Live or Die
1969 Love Poems
1971 Transformations
1972 The Book of Folly

Published after she died

1975 The Awful Rowing Toward God
1976 45 Mercy Street

SHAKESPEARE, William

English playwright and poet

Born c. Apr. 23, 1564
Died Apr. 23, 1616
Age at death c. 52

Shakespeare is considered the greatest playwright and poet in the English language. Some of his plays, such as *Hamlet* and *Romeo and Juliet*, are among the most famous literary works in the world. With great insight into human nature, he created memorable characters from all walks of life.

Shakespeare was born in Stratford-upon-Avon, a small country town in England. His father became the town mayor, and his mother was the daughter of a local landowner. Very little is known about Shakespeare's early life, but it is likely that he was educated at Stratford Grammar School. At age 18, he married a local woman, Anne Hathaway, and together they had three children.

By the end of 1592, Shakespeare, then 28, was in London working

Publications

Approximate dates

1593 The Taming of the Shrew
1594 Romeo and Juliet

as an actor and a playwright. He had already written several successful plays by this time, although the exact dates are not known. From 1594 to about 1612, he was a partner in a theater group called first The Chamberlain's Men and later The King's Men. He wrote many great plays for the group, and by 1599 their success had allowed them to build a new theater called The Globe. In 1609, a collection of 154 sonnets written by Shakespeare was published. They include some of the finest poems ever written.

By the time he was 49, Shakespeare had retired from writing and returned to Stratford to be with his family. He had written at least 37 plays, ranging from hilarious comedies to dark tragedies, which established his reputation as the best playwright of his time. Almost all of his plays are still performed today, more than 400 years later.

1595	*A Midsummer Night's Dream*
1596	*The Merchant of Venice*
1599	*Julius Caesar*
1599	*As You Like It*
1601	*Twelfth Night*
1602	*Hamlet*
1604	*Othello*
1605	*King Lear*
1605	*Macbeth*
1606	*Antony and Cleopatra*
1611	*The Tempest*

SHANGE, Ntozake

American playwright, poet and novelist

Born Oct. 18, 1948

Ntozake Shange is a celebrated playwright best known for her dramatic poem *For Colored Girls Who Have Considered Suicide / When the Rainbow Is Enuf*, which took Broadway by storm when she was just 28.

Shange was born Paulette Williams in Trenton, New Jersey. As a child she was surrounded by positive role models of creative and professional African Americans: her father was the local doctor, and her mother was a social worker and teacher. Visitors to the house included the writer W.E.B. Du Bois and the musicians Duke Ellington and Dizzy Gillespie. When Shange was eight, the family moved to St. Louis, and she describes their community there as a vibrant multicultural mix. But Shange, who was a bright student, was sent to a mostly white school, and there she came up against racism and segregation. When she went to Barnard College in New York, she began to find her own way: in poetry and in the Black Power and anti-Vietnam War movements. She graduated in 1970, and the following year, at age 23, she adopted her African name.

For Colored Girls, described by Toni Cade Bambara as a celebration of "women's loyalties to women," uses music, dance and poetry to describe the growing up of a young African-American woman. It is full of anger, pain and triumph. The play won an Obie Award for drama and was received enthusiastically by critics. Other works include her first novel, *Sassafrass, Cypress & Indigo*, published when she was 34, and the poetry collections *Nappy Edges* and *A Daughter's Geography*. Shange has one daughter, Savannah, and lives and teaches in Houston, Texas.

Publications

1975	*For Colored Girls Who Have Considered Suicide / When the Rainbow Is Enuf*
1978	*Nappy Edges*
1981	*Three Pieces*
1982	*Sassafrass, Cypress & Indigo*
1983	*A Daughter's Geography*
1991	*The Love Space Demands*
1994	*Liliane*

SHAPIRO, Karl

American poet and critic

Born Nov. 10, 1913
Died May 14, 2000
Age at death 86

Karl Shapiro is a leading American poet who uses both traditional and experimental styles in his poems, which attack the values of the middle classes.

Shapiro was born into a Jewish family in Baltimore, Maryland, and attended both the University of Virginia and Johns Hopkins in Baltimore before serving in the US Army during World War II. Although he had already published his first collection of poems at age 22, he began his working life in the family-run business.

By 1948, however, Shapiro was pursuing an academic career that took him to several universities. During this time he wrote many volumes of poetry, essays and criticism, notably *In Defense of Ignorance*, in which he attacks the highly learned verse of poets like Ezra Pound and T.S. Eliot.

Shapiro was not an optimistic poet, and he did not use his poetry to rouse people to action. Instead, his work described, sometimes with shocking detail, middle-class values and false beliefs. Shapiro's style changed over the course of his career. His early works are formal, such as *V-Letter and Other Poems*, which won the Pulitzer Prize in 1945. This collection includes some of the best war poems ever written by an American. However, in the 1950s and '60s, he turned against traditional forms. The best example from this period is *The Bourgeois Poet*, which was written in an experimental style more like prose than poetry. His more recent writing showed a return to traditional forms such as the sonnet, which give added structure to his often mocking and satirical poetic voice.

Publications

1935 Poems
1944 V-Letter and Other Poems
1960 In Defense of Ignorance
1964 The Bourgeois Poet
1968 Selected Poems
1976 Adult Bookstore
1978 Collected Poems 1940–78
1987 New and Selected Poems 1940–86
1994 A Day's Portion

SHAW, George Bernard

Irish playwright, critic and essayist

Born Jul. 26, 1856
Died Nov. 2, 1950
Age at death 94

George Bernard Shaw is probably Ireland's most famous playwright. During his long life he wrote over 50 plays. A powerful public speaker and a great wit, he was awarded the Nobel Prize for Literature in 1925.

Born in Dublin, Shaw had a troubled childhood. His father drank heavily, and his mother eventually left the family home to teach music in London. This, and a strong religious education, shaped many of his views. He was a teetotaller, a vegetarian, a supporter of women's rights and a strong critic of Victorian society. He defends his views in his essays, which are noted for their clarity of expression and wit.

When he was 20, Shaw joined his mother in London, where he

became a respected critic. It was during this time that he encountered the work of the playwright Henrik Ibsen, whose realistic dramas were a great influence on his thinking.

When he was 36, Shaw wrote his first play, *Widower's Houses*, which criticizes slum landlords. This was the first of three plays that together Shaw labeled "Plays Unpleasant" because they dealt with subjects that many people wanted to ignore. A lifelong socialist, Shaw helped found the Fabian Society, which believed in reforming society in a way that was fair to all people.

Pygmalion is probably Shaw's best-known play. The story, which criticizes the British class system, was the basis for the popular musical *My Fair Lady*. However, *Saint Joan*, which tells the story of Joan of Arc, is widely regarded as his masterpiece.

Publications

1891	*The Quintessence of Ibsenism*
1892	*Widower's Houses*
1894	*Arms and the Man*
1902	*Mrs. Warren's Profession*
1903	*Man and Superman*
1912	*Pygmalion*
1913	*Androcles and the Lion*
1919	*Heartbreak House*
1921	*Back to Methuselah*
1923	*Saint Joan*

SHELDON, Sidney

American novelist, playwright and screenwriter

Born Feb. 11, 1917

Sidney Sheldon is one of the most popular authors in the world. As well as novels, he has written and produced plays, screenplays and television shows.

Sheldon was born in Chicago and studied at Northwestern University for a year then, in 1941, served briefly in the US Air Force. His career in the media started when he worked as a script reader for Universal Studios in Hollywood. He then began writing his own screenplays, starting with *Borrowed Hero* when he was 24. In his late 20s, Sheldon started writing plays for the theater, and he continued to write screenplays and stageplays for the next 20 years. Many won awards, including an Oscar, two Screen Writers' Guild awards and a "Tony" award. His successful television shows included *I Dream of Jeannie*, which won an Emmy, and *Hart to Hart*.

Sheldon started writing novels when, at the age of 50, he had an idea that would not have worked as a screenplay. This idea was to become his first novel, *The Naked Face*, published when he was 53. It did not sell very well but received an Edgar Award from The Mystery Writers of America. He went on to write *The Other Side of Midnight*, which has since sold over seven million copies. Nearly all of his books after this became bestsellers. Many critics say that Sheldon's work is not "great literature," but he does write exciting stories with great plots, strong female heroines, and exotic locations, which explains why he has such a large following. Sheldon now has a star on Hollywood's Walk of Fame.

Publications

1943	*The Merry Widow*
1959	*Redhead*
1970	*The Naked Face*
1974	*The Other Side of Midnight*
1976	*A Stranger in the Mirror*
1977	*Bloodline*
1980	*Rage of Angels*
1988	*Windmills of the Gods*
1992	*The Stars Shine Down*
1995	*Morning, Noon, and Night*

SHELLEY, Mary

English horror writer

Born Aug. 30, 1797
Died Feb. 1, 1851
Age at death 53

Mary Shelley is best known as the author of the novel *Frankenstein*, one of the first horror stories.

Born Mary Wollstonecraft Godwin in London, she was the daughter of William Godwin and Mary Wollstonecraft. Her father was a political writer and novelist who had revolutionary attitudes to most social institutions, including marriage. Her mother, also a famous writer, was one of the first feminists; she died 11 days after Mary's birth.

Educated at home, where she met her father's literary friends, Mary eloped to France with the poet PERCY BYSSHE SHELLEY when she was 16. Their first child, a daughter, died in Venice, Italy, a few years later. They returned to England, where their son, William, was born. They married after Percy's first wife committed suicide. Tragedy was never far from their lives. After their return to Italy, William died in 1819.

Frankenstein, Shelley's first novel, was published when she was 21. In the style of the gloomy and sinister gothic novels popular at the time, it deals with the ambitions of a young scientist to be the creator of life, the horrors that follow his experiment, and his destruction by the monster he creates. It was immediately successful and has retained its fascination, becoming the subject of many movies and plays.

After her husband's death in 1822, Shelley returned to England. Her second novel, *Valperga*, was published when she was 26. She also wrote verse, accounts of her travels, and four more novels, including one set in the future about the destruction of the human race, *The Last Man*. None achieved the success of *Frankenstein*.

Publications

- *1817 History of a Six Weeks' Tour*
- *1818 Frankenstein*
- *1823 Valperga*
- *1826 The Last Man*
- *1830 The Fortunes of Perkin Warbeck*
- *1835 Lodore*
- *1837 Falkner*
- *1844 Rambles in Germany and Italy*

Published after she died

- *1987 The Journals of Mary Shelley* (2 vols)

SHELLEY, Percy Bysshe

English poet, novelist and essayist

Born Aug. 4, 1792
Died Jul. 8, 1822
Age at death 29

Percy Bysshe Shelley was one of England's greatest Romantic poets.

Shelley was born into a wealthy noble family. He was educated at Eton College, where his radical views on politics and religion earned him the nickname "Mad Shelley." While still at Eton and aged just 18, he published his first book, a gothic horror novel called *Zastrozzi*. In 1811, he was expelled from Oxford University for writing an anti-Christian pamphlet.

That same year 19-year-old Shelley shocked his family even more by secretly marrying 16-year-old Harriet Westbrook. This was the start of Shelley's adventurous life of elopements and restless travels. Three years later, Shelley eloped with Mary Wollstonecraft Godwin, who became MARY SHELLEY and who wrote the famous novel

Frankenstein. Harriet killed herself in 1816, and Shelley married his new love. Mary and Shelley moved around constantly; they traveled around Europe and lived in many different towns in England. Shelley wrote his poetry in short bursts of intense creativity. His poems, such as *Alastor* and "Ozymandias," overflow with intense emotion and radical ideas that were not always appreciated by readers of his time.

In 1818, Shelley and Mary left England to live in Italy. He completed some of his greatest poetry there, including his masterpiece *Prometheus Unbound*. A few years later, on a short sea voyage along the Italian coast, Shelley's small sailboat was caught in a storm and he was drowned. He was just 29 years old, but he had written poetry that established him as one of the greatest English poets.

Publications

1810 Zastrozzi
1813 Queen Mab
1816 Alastor
1818 The Revolt of Islam
1818 "Ozymandias"
1819 The Cenci
1820 Prometheus Unbound
1821 Adonais

Published after he died

1824 The Triumph of Life

SHEPARD, Sam

American playwright, novelist and short-story writer

Born Nov. 5, 1943

Sam Shepard is one of America's most successful playwrights, and he has written more than 40 plays since the mid-1960s.

Shepard was born in Fort Sheridan, Illinois. His father was a bomber pilot in World War II, which meant that the family moved around between various army bases, eventually settling on a ranch in California where Shepard played drums and began to enjoy rock and roll music. After graduating from secondary school and trying university for a year, Shepard decided to leave home and joined a touring theater company. He arrived in New York City at the age of 19. His first complete play, *Cowboys*, was based on his life there with his roommate. The Theater Genesis in New York produced this play when Shepard was just 21. Between 1964 and 1968, he wrote quickly and successfully, mostly one-act plays, and won 6 of his 11 Obie drama awards. In 1979 he won a Pulitzer Prize for his play *Buried Child* – a tale of incest and murder in America's heartland.

Shepard has acted in many films since the late 1970s. He starred in the movie version of his well-known play *Fool for Love* and was also nominated for an Oscar for his starring role in the film *The Right Stuff*, about the test pilot Chuck Yeager. He wrote the screenplay for the film *Paris, Texas*, which was loosely based on his book *Motel Chronicles*. Some critics feel that Shepard's plays portray women unfavorably, and others do not like the images of Western culture in his plays, which emphasize rock and roll, drugs and television. Nevertheless, his work has continued to be popular.

Publications

1964 Cowboys
1965 Chicago
1965 Icarus's Mother
1966 Red Cross
1967 La Turista
1967 Forensic and the Navigators
1978 Buried Child
1982 Motel Chronicles
1983 Fool for Love
1993 Simpatico

SHERIDAN, Richard Brinsley

Irish playwright

Born Oct. 31, 1751
Died Jul. 7, 1816
Age at death 64

The playwright Richard Brinsley Sheridan is best known for his comedies of manners.

Sheridan was born in Dublin, and the theater was in his blood. His father was an actor, and his mother had written novels and plays. However, his family had money problems, and while Sheridan was away in England being educated, the family moved to France to avoid debtors.

When Sheridan was 19, the family moved back to England, and he joined them in the city of Bath. While there he became involved in a scandal concerning a well-known singer, Elizabeth Anne Linley, over whom he later fought two duels. They were married in 1773 and then moved to London.

Once in London, Sheridan became friends with a group of writers, including DR. JOHNSON and OLIVER GOLDSMITH. Although Elizabeth's singing career could easily have supported them both, Sheridan decided to earn a living from writing. His first play, *The Rivals*, was written when he was 23. Two more followed later that year. The success of these plays led directly to Sheridan being offered the job of actor-manager of a London theater.

Sheridan's *The School for Scandal* is considered one of the most brilliant comedies of the 18th century. Like all of his plays, it makes fun of types of people Sheridan felt were cruel, stupid or self-important.

Sheridan's theatrical skills made him a natural public speaker. He became a member of the British parliament and served as a minister.

Publications

1775 The Rivals
1775 St. Patrick's Day
1775 The Duenna
1777 The School for Scandal
1779 The Critic

SHERWOOD, Robert E.

American playwright and novelist

Born Apr. 4, 1896
Died Nov. 14, 1955
Age at death 59

Robert E(mmet) Sherwood was an antiwar playwright and novelist whose work reflects the anxieties of America in the 1920s and '30s. He was awarded the Pulitzer Prize four times and won an Oscar for his screenplay *The Best Years of Our Lives*.

Sherwood was born in New Rochelle, New York. He studied at Harvard, and he then served in a Canadian regiment in World War I, during which he was wounded in both legs. His experiences left him with extreme antiwar feelings.

One of Sherwood's first plays, *The Road to Rome*, produced when he was 31, deals lightheartedly with these feelings. In it, the ancient general Hannibal tries to delay his march to Rome, preferring a peaceful solution. In his last important play, the Pulitzer Prize-win-

Publications

1927 The Road to Rome
1928 The Queen's Husband

ning *There Shall Be No Night*, the main character, a scientist, fights for freedom, even though he risks everything.

One of Sherwood's major themes is humankind's willingness to make personal sacrifices. He often uses a background of war and violence to show up the moral values of his characters.

Sherwood also experimented with other types of writing. During World War II, he was one of President Franklin D. Roosevelt's favorite speechwriters. He wrote about his experiences in his Pulitzer Prize-winning biography, *Roosevelt and Hopkins*, about the president and his personal assistant, Harry L. Hopkins.

Because Sherwood wrote about topical events, his work gives an interesting picture of American life in the first half of the 20th century.

1930 Waterloo Bridge
1931 Reunion in Vienna
1935 The Petrified Forest
1936 Idiot's Delight
1938 Abe Lincoln in Illinois
1940 There Shall Be No Night
1946 The Best Years of Our Lives
1948 Roosevelt and Hopkins

SHIELDS, Carol

American-born Canadian novelist, short-story writer and poet

Born Jun. 2, 1935

Novelist Carol Shields has only recently become known outside Canada, although she has been writing for more than two decades. Her bestselling book *The Stone Diaries* won a Pulitzer Prize in 1995.

Shields was born Carol Warner in Oak Park, near Chicago. At age 22, she graduated from Hanover College in Indiana and married a Canadian whom she had met on a visit to England. She and her husband moved to Canada, and Shields became a Canadian citizen in 1971. In 1975, she earned a Master's degree from the University of Ottawa. At age 37, she published her first volume of poetry, *Others*, followed by *Intersect* two years later.

Shields began writing about women's friendships – a subject she was interested in reading about but could not find many books on. She also wanted to explore the intellectual lives of women. Her first novel, *Small Ceremonies*, was published when she was 41. As in many of her books, the main character is a middle-aged woman, the wife of a professor but also a writer herself. Biography and autobiography feature in much of Shields's work, as do family life and marriage. In 1977, *Small Ceremonies* won the Canadian Authors' Association Award for best novel.

With *Swann: A Mystery*, which came out when she was 52, Shields's reputation became international. *The Stone Diaries*, published when she was 58, established her as a major writer. It is the fictional biography of a wife, mother and widow and explores issues such as loneliness and regret.

Publications

1972 Others
1974 Intersect
1976 Small Ceremonies
1977 The Box Garden
1980 Happenstance
1986 Various Miracles
1987 Swann: A Mystery
1989 The Orange Fish
1992 The Republic of Love
1993 The Stone Diaries
1997 Larry's Party

SHIMAZAKI, Toson

Japanese novelist and poet

Born Feb. 17, 1872
Died Aug. 22, 1943
Age at death 71

Shimazaki Toson is noted for his novels of an intensely personal nature that reveal in great detail the states of mind and emotion of the narrator. These books also illustrate the mental and emotional upheaval caused by the conflicts between traditional Japanese values and the pressures of modernization around the late 19th and early 20th centuries. His best-known work is the novel *Before the Dawn*, which has been described as one of the masterpieces of modern Japanese literature.

Shimazaki Toson was the pen name of Shimazaki Haruki, the son of a poet who was born in a village in Nagano Prefecture in the west of Japan. He was educated in Tokyo. While working as a teacher in his early 20s, he began to write poetry of a romantic type then popular with some younger writers. These poems proved immediately successful in Japan. He then turned to novel writing. His first important work, *The Broken Commandment*, was published when he was 34. It describes the struggle of a young teacher for self-realization. Groundbreaking for its realism and treatment of social issues, this book was one of Japan's first naturalistic novels. *The Family* explores the internal stresses in two rural families caused by the movement toward modernization in Japan.

One of Toson's finest works, *Before the Dawn*, recounts the effects of the social and political upheavals at the time of the Meiji Restoration of 1868, which brought back Japan's monarchy and launched the country's modern era. The hero is a tragic figure whose life ends in disillusionment and bitterness.

Publications

1897 Collection of Young Leaves
1898 Summer Grass
1906 The Broken Commandment
1908 Spring
1910–11 The Family
1912 After a Meal
1913 Gentle Breeze
1914–18 When the Cherries Ripen
1918–19 New Life
1935 Before the Dawn

SHOLOKHOV, Mikhail

Russian novelist

Born May 24, 1905
Died Feb. 21, 1984
Age at death 78

Mikhail Sholokhov is best known for his stories about the Don Cossacks, the fiercely independent horsemen of southwestern Russia. He was awarded the Nobel Prize for Literature in 1965.

Sholokhov was born in a Cossack village near the Don River. He was educated in Moscow but returned to his native village, where he lived during the Russian Revolution of 1917 and the bitter years of fighting that followed it. He later served in the communist Red Army and became a member of the Russian Communist Party.

Sholokhov began writing when he was 17. His first published book was a collection of short stories, *Tales of the Don*. He then began his most famous work, *The Quiet Don*. The first part was published when he was 23 as *And Quiet Flows the Don* and the second as *The*

Don Flows Home to the Sea, when he was 35. Set in the years 1912–22, *The Quiet Don* traces the effects of World War I, the Russian Revolution, and the Civil War on the lives of the Don Cossacks. Written with great beauty, and containing memorable characters, this epic work describes how the Don Cossacks struggled to keep their independence against the new communist government. It became the most widely read novel in Russia, and the government honored Sholokhov as a great writer.

Sholokhov wrote other novels, including *Virgin Soil Upturned*, about the impact of communist farming policies on the Don Cossacks, and *They Fought for Their Country*, a moving account of the Russian defense of St. Petersburg (then called Leningrad) during World War II.

Publications

1925 Tales of the Don
1928–40 The Quiet Don (2 parts)
1932–33 Virgin Soil Upturned
1944 They Fought for Their Country
1957 The Fate of Man
1960 Harvest on the Don
1973 Stories

SHUTE, Nevil

English-Australian novelist

Born Jan. 17, 1899
Died Jan. 12, 1960
Age at death 60

In writing his many popular novels, Nevil Shute drew on his technical expertise as an engineer and his experiences of war to tell exciting, realistic adventure stories.

Until 1938, Shute had two careers – engineer and writer. After military service in the later stages of World War I, he graduated from Oxford University and became an aeronautical engineer. He helped in the design and construction of one of the last of the British airships, the *R100*, and twice flew to America aboard it. Later, he started a company to make conventional airplanes and, at the outbreak of World War II, he became involved in the design of top-secret, specialized weapons.

Shute published his first book, *Marazan*, when he was 27. Although his books are mainly adventure stories, they are also about the morality of war. *Ordeal* imagines the effects on an English city of the deliberate bombing of civilians, a practice that had recently been seen for the first time in the Spanish Civil War.

After the war, Shute emigrated to Australia. One of his most popular books, *A Town Like Alice* (or *The Legacy*), is set in Malaya during World War II and in Australia. It was made into a movie in 1956. His later novels were all set in Australia, including perhaps his most successful book, *On the Beach*, about the survivors of a nuclear war. It sold more than two million copies and was also made into a movie. The title of Shute's autobiography, *Slide Rule*, is the name of a calculating device used by engineers before computers were developed.

Publications

1926 Marazan
1928 The Mysterious Aviator
1939 Ordeal
1942 Pied Piper
1945 Most Secret
1947 The Chequer Board
1948 No Highway
1949 A Town Like Alice (or *The Legacy*)
1954 Slide Rule
1957 On the Beach

SIDNEY, Sir Philip

English poet and essayist

Born Nov. 30, 1554
Died Oct. 17, 1586
Age at death 31

Sir Philip Sidney was one of the finest English poets of the 16th century. He was regarded as the ideal gentleman of the time. He was so much admired that the tombstone of his biographer, Fulke Greville, had the inscription "friend to Sir Philip Sidney."

Sidney came from a family of important aristocrats. After studying at Oxford University, he spent three years traveling in Europe, becoming fluent in French, Italian and Latin – then the international language. When he was 21, Queen Elizabeth gave him a minor court appointment, and soon after she sent him as an ambassador to the German emperor Rudolf II.

By Sidney's own wish none of his work was published during his lifetime. His first work, written when he was 24, was *The Lady of May*, a short play dedicated to the queen. Soon after he wrote a long prose romance for his sister Mary, Countess of Pembroke. His greatest work was a set of sonnets, *Astrophel and Stella*, which are about his love for a married lady, Penelope Devereux, the "Stella" of the poems. His *Apologie for Poetrie*, in simple, direct and lyrical prose, was a defense of all forms of literature; he argues in it that literature can move the reader toward wisdom.

Sidney was given the title "Sir" in 1583. Two years later, he went as part of an army to the Netherlands to help the Dutch win their freedom from Spain and became governor of the town of Flushing. He was fatally wounded in a battle at Zutphen, leading a charge against the Spaniards. As he was carried away, he handed his water bottle to a dying soldier with the words: "Thy necessity is yet greater than mine."

Published after he died

1590	*The Countess of Pembroke's Arcadia*
1591	*Astrophel and Stella*
1595	*Apologie for Poetrie*
1598	*The Lady of May*
1912–26	*The Complete Works* (4 vols.)

SIENKIEWICZ, Henryk

Polish novelist and short-story writer

Born May 4, 1846
Died Nov. 15, 1916
Age at death 70

Henryk Sienkiewicz, the Polish author of the bestselling novel *Quo Vadis?* was the winner of the 1905 Nobel Prize for Literature.

Sienkiewicz was born to a well-to-do family in the village of Wola Okrzejska in a part of Poland then under Russian rule. He was educated at school and university in Warsaw. Becoming a freelance journalist and story writer, Sienkiewicz divided his time between writing and traveling in Europe, Africa, Asia and the US. He lived in America from 1876 to 1878.

Sienkiewicz began his writing career with a novel, *In Vain* – published when he was 30 and based on his university experience – and a short novel, *The Old Servant*. Collections of short stories followed, but it was with the trilogy of novels *With Fire and Sword*, *The*

Deluge, and *Pan Michael* that he first made a name for himself as a writer.

Many other novels followed, the most famous of which, *Quo Vadis?*, became an international bestseller and has been filmed several times. The book is a fine re-creation of ancient Rome in the time of the emperor Nero and deals with the conflict between early Christianity and paganism. Other notable novels include *The Knights of the Cross*, *On the Field of Glory* and *The Whirlpools*.

All his books are carefully researched and are written in an exciting, fast-paced style. Despite the broad popular appeal of his work, Sienkiewicz is still regarded as a serious and important novelist.

Publications

1876 In Vain
1880 The Old Servant
1884 With Fire and Sword
1886 The Deluge
1888 Pan Michael
1895 Children of the Soil
1896 Quo Vadis?
1900 The Knights of the Cross
1906 On the Field of Glory
1910 The Whirlpools

SILKO, Leslie Marmon

American novelist and short-story writer

Born Mar. 5, 1948

With the publication of her first novel Leslie Silko became one of the first Native American women to receive widespread popularity as a novelist. Part Laguna Pueblo, she writes of the conflicts between Native American and white Anglo-American cultures.

Silko was born in Albuquerque, New Mexico. Although her heritage is a mix of Mexican, Laguna Pueblo and white, her childhood was spent on a reservation where she was told folklore stories – Laguna Pueblo legends and myths – by her grandmother and great-grandmother. These made a deep impression on her and appear in much of her writing.

After graduating from the University of New Mexico and briefly attending law school, Silko began to teach and write. At age 26, she published a poetry collection, *Laguna Woman*. Her successful first novel, *Ceremony*, is about a young World War II veteran, half Native American and half white, who is on the edge of a mental breakdown when he returns to his reservation after the war. The novel explores the pain of losing one's heritage and the healing power of tribal rituals, and it includes many of the stories Silko learned as a child, which she feels continue to give relevant lessons about human behavior. These stories also appear, combined with her own family photos, in her book *Storyteller*.

Silko spent more than 12 years writing her second novel, *Almanac of the Dead*. A large book with a huge cast of characters, it describes a revolution by Native Americans who triumph over the Anglo-American culture that has dominated them.

Publications

1974 Laguna Woman
1976 Lullaby
1977 Ceremony
1981 Storyteller
1986 The Delicacy and Strength of Lace: Letters between Leslie Marmon Silko and James A. Wright
1991 Almanac of the Dead

SILLANPÄÄ, Frans Eemil

Finnish novelist and short-story writer

Born Sep. 16, 1888
Died Jun. 3, 1964
Age at death 76

Frans Eemil Sillanpää is noted principally for a powerful novel, *Meek Heritage*, that established him as the outstanding Finnish novelist of his time and which, with other work, earned him the Nobel Prize for Literature in 1939. He was the first Finnish writer to earn this award.

Sillanpää was born into a humble peasant family in Hameenkyro, Finland, and never forgot his origins. He borrowed money to study science at the University of Helsinki but, at the age of 25, returned to his country home and began to write short stories for magazines, the first being published when he was 27. His first novel, *Life and Sun*, was published a year later. It is a love story showing how people are a part of nature and are driven by instincts to fulfill life's hidden purpose.

At age 31, he published *Meek Heritage*, a novel about the Finnish Civil War of 1918 between the revolutionary, left-wing Red Guards and the right-wing White Army. The war had deeply disturbed Sillanpää. The book, his most substantial work, describes how a simple country worker becomes involved with the Red Guards without clearly understanding the politics involved.

From 1924 to 1927, Sillanpää worked for a publishing company and in the late 1920s wrote several collections of short stories. These were followed by a sequence of fine novels, including his internationally famous work *The Maid Silja* and the poetic novel *People in the Summer Night*. He also published his memoirs, *The High Moment of the Day* and *Telling and Describing*.

Publications

1916 Life and Sun
1919 Meek Heritage
1923 Hilda and Ragnar
1931 The Maid Silja
1932 Way of a Man
1934 People in the Summer Night
1953 Telling and Describing
1956 The High Moment of the Day

SILLITOE, Alan

English novelist, short-story writer and playwright

Born Mar. 4, 1928

Alan Sillitoe's best-known books are his earliest works, *Saturday Night and Sunday Morning* and *The Loneliness of the Long-Distance Runner*. As with much of his work, they focus on the stark lives of working-class people and the difficulties they face.

Sillitoe was born in the industrial city of Nottingham in central England. His father was an unskilled laborer, and the family was poor. When he was 14, Sillitoe left school to work in factories. Within a couple of years, he became a lathe operator at a small engineering firm. At the age of 18, he joined the Royal Air Force, happy to escape his boring job and hoping to see the world. He was posted to Malaysia and trained as a radio operator. After being diagnosed with tuberculosis, he spent a year in an army hospital.

It was while he was recovering that Sillitoe decided to educate himself. He began by reading translations of ancient Greek and Roman classics and writing imitations of the books that most influenced him. This period of self-education lasted for ten years. He finished writing *Saturday Night and Sunday Morning* in 1957, but it took him a year to find a willing publisher. Set in Nottingham, it features a factory worker's life described in a realistic fashion. It was an immediate popular success. At the age of 31, Sillitoe became a full-time writer when his second book, a collection of short stories, *The Loneliness of the Long-Distance Runner*, was also a success. The title story, considered by many to be his masterpiece, is about the thoughts of a boy athlete who is at a school for young offenders.

Publications

1958 Saturday Night and Sunday Morning
1959 The Loneliness of the Long-Distance Runner
1960 The General
1960 The Rats and Other Poems
1978 Three Plays
1979 The Storyteller
1982 Her Victory
1995 Life without Armor

SILVERBERG, Robert

American science fiction writer

Born Jan. 15, 1935

Robert Silverberg is one of the busiest and most versatile writers of science fiction.

Silverberg was born in New York City, a clever, rather solitary only child. He enjoyed reading science fiction stories and by the age of 14, had started a fan magazine called *Starship*. At 18, he made his first professional sale as a writer with an article in the magazine *Science Fiction Adventures*. In the following year he sold his first piece of fiction, a short story called "Gorgon Planet."

While a student at Columbia University, Silverberg moved into a flat and found himself living next door to Randall Garrett, an established science fiction writer. Garrett introduced him to many important editors and wrote stories with him, often under the name Robert Randall.

Silverberg's first novel, *Revolt on Alpha C*, was published when he was 20. He then began to write at an astonishing rate. Between 1957 and 1959, using various pen names, he published over 220 short stories and 11 novels. He could write any kind of story: magazine editors would phone him with a request for a story of a given length or theme, and he would always produce it on time. Not surprisingly, much of his work from this period was written to a formula and lacked depth. In 1975, Silverberg announced his retirement and for four years just looked after his garden. Financial needs forced him back into writing, and he published a massive novel, *Lord Valentine's Castle*, for a record fee to a science fiction author. His later work has stronger characters and more complex plots, and shows his true ability as a writer and thinker.

Publications

1955 Revolt on Alpha C
1957 The 13th Immortal
1961 Collision Course
1968 Hawksbill Station
1970 Downward to the Earth
1971 The World Inside
1972 Dying Inside
1976 Shadrach in the Furnace
1980 Lord Valentine's Castle
1994 Hot Sky at Midnight

SIMAK, Clifford D.

American science fiction writer

Born Aug. 3, 1904
Died Apr. 25, 1988
Age at death 83

Clifford D(onald) Simak is one of the fathers of modern science fiction.

Simak was born in Millville Township, Wisconsin, on his grandfather's farm. He later set much of his fiction in this rugged countryside, drawing inspiration from its people to create one of his favorite character types: the old farmer more at home on the land with his animals than with other people.

After leaving university, Simak began a career as a journalist. His first job was as a reporter, and he then went on to become a news editor. His experience as a journalist also inspired another favorite fictional character, the inquisitive reporter who looks beneath the surface to find out the truth.

In 1931, when he was 27, Simak had a story, "The World of the Red Sun," accepted by the magazine *Amazing Stories*. Four years later, a long story, "The Creator," was published in *Marvel Tales*. The story proved popular with readers, and Simak went on to become one of the most important science fiction writers of his day.

One of Simak's best known works is *City*, a set of tales about a world in which human beings have handed over power to a new race of intelligent dogs. The dogs create a civilized society based on cooperation rather than violence, but are attacked by an alien race of ants. The moral dilemma of the story is how to save the dogs' civilization without reintroducing violence by killing the ants, and it raises the question of how we can protect ourselves without going to.

Publications

1946 The Creator
1950 Cosmic Engineers
1952 City
1963 Way Station
1965 All Flesh Is Grass
1970 Out of Their Minds
1973 Cemetery World
1975 Enchanted Pilgrimage
1978 Mastodonia
1979 The Visitors

SIMENON, Georges

Belgian-born French crime writer

Born Feb. 13, 1903
Died Sep. 4, 1989
Age at death 86

Georges Simenon is famous as the creator of the French detective Inspector Jules Maigret. Simenon's stories do not belong to any particular school of crime writing but are in a class of their own.

Born in Liège, Belgium, Simenon worked as a reporter on the *Gazette de Liège* before moving to Paris in 1922. His first marriage ended in divorce and his second in separation. His love life was very eventful: he once boasted that he had slept with over 1,000 women. He had three sons and one daughter who, to his great sadness, committed suicide.

At age 21, Simenon became a full-time writer. He wrote serious novels and crime stories under several pen names as well as under his own. He was a great self-publicist who once wrote an entire novel while sitting on display in a large glass box. His character Inspector Maigret is a police detective, but he does not operate like most detectives, looking for clues and gathering evidence. Instead, he visits the scene of the crime and watches people going about their daily lives, trying to imagine what might have happened. When he finally solves the mystery, he often feels sorry for the culprit rather than happy that justice has been done. In this respect, Maigret's role is very different from that of most thriller heroes. Maigret is there to witness the pain and sadness of human life rather than to avenge a crime.

Simenon's Maigret stories have been translated into many languages, and he continues to be one of the most popular crime writers of all time.

Publications

1931 Maigret Keeps a Rendezvous
1931 Maigret Abroad
1932 The Triumph of Inspector Maigret
1948 Maigret on Holiday
1951 Maigret's Memoirs
1953 Maigret Afraid
1955 Maigret Sets a Trap
1962 Maigret and the Black Sheep
1972 Maigret and Monsieur Charles

SIMIC, Charles

Yugoslavian-born American poet

Born May 9, 1938

Charles Simic is considered to be one of the finest modern American poets.

Simic was born in Yugoslavia just before the start of World War II. German forces occupied Yugoslavia, and Simic's family regularly had to escape from bombing and fighting. Despite this Simic describes his childhood as a happy time. His family moved first to Paris, then to New York City. In 1949, he and his mother moved to Chicago, joining Simic's father, who'd already found employment there. It was in Chicago that Simic first encountered American jazz and poetry. He served in the US Army for two years and earned a Bachelor's degree from New York University in 1966. After editing a photography magazine for eight years, he joined the staff of the University of New Hampshire in 1974, eventually becoming a professor of English.

Simic's first volume of poems, *What the Grass Says*, was published in 1967 when he was 29. Selections from this and a second volume were published together in *Dismantling the Silence*, which received praise from the critics. They were impressed with his spare, pared-down language and powers of observation that endowed everyday objects like a fork or a stone with an almost mythical quality. Later poems draw on the folklore of his Eastern European background combined with American jazz and blues influences and dream sequences inspired by the work of the psychoanalyst Sigmund Freud.

In 1990, Simic was awarded the Pulitzer Prize for his collection of prose poems *The World Doesn't End*.

Publications

1967 What the Grass Says
1971 Dismantling the Silence
1974 Return to a Place Lit by a Glass of Milk
1977 Charon's Cosmology
1986 Unending Blues
1989 The World Doesn't End
1990 The Book of Gods and Devils
1992 Hotel Insomnia
1994 A Wedding in Hell
1995 Walking the Black Cat

SIMON, Claude

French novelist

Born Oct. 10, 1913

Claude Simon is best known for the novels that earned him the 1985 Nobel Prize for Literature.

Simon was born to French parents in Antananarivo, the capital of the island of Madagascar off the east coast of Africa. Madagascar was then a French colony. The son of an army officer who was killed in World War I, Simon was raised by his mother in Perpignan, in the south of France.

Having completed his education in Paris and at Oxford and Cambridge universities in England, Simon studied painting and traveled widely. He then enlisted in the French army and fought in World War II. In 1940, he was captured by the Germans. He escaped, however, and joined the French freedom fighters (the Resistance) against the Germans, who by then were occupying France. Later, he returned to Perpignan to grow grapes and make wine.

By the end of the war, Simon had completed his first novel, *The Trickster*. It was published when he was 33. Simon's concern with "creating a succession of images born from the memory of one event" is not obvious in his early books, they are largely traditional in form, having a logical plot and identifiable characters. His first important book, *The Wind*, was published when he was 44. In this and following novels, Simon developed the style that won him the Nobel Prize. Often the plot is little more than one main event seen from different angles as a central character seeks to understand it using memory, imagination and other devices that fuse past and present together. Sentences can be several pages long, and it is often difficult to tell why, how or when events occur.

Publications

1946 The Trickster
1954 The Rite of Spring
1957 The Wind
1958 The Grass
1960 The Flanders Road
1962 The Palace
1967 Histoire
1969 The Battle of Pharsalus
1973 Triptych
1987 The Invitation

SIMON, Neil

American playwright and screenwriter

Born Jul. 4, 1927

Neil Simon is one of America's most popular and successful playwrights. He has written many plays for Broadway as well as screen adaptations and original screenplays. Simon has won several awards, including a 1991 Pulitzer Prize for his play *Lost in Yonkers*.

Simon was born into a Jewish family in the Bronx, New York City. He attended both New York University and the University of Denver. After working as a post room clerk for a while and briefly serving in the army, Simon launched his career as a professional writer in the late 1940s. With his older brother, Danny, he wrote comedy sketches for the radio personality Goodman Ace. The pair soon moved on to television, writing for Phil Silvers and Sid Caeser.

Simon came to hate the control television executives had over his writing, so after ten years he switched to writing for the theater. His first play, and the first of many successes, *Come Blow Your Horn*, came out when he was 33. Few of Simon's plays have been financial failures, and he is now one of the richest playwrights alive. His plays are mostly set in New York, often within one room or flat, and deal humorously with family life or friendships. *Barefoot in the Park* is about a newly married couple coming to terms with their differences. *The Odd Couple* is about two divorced friends who move in together and drive each other crazy for exactly the same reasons that they drove their wives away.

Although Simon's early plays were always popular for the way they combined both tragedy and comedy, with his later plays he has become recognized as a major, serious playwright.

Publications

1960	*Come Blow Your Horn*
1962	*Barefoot in the Park*
1965	*The Odd Couple*
1968	*Plaza Suite*
1969	*Last of the Red Hot Lovers*
1976	*California Suite*
1982	*Brighton Beach Memoirs*
1984	*Biloxi Blues*
1986	*Broadway Bound*
1991	*Lost in Yonkers*

SIMPSON, Louis

Jamaican-born American poet and novelist

Born Mar. 27, 1923

Louis Simpson is a well-known poet who received the 1964 Pulitzer Prize for his collection of poems *At the End of the Open Road*.

Simpson was born in Jamaica in the West Indies. His father was of Scottish descent, his mother was Polish Jewish: his family background and Jamaican childhood are important influences in his poetry. Simpson moved to New York to attend Columbia University when he was 17. At 20, he joined the US Army and received awards for bravery in World War II. After the war, he returned to Columbia, earning his Bachelor's degree in 1948. From 1967, he taught at the State University of New York at Stony Brook.

When he was 26, Simpson published his first book of poems, *The Arrivistes*, at his own expense. The theme of this collection, and of many later poems, is the effect of war on a sensitive young man. "Carentan O Carentan" is one of the most famous American war poems and tells of a German ambush on an American patrol. Further volumes continue his interest in the war and also in post-war American life. In his Pulitzer Prize-winning collection, *At the End of the Open Road,* Simpson began to experiment with new forms of verse writing. Some of the poems explore his childhood and adolescent memories; others criticize American society.

Simpson's *Collected Poems*, published in 1988, draws on four decades of writing. The personal viewpoint of his own wartime experiences shifts to observations about other conflicts, and his later poems evoke the belief that poetry can help fire the imagination of a country, not just criticize it.

Publications

1949	*The Arrivistes*
1963	*At the End of the Open Road*
1971	*Adventures of the Letter I*
1983	*The Best Hour of the Night*
1983	*People Live Here*
1988	*Collected Poems*
1990	*In the Room We Share*
1994	*The King My Father's Wreck*
1994	*Ships Going into the Blue*
1995	*There You Are*

SINCLAIR, Upton

American novelist

Born Sep. 20, 1878
Died Nov. 25, 1968
Age at death 90

Upton Sinclair was a famous muckraker, one of a group of American writers who exposed scandal and corruption during the first half of the 20th century.

Sinclair was born in Baltimore, Maryland, the son of a liquor salesman whose addiction to alcohol left his son with a dislike of drink – a fact reflected in his novel *The Wet Parade*. He was educated at the College of the City of New York and Columbia University, working his way through by writing poorly paid stories for magazines.

Sinclair's first successful novel, *The Jungle*, was published when he was 28 and became a bestseller. It describes the appallingly dirty conditions in the Chicago stockyards. Influencing the passage of landmark food inspection laws, it also set the tone for all Sinclair's later work. In the following decades, he wrote about a number of social injustices of the day: sexually transmitted diseases, the behavior of journalists, Christian hypocrisy, and the trial and execution of two immigrants, Sacco and Vanzetti, which caused widespread outrage in the 1920s.

A member of the Socialist Party since the age of 24, he tried to put his socialism into practice by founding a cooperative colony called Helicon Hall in Englewood, New Jersey, but it was destroyed by fire, and he lost most of his money.

Sinclair won a Pulitzer Prize in 1943 for *Dragon's Teeth*, a novel about the rise to power of the German Nazi leader Adolf Hitler. The book is part of a series of 11 novels featuring Lanny Budd, beginning with *World's End*. Budd is a character who always manages to be around at decisive moments in history.

Publications

1906 The Jungle
1913 Damaged Goods
1917 King Coal
1919 The Brass Check
1923 The Goose-Step
1927 Oil!
1928 Boston
1931 The Wet Parade
1940 World's End
1942 Dragon's Teeth

SINGER, Isaac Bashevis

Polish-American novelist, short-story writer and essayist

Born Nov. 21, 1904
Died Jul. 24, 1991
Age at death 86

Isaac Bashevis Singer is considered by many critics to be the greatest writer in the Jewish language Yiddish.

Singer was born in a village near Warsaw, Poland. He was the son and the grandson of a rabbi and was supposed to become a rabbi himself, but his interests were literary rather than religious and he resisted. For ten years, he worked as a translator and proofreader, and during that time he wrote his first novel, *Satan in Goray*. His older brother had emigrated to the United States, and when he was 31, soon after his novel was published, Isaac followed and got a job with his brother on a Yiddish newspaper, the *Jewish Daily Forward*. In 1943, he became a US citizen.

Singer wrote almost entirely in Yiddish, which few people could

Publications

1935 Satan in Goray
1950 The Family Moskat

read. Most of his works were translated into English, however, and attracted a wide readership. His stories and novels are largely concerned with Jewish life in Poland and America before the Holocaust and are filled with Jewish legends and folklore.

Singer's major novels, *The Manor* and *The Estate,* are sagas describing generations of a Jewish family and the changes brought about by modern living and the decline in religious faith. Singer's stories reveal the depth of his understanding of the frailty of human nature. He also wrote much-loved children's stories. The high literary quality of his work earned him the Nobel Prize for Literature in 1978.

1957 Gimpel the Fool and Other Stories
1960 The Magician of Lublin
1961 The Spinoza of Market Street
1967 The Manor
1969 The Estate
1972 Enemies: A Love Story
1973 A Crown of Feathers

SITWELL, Edith

English poet, novelist and critic

Born Sep. 7, 1887
Died Dec. 9, 1964
Age at death 77

Edith Sitwell, one of England's finest 20th-century poets, had a reputation for eccentricity. She dressed in exotic clothes, colorful capes and turbans, and wore a great deal of jewelry. She and her brothers Osbert and Sacheverell were the children of an even more eccentric baronet, Sir George Sitwell.

The three Sitwells spent much of their time attacking pompous minor literary figures. Edith Sitwell's poetry ranges from the comic to the grand and tragic and was partly inspired by the work of W.B. YEATS and T.S. ELIOT. Her earliest book of poems, *The Mother and Other Poems*, appeared when she was 28.

Between 1916 and 1921, Sitwell edited an annual anthology of new poetry called *Wheels*. She first came to public attention at the age of 36 with *Facade*, a revolutionary poetical performance with music composed by William Walton. Sitwell recited her lively verse through a megaphone from behind a screen. World War II inspired her to write several more volumes of poetry, among them *Green Song* and *Song of the Cold*.

Sitwell's prose works show her scholarship at its best. They include a book on ALEXANDER POPE and a study of the girlhood of Queen Elizabeth I, *A Fanfare for Elizabeth*, which was later made into a film. Sitwell went to Hollywood to work on the film script herself. She wrote only one novel, *I Live Under a Black Sun*, which was based on the life of JONATHAN SWIFT. In 1954, she was made a Dame of the British Empire, a title equivalent to knighthood. Her autobiography, *Taken Care Of*, was published after she died.

Publications

1915 The Mother and Other Poems
1923 Facade
1937 I Live Under a Black Sun
1942 Street Songs
1944 Green Song
1945 Song of the Cold
1946 A Fanfare for Elizabeth
1962 The Outcasts

Published after she died

1965 Taken Care Of

SMILEY, Jane

American novelist and short-story writer

Born Sep. 26, 1949

Jane Smiley is a modern American writer best known for her novel *A Thousand Acres*, which won a Pulitzer Prize in 1992.

Smiley was born in Los Angeles, but grew up in St. Louis, Missouri. She was educated at Vassar College in New York and at the University of Iowa. Since 1981, she has taught English literature at Iowa State University.

While still a university student, Smiley decided to become a writer. She joined Iowa's Writers' Workshop and wrote a number of stories. However, she did not publish her first novel, *Barn Blind*, until she was 31. Like much of her work it focuses on family life. In this case the story is about the awkward relationships a mother has with her four teenage children. Smiley's fifth novel, *The Greenlanders*, is an epic tale of 14th-century Viking colonies on Greenland. Inspired by a 1976 trip to Iceland, it took five years to research and write. Smiley blended fact and fiction to contrast the failure of these ancient Viking colonies with the problems of modern society.

A Thousand Acres has since overshadowed *The Greenlanders*. It is a feminist reworking of WILLIAM SHAKESPEARE'S *King Lear*. In Shakespeare's play an old king divides his kingdom between his three daughters, who then turn on him and drive him mad. In Smiley's novel the "old king" is an Iowa farmer, and his "kingdom" is his farm. Unlike in the original, however, the women are not portrayed as wicked and selfish but as real people who have good reason for hating their father.

Publications

1980 Barn Blind
1981 At Paradise Gate
1984 Duplicate Keys
1987 The Age of Grief
1988 The Greenlanders
1989 Ordinary Love and Good Will
1990 The Life of the Body
1991 A Thousand Acres
1995 Moo
1998 All-true Travels and Adventures of Lidie Newton

SMITH, Betty

American novelist

Born Dec. 15, 1896
Died Jan. 17, 1972
Age at death 75

When Betty Smith's book *A Tree Grows in Brooklyn*, about life in a New York slum, became an overnight success, some reviewers criticized the story's "unrealistic" rags-to-riches ending. But Smith, who based the novel on her own childhood, was proof that fairy tales can come true. She'd always dreamed of having money, and the profits from her first novel made her rich.

Born in Brooklyn, New York City, Smith was the daughter of German immigrants, and she left school at 14 when her father died. She helped support the family by taking factory and office jobs, but her hobby was acting. Smith started writing plays after marrying her first husband when she was 17, and had more than 30 published before becoming a novelist at the age of 47.

After studying at Yale Drama School, Smith, who also worked as a journalist and university lecturer, moved to North Carolina with her two daughters and started writing her first book.

A Tree Grows in Brooklyn was an immediate hit on its publication when Smith was 47. Eventually it sold more than four million copies. People were captivated by the heartwarming story of Francie Nolan, a bright and sensitive girl who dreams of a better life.

Smith wrote two more novels set in Brooklyn: *Tomorrow Will Be Better* and *Maggie – Now*. Both feature similar female characters, but neither was as successful as her first. For her last book, *Joy in the Morning*, published nine years before her death, Smith drew on her experiences as a poor but hopeful young wife of a Michigan University student.

Publications

1943 A Tree Grows in Brooklyn
1948 Tomorrow Will Be Better
1958 Maggie – Now
1963 Joy in the Morning

SMITH, Clark Ashton

American horror/ science fiction writer

Born Jan. 13, 1893
Died Aug. 14, 1961
Age at death 68

Clark Ashton Smith is one of the most original voices in horror fiction.

Smith was born in Long Valley, California, and attended a local school. He also educated himself by reading encyclopedias, developing a style of writing using long, unusual words. By the age of 17, he was already writing short stories and poems. His first collection of verse, *The Star-Treader and Other Poems*, was published when he was 19. He was hailed as a great new poet but, only a few years later, was unable to find a publisher because his romantic style of poetry had gone out of fashion.

For many years Smith worked at a variety of jobs, from journalist to fruit picker, until a friend, the horror writer H.P. LOVECRAFT, encouraged him to write stories for the "pulps" – cheap and popular fiction magazines. The magazine *Weird Tales* published one of Smith's first stories, and he became, along with Lovecraft and ROBERT E. HOWARD, one of the great horror writers of the period.

Smith's stories are full of alien beings causing death and destruction. For example, one of his stories, "The Dweller in the Gulf," describes a race of blind underground creatures who worship a monster that eats them. Smith also created several imaginary worlds: the continent Zothique; the prehistoric land Hyperborea, where people worship the demon-god Tsathoggua; and Averoigne, a province in medieval France full of witches and sorcerers.

After Lovecraft died, Smith began to write poetry again. He also became a sculptor and painter, creating weird images from his stories.

Publications

1912 The Star-Treader and Other Poems
1922 Ebony and Crystal
1933 The Double Shadow
1942 Out of Space and Time
1944 Lost Worlds
1960 The Abominations of Yondo

Published after he died

1970 Zothique
1988 A Rendezvous in Averoigne

SMITH, Dodie

English children's writer, playwright and novelist

Born May 3, 1896
Died Nov. 24, 1990
Age at death 94

Dodie Smith was a successful playwright and novelist who is best known as the author of *The Hundred and One Dalmatians*. This children's story was made into a Walt Disney cartoon movie.

Dodie Smith was born Dorothy. Her father died when she was 18 months old, and she and her mother went to live at the lively home of her grandparents, three uncles, and two aunts in Manchester. The city had flourishing theaters, and one uncle was an actor. Smith decided to become an actress. She studied at the Royal Academy of Dramatic Art in London and joined a theater company.

After World War I, Smith left the stage and worked for a furniture store, writing plays in the evenings. *Autumn Crocus*, her first play for the professional stage, was produced when she was 35. She used the pen name C.L. Anthony for this and her next two plays. Her first play under her own name, *Call It a Day*, was a great success all over Europe, and it made her financially independent.

Smith went to America with another London success, *Dear Octopus*, and while there married her business manager. The couple stayed in America for 15 years and kept nine dalmatians – the inspiration for her later books. At the age of 52, she wrote *I Capture the Castle*, the first of her six novels. On returning to England she turned the novel into another successful play and wrote her famous book for children, *The Hundred and One Dalmatians*.

Smith wrote two more children's books, *The Starlight Barking* – a sequel to *The Hundred and One Dalmatians* – and *The Midnight Kittens*.

Publications

1931	*Autumn Crocus*
1935	*Call It a Day*
1938	*Dear Octopus*
1948	*I Capture the Castle*
1956	*The Hundred and One Dalmatians*
1962	*Amateur Means Lover*
1963	*The New Moon with the Old*
1967	*The Starlight Barking*
1974	*Look Back with Love*
1978	*The Midnight Kittens*

SMITH, E.E. "Doc"

American science fiction writer

Born May 1, 1890
Died Aug. 31, 1965
Age at death 75

E.E. Smith, otherwise known as "Doc" Smith, has been called the father of "space opera." He was not the first to set a science fiction story in space, but his adventures were unique at the time for their sheer vastness of scale. Smith's characters travel beyond the known galaxy, and his stories cover millions of years and light-years. Plots involve not only a "good guy" versus a "bad guy" but whole civilizations pitted against each other. Spaceships and weapons through the series become bigger, faster and more powerful. This extravagant style came to be known as space opera.

Edward Elmer Smith was born in Sheboygan, Wisconsin. He studied chemistry at university, and his first career was as a chemist for the US Bureau of Standards. After returning to university to take a further degree in food chemistry, Smith became chief chemist for a doughnut manufacturer. During World War II, he worked for the army. He then returned to his previous career in 1945, retiring in 1957.

Smith's first novel, *The Skylark of Space*, was serialized in a paper when he was 38. It was the first ever space opera and the first in a whole Skylark series. It features a genius inventor who battles against an evil foe and various aliens in a huge interstellar war.

The Lensman series – a second series by Smith – has even greater scope than the Skylark books. They feature superhumans bred by good aliens to defeat a race of evil aliens. Each book ends with the defeat of the aliens, but the next in the series starts with the discovery that there is another group of even stronger aliens to destroy.

Publications

1928 The Skylark of Space
1930 Skylark Three
1949 Skylark of Valeron
1950 First Lensman
1954 Children of the Lens
1959 The Galaxy Primes
1960 The Vortex Blaster
1960 Subspace Explorers

Published after he died

1979 Lord Tedric: The Space Pirates

SMITH, Stevie

English poet and novelist

Born Sep. 20, 1902
Died Mar. 7, 1971
Age at death 68

Stevie Smith is famous for her poetry, which is written in an amusing way but deals with serious themes.

She was born Florence Smith in the northern city of Hull and moved with her parents to London when she was three. She lived there for the rest of her life. After leaving school, she went to work for a London publisher. She also wrote poems and, when she was 33, submitted them to another publisher. He advised her to write a novel instead, so her first publication was the humorous *Novel on Yellow Paper*. It was a success, so she wrote another in the same style.

Smith had not stopped writing poetry, however, and she published her first collection of verse, *A Good Time Was Had by All*, when she was 35. Her style is chatty and amusing, but often has deep undertones. Her subject matter was usually drawn from suburban life and her own experiences and religious beliefs. A recurring subject is loneliness, as in the poem "Not Waving but Drowning." She could draw as well as write and often used her drawings to illustrate poems. The drawings were published on their own in *Some Are More Human than Others* in 1958.

Smith never married nor set up home on her own but continued to live with her elderly aunt, whom she nursed in old age. During the 1960s, with her reputation well established, she was much in demand for poetry readings. *Scorpion and Other Poems* was published in 1972 after she died, and her reputation remains high.

Publications

1936 Novel on Yellow Paper
1937 A Good Time Was Had by All
1938 Over the Frontier
1942 Mother, What Is Man?
1949 The Holiday
1950 Harold's Leap
1957 "Not Waving but Drowning"
1962 Selected Poems
1969 The Best Beast

SMOLLETT, Tobias

Scottish novelist, poet and playwright

Born Mar. 1721
Died Sep. 17, 1771
Age at death 50

One of the 18th-century's greatest writers, Tobias Smollett is remembered for his comic novels of travel and adventure, notably *The Expedition of Humphrey Clinker.*

The son of a distinguished Scottish landowner, Smollett studied medicine and joined the British Royal Navy as a surgeon's mate. He saw service in South America and the Caribbean, where he met and married an English heiress, Anne Lassells.

Back in Britain, Smollett set up as a surgeon in London. He began his literary career by writing poems about London life and the plight of Scotland after the 1745 rebellion against King George II. The success of his first novel, *The Adventures of Roderick Random*, shot the 27-year-old Smollett to fame. This witty and angry satire follows the adventures of its hero, who serves in the navy as Smollett himself did. Several other comic novels followed.

For a time, Smollett was editor of the *Critical Review*, a magazine devoted to politics and book reviews. Various ventures, such as writing a history of England, brought him financial security. But the death of the Smollett's only child, a girl of 15, led them to travel abroad again; they eventually settled in Italy.

Smollett's final novel, *The Expedition of Humphrey Clinker*, was published when he was 50. It is considered his best. This comic romance describes the adventures of a family traveling in England and Scotland and was very popular with both readers and critics. Smollett, however, did not live long enough to enjoy this success – he died three months after it was published.

Publications

1748 The Adventures of Roderick Random
1751 The Adventures of Peregrine Pickle
1753 The Adventures of Ferdinand Count Fathom
1762 The Adventures of Sir Launcelot Greaves
1769 The History and Adventures of an Atom
1771 The Expedition of Humphrey Clinker

SNODGRASS, W.D.

American poet

Born Jan. 5, 1926

Known for exploring his emotions in his work, W.D. Snodgrass's first collection of poems, *Heart's Needle*, won a Pulitzer Prize in 1960.

William DeWitt Snodgrass was born in Wilkinsburg, Pennsylvania, and attended local schools. His education was interrupted by World War II, during which he served in the navy. In 1949, he went to the University of Iowa's Writers' Workshop to study playwriting. He found, however, that he was unable to write good plays and chose instead to focus on poetry. He stayed on at Iowa for a further four years, studying French poets of the 1800s and English poets of the 1600s. Snodgrass has since taught at a variety of universities, including Cornell University, New York. From 1968, he was Professor of English at Syracuse University, New York.

Snodgrass published *Heart's Needle* at the age of 33. The poems explore the breakup of his first marriage and his painful separation from his daughter. The book was a great success. After this work, however, he did not publish any poems under his own name for nearly ten years. Using the pen name S.S. Gardons, he published several that he felt were not as good as those in *Heart's Needle*. Since the poems were still very personal, he also wanted to avoid hurting people. His second collection of poetry, *After Experience*, deals with the effects of the breakup of his second marriage. His fourth collection, *The Führer Bunker*, is a series of poems written from the point of view of Nazis in the last days of World War II. Snodgrass was interested in portraying them as people, but he was criticized by some for making them seem too normal.

Publications

1959 Heart's Needle
1968 After Experience
1970 Remains
1977 The Führer Bunker
1983 Six Minnesinger Songs
1987 Selected Poems 1957–87
1989 W.D.'s Midnight Carnival (with Deloss McGraw)
1989 The Death of Cock Robin
1993 Each in His Season

SNYDER, Gary

American poet

Born May 8, 1930

Gary Snyder expresses love for family and friends and his concerns for the natural environment in poems that are deeply influenced by his studies of Asian and Native American cultures. Though only briefly involved, he was also an important figure in the beat generation of the 1950s.

Snyder was born in San Francisco and received his anthropology degree from Reed College. He studied Asian languages at Berkeley at a time when the beat generation first flourished. Members of the beat generation rejected convention and celebrated artistic freedom. They were attracted to jazz, drugs, sex and, most important for Snyder, Buddhism and other Asian religions. Between 1956 and 1968, Snyder often visited Japan to study Zen Buddhism, and he has translated Japanese poetry. Otherwise, he spent most of his time in the Pacific Northwest working in outdoor manual laboring jobs; his first volume of poetry, *Riprap*, published when he was 29, was based on these experiences.

Snyder's poems celebrate simple living, hard physical work, and living in harmony with the Earth. He believes that societies such as the Native Americans have a positive relationship with the Earth that modern societies have lost. *Earth House Hold*'s poems focus on environmental destruction by business and technology; in *Regarding Wave* he writes about becoming a father at the age of 38 and of his joy in family life. *Turtle Island* won the Pulitzer Prize for poetry in 1975. The title derives from the Native American belief that the Earth rides on the back of a great turtle.

Publications

1959 Riprap
1969 Earth House Hold
1970 Regarding Wave
1974 Turtle Island
1977 The Old Ways
1980 The Real Work
1983 Axe Handles
1986 Left Out in the Rain
1992 No Nature
1995 A Place in Space

SOFALA, Zulu

Nigerian playwright

Born 1935

Zulu Sofala was Nigeria's first female playwright. For many years she was also Nigeria's only female dramatist, but her work has inspired other women in her country to write plays.

Sofala was born into an Igbo family in midwestern Nigeria (West Africa), which was then a British colony. The Igbos are one of Nigeria's largest ethnic groups. She grew up in the United States, however, and spent her early adulthood there. While in America she studied English at Virginia Union University and drama at the Catholic University of America in Washington, DC. As part of her degree, she wrote a thesis on the dramatic elements of Igbo ceremonies.

When she was in her early 30s, Sofala returned to Nigeria and took a job teaching in the University of Ibadan's department of theater arts, where she also earned a doctorate in drama. She was made head of performing arts at the University of Ilorin, Nigeria.

Sofala has written many dramas and plays for both theater and television. She has refused to limit herself to any particular style. As a result her work ranges from domestic comedy, as in *The Sweet Trap*, to historical tragedy. Her knowledge of Igbo culture has influenced much of her writing. She often deals with Igbo traditions in a way that reflects life in present-day Nigeria. Sofala's most frequently performed plays are *The Sweet Trap* and *Wedlock of the Gods* – about a woman who decides to marry against the customs of her people. She and her new husband are hunted down, and the woman is killed. *The Sweet Trap* makes fun of Nigerians who try to live and speak as Westerners.

Publications

1970	*Wedlock of the Gods*
1971	*The Disturbed Peace of Christmas*
1974	*King Emene*
1976	*The Wizard of Law*
1977	*The Sweet Trap*
1981	*Old Wines Are Tasty*
1986	*Memories in the Moonlight*
1991	*Song of a Maiden*

SOLZHENITSYN, Aleksandr

Russian novelist

Born Dec. 11, 1918

Aleksandr Solzhenitsyn is probably the greatest Russian writer of the 20th century. He is famous for his books based on his own experiences of life under the communist dictator, Joseph Stalin. In 1970, he was awarded the Nobel Prize for Literature.

Solzhenitsyn was born in the mountainous region of central Russia. He did well at school, then graduated in math and physics. In 1945, he was arrested for criticizing the Russian leader Stalin in letters to a friend. He served eight years' hard labor in a prison camp, followed by three years' exile in Kazakhstan, a desolate region of the Soviet Union. When he was 38, he came out of exile and began writing. His first novel, *One Day in the Life of Ivan Denisovitch*, appeared in 1962. Written in a clear and direct style, it describes the horrors of just one day in a labor camp. It was an enormous success, but within a year Solzhenitsyn's work was banned in Russia. His major books, *The First Circle*, about imprisoned research scientists forced to work for the secret police, and *Cancer Ward*, which was based on his treatment for cancer, had to be smuggled out of Russia and published abroad.

In 1973, the first volume of *The Gulag Archipelago* appeared – a detailed account of the vast network of prison and labor camps in Stalin's Russia. It angered the Soviet authorites, and Solzhenitsyn was deported. He settled in the United States, where he continued writing but was critical of the West's concern with wealth. In 1994, after communism collapsed, Solzhenitsyn returned to Russia a hero.

Publications

1962	*One Day in the Life of Ivan Denisovitch*
1968	*The First Circle*
1968	*Cancer Ward*
1971	*August 1914*
1973–75	*The Gulag Archipelago* (3 vols.)
1980	*The Oak and the Calf*
1991	*Rebuilding Russia*
1996	*Invisible Allies*
1999	*November 1916*

SONTAG, Susan

American critic, novelist and screenwriter

Born Jan. 16, 1933

Susan Sontag is a leading commentator on modern culture in many mediums, including novels, films, short stories, and in the essays for which she is best known. She had a great impact on experimental art in the 1960s and 1970s, and she has introduced many new ideas to American culture.

Sontag was born in New York City but raised in Tuscon, Arizona, and Los Angeles. She entered the University of California when she was just 15, transferring to the University of Chicago after one year. While still in her 20s, she studied English literature and philosophy at Harvard University and then attended Oxford University, and the Sorbonne in Paris. She has since taught at several universities in the United States.

Sontag published her first novel, *The Benefactor*, when she was 30. The story is told by Hippolyte, who decides to act out his dreams. He finds attempts to interpret his dreams unsatisfying and prefers instead to take them at face value. By totally rejecting outside definitions of his real/dream life, Hippolyte finally achieves complete freedom from interpretation by living in silence. Sontag further explored this theme in her famous *Against Interpretation* essays. She argued that people should not attempt to find the "meaning" in a work of art but to experience it as a thing in itself. Her next novel, *Death Kit*, explores similar themes. Sontag's fiction has been condemned for being too obviously critical rather than creative. Her recent novel, *The Volcano Lover*, is a romance and a departure from her previous works.

Publications

1963	*The Benefactor*
1966	*Against Interpretation*
1967	*Death Kit*
1969	*Styles of Radical Will*
1977	*On Photography*
1978	*I, Etcetera*
1978	*Illness as Metaphor*
1980	*Under the Sign of Saturn*
1988	*AIDs and Its Metaphors*
1992	*The Volcano Lover*

SOPHOCLES

Greek playwright

Born c. 496 BC
Died c. 406 BC
Age at death c. 90

Publications

c. 450 BC Ajax
c. 442 BC Antigone
c. 430 BC Oedipus the King
c. 420 BC Women of Trachis
c. 413 BC Electra
409 BC Philoctetes

Published after he died

401 BC Oedipus at Colonus

Sophocles was one of the great playwrights of ancient Greece. He developed the art of tragic drama from the work of the first tragic playwright, AESCHYLUS. Sophocles was born into a wealthy family at Colonus, near the city of Athens. He was well educated and mixed with some of the most powerful figures of his day.

Drama was an important part of ancient Athenian society. There were regular drama competitions that were attended by most of the city's citizens, and winners were highly regarded. Plays were treated as a kind of public political and religious discussion. Playwrights addressed important issues of the day by presenting stories from mythology that contained problems or dilemmas similar to the ones being faced by the city.

During Sophocles's lifetime, Athens fought a long and bitter war, called the Peloponnesian War, with its archrival, the city of Sparta. Many of Sophocles's plays reflect the patriotic mood of the Athenian people and, later, their desire for peace. His play *Antigone*, which is about the moral dilemmas faced by people in a war, so impressed the Athenians that they elected him to be a general in the army.

In 468 BC, Sophocles entered the most important Athenian drama competition of the year for the first time. AESCHYLUS, by then a well-established and respected figure, regularly won the competition, but amazingly the unknown Sophocles beat him to first place. The result caused great excitement in Athens. Sophocles wrote over 120 plays in his lifetime and went on to win first place 24 times. Only seven of his plays have survived to the present day.

SOUTHERN, Terry

American novelist and screenwriter

Born May 1, 1924
Died Oct. 29, 1995
Age at death 71

Terry Southern is famous for writing strange, comical novels in which he makes fun of various institutions as well as character types. His best-known novel is *Candy*, written under the pen name Maxwell Kenton with Mason Hoffenberg.

Southern was born in Alvarado, Texas. He received his first degree from Northwestern University in 1948, and went on to study at the Sorbonne in Paris for two years. From 1943 to 1945, he served in the US Army.

With his first novel, *Flash and Filigree*, published when he was 34, Southern established a style, theme and character type that would dominate his future work: a sketchy storyline, two parallel plots that work side by side and only occasionally come together, and perhaps most important, an innocent central character. Like *Flash and Filigree*, Southern's second novel, *Candy*, is concerned with sex; as well as following the title character as she wanders through a series of bizarre but hilarious sexual encounters, Southern pokes fun at a number of his favorite targets, including social do-gooders, academics and doctors.

Critical opinion of Southern's work is mixed. His early novels were considered promising for a young writer, but some critics were disappointed that he did not move on to explore broader themes. In addition to novels he has written a number of screenplays, often with a coauthor. He was twice nominated for an Academy Award for his screenplays: in 1964 for *Dr. Strangelove or How I Learned to Stop Worrying and Love the Bomb* and in 1968 for *Easy Rider*.

Publications

1958	*Flash and Filigree*
1958	*Candy*
1964	*Dr. Strangelove or How I Learned to Stop Worrying and Love the Bomb*
1965	*The Journal of the Loved One*
1967	*Red-Dirt Marijuana*
1968	*Easy Rider*
1991	*Texas Summer*
1995	*Virgin*

SOUTHEY, Robert

English poet and prose writer

Born Aug. 12, 1774
Died Mar. 21, 1843
Age at death 68

Robert Southey wrote several major ballads, including "The Battle of Blenheim," and was made Poet Laureate in 1813. However, he is probably best remembered for his lifelong friendship with the poet SAMUEL TAYLOR COLERIDGE.

Southey was born in Bristol, and studied at Westminster School, London, where he wrote an article for the school magazine condemning the practice of whipping, for which he was expelled. He went to Oxford University but left without a degree. It was at Oxford that he first met Coleridge. At 21, Southey secretly married Edith Fricker, and soon afterward Coleridge married her sister.

Having tried to study law and finding himself unsuited to it, Southey decided to make his living by writing. Inspired by the French Revolution, he celebrated it by writing an epic poem, *Joan of Arc*, which was published when he was 22. His clear prose style made him popular with newspaper editors, and he wrote many articles and reviews. At the same time, he produced many fine ballads and short poems.

When he was 29, Southey and his family paid a visit to the Coleridges in Keswick in the Lake District. They remained there for life. The following year Coleridge, then addicted to opium, abandoned his family, so Southey, with seven children of his own, accepted responsibility for them all. He was forced to work long, hard hours writing for newspapers, including some 100 articles for the *Quarterly Review*. He also wrote several biographies, including *The Life of Nelson*, and a prose collection, *The Doctor*, that made famous the fairy tale "The Three Bears."

Publications

1796	*Joan of Arc*
1798	"The Battle of Blenheim"
1801	*Thalaba the Destroyer*
1805	*Madoc*
1811	*The Curse of Kehama*
1813	*The Life of Nelson* (2 vols.)
1814	*Roderick: The Last of the Goths*
1817	*Wat Tyler*
1821	*A Vision of Judgment*
1834–47	*The Doctor* (7 vols.)

SOYINKA, Wole

Nigerian playwright, poet and novelist

Born Jul. 13, 1934

In 1986, Wole Soyinka, one of Africa's most important writers, became the first African to win the Nobel Prize for Literature. He is now famous worldwide.

Soyinka was born in Abeokuta, southwestern Nigeria (West Africa), which was then a British colony. He studied in Nigeria before traveling to Britain to study English at Leeds University. After graduating, he wrote plays for the Royal Court Theater in London. *The Swamp Dwellers* – his first play, performed when he was 24 – and *The Lion and the Jewel* were staged in London. They explore the clash between African and Western cultures. In *The Lion and the Jewel* a Westernized school teacher and an African chief compete for a young woman. The chief, who turns out to be more progressive, wins her heart.

Soyinka returned to Nigeria in 1960 to study African drama. During the 1960s, he taught literature and drama at various universities, founded two theaters, and wrote many plays, including *A Dance of the Forests* for Nigeria's independence celebrations. Like much of his work, it combines Western forms with African techniques such as singing, drumming, and the retelling of myths and legends from African folklore.

During the Biafran War (a civil war in Nigeria), he was imprisoned for two years, from 1967 to 1969, for pro-Biafran activities. While in prison, he wrote several poems for *A Shuttle in the Crypt* and *The Man Died* that describe his time in jail. After his release Soyinka lived in England for seven years before returning home. He has often criticized the Nigerian government, and he had to flee Nigeria after his passport was taken by officials in 1994.

Publications

1958 The Swamp Dwellers
1959 The Lion and the Jewel
1960 A Dance of the Forests
1963 The Strong Breed
1965 The Interpreters
1972 A Shuttle in the Crypt
1972 The Man Died
1984 A Play of Giants
1990 Mandela's Earth
1995 Ibadan

SPARK, Muriel

Scottish novelist, short-story writer and biographer

Born Feb. 1, 1918

Muriel Spark's most famous work is her novel *The Prime of Miss Jean Brodie*. It is the disturbing story of an eccentric teacher at a girls' school in Edinburgh, seen through the eyes of one of her students. The novel shows how the girl's initial admiration for Miss Brodie gradually turns to disappointment. It has been successfully adapted for theater and film.

Spark was born and educated in Edinburgh, and she is of Jewish and Italian ancestry. As a teenager, she traveled to central and southern Africa, where she married in 1938. The marriage was not a success, and Spark returned to Britain in 1944 to work in the intelligence department of the Foreign Office during World War II.

After the war, Spark began her literary career as an editor with the

British Poetry Society. At age 33, she won a short-story competition in a British national newspaper and decided to concentrate on fiction.

In the early 1950s, Spark became a Roman Catholic. Many of the characters in her novels are Catholics, although she often portrays them as eccentric and of dubious morals. Her stories are often short and bizarre satires on modern life. *The Abbess of Crewe* is a satirical fantasy about politics. *Loitering with Intent* examines good, evil and the mind of the writer, while *The Only Problem* is a humorous reflection on the Old Testament Book of Job.

Most of Spark's writing is set in Britain, Italy (where she has lived for many years) and Africa. An exception is *The Mandelbaum Gate*, a story of tensions in the Middle East.

Publications

1957 *The Comforters*
1959 *Memento Mori*
1961 *The Prime of Miss Jean Brodie*
1965 *The Mandelbaum Gate*
1971 *Not to Disturb*
1973 *The Abbess of Crewe*
1981 *Loitering with Intent*
1984 *The Only Problem*
1990 *Symposium*
1993 *Curriculum Vitae*

SPENDER, Stephen

English poet and critic

Born Feb. 28, 1909
Died Jul. 17, 1995
Age at death 86

Stephen Spender was a leading English poet in the first half of the 20th century. He was born in London, the son of a well-known liberal journalist and lecturer.

At Oxford University, Spender mixed with other leading poets of his generation, including W.H. AUDEN, CECIL DAY-LEWIS, and LOUIS MACNEICE. He shared their determination to turn away from the difficult work written by poets of the previous generation, such as T.S. ELIOT, and to write openly about political and social issues. Events such as the Spanish Civil War, the Great Depression, and the rise of fascism in Europe were Spender's inspiration in the 1930s.

After leaving university, he visited Germany with the novelist CHRISTOPHER ISHERWOOD. His interest in politics grew, and he briefly became a communist. With the outbreak of World War II, he came to believe less in the importance of politics and started to write about more personal subjects. He refused to fight during the war because he was a pacifist and served in the volunteer fire service instead.

After the war, Spender worked for UNESCO, a United Nations department dedicated to spreading education and understanding. In 1951, he published his autobiography, *World within World*, which gives fascinating insights into the lives of the famous literary figures he knew in the 1930s.

Spender continued writing poetry all his life, his last volume, *Dolphins*, was published a year before he died. He also wrote works of literary criticism, translations, plays, and two novels. In 1983, he was given the honorary title "Sir."

Publications

1933 *Poems*
1934 *Vienna*
1938 *Trial of a Judge*
1949 *The Edge of Being*
1951 *World within World*
1974 *Love-Hate Relations*
1978 *The Thirties and After*
1985 *Collected Poems 1928–85*
1994 *Dolphins*

SPENSER, Edmund

English poet and satirist

Born c. 1552
Died Jan. 16, 1599
Age at death c. 47

Edmund Spenser was a leading English poet in the time of Queen Elizabeth I. He was born in London, where his father was a clothmaker, and educated at Merchant Taylors' School and Cambridge University.

After finishing his studies, Spenser became an assistant to a powerful aristocrat, the Earl of Leicester. He mixed with important people and got to know the poet SIR PHILIP SIDNEY. Spenser dedicated his first important work, a series of 12 long poems called *The Shepheardeꞌs Calendar*, to Sidney, and they became lifelong friends.

In 1580, Spenser was appointed secretary to Lord Grey, Lord Deputy to Ireland. Spenser went with him to Ireland and became involved in the forced seizure of land from the Irish. For this, the Queen gave him Kilcolman Castle in southern Ireland. Spenser did not like being away from London but felt he could not refuse this gift. He settled into his new home and devoted his time to writing his greatest poem, *The Faerie Queene.*

The first three books of *The Faerie Queene* were published when Spenser was 38. He dedicated them to Queen Elizabeth, hoping to receive an invitation to return from Ireland and serve at her court. No such invitation came. Spenser expressed his disappointment with a satire on court life in his book *Colin Clouts Come Home Againe*. Spenser finished the last three books of *The Faerie Queene* in Ireland.

In 1598, an Irish rebellion broke out, and Kilcolman Castle was burned to the ground. Spenser managed to escape to London with his family, but he lived for only a short time to enjoy his return home.

Publications

1579 The Shepheardeꞌs Calendar
1590 The Faerie Queene (Books 1–3)
1591 Complaints
1595 Colin Clouts Come Home Againe
1596 The Faerie Queene (Books 4–6)

Published after he died

1633 Viewe of the Present State of Ireland

SPILLANE, Mickey

American crime writer

Born Mar. 9, 1918

Mickey Spillane was one of the most popular crime writers of the 1950s, known for the sex and violence of his stories.

He was born Frank Morrison Spillane in Brooklyn, New York City. During World War II, he served in the US Army. His career as a writer began with comic books such as *Captain Marvel* and *Captain America*. At age 29, when one of his comic-book stories was rejected, he rewrote it and sold it as his first novel: *I, the Jury.* It was the first of many novels featuring his hard-boiled fictional detective Mike Hammer.

Spillane became the most successful writer in the commercial paperback industry of the 1950s. This was a period when public taste for stories of crime, sex and violence was exploited to the full in cheap paperbacks with shocking covers. In general, the stories had plots that followed the same formula and characters that were stereotypes rather than individuals.

Despite being ignored by the critics, Spillane's books sold in the millions. Several of his novels were made into Hollywood films, including *Kiss Me, Deadly* in 1955. Today, the view that his work is of no literary merit is being revised. It is argued that his books were popular partly because they reflected the world view of the period. The time in which he was writing was a repressive one; Americans were filled with anxiety about communism, sex and morality. While Spillane's books do not deeply explore the thoughts and feelings of his characters, they are forceful and accurate in revealing the guilt-ridden attitude of people in the 1950s.

Publications

1947 I, the Jury
1950 My Gun Is Quick
1950 Vengeance Is Mine!
1951 The Big Kill
1951 One Lonely Night
1952 Kiss Me, Deadly
1962 The Girl Hunters
1965 The Death Dealers
1970 Survival: Zero
1989 The Killing Man

SPITTELER, Carl

Swiss poet, novelist, and essayist

Born Apr. 24, 1845
Died Dec. 29, 1924
Age at death 79

Carl Spitteler, a German-speaking Swiss writer of epic poems, was awarded the Nobel Prize for Literature in 1919.

Born at Liestal in northern Switzerland, Spitteler studied at the universities of Basel in Switzerland and Heidelberg in Germany. He then spent eight years in Russia and Finland working as a private tutor. He continued to earn his living by teaching and working as a journalist but, at the age of 36, he turned to poetry and published his first work. A second volume followed two years later. These highly individual and original epics in the form of lyrical prose-poems are *Prometheus and Epimetheus* and *Extramundana*. They were published under the pen name Felix Tandem, but later works were published in his own name.

When Spitteler was 47, he inherited a small fortune and was able to settle in Switzerland, where he remained for the rest of his life. It was here that his writing began to show remarkable versatility. He produced a witty collection of satirical essays, *Laughing Truths*, which highlight the follies of contemporary life, and he published the powerful novel *Conrad the Lieutenant*. Then came his most impressive and distinctive work, *Olympian Spring*. This extraordinary epic poem uses subjects from classical mythology to address universal concerns about life. It was published in five parts and earned him the Nobel Prize. Spitteler continued to produce outstanding work and, at the outbreak of World War I, wrote an eloquent and balanced statement on the Swiss attitude to the war.

Publications

1881 Prometheus and Epimetheus
1883 Extramundana
1898 Laughing Truths
1898 Conrad the Lieutenant
1900–05 Olympian Spring
1906 Imago
1914 Our Swiss Viewpoint
1914 My Earliest Experiences
1922 The Little Misogynists
1924 Prometheus the Sufferer

STAËL, Madame de

French writer

Born Apr. 22, 1766
Died Jul. 14, 1817
Age at death 51

Madame de Staël is an important figure in the history of French literature. Her novels and nonfiction works had a great influence on French culture at a time when few women had the opportunity for self-expression.

Madame de Staël was born in Paris. Her father, an aristocratic Swiss banker, became a powerful minister at the court of the French king, and she enjoyed an extremely privileged upbringing. At the age of 20, she married the Swedish ambassador to France and soon established herself as a leading figure in Parisian society. Like other wealthy and educated women of the time she organized a salon – a kind of private club where intellectuals and artists met to discuss art and politics.

These were exciting and dangerous times in France – when Madame de Staël was 23, the French Revolution began. She was deeply involved in the power struggles that followed the overthrow of the king, but had to leave France when the revolutionaries began executing all aristocrats. She escaped to Switzerland and lived in England before returning briefly to Paris when the future emperor Napoleon came to power.

At age 34, Madame de Staël published *The Influence of Literature upon Society*, a nonfiction study of the role of political ideas in fiction. Her first novel, *Delphine*, followed two years later. Like her later novel, *Corinne*, it is regarded by scholars as one of the first works of French literature in the Romantic style of writing. She later wrote an influential history of the French Revolution.

Publications

1800	*The Influence of Literature upon Society*
1802	*Delphine*
1807	*Corinne*
1813	*Germany*

Published after she died

1818	*Memoirs of the Private Life of My Father*
1818	*Considerations on the Principal Events of the French Revolution*

STAFFORD, Jean

American short-story writer and novelist

Born Jul. 1, 1915
Died Mar. 23, 1979
Age at death 63

Best known as a short-story writer, Jean Stafford was also a novelist and children's writer. In 1970, she won the Pulitzer Prize for her *Collected Stories*.

Stafford was born in California but, at age six, she moved to Colorado. She remembers her childhood as an unhappy one. Her father, John Stafford, wrote Westerns, but young Jean kept her writing a secret. After receiving both an undergraduate and Master's degree from the University of Colorado, she moved to Missouri, where she taught university. When she was 25, Stafford married the poet ROBERT LOWELL, with whom she spent an unhappy eight years before divorcing. After the marriage collapsed, she was hospitalized for a mental breakdown.

At age 29, Stafford published her first novel, *Boston Adventure*, about the daughter of immigrants who observes wealthy Boston society from her position as a private secretary. Three years later, she published *The Mountain Lion*, a novel about childhood through the eyes of a brother and sister growing up on a ranch in Colorado. The mountain lion represents the powerful, untamed natural world in which the two children find themselves. Much of Stafford's writing explores the solitude of childhood, either through the eyes of the children themselves or through those of an adult remembering her youth.

In the early 1950s, Stafford began to publish short stories in magazines, including the *New Yorker* and *Saturday Evening Post*. She also wrote two children's books, but it was for her stories that she became well known and loved.

Publications

1944 Boston Adventure
1947 The Mountain Lion
1952 The Catherine Wheel
1953 Children Are Bored on Sunday
1962 Elephi, the Cat with the High I.Q.
1964 Bad Characters
1966 A Mother in History
1969 Collected Stories

STAPLEDON, Olaf

English science fiction writer

Born May 10, 1886
Died Sep. 6, 1950
Age at death 64

Olaf Stapledon is known for the huge scope of his vision as a science fiction writer. He does not write from the point of view of human history but describes the evolution of the Universe over billions of years.

Born near Liverpool, into a wealthy family of traders, Stapledon spent much of his childhood in Port Said, Egypt, where his father was working. He received a typical British middle-class education at public school and then at Oxford University. After graduating, he had various teaching jobs and worked in a shipping office. During World War I, he worked as an ambulance driver, witnessing some horrifying incidents on the battlefields of France. After the war, he taught at the University of Liverpool and wrote a book on philosophy. He then began to write science fiction.

Stapledon's first and probably most successful novel, *Last and First Men*, was published when he was 44. In it, he describes the progress of the human race over two billion years of imagined history. The "first men" of the title are human beings today, continually at war with one another. The "last men" are more evolved beings living in the distant future. In his second novel, *Last Men in London*, Stapledon imagines that one of the last men comes back to help the first men, but the experiment is doomed to failure.

Stapledon's books never gained great popularity, partly because he dealt with such large concepts. However, the extraordinary breadth of his imagination has made him one of the most admired and influential science fiction writers of this century.

Publications

1930 Last and First Men
1932 Last Men in London
1934 Waking World
1935 Odd John
1937 Star Maker
1942 Darkness and the Light
1944 Sirius
1946 Death into Life
1947 Flames, a Fantasy
1950 Man Divided

STEAD, Christina

Australian novelist and short-story writer

Born Jul. 17, 1902
Died Mar. 31, 1983
Age at death 80

Publications

1935 Seven Poor Men of Sydney
1940 The Man Who Loved Children
1944 For Love Alone
1966 Dark Places of the Heart
1973 The Little Hotel
1982 Miss Herbert (The Suburban Wife)

Published after she died

1987 I'm Dying Laughing

The majority of Australian-born Christina Stead's works were originally published in England and the US; she remained largely unknown in her native land during her life. She is now acknowledged as one of Australia's greatest writers for her portrayals of women facing the choices of artistic freedom and complex family relationships.

Stead was born in Sydney. Her socialist father was a renowned naturalist and talented storyteller. Stead attended Sydney Teachers' College and taught children with special needs. By 1928, she had saved enough money to travel to Europe, where she worked as a secretary in London and Paris. She lived with William J. Blake, an American economist, eventually marrying him in 1952.

In the 1930s and '40s, they lived in the US, where she wrote movie scripts and taught at New York University. Her earliest major work was *The Man Who Loved Children*, which initially was poorly received. When rereleased in 1965, the novel gained critical acclaim for its sensitive fictional account of her own adolescent love-hate relationship with her father. Her second autobiographical novel, *For Love Alone*, is the story of a young woman who wants to write but is worried her desire for love and marriage will get in the way of her ambitions. Many of Stead's female characters were ahead of their time in their independence.

In 1968, she returned to Australia after her husband's death and, in 1974, was the first recipient of the PATRICK WHITE Award.

STEGNER, Wallace

American novelist and short-story writer

Born Feb. 18, 1909
Died Apr. 13, 1993
Age at death 84

Wallace Stegner's best-known novels are *The Big Rock Candy Mountain* and *Angle of Repose*, for which he was awarded the Pulitzer Prize in 1972.

Stegner was born in Lake Mills, Iowa. His family moved frequently because his father – unsuccessfully seeking to make the "American Dream" a reality – was always looking for get-rich-quick schemes.

Stegner began writing as a student at the University of Utah, but it was not until he received a Ph.D in literary studies that he considered himself a writer. While pursuing his degree, he began teaching courses as a graduate assistant. This was the beginning of an outstanding teaching career that reached its peak in the successful and prestigious writing program at Stanford University.

While writing his first four novels, Stegner was also working on *The Big Rock Candy Mountain*, a novel of far larger scope than any he had written before. The book is a family saga; its central characters are based on Stegner's own family. Its settings – North Dakota, Washington, Canada and the Salt Lake valley – were all places to which his father had taken the family. *Angle of Repose* is also a novel concerned with family relationships, especially the complex emotional ties that bind parents and children, husbands and wives.

Like his previous books and those that followed, these two novels explore the question most vital to Stegner: how an individual can achieve a sense of identity, permanence, and a feeling of belonging in a place like America where rootlessness is part of the culture.

Publications

1940 *On a Darkling Plain*
1942 *Mormon Country*
1943 *The Big Rock Candy Mountain*
1950 *The Women on the Wall*
1961 *A Shooting Star*
1967 *All the Little Live Things*
1971 *Angle of Repose*
1976 *The Spectator Bird*
1979 *Recapitulation*
1987 *Crossing to Safety*

STEIN, Gertrude

American writer

Born Feb. 3, 1874
Died Jul. 27, 1946
Age at death 72

Even though she lived most of her life in Paris, Gertrude Stein is an important figure in American literature.

Stein was born in Allegheny, Pennsylvania, and lived in Austria and France as a child. Her father had become wealthy through his investments in street railroads and real estate. She studied at Radcliffe College and Johns Hopkins University, where she was a medical student.

Stein was devoted to her artistic brother Leo, and when he went to live in Paris, she deliberately failed her exams so that she could leave university and follow him. In Paris, they established a famous salon – a kind of private club where intellectuals and artists met to discuss new ideas in art and politics. These were exciting times in Paris; artists such as Paul Cézanne, Henri Matisse and Pablo Picasso were experimenting with new forms of painting. Stein wanted to create a literary version of the new art. *Three Lives*, Stein's first novel and her first attempt to achieve this new form of literature, was published when she was 35.

Stein and her brother, Leo, gradually drifted apart. Another American woman writer living in Paris, ALICE B. TOKLAS, moved in with Stein and became her lifelong companion. Their apartment was a center of Parisian culture in the years between World Wars I and II. Important American writers such as F. SCOTT FITZGERALD, SHERWOOD ANDERSON and ERNEST HEMINGWAY were regular visitors. Stein wrote about this time in her experimental book *The Making of Americans*.

Publications

1909 *Three Lives*
1925 *The Making of Americans*
1930 *Lucy Church Amiably*
1933 *The Autobiography of Alice B. Toklas*
1934 *Four Saints in Three Acts*
1935 *Lectures in America*
1945 *Wars I Have Seen*
1946 *Brewsie and Willie*

Published after she died

1947 *The Mother of Us All*

STEINBECK, John

American novelist and short-story writer

Born Feb. 27, 1902
Died Dec. 20, 1968
Age at death 66

John Steinbeck is famous for his compassionate depiction of people at the bottom of American society. His attention to detail and sense of social justice gave a human face to people many readers had rarely encountered before: fruit pickers, migrant workers and hobos. Several of his novels were made into films and, in 1962, he received the Nobel Prize for Literature.

Born in Salinas, California, Steinbeck attended Stanford University and studied marine biology, but he never gained a degree. He wanted to be a writer and worked his way on a freighter to New York to find his literary fortune, only to return soon after, unsuccessful. In 1928, Steinbeck moved to San Francisco to be with his girlfriend, who he married two years later. Eventually, he settled in California and was married three times.

Steinbeck's first novel, *Cup of Gold*, came out when he was 27. It was not a great success, but the income from its sales allowed him to carry on writing. Finally, his fourth novel, *Tortilla Flat* – a story about Mexican-American farmhands – was his first popular success. *The Grapes of Wrath*, his most famous book, is a portrait of poor Oklahoma farmers forced off their land and onto the road by drought, a frequent occurrence during the Great Depression of the 1930s. This novel, a strong voice of social protest, won the Pulitzer Prize in 1940. *Of Mice and Men*, one of Steinbeck's best works, is a tragic story that celebrates simple human values. It explores the close bond between George, a physically strong but mentally impaired farmhand, and his friend and guardian, Lennie.

Publications

1929	*Cup of Gold*
1935	*Tortilla Flat*
1936	*In Dubious Battle*
1937	*Of Mice and Men*
1939	*The Grapes of Wrath*
1942	*The Moon Is Down*
1945	*Cannery Row*
1950	*Burning Bright*
1952	*East of Eden*
1961	*The Winter of Our Discontent*

STENDHAL

French novelist

Born Jan. 23, 1783
Died Mar. 23, 1842
Age at death 59

Stendhal was the pen name used by the French writer Marie-Henri Beyle, who is mainly known for two great novels, *The Red and the Black* and *The Charterhouse of Parma*.

Stendhal was born in Grenoble, France, the son of a lawyer. His mother died when he was a child, and rebelling against his father, he went to study in Paris at the age of 16. He wanted to be a playwright but joined the army of the great French leader Napoleon and went to fight in Italy, Germany and Russia. After the final defeat of Napoleon in 1815, Stendhal lived in Italy and Paris and became a writer. During the years spent in Italy, a country he loved, Stendhal wrote books on painting and travel as well as some fiction. One of his early works, a study of Italian life called *Rome, Naples, and*

Florence, brought him success. But he didn't gain recognition as a novelist until he was 47, when he published *The Red and the Black*. It attacks the false values of France during the period 1815–30.

After King Louis-Philippe came to power in France in 1830, Stendhal became a diplomat in Italy and while there wrote his other masterpiece, *The Charterhouse of Parma*, published when he was 56. It depicts the intellectual and moral climate of France after Napoleon's defeat. Then, bad health forced Stendhal to return to Paris, where he died.

Stendhal's genius as a novelist stems from his great originality, sharp sensibility and passion for examining things in detail. He also wrote a number of autobiographical works, including *Memoirs of an Egotist*, in which he used a new way of writing about his own life and experience.

Publications

1817 Rome, Naples, and Florence
1822 On Love
1829 Promenades in Rome
1830 The Red and the Black
1838 Memoirs of a Tourist
1839 The Charterhouse of Parma

Published after he died

1889 Lamiel
1892 Memoirs of an Egotist
1894 Lucien Leuwen

STERNE, Laurence

English novelist

Born Nov. 24, 1713
Died Mar. 18, 1768
Age at death 54

Laurence Sterne was one of the cleverest and most original English writers of the 18th century. He is remembered as the author of *The Life and Opinions of Tristram Shandy* (known as *Tristram Shandy*) – a comic novel that introduced new ways of writing.

Sterne was born in Ireland, where his father was serving as a soldier. When Sterne was two, his father died, and he was sent to England to be educated. He studied to become a priest at Cambridge University and, in 1738, was ordained and sent to take up a post in Yorkshire, in the north of England. He lived there for the next 21 years.

Sterne soon became known for the unusual and amusing sermons he gave in church. He also began writing. When he was 46, the first two volumes of *Tristram Shandy* were published. They were an immediate success, and Sterne expanded the work to nine volumes in the years that followed.

The comedy in *Tristram Shandy* is strongly influenced by the writings of FRANÇOIS RABELAIS and MIGUEL DE CERVANTES, whom Sterne admired and read constantly. Sterne's novel was new and unusual because it followed the inner thoughts of its characters. This technique later became known as stream-of-consciousness writing, but it was not widely used by other authors until the 20th century. Sterne also used flashbacks to tell his story, another new idea that was used by other writers much later.

Sterne became ill and traveled to the warmth of southern Europe. He wrote *A Sentimental Journey through France and Italy* before dying in London.

Publications

1759 The History of a Good Warm Watchcoat
1759–67 The Life and Opinions of Tristram Shandy
1761 Sermons of Mr. Yorick
1767 Journal to Eliza
1768 A Sentimental Journey through France and Italy

STEVENS, Wallace

American poet and essayist

Born Oct. 2, 1879
Died Aug. 2, 1955
Age at death 75

Publications

1923 Harmonium
1935 Ideas of Order
1937 The Man with the Blue Guitar
1942 Notes Toward a Supreme Fiction
1950 The Auroras of Autumn
1951 The Necessary Angel
1954 Collected Poems

Published after he died

1957 Opus Posthumous
1977 Souvenirs and Prophecies

Wallace Stevens wrote some of the finest poems in English in the 20th century. His most important poems were not composed until he was nearly 50 years old.

Stevens was born in Reading, Pennsylvania, into a deeply religious family. His father was a lawyer, and his mother had been a schoolteacher. At Harvard University, Stevens lost his religious faith and developed his belief in what he called the "Supreme Fiction": poetry as a response of the creative imagination to the external world that brings us to higher spiritual wisdom.

Stevens realized, however, that he wanted a more financially secure life than being a poet could provide. He enrolled in New York Law School, but kept in contact with a thriving artistic community in New York. Eventually, he joined an insurance company in Hartford, Connecticut, in 1916, serving as vice-president from 1934 until his death.

Stevens's first volume of poetry, *Harmonium*, was published to critical acclaim when he was 44. The thread running through his work is the need to create artistic order out of the chaos of nature and that the imagination responds to the disorder of reality by creating art. In 1951, he published a series of essays on this subject called *The Necessary Angel*. In 1955, he received the Pulitzer Prize for his *Collected Poems*. Despite this and other honors, his coworkers knew little of his writing and thought it was simply a hobby.

After his death from cancer, Stevens's daughter Holly found and published his diaries, which reveal the creative process of a very private man.

STEVENSON, Robert Louis

Scottish novelist, essayist and short-story writer

Born Nov. 13, 1850
Died Dec. 3, 1894
Age at death 44

Publications

1878 An Inland Voyage
1879 Travels with a Donkey in the Cevennes

Robert Louis Stevenson is the author of the classic Victorian novels *Treasure Island* and *The Strange Case of Dr. Jekyll and Mr. Hyde*.

Stevenson was born in Edinburgh. He was a sickly child and suffered from poor health all his life. At Edinburgh University, he studied engineering but switched to law. After leaving university, he decided not to practice law, and became a writer instead. His first book, *An Inland Voyage* – about a river trip he made in France – was published when he was 28.

In France, Stevenson met an American woman who was studying art in Paris. He went with her to America and married her in 1880. After returning to Scotland with his new wife and stepson, Stevenson began working on *Treasure Island*, an adventure story set among pirates. Published when he was 33, it established him as a popular writer. Three years later Stevenson's novel *Kidnapped* appeared – a tale based on a true Scottish murder case. He wrote several more exciting adventure stories and, at age 36, produced *The Strange Case of Dr. Jekyll and Mr. Hyde*, about a scientist who becomes evil when he drinks an experimental potion. Many regard this as his greatest work.

In 1886, Stevenson returned to America and entered a hospital because of his poor health. Once he had recovered his strength, he set off with his family on a four-year voyage around the South Pacific. Eventually they settled on the island of Samoa, where Stevenson built a house and continued writing. His last novel, *Weir of Hermiston*, was never finished.

1883 Treasure Island
1885 A Child's Garden of Verses
1886 Kidnapped
1886 The Strange Case of Dr. Jekyll and Mr. Hyde
1889 The Master of Ballantrae

Published after he died
1896 Weir of Hermiston

STOKER, Bram

Irish horror writer

Born Nov. 8, 1847
Died Apr. 20, 1912
Age at death 64

Bram Stoker is best known as the author of *Dracula*, the most famous of all vampire stories.

Stoker was born in Dublin. He was a sickly child who could not even stand upright until he was seven. His father had a large library, so he read widely as well as enjoying the horror stories from Irish folklore that his mother used to tell him. Stoker overcame his disabilities to become a champion athlete when he was at Dublin University. After graduation, he worked for the Irish government for ten years, while writing reviews and stories for local newspapers. At age 31, he left Ireland to work as manager for Sir Henry Irving, a famous English actor, and he held this position for 30 years.

Stoker continued to write in his spare time, and his first full-length novel, *The Snake's Pass*, a romantic adventure set on the Irish coast, was published when he was 43. Seven years later came *Dracula*, the book that made him famous. It is a bloodcurdling story about the vampire Count Dracula who drinks the blood of his victims. This causes them to die and then rise from the dead as vampires themselves. Stoker based the story on a Transylvanian myth. In this century, Stoker's version, in which Dracula leaves Transylvania and visits an ordinary English town, Whitby, has been retold hundreds of times and made into dozens of movies.

The Lair of the White Worm, Stoker's last novel, tells the story of Lady Arabella, who is also a vampire and has the ability to turn herself into a huge white serpent. None of Stoker's other novels, however, has had the same success as *Dracula*.

Publications
1882 Under the Sunset
1890 The Snake's Pass
1897 Dracula
1902 The Mystery of the Sea
1903 The Jewel of the Seven Stars
1906 Personal Reminiscences of Henry Irving
1909 The Lady of the Shroud
1911 The Lair of the White Worm

STOPPARD, Tom

Czech-born British playwright, screenwriter and novelist

Born Jul. 3, 1937

Tom Stoppard is one of the major 20th-century British playwrights.

Stoppard was born Tomas Straussler in what is now the Czech Republic. His family traveled extensively during his early life. With World War II raging in Europe, they settled first in Singapore and then in India – where Tom's father was killed. His mother married a British army officer, and Tom took his stepfather's name, Stoppard. In 1945, the family moved to England, where Tom was educated.

When he was 17, Stoppard got his first job as a reporter. Six years later, he suddenly decided to commit himself seriously to creative writing. He resigned from his job and moved to London, where he was soon working for radio. When he was 26, he sold his first play, *A Walk on the Water*, which was produced for television.

Four years later, Stoppard wrote his most famous play, *Rosencrantz and Guildenstern Are Dead*. It was an immediate success and won him the New York Drama Critics' Circle Award. The play features two minor characters from WILLIAM SHAKESPEARE's play *Hamlet* who are caught up in events they do not understand. This was the first of a string of award-winning works, including *Travesties*. During this time, he married his second wife, who is now the well-known writer and physician, Dr. Miriam Stoppard.

Perhaps because of such a wide range of experiences in early life, Stoppard's writing is always original, often blending ideas about science, art and religion. Recently, he has written several successful screenplays adapted from books by other authors.

Publications

1963 A Walk on the Water
1967 Rosencrantz and Guildenstern Are Dead
1968 The Real Inspector Hound
1970 After Magritte
1974 Travesties
1978 Night and Day
1982 The Real Thing
1993 Arcadia
1995 India Ink

STOUT, Rex

American crime writer

Born Dec. 1, 1886
Died Oct. 27, 1975
Age at death 88

Rex Stout is best known for his mystery stories about Nero Wolfe, a classic detective in the tradition of ARTHUR CONAN DOYLE's Sherlock Holmes.

Stout was born in Noblesville, Indiana, and educated in Kansas. He did his military service in the US Navy as a yeoman on President Theodore Roosevelt's yacht. On leaving the navy, he worked as an office boy, store clerk, bookkeeper and hotel manager until he became a full-time writer at the age of 41.

Stout wrote many kinds of fiction, but his most famous work is a series of 40 mystery novels and stories featuring Nero Wolfe, an eccentric character who lives in a big Manhattan brownstone house on West 35th Street, New York City. Wolfe is a fat, middle-aged man who loves eating good food and drinking beer. He likes to read and spends a lot of his time growing rare orchids. He is clever at solving problems, especially murder puzzles, but he is also rather lazy and hates to leave the house. His best friend is Archie Goodwin, a private detective who seeks advice on how to solve crimes. Archie is younger, more handsome and more energetic than Nero, but not as clever. Between them, the pair are able to follow the twists and turns of the murderer's trail until they finally find the culprit.

Stout's plots are full of intrigue and suspense, but it is the way he describes his characters, Nero and Archie, and their witty conversations together, that make his books memorable.

In 1959, Stout received the Mystery Writers of America Grand Master Award.

Publications

1934 Fer-de-Lance
1935 The League of Frightened Men
1940 Where There's a Will
1947 Too Many Women
1951 Murder by the Book
1956 Three Witnesses
1958 Champagne for One
1964 A Right to Die
1971 Three Aces
1975 A Family Affair

STOWE, Harriet Beecher

American novelist

Born Jun. 14, 1811
Died Jul. 1, 1896
Age at death 85

Harriet Beecher Stowe wrote one of the most powerful antislavery novels in the world, *Uncle Tom's Cabin*.

Born in Litchfield, Connecticut, Stowe had one sister and six brothers, and she was the daughter of a church minister. Her mother died when she was four, and the family moved to Cincinnati. Later, Stowe started teaching at a girls' school and wrote stories for magazines in her spare time.

After her marriage in 1836, she got a chance to visit the South and see for herself how cruel slavery was. Over the next 14 years, Stowe had 7 children, which didn't leave much time for writing. Nevertheless, she began work on *Uncle Tom's Cabin*, which was eventually published when Stowe was 41. It caused an immediate sensation, selling 300,000 copies within a year. *Uncle Tom's Cabin* tells the heart-rending story of a slave, the "Uncle Tom" of the title, who is bought and sold three times in his life and is finally beaten to death by his last owner.

In the northern states, the book stirred up such strong feelings of disgust against slavery that when the American Civil War started, President Lincoln was said to have jokingly told Stowe it was her fault!

Stowe made a lot of money from her novel and was able to go on speaking tours in Europe. She published one more novel about slavery and then concentrated on stories about her native New England, none of which were as popular. Although Stowe believed in the equality of all people, *Uncle Tom's Cabin* has been criticized because its main character seems happy to be serving his kind owners.

Publications

1852 Uncle Tom's Cabin
1853 The Key to Uncle Tom's Cabin
1856 Dred: A Tale of the Great Dismal Swamp
1859 The Minister's Wooing
1862 The Pearl of Orr's Island
1869 Oldtown Folks
1875 We and Our Neighbors
1880 A Dog's Mission

STRINDBERG, August

Swedish playwright and novelist

Born Jan. 22, 1849
Died May 14, 1912
Age at death 63

August Strindberg is regarded as one of the leading playwrights of the 20th century. He ranks among Sweden's most famous literary figures.

Born in Stockholm, the son of a bankrupted gentleman and a waitress, Strindberg had a poor and miserable childhood. He attended Uppsala University for five years but returned to Stockholm without a degree, supporting himself by acting, teaching and journalism as he began his writing career.

A controversial figure who rebeled against the sentimental style of writing popular at the time, his difficult personal and public relationships influenced his life and work. His first major work was a historical play, *Master Olof*, which was first performed when he was 26. But fame didn't come until seven years later with the publication of his novel, *The Red Room*, a satire on Stockholm society. After the publication of his short-story collection *Married*, he was prosecuted for blasphemy but acquitted.

Strindberg was married unhappily three times, and some of his most important plays deal with conflicts between husband and wife. The most famous of these is *Miss Julie*. After his first two marriages failed, he struggled with mental illness and began to write in a new, experimental style that included elements of mysticism and dream-like scenes. His work has been a major influence on modern theater.

Strindberg wrote more than 70 plays as well as novels, short stories and studies of Swedish history.

Publications

1875	*Master Olof*
1879	*The Red Room*
1884	*Married*
1886	*The Son of a Servant*
1888	*Miss Julie*
1892	*The Keys of Heaven*
1897	*Inferno*
1898–1904	*The Road to Damascus*
1901	*The Dance of Death*
1907	*The Ghost Sonata*

STURGEON, Theodore

American science fiction/horror writer

Born Feb. 26, 1918
Died May 8, 1985
Age at death 67

Theodore Sturgeon wrote unusual science fiction. He combined science fiction writing with elements of fantasy and horror to express his ideas about how human beings can overcome evil through love.

Born Edward Hamilton Waldo, he became known as Theodore Sturgeon when he took his stepfather's surname and invented a new first name for himself. His relationship with his stepfather was troubled and prompted a later concern in his writing with the cruel, uncaring way adults can sometimes treat children.

Sturgeon's career as a writer began when he was 20 with stories for the magazines *Unknown* and *Weird Tales*. His early stories were mostly tales of mischief that mixed horror with humor. He then moved toward pure horror with memorable stories such as "It," about a hideous monster seeking to transform itself, and "Bianca's Hands," about a deformed young woman whose hands have a life and will of their own.

Sturgeon's first novel was published when he was 32. *The Dreaming Jewels* is the story of a boy who is persecuted by a cruel stepfather and runs away to a carnival. There he finds happiness, and it emerges that he is no ordinary child but a shapeshifter "dreamed" into life by a race of aliens who resemble jewels. In his later novels, such as *More Than Human* and *Venus Plus X*, Sturgeon returned to this theme of the joy, wonder and freedom of the human spirit trapped in the often joyless conditions of the mortal world.

Sturgeon also wrote some episodes of the TV series *Star Trek* and was awarded, after his death, the World Fantasy Award for his contribution to science fiction.

Publications

1950 *The Dreaming Jewels*
1953 *More Than Human*
1953 *E Pluribus Unicorn*
1958 *A Touch of Strange*
1960 *Venus Plus X*
1979 *The Golden Helix*
1982 *Slow Sculpture*
1984 *Alien Cargo*

Published after he died

1986 *Godbody*

STYRON, William

American novelist and short-story writer

Born Jun. 11, 1925

William Styron is best known for two novels: *The Confessions of Nat Turner* and *Sophie's Choice*.

Born in Newport News, Virginia, Styron was educated at two Southern colleges: Davidson and Duke. After graduating in 1947, he moved to Greenwich Village in New York where he wrote his first novel, the much-acclaimed *Lie Down in Darkness*.

Styron's novels are about individuals who have to battle to maintain their own principles and ideals in the midst of the chaos and pretenses of the modern world. He is a perfectionist who struggles with every sentence and paragraph until it is flawless. By the time *The Confessions of Nat Turner* was published, he was 42 and the public had waited 7 years since his previous novel. The idea of writing a book about Turner, who had led the most successful slave rebellion in American history, first occurred to Styron in the early 1940s. The racial tensions of the 1960s brought the rebellion to mind again, and Styron decided to write Turner's story in the first person – as if Turner himself were writing his "confession" before being executed. The book was a great success and won the Pulitzer Prize in 1968. *Sophie's Choice* also tells a harrowing story, this time about a woman trying to live with the memory of being forced by the Nazis to choose between the lives of her young son and her young daughter. The book was filmed in 1982.

Although inventive and gifted, Styron does not find writing easy. In addition to novels, he has produced a few short stories and, since the 1950s, has published excerpts from his novels-in-progress.

Publications

1951 *Lie Down in Darkness*
1953 *The Long March*
1960 *Set This House on Fire*
1967 *The Confessions of Nat Turner*
1973 *In the Clap Shack*
1979 *Sophie's Choice*
1990 *Darkness Visible*
1993 *A Tidewater Morning*

SULLY-PRUDHOMME

French poet, essayist and translator

Born Mar. 16, 1839
Died Sep. 7, 1907
Age at death 68

Sully-Prudhomme was a French poet. Although little known today, he was the winner of the very first Nobel Prize for Literature, which was awarded in 1901.

Sully-Prudhomme was born René François Armand Prudhomme in Paris, France, and he studied science and philosophy at university. His knowledge of these subjects greatly influenced his writing after a severe eye disorder caused him to abandon science and turn to a literary life. He started work as a clerk in a factory but, at the age of 21, took up the study of law. His first substantial work, *Stanzas and Poems*, was published when he was 26, after an unhappy love affair. This collection contains his best-known poem, "The Broken Vase." At the age of 30, he published a verse translation of the first volume of *On the Nature of Things*, a poem by the Roman poet and philosopher LUCRETIUS, a work ideally suited to Sully-Prudhomme's tastes. Lucretius was a great influence on the French poet.

Sully-Prudhomme wanted to correct the excessive Romanticism of the poetry of his time and to restore classical standards of elegance. His principal concern, especially in his later work, however, seems to have been to try to express philosophical thoughts in poetic form. In this, he was not entirely successful, and his work is sometimes difficult to understand. Critics have also suggested that his lyrical gifts were limited. These alleged shortcomings, however, did not prevent him from being elected to the French Academy, a group of top scholars and writers, in 1881. Sully-Prudhomme was seriously disabled by paralysis during the last few years of his life.

Publications

1865	*Stanzas and Poems*
1866	*Trials*
1869	*Solitude*
1878	*Justice*
1888	*Happiness*
1901	*Poetical Testament*
1905	*The True Religion According to Pascal*

SUSANN, Jacqueline

American novelist

Born Aug. 20, 1921
Died Sep. 21, 1974
Age at death 53

Jacqueline Susann is remembered for her shocking 1966 bestseller, *Valley of the Dolls*, a tale of immorality and death in the world of show business.

Susann was born in Philadelphia. Her father was a portrait artist and her mother a teacher. Not much is known about her early life, except that she worked for many years as a Broadway actress before turning to writing fiction in her early 40s. She was 45 when she published *Valley of the Dolls*. It is "escapist" literature with a highly absorbing plot, featuring glamorous characters living in the fast lane. But it is also highly critical of the show business world and its lack of morality – a fact that was often lost in the torrent of criticism that followed its publication. The book has since been referred to as a modern-day *Charlotte Temple*, the morality tale by 18th-century novelist SUSANNA ROWSON.

Valley of the Dolls was criticized for its sexually graphic scenes and rude language. It became a bestseller, however, as did her second novel, *The Love Machine*, which was also groundbreaking in its references to breast cancer, which at the time was rarely mentioned in popular fiction.

Susann set out to write fiction that was popular, not literary, and in that she certainly achieved her aims. *Valley of the Dolls* was made into a successful movie and is now a cult classic, and Susann became one of America's wealthiest women novelists.

Susann died of cancer age 53. The year she died her third novel, *Once Is Not Enough*, was published, and *Dolores* was published after her death.

Publications

1966 Valley of the Dolls
1969 The Love Machine
1974 Once Is Not Enough

Published after she died

1976 Dolores

SUTCLIFF, Rosemary

English novelist

Born Dec. 14, 1920
Died Jul. 23, 1992
Age at death 71

The English author Rosemary Sutcliff wrote popular novels for young adult readers. All her books have historical settings and most are set in the distant past of England and Ireland.

Sutcliff was born in a small town near London. She had an isolated childhood – her father was a Naval officer and often away from home, her mother was extremely protective and did not allow her daughter many companions, and Rosemary herself suffered from a debilitating bone disease. After leaving school, Sutcliff trained at art college to become a miniature painter, more because her mother desired it than because she had any talent or interest. It wasn't until she had left home and established her own life, that Sutcliff discovered her talent for writing.

Sutcliff's first book *The Chronicles of Robin Hood*, was written for children and published when she was 30. It established the pattern of her most successful work – a strong story interwoven with carefully researched historical details that make the characters and locations come alive. *The Eagle of the Ninth*, the first book of Sutcliff's famous trilogy set in Britain during the period of Roman rule, was published four years later. It tells the story of a young Roman soldier and his search for his missing father in 2nd century BC Britain.

Other successful series followed. *The Light Beyond the Forest* was the first of Sutcliff's three novels retelling the legends of King Arthur. In all her stories, Sutcliff shows how people overcome hardships through courage and integrity.

Publications

1950 The Chronicles of Robin Hood
1954 The Eagle of the Ninth
1956 The Shield Ring
1957 The Silver Branch
1959 The Lantern Bearers
1979 The Light Beyond the Forest
1981 The Sword and the Circle
1981 The Road to Camlann
1986 Flame-Colored Taffeta
1990 The Shining Company

SUTHERLAND, Efua

Ghanaian poet, playwright and children's author

Born Jun. 27, 1924
Died Jan. 2, 1996
Age at death 71

Efua Sutherland was one of Ghana's leading playwrights. She had a major influence on the development of playwriting in Ghana through the many theaters and studios she founded.

Sutherland was born in the Cape Coast region of Ghana (West Africa), which was then the British colony of the Gold Coast. After finishing school, she trained as a teacher at Cambridge University, and then studied at London University. On returning to Ghana in 1951, she taught at various schools before settling in Accra, the capital.

In 1958, Sutherland started the Experimental Theater. It traveled around Ghana performing on the streets of many towns. The aim was to inspire both young and old to take part in newly independent Ghana's future. By using drama instead of the written word, Sutherland was able to reach people who could not read.

In 1960, Sutherland founded the Drama Studio at Accra as a workshop for children's writers. The studio became an important training ground for Ghanaian playwrights.

Sutherland's plays are often based on the myths and legends of African folklore. They focus on the nature of power and the need for change. In particular, she writes about the role that women can take. In *Foriwa,* a princess and a prince are needed to wake up the sleeping Kyerefaso, who represents Ghana. The play condemns the lack of progress made after independence. In *The Marriage of Anansewa,* a cunning and dishonest father tries to wed his daughter to the highest bidder.

Publications

1961 The Roadmakers
1962 Playtime in Africa
1967 Edufa
1967 Foriwa
1968 Vulture! Vulture!
1968 Tahinta
1977 The Marriage of Anansewa
1983 Nyamekye
1983 The Voice in the Forest

SVEVO, Italo

Italian novelist and short-story writer

Born Dec. 19, 1861
Died Sep. 13, 1928
Age at death 66

Italo Svevo's reputation rests mainly on one work – *Confessions of Zeno*, considered to be one of the greatest comic novels of modern times.

Svevo (whose real name was Ettore Schmitz) was born in Trieste, Italy, of a German-Jewish father and an Italian mother. He studied at a commercial school in Trieste but had to take a job as a bank clerk when his father's glassware business failed. Svevo really wanted to be a writer and, at age 31, he produced his first novel, *A Life*. This was a complete failure, as was his second, *As a Man Grows Older*. So Svevo gave up writing and began to make a success of his father's new business in underwater paint.

At this point, Svevo met the young JAMES JOYCE, who was working as a private tutor in Trieste and who gave him English lessons. Joyce read Svevo's two novels, declared them excellent, and encouraged him to continue writing. Svevo then wrote *Confessions of Zeno*, which he published, aged 62, at his own expense. This, too, was a failure. A few years later Joyce, now important enough to be influential, introduced Svevo's work to two important French critics who greatly praised it. As a result, Svevo came to be known and widely appreciated – except in Italy.

Confessions of Zeno is a comic novel in the form of a long statement that a revengeful psychoanalyst has "stolen" from one of his patients. It is written in terrible Italian (German was Svevo's first language) and makes fun of Sigmund Freud's theories of pschyoanalysis but builds up to a terrifying climax. Svevo was working on a sequel to this remarkable novel when he was killed in an automobile accident.

Publications
- 1892 *A Life*
- 1898 *As a Man Grows Older*
- 1923 *Confessions of Zeno*

Published after he died
- 1930 *The Nice Old Man and the Pretty Girl*
- 1949 *Short Sentimental Journey and Other Stories*
- 1969 *Further Confessions of Zeno*

SWIFT, Jonathan

Irish satirist and poet

Born Nov. 30, 1667
Died Oct. 19, 1745
Age at death 77

Jonathan Swift was one of the greatest satirists to write in the English language. He is best known as the author of the brilliant satire *Gulliver's Travels*. Swift's rebellious nature drove him to attack a whole range of unjust laws and ridiculous customs with his writings.

Swift was born in Dublin and lived in Ireland for most of his life, although his parents were English. His dislike of authority got him into trouble from an early age. Trinity College, Dublin, almost refused to award him a degree because he broke the rules so often. Swift was ordained as a priest in 1694, and for a while he was employed as secretary to a famous scholar and politician of the day, Sir William Temple. Swift published his first important satires, *Battle of the Books* and *A Tale of a Tub*, when he was 37. The former makes fun of arguments between scholars, and the latter mocks certain religious beliefs. As Swift grew older, he became more interested in serious political issues, and his satires became more savage. In a famous satire against English rule in Ireland called *A Modest Proposal*, he suggested that Irish children should be sold as slaves or eaten to prevent them growing up in poverty! The horror of this idea was supposed to make readers aware that the English cared little about Irish problems.

Swift published *Gulliver's Travels* when he was 60. Although the book is enjoyed for the incredible adventures of its hero, Swift wrote it to ridicule human weaknesses and cruelties. Some critics have said that he hated humanity, but throughout his life Swift donated a third of his income to charity and, when he died, he left money to build a hospital.

Publications
- 1704 *Battle of the Books*
- 1704 *A Tale of a Tub*
- 1710–13 *Journal to Stella*
- 1713 *Cadenus and Vanessa*
- 1713 *On the Conduct of Allies*
- 1724 *Drapier's Letters*
- 1726 *Gulliver's Travels*
- 1729 *A Modest Proposal*
- 1739 *Verses on the Death of Dr. Swift*

SWINBURNE, Algernon Charles

English poet, playwright and critic

Born Apr. 5, 1837
Died Apr. 10, 1909
Age at death 72

Algernon Charles Swinburne was one of the last poets of the Romantic movement. His attacks on Victorian morals and beliefs now seem less important than his rich, melodious use of words.

Swinburne was born in London, the son of an admiral. He was educated at Eton College, and he also studied at Oxford University, where he helped start a club that rejected religion and favored a republican government. Swinburne left Oxford without a degree. Supported by his father's allowance, he took up writing in London, where his friends included the writers DANTE GABRIEL ROSSETTI, WILLIAM MORRIS and GEORGE MEREDITH.

Two verse plays, *The Queen Mother* and *Rosamond*, appeared when Swinburne was 23. At age 28, his verse play *Atalanta in Calydon* won praise for its musical poetry. Next year, the first series of *Poems and Ballads*, with its lush verses praising physical love, made Swinburne notorious. In his mid-30s, his *Songs before Sunrise* glorified revolution and democracy. Swinburne's poems used long lines and cleverly varying rhythms and rhyme patterns. Ancient Greek poets and others inspired much of his writing. Some of this challenged Victorian ideas of what people should believe in and how they ought to behave.

The poet's own wild, drunken lifestyle began wrecking his health. After a breakdown at 42, a friend looked after him for the rest of his life. In his later years, he wrote nearly two dozen books of poetry, verse drama and literary criticism.

Publications

1860	*The Queen Mother*
1860	*Rosamond*
1865	*Atalanta in Calydon*
1866	*Poems and Ballads, first series*
1871	*Songs before Sunrise*
1876	*Erechtheus*
1877	*Love's Cross-Currents*
1878	*Poems and Ballads, Second Series*
1882	*Tristram of Lyonesse*

SYNGE, John Millington

Irish playwright

Born Apr. 16, 1871
Died Mar. 24, 1909
Age at death 37

John Millington Synge was one of Ireland's most original playwrights, specializing in a form of drama that combined both comedy and tragedy. Born near Dublin, the son of a lawyer, Synge was well educated and, after graduating from university, traveled in Europe to study music.

Synge was interested in folklore and spent much of his time living among the poor, listening to their stories. While living in a Paris slum he met the poet W.B. YEATS. At Yeats's suggestion, he went to live on the remote Aran Islands, off the Irish coast. Synge was particularly impressed by the rich and colorful language used by the islanders. The characters he met and experiences he had there formed the basis for most of his writing.

His first play, *In the Shadow of the Glen*, written when he was 32, was an immediate success. When it was performed in London, one member of the audience was so impressed that she provided the funds to found the Abbey Theater in Dublin, so that Irish drama would at last have its own permanent venue. It was here that Synge met the actress Maire O'Neill, to whom he was engaged when he died.

Between 1904 and 1909, Synge wrote five more plays, before his untimely death from cancer. The most famous of these is *The Playboy of the Western World*.

Despite success elsewhere, Synge's work was not well received in Ireland during his lifetime. His characters are simple people who live a harsh and unglamorous life. Many felt that his plays insulted the Irish, portraying them as stupid and ugly. His plays still cause controversy today.

Publications

1903 In the Shadow of the Glen
1904 Riders to the Sea
1905 The Well of the Saints
1907 The Playboy of the Western World
1907 The Aran Islands
1908 The Tinker's Wedding

Published after he died

1910 Deirdre of the Sorrows

TAGORE, Rabindranath

Indian poet, short-story write, and playwright

Born May 7, 1861
Died Aug. 7, 1941
Age at death 80

Rabindranath Tagore was the first Indian to receive the Nobel Prize for Literature. He is one of India's greatest literary figures.

Tagore was born in Calcutta, India, into a wealthy Hindu family and was educated partly in England. His first book, a collection of poems called *A Poet's Tale*, was published when he was 17. At the age of 30, he went to manage two family estates in East Bengal (now Bangladesh), where he collected local legends and folklore that he was later to use in his writings.

Tagore abandoned the ancient form of the Indian language Sanskrit traditionally used for literature and wrote in the common language of the people. This made him enemies among Indian scholars, but it meant he was able to introduce many aspects of Indian culture to the West and introduce Western culture to India. For a time he was a cult figure in America and Britain. In 1901, he set up a school dedicated to merging Western and Indian philosophy and education. This developed into Visva-Bharati University. Tagore believed in what he called "unity consciousness" and had a vision of all creation as "one." He was an early and eloquent advocate of independence for India at a time when the country was ruled by the British.

Tagore wrote poems, plays, novels and philosophical works. The book that earned him the Nobel Prize in 1913 was the set of romantic lyrics called *Gitanjali*, published when he was 49. Tagore also wrote the music for over 2,000 songs, many of which are still popular in Bangladesh. At 70, Tagore took up painting and produced some excellent work.

Publications

1878 A Poet's Tale
1894 The Golden Boat
1902 Binodini
1910 Gitanjali
1910 Gora
1914 Chitra
1916 The Home and the World
1931 The Religion of Man
1939 Shyama
1940 My Boyhood Days

TAN, Amy

American novelist and children's writer

Born Feb. 19, 1952

Amy Tan became an instant success with her first novel, *The Joy Luck Club*, which has since been made into a film that she cowrote. With the publication of several equally successful novels and two children's books, Tan has become a leading Chinese-American writer.

Tan was born in Oakland, California. She went to school in Europe before attending San Jose State University. After graduating in 1973, she studied at the University of California, Berkeley. Tan then spent four years developing programs for disabled children before launching a career in publishing. She became managing editor and then associate publisher of *Emergency Room Reports* but resigned in 1983 to work as a freelance technical writer.

Tan became a novelist almost by accident. She found herself working very long hours as a freelancer and went into therapy to try and control the amount of time she worked. She knew therapy wasn't working when her therapist fell asleep, and she decided to take up writing as a hobby instead. This hobby developed into a career with the publication of *The Joy Luck Club* when she was 37. Like her second novel, *The Kitchen God's Wife*, it is about the relationship between American-born women and their Chinese-born mothers. It explores the difficulties different generations have in understanding each other while celebrating the women's strength and courage – in particular of the mothers, who had faced great hardships in China. Tan herself says that she found writing the books helped her accept her Chinese roots, which she had previously tried to ignore.

Publications

1989 The Joy Luck Club
1991 The Kitchen God's Wife
1992 The Moon Lady
1994 The Chinese Siamese Cat
1995 Hundred Secret Senses
1995 The Year of No Flood

TANIZAKI Junichiro

Japanese novelist and playwright

Born Jul. 24, 1886
Died Jul. 30, 1965
Age at death 79

Tanizaki Junichiro is an important Japanese author known for his novels about the conflict between traditional Japanese culture and the influence of the West in the 20th century. He often explored this conflict in his writings about sexual relationships.

Tanizaki was born in Tokyo. His family, although once wealthy, had fallen on hard times. He had to leave the University of Tokyo after two years because his fees could not be paid.

At the age of 24, Tanizaki published his first important work, the short story "The Tattoo." It is a study of a young Japanese woman whose character changes after she has a tattoo. In this and other stories written around this time, Tanizaki established the main themes of his work – a fascination with feminine beauty and the way that beauty and goodness do not always go together. His short story "Whirlpool" is about a beautiful girl who, although she poses for an artist's drawing of a Buddhist saint, is actually evil and destructive.

In 1923, Tokyo was devastated by an earthquake, and Tanizaki moved to the Osaka region of Japan, which was much more old fashioned. There he found the inspiration to write one of his best-known works, *The Makioka Sisters*. This three-volume novel, published when he was in his 60s, is a complex study of an Osaka family in the 1930s. It shows how one daughter's rejection of traditional values leads to her destruction.

Tanizaki is also famous for his modern version of *The Tale of Genji*, a classic of Japanese literature written in the 11th century by MURASAKI SHIKIBU.

Publications

1910 "The Tattoo"
1928 "Whirlpool"
1929 *Some Prefer Nettles*
1933 *A Portait of Shunkin*
1937 *Arrowroot*
1939–41 *The Tale of Genji*
1946–48 *The Makioka Sisters* (3 vols.)
1956 *The Key*
1962 *Diary of a Mad Old Man*

TARKINGTON, Booth

American novelist, short-story writer and playwright

Born Jul. 29, 1869
Died May 19, 1946
Age at death 76

Booth Tarkington was a popular and successful writer of stories, novels and plays. His work celebrates middle-class conservative values.

Tarkington was born in Indianapolis, the son of a lawyer in what was then a small, quiet city. He was a frail child whose closest friend was his elder sister, to whom he dictated his first novels at the age of six. He attended a school in Lafayette, Indiana, and went on to Purdue University and later to Princeton. Tarkington never graduated, but in spite of this Princeton later awarded him two honorary degrees.

Tarkington's boyhood dream was to become an illustrator. Although he did sell a drawing to *Life* magazine, it was clear that his talents lay in writing. His Indiana boyhood as well as the broader horizons he experienced at university formed the basis of many of his books. For instance, his first novel, *The Gentleman from Indiana*, published when he was 30, was inspired by his interest in politics – he served for a term in the Indiana House of Representatives as a Republican. His next work, *Monsieur Beaucaire*, made him a household name.

Tarkington's "Penrod" stories about a boy growing up in middle America became his best-known work. They were collected in three hugely popular volumes. Other famous books, *The Magnificent Ambersons* and *Alice Adams*, won him two Pulitzer prizes, the first in 1919 and the second in 1922.

During his career, Tarkington produced nearly 200 stories, 21 novels, and 19 full-length plays. He was the third writer to be awarded the gold medal of the American Institute of Arts and Sciences.

Publications

1899 *The Gentleman from Indiana*
1900 *Monsieur Beaucaire*
1914 *Penrod*
1916 *Seventeen*
1916 *Penrod and Sam*
1918 *The Magnificent Ambersons*
1921 *Alice Adams*
1927 *Growth* (3 vols.)
1929 *Penrod Jashber*
1937 *Rumbin Galleries*

TASSO, Torquato

Italian poet, playwright and essayist

Born Mar. 11, 1544
Died Apr. 25, 1595
Age at death 51

Torquato Tasso was an important Italian Renaissance poet. Pope Clement VIII wished to appoint him to be Italy's Poet Laureate, but Tasso died before he could accept this honor.

Tasso was born in Sorrento, Italy. His father, Bernardo, was a poet at the court of the Duke of Mantua. Tasso attended a Jesuit school in Naples, followed by law studies at the University of Padua. After leaving university, he entered the service of Duke Alfonso II as poet-in-residence.

When he was 18, Tasso published his first work, *Rinaldo*, a romantic epic poem that was very well received. His pastoral drama, *Aminta*, which he himself directed aged 29, also much impressed the court. His masterpiece, *Jerusalem Delivered*, tells the story of the First Crusade, when Christian knights attempted to capture the holy city of Jerusalem, then ruled by Muslims. It is a rich mixture of adventure, religion and drama that made him famous.

Hard working and ambitious, Tasso aimed for perfection in his work and worried endlessly about how it would be received, particularly by the authorities in the Catholic Church. By 1577, very depressed and unhealthy, Tasso began to show signs of mental illness. He was confined for his own safety two years later in the prisonlike asylum of St. Anna.

The image of the tortured genius caught the imagination of readers and led to his release after seven years in 1586. Although he never totally regained his sanity, Tasso continued to write, producing nearly 2,000 poems of great beauty.

Publications

1562 Rinaldo
1573 Aminta
1575 Jerusalem Delivered
1586 Torrismondo
1593 Jerusalem Conquered
1593 The Tears of Christ
1594 The Creation of the World in Seven Days
1594 Discourses on the Heroic Poem

TAYLOR, Mildred D.

American young-adults' writer

Born Sep. 13, 1943

Mildred D. Taylor is the author of the outstanding novel for young adults, *Roll of Thunder, Hear My Cry*. It is one of a series of popular books about the Logans, an African-American family living in rural Mississippi in the 1930s to '50s.

Mildred Delois Taylor was born in Jackson, Mississippi, but her family moved north to Toledo, Ohio, to escape the racism of the South. They lived in one of Toledo's all-white suburbs, and Taylor was the only African American in her class. Although she was an excellent student, her school life was difficult. On graduating from secondary school, she trained to be a teacher at the University of Toledo. After this she spent two happy years in Ethiopia, East Africa, teaching English and history. On her return to the US, she studied journalism in university and became involved with the Black Power movement. She fought to improve the teaching of black history and culture.

In 1971, Taylor moved to Los Angeles to concentrate on writing. Her first novel, *Song of the Trees*, told by clever and brave eight-year-old Cassie Logan, came out when she was 32. In this and her other novels about the Logans, Taylor describes a family in which the children grow up with love, self-respect and pride in the face of a racist and bigoted society. She drew on her childhood visits to the South and the stories told her by her father, a master storyteller who taught his daughters about their heritage. It was her father who most inspired her to write, and Taylor's own experiences encouraged her to correct the lack of positive images of black people available to children.

Publications

1975 Song of the Trees
1976 Roll of Thunder, Hear My Cry
1981 Let the Circle Be Unbroken
1987 The Friendship
1987 The Gold Cadillac
1990 The Road to Memphis
1990 Mississippi Bridge
1995 The Well: David's Story

TEASDALE, Sara

American poet

Born Aug. 8, 1884
Died Jan. 29, 1933
Age at death 48

Sara Teasdale, who typically wrote about love from a woman's point of view, was one of America's most popular poets during the early 20th century. Although she only published seven collections of poems in her lifetime, they were highly thought of by other poets. Her collection *Love Songs* won the first ever Pulitzer Prize for poetry in 1918 (then called the Columbia Poetry Prize).

Teasdale was born in St. Louis, Missouri. She was educated in private schools and made to believe by her doting mother that she was frail and needed constant care. At 28 and still dependent on her parents, she made the first of many trips to Europe and started to distance herself from her oppressive home life.

Teasdale's first collection of poetry, *Sonnets to Duse and Other Poems*, was published privately when she was 23. This was followed by *Helen of Troy and Other Poems*, which includes the fine poem "Union Square," about a woman unable to express her love to a man who is already aware of it. Many of Teasdale's poems are about love and the conflict it can bring; her own marriage to a businessman was unhappy. *Rivers to the Sea* was followed by the prizewinning collection *Love Songs*. During this productive period, she also published the 20th century's first collection of poetry written by women, *The Answering Voice* (1917).

For much of her life, Teasdale battled with the effects of her sheltered unbringing. Her shyness conflicted with her professional ambition and search for self-identity. At age 48, after suffering from depression, she killed herself.

Publications

1907 Sonnets to Duse and Other Poems
1911 Helen of Troy and Other Poems
1915 Rivers to the Sea
1917 Love Songs
1920 Flame and Shadow
1926 Dark of the Moon

Published after she died

1933 Strange Victory
1984 Mirror of the Heart

TENNYSON, Alfred

English poet

Born Aug. 6, 1809
Died Oct. 6, 1892
Age at death 83

Alfred Tennyson was the most important English poet of the Victorian era and one of the finest lyric poets in the English language.

Tennyson was the son of a clergyman. He was educated by his father, who encouraged his interest in poetry. Before age 15, he was writing verse plays and poetry in the style of Lord Byron. When he was 18, Tennyson entered Cambridge University. That year, some of his childhood poetry was published, along with poems by his brothers, in *Poems by Two Brothers*. At Cambridge, Tennyson continued to write poetry and became close friends with Arthur Hallam.

Tennyson's second volume of poetry, *Poems, Chiefly Lyrical*, was criticized by reviewers, although it contained the popular "Mariana." In his next collection, are poems now regarded as being among his best, including "The Lady of Shalott" and "The Lotus-eaters." The following year, Hallam died. Tennyson was deeply depressed, and he published little for ten years, but continued to write.

The two-volume *Poems* of 1842 immediately established Tennyson as the most popular poet of the day. The new work included "Morte d'Arthur" and "Ulysses." In 1850, Tennyson was appointed Poet Laureate. The same year he published his greatest work, "In Memoriam," a tribute to the memory of Arthur Hallam. The famous "Charge of the Light Brigade" was published in the collection *Maud*. In his later years, Tennyson devoted himself to writing his epic *Idylls of the King*, based on the legends of King Arthur. One of his last poems, a farewell, was "Crossing the Bar."

Publications

1827 Poems by Two Brothers
1830 Poems, Chiefly Lyrical
1832 Poems
1842 Poems (2 volumes)
1847 The Princess
1850 "In Memoriam"
1855 Maud
1859–85 Idylls of the King
1884 Beckett
1892 The Foresters

TERENCE

Roman playwright

Born c. 195 BC
Died c. 159 BC
Age at death c. 36

Terence was a Roman comic playwright. He was born in the North African city of Carthage and first came to Rome as the slave of a wealthy Roman politician called Terentius Lucanus. His master recognized Terence's intelligence and made sure that he was well educated. Later, he made Terence a free man and encouraged him in his career as a writer.

Talent, intelligence, and a friendly personality made Terence a favorite in sophisticated Roman social circles, and he enjoyed the friendship of some of Rome's most important political figures.

Terence's plays were based on earlier works by Greeks, particularly the Athenian comic playwright Menander, from the 4th century BC. Terence adapted the stories to suit a Roman audience of his day.

Terence set his stories among the wealthy and refined upper classes of Roman society, which he knew well. His style of writing is elegant and appealed to a highly educated section of society. His plays were never popular with the ordinary people.

All of Terence's plays have a romantic theme. Their humor comes from characters misunderstanding each other or breaking the rules of social convention. This style of writing had a great influence on later European comedy. The great 17th-century French playwright MOLIÈRE regarded Terence as one of the best ancient writers. Through Molière's influence Terence's plays became the inspiration for the style of 18th- and 19th-century drama known as comedy of manners.

Publications

166 BC	*The Girl from Andros*
165 BC	*The Mother-in-Law*
163 BC	*The Self Punisher*
161 BC	*The Eunuch*
161 BC	*Phormio*
160 BC	*The Brothers*

THACKERAY, William Makepeace

English novelist

Born Jul. 18, 1811
Died Dec. 24, 1863
Age at death 52

William Makepeace Thackeray was one of the finest English novelists of the 19th century. His best stories are funny and carefully observed studies of the society he lived in.

Thackeray was born in India, the only son of a British civil servant. He was educated in England – in London and then at Cambridge University, which he left without a degree. Later, he studied law in London and art in Paris. In 1836, he married a poor Irish girl, Isabella Shaw. Together they had three daughters, but Isabella became insane, and the family split up.

Meanwhile Thackeray had lost an inherited fortune. To earn money he became a full-time journalist. For magazines, he wrote book reviews, stories and amusing articles, often using absurd pen names such as Fitz-Boodle. His humorous sketches of London characters written for the famous satirical magazine *Punch* reappeared in 1848 as *The Book of Snobs*.

Vanity Fair was the novel that made Thackeray famous. This tale of two middle-class London families has two heroines: scheming, ambitious Becky Sharp and gentle, good-natured but "silly" Amelia Sedley. There is no ideal hero or heroine because Thackeray believed that no one is perfect. The book was published when he was 37.

Thackeray's books were more realistic than most other novels of the time. He showed his characters to have bad points as well as good. As in real life, the bad characters sometimes succeed and prosper more than the good ones.

Publications

1839–40	*Catherine*
1840	*The Paris Sketchbook*
1844	*The Luck of Barry Lyndon*
1847–48	*Vanity Fair*
1848	*The Book of Snobs*
1848–50	*The History of Pendennis*
1852	*The History of Henry Esmond Esq.*
1853–55	*The Newcomes*
1857–59	*The Virginians*

THEROUX, Paul

American novelist, travel writer and short-story writer

Born Apr. 10, 1941

Publications

1967 *Waldo*
1971 *Jungle Lovers*
1973 *Saint Jack*
1974 *The Black House*
1975 *The Great Railway Bazaar*
1976 *The Family Arsenal*
1978 *Picture Palace*
1982 *The Mosquito Coast*
1990 *Chicago Loop*
1992 *The Happy Isles of Oceania*
1998 *Sir Vidia's Shadow: A Friendship Across Five Continents*

Paul Theroux is a popular American writer best known for his travel books, although he also writes novels.

Theroux was born into an ordinary family in a quiet suburb of Boston. He attended the University of Massachusetts, where he made a name for himself by leading antiwar demonstrations. Aged 22 Theroux joined the Peace Corps, a voluntary youth organization, and was sent to Malawi in central Africa to teach English. While there he became involved in the unstable politics of the country, was eventually accused of spying, and had to leave. Theroux continued to live in Africa. In 1966, he met the Caribbean writer V.S. NAIPAUL, who inspired him to take his writing seriously.

Waldo, Theroux's first novel, was published when he was 26. It was not well received, and Theroux went to live in Singapore for a time. His novel *Saint Jack* was based on his experiences of that country, and it established his reputation as an important writer.

In 1974, when he was living in London, Theroux set off on an epic train journey across Asia. He recorded his adventures in *The Great Railway Bazaar*, which became one of the bestselling travel books ever. Since then he has made many more incredible journeys and written successful books about what he saw, thought and felt.

Theroux has also continued to write novels. Like his travels his novels never cover the same ground twice. He constantly surprises readers with new settings and ideas for his stories.

THOMAS, Audrey

Canadian short-story writer and novelist

Born Nov. 17, 1935

Audrey Thomas's fiction explores, as she herself has said, "modern women with their particular dreams, delights, despairs."

Born Audrey Callahan in Binghamton, New York, Thomas loved to read as a child. She worked one summer in a mental hospital, an experience she used in her novel, *Songs My Mother Taught Me*. Thomas often weaves aspects of her own life into her fiction.

Thomas went to boarding school in New Hampshire, then to Smith College. While studying for a year in Scotland, she met the sculptor Ian Thomas. They married and moved together to Canada, settling in Vancouver. She has been a visiting professor at a number of Canadian universities.

In the mid-1960s, she and her husband lived in Ghana, West

Africa. There Thomas had a pregnancy that ended in miscarriage, a horrific experience that required her to spend months in the hospital. She used it as the basis for her first short-story collection, *Ten Green Bottles*, published when she was 32. The African landscape and the trauma of miscarriage also feature in her first published novel, *Mrs. Blood*. The main character in *Mrs. Blood*, an unhappy woman living in West Africa and, like Thomas herself, suffering the loss of a pregnancy, also appears in Thomas's experimental novel *Blown Figures*. Common themes in Thomas's novels and short stories include relationships between men and women, the experience of women dealing with tragedy and living alone, and the fine line between madness and sanity.

Publications

1967	*Ten Green Bottles*
1970	*Mrs. Blood*
1972	*Munchmeyer & Prospero on the Island*
1973	*Songs My Mother Taught Me*
1974	*Blown Figures*
1984	*Intertidal Life*
1986	*Goodbye Harold, Good Luck*
1990	*The Wild Blue Yonder*
1993	*Graven Images*

THOMAS, Dylan

Welsh poet and short-story writer

Born Oct. 27, 1914
Died Nov. 9, 1953
Age at death 39

Dylan Thomas is perhaps the most famous Welsh writer of the 20th century and one of Britain's best modern poets. Much of his writing depicts life in Wales and, although in English, captures the musical quality of the Welsh language. A prime example is his best-known work, the radio play *Under Milk Wood* – an affectionate portrayal of a small Welsh coastal town. It was made into a successful film starring Elizabeth Taylor and Richard Burton in 1971.

Thomas was born in Swansea, west Wales, and educated at Swansea Grammar School, where his father taught English. He edited the school magazine and wrote poetry but was a lazy student. After leaving school at 16, he became a trainee newspaper reporter but left after a year to become a full-time poet. His first book, *Eighteen Poems*, was published when he was 20. At around this time, Thomas moved to London, where he soon became well known.

In 1937, Thomas married Caitlin Macnamara, and they settled in Wales. The couple had three children, but it was a difficult, violent marriage. Thomas managed money badly, and he and his family were poor. He often made ends meet by borrowing from his friends; unfortunately, he treated many of them badly in return.

After World War II, during which Thomas worked as a screenwriter, he became known as a broadcaster and, in 1950, went on a successful lecture tour of the United States. When he was only 38, however, his health began to fail as a result of years of heavy drinking. His death during his fourth American tour was related to drug and alcohol abuse.

Publications

1934	*Eighteen Poems*
1936	*Twenty-Five Poems*
1939	*The Map of Love*
1940	*Portrait of the Artist as a Young Dog*
1952	*Collected Poems, 1934–1952*
1953	*Under Milk Wood*

Published after he died

1955	*Adventures in the Skin Trade*

THOMPSON, Hunter S.

American writer

Born Jul. 18, 1939

Hunter S. Thompson is one of America's most famous and notorious journalists.

Hunter Stockton Thompson was born and educated in Louisville, Kentucky. At the age of 20, he joined the staff of the *New York Herald Tribune* as Caribbean correspondent, later working for the *National Observer* and, finally, *Rolling Stone* magazine from 1970 to 1984. During this period, Thompson became a leading figure in a movement known as New Journalism, in which the facts of the story take second place to the thoughts and feelings of the journalist. Thompson became the most extreme writer of New Journalism – in his work the story disappears almost completely under the wild opinions and adventures of Thompson himself. He called this style Gonzo Journalism.

Thompson's books are enlarged versions of his journalistic pieces, often with a fictional character taking Thompson's place as the narrator. His first book, *Hell's Angels: A Strange and Terrible Saga*, was published when he was 27. He lived with the Hell's Angels in California for a year in order to give an accurate picture of the motorcycle gang, which had been sensationalized in the press. *Fear and Loathing in Las Vegas*, published when Thompson was 33, is his most famous book. The narrator, Raoul Duke, has been sent to Las Vegas by *Rolling Stone* to cover a motorcycle race and a law-enforcement convention on dangerous drugs. The novel chronicles the drug-induced, nightmarish adventures of Duke and his sidekick Dr. Gonzo in a Las Vegas that becomes the symbol of an empty society obsessed with money and possessions.

Publications

1966 Hell's Angels: A Strange and Terrible Saga
1972 Fear and Loathing in Las Vegas
1973 Fear and Loathing on the Campaign Trail '72
1979 The Great Shark Hunt
1984 Silk Road
1988 Generation of Swine
1993 Better than Sex
1997 The Proud Highway

THOMPSON, Jim

American crime writer

Born Sep. 27, 1906
Died Apr. 7, 1977
Age at death 70

Jim Thompson's novels are some of the most disturbing in American crime fiction.

Thompson was born in Oklahoma, the son of a county sheriff. His father lost his job in a financial scandal and went into the oil business before going bankrupt. In his teens, Thompson worked as a bellboy in a hotel. This was during Prohibition in the 1920s, when trading in liquor was illegal. He got to know the local gangsters, and it is this world that he later described in his novels.

In the Great Depression of the 1930s, Thompson wandered America looking for work. He became a communist and made friends with other political activists, such as folk singer Woody Guthrie. He also helped run a writers' project in Oklahoma, the

Federal Writers' Program. He then wrote two novels, but they did not sell well.

In his mid to late 40s, Thompson turned to crime fiction as a way of making money. His bleak, savage stories full of fast action and witty dialogue are better than many being written at the time. His novels were influenced by the classics of modern literature, and he was an admirer of the great Russian novelist FYODOR DOSTOEVSKY. Today, Thompson's work is a big influence on filmmakers such as Quentin Tarantino.

In later years, Thompson became a film and TV writer. By the time he died, his books were out of print in the US. However, he predicted that ten years after his death he would be famous, and so he is. His novels have all been reissued, and several of them, such as *The Grifters*, made into movies.

Publications

1949 Nothing More than Murder
1953 The Killer inside Me
1953 Savage Night
1954 A Hell of a Woman
1954 The Golden Gizmo
1955 After Dark, My Sweet
1957 The Kill-Off
1959 The Getaway
1963 The Grifters
1964 Pop. 1280

THOREAU, Henry David

American writer

Born Jul. 12, 1817
Died May 6, 1862
Age at death 44

Henry David Thoreau was an American writer known for his belief in the importance of the individual and for his strong political views.

Thoreau, the son of a pencil maker, was born in Concord, Massachusetts, and educated at Harvard University. He graduated in 1837, the year RALPH WALDO EMERSON gave his famous address, urging American scholars to create a new culture separate from European influences. Thoreau became a friend and follower of Emerson.

In 1845, Thoreau built a small cabin on Walden Pond near Concord, where he lived alone for over two years. There he recorded his daily thoughts and activities and described the environment around the pond. These observations became the source of one of his most important works, *Walden*, published when he was 37. The book was not just a journal of how he spent his time. It called for people to live simple lives, without many possessions, in harmony with nature.

When Thoreau was 29, he was imprisoned briefly for refusing to pay his taxes, which he did to express his opposition to slavery. This experience prompted him to write his essay "Civil Disobedience," in which he explained his belief that the individual is more important than the government. He said that people should refuse to obey laws they thought were wrong. Thoreau's ideas were adopted by many 20th-century reformers. Martin Luther King, Jr., used them during the 1960s civil rights movement.

Thoreau died of tuberculosis when he was 44. Many of his works were published only after his death.

Publications

1849 A Week on the Concord and Merrimack Rivers
1849 "Civil Disobedience"
1854 Walden

Published after he died

1865 Cape Cod
1866 A Yankee in Canada
1884 Summer
1887 Winter

THURBER, James

American writer

Born Dec. 8, 1894
Died Nov. 2, 1961
Age at death 66

James Thurber is one of the best-loved American humorists of all time.

Thurber was born in Columbus, Ohio. His father Charles, who had dreams of being an actor or lawyer, was said to have been the basis of the typical small, slight man of Thurber's short stories. By contrast, his mother Mary was a strong-minded woman who was a model for the typical strong Thurber woman.

Thurber began writing at secondary school and continued while at Ohio State University on the literary and humor magazines there. He was projected to fame when, after meeting Harold Ross, the founder of the *New Yorker* magazine, he was made managing editor at age 31, then demoted himself to staff writer. Thurber was also a cartoonist, and his comical drawings of animals and people accompany his stories.

Thurber said that his ideas were influenced by the Midwestern atmosphere of Columbus and movies and comic strips. He had a clear, straightforward style that was funny and showed great sensitivity to human fears and follies. Nowhere is this more so than in his famous short story "The Secret Life of Walter Mitty" (part of *My World and Welcome to It*). This story, about a daydreamer with fantasies of greatness, is so well-loved that even today the name "Walter Mitty" is used to describe dreamers with grand ideas.

Due to an eye accident when he was a child, Thurber's sight deteriorated until he was almost blind at the age of 46. Nevertheless, he continued to compose stories in his head, and he played himself in 88 performances of the play *A Thurber Carnival*.

Publications

1929 Is Sex Necessary?
1933 My Life and Hard Times
1942 My World and Welcome to It
1945 The Thurber Carnival
1949 The Beast in Me and Other Animals
1955 Thurber's Dogs
1959 The Years with Ross
1960 A Thurber Carnival

TLALI, Miriam

South African novelist, journalist and short-story writer

Born c. 1930

Miriam Tlali is the author of novels that were banned by the former South African government because they criticized its policies.

Tlali was born near Johannesburg, South Africa, at a time when the government and all the major industries were controlled by white people. Laws restricted where black people lived and what work they could do. Tlali went to the University of Witwatersrand (Johannesburg) until it was closed to black people. She then studied at a university in Lesotho (an independent African kingdom).

Muriel at Metropolitan, Tlali's first book, was written when she was in her 30s. Based on the time she worked in a white-owned shop, it is about a black woman who is insulted by her white bosses as well as by other black people who think she is trying to make money from them. The book was finished in 1968 but not published until 1975. It was groundbreaking in the way that it deals with the day-to-day effects of the government's racist apartheid system.

Tlali lives in the township of Soweto, Johannesburg. Townships were set up by the old government to house black people evicted from "white" cities. She wrote a series of articles called *Soweto Speaking* that highlighted the poor conditions in townships. In 1976, the citizens of Soweto, led by schoolchildren, rebelled against the plan to teach in Afrikaans, the language of the white rulers. The police killed, tortured or imprisoned many protesters, including children. Tlali's second book, *Amandla!* ("Power!"), is about the Soweto uprisings. Its title is the battle cry that was used to unite and rally the people.

Publications

1975	*Muriel at Metropolitan*
1980	*Amandla!*
1984	*Mihloti*
1989	*Footprints in the Quag*

TOKLAS, Alice B.

American writer

Born Apr. 30, 1877
Died Mar. 7, 1967
Age at death 89

Alice B. Toklas was famous for her friendship with the writer Gertrude Stein and later for her own book, *The Alice B. Toklas Cookbook*.

Toklas was born in San Francisco into a middle-class Jewish family and educated in private schools and at the University of Seattle. After the death of her mother, she was forced to become housekeeper for a group of male relatives. At age 29, she was living a dreary life, but all this changed when she met the brother of Gertrude Stein, an American writer living in Paris, France. Thrilled by his descriptions of Paris, she decided to go there.

Toklas and Gertrude Stein were obsessed with each other from the moment they met. Before long, the two women were living together in what was, in effect, a marriage. Together they were at the center of one of the most famous artistic and intellectual circles in Paris in the 1920s and '30s, surrounded by artists and writers such as Pablo Picasso and Ernest Hemingway. Toklas ran the household and helped publish Stein's books; Stein later bizarrely titled her own autobiography *The Autobiography of Alice B. Toklas*.

Toklas published her first book, *The Alice B. Toklas Cookbook*, when she was 77 – eight years after Stein's death. The book became famous because one recipe, given by a friend, was for hashish fudge; unfortunately, Toklas had not tested the recipe, so did not realize what the ingredients were.

When she was 80, Toklas converted to Catholicism, hoping, she told friends, to be reunited with Gertrude Stein in heaven.

Publications

1954	*The Alice B. Toklas Cookbook*
1958	*Aromas and Flavors of Past and Present*
1963	*What Is Remembered*

TOLKIEN, J.R.R.

English fantasy writer

Born Jan. 3, 1892
Died Sep. 2, 1973
Age at death 81

J.R.R. Tolkien is famous as the author of the fantasy novels, *The Hobbit* and *The Lord of the Rings*.

John Ronald Reuel Tolkien was born in Bloemfontein, South Africa, of English parents. He moved with his mother to England when he was three. As a young man, he fought in World War I and, after the war, he studied early forms of language. At age 33, he became Professor of Anglo-Saxon at Oxford University. He stayed at Oxford until he retired.

At Oxford, Tolkien made friends with other writers, including C.S. Lewis, author of the *Narnia Chronicles.* He formed a writers' group called "The Inklings"; all the members were Christians, and all had an interest in storytelling. At their meetings,they would read aloud early versions of their work.

Tolkien published his first book, *The Hobbit*, when he was 45 years old. It is a children's story about the adventures of a timid, humanlike creature, set in an imaginary world called Middle Earth. Tolkien then further developed the history of Middle Earth in the three volumes of *The Lord of the Rings*.

The Lord of the Rings is an epic story on a vast scale. It is about the final conflict between good and evil in a world populated by elves, dwarves, magicians and evil monsters. No other writer has created such a detailed and realistic imaginary world – Tolkien even made up languages for the races that inhabit his world. His knowledge as a scholar helped him create a believable fantasy realm with a complex history, geography and society of its own.

Today, there is a worldwide community of Tolkien fans dedicated to furthering interest in his works.

Publications

1937 The Hobbit
1949 Farmer Giles of Ham
1954–56 The Lord of the Rings (including *The Fellowship of the Ring, The Two Towers, and The Return of the King*)
1964 Tree and Leaf
1967 Smith of Wooton Manor

Published after he died

1977 The Silmarillion

TOLSTOY, Alexei

Russian novelist, playwright, and short-story writer

Born Jan. 10, 1883
Died Feb. 23, 1945
Age at death 62

Alexei Tolstoy is best known for his stories about the effect of the Russian Revolution on Russian society.

Tolstoy was born in the Russian port of Nikolayevsk. He was the son of a Russian count and was distantly related to the great novelist Leo Tolstoy. He first studied engineering but gave it up to become a writer, publishing his first novel, *The Eccentrics*, a humorous account of the decline of the Russian gentry, when he was 27. Tolstoy opposed the communists during the Russian Revolution and, in 1919, he left Russia and lived as a political exile in Paris, France, for four years. During these years, he wrote one of his finest works, the novel *Nikita's Childhood*, a delightful account of a small boy's life in Russia, partly based on Tolstoy's own childhood.

By 1923, Tolstoy was homesick for his country. The communist authorities gave him permission to return and, once back in Russia, he accepted the communist system. He wrote many books and was honored as a leading Russian writer. His books included science fiction, children's stories, thrillers, and more than 20 plays. One of his most important works is *The Road to Calvary* – a trilogy published over a 20-year period. *The Road to Calvary* describes Russia before, during, and after the revolution. It follows the stories of four intellectuals who, like Tolstoy, gradually accept the changes in Russia caused by the revolution and become communists. When Tolstoy died, he was working on a historical novel about the 18th-century emperor of Russia, Peter the Great.

Publications

1910 The Eccentrics
1912 The Lame Squire
1920–41 The Road to Calvary (3 parts)
1921 Nikita's Childhood
1922 Aelita
1929–45 Peter the First
1937 Bread
1943 Ivan the Terrible

TOLSTOY, Leo

Russian novelist and philosopher

Born Sep. 9, 1828
Died Nov. 20, 1910
Age at death 82

Leo Tolstoy was one of Russia's finest writers. He is best known for his novels *War and Peace* and *Anna Karenina*, which are considered to be among the greatest of all time.

Tolstoy's family were wealthy landowners, and he was born on a huge estate, Yasnaya Polyana, near Moscow. His parents died when he was young, and his aunts brought him up. According to his writings, he had a happy childhood. He was taught at home, then studied law and Asian languages in college. A dreamy young man, he failed to graduate, and moved to Moscow, where he lived a fairly wild life.

When he was 23, Tolstoy joined the army serving in the Crimean War. He published his autobiography and *Sevastapol Sketches*, a view of war as soldiers see it. He toured Europe as a literary celebrity but returned to Russia, where he set up a school for peasant children on his estate.

When he was 34, he married 18-year-old Sofya Behrs. They were happy and had 10 surviving children. Tolstoy devoted himself to his family, his writing and improving the lives of the peasants who lived on his estate. During these years, he produced his two literary masterpieces. *War and Peace* is a huge and complicated novel set in Russia during the Napoleonic Wars. It was followed by *Anna Karenina*, the story of doomed love.

Late in life, Tolstoy went through a "spiritual crisis" that he described in *My Confession*. He rejected materialism, war, the Church, and his own wealth in favor of a simple, peasantlike life.

Publications

1852 Childhood
1855–56 Sevastapol Sketches
1865–69 War and Peace
1875–7 Anna Karenina
1884 My Confession
1886 How Much Land does a Man Need?
1886 The Death of Ivan Ilyich
1895 Master and Man
1899 Resurrection

TOOMER, Jean

American novelist and poet

Born Dec. 26, 1894
Died Mar. 30, 1967
Age at death 72

Jean Toomer is known for his novel *Cane*, a groundbreaking blend of poetry and prose honoring the African-American culture of the South.

Toomer was born in Washington, DC. His father, a plantation owner from Georgia, left Toomer's mother when he was a baby. They lived with Toomer's mother's father, an important African-American politician from Louisiana and, for many years, Toomer used his grandfather's surname of Pinchback.

After his mother remarried, when Toomer was 11, his life became unstable. For many years, he roamed from college to college, trying out and then abandoning different areas of study. When he was 26, and with his aging grandparents needing help, he returned to Washington, DC, to write. A year later he took up a short-term offer to teach black children in Georgia, pleased to have a chance to learn something about this part of his heritage. While there he was inspired to write his first novel, *Cane*, which was published when he was 29.

Cane was highly praised, but against Toomer's wishes he was called a new member of the Harlem Renaissance. Seeing himself as simply a member of the human race, he rejected the racial distinctions that separated out "black" literature and instead identified with poet WALT WHITMAN's vision of a racially unified country.

Toomer continued to write, but none of his later works was nearly as successful as *Cane*. After marrying a second time (his first wife had died in childbirth), he moved to Pennsylvania and became a Quaker, living the last years of his life as a recluse.

Publications

1923 *Cane*
1929 "Reflections"
1929 "White Arrow"
1931 *Essentials*
1936 "Blue Meridian"

Published after he died

1980 *The Wayward and the Seeking*
1988 *Collected Poems*
1993 *A Jean Toomer Reader*

TRAVEN, B.

American-born Mexican writer

Born Mar. 5, 1890
Died Mar. 26, 1969
Age at death 79

B. Traven is one of the pen names used by a writer who wanted to keep his real name a secret. To this day it is not known for sure who he really was. Although he is usually identified as the American writer Berick Traven Torsvan, very little is known about him. His most famous novel is *The Treasure of the Sierra Madre*, which was set in Mexico and made into a film starring Humphrey Bogart in 1947.

Traven was probably born in Chicago of American-Scandinavian parents. He lived in Germany during World War I, moved to Mexico during the 1920s or '30s, and took Mexican citizenship in 1951; six years later he married his literary agent, Rosa Elena Luján. Some think Traven was a German who invented his American past.

He became a writer relatively late in life, at the age of 36, and all his books were written in German before being translated into English. He became a bestselling author in the German-speaking countries of Europe with his first novel, *The Death Ship*, but was not well known in the US until the late 1960s and early '70s. This was because he would not allow American publishers to advertise his books or to put any information about him on the dust jackets.

Although Traven's novels are exciting adventure stories, they also show his concern about the power the very rich have over the very poor. His heroes are always underdogs, those on the run from the law, or those who, as a result of war, have lost their papers – and their identities. He also used the characters in his novels to demonstrate that the poorest person is often spiritually the richest.

Publications

1934 The Death Ship
1935 The Treasure of the Sierra Madre
1935 The Carreta
1938 The Bridge in the Jungle
1952 The Rebellion of the Hanged
1954 General from the Jungle
1956 The Cotton Pickers
1961 March to Caobaland
1965 The White Rose

TRAVERS, P.L.

P.L. Travers is not nearly as famous as the character that she wrote about – Mary Poppins, the magical English nanny.

Pamela Lyndon Travers was born in northeastern Australia in Maryborough, Queensland. Her father was Irish and her mother Scottish, and she grew up hearing of the myths and legends of her parents' homelands. When Travers was seven, her much-loved father died, and the family moved to New South Wales. Travers was sent to boarding school, where she turned into a budding actress. Although she was offered a scholarship to study in university, Travers started work right after leaving school at age 16 so that she could help her mother financially. She took a variety of jobs, including acting and reporting. She also published several poems and articles in newspapers.

When she was 25, Travers traveled to London, where she lived for much of her life. She sent one of her poems to the Irish poet and publisher George William Russell, who became a lifelong friend and encouraged her to write. *Mary Poppins* was published when Travers was 35. She always insisted that she did not create Mary Poppins but that the character had a life of her own. Travers (who became an expert on mythology) found she had invented her own mythical character when she wrote Mary Poppins into existence. Mary Poppins not only had magical powers but was stern yet loving, wise yet vain, and very disagreeable. The popular 1964 film version, which Travers hated, turned this rather scary person into a sweet, kind and pretty gentlewoman.

Australian-born English children's writer

Born Aug. 9, 1899
Died Apr. 23, 1996
Age at death 96

Publications

1934 Mary Poppins
1935 Mary Poppins Comes Back
1943 Mary Poppins Opens the Door
1952 Mary Poppins in the Park
1962 Mary Poppins from A to Z
1980 Two Pairs of Shoes
1982 Mary Poppins in Cherry Tree Lane
1989 Mary Poppins in the House Next Door

TROLLOPE, Anthony

English novelist

Born Apr. 24, 1815
Died Dec. 6, 1882
Age at death 67

Anthony Trollope was a popular 19th-century English novelist best known for his stories set in the imaginary English county of Barsetshire.

Trollope was born in London and educated at two famous public schools. His mother earned money by writing novels and travel books. His father was a failed lawyer and farmer. Sometimes they could not afford to pay their son's school fees.

At 19, Trollope became a post office clerk in London and, at 26, he was made a deputy postal surveyor in Ireland. He worked for the post office for 33 years and first introduced the red British mail boxes known as pillar boxes. He lived mainly in England and Ireland, but his work also took him to Africa and America.

Soon after marrying in 1844, Trollope began writing in his spare time to earn extra money. He regularly produced 1,000 words an hour before breakfast. He was 32 when *The Macdermots of Ballycloran*, his first book, was published and 40 when his first successful story appeared. *The Warden* is about a clergyman accused of misusing money meant for the old people's home he looks after. This was the first of the six Barchester novels about people living in the imaginary cathedral city of Barchester. With humor and gentle satire, Trollope told stories of ordinary men and women with human weaknesses. He wrote nearly 50 novels altogether. Many of his later works are about power and politics; they involve an invented family of nobles called the Pallisers.

Publications

1847 The Macdermots of Ballycloran
1855 The Warden
1857 Barchester Towers
1858 Doctor Thorne
1861 Framley Parsonage
1864 The Small House at Allington
1864 Can You Forgive Her?
1867 The Last Chronicle of Barset
1869 Phineas Finn
1875 The Way We Live Now

TSUSHIMA, Yuko

Japanese short-story writer and novelist

Born Mar. 30, 1947

Tsushima Yuko is one of Japan's best-known feminist writers. Her short stories and novels have been awarded many prizes.

Tsushima was born in Tokyo, Japan. Her father, Osamu Dazai, was an important novelist and a wild and unstable person. He committed suicide with one of his lovers when Tsushima was only eight months old. Her elder brother, to whom she was very close, had Down's syndrome and died when Tsushima was 13. These two tragedies affected her deeply, and she often draws on her experiences of loss in her writings.

Tsushima attended a Catholic girls' school and, at age 18, enrolled in the English literature department of Shirayuri Women's University, where she started to write. After graduating, she entered

Meiji University but did not complete her course.

"A Birth," Tsushima's first short story, was published when she was 20. Its theme is taken from her own family situation and tells of a mentally retarded boy's relationship with his guilt-ridden father and loving sister. Tsushima's first full-length novel was *The House Where Living Things Gather* – about a young woman's search for memories of her dead father.

Tsushima's acclaimed prizewinning novel *Child of Fortune* was published when she was 30 and again draws heavily on events in her own life. Much of her work reflects her experiences as a lone parent raising children in Japan. There was further tragedy in Tsushima's life when, in 1985, her eight-year-old son died while in the bath. She expresses her sorrow in the tender novel *Pursued by the Light of the Night*.

Publications

1967	"A Birth"
1971	*Carnival*
1973	*The House Where Living Things Gather*
1978	*Child of Fortune*
1980	*Woman Running in the Mountains*
1986	*Pursued by the Light of the Night*
1988	*A Record of Dreams*
1988	*The Shooting Gallery*
1994	*The Age of Glimmering Waters*

TSVETAYEVA, Marina

Russian poet

Born Oct. 8, 1892
Died Aug. 31, 1941
Age at death 48

Marina Tsvetayeva was one of the finest Russian poets of the 20th century, but she was exiled from her homeland because of her political views.

Tsvetayeva was born in Moscow. Her mother was a talented pianist, her father a university professor. They traveled a great deal, and Tsvetayeva studied at the Sorbonne in Paris. *Evening Album*, her first collection of poems, was published when she was 18. It established her reputation as a powerful new talent.

Tsvetayeva hated the Russian Revolution. Her husband, Sergei Efron, whom she had married in 1912, fought against the communists. During these years, she wrote a series of lyrical poems, *The Demesne of the Swans*, which glorified those who fought against the communists. The collection was not published in its entirety until 1957, 16 years after she died.

In 1922, after the communists had won complete power, Tsvetayeva followed her husband to Prague (now in the Czech Republic), and then Paris, where they spent the next 18 years living the life of political exiles. Tsvetayeva became a symbol for Russians in exile and wrote several volumes of poetry, including *After Russia,* the last of her poems to be published during her life. She corresponded regularly with the Russian writer Boris Pasternak, who greatly admired her work.

In 1939, Tsvetayeva returned to Moscow. Later, her husband was shot and her daughter was arrested. In despair, Tsvetayeva hanged herself.

Publications

1910	*Evening Album*
1922	*Poems to Blok*
1922	*Tsar-Maiden*
1922	*Parting*
1924	*The Swain*
1928	*After Russia*

Published after she died

1957	*The Demesne of the Swans*
1971	*Selected Poems*
1980	*A Captive Spirit*

TURGENEV, Ivan

Russian novelist, short-story writer and dramatist

Born Oct. 28, 1818
Died Sep. 3, 1883
Age at death 64

Publications

1852 A Sportsman's Sketches
1856 Tales and Stories
1859 Home of the Gentry
1860 On the Eve
1860 First Love
1862 Fathers and Sons
1869 A Month in the Country
1870 A Lear of the Steppe
1872 Torrents of Spring
1877 Virgin Soil

Ivan Turgenev wrote stories about the everyday lives of Russians and the conflicts in Russian society during the 19th century. They are famous for their detailed descriptions of ordinary life.

Turgenev was born into a wealthy family in the Ukraine region of Russia. He attended universities in Moscow, St. Petersburg, and in the German city of Berlin, where he met radical political thinkers of the time. Back in St. Petersburg, Turgenev worked for the Russian civil service for a short time before the success of two of his story-poems encouraged him to become a full-time writer.

Turgenev's first important work was *A Sportsman's Sketches*, published when he was 34. They are short pieces written from the point of view of a young nobleman who is surprised to find the qualities of intelligence and morality among the peasants who live on his family's estates. Turgenev was one of the first Russian authors to write realistically about the lives of peasants and to portray them as worthwhile human beings.

In 19th-century Russia, peasants were little more than slaves, and all power lay with the czar (emperor). Turgenev believed that reforms had to be made and wrote many novels on this theme. In his most famous novel, *Fathers and Sons*, he shows the conflict between the older generation, who respect tradition, and the youth, who want change.

Disappointed at the lack of reform, Turgenev left Russia and settled first in Germany and then in France. Away from his homeland his work lost touch with the reality of Russia.

TUTUOLA, Amos

Nigerian novelist and short-story writer

Born Jun. 20, 1922
Died Jun. 8, 1997
Age at death 74

Publications

1952 The Palm-Wine Drinkard

Amos Tutuola achieved international fame with his remarkable novel *The Palm-Wine Drinkard*, which is widely considered to be the first modern African novel written in English.

Tutuola was born in Abeokuta, a town in Nigeria, West Africa. At the age of seven, he was sent to live with a family friend, Moru, as a domestic servant. In return for his labor, Moru paid Tutuola's school fees. In 1936, he moved with Moru to nearby Lagos, the capital city, but returned home two years later. When his father died in 1939, he had to leave school because the family had no money. He went back to Lagos and trained as a coppersmith. During World War II, he served in the Royal Air Force.

After the war, Tutuola found a job with the government's Department of Labor as a messenger. He wrote his first novel, *The Palm-Wine Drinkard*, during this time. Set in a fantasy world, the book draws on Nigerian folklore and legends. The hero tells of his search for a dead companion in a land of ghosts and the lessons he learns on the way. Having failed to get beyond primary school, Tutuola writes in the imperfect English spoken on the streets of West Africa, and his work has been described as translating oral tradition into literary art.

Despite the book's great success and its adaptation into a play and an opera, Tutuola never became a full-time writer. In the 1960s and '70s, he worked for the Nigerian Broadcasting Corporation as a storekeeper, continuing to write in his spare time. His later works share similar themes – a hero or heroine journeying through strange and fabulous lands.

1954 My Life in the Bush of Ghosts
1956 Simbi and the Satyr of the Dark Jungle
1958 The Brave African Huntress
1962 The Feather Woman of the Jungle
1967 Ajaiyi and His Inherited Poverty
1982 The Witch-Herbalist of the Remote Town
1987 Pauper, Brawler, and Slanderer

TWAIN, Mark

American children's writer

Born Nov. 30, 1835
Died Apr. 21, 1910
Age at death 74

Mark Twain is one of America's great humorous writers. He created two famous characters – Tom Sawyer and Huckleberry Finn.

Twain was born Samuel Leghorne Clemens in Florida, Missouri, the fifth of six children. His father suffered ill health, and the family was poor. In 1839, they moved to Hannibal, a rapidly growing town on the Mississippi River, where Twain went to the local school. When he was 12, his father died and Twain had to leave school to find work.

At age 22, Twain became a river pilot at a time when there were 1,000 boats a day on the Mississippi. He followed this trade for four years and loved it, but river traffic ended during the American Civil War.

Becoming a full-time reporter in 1862, he soon began to use the pen name Mark Twain. He published his first important story at age 32, and his first successful novel, the humorous travel book *The Innocents Abroad*, when he was 34.

In 1870, Twain married Olivia Langdon, with whom he had five children. He wrote his classic children's stories, *The Adventures of Tom Sawyer* and *The Adventures of Huckleberry Finn*, in his 40s. Twain had become increasingly disillusioned by modern life and personal tragedies, and the books provided an opportunity for him to relive the "golden days" of his boyhood on the Mississippi. Both stories give a realistic picture of life around the Mississippi and are full of adventure and humor. *The Adventures of Huckleberry Finn*, considered his masterpiece, is noted for its accurate and sympathetic depiction of adolescent life.

Publications

1867 The Celebrated Jumping Frog of Calaveras County and Other Sketches
1869 The Innocents Abroad
1872 Roughing It
1876 The Adventures of Tom Sawyer
1881 The Prince and the Pauper
1884 The Adventures of Huckleberry Finn
1894 Pudd'nhead Wilson: A Tale

TYLER, Anne

American novelist and short-story writer

Born Oct. 25, 1941

Novelist Anne Tyler says that she has been "fascinated all my life by the tension between the wish to fly and the resolve to stay earthbound." This tension is present in all her work, which explores the day-to-day lives of middle-class American women.

Although born in Minneapolis, Tyler was raised in Quaker communities in North Carolina and elsewhere. She loved to read, and she describes her childhood as being spent "sitting behind a book waiting for adulthood to arrive." She earned a degree in Russian from Duke University in 1961, having already won awards for her writing, and she published her first novel, *If Morning Ever Comes*, at age 23. She continued her Russian as a graduate student at Columbia University in New York, and she worked for some time as a librarian. In 1963, Tyler married. She and her husband have two daughters.

Although Tyler now lives in Baltimore, much of her work is based in the South of her childhood, and she is often considered a Southern writer. She has been influenced by EUDORA WELTY, who also writes about life in the South. Tyler's fiction explores the conflicts of family life and the urge to escape. Her characters often look back to the past, longing to flee their present lives. Her 1985 novel *The Accidental Tourist* was made into a Hollywood movie; it uses an accident as a way to explore life's possibilities.

In 1989, Tyler won the Pulitzer Prize for *Breathing Lessons*. In this, her eleventh novel, Tyler examines the love and regrets of a couple who have been married for 28 years. It is written with typical humor and sensitivity.

Publications

1964	*If Morning Ever Comes*
1974	*Celestial Navigation*
1976	*Searching for Caleb*
1977	*Earthly Possessions*
1980	*Morgan's Passing*
1982	*Dinner at the Homesick Restaurant*
1985	*The Accidental Tourist*
1988	*Breathing Lessons*
1991	*Saint Maybe*
1995	*Ladder of Years*
1998	*A Patchwork Planet*

ULASI, Adaora Lily

Nigerian crime writer and journalist

Born c. 1932

Adaora Lily Ulasi was the first Nigerian to write crime novels in English.

Ulasi was born in Aba, southeastern Nigeria (West Africa), which was then a British colony. Her father was a high-ranking Igbo chief who worked as a judge. As a child, Ulasi listened to the stories her father told about the courtroom. She later based her crime novels on some of these stories.

Ulasi studied journalism in Los Angeles, California, graduating in 1954. After returning to Nigeria, she had a successful career as a women's page editor. She then moved to England with her new husband, where she had three children.

Ulasi's first novels, *Many Thing You No Understand* and its sequel *Many Thing Begin for Change*, were published when she was in her 30s. They are set in British-ruled Nigeria. The first is about a British official's investigation into the killing of people for an Igbo ruler's funeral. It ends with the official's death. The second book deals with the investigation into his death. Ulasi's crime novels have a uniquely African point of view – they include references to African religions and rituals, and characters speak in the pidgin ("broken") English used on the streets of West Africa. By contrast, her novel *The Night Harry Died* is set in the American South of the early 1900s.

Ulasi returned to Nigeria after her marriage broke up in 1972 and became editor of the popular magazine *Woman's World*. In 1976, she went back to England and devoted herself to journalism and writing.

Publications

1970	*Many Thing You No Understand*
1971	*Many Thing Begin for Change*
1974	*The Night Harry Died*
1978	*Who Is Jonah?*
1978	*The Man from Sagamu*

UNDSET, Sigrid

Norwegian novelist

Born May 20, 1882
Died Jun. 10, 1949
Age at death 67

Sigrid Undset is regarded as one of the greatest Norwegian novelists of the 20th century. In 1928, in recognition of her contribution to literature, she was awarded the Nobel Prize.

Undset was born in Kalundborg, Denmark, the daughter of a Norwegian archeologist from whom she derived a keen interest in historical Norway and the country's legends and folklore. When she was 11, her father died and, at age 16, she had to get a secretarial job in an office, where she worked for the next 10 years. During that time, Undset became concerned about the status of women in society and decided to write about it. Her work experiences provided excellent material and, at the age of 25, she published her first novel, *Mrs. Marta Oulie*. Four years later her third novel, *Jenny,* the story of a promising young artist who commits suicide, caused a storm.

The novels that followed include two long, multivolume historical novels of the Middle Ages, the first of which, *Kristin Lavransdatter*, is a dramatic story of love and religion in 14th-century Norway. This is usually considered her masterpiece. Later she became a Roman Catholic and turned to writing books in a realistic contemporary setting that reflect her new attitudes to life and deepening interest in religion.

During World War II, Undset, who was an outspoken critic of the Nazis, had to flee from Nazi-occupied Norway to the US. While in America, she lectured and wrote in support of her much-abused country and its exiled government. She returned home at the end of the war and died a few years later.

Publications

1907	*Mrs. Marta Oulie*
1909	*Gunnar's Daughter*
1911	*Jenny*
1920–22	*Kristin Lavransdatter*
1925–27	*The Master of Hestviken*
1929	*The Wild Orchid*
1930	*The Burning Bush*
1934	*The Longest Years*
1936	*The Faithful Wife*
1939	*Madame Dorthea*

UPDIKE, John

American novelist, short-story writer and critic

Born Mar. 18, 1932

Publications

1960 Rabbit, Run
1963 The Centaur
1966 The Music School
1968 Couples
1971 Rabbit Redux
1981 Rabbit Is Rich
1984 The Witches of Eastwick
1990 Rabbit at Rest
1996 In the Beauty of the Lillies
1997 Toward the End of Time
1998 Bech at Bay
2000 Gertrude and Claudius

John Updike is a prolific writer whose fiction strips away the respectable surface of suburban American families to reveal the painful feelings of inadequacy and unfulfilled dreams lurking beneath. His tone is not condemning but sympathetic and often humorous. He once said that his ambition was to be a cartoonist.

Updike was born in Shillington, Pennsylvania but, while still young, he moved from town to an isolated farm, where he was very lonely. His early stories tend to draw on his youth and the longing for escape while fearing its consequences. However, his first novel, published when he was 27, has a more unusual concern – it is about the residents of an old people's home who have reached the end of their life's journey.

After studying at Harvard and spending a year at the Ruskin College of Art in Oxford, Updike worked on the staff of the *New Yorker* magazine from 1955 to 1957. He has continued to contribute to the magazine ever since.

At 28, Updike created his most famous character – Rabbit Angstrom, a typical suburban male whose life is explored over four novels. Starting with a young man confused by the demands of his growing family, Updike chronicles Rabbit's progress through the turbulent 1960s to wealthy, but spiritually empty, middle age. The third novel, *Rabbit Is Rich*, won the Pulitzer Prize in 1982. The last novel in the series, *Rabbit at Rest*, depicts Rabbit in retirement and, in 1991, it also won a Pulitzer Prize.

Updike has also published collections of poems, short stories, essays and criticism.

URIS, Leon

American novelist and screenwriter

Born Aug. 3, 1924

Leon Uris is known for his bestselling adventure novels based on recent historical events.

Uris was born in Baltimore, Maryland, and served in the US Marine Corps during World War II. He worked as newspaper driver for the *San Francisco Call-Bulletin* until he became a full-time writer at age 26.

Uris achieved immediate success with his first novel, *Battle Cry*, which was published when he was 29. Drawing on his own experience, he wrote about how marines trained and fought in World War II. When he was 34, he published one of his most famous, and successful, novels, *Exodus*, which traces the history of European Jews from the 19th century to the founding of the state of Israel in 1948.

Both works have been made into popular movies.

Uris's later works follow the pattern of his earlier novels. In each case, he sets a fictional main character in the center of a real historical event. Based on his careful research, Uris not only tells the story of his hero but also skillfully develops the history of a major event. He makes the story easily understandable to his audience without leaving out the real complexity. In his later novels, he explores such subjects as the 1948 Berlin airlift (in *Armageddon*) – during which the Russians blockaded the city and supplies had to be flown in; the conflicts in Northern Ireland, in *Trinity*; and in *Mila 18,* the 1943 Warsaw ghetto uprising in which 60,000 Jews rebeled against the Nazis.

Uris has also written a number of screenplays, the most famous of which was for the 1957 movie *Gunfight at the OK Corral*.

Publications

1953 Battle Cry
1955 The Angry Hills
1958 Exodus
1960 Mila 18
1964 Armageddon
1967 Topaz
1970 QB VII
1976 Trinity
1984 The Haj
1988 Mitla Pass

VALÉRY, Paul

French poet and essayist

Born Oct. 30, 1871
Died Jul. 20, 1945
Age at death 73

Even though he wrote poetry for only a few years of his life, Paul Valéry is regarded as one of the greatest French poets of the last 100 years. He was brought up in the south of France, and his poetry reflects his love of the Mediterranean Sea, sky and sun.

Valéry's first creative period was as a young man between the ages of 17 and 20. Several of his poems from this period were published in literary magazines. At age 21, he stopped writing because of an unhappy love affair. He made his decision during a violent thunderstorm that, he later reported, made him reject the personal nature of poetry.

Valéry was intensely interested in education, politics, culture and especially in science and mathematics. He read very widely and met many famous scientists. From age 23 onward, he got up at dawn every day to read and think about science and philosophy. He wrote his thoughts and ideas down in notebooks, which were published after his death. His poems reflect his intellectual interests but at the same time are very lyrical and full of feeling.

After his early 20s, Valéry did not publish any poetry again until he was 46. In that year, he finished *The Young Fate*, a 500-line poem that had taken him five years to write. *Charms*, his last major poetry collection, appeared when he was 51.

Throughout his life, Valéry wrote essays on many different literary and cultural subjects. Toward the end of his life, he became a national celebrity and lectured all over Europe. He became a professor of poetry and was given a state funeral when he died.

Publications

1896 An Evening with Monsieur Teste
1917 The Young Fate
1920 The Album of Early Verse
1922 Charms
1924 Dance and the Soul
1931 Regarding the Real World
1932 Eupalions: or, the Architect

Published after he died

1946 The Graveyard by the Sea
1957–60 Notebooks

Van DOREN, Mark

American poet and critic

Born Jun. 13, 1894
Died Dec. 10, 1972
Age at death 78

Publications

- *1920 The Poetry of John Dryden*
- *1924 Spring Thunder and Other Poems*
- *1926 7 P.M. and Other Poems*
- *1928 Now the Sky and Other Poems*
- *1931 Jonathan Gentry*
- *1935 The Last Look and Other Poems*
- *1939 Collected Poems 1922–38*
- *1953 Mortal Summer*
- *1960 Morning Worship and Other Poems*

Mark Van Doren published over a dozen collections of poetry during his long life and was awarded the Pulitzer Prize in 1940 for his *Collected Poems 1922–38*.

Van Doren was born in Hope, Illinois, moving to Urbana when he was six. He attended secondary school before going to the University of Illinois and taking his degree in 1915. He followed his brother to Columbia University but interrupted his studies to serve in the army during World War I. At 26, he completed a book on the poetry of John Dryden, who was a major influence on his writing style. His brother offered him the job of literary editor on the *Nation*, then a famous magazine. There he met his wife, and they were married in 1922.

Van Doren's first book of short poems, *Spring Thunder and Other Poems*, published when he was 30, celebrates the rural life he and his wife shared on their farm in northwest Connecticut, as do two further collections *7 P.M. and Other Poems* and *Now the Sky and Other Poems*. *The Last Look and Other Poems* records in great detail a long vacation spent on the farm in 1932.

Van Doren's other work included editing *An Anthology of World Poetry* (1928) and *The Oxford Book of American Prose* (1932) as well as studies on Walt Whitman, Ralph Waldo Emerson, and William Wordsworth. On his retirement, Van Doren took more time to travel and write. His later collections of poems, *Mortal Summer* and *Morning Worship and Other Poems*, take a greater concern with religion and death.

Van DUYN, Mona

American poet

Born May 9, 1921

Mona Van Duyn is one of America's most distinguished poets. In 1992, aged 71, she became the first female Poet Laureate of the United States.

Van Duyn was born in Waterloo, Iowa, and attended teaching college and Iowa State University. She taught at the well-known writers' workshop at the University of Iowa and, in 1947, she founded *Perspectives*, a literary journal that she edited for over 20 years. She has also taught at other universities and writers' workshops around the country. In 1950, she moved with her husband to St. Louis, Missouri, where they have lived ever since.

Van Duyn published her first collection of poetry, *Valentines to the Wide World*, when she was 38. In 1971, she won the National Book

Award for *To See, To Take*. Other awards include the Liones Prize from the National Institute of Arts and Letters in 1976 and a fellowship from the Academy of American Poets.

Many of Van Duyn's poems use what is sometimes called "domestic" imagery: they feature home related activities such as cooking, cleaning, and gardening. She dislikes the fact that women poets are often called "domestic" in a dismissive way. Her poems explore universal themes with thoughts about our world and the way we view it and about how we interact with one another. They are often humorous and sometimes painful. *Letters from a Father* is dedicated to her parents, who both died in 1980, and a number of its poems refer to their aging and to her memories of them. Her collection *Near Changes* won the Pulitzer Prize in 1991.

Publications

1959 Valentines to the Wide World
1964 A Time of Bees
1970 To See, To Take
1972 Bedtime Stories
1973 Merciful Disguises
1982 Letters from a Father
1990 Near Changes
1993 Firefall

Van VOGT, A.E.

American science fiction writer

Born Apr. 26, 1912

A.E. van Vogt is a unique and popular writer of science fiction.

Alfred Elton van Vogt was born in Winnipeg, Canada, to Dutch parents. The family moved to rural Saskatchewan, returning to Winnipeg when van Vogt was 14. The move unsettled him, and he became a loner. At 19, he began working as a government employee and took a course in creative writing. Soon he was writing stories himself.

Van Vogt's first published science fiction story, "The Black Destroyer," appeared when he was 27. It is about a catlike creature that boards a spaceship and kills the crew. Another story, "The Vault of the Beast," describes a shapeshifting monster, again on a spaceship, who seeks the answer to a mathematical problem. The plot of the story is overcomplicated, but it contains fascinating ideas about mathematics and human psychology.

The following year van Vogt's first novel, *Slan*, appeared. It describes the adventures of Johnny Cross, a human mutant with great powers of endurance and the ability to read minds. The novel raises many questions about human evolution and became one of the most successful science fiction novels ever published.

In the 1950s, van Vogt became fascinated with dianetics, a theory about human potential devised by L. Ron Hubbard, and for many years he reworked old ideas instead of publishing original science fiction. Eventually, he returned to writing novels that explored the outer limits of the world of ideas while entertaining readers with action-packed plots.

Publications

1946 Slan
1947 The Weapon Makers
1948 The World of A–
1951 The Weapon Shops of Isher
1952 Away and Beyond
1956 Empire of the Atom
1969 The Silkie
1971 The Battle of Forever
1984 Null-A Three

VARGAS LLOSA, Mario

Peruvian novelist, short-story writer and playwright

Born Mar. 28, 1936

Mario Vargas Llosa is known both for his literary work and for running for president of Peru.

Vargas Llosa was born in Arequipa, Peru, and was educated initially in Cochabamba, Bolivia, where his grandfather was the Peruvian consul. He continued his schooling in Peru and at age 14 entered a military school in the capital, Lima.

Vargas Llosa wasted no time in becoming a writer, and his first published work, a three-act play called *The Escape of the Inca*, appeared when he was only 16. He then wrote stories for Peruvian literary magazines and produced two books about literature. He continued his education at the University of Madrid in Spain and worked as a journalist and broadcaster. When he was 23, he moved to Paris, where he lived until he was 30. He has also lived in London, Washington and Barcelona.

Vargas Llosa's first novel, *The Time of the Hero*, published when he was 27, was based on his experiences in military school. It was a great success and has been translated into many languages. Later novels deal with the frustrations of Peruvians living under a military dictatorship. At age 41, Vargas Llosa published the comic autobiographical novel *Aunt Julia and the Scriptwriter*, which has since been made into a movie.

Vargas Llosa is also a major literary critic and has written important studies of writers Gabriel García Márquez and Albert Camus, among others. In 1990, Vargas Llosa came close to being elected president of Peru but was defeated.

Publications

1963 The Time of the Hero
1966 The Green House
1969 Conversation in the Cathedral
1977 Aunt Julia and the Scriptwriter
1981 The War of the End of the World
1987 The Storyteller
1991 A Writer's Reality
1994 A Fish in the Water

VERLAINE, Paul

French poet

Born Mar. 30, 1844
Died Jan. 8, 1896
Age at death 51

One of the most gifted of France's 19th-century poets, Paul Verlaine's work is full of feeling and desire. He always tried to use simple, musical language.

Throughout his life Verlaine was an extremely unstable person. Sometimes he was very rebellious and angry, sometimes ordered and loving. Born in Metz, northeast France, he started studying law in Paris at age 18, but gave up two years later. His father refused to finance him any longer because he spent so much time drinking and writing. Instead, he worked as a clerk. When he was 22, his first book, *Saturnine Poems*, appeared.

Four years later Verlaine married Mathilde Mauté, and they had a son. The marriage was not happy and, after two years, Verlaine left his wife and child. He had fallen in love with a younger poet, ARTHUR RIMBAUD. The two men lived together in London and Brussels, but in 1873 they quarreled. Verlaine shot and wounded Rimbaud, and he was arrested and imprisoned for 18 months.

The next few years were quieter. Verlaine returned to his religious faith, Catholicism, and worked as a schoolteacher. He adopted a pupil, Lucien Létinois, and they ran a farm together. Lucien died of typhus in 1883. In *Wisdom,* Verlaine reflected on his earlier life, and *Love* was inspired by Lucien's death.

For the rest of his life, Verlaine lived in poverty in Paris. He was often ill, partly because he drank so much, and he spent long periods in the hospital. But his poetry became famous, and he lectured in several countries. In 1894, he was elected France's Prince of Poets. Despite his fame Verlaine died in poverty.

Publications

1866 *Saturnine Poems*
1869 *Gallant Parties*
1874 *Romances without Words*
1880 *Wisdom*
1884 *Accursed Poets*
1884 *Long Ago and Not So Long Ago*
1888 *Love*
1889 *In Parallel*
1892 *Intimate Liturgies*
1893 *Elegies*

VERNE, Jules

Jules Verne is famous for his imaginative adventure novels, which are the first examples of science fiction.

Born in the port of Nantes, western France, the son of a lawyer, Verne went to Paris to study law. There his uncle introduced him into literary circles, and he met ALEXANDRE DUMAS. During this time, he was busily writing plays but managed to pass his law degree. His one-act comedy, *The Broken Straws,* was performed in Paris when he was 22 and, the following year, he published some short stories. At age 28, he married a young widow, Honorine de Viane, acquiring two step-children, and became a stockbroker to provide a secure income; but he managed to write as well and achieved his first real popularity with *Five Weeks in a Balloon* when he was 35. Verne was a better writer than stockbroker, and after the success of *A Journey to the Center of the Earth* when he was 36, he devoted himself to writing.

Verne's books describe incredible adventures in intriguing machines, influencing later writers like H.G. WELLS. His bizarre stories caught the imagination of 19th-century readers, who were themselves enthralled by scientific progress and recent inventions such as the airplane. Machines that hadn't been invented, such as spacecraft, were imagined by Verne, and his descriptions made them sound believable. His two most successful works are *Twenty Thousand Leagues under the Sea*, about Captain Nemo, who travels in a submarine under the oceans, and *Around the World in Eighty Days*, about the journey of Phileas Fogg around the Earth in the then incredible time of just 80 days.

French science fiction writer

Born Feb. 8, 1828
Died Mar. 24, 1905
Age at death 77

Publications

1863 *Five Weeks in a Balloon*
1864 *A Journey to the Center of the Earth*
1865 *From the Earth to the Moon*
1870 *Twenty Thousand Leagues under the Sea*
1873 *Around the World in Eighty Days*
1904 *The Master of the World*

Published after he died

1994 *Paris in the 20th Century*

VIDAL, Gore

American novelist, playwright and essayist

Born Oct. 3, 1925

Gore Vidal is best known for his many satires about politics and politicians.

Eugene Luther Vidal was born at the military academy in West Point, New York, where his father was an instructor. He spent much of his childhood in Washington, DC, with his grandfather Senator Thomas Gore, a witty and scholarly man from whom he learned about political life. When he was a teenager he adopted the first name Gore.

At the age of 18, during World War II, Vidal served on an army supply ship in the Aleutian Islands, near Alaska. This experience became the background of his first novel, ***Williwaw***, published to critical acclaim when he was only 21. Two years later his writing career suffered a setback when ***The City and the Pillar*** was published. This novel, about a young man satisfactorily coming to terms with his homosexuality, proved too controversial for the general public. Though still writing, he found additional work as a TV dramatist and political commentator.

In 1960, Vidal ran for Congress, lost, and returned to writing novels, many of whose characters are real historical figures. For example, ***Julian*** depicts the Roman emperor's struggle against the new Christian religion in the fourth century AD. ***Lincoln*** is a carefully researched novel about Abraham Lincoln and is part of a series of novels about American history. In ***Live from Golgotha,*** Vidal portrays events in the Bible as though they are being reported on television.

Vidal recollects his early life and his friendship with, among others, President Kennedy's family in his memoirs, ***Palimpsest***.

Publications

1946 Williwaw
1948 The City and the Pillar
1960 The Best Man
1964 Julian
1967 Washington, DC
1968 Myra Breckinridge
1976 1876
1984 Lincoln
1992 Live from Golgotha
1995 Palimpsest

VILLON, François

French poet

Born 1431
Died c. 1463
Age at death c. 32

Although the poetry of François Villon ranks among the most fascinating and romantic of the medieval period, he is probably best remembered for his disgraceful life of crime.

Born François de Montcorbier, he took the name of his guardian – a priest who supported him until he had graduated from university. While he was a student, Villon got into bad company. After becoming a master of arts at the age of 21, he killed a priest in a street brawl and had to flee from Paris a few years later.

When he was 25, Villon was given a pardon and returned to Paris. He then wrote a remarkable set of poems called the ***Petit Testament***. It was not long before he was again in trouble. He took part in a robbery of funds from a university in Navarre on the border between France and Spain and then fled to central France. There the 30-year-old Villon began writing his masterpiece, *Grand Testament*, a long poem and series of ballads. He was forgiven for the robbery, but shortly afterward he was sentenced to death, for another crime, then pardoned again. When he was 31, he was arrested for theft and brawling and again sentenced to death. This time the sentence was changed to permanent exile, and he left Paris. Nothing is known of what happened to him after that.

Villon's poetry is deeply moving. Drawing from his own colorful life, he uses vivid language and irony to create striking images. He wrote about prostitutes and drunkenness, but he also dealt with love and morality, death, compassion for suffering and deep regret for his wasted life. His poem "Ballad of Hanged Men" was written as he reflected on his own death sentence.

Publications

1456 *Petit Testament*

1462 "Ballad of Hanged Men"

Published after he died

1489 *Grand Testament*

VIRGIL

Roman poet

Born Oct. 15, 70 BC

Died Sep. 21, 19 BC

Age at death c. 50

Virgil was the greatest poet of ancient Rome and one of the greatest literary figures in history. He was born near the city of Mantua in northern Italy, where his family owned a small farm. His rural childhood left him with a lifelong love of the countryside that he often expressed in his poems.

During Virgil's lifetime, the Roman Republic (a form of government that had ruled the Roman people for centuries) collapsed, and a man called Augustus became the first Roman emperor. This was a time of enormous social and political change in the Roman world. Virgil and other poets of the time tried to write new works that reflected their excitement and high hopes about the future of the Roman people.

Virgil wanted to show that Rome had become the new center of the world and that the Roman language, Latin, had replaced Greek as the language of learning and culture. When he was 41, he completed the *Georgics*, a long poem in four books about farming life. It was directly inspired by the ancient Greek poet HESIOD's *Works and Days*, which was regarded as a great classic even in Virgil's time.

Virgil spent the last ten years of his life composing his greatest work, the *Aeneid*. It was written at the request of the emperor, who wanted an epic poem for the Romans that would rival HOMER'S poem, the *Iliad*. The *Aeneid* is a sequel to the *Iliad*. Its 12 books tell the story of Aeneas, a survivor of the Trojan Wars who, after many adventures and tragedies, becomes the founder of Rome. It became one of the most influential works in European literature.

Publications

37 BC *Eclogues* (or *Bucolics*)

29 BC *Georgics* (or *Art of Husbandry*)

19 BC *Aeneid*

VITTORINI, Elio

Italian novelist and essayist

Born Jul. 23, 1908
Died Feb. 13, 1966
Age at death 57

Elio Vittorini wrote highly realistic novels about the lives of ordinary people. He wrote in a very direct style that presents events without making any comment or judgment about them.

The son of a railway worker, Vittorini was born in Siracusa on the Italian island of Sicily. Intensely unhappy, he ran away from home three times while still in his early teens. Because of this he was mainly self-taught, and he developed an early love of foreign literature. He strongly rejected the "provincial" atmosphere that dominated Italian writing at the time and was influenced by the work of the American novelists Ernest Hemingway and John Steinbeck.

At age 22, Vittorini moved to Florence, Italy, where he worked as an editor. After teaching himself English, he began translating the works of foreign authors, doing much to introduce new literature to the Italian public. When he was 23, he published his first book, *Petty Bourgeoisie*. *The Red Carnation* followed two years later and showed clearly his developing ideas about social and economic injustice.

When he was 33, Vittorini published the book that made him famous, *In Sicily*. This novel tells of an ordinary man's journey back to his hometown. It was seen as a celebration of the individual against the state and was praised by groups fighting fascism throughout Europe.

During World War II, Vittorini became increasingly involved in politics. He joined the communists fighting against fascist forces in Italy. After the war, he became a leading figure in promoting the work of new Italian authors.

Publications

1931 Petty Bourgeoisie
1933 The Red Carnation
1936 Voyage to Sardinia
1941 In Sicily
1947 The Twilight of the Elephant
1949 Women of Messina
1956 The Dark and the Light
1957 Public Diary

Published after he died

1967 Two Tensions

VOLTAIRE

French satirist and philosopher

Born Nov. 21, 1694
Died May 30, 1778
Age at death 83

Voltaire was one of the leading thinkers of the 18th century. He wrote poetry, plays and books on politics, history and philosophy that had a great influence on European society long after his death.

Voltaire was born François Marie Arovet in Paris. He went to a college run by Jesuit priests and studied law before becoming a writer. Tall, thin and odd-looking, he suffered from poor health but had great energy, stimulated by endless cups of coffee. His written attacks on opponents could be savage, but he was also a loyal friend and believed passionately in the rights of the individual, including free speech. According to legend he famously declared, "I disagree with what you say, but I will defend to the death your right to say it."

His constant criticism of the French government and the Catholic

Church soon got Voltaire into serious trouble and, when he was 22, he was put in jail. Later, he moved to England for three years to avoid trouble. Back in Paris in 1733 he published *Philosophical Letters*, which contrasts the French system of government with the democratic system he had seen in England. The authorities banned this book and, once again, Voltaire had to flee Paris.

Eventually Voltaire settled in the small French town of Ferney, from where he could easily escape across the border into Switzerland if necessary. There, aged 65, he wrote his best-known book, *Candide*, a satire about an optimist who goes on believing that everything is for the best despite living through a series of disasters.

Publications

1718 *Oedipus*
1728 *The Henriade*
1730 *Brutus*
1731 *Charles XII*
1733 *Philosophical Letters*
1748 *Sémiramis*
1751 *The Century of Louis XIV*
1759 *Candide*
1760 *Tancrèdi*
1778 *Irène*

VONNEGUT, Kurt, Jr.

American novelist and science fiction writer

Born Nov. 11, 1922

Kurt Vonnegut, Jr., is an original and thought-provoking writer who often writes stories with science fiction settings, although he denies that he is a science fiction writer.

Born in Indianapolis, the son of an architect, Vonnegut wrote for his secondary school newspaper before going to Cornell University, where he studied chemistry. America entered World War II when Vonnegut was 20; he joined the army and was sent to Europe. Within a few days of reaching the front line, he was captured by the Germans and sent to work in a factory in the German city of Dresden. In 1945, Dresden was utterly destroyed by Allied bombers, and Vonnegut was one of the few people to survive.

After returning from the war, Vonnegut continued his studies at the University of Chicago, then worked for a news agency and for a large multinational company as a public relations officer. His first novel, *Player Piano*, was published when he was 30. It is set in a future where scientists and corporate engineers have attempted to automate everything. His second novel, *Cat's Cradle*, is about a scientist working on the atomic bomb who absentmindedly creates a chemical that turns all water into ice and brings about the end of the world.

Vonnegut's best-known book, *Slaughterhouse-Five*, is based on his wartime experiences. It is about an American prisoner in Dresden who survives the bombing and is transported through time by a race of superintelligent beings from a distant planet who eventually put him in a zoo.

Publications

1952 *Player Piano*
1963 *Cat's Cradle*
1968 *Welcome to the Monkey House*
1969 *Slaughterhouse-Five*
1973 *Breakfast of Champions*
1976 *Slapstick*
1985 *Galápagos*
1987 *Bluebeard*
1990 *Hocus Pocus*
1997 *Timequake*

VOZNESENSKY, Andrei

Russian poet

Born May 12, 1933

Andrei Voznesensky was a leading Russian poet in the period after the death of the dictator Joseph Stalin in 1953.

Voznesensky was born in Moscow. He grew up during World War II, when the suffering in Russia, under attack by the Germans, was severe. His experience of war is reflected in some of his poetry; his famous poem "Goya," published when he was 27, is a powerful vision of the horrors of war. He trained as an architect but while still a student sent some of his poems to the novelist BORIS PASTERNAK, who encouraged and advised him for several years.

Voznesensky's first published poems appeared when he was 26. In the late 1950s and early '60s, public poetry readings became very popular in Russia. Voznesensky soon became a star performer and would give readings in sports stadiums before thousands of listeners. He used his reputation to lead a revolt against the censorship of literature in Soviet Russia and fell out of favor with the government, which accused him of not having the right attitude to communist ideas.

While on tour in the US during the 1960s and '70s, Voznesensky gained an international reputation and greatly impressed the poets ROBERT LOWELL and W.H. AUDEN. They praised his clever, experimental and often comic work. The trip was the inspiration for Voznesensky's series of poems called *The Triangular Pear*, which caused uproar in Soviet Russia.

Publications

1959 "The Masters"
1960 *Mosaic*
1960 *Parabola*
1960 "Goya"
1962 *The Triangular Pear*
1964 *Selected Poems*
1966 *An Achilles Heart*
1974 *Story under Full Sail*
1978 *Nostalgia for the Present*
1987 *An Arrow in the Wall*

WALCOTT, Derek

St. Lucian poet and playwright

Born Jan. 23, 1930

In his poems and plays, writer Derek Walcott explores the tortured route from slavery to independence and the resulting multicultural mixture of identities. He blends the traditions of Caribbean storytelling with European and other literary traditions.

Walcott was awarded the Nobel Prize for Literature in 1992. His success as a writer has inspired many young Caribbean writers. Born on the island of St. Lucia, Walcott was raised by his mother to love literature and the theater, his father having died when Derek was a baby. Walcott's twin brother is also a playwright. In a mostly Catholic, French-speaking community, Walcott, of both African and European ancestry, was brought up as a Methodist and was interested in the English language. In university, he was introduced to

European literature, especially the works of JAMES JOYCE, W.B. YEATS, and JOHN MILLINGTON SYNGE.

Walcott was an ambitious author: at age 18 he borrowed $200 from his mother to have his first book, *Twenty-Five Poems*, privately printed. He sold the book on street corners and it attracted the praise of critics.

Walcott received a scholarship to the University of the West Indies in Jamaica. His first play, *Henri Christophe*, was performed when he was only 20. In 1959, he founded the Trinidad Theater Workshop. Today he has homes in Trinidad and in Boston, where he teaches at Boston University. His epic poem *Omeros* is loosely based on the ancient Greek poet HOMER's *Odyssey*. Set in the Caribbean, *Omeros* explores the relationship between personal and collective memories.

Publications

1962 In a Green Night
1967 Dream on Monkey Mountain
1973 Another Life
1976 Sea Grapes
1977 The Star-Apple Kingdom
1984 Midsummer
1984 Collected Poems 1948–84
1987 The Arkansas Testament
1990 Omeros

WALKER, Alice

American novelist, poet and short-story writer

Born Feb. 9, 1944

Alice Walker is one of America's most respected contemporary writers. Much of her work describes the oppression of African-American women, but always with a sense of the will to survive and thrive.

Walker was born in Eatonton, Georgia, the youngest of eight children of a poor sharecropping family. She lost her vision in one eye when one of her brothers accidentally shot her with a BB gun and, after that, she spent much of her time alone, reading. Walker says that her mother gave her three gifts when she was growing up: a sewing machine, a suitcase and a typewriter – gifts symbolic of the independence she wanted for her daughter.

After studying in Atlanta, Walker went to university in New York, which broadened her range of experiences beyond her native South. She published her first book, the poetry collection *Once*, when she was just 24.

Walker went back to the South to work in the voter registration drive of the late 1960s. Still in the South, she married a fellow civil rights worker, gave birth to her daughter Rebecca, and completed her first novel, *The Third Life of Grange Copeland*.

Although already well known, she became an international bestseller at age 38, when her novel *The Color Purple* was published. Through letters it tells the story of a young, poor black woman, abused by her family and husband, whose close friendship with another black woman leads to happiness. It was a huge success and was made into a movie. The book also won Walker both the Pulitzer Prize and the National Book Award in 1983.

Publications

1968 Once
1970 The Third Life of Grange Copeland
1979 Good Night, Willie Lee, I'll See You in the Morning
1982 The Color Purple
1985 Horses Make a Landscape Look More Beautiful
1989 The Temple of My Familiar
1996 The Same River Twice: Honoring the Difficult
1998 By the Light of My Father's Smile

WALKER, Margaret

American poet and novelist

Born Jul. 7, 1915

Margaret Walker's first book of poetry, *For My People*, marked a milestone in African-American literary history. In 1942, it was rare for a black woman poet to be published, and this book brought her recognition as an important new talent.

Walker was born in Birmingham, Alabama. Her mother was a music teacher, and her father was a minister who spoke several languages. The young Walker was surrounded by a love of learning, and she was an early achiever – reading by age 4, finishing university by 19. The family moved to New Orleans, where her parents began teaching at the university. It was in college there that 16-year-old Walker showed her work to the poet LANGSTON HUGHES, who was giving a reading and who encouraged her to continue.

Later, after moving to Chicago, Walker met W.E.B. DU BOIS at Northwestern University and then worked with GWENDOLYN BROOKS and RICHARD WRIGHT at the Federal Writers' Project, part of President Roosevelt's Works Progress Administration. Walker's *For My People*, published when she was 27, earned her widespread recognition, and she became the first black poet to win the Yale Younger Poets' Award. She spent the next two decades teaching to support her family, and it wasn't until she was 51 that she published again. She had just finished her Ph.D., for which she submitted the novel *Jubilee*. Her best-known work, it retells the story of Walker's great-grandmother, who went from slavery to freedom. The novel was hugely popular and was made into an opera and translated into several languages.

Publications

1942 For My People

1966 Jubilee

1966 Ballad of the Free

1970 Prophets for a New Day

1973 October Journey

1986 For Farish Street Green

1989 This Is My Century

1990 How I Wrote Jubilee and Other Essays on Life and Literature

WALLACE, Edgar

English novelist and crime writer

Born Apr. 1, 1875

Died Feb. 10, 1932

Age at death 56

Edgar Wallace was one of the creators of the modern thriller. Rather than concentrating on plot and character, his stories rely on action, excitement and sensational events.

Wallace was abandoned as a baby, and he was brought up by a poor family in London. He left school at 12 years old and did a number of jobs; he was, at various times, a merchant seaman, a plasterer, a printer, a milk-delivery boy and a rubber-factory worker. His early life on the streets of London helped him create believable characters when he became a writer.

When he was 18, Wallace joined the Army and went to fight in South Africa in the Boer War. In 1899, he left the Army and got a job as a war correspondent. Back in England he continued to work as a journalist, becoming also a racing correspondent and a drama critic. He also began writing novels and plays. Wallace's first book, *The Mission that Failed!*, was published when he was 23. Seven years later his first success came with the mystery novel *The Four Just Men*. Unable to find a publisher, Wallace financed the book himself. The first edition lacked the final chapter, and readers were asked to solve the mystery in order to win a prize.

Wallace's output as a writer was enormous. As well as his journalism, he wrote poetry, plays, 175 novels, and a ten-volume history of World War I. It was his novels that caught the public imagination, and he became a very popular mystery writer. The speed at which Wallace wrote was legendary – it was said that he wrote the novel *The Coat of Arms* over a weekend.

Publications

1898	*The Mission that Failed!*
1905	*The Four Just Men*
1911	*Sanders of the River*
1918	*The Man Who Knew*
1922	*The Angel of Terror*
1923	*The Clue of the New Pin*
1927	*The Man Who Was Nobody*
1931	*The Coat of Arms*
1932	*The Case of the Frightened Lady*

WALPOLE, Horace

English writer

Born Sep. 24, 1717
Died Mar. 2, 1797
Age at death 79

Horace Walpole achieved lasting literary fame for the 4,000 personal letters he wrote during his lifetime; many consider these the finest collection of private letters in the English language.

Born in London, Walpole was the son of Britain's longest-serving prime minister, Robert Walpole. At age nine, he was sent to the famous Eton College, where he stayed until he was 17. From Eton he went on to Cambridge University and, at age 24, he was elected to parliament just as his father was being forced to resign as prime minister. Although he went on to serve for 17 years in parliament, the younger Walpole soon became bored with politics.

In addition to many hundreds of letters, Walpole wrote a pioneering novel, *The Castle of Otranto*, published when he was 48, which was the first gothic novel. He also composed satirical verses and produced a poetic tragedy, *The Mysterious Mother*. These were not his main achievements, however. His most valuable contribution to literature lies first in his outstanding series of historical memoirs and second in his personal letters, which give details of almost every aspect of English national life – from politics and entertainment to crime, sports, theater and art. In addition, he compiled *Anecdotes of Painting in England*, the first work of art history in the English language.

Walpole was also a printer and, in his 30s, he published, among other work, several poems by his good friend the poet THOMAS GRAY.

Publications

1748	*Aedes Walpolianae*
1757	*A Letter from Xo Ho*
1762–71	*Anecdotes of Painting in England*
1765	*The Castle of Otranto*
1768	*Historic Doubts on the Life and Reign of King Richard the Third*
1768	*The Mysterious Mother*
1785	*Hieroglyphic Tales*

WAMBAUGH, Joseph

American crime writer

Born Jan. 22, 1937

Joseph Wambaugh is one of the first serving policemen to become a successful crime writer. Rather than writing detective stories about a private individual solving crimes, his novels are realistic "police procedurals" – that is, they are about the day-to-day work of officers in a police department.

Wambaugh was born in East Pittsburgh, Pennsylvania, and later moved to California, where he completed his education. After serving in the US Marine Corps, he joined the Los Angeles Police Department, where he became a detective sergeant. After more than ten years in the department, he became a full-time writer.

Wambaugh based his books on the knowledge he gained as a police officer. There are many themes in his stories. A major theme concerns the psychological effects of police work on individuals. He shows how coping with violence and horror on a daily basis often makes policemen emotionally isolated and withdrawn. Another theme concerns the way in which luck and chance, as well as careful police work, play a part in solving crimes. As Wambaugh's writing developed, this theme became more important, so that the absurd aspects of horrific situations are played up.

Wambaugh also wrote several stories based on true crimes. The first of these, *The Onion Field*, tells the story of a police officer who is kidnapped by two criminals. When the criminals kill the officer's colleague, the officer has a mental breakdown. Later, true crime stories such as *Lines and Shadows* also explore the psychology of policemen trapped in impossible situations.

Publications

1971 The New Centurions
1972 The Blue Knight
1973 The Onion Field
1975 The Choirboys
1978 The Black Marble
1983 The Delta Star
1984 Lines and Shadows
1990 The Golden Orange
1992 Fugitive Nights
1996 Floaters

WARREN, Robert Penn

American poet, novelist, and critic

Born Apr. 24, 1905
Died Sep. 15, 1989
Age at death 84

Robert Penn Warren was a distinguished writer who made an immense contribution to American literature. He became America's first Poet Laureate and won the Pulitzer Prize three times.

Born in Guthrie, Kentucky, Warren had a keen interest in natural history, and this shaped his interest in writing, as did the war stories told by his grandfather. Prevented from enrolling in naval college because of a hunting accident in which he lost an eye, he started writing his first book, *John Brown: The Making of a Martyr*, while studying at Berkeley and Yale. This harsh analysis of the abolitionist's life and politics was published when Warren was 24.

Warren began writing poetry in the early 1920s. Many of the ideas in his poems draw from his rural Southern roots. The poems often contain bizarre images and a lyrical mixture of formal and informal language; Warren believed that this contrast in language created more realistic poetry. In 1922, he joined a group of poets known as the Fugitives and, in 1930, he contributed to their manifesto, *I'll Take My Stand*. His contribution was an attack on northern industrialism in America; he believed that black workers were being taken from the land only to be exploited in factories instead.

Warren twice won a Pulitzer Prize for poetry. First in 1958 for *Promises: Poems 1954–56* and again, in 1979, for *Now and Then: Poems 1976–78*. He also won a Pulitzer in 1947 for his novel *All the King's Men*. This story of a Louisiana governor's rise to power and his assassination is considered a modern classic.

Publications

1929	*John Brown: The Making of a Martyr*
1935	*Thirty-Six Poems*
1939	*Night Rider*
1946	*All the King's Men*
1957	*Promises: Poems 1954–56*
1959	*The Cave*
1975	*Democracy and Poetry*
1978	*Now and Then: Poems 1976–78*
1985	*New and Selected Poems*

WASHINGTON, Booker T.

American essayist and biographer

Born Apr. 5, 1856
Died Nov. 14, 1915
Age at death 59

As a writer and educator, Booker T. Washington was one of America's most important African-American leaders in the early 20th century. His bestselling autobiography *Up from Slavery*, written when he was 45, is a classic of American literature.

Booker Taliaferro Washington was born into slavery on a small plantation near Roanoke, Virginia. His mother was a cook, and it is thought that his father was a member of the planter's family. After the American Civil War, slavery was abolished, and Washington and his mother were freed. They moved to Malden, West Virginia, to live with his mother's new husband. Still a child, Washington worked in salt furnaces and coal mines and as a houseboy to help support his family. He began to educate himself, learning to read and studying at night with a local teacher. At the age of 16, he set off on a 500-mile journey to a school for African Americans that had recently been set up in Virginia. He walked most of the way.

After graduating in 1875, Washington was given the job of headmaster in Tuskegee, Alabama. He found there were neither buildings nor money, so he began classes in a donated shanty. After 34 years, Washington had transformed the Tuskegee Institute into a leading school. He also became a famous speaker on racial issues and an advisor to presidents Roosevelt and Taft. Publicly, he focused on economic advancement for blacks – he believed that economic equality would lead to social equality.

Publications

1899	*The Future of the American Negro*
1900	*The Story of My Life* (with Edgar Webber)
1901	*Up from Slavery* (with Max Bennett Thrasher)
1904	*Working with the Hands*
1913	*The Story of Slavery*

WASSERSTEIN, Wendy

American playwright

Born Oct. 18, 1950

Publications

1973 Any Woman Can't
1974 Happy Birthday, Montpelier Pizz-zazz
1975 When Dinah Shore Ruled the Earth
1975 Uncommon Women and Others
1981 Isn't It Romantic
1986 The Man in a Case
1988 The Heidi Chronicles
1993 The Sisters Rosensweig

Wendy Wasserstein won the Pulitzer Prize in 1989 for her play *The Heidi Chronicles*, a reflection on the achievements and the failures of the women's movement.

Wasserstein was born in Brooklyn, New York City, the youngest of four children in a middle-class family. She says she "grew up going to the theater," and she began writing at the exclusive public school she attended. She graduated from Mount Holyoke College in 1971, then attended playwriting workshops in New York. At age 23, her first play, *Any Woman Can't,* was produced off-Broadway. Wasserstein then went to Yale Drama School, where she wrote two more plays – *Happy Birthday*, *Montpelier Pizz-zazz* and *When Dinah Shore Ruled the Earth*. She earned her Master's degree from Yale in 1976.

Much of Wasserstein's work is about women of her own generation, university educated but faced with having to choose between career and marriage. *Uncommon Women and Others* is a play featuring five university friends in the 1970s as they examine the choices they have made about their lives in the years following their graduation. Wasserstein returned to this theme and to a portrayal of women's friendship in *Isn't It Romantic*.

Wasserstein's work is characterized by its sharp insights into human nature and her use of comedy to explore serious themes. Her Pulitzer Prize-winning *The Heidi Chronicles* – in which a professor, determined not to be submissive to men, finds fulfillment on her own – also won a Tony Award and had a long run on Broadway.

WAUGH, Evelyn

English novelist

Born Oct. 28, 1903
Died Apr. 10, 1966
Age at death 62

Many people think that the English writer Evelyn Waugh was the most brilliant satirist of his day.

Waugh was born in London into a comfortable middle-class family. He was educated at Oxford University and began his career teaching, which he hated. But the experience gave him the material for his first novel, *Decline and Fall*, published when he was 25. It was an immediate success, and several more riotously funny books followed.

In 1936, Waugh went to Ethiopia as a newspaper reporter to cover the Italian invasion. From this experience he wrote *Scoop*, in which a writer of nature notes is confused with a hard-bitten novelist and sent to cover a similar war. Soon Waugh himself was involved in

World War II. He served on a British military mission to aid the resistance movement in Yugoslavia.

From his wartime experiences came a three-novel series – *Men at Arms*, *Officers and Gentlemen*, and *Unconditional Surrender* – in which he reflects on army life and the struggle between good and evil.

When he was 27, Waugh became a Roman Catholic, and his religion played a part in several books, including *Brideshead Revisited*, which is about a Roman Catholic family living in a large country house. He returned to his earlier satirical style with the novel *The Loved One*, which makes fun of the work of morticians in California.

Waugh passed his later years living quietly in the country. In addition to his novels, he wrote biographies and travel books, and an incomplete autobiography, *A Little Learning*.

Publications

1928	*Decline and Fall*
1930	*Vile Bodies*
1932	*Black Mischief*
1938	*Scoop*
1942	*Put Out More Flags*
1945	*Brideshead Revisited*
1948	*The Loved One*
1955	*Men at Arms*
1955	*Officers and Gentlemen*
1961	*Unconditional Surrender*

WEBSTER, John

John Webster was a 17th-century English playwright. He is remembered as the author of two powerful tragedies, *The White Devil* and *The Duchess of Malfi*.

Webster was born in London, but little else is known about his life. Some think he once studied law or was an actor who later turned playwright. By his early 20s, he seems to have written and cowritten several plays for the London theaters. In his mid-20s, Webster wrote the comedy *Westward Ho!* with Thomas Dekker.

It was probably in his early 30s, that Webster wrote his two gloomy plays about passion and violent death. In *The White Devil,* a husband and wife are killed so that two lovers can be together. In *The Duchess of Malfi,* two brothers kill their sister, the duchess, to inherit her fortune. In both plays, the villains also die in the end.

Both tragedies are set in the courts of dukes ruling the small states that made up Renaissance Italy. Like other dramatists, Webster borrowed plots from earlier stories. He based *The White Devil* on a true episode of the 1580s. For *The Duchess of Malfi,* he used an Italian tale translated into English in the 1560s. Like many popular plays of the time, they feature bloodthirsty murder, torture, treachery and revenge. But Webster's poetic language and the subtle way in which he creates main women characters lift his plays out of the ordinary.

For most of his later plays, Webster worked with other authors, including Thomas Middleton, Thomas Heywood and William Rowley. Eight plays wholly or partly by Webster survive.

English playwright

Born c. 1580
Died c. 1634
Age at death c. 54

Publications

c. 1604	*Westward Ho!* (with Thomas Dekker)
c. 1605	*Northward Ho!* (with Thomas Dekker)
c. 1607	*The Famous History of Sir Thomas Wyatt* (with Thomas Dekker)
c. 1612	*The White Devil*
c. 1613	*The Duchess of Malfi*
c. 1620	*The Devil's Law-Case*
1625	*A Cure for a Cuckold* (with William Rowley)

WEISS, Peter

German playwright, poet and novelist

Born Nov. 8, 1916
Died May 10, 1982
Age at death 65

Peter Weiss is considered to be one of the most important German authors since World War II. He is particularly known for "documentary theater," in which historical events are presented to the audience without comment from the playwright.

Weiss was born in a wealthy suburb of Berlin, Germany. His childhood was a time of despair. Although he was desperate to study art, his family, who made a good living from the textile trade, insisted instead on a practical education. When Weiss was 21, his parents finally agreed to let him study at the Academy of Art in Prague, Czechoslovakia (now the Czech Republic). The German invasion the following year forced him to move to Sweden, and he became a Swedish citizen in 1945.

In his 30s, Weiss began to write; his short stories in Swedish received critical acclaim. In his mid-30s, he began writing in German, producing a number of novels before turning to drama. Many of his early plays are very complex and little known today. It is for *Marat/Sade*, first staged when Weiss was 48, that he is best remembered. The play was a sensation, and it won the New York Drama Critics' Circle Award in 1965. Set in a mental hospital, *Marat/Sade* is a play within a play. An inmate of the hospital, the MARQUIS DE SADE, is staging a play about the assassination of French radical Jean-Paul Marat during the French Revolution. Weiss's play explores the conflict between the ideals of revolution and personal freedom.

In 1965, Weiss declared his belief in communism, and many of his later works deal exclusively with political issues.

Publications

- 1960 *The Shadow of the Coachman's Body*
- 1961 *The Leavetaking*
- 1962 *The Exile*
- 1963 *The Conversation of the Three Walkers*
- 1964 *Marat/Sade*
- 1965 *The Investigation*
- 1967 *Discourse on the Progress of the Prolonged War of Liberation in Vietnam*

WELDON, Fay

English novelist and screenwriter

Born Sep. 22, 1931

Fay Weldon is known for her strong novels and plays about women's lives.

Born Fay Birkinshaw in the village of Alvechurch, in western England, she emigrated to New Zealand with her parents and attended school in Christchurch. She returned to England when she was 14 to live with her mother (who was a writer, too), grandmother and sister. Her parents had divorced when she was six, and female households would later figure strongly in her writing. She graduated from St. Andrews University in 1952 with a Master's degree in economics and psychology. Three years on, she had a son; the life of the unwed mother has also featured in her books. In 1960, she married Ronald Weldon and went to live in London.

Publications

- 1967 *And the Wife Ran Away*

From early days Weldon held feminist ideals – but she says emphatically that she never regarded man as the enemy. As well as raising another three children in the 1960s and '70s, she worked as an advertising copywriter and also wrote successful plays for radio and television. Her first novel, *And the Wife Ran Away*, published when she was 36, was originally a TV drama.

Weldon's books and plays examine the lives of women in a male-dominated society; she makes her points with wit and comedy, sometimes using bizarre plots. The female characters, although often traditional stereotypes, are full of life (and sometimes vengeful, as in *The Life and Loves of a She-Devil*), but her male characters can seem rather uninspiring. She has completed a large body of work and continues to write about the experiences of women.

1971	*Down among the Women*
1974	*Female Friends*
1976	*Remember Me*
1978	*Praxis*
1980	*Puffball*
1983	*The Life and Loves of a She-Devil*
1987	*The Heart of the Country*
1989	*The Cloning of Joanna May*
1997	*Big Women*

WELLS, H.G.

English science fiction writer and novelist

Born Sep. 21, 1866
Died Aug. 13, 1946
Age at death 79

The English writer H.G. Wells is often regarded as the father of modern science fiction.

Herbert George Wells was born in Bromley, in the south of England. His family was not wealthy, and he only escaped a career as a shop assistant by winning a scholarship to a science school in London. In college, his tutor was Thomas Huxley, a famous scientist who taught him about Darwin's theory of evolution, which states that animals evolve in response to changes in their environment. Wells was fascinated by what this idea might mean for the future of humanity and explored it in many novels.

Wells worked as a bookkeeper, tutor and journalist until he was 29, when he became a full-time writer. In his career, he wrote over 80 stories and novels. Some of these were science fiction; some were novels about political and social ideas. Wells also wrote a popular history book, *The Outline of History*.

The Time Machine, Wells's first novel, is one of his best-known works. It is about a time traveler who journeys to the future and witnesses the dying moments of the planet Earth. Wells describes how, in the future, human beings have evolved into two species, the useless Eloi and the practical Morlocks. In another famous novel, *The War of the Worlds*, Wells describes how Martians invade the Earth and are only defeated by common human germs.

Wells had great faith in the potential of science and technology to solve the problems of the human race. However, as he grew older, he began to feel that human beings are too cruel and selfish to use technology for good rather than for evil.

Publications

1895	*The Time Machine*
1896	*The Island of Dr. Moreau*
1897	*The Invisible Man*
1898	*The War of the Worlds*
1899	*When the Sleeper Awakes*
1901	*The First Men in the Moon*
1908	*The War in the Air*
1920	*The Outline of History*
1933	*The Shape of Things to Come*
1939	*The Holy Terror*

WELTY, Eudora

American novelist and short-story writer

Born Apr. 13, 1909

Eudora Welty is known for her fiction set in the American South. She writes about people trying to find their place within Southern society, particularly women defying the stereotype of "Southern belle."

Welty was born and raised in Jackson, Mississippi, which was then a small town. She loved the stories told by her family's friends and neighbors and was writing her own stories by the time she was 16. She received her undergraduate degree from the University of Wisconsin, then went to New York City to study advertising at Columbia University. After the death of her father, and with the start of the Great Depression, she returned to Jackson, where she lived for most of her life.

Welty's first collection of short stories, *A Curtain of Green*, was published when she was 32. It was introduced by the writer KATHERINE ANNE PORTER, who was nearly 20 years older than Welty and helped establish the younger writer's career. The following year Welty published her first novel, *The Robber Bridegroom*, a partly comical, partly romantic story set during America's frontier days. For the settings of her other four novels and most of her short stories, however, Welty returned to the Mississippi of her childhood, creating comic but thoughtful stories that celebrate life and human relationships.

Written when she was in her 60s, Welty's last two novels, *Losing Battles* and *The Optimist's Daughter*, are widely regarded as her best. She won the Pulitzer Prize in 1973 for *The Optimist's Daughter* – a masterpiece of social observation set in the world of small-town Mississippi that she knew so well.

Publications

1941 A Curtain of Green
1942 The Robber Bridegroom
1946 Delta Wedding
1949 The Golden Apples
1954 The Ponder Heart
1955 The Bride of Innisfallen
1970 Losing Battles
1972 The Optimist's Daughter
1980 Collected Stories
1984 One Writer's Beginnings

WEST, Nathanael

American novelist, playwright and screenwriter

Born Oct. 17, 1903
Died Dec. 22, 1940
Age at death 37

Nathanael West became famous for his last novel, *The Day of the Locust*, which is about characters living on the fringes of Hollywood's movie industry.

Born Nathan Weinstein, son of immigrant German Jews from Lithuania, West did not do well at school, and it was only in secondary school that his future promise began to show. Two years after graduating from Brown University with a Ph.D. he changed his name legally to Nathanael West, some say to give himself an American – rather than a Jewish – identity. Having been treated as an outsider himself, he came to identify with others who had also suffered from ignorance and prejudice.

Because West believed that society was decaying, the main theme in his novels is the breakdown of religion, art and morality. The aim of all his books is to show that the American dream of wealth and freedom is a myth. He wrote only four books, one of which, *Miss Lonelyhearts*, is now acknowledged to be a masterpiece. His first three books did not sell well, so, to make enough money to go on writing, he went to Hollywood as a screenwriter in 1935. There he began to gather material for what would be his last novel, *The Day of the Locust*.

In 1939, the reviews of *The Day of the Locust* turned out to be good. West's financial situation was stable, and he had high hopes for the future. He married in early 1940, but sadly within 9 months both West and his new wife were killed in an automobile accident.

Publications

- 1931 *The Dream Life of Balso Snell*
- 1933 *Miss Lonelyhearts*
- 1934 *A Cool Million: The Dismantling of Lemuel Pitkin*
- 1939 *The Day of the Locust*

WEST, Rebecca

Anglo-Irish novelist and journalist

Born Dec. 21, 1892
Died Mar. 15, 1983
Age at death 90

Rebecca West had two reputations: as a novelist who wrote from a feminist point of view, and as a journalist who covered the trials of Nazi war criminals in Nuremberg, Germany, after World War II. She also wrote many articles supporting the cause of votes for women.

West was born Cicily Isabel Fairfield in Ireland. The name of Rebecca West was adopted by her when she was 19. She trained for the stage, then turned to journalism and joined the women's movement. West became a well-known writer of witty articles on subjects ranging from social issues to book reviews. Her first book, published when she was 24, was a biography of the writer HENRY JAMES. Around that time she became one of the many lovers of the novelist H.G. WELLS, by whom she had a son.

West's first novel, *The Return of the Soldier*, was published when she was 26. Its hero is a soldier suffering from shell shock after fighting in World War I. He cannot remember the last 15 years of his life, including his marriage. Several more novels followed, but then there was a long gap of 20 years before she produced the bestseller *The Fountain Overflows*. Partly based on her own early years, the story is told by a child, Rose, who describes the day-to-day events of her life in a wealth of detail.

West's best-known book is *The Meaning of Treason*, a balanced account of the trials for treason of Britons who worked for Germany during World War II. Her reports on the Nuremberg trials were issued in book form as *A Train of Powder*. She continued to write until shortly before she died at age 90.

Publications

- 1916 *Henry James*
- 1918 *The Return of the Soldier*
- 1922 *The Judge*
- 1929 *Harriet Hume*
- 1936 *The Thinking Reed*
- 1949 *The Meaning of Treason*
- 1955 *A Train of Powder*
- 1956 *The Fountain Overflows*
- 1966 *The Birds Fall Down*
- 1982 *The Young Rebecca*

WHARTON, Edith

American novelist and short-story writer

Born Jan. 24, 1862
Died Aug. 11, 1937
Age at death 75

If Edith Wharton had done what was expected of someone born into New York's rich, upper-class society, she would have spent all her life going to parties. Instead, she had a nervous breakdown and wrote a book as a form of therapy. So began the career of one of the great masters of the American novel. Her best works satirized New York's class structures; in particular the clash of old monied families and the "nouveau riche," who had made their fortunes in more recent years.

Educated at home, Wharton once said her ambition was to become "the best dressed woman in New York." She wrote poems in her teens but did little if any writing during the first years of her marriage, at age 23, to wealthy Edward Wharton.

Following a nervous breakdown when she was 32, Wharton was advised that writing might help her recover. Three years later she published a nonfiction book, *The Decoration of Houses*, that launched her writing career. Her first successful novel, *The House of Mirth*, was published when she was 43. It is the story of a beautiful but poor young woman trying to survive in New York City.

In 1910, Wharton moved to France and later became involved in World War I, writing reports for American newspapers and helping refugees. At age 58, Wharton published *The Age of Innocence*, which deals with New York high society, and it won a Pulitzer Prize in 1921.

Wharton, who was a friend of the American novelist HENRY JAMES, wrote more than 35 books. She was one of the first women to receive an honorary degree from Yale University.

Publications

1905 The House of Mirth
1910 Tales of Men and Ghosts
1911 Ethan Frome
1913 The Custom of the Country
1918 The Marne
1920 The Age of Innocence
1924 Old New York
1925 The Mother's Recompense
1927 Twilight Sleep
1936 The World Over

WHEATLEY, Dennis

English thriller/crime writer

Born Jan. 8, 1897
Died Nov. 11, 1977
Age at death 80

Dennis Wheatley has been described as the prince of thriller writers. As well as thrillers, he wrote spy stories, detective novels, historical romances, adventure stories and books on devil worship and other aspects of the occult. In total, he wrote over 60 books that altogether sold more than 45 million copies worldwide, making him one of the 20th century's busiest and bestselling authors.

Wheatley was born in London. He served in the army during World War I, but was discharged after being injured in a gas attack. He then joined the family wine firm, of which he became the sole owner after his father's death in 1927. Badly hit by the Great Depression of the 1930s, the business collapsed, leaving Wheatley several hundred thousand pounds in debt. Facing poverty, he was encouraged by his wife to write a thriller. His first novel, *The Forbidden Territory*, came out when he was 36. Determined that it would be a success, he paid for 2,000 advertising postcards to be printed himself; the book became a worldwide bestseller.

Wheatley went on to write many other successful books, including a whole series based on a character called Sallust. So convincing were his stories set in wartime that during World War II, the British secret service asked him to advise on what to do if Britain were invaded. He also wrote detective stories that asked the reader to solve the crime. Photographs of clues were included in the books, and the solution given in a sealed envelope. Wheatley often wrote in an offensive way about women and black people, however, and his work has become less popular.

Publications

1933 The Forbidden Territory
1934 The Devil Rides Out
1936 Murder off Miami
1939 Herewith the Clues!
1940 The Black Baroness
1947 The Launching of Roger Brook
1950 The Second Seal
1957 The Prisoner in the Mask
1957 The Devil and All His Works
1974 The Satanist

WHEATLEY, Phillis

African-born American poet

Born c. 1754
Died Dec. 5, 1784
Age at death c. 30

Phillis Wheatley was one of the first African-American poets. Born in West Africa, she was kidnapped by slave traders at the age of seven and brought to America, where she was purchased by John and Susanna Wheatley at the Boston slave market.

Wheatley had a thirst for learning that extended far beyond ordinary reading and writing. Encouraged by the Wheatleys, she achieved a level of education that in those days was only to be found among a handful of male university graduates.

Her first poem was published when she was just 13, but it was her poem lamenting the death of a famous minister that brought Wheatley public recognition when she was 16. Three years later her fame spread to England with the publication of *Poems on Various Subjects, Religious and Moral*.

A devout Christian, Wheatley was also a staunch supporter of the American Revolution. In 1776, she became the first person to have a poem published in praise of George Washington.

Many of Wheatley's poems were written to celebrate public events or in memory of famous people who had died; they are mostly formal in style and tone. However, her best-known poem, "On Being Brought from Africa to America," written when she was 18, is a personal account of the sorrow her parents must have felt when she was kidnapped.

Wheatley was legally set free in 1774, but she continued to live with her former masters until 1778, when she married another ex-slave, John Peters. Life was hard for "free blacks," and Wheatley, who had three children, died in great poverty at an early age.

Publications

1770 An Elegiac Poem, on the Death of the Rev. George Whitefield
1773 Poems on Various Subjects, Religious and Moral
1784 An Elegy, to the Memory of the Rev. Samuel Cooper
1784 Liberty and Peace

Published after she died

1916 Life and Works of Phillis Wheatley

WHITE, E.B.

American essayist, children's writer and poet

Born Jul. 11, 1899
Died Oct. 1, 1985
Age at death 86

E.B. White was an elegant prose writer whose essays and stories range from satire to children's fiction.

Elwyn Brooks White was born in Mt. Vernon, New York. Before attending Cornell University, he served in the army during World War I. After graduating, he began his writing career, first as a reporter on the *Seattle Times*, then as a writer for the *New Yorker* magazine. There he met his wife, Katharine Sergeant Angell, who was the magazine's literary editor. For more than a decade, he wrote the famous column "Talk of the Town." During this period, at age 30, he collaborated on a satirical book with JAMES THURBER, *Is Sex Necessary?*, which is a spoof on the popular self-help books of the day.

At age 39, White moved with his wife to North Brooklin, Maine, where he continued to contribute columns for well-known magazines, most notably "One Man's Meat" for *Harper's* (later collected into a book of the same name).

White's best-known works belong to two very different sorts of literature. *The Elements of Style* (his famous 1959 revision of a book by William Strunk, Jr.) is still the standard guide to written English. In contrast, *Stuart Little*, *Charlotte's Web* and *The Trumpet of the Swan* are classic children's books. *Charlotte's Web*, perhaps the most famous, is about a spider who saves her friend, a pig, from slaughter.

The National Institute of Arts and Letters awarded White a gold medal in 1960 for his essays and criticism. In 1963, he received the Presidential Medal of Freedom and in 1978 was awarded a special Pulitzer Prize.

Publications

1929 The Lady Is Cold
1929 Is Sex Necessary? (with James Thurber)
1934 Every Day Is Saturday
1939 Quo Vadimus?
1942 One Man's Meat
1945 Stuart Little
1952 Charlotte's Web
1962 The Points of My Compass
1970 The Trumpet of the Swan

WHITE, Patrick

Australian novelist, short-story writer and playwright

Born May 28, 1912
Died Sep. 30, 1990
Age at death 78

Patrick White's work explores the theme of isolation in his characters, who are often separated from society by age, sexuality, race or geography. Worldwide he is regarded as an important writer but was unpopular in his native land because of his often cruel depictions of the Australian middle class as materialistic and soulless. He was awarded the Nobel Prize for Literature in 1973.

White was born while his Australian parents were on vacation in London. At the age of 13, he was sent back to England to attend Cheltenham College, which he hated. He began to write plays and stories. After a few years on remote sheep ranches in Australia, at the age of 20, he returned to England to attend Cambridge University.

During World War II, White served in the RAF in Greece and the Middle East. Following the war, he eventually settled on a farm near Sydney, Australia, with his partner Manoly Lascaris. There he wrote his first important work, *The Aunt's Story* – the reminiscences of an elderly woman. *The Tree of Man*, about the struggles of a small farmer, and *Voss*, about the early days of Australian exploration, also received critical acclaim. One of his most important novels, *The Eye of the Storm*, was published when he was 61. It is about a city dweller who remembers the most significant time of her life, when she was stranded on a tropical island.

In his memoirs, *Flaws in the Glass: A Self-Portrait*, White focuses on his life as a writer and a homosexual in Australian society. He died in Sydney after a long illness.

Publications

1939 Happy Valley
1948 The Aunt's Story
1955 The Tree of Man
1957 Voss
1961 Riders in the Chariot
1966 The Solid Mandala
1973 The Eye of the Storm
1980 The Twyborn Affair
1981 Flaws in the Glass: A Self-Portrait

WHITE, T.H.

English fantasy writer

Born May 29, 1906
Died Jan. 17, 1964
Age at death 57

T.H. White is best known for his four books about Arthur, the legendary medieval king of Britain.

Born in Bombay, India, Terence Hanbury White was the son of an English police officer. His childhood was unhappy (his parents argued a lot and eventually divorced). He went to Cambridge University, where he was popular with his tutors but had to interrupt his studies and visit Italy to recover from a bout of tuberculosis. When he was 23, his first collection of poetry, *Loved Helen*, was published.

After graduating, White became an English teacher. He soon tired of teaching, however, and retired to live in a cottage and follow his favorite pursuits of hunting and fishing. His popular book *England Have My Bones* is based on his experience of life in the cottage.

Around this time White read SIR THOMAS MALORY'S *The Death of Arthur*, a 15th-century account of King Arthur. He was so inspired that he decided to write an introduction to Malory's book. *The Sword in the Stone*, White's first book about Arthur, was published when he was 32. It is the story of Arthur's youth, depicted as a perfect childhood guided by an ideal teacher – the magician Merlyn. The book was well received, and White wrote three more volumes. The complete set was published as *The Once and Future King* when White was 52. *Camelot*, a musical by Alan Jay Lerner and Frederick Loewe based on the King Arthur books, followed soon after and was very popular.

Despite his successes and his many friends, White was often unhappy, finding consolation in alcohol. He always lived alone except for his dogs and hawks, creating fantasy worlds in his imagination.

Publications

1929 Loved Helen
1935 Earth Stopped
1936 England Have My Bones
1938 Burke's Steerage
1938 The Sword in the Stone
1939 The Queen of Air and Darkness
1940 The Ill-Made Knight
1958 The Once and Future King (4 parts)

Published after he died

1977 The Book of Merlyn

WHITMAN, Walt

American poet and journalist

Born May 31, 1819
Died Mar. 26, 1892
Age at death 72

Walt Whitman was America's greatest 19th-century poet. He wrote one of the finest works of American literature, the poetry collection *Leaves of Grass*.

Whitman was born in West Hills, Long Island, and grew up in Brooklyn. His father was a Quaker carpenter. As a youth, Whitman attended rural schools, trained to be a printer, and spent his summers on Long Island, where he developed a love of nature that was to dominate his writing.

For most of his life, Whitman worked as a journalist. He began working on newspapers in New York, but as a young man he traveled to New Orleans to work on a paper there and saw the huge size and diversity of America for the first time. Back in New York he witnessed the rapid growth of the city as hundreds of thousands of people arrived from all over the world to make a better life. Whitman wanted to write a new kind of poetry that could express his excitement at this amazing mix of people and their hopes for freedom.

The first edition of *Leaves of Grass* was published at Whitman's own expense when he was 36 – no publisher would accept his poems because they were so unusual. They are celebrations of nature, of the individual, of freedom and of the kinship of all humanity. He was widely criticized for his use of blank verse and his openness about sexuality.

During the American Civil War, Whitman worked as a nurse. After the war, he published *Drum-Taps* – poems about his experience of war – and one of his most famous poems, "O Captain! My Captain!," about the death of President Abraham Lincoln.

Publications

1855 Leaves of Grass
1865 Drum-Taps
1865–66 Sequel to Drum-Taps (including "O Captain! My Captain!")
1871 Democratic Vistas
1875 Memoranda during the War
1882 Specimen Days and Collect

WHITTIER, John Greenleaf

American poet

Born Dec. 17, 1807
Died Sep. 9, 1892
Age at death 84

John Greenleaf Whittier was one of the best-loved nature poets of his generation. He was also an active antislavery campaigner and used his poetry to call for an end to the tyranny and suffering caused by slavery.

As a child growing up in a Quaker family on a farm in Massachusetts, Whittier was mostly self-taught. He loved to read and was greatly influenced by the work of the great Scottish poet ROBERT BURNS. The owner of the newspaper that first published his poems helped him obtain a job on a Boston newspaper. Whittier's first book of poetry, *Legends of New-England in Prose and Verse*, was published when he was 24.

By the mid-1830s, Whittier had become involved in the antislavery movement, and his poetry became more political. Among the works from this period are *Poems Written During the Progress of the Abolition Question* and *Voices of Freedom*. Whittier was an important voice in the abolitionist movement. At age 28, he was elected to the Massachusetts legislature; he also wrote political essays and formed a new political party, the Liberty Party. The American Civil War inspired him to write *In War Time and Other Poems*, containing the well-known poem "Barbara Frietchie."

When the Civil War ended and slavery had been abolished, Whittier settled into a quiet life and returned to his theme of the New England countryside. He had matured as a poet and wrote more thoughtful poetry, including the well-received book *Snowbound*, in which he recalls his childhood and his recently deceased sister Elizabeth.

Publications

1831	*Legends of New-England in Prose and Verse*
1838	*Poems Written During the Progress of the Abolition Question*
1843	*Lays of My Home and Other Poems*
1846	*Voices of Freedom*
1850	*Songs of Labor*
1864	*In War Time and Other Poems*
1866	*Snowbound*
1890	*At Sundown*

WIGGIN, Kate Douglas

American children's writer

Born Sep. 28, 1856
Died Aug. 24, 1923
Age at death 66

Kate Douglas Wiggin became famous for her sentimental children's novels – especially *Rebecca of Sunnybrook Farm* – and also for her popular travel books and tireless efforts in nursery education.

Wiggin was born in Philadelphia. Her father died when she was three, and she moved with her mother and sister to Maine soon after. She spent most of her early and later life in Maine and was to write many of her books there. After the death of her mother's second husband, the family was left without any money, and Wiggin and her sister went to work. Her first published story appeared in a magazine when she was 20. Wiggin then got involved in the development of early education, helping to found the first free nursery west of the Rocky Mountains. In 1883, she wrote her first novel, *The Story of Patsy*, to raise money for the school.

Rebecca of Sunnybrook Farm, probably Wiggin's best and definitely her most famous book, came out when she was 47. It is about young Rebecca, who is sent to live with two aunts after the death of her father. The novel stands out from Wiggin's other books since it re-creates the world from a child's point of view rather than from an adult's view of what childhood should be like. It is still read today for its memorable and often amusing characters such as lively, clever, headstrong Rebecca and her two aunts – gentle and kind Aunt Jane and Aunt Miranda, who, although bullying and strict at first, comes to love Rebecca. Set in Maine, the book also gives one of the first realistic portrayals of rural life in that state.

Publications

1876	*Half a Dozen Housekeepers*
1883	*The Story of Patsy*
1887	*The Birds' Christmas Carol*
1890	*Timothy's Quest*
1895	*Froebel's Gifts*
1900	*Penelope's English Experiences*
1903	*Rebecca of Sunnybrook Farm*
1911	*Mother Carey's Chickens*

WILBUR, Richard

American poet, critic and translator

Born Mar. 1, 1921

Richard Wilbur was appointed America's Poet Laureate in 1987. His poetry is noted for its skill, humor and traditional forms.

Although born in New York City, Wilbur grew up in the New Jersey countryside. His father was a painter, and his mother came from a family of journalists. He was educated at Amherst College, where the poet ROBERT FROST worked as a visiting lecturer. After graduating, Wilbur served with the US military in Italy and France during World War II. At the end of the war, he returned to Harvard to study poetry. His first two collections of poems, *The Beautiful Changes* and *Ceremony and Other Changes*, were published while he was a university student in his mid-20s. At age 33, he became a professor of English at Wellesley College, where he published a third collection, *Things of This World*. This won the Pulitzer prize in 1957. He won a second Pulitzer in 1989 for *New and Collected Poems*.

Wilbur has rejected the hermitlike, isolated way of life preferred by the likes of T.S. ELIOT and WALLACE STEVENS. In contrast, he calls himself a "poet-citizen" who works as part of a growing community of poets. Wilbur's skill has been to inject wit into traditional forms of poetry. His early verse includes several poems about the chaos and destruction of war. Other poems celebrate the beauty and mystery of nature. He has also explored themes such as the importance of the imagination and of order and beauty. Wilbur has published collections of poetry for children, including *Loudmouse* and *Opposites*. He has also developed a reputation as a critic and as a translator of plays by the French playwright MOLIÈRE.

Publications

1947 The Beautiful Changes
1950 Ceremony and Other Changes
1956 Things of This World
1961 Advice to a Prophet
1963 Loudmouse
1973 Opposites
1976 The Mind-Reader
1988 New and Collected Poems

WILDE, Oscar

Irish playwright, novelist and poet

Born Oct. 16, 1854
Died Nov. 30, 1900
Age at death 46

A celebrated poet and playwright, Oscar Wilde was famous for his wit.

Born in Dublin, Wilde was the second son of a surgeon; his mother was a poet. Wilde was a natural scholar, and he did well at university in Dublin and Oxford. With his charm and flamboyant dress he was soon well known in London society.

In 1884, Wilde married Constance Lloyd. They had two sons, Cyril and Vyvyan. During this time, Wilde worked as a journalist, and it was not until he was 34 that he had literary success with *The Happy Prince and Other Tales*, a book of children's fables.

Wilde's only novel, *The Picture of Dorian Gray*, was also written in the form of a fable but tells a much darker story. The central

Publications

1888 The Happy Prince and Other Tales

WILDER, Thornton

American playwright and novelist

Born Apr. 17, 1897
Died Dec. 7, 1975
Age at death 78

Thornton Wilder is best known as a playwright who wrote about the extraordinary qualities people show in the ordinary events of life.

The son of a journalist and diplomat, Wilder was born in Wisconsin but raised in China and California. He attended Oberlin College in Ohio and Yale University. After university, he embarked on a teaching career while writing. At age 29, he published his first book, *The Cabala*, an ironic novel about decadent Italian nobility. That same year his first play, *The Trumpet Shall Sound*, was also produced.

When he was 30, Wilder achieved wide popularity and, a year later, a Pulitzer Prize for his novel *The Bridge of San Luis Rey*. It is about a friar who examines the lives of people who die suddenly after a bridge collapses. Each victim had become separated from humanity by obsessive and unrequited love.

A busy playwright, Wilder is best known for three works: *Our Town*, *The Skin of Our Teeth*, and *The Matchmaker*. Using experimental staging techniques, *Our Town* shows how the ordinary lives of simple folk are linked to universal themes. It won a Pulitzer in 1938. *The Skin of Our Teeth*, which also won a Pulitzer, in 1943, uses situations from history to applaud humanity's ability to survive disaster. *The Matchmaker* is a lighthearted comedy about a stingy merchant who wishes to marry a young girl. It became the basis for the musical *Hello Dolly!*

When he was 70, Wilder returned to the novel, publishing *The Eighth Day*, the chronicle of a Midwestern family that won the National Book Award in 1968.

Publications

1926 The Trumpet Shall Sound
1926 The Cabala
1927 The Bridge of San Luis Rey
1931 The Long Christmas Dinner
1934 Heaven's My Destination
1938 Our Town
1939 The Merchant of Yonkers
1942 The Skin of Our Teeth
1957 The Matchmaker
1967 The Eighth Day

WILLIAMS, John A.

American novelist

Born Dec. 5, 1925

John A(lfred) Williams is known for his angry novels about the African-American experience.

Williams was born in Mississippi and raised in Syracuse, New York. He served in the navy during World War II. A member of the medical corps, he was assigned to a land force because African Americans were not wanted aboard ships. The racism he faced had a profound impact on his writing. Williams graduated from Syracuse University at age 25 and then held jobs in public relations and publishing.

Williams's first novel, *The Angry Ones*, was published when he was 35. It is a bitter book about a young, ambitious black man dealing with racial prejudice. Its themes are ones Williams returned to character, who is addicted to good living, has a dreadful secret; he remains young and handsome, but his portrait grows ugly as a result of his moral decline.

Between 1879 and 1895, Wilde wrote nine plays. His most popular is the comedy of manners *The Importance of Being Earnest*. This hilarious satire hinges on the double lives of two would-be bridegrooms. However, while his professional life was at a peak, Wilde's private life was unhappy. He had been having an affair with Lord Alfred Douglas. At the time, homosexuality was illegal in Britain, and Wilde was sent to prison in 1895. *The Ballad of Reading Gaol*, a narrative poem, records his thoughts about imprisonment.

After his release in 1897, Wilde went to live in France. However, his reputation and health were ruined. He died three years later in Paris.

1890 The Picture Gray
1891 Lord Arthur Crime
1892 Lady Winde Fan
1893 A Woman o Importance
1895 The Importa Being Earne
1895 An Ideal Hu
1896 Salome
1898 The Ballad Reading Ga

WILDER, Laura Ingalls

Laura Ingalls Wilder is one of the most popular American children's writers of the 20th century. She is best remembered as the author of *Little House on the Prairie*.

Born in Big Woods, Wisconsin, Wilder was the daughter of a farmer who moved his family around Kansas, Minnesota, Iowa and Dakota Territory (now South Dakota) in his struggle to support them. She attended school whenever there was one and worked after school to help family finances. She married another farmer, Almanzo Wilder, in 1885.

Life on her husband's farm in Dakota Territory was hard. After years of illness, crop failures and the death of their baby son, they traveled to Missouri with their daughter Rose and bought a site at Rocky Ridge. This farm was more successful.

At the age of 44, Wilder started to write about farm life in a local newspaper. Rose, who had also become a writer, sold her mother's first story, *Little House in the Big Woods*, to a publisher more than 20 years later, when Wilder was 65.

The "Little House" books are set in the places where Wilder lived and are based on her experiences. The adventures and difficulties of pioneer life are vividly presented in the seven books. The novels reveal her close observation of family relationships, as well as the importance she placed on moral values.

The books were immediately and lastingly successful. The television series *Little House on the Prairie* is based on them. In 1954, the Laura Ingalls Wilder Award for children's writers was established.

American child writer

Born Feb. 7, 1867
Died Feb. 10, 1957
Age at death 90

Publications

1932 Little House Big Woods
1933 Farmer Boy
1935 Little House Prairie
1937 On the Bank Creek
1939 By the Shore Silver Lake
1940 The Long Wi
1941 Little Town o Prairie
1943 These Happy Years

Published after s

1971 The First Fou

in later works – relationships between black men and women, blacks in the military, and racism in institutions like law and medicine.

Williams's novels can be divided into three phases. The first works, *The Angry Ones*, *Night Song* and *Sissie*, are about African Americans in white society. They are cautiously optimistic about the black struggle. The works in his second phase, *The Man Who Cried I Am*, *Sons of Darkness, Sons of Light* and *Captain Blackman*, see blacks as tools of white society. They reflect Williams's vision of black revolutionaries and the white reaction. Williams's later novels, *Mothersill and the Foxes*, *The Junior Bachelor Society* and *!Click Song*, reflect an awareness of emerging African-American unity.

Williams has also written nonfiction works, including biographies of the black novelist Richard Wright and of Martin Luther King, Jr.

Publications

1960 *The Angry Ones*
1961 *Night Song*
1963 *Sissie*
1967 *The Man Who Cried I Am*
1969 *Sons of Darkness, Sons of Light*
1972 *Captain Blackman*
1975 *Mothersill and the Foxes*
1976 *The Junior Bachelor Society*
1982 *!Click Song*
1991 *Flashbacks 2: A Diary*

WILLIAMS, Tennessee

American playwright, novelist and poet

Born Mar. 26, 1911
Died Feb. 25, 1983
Age at death 71

Tennessee Williams is widely considered to be one of America's finest playwrights since World War II. His plays deal sensitively with emotionally damaged people trying to survive in a hostile world.

Williams was born in Columbus, Mississippi, and brought up in his grandfather's home, where his parents lived. The family moved to St. Louis when he was 12, but neither Williams nor his sister adjusted to city life. In school, they were made fun of for their poverty and Southern accents. In 1929, he entered the University of Missouri, but the family's lack of funds forced him to leave without graduating. He eventually earned a degree in playwriting when he was 27.

Williams's first play was *American Blues*, produced when he was 28. His breakthrough came with *The Glass Menagerie*, which ran on Broadway for over a year and won Williams the first of his four New York Drama Critics' Circle Awards. This was followed by *A Streetcar Named Desire* – the story of a Southern belle, Blanche Du Bois, whose privileged upbringing does not prepare her for the harsh realities of life. The play won Williams his first Pulitzer Prize, in 1948. *Cat on a Hot Tin Roof* – about the moral decay of a Southern family – was also a great triumph and gained him his second Pulitzer Prize, in 1955. It was made into a memorable movie, as have many of Williams's plays.

Later works disappointed the critics. Williams was in poor health during the 1960s, caused by a dependence on drink and sleeping pills that led to a breakdown in 1969. After this, he struggled to overcome his addictions.

Publications

1939 *American Blues*
1944 *The Glass Menagerie*
1945 *Battle of Angels*
1947 *A Streetcar Named Desire*
1950 *The Roman Spring of Mrs. Stone*
1951 *The Rose Tattoo*
1953 *Camino Real*
1955 *Cat on a Hot Tin Roof*
1959 *Sweet Bird of Youth*
1961 *The Night of the Iguana*

WILLIAMS, William Carlos

American poet, short-story writer and novelist

Born Sep. 17, 1883
Died Mar. 4, 1963
Age at death 79

Publications

1909 Poems
1923 The Great American Novel
1923 Spring and All
1925 In the American Grain
1937 White Mule
1938 The Collected Early Poems
1946–58 Paterson
1950 The Collected Later Poems
1961 Many Loves and Other Plays
1962 Pictures from Brueghel

William Carlos Williams was a prolific poet and writer who passionately believed that American art should reflect the American experience.

Williams was born in Rutherford, New Jersey began his studies at the University of Pennsylvania Medical School in 1902. At age 26, he paid for his first collection of poetry, *Poems*, to be published. All his life he combined his medical practice with the prolific production of over 40 volumes of poetry, fiction, plays and essays.

As both doctor and writer, Williams believed it was his duty to improve society. He argued that complex ideas could be expressed in simple ways. His easily understandable way of writing was influenced by his friend, the poet EZRA POUND; it contrasted with the complex approach of some of his contemporaries, including T.S. ELIOT and JAMES JOYCE. Williams wrote in an everyday language he called "the American idiom." His five-volume epic poem *Paterson*, about his boyhood home, is an example of the way he explored important themes, like love and friendship, through writing about ordinary things. *White Mule*, the story of a poor immigrant family, is another example of the power of ideas presented in a straightforward way.

Williams's influence on younger poets, such as ALLEN GINSBERG and ROBERT LOWELL, was evident long before he was nationally recognized in 1950, when he won the National Book Award for poetry. Just after he died, he won the 1963 Pulitzer Prize for poetry for his *Pictures from Brueghel*.

WILSON, August

American playwright

Born 1945

Since the mid-1980s, August Wilson has been recognized as an important American playwright. He is famous for plays that describe the experiences of African Americans, especially the conflict between those who accept the American way of life and those who prefer to celebrate their African heritage.

Wilson was born in Pittsburgh, Pennsylvania. He had little formal education, dropping out of school when he was 14; his teacher, who regarded his work as too good to be from an African-American student, had accused him of copying the work of famous writers. He continued his education away from the school system and became influenced by African-American writers like RALPH WALDO ELLISON and LANGSTON HUGHES.

At age 23, Wilson founded a community theater called Black

Horizon in Pittsburgh. Later, he began writing plays for another black theater in St. Paul, Minnesota. His first major work, *Ma Rainey's Black Bottom*, won the New York Drama Critics' Circle Award for best play. It relates the exploitation of the founder of blues music, Ma Rainey, by studio bosses, all of whom were white. The characters do little more than talk to each other. But this talk leads to murder.

Wilson, aged 42, won his first Pulitzer Prize for his play *Fences*. It tells the story of a brilliant baseball player, ignored by the major leagues because of his race, who is in conflict with his son, who wants to accept a sports scholarship. In 1990, *The Piano Lesson* won him a second Pulitzer Prize. It is the painful tale of a family at war over the sale of a piano that was traded for their enslaved grandparents.

Publications

1979 The Homecoming
1979 The Coldest Day of the Year
1981 Black Bart and the Sacred Hills
1982 Jitney
1984 Ma Rainey's Black Bottom
1985 Fences
1986 Joe Turner's Come and Gone
1987 The Piano Lesson
1990 Two Trains Running
1995 Seven Guitars

WILSON, Harriet E.

American novelist

Born c. 1827
Died c. 1863
Age at death c. 36

Harriet E. Wilson is thought to be the first African-American woman to publish a novel.

Wilson was born Harriet E. Adams. Her birth date is given as 1827/1828 in official records in New Hampshire. As a child, she was made to work very hard, damaging her health. She worked as a straw sewer in a hat factory and lived with a white family as a servant in her early 20s. In 1851, she married Thomas Wilson, a former slave, and the following year she had a son, George. Soon after the birth her husband abandoned them, and Wilson was forced to place her child with foster parents. At about age 32, in an effort to earn enough money to get back her son and support them both, Wilson wrote *Our Nig*.

For many years, *Our Nig* was thought to be a nonfictional autobiography, and FRANCES E.W. HARPER'S 1892 novel, *Iola Leroy*, was regarded as the first by an African-American woman. But when *Our Nig* was rediscovered in the 1980s, it was recognized as a work of fiction. Although the story is loosely based on her own life, Wilson had invented a new form of novel. She used a popular plot among white female readers – sentimental, involving seduction and marriage – along with the story of rebellion and strength that featured in many slave writings. But *Our Nig* is about racism in the antislavery North. That, and its description of a marriage between a black man and a white woman, which was shocking at the time, may be why the book went unread for more than a century and a half. Sadly, Wilson's son George – her reason for writing the novel – died within a year of its publication.

Publications

1859 Our Nig

WILSON, Margaret

American novelist, poet and short-story writer

Born Jan. 16, 1882
Died Oct. 6, 1973
Age at death 91

Publications

1923	*The Able McLaughlins*
1925	*The Kenworthys*
1926	*The Painted Room*
1928	*Daughters of India*
1929	*Trousers of Taffeta*
1931	*The Crime of Punishment*
1933	*The Valiant Wife*
1936	*The Law and the McLaughlins*
1939	*The Devon Treasure Mystery*

Margaret Wilson had published many short stories before her first novel, *The Able McLaughlins*, won the Pulitzer Prize in 1924, making her famous.

Born of Scottish Presbyterian parents in a farming community in Iowa, Wilson attended state schools in Chicago and graduated from the University of Chicago. She then served as a missionary in India for 12 years until emotional stress brought her back to the US. At age 41, she married George Turner, an Englishman whose views on crime and punishment were to influence her deeply.

Wilson's novels have three main themes: the effects of rigid religious beliefs on individuals and communities, the lowly position of women in society, and the failings of the prison system. In *The Able McLaughlins*, published when she was 41, she focuses on the harsh judgments made by a Scottish Presbyterian community when one of its members becomes pregnant. In this and other works, Wilson calls for greater understanding and compassion by society. Other novels include two based on her experiences as a missionary and several concerned with crime and punishment.

Wilson's work was popular during her lifetime but has since been neglected. Her books reflect her belief in the basic goodness of human beings; unlike THEODORE DREISER and other novelists of the time, she preferred an optimistic, compassionate point of view. Her feminist themes ensure her place among the serious feminist writers of the early 20th century.

WODEHOUSE, P.G.

Anglo-American writer

Born Oct. 15, 1881
Died Feb. 14, 1975
Age at death 93

P.G. Wodehouse was one of the most popular comic novelists of his time. He wrote more than 110 books in which he created such characters as Jeeves and Wooster. The perfect "gentleman's gentleman," Jeeves serves upper-class bachelor Bertie Wooster as a valet. His tasks include running the house, dressing his master and saving Wooster's life when required. Wodehouse also wrote short stories, plays, lyrics for musical shows, and many film scripts. Among his greatest lyrics is "Bill," a hit in the musical *Show Boat*.

Pelham Grenville Wodehouse was the son of a British judge serving in Hong Kong. His first job was in a bank, but he gave it up to write and joined a London evening newspaper. He began writing school stories for boys, and among his earliest novels were *A*

Prefect's Uncle, published when he was 22, and *Mike*, one of the best school stories ever written.

After 1909, Wodehouse spent most of his life in the United States, with periods in France. He introduced Bertie Wooster and his man Jeeves when he was 36 in the short novel *The Man with Two Left Feet* and was still writing about them in the 1970s. His stories are always beautifully written, with complicated plots.

Wodehouse was captured by the Germans in France during World War II and held prisoner. He unwisely made some humorous broadcasts to America for the Germans, which made him deeply unpopular in bomb-ravaged Britain. After the war, he returned to America and took US citizenship in 1955. In due course, the British largely forgave him. He received a knighthood a few weeks before he died.

Publications

1902 The Pothunters
1903 A Prefect's Uncle
1909 Mike
1915 Something New
1915 Psmith, Journalist
1917 The Man with Two Left Feet
1934 Right Ho, Jeeves
1949 The Mating Season
1963 Stiff Upper Lip, Jeeves
1971 Much Obliged, Jeeves

WOLF, Christa

German novelist, short-story writer and essayist

Born Mar. 18, 1929

Internationally famous novelist Christa Wolf wrote about ordinary people living in the communist state of East Germany after World War II.

Wolf was born in Landsberg an der Warthe, Germany (now in Poland). She attended universities in Jena and Leipzig, after which she worked for several years as a critic and editor before becoming a full-time writer at the age of 33.

Wolf established her reputation at age 34 with *Divided Heaven*, a novel about a love affair set in East Germany – the affair ends when the man, disillusioned with the regime in his homeland, decides to move to the West. This was followed by *The Quest for Christa T.*, which questions East German values and ideals, and *A Model Childhood* – a long autobiographical novel based on her childhood in a provincial town.

In her early years, Wolf was an idealistic believer in communism and supported the creation of East Germany after World War II. By the late 1960s, she had begun to oppose the regime because she felt it stifled freedom of speech and oppressed ordinary people. When, in 1989, the East German government fell, Wolf argued against joining together the two halves of Germany, which had been divided since 1949. In 1993, she admitted to having worked with the East German secret police when she still supported the communist state. Later, she and her husband were themselves investigated by the authorities. *What Remains and Other Stories* reflects her mixed feelings about communism and democracy.

Publications

1961 Moscow Novella
1963 Divided Heaven
1968 The Quest for Christa T.
1976 A Model Childhood
1979 No Place on Earth
1983 Cassandra
1987 Accident: A Day's News
1990 What Remains and Other Stories
1993 The Author's Dimension

WOLFE, Tom

American journalist and novelist

Born March 2, 1931

Publications

1965	*The Kandy-Kolored Tangerine-Flake Streamline Baby*
1968	*The Electric Kool-Aid Acid Test*
1970	*Radical Chic & Mau-Mauing the Flak Catchers*
1973	*The New Journalism*
1975	*The Painted Word*
1979	*The Right Stuff*
1980	*In Our Time*
1981	*From Bauhaus to Our House*
1987	*The Bonfire of the Vanities*
1998	*A Man in Full*

Tom Wolfe, the author of many books and collections of essays dealing with aspects of American popular culture, has been instrumental in the development of the literary style known as "New Journalism," an aural style which blends a number of literary devices as a way of involving the reader in the events described.

Tom Wolfe (Thomas Kennerly, Jr.) was born in Richmond, Virginia,. in 1931, the son of Helen Wolfe and Thomas Kennerly, a scientist and businessman. He graduated from Washington and Lee University in 1951 and gained a Ph.D. from Yale in 1957. He has worked as a journalist and social commentator.

In 1963, Esquire published 49 pages of Wolfe's notes on car customizers, "There Goes (Varoom! Varoom!) That Kandy Kolored Tangerine-Flake Baby," allowing his random thoughts and sensory perceptions to appear unedited. Wolfe has written about various aspects of popular American culture such as the drug scene in California and American art and architecture. The astronauts of the Mercury space program are the subject of *The Right Stuff*. *The Bonfire of the Vanities*, a satire on greed and ambition in New York City, was one of the top ten bestselling books of the 1980s. Both of these novels were made into successful films.

Wolfe also illustrates most of his own books and has held exhibitions of his drawings. Known for his elegant appearance, he usually dresses in a three-piece white suit. Wolfe has added such phrases to the American vocabulary as "The Me Decade" and "Radical Chic."

WOOLF, Virginia

English novelist, critic and journalist

Born Jan. 25, 1882
Died Mar. 28, 1941
Age at death 59

Virginia Woolf was a founder of the Bloomsbury Group of writers and artists. She developed the stream-of-consciousness method of writing, in which the reader follows the internal thoughts of the characters as the story unfolds.

Woolf was born Adeline Virginia Stephen into a distinguished literary family. She married Leonard Woolf, a social reformer, when she was 30 and published her first novel, *The Voyage Out*, three years later. By this time, she was suffering from occasional mental illness. In 1917, Woolf and her husband founded the Hogarth Press, a small company that published new and experimental work, such as the poems of T.S. ELIOT.

In her third novel, *Jacob's Room*, published when she was 40,

Woolf began experimenting with the stream-of-consciousness method. She continued this style of writing in her novels *Mrs. Dalloway*, *To the Lighthouse* and *The Waves*. In *Orlando,* she wrote about a character who lived through several centuries and changed from male to female and back again several times. Her style of writing had a very significant influence on the development of the novel in the 20th century.

Woolf was a pioneer of feminism. She described the problems of women in a male-dominated world in *A Room of One's Own*. Shortly after finishing her last novel, *Between the Acts*, her mental illness returned. She became very depressed and drowned herself in a river near her home.

Since her death Woolf's literary essays have been published in several volumes, such as *The Common Reader* (1925).

Publications

1915 The Voyage Out
1919 Night and Day
1922 Jacob's Room
1925 Mrs. Dalloway
1927 To the Lighthouse
1928 Orlando
1929 A Room of One's Own
1931 The Waves
1937 The Years
1941 Between the Acts

WOOLSEY, Sarah Chauncy

American children's writer

Born Jan. 29, 1835
Died Apr. 9, 1905
Age at death 70

Under the pen name Susan Coolidge, Sarah Chauncy Woolsey published the famous series of five "Katy" books, beginning with *What Katy Did*.

Woolsey was born into a wealthy family in Cleveland, Ohio. She went to local public schools and to a boarding school in Hanover, New Hampshire. The whole family moved to New Haven, Connecticut, when Woolsey was 20. During the American Civil War, she worked in hospitals. From 1870 to 1872 the Woolseys traveled around Europe. On their return, they settled in Newport, Rhode Island, where Woolsey spent the rest of her life.

Woolsey's first book, *The New-Year's Bargain*, did not come out until she was 37. Like much of her fiction, it was largely aimed at young girls. She probably began writing at this late stage in her life because her father had recently died, and the family needed extra money. In the next two years, the first two Katy books came out. In *What Katy Did* the Carr family's mother has just died leaving behind five children. Katy, the eldest, tries to take the place of her mother and look after her brothers and sisters. *What Katy Did at School* recounts Katy's year at boarding school. The third Katy book, *What Katy Did Next*, did not come out until 12 years later. During this time, Woolsey wrote many short stories and poems for children and traveled in Europe and the US. Her heroine followed suit in the third book by also traveling in Europe. The last two Katy books, *Clover* and *In the High Valley*, focus on Katy's brothers and sisters.

Publications

1872 The New-Year's Bargain
1873 What Katy Did
1874 What Katy Did at School
1879 Eyebright
1880 Verses
1886 What Katy Did Next
1888 Clover
1890 In the High Valley
1893 The Barberry Bush
1904 The Rule of Three

WORDSWORTH, William

English poet

Born Apr. 7, 1770
Died Apr. 23, 1850
Age at death 80

William Wordsworth was the first and greatest of the English Romantic poets. He became England's Poet Laureate in 1843.

Wordsworth was born in the Lake District. The region's magnificent landscape gave him a love of nature that deeply affected his life. He was orphaned at 13, but two uncles had him educated at a good local school and at Cambridge University. At age 23, his first poems were published. *An Evening Walk* and *Descriptive Sketches* were inspired by a walking vacation in France and Switzerland.

In 1795, Wordsworth met SAMUEL TAYLOR COLERIDGE and, in 1798, they produced *Lyrical Ballads* together. Most of the poems were Wordsworth's. He used ordinary words to express strong personal feelings about remembered scenes and events. His imagination could make even everyday countryside scenes seem full of meaning. By the time he was 36, Wordsworth had written his best poetry, including a first version of *The Prelude*. In this long poem, he tells how he came to love nature and see himself as a part of the natural world. All this was new at a time when many poets still wrote about ancient Greek and Roman heroes in a flowery language that no one actually spoke.

For years, Wordsworth shared a Lake District home with his sister Dorothy. Scenes described in her diary inspired some of his most famous lines. In 1802, Wordsworth married Mary Hutchinson.

Publications

1793 *An Evening Walk*
1793 *Descriptive Sketches*
1798 *Lyrical Ballads* (with Samuel Taylor Coleridge)
1807 *Poems in Two Volumes*
1814 *The Excursion*
1815 "Surprised by Joy"
1819 *The Waggoner*

Published after he died

1850 *The Prelude*

WOUK, Herman

American novelist and playwright

Born May 27, 1915

Herman Wouk is most famous for *The Caine Mutiny*, which won the Pulitzer Prize in 1952.

Born in New York, Wouk was educated at Columbia University and started his career writing jokes for radio comedians. By 1936, he was a scriptwriter for the comedian Fred Allen, and he kept this job until 1941. In that year, he also wrote radio broadcasts to promote sales of war bonds. Wouk was married in 1945 to Betty Sarah Brown, and they had three children.

During World War II, Wouk served in the US Navy as an officer on destroyers and minesweepers in the Pacific. Many of the experiences of this period helped him to write *The Caine Mutiny*, which was published when he was 46. The story tells how a group of officers aboard the navy ship *Caine* rebel against their captain, Queeg, because of his strange behavior. By 1953, this book had sold nearly 2 million copies, and it was made into a hit Broadway play starring Henry Fonda and a film. It has been translated into more than a dozen languages. More novels and plays followed, including the bestselling novel *Marjorie Morningstar* and *This Is My God*, a study of the Jewish religion. Wouk's other popular novels include *Winds of War* and *War and Remembrance*. Both have been made into successful serial films for television.

Wouk's style is praised for being direct and straightforward. It has been compared to that of MARK TWAIN. Influence came from the novelist ANTHONY TROLLOPE, whose work, Wouk has said, taught him discipline. Wouk uses traditional storytelling methods and traditional characters who stand for honor, valor and patriotism.

Publications

1947	*Aurora Dawn*
1948	*The City Boy*
1949	*The Traitor*
1949	*Slattery's Hurricane*
1951	*The Caine Mutiny*
1955	*Marjorie Morningstar*
1959	*This Is My God*
1965	*Don't Stop the Carnival*
1971	*Winds of War*
1978	*War and Remembrance*

WRIGHT, James

American poet and translator

Born Dec. 13, 1927
Died Mar. 25, 1980
Age at death 52

James Wright's poems tell of his encounters with both human suffering and natural beauty and of his attempts to express the significance of both.

Born in Martins Ferry, Ohio, a steel-mill town, Wright spent part of his childhood on a nearby farm. Both farm and town are frequent settings for his poems. He served in the US Army in Japan in World War II. After the war, he graduated from Kenyon College and then studied with THEODORE ROETHKE at the University of Washington in Seattle. Throughout his life he taught at various universities, his final position lasting 14 years at Hunter College in New York City.

The Green Wall, Wright's first book of poems, was published when he was 30. His early poetry was written in rhyme, but in the early 1960s, he was influenced by the work of PABLO NERUDA and other poets. Neruda's sharp, immediate imagery and visions of nature inspired Wright to abandon traditional poetic forms, and to write in the rhythm of ordinary speech.

Wright's poems belong to the "deep image" poetry of the 1960s and '70s, in which images are used to convey emotional meaning. Typical of this style are his lines "When I stand upright in the wind / My bones turn to dark emeralds."

He wrote with compassion about the outcasts of society – tramps, prostitutes, drunks – and of his concern about technology's effect on the natural world. He also drew inspiration from great works of art and poetry. In 1972, Wright won the Pulitzer Prize for his *Collected Poems*.

Publications

1957	*The Green Wall*
1959	*Saint Judas*
1963	*The Branch Will Not Break*
1968	*Shall We Gather at the River*
1971	*Collected Poems*
1973	*Two Citizens*
1974	*I See the Wind*
1977	*To a Blossoming Pear Tree*

Published after he died

1982	*This Journey*

WRIGHT, Richard

American novelist

Born Sep. 4, 1908
Died Nov. 28, 1960
Age at death 52

Richard Wright was one of the first modern authors to write realistically about African Americans in both rural and urban America. His efforts to understand black culture and its strength in a hostile world made him one of the leading writers of his time.

Wright was born on a plantation near Natchez, Mississippi, the son of a sharecropper and a schoolteacher. Wright's father moved his wife and child to Memphis, Tennessee, when Wright was three years old, and then abandoned them. His mother was frequently ill, and he was brought up by relatives.

Wright had little formal education, and he left school early to get a job. He continued to teach himself, secretly borrowing books from the whites-only library in Memphis. At 19, he moved to a better job in Chicago, where he joined the Communist Party. Ten years later he moved to New York City, where his first book, *Uncle Tom's Children,* a collection of four short novels, was published. He was then 30.

The award of a Guggenheim fellowship enabled Wright to complete another novel, *Native Son*, about a black man who murders a white woman. He recorded his early life of poverty in *Black Boy*.

Wright emigrated to Paris, where he spent the last 14 years of his life and made friends with JEAN-PAUL SARTRE and SIMONE DE BEAUVOIR. He had long broken with the communists but believed in the teachings of Karl Marx, the founder of communism. He was deeply concerned about Africa and traveled to the Gold Coast (now Ghana) to study conditions on the continent at first hand. He described his visit in *Black Power.*

Publications

1938 Uncle Tom's Children
1940 Native Son
1941 Twelve Million Black Voices
1945 Black Boy
1953 The Outsider
1954 Black Power
1957 White Man, Listen!

Published after he died

1963 Lawd Today
1977 American Hunger

WU CHENGEN

Chinese poet and novelist

Born c. 1500
Died c. 1582
Age at death 82

Wu Chengen wrote *Journey to the West* (or *Monkey*), a classic of ancient Chinese literature.

Little is known about Wu Chengen's life. He was born in what is now Jiangsu Province, China, into a comfortable merchant family. At that time, China had a highly organized and complex system of government in which thousands of civil servants carried out the authority of the emperor. Like many educated young men, Wu Chengen took the examinations required to work for the civil service, but he failed and turned to writing as a way of earning money. Later in life he held minor government posts in the city of Nanjing.

It is known that Wu Chengen wrote poems and satirical plays, but the novel *Journey to the West* is his only major work to have survived. Based on the legendary journey of a Chinese Buddhist monk named Tripitaka from China to India, *Journey to the West* is a retelling of very old tales from Chinese folklore. Tripitaka is accompanied by magical helpers, and every step of his journey is delayed by gods and demons who create problems and dangers to test the strength of his belief.

One of Tripitaka's companions is a monkey king who has angered the gods by stealing the secret of immortality and must make the journey to pay for his crime. In many ways, Monkey becomes the central character of the story; he is witty, brave and mischievous – always getting into trouble but always saving the day. The story is as much about the way he learns to become a good person as it is about the journey to India.

Published after he died

1592 Journey to the West

WYNDHAM, John

English science fiction writer

Born Jul. 10, 1903
Died Mar 11, 1969
Age at death 65

John Wyndham is known for his science fiction novels and short stories.

Wyndham was born John Beynon Harris in a small rural town in the south of England. His father was a lawyer. His parents separated when he was eight, and he was sent away to private school. He tried various careers: the law, farming, commercial art, advertising, but he did not persevere in any of them.

An admirer of the novels of H.G. WELLS, Wyndham began to write science fiction stories in his 30s. He sold his first ones to American magazines under his own name. At age 32, he sold a serial – a story published in several parts, continuing from one issue of a magazine to the next – to an English magazine, this time using the name John Beynon. *The Secret People* was published as a book in the same year.

World War II interrupted Wyndham's writing career, and he served in the civil service and the British Army. After the war, he joined an exclusive London club, where he met a publisher who advised him on his next novel. *The Day of the Triffids* was published when he was 48 under the name that was to make him famous – John Wyndham. The novel is about giant mutant plants that take over the Earth after almost everybody is blinded by a freak meteor shower. Wyndham's success was international and contributed to the growing science fiction genre. He had an educated English style and an ability to explore his ideas in a way that makes them believable. His best novels were written during the 1950s, when he also produced powerful and original short stories that grip the imagination.

Publications

1935 The Secret People
1936 Planet Plane
1951 The Day of the Triffids
1953 The Kraken Wakes
1954 Jizzle
1955 The Chrysalids
1956 The Seeds of Time
1957 The Midwich Cuckoos
1959 The Outward Urge
1961 Consider Her Ways

WYSS, Johann David and Johann Rudolf

Swiss children's writers

Johann David Wyss
Born 1743
Died 1818
Age at death c. 75

Johann Rudolf Wyss
Born 1781
Died 1830
Age at death c. 49

Father and son, Johann David and Johann Rudolf Wyss wrote the famous children's classic *The Swiss Family Robinson*. This still-popular adventure story about a family shipwrecked on a desert island was Switzerland's first children's book to become internationally famous.

Johann David Wyss was a chaplain in the Swiss Army. At the time, his four sons were growing up, the English writer DANIEL DEFOE'S novel *Robinson Crusoe* was extremely popular. This story of a man shipwrecked on a desert island inspired many imitations (known as "Robinsonnades") in the 18th and 19th centuries. Johann David first made up his own "Robinsonnade" to entertain and teach his four sons about natural history, biology and other branches of science. It is about a Swiss pastor, his wife, and their four sons who have to learn how to survive alone on a deserted island. He wrote the story down, and one of his sons, Johann Emmanuel, illustrated it, but the manuscript was disorganized and incomplete.

Johann Rudolf Wyss grew up to become an expert on Swiss folklore and was a professor of philosophy at a university in Bern, Switzerland, from 1805. He also wrote the words to the Swiss national anthem. In the early 1800s, he rediscovered his father's story and revised, edited, and enlarged it for publication. *The Swiss Family Robinson* first came out when he was 31 and his father was 69. Over the years editors have added their own episodes. So the story as it is known today is very much a collective effort.

Publications
1812–13 The Swiss Family Robinson

YEATS, W.B.

Irish poet and playwright

Born Jun. 13, 1865
Died Jan. 28, 1939
Age at death 73

W.B. Yeats was a great Irish poet and one of the most influential writers of the 20th century; T.S. ELIOT called him the greatest poet of his time. In 1923, he won the Nobel Prize for Literature.

William Butler Yeats was born in Dublin. For much of his early life, he lived sometimes in London and sometimes in Ireland, but he was always attached to his homeland. In London, he became increasingly interested in Asian religions, the supernatural and Irish folklore. Such themes inspired *The Wanderings of Oisin and Other Poems*, published when he was 24. This poetry is beautiful and filled with sad longings.

In 1889, Yeats met and fell in love with Maud Gonne, a beautiful Irish actress who was involved in the political struggle to end

English rule in Ireland. As a result, Yeats became interested in Irish politics, and this was reflected in his poetry. He believed in the power of poetry and plays to bring a sense of unity to Ireland. In *The Celtic Twilight* and *The Secret Rose,* he collected Irish legends and myths.

In 1896, Yeats returned to live permanently in Ireland. He met LADY GREGORY, a wealthy aristocrat whose interest in Irish traditions matched his own. Together in 1904 they formed the Abbey Theater group, which became famous. Yeats's most popular plays were *Cathleen ni Houlihan* and *The Land of Heart's Desire*.

In *A Vision,* Yeats set out his philosophy, his belief in myths and the meanings of the symbols he used. His writing became stronger and more solid as he aged: his best work is in *The Tower*, *The Winding Stair* and *Last Poems and Plays*.

Publications

1889 The Wanderings of Oisin and Other Poems
1893 The Celtic Twilight
1894 The Land of Heart's Desire
1897 The Secret Rose
1902 Cathleen ni Houlihan
1925 A Vision
1928 The Tower
1933 The Winding Stair
1936–39 Last Poems and Plays

YEVTUSHENKO, Yevgeny

Russian poet, playwright and novelist

Born Jul. 18, 1933

Yevgeny Yevtushenko is an internationally famous Russian poet. His poems, which are often autobiographical, are concerned mainly with the need for truth. A fearless fighter for artistic freedom, he publicly supported the writer ALEKSANDR SOLZHENITSYN when he was forced into exile and has been a role model for Soviet youth.

Yevtushenko was born into a peasant family in the remote town of Zima, Siberia, and even as a small child made up verses for the family. In 1944, he moved with his mother to Moscow. He went to the Moscow Literary Institute and, at 19, his first book of poems was published.

During his 20s, Yevtushenko wrote extensively, producing three volumes of poetry in three years. In many poems, he attacked the propaganda of the Stalin years, when truth had been distorted to meet the needs of the authorities. His verses were fresh and imaginative, and his poetry was extremely popular, particularly with the young. He traveled through the United States and Europe, giving readings. Everywhere crowds greeted him with enthusiasm, seeing him as a symbol of a new freedom in the Soviet Union.

Two of Yevtushenko's best-known poems date from this period. They are *Zima Junction,* a long narrative about his childhood in Siberia, and *Babi Yar*, a moving poem about the Nazi slaughter of Jews, which also criticized anti-Jewish feelings in the Soviet Union. In recent years, he has produced plays and novels.

Publications

1956 Zima Junction
1962 Babi Yar
1963 A Precocious Autobiography
1966 Bratsk Station
1971 Stolen Apples
1972 Under the Skin of the Statue of Liberty
1982 Dove in Santiago
1982 Wild Berries
1995 Don't Die before You're Dead

ZAMYATIN, Yevgeny

Russian science fiction/ fantasy writer

Born Feb. 1, 1884
Died Mar. 10, 1937
Age at death 53

Yevgeny Zamyatin was one of the most brilliant Russian writers of the 20th century.

Born in Lebedyan, Russia, as a child Zamyatin absorbed the folklore and storytelling traditions of this rural area. Later, as a writer he drew inspiration from the inventive way Russian folklore interweaves fact with fantasy and from its playful mocking of powerful figures in society.

As a young man, Zamyatin trained as a naval architect and became involved with a political movement that opposed the czar (emperor) of Russia. He was arrested and jailed for his activities. He then began writing stories, plays and poems. His first major story, *A Provincial Tale*, was published when he was 27. Soon afterward he wrote a short novel, *At the World's End*, making fun of army officers, which again brought him into conflict with the authorities.

During World War I, Zamyatin worked in England, designing icebreaking ships for the Russian navy. In 1917, he returned to Russia, excited by the recent Russian Revolution, but he soon became a critic of the new communist regime. In his 30s, he wrote his most famous work, *We*, a novel that predicted how the communist regime in Russia could result in a mechanized, antihuman future. The novel never appeared in communist Russia, although it influenced British writers such as George Orwell.

Zamyatin continued to write, encouraged by fellow writers like Maksim Gorky. However, he was hounded by the Russian authorities until, in 1931, he left the country. He settled in Paris, where he lived in poverty until he died.

Publications

1911 A Provincial Tale
1914 At the World's End
1917 Islanders
1922 The Cave
1922 We
1923 The Fires of St. Dominic

ZELAZNY, Roger

American science fiction writer and poet

Born May 13, 1937
Died Jun. 16, 1995
Age at death 58

Roger Zelazny is one of the most important science fiction writers to emerge in the 1960s.

Zelazny was born in Euclid, Ohio. He graduated from Columbia University, New York, with a Master's degree in English. After leaving university, he briefly enlisted with the Ohio National Guard and then worked for the Social Security administration, writing in his spare time.

Zelazny's first story, "Passion Play," was published when he was 25. He was part of a group of science fiction writers in the 1960s known as the "New Wave." Up until that time, science fiction had been mostly action–adventure stories set in space; new wave writers explored the thoughts and feelings of characters in strange alien settings. Many of the characters in Zelazny's fiction were inspired by the mythology of various cultures: for example, *Lord of Light* is based on the Hindu religion, and *Creatures of Light and Darkness* is inspired by the gods of ancient Egypt.

Zelazny went on to publish 150 more short stories and 50 novels. He also won several important science fiction awards. When he was 33, *Nine Princes in Amber* appeared, the first in a series of novels about Amber, a place on a higher, more intense plane than Earth where a godlike race of beings lives. The Amber series is full of action and was very popular. The stories have been adapted for comics and used as the basis for a computer game.

Zelazny also published three collections of poetry. One of his novels, *Damnation Alley*, was made into a movie. When he was 38, he moved to Santa Fe, where he lived until his death.

Publications

1966	*This Immortal*
1966	*The Dream Master*
1967	*Lord of Light*
1969	*Creatures of Light and Darkness*
1969	*Damnation Alley*
1970	*Nine Princes in Amber*
1971	*The Doors of His Face, the Lamps of His Mouth*
1979	*Roadmarks*
1990	*Home Is the Hangman*

ZINDEL, Paul

American young-adults' writer and playwright

Born May 15, 1936

Paul Zindel has written many popular novels for young people and a Pulitzer Prize-winning play for adults called *The Effect of Gamma Rays on Man-in-the-Moon Marigolds*.

Zindel was born on Staten Island in New York City. His parents separated when he was only two years old, and he had a troubled childhood, rarely seeing his father. His relationship with his mother, a nurse, was difficult. She took a variety of jobs and moved house almost every year. Zindel felt lonely and unloved a lot of the time. With few friends and only able to express his true feelings in private, he began to write. When he was 16, he wrote his first play, about the year he spent recovering from tuberculosis in a hospital.

After finishing secondary school, Zindel studied chemistry at Wagner College and took a creative writing course taught by EDWARD ALBEE. Working as a school science teacher from 1959 to 1969 taught Zindel a lot about the problems and lives of young people. He had his first success as a playwright at age 29 with *The Effect of Gamma Rays on Man-in-the-Moon Marigolds*, a story reflecting his own troubled childhood. Based on the realism of the young characters in the play, Zindel was asked by a publisher to write a book for young adults. The result was *The Pigman*, a story of two teenagers who take advantage of a sick old man. It was highly praised for its realism and the way it tackles difficult subjects usually avoided in books for young people. Zindel has since written more than 20 books for young readers, many of which have become bestsellers.

Publications

1959	*Dimensions of Peacocks*
1965	*The Effect of Gamma Rays on Man-in-the-Moon Marigolds*
1968	*The Pigman*
1969	*My Darling, My Hamburger*
1976	*Pardon Me, You're Stepping on My Eyeball!*
1989	*Amulets against the Dragon Forces*
1993	*Attack of the Killer Fishsticks*

ZOLA, Émile

French novelist, critic and journalist

Born Apr. 2, 1840
Died Sep. 29, 1902
Age at death 62

Émile Zola was a major 19th-century novelist known for his realistic novels that deal with working-class life.

Zola was born in Paris but grew up in Aix-en-Provence, southeast France. When he was seven, his father died, leaving the family with money problems. He moved with his mother to Paris when he was 18. After failing his final school exam, he went to work for a publisher. He began writing novels and achieved his first success with *Thérèse Raquin*, which was published when he was 27.

Zola was also a political journalist who was critical of the French Emperor Napoleon III and his Second Empire. At age 31, Zola began the great *Rougon-Macquart* series of 20 novels about "the natural and social history of a family under the Second Empire," which he did not complete until 22 years later. Each book in the series describes the life and adventures of one or more members of the family. In this way, Zola wrote about all levels of French society, from prostitutes (in *Nana*) to coal miners (in *Germinal*) and poor farm workers (in *The Soil*).

Zola wrote two more series of novels, *The Three Cities* and *The Four Gospels*. His novels portray the harsh realities of life, but they also reflect his attachment to humane values and the need to defend them. It was this that inspired his defense of Jewish soldier Alfred Dreyfus in his famous letter *I Accuse!* to the president of France in 1898. Dreyfus had been falsely accused of treason. It may also have led Zola's enemies to block the chimney of his Paris apartment, causing poisonous fumes to build up and kill him.

Publications

1867	*Thérèse Raquin*
1873	*The Belly of Paris*
1877	*The Grog Shop*
1880	*Nana*
1885	*Germinal*
1887	*The Soil*
1890	*The Human Animal*
1894–98	*The Three Cities* (3 vols.)
1898	*I Accuse!*
1899–1902	*The Four Gospels* (4 vols.)

ZWEIG, Arnold

German novelist and playwright

Born Nov. 10, 1887
Died Nov. 26, 1968
Age at death 81

During his lifetime, Arnold Zweig was the most celebrated author in East Germany (now part of Germany). He was most famous for his antiwar and antifascist novels.

Zweig was born into a Jewish family in the town of Glogów (now in Poland). He studied at several institutions, including the universities of Breslau, Munich and Berlin. During World War I, he served in the German Army. After this war, the anti-Jewish Nazi party led by Adolf Hitler grew more popular. Zweig, who supported the idea of an independent Jewish state (Israel), began to receive death threats. He left Germany before World War II broke out, and lived in Palestine for 14 years. Unhappy with the treatment of incoming Jews and the Arab Palestinians by settled Jews, he moved to East Germany in 1948.

While still a 24-year-old university student, Zweig published his first book, *Notes about a Family Named Klopfer*. When he was 40, he published his best-known novel, *The Case of Sergeant Grischa*. In this antiwar tale set during World War I, a German held prisoner by the Russians escapes to his own lines only to find himself accused of being a Russian spy. The mistake is uncovered, but he is still executed. Only one of Zweig's books was set during World War II – *The Axe of Wandsbek*. This anti-Nazi tale is based on the true story of a Nazi executioner who commits suicide.

Zweig was a friend of the famous doctor, Sigmund Freud, who developed new theories on how the mind works. Zweig tried to work Freud's theories of psychoanalysis into his books, showing the effects events had on his characters mentally.

Publications

1911	*Notes about a Family Named Klopfer*
1912	*Claudia*
1927	*The Case of Sergeant Grischa*
1931	*Young Woman of 1914*
1932	*De Vriendt Goes Home*
1935	*Education before Verdun*
1947	*The Axe of Wandsbek*
1957	*The Time Is Ripe*

ZWEIG, Stefan

Austrian novelist, playwright and biographer

Born Nov. 28, 1881
Died Feb. 23, 1942
Age at death 60

Stefan Zweig is remembered mainly for his psychological novels and biographies.

The son of wealthy Jewish parents, Zweig was born in Vienna, the capital city of Austria. He studied in Germany and Austria and traveled worldwide before returning to Austria in his early 30s. He had published his first verses by the time he was 20.

Zweig's travels and World War I made him hate war and champion the idea of international culture and a Europe united under one government. During World War I, he condemned war in his play *Jeremias*.

Zweig was strongly influenced by psychoanalyst Sigmund Freud's theories about how people's minds work. He became one of the first writers to put such ideas in biographies. At age 39, he produced *Three Masters*, character-study essays on the writers HONORÉ DE BALZAC, CHARLES DICKENS and FYODOR DOSTOEVSKY. Five brief historical portraits called *The Tide of Fortune* appeared when he was 47; they helped make Zweig known worldwide. In his 40s and 50s, he wrote full-length lives of the 18th-century French queen, Marie Antoinette, the medieval philosopher, ERASMUS, and other famous historical figures. In those years, he also wrote novels, of which the best known are *Amok*, *Conflicts* and *Beware of Pity*.

At 53, the Nazis' hatred of Jews forced Zweig to leave Austria. For six years, he lived in London before moving to the US and then to Brazil. Zweig and his wife killed themselves there, so deeply depressed were they by the way World War II was destroying civilization in Europe. Both world wars figure in Zweig's autobiography, *The World of Yesterday*.

Publications

1917	*Jeremias*
1920	*Three Masters*
1922	*Amok*
1925	*Master Builder*
1927	*Conflicts*
1928	*The Tide of Fortune*
1932	*Marie Antoinette*
1935	*The Queen of Scots*
1938	*Beware of Pity*
1941	*The World of Yesterday*

INDEX

Authors' names appear under headings that indicate period, nationality, and kind of work: William Shakespeare, for example, appears by period under **SIXTEENTH-CENTURY WRITERS**, by nationality under **BRITISH AND IRISH WRITERS**, and by kind of work under both **PLAYWRIGHTS** and **POETS**. The authors' names also appear in their chronological order.

Period

Nationality

Genre

SCIENCE FICTION WRITERS

PRE-1940

POST-1940

CHRONOLOGICAL LIST OF AUTHORS

1900